PASOLINI OLD AND NEW

PASOLINI
OLD AND NEW

Surveys and Studies

edited by

ZYGMUNT G. BARAŃSKI

Published for
The Foundation for Italian Studies
University College Dublin

FOUR COURTS PRESS · DUBLIN

Publication of this book was assisted by financial help from

The Humanities Research Board of the British Academy
The University of Reading Department of Italian Studies

Printed and bound by MPG Books, Bodmin, England

First published 1999

by

Four Courts Press
Fumbally Court
Fumbally Lane
Dublin 8
Ireland

A catalogue record for this book is available from the British Library

ISBN 1 85182 436 7

For Giulio Lepschy

PREFACE

It is now generally acknowledged that Pier Paolo Pasolini stands as Italy's major post-war intellectual. Since his murder in November 1975, the importance of his richly varied career—a career which embraced poetry and the cinema, the novel and the critical essay, journalism and the theatre, the scholarly anthology and semiotic theory—has increasingly been recognized. The last twenty or so years have seen not only the posthumous appearance of a large number of Pasolini's previously unpublished works which have cast new light on his life and art, but also the publication of a huge body of critical writing on the artist. Although some of this work has been of a very high standard (especially that written in recent years by younger scholars working outside Italy), much of it has also been anecdotal, fragmentary, or coloured by the same biases as characterized most reactions to Pasolini during his life. In particular, there have been no serious attempts to look at Pasolini's highly complicated intellectual and artistic career as a whole.

The present collection of essays, without claiming to provide an overall assessment of Pasolini, does aim to offer a clear sense of the range and complexity of his achievements. It suggests, in fact, the kind of directions which a historically sensitive and text-based comprehensive study might take. The book is divided into two sections. "Surveys" examines some of the major large-scale components of Pasolini's cultural experience: his obsession with himself, with language, with reality, and with rewriting; his problematic assimilation of Italy's two greatest modern thinkers, Benedetto Croce and Antonio Gramsci; and his work as a cultural theorist. "Studies" provides detailed analyses of some of his most important works: his dialect verse, his Friulan and Roman prose, his film adaptations from St Matthew and from Chaucer, his plays, and his late polemical journalism. These texts have been chosen to reflect the whole of his career, from the early 1940s to 1975, and to focus on different areas of his artistic and intellectual activity. It is hoped that, in this way, the two parts of the book can integrate and offer a broad insight into Pasolini's career. The Introduction, by exploring the extent and nature of Pasolini's reception since his death, sets the tone for the collection's attempt to merge the general with the particular.

Unlike the chapters of other books which can be used as "companions" to an artist, the essays of *Pasolini Old and New* are the result of original research and do not simply synthesize existing scholarship. They have been written by the authors of some of the best recent studies of Pasolini (Francese, Gordon, Rohdie, Rumble, and Ward), by an emerging scholar of great promise (Meekins), and by critics with a long-established interest in the writer (Barański, Caesar, De Mauro, Wagstaff and Welle). Five of the essays—the ones by Barański, Caesar, De Mauro and Wagstaff—are revised versions of articles published in the highly successful and influential 1985 issue of *The Italianist* on Pasolini (now long out of print), while the remainder have been specifically commissioned for this collection (though versions of the essays by Rumble and Ward have now appeared in their excellent books). Of the revised articles, the ones on Pasolini's early Roman prose writings and on his critical theory may be said almost to constitute new pieces of work. The title of the book is designed, in part, to reflect the make-up of its content. More specifically, however, it is intended to highlight the fact that the volume approaches "old" questions in Pasolini studies from new directions, or that it examines his work from perspectives which have been largely ignored.

I should like to record my thanks to John Barnes for having agreed to publish the book in his prestigious series and for all the help he has given me in preparing the collection for publication. It is always a pleasure to work with a close friend. I am also indebted to Laura Betti and to Giuseppe Iafrate of the Fondo Pier Paolo Pasolini for their support. Long may their indispensable archive flourish. This book could not have been published without a generous contribution from the Humanities Research Board of the British Academy, for which I am deeply grateful.

I should like to express special thanks to all the contributors not only for their excellent essays, but also, and more specifically, for their patience. As they well know, this has not been a straightforward project.

Finally, and as has now been the case for many years, my greatest debts are to Giulio Lepschy. His support, advice and exceptional scholarly knowledge and expertise have accompanied me at every stage of this project. It seems more than appropriate that, as Giulio prepares to retire from full-time university work, this book should be dedicated to him.

The following abbreviations are used:

Alí	*Alí dagli occhi azzurri*
BB	*Le belle bandiere*
EE	*Empirismo eretico*
LL	*Lettere luterane*
LNG	*La nuova gioventú*
P	*Petrolio*
PI	*Passione e ideologia*
PM	*Il portico della morte*
PS	*Pasolini e "Il setaccio"*
PTP	*Un paese di temporali e di primule*
SC	*Scritti corsari*
SCD	*Storie della città di Dio: racconti e cronache romane (1950–1966)*
T	*Teatro*
TLP	*Bestemmia: tutte le poesie*
V	*Il Vangelo secondo Matteo* [screenplay]

In each essay, unless otherwise indicated, translations are by the essay's author.

CONTENTS

STUDIES

INTRODUCTION:
THE IMPORTANCE OF BEING
PIER PAOLO PASOLINI

Zygmunt G. Barański

> Pier Paolo è in contatto con tutto il
> mondo.
> [Pier Paolo is in contact with the
> whole world.]
> (Laura Betti on 1 July 1997)

As I was putting the final touches to this book in August 1997, I found myself entangled in a slightly bizarre event. Without my knowing it I had been assigned a minor role in yet another *caso Pasolini*. In July rumours had begun to circulate in Italy to the effect that, if adequate funding from the public purse were not found to continue subsidizing the activities of the Fondo Pier Paolo Pasolini, the archive would be transferred to the University of Reading. Although both the University and my Department issued statements denying any knowledge of the proposed move, the rumour quickly became headline news in Italy. The threat of the possible loss of the Fondo—a threat which, once it took on the "legitimacy" of a *fatto di cronaca*, brought about a quite intense public reaction—had the desired outcome: almost immediately money was found to ensure that Laura Betti and her collaborators could carry on with their important work.[1]

Despite the problems and perplexities which the rumour caused us in Reading, personally I am not vexed by the unwitting role I was obliged to play in this latest in a long line of Pasolinian "dramas" (to be "used" in a good cause...); indeed, I am pleased about how things turned out. That the Fondo should be located anywhere but in Rome is unthinkable.[2] At the same time, the episode of the fantastic transfer to my University did bring to mind a host of other thoughts. In particular, it has made me reflect on the nature of Pasolini's legacy, specifically on the intriguing question of his standing in present-day Italy. There is something slightly surreal in the fact that a relatively minor problem connected with the running of a foundation dedicated to an aggressively individualistic, not to say eccentric, artist-intellectual, dead for over twenty years, should today still be deemed the stuff of front-page news. What this state of affairs inescapably points to is the sway which Pasolini continues to exert over the cultural and emotional sensibilities of his compatriots. That sway is all the more remarkable given the many political and social changes that Italy has undergone since Pasolini's murder in 1975, and given the fact that much of his work is closely tied to the historical moment of its production. And yet, despite such restrictions, there seems little doubt that Pasolini continues to be a "living" and authoritative force in Italy.

What is more difficult to assess and define is the reasons for this lasting influence, as well as its precise nature: the why and the how of Pasolini's reception in Italy since his death—a reception whose tangled roots go back to the difficult years of the author's lifetime, and which, revealingly, is often subsumed under, and hence defined by, the tag *il mito Pasolini* (the main feature of the "myth" being the idea that Pasolini is a privileged source of "truth"). In this short Introduction, I should like to draw a preliminary sketch of what I perceive to be some of the salient features of Pasolini's *fortuna* during the last twenty years or so. My discussion is inevitably selective, and possibly partial, since it is based on material I have been collecting, somewhat haphazardly, over the last few years; it is further constrained by attempting to touch on matters which have received little serious critical attention.[3] Yet despite these limitations I believe it is important to preface the present volume with an essay which seeks, however tentatively, to delineate some of the ways in which Pasolini's presence has continued to be felt in Italy, given that, as I shall endeavour to demonstrate, his general reception has fundamentally affected the ways in which he has been studied. Thus a book such as this, which aims to give a historically and textually sensitive assessment of the range and complexity of Pasolini's career, needs to be aware of how non-scholarly concerns can interfere with critical judgements. Too much academic work on Pasolini—it is my contention—has ignored this basic fact; too many studies have examined both Pasolini and his *œuvre* in an anecdotal, fragmentary and subjective manner—a critical tradition, as we shall see, which has helped to create and sustain *il mito Pasolini* during the last two decades, and which, concurrently, has been profoundly affected and constrained by that very same "myth". It goes without saying that our collection hopes to stand in opposition to this way of analysing the poet, recognizing instead that any philologically based assessment of Pasolini's career needs to acknowledge the presence of the *mito* and to look beyond it.[4]

At one level it should not come as a surprise that considerable interest surrounds the artist and his work. Pasolini is almost certainly Italy's major post-war intellectual, and hence deserves careful and enduring consideration; and the number, if not always the quality, of critical works on him bears clear testimony that other intellectuals tend to have few doubts about his importance.[5] It is not the question of whether or not Pasolini deserves to be studied and remembered that is at stake here. Rather it is the ways in which he has been studied, remembered and assimilated that are problematic and intriguing. In particular, as I have already mentioned, the key question arises of the nature of the relationship between the flourishing scholarly work on Pasolini and his iconic status as a figure worthy of media attention—specifically, the issue of the relative sway which academia and the press have exerted on each other. It is, of course, the case that, as a rule, academics in Italy are able to wield greater influence over public opinion than their counterparts in English-speaking countries, not least because they are given greater access to the mass media.[6] Thus in the days, weeks and months after Pasolini's murder, it was intellectuals—authors, artists and scholars—writing in or quoted by the press who were largely responsible for establishing the principal lineaments of the *mito pasoliniano*.[7] Nevertheless, the fact of media access cannot of itself explain, first, why the "myth" took on the traits that it did; second, why the concerns and preoccupations of a high-brow élite became a source of fascination for the readers of newspapers (and also, as I shall note, for film-makers and their audiences); or, third, why, rather than academic criteria, it has been Pasolini's public, largely media-fabricated image that has exerted a determining ascendancy on how he has been studied and how his works have been read, and, just as importantly, on how his works have been marketed. Most of all, the means by which the *mito* was first promulgated—in contrast, as we shall see, to the context, the historical moment, of its dissemination—do not explain why it is specifically Pasolini who has been accorded "mythic" status. Other important contemporary artists and thinkers have not been treated in the same way; in particular, those who, like Pasolini, have been dead for some time do not generate the same kind of enduring reaction in the mass media and elsewhere that he still manages to provoke.

One fact regarding Pasolini's reception since his death is eye-catching. When one considers his publishing, critical, cultural and social successes since 1975, the impression can easily be gained that, far from dead, he is still very much alive. This is especially so as far as Pasolini's relationship with the press is concerned. During the last twenty or so years of his life, he was regularly present in its pages either as a trenchant commentator or as the protagonist of a series of "scandals" and *casi* which reached its climax in the media circus that accompanied his murder.[8] In the twenty or so years since his death, he has continued to "speak" in the press as unpublished or little-known writings have been excerpted or printed in full, and he has continued to "make news" as the protagonist of controversy and scandal—from the shocked re-actions to the appearance of *Salò* in the immediate aftermath of his murder to the relentless publicity campaign which in 1992 paved the way for the publication of *Petrolio*, and to the recent spat involving the Fondo.

This is an extraordinary continuity—one which provides a first tangible clue to the concrete means by which Pasolini has managed to remain at the forefront of the consciousness of so many Italians. While the press appears to have offered Pasolini an effective mode of life-support, however, the question of why it should have felt compelled to provide that service remains unanswered. The prob-lem is all the more pressing since such an outcome seems far from obvious when one remembers Pasolini's position in Italy in the years before his death. It is now well established that, as his view of the modern world had become ever more doom-laden and apocalyptic after the failure of the *centro-sinistra* and the events of

1968, so Pasolini had become an increasingly isolated figure.[9] He may have been offered the prestigious pulpit of the *Corriere della sera*'s front page, but his views on abortion, divorce, sexuality, young people, education, the environment, Fascism, and so on, drew little support while eliciting considerable antipathy, shock or just bemused disbelief. Pasolini had neither a popular constituency ready to back his positions nor the active support of influential sections of the political, economic or cultural establishment. He was granted a public voice less so that he could contribute meaningfully to contemporary debates than as a source of vicarious titillation. Even then he could sell newspapers. His ideas were rarely deemed worthy of serious consideration, nor were they generally perceived as the fruit of serious reflection (even though, as Michael Caesar demonstrates elsewhere in this volume, there is much that is serious in them). Indeed, it would not be an exaggeration to say that by November 1975 Pasolini had managed to alienate and offend most, if not all, strands of Italian opinion; and the aura of scandal, accompanied by the inevitable right-thinking tut-tutting, which surrounded him was bolstered by the ever more prominent position which sex played in his art and thought: from the obsessive representations of nudity and sexual behaviour in the *Trilogia della vita* to his essays criticizing heterosexuality, which were accompanied by a concomitant increase in positive assessments of homosexuality, a topic which previously, in public at least, he had studiously avoided or had presented in an unflattering light, as in the Roman stories. Nor was the status of the "outsider" something that Pasolini had allowed to be imposed on him against his will. As Robert Gordon has effectively shown,[10] Pasolini actively collaborated in presenting himself as "other"—this was in fact a position which he always found to his liking, since it allowed him to give primacy to his main obsession: the self and its needs. And yet, nearly twenty-three years after his death, this alienated, self-centred and self-serving "misfit", this latter-day prophetic "voice in the wilderness", this eccentric middle-class iconoclast keen to *épater les bourgeois*, has acquired a significance and a legitimacy in the Italy of today which he never achieved, and probably never wanted, during his lifetime. Since his death Pasolini has moved from the margins to the centre, and in the process both he and his work have taken on meanings and values which largely eluded them while he was still alive. How did this happen?

The blunt and shocking answer is that Pasolini died. And the fact that he died unexpectedly, in brutal and ambiguous circumstances, made it much easier for the process of revision to take place. There is no doubt that Pasolini's murder caused immediate and widespread consternation. This was not so much because the death, especially the violent death, of any well-known personality creates ripples in the social order, but because the actual, almost certainly erotic, conditions of his murder were sidelined by the invention of more sinister yet somehow less troubling explanations—explanations, it must be added, for which, to this day, there has never been any real evidence, but which conformed remarkably well to the sombre, anxious mood of the era.[11] The early 1970s in Italy were violent, bewildering, crisis-ridden years. The fabric of post-war society appeared to have been permanently torn; the possibility of achieving any sort of national consensus seemed to be a pipedream, not least because of the lack of any meaningful political leadership. Instead Italy was filled with conflict and rumour, as a thick shroud of paranoia descended upon the country. In fact the most revealing feature of Pasolini's journalism of this period—with its obsessive apocalypticism and bleakness, its incapability of viewing things in other than negative and accusatory terms—is the degree to which his articles, regardless of their actual content, succeed in capturing the mood of this darkly troubled moment in recent Italian history. Thus when Pasolini was killed the manner of his demise not only helped bolster the general sense of disquiet, but made it easy for his death to become confused with his socio-political writings. The terrors which Pasolini depicted in the *Corriere* had escaped the printed page to destroy him. Given that, for years, Pasolini had been vehemently warning his fellow-citizens that the world in general and Italy in particular were swiftly speeding to disaster, there seemed to be a powerful "logic" to the theory that he had become a victim of the times—specifically, that he had been killed because of his opinions. Credit began to be given to the idea that Pasolini had been silenced because he had been telling the "truth", thereby making things difficult for the "hidden" forces, the "invisible fascisms", as he would have put it, which were drawing huge advantage from the contemporary chaos. One or more of the many targets of his attacks had retaliated; and their actions had confirmed the "veracity" and pertinence of Pasolini's views.

In the light of the irritation, disbelief and condescension with which Pasolini's socio-political analyses had been greeted when he was alive, this was a remarkable turn of affairs. Of course, paranoid times evoke paranoid solutions; in late 1975, however, with the scandals involving the clandestine activities of the Christian Democrats, of the petrol companies and of the secret services fresh in people's minds,[12] the suggestion that Pasolini, on account of the forthrightness of his views, had been the target of a shadowy and powerful conspiracy sounded all too plausible (and reassuring). Tellingly, such an explanation also fitted in rather well with the image which Pasolini had constructed for himself—most famously through the figure of Christ—of the persecuted *iustus* bravely proclaiming his uncomfortable convictions to a hostile and uncaring world. And the theory of a plot to take Pasolini's life served other ends too. It provided a handy and comforting bulwark against the shock of his sudden disappearance by giving his death a meaning which elevated it above the squalor of a darkened field on the periphery of Rome. While I do not wish to indulge in facile psychologizing, it is difficult to escape the impression that what also powered the "myth" of Pasolini's murder was a sense of guilt, especially among those who had been close to or critical of the writer—a way of countering the nagging feeling of somehow having contributed to the artist's demise by not giving him the attention and support he deserved. Transforming Pasolini's killing into an act of political martyrdom was a means of making amends. The revisionary implications of such an act of recompense, however, went far beyond the circumstances of his death. If Pasolini had been eliminated because of his opinions, then these needed drastic reconsideration. They could no longer be dismissed as the rantings of a crank; indeed, the whole of his career needed to be revalued. In particular, Pasolini's claims that all his artistic and intellectual activity, especially his striving after "realism", was driven by a profound sense of commitment, in which the public and the private, as well as life and art, merged, could no longer be as readily challenged by critics who were quite rightly disquieted by the aestheticizing and self-serving strains in his work.[13] A simpler, less troubling and more coherent Pasolini began to emerge, one whose ambiguities—artistic, moral, political, sexual—were conveniently forgotten or reshaped (for instance, the "scandalous" character of his work became associated with his perceived "truthfulness", thereby ensuring that even what was "problematic" in his *œuvre* could be adapted to the needs of the *mito*). Pasolini was transformed into a national "hero", the persecuted witness, the "honest" conscience of a "dishonest" society, a privileged source of truth and authority on both life and art, a veritable character of myth.[14]

To be accepted, Pasolini had to die; and, returning to my earlier conceit—the key one as far as I am concerned for understanding the lasting force of Pasolini's appeal—, he had to die in order to continue living.[15] More specifically and prosaically, control over his life and art had to pass to others (and, as we have been seeing and shall soon see again, issues of control play a key part in conditioning Pasolini's *fortuna* since his demise). Alive, he was too unpredictable, confrontational and eccentric ever to be a figure of consent and consensus. In such circumstances it should come as no surprise that Pasolini's death (and the events attending it)—the focus of three films, a wealth of books and persistent hypotheses— has not just fascinated in the manner of all whodunnits,[16] but has also been placed at the very heart of the interpretative strategies which have fashioned the *mito pasoliniano*,[17] since the "myth" is crucially built on the idea that proper understanding of the poet's significance was only achieved after his murder. Dead, he could be moulded into someone both less threatening and more "useful"; and it is striking how the "Pasolini myth" was not the creation of any one group, but may be said to express and embrace the sentiments and views of people of differing opinion.[18] In the climate of doubt, confusion and leaderlessness of the 1970s, the image of Pasolini as ethical guide to the community satisfied a deeply felt and widespread need for some form of societal co-hesion; in any case the poet was simply being assigned a role which Italians, given the vicissitudes of their fragmented history, have frequently been keen to impose on their writers, from Dante to d'Annunzio. Thus to this day, given the continuing tensions in Italian political and social life, the mantle of upright and ultimately non-partisan moral authority—Pasolini may well have declared himself a "Marxist", but his Marxism was "heretical" and not at the service of any party—continues to be draped over his shoulders. His name can be invoked both by the Italian left and by Bossi's *leghisti* to justify their policies, while the threat to the funding of the Fondo can be presented as an act of national disloyalty.[19] In addition, it is something of a commonplace to declare that Pasolini's *saggistica* has continued to be as relevant in the years since his death as it was in the 1960s and 1970s. The view appears to have gained currency—even though, as far as I am aware, it has not been critically tested—that his essays transcend both the time when they were written and the specific problems which they originally addressed.[20] Pasolini is thus allowed to express his opinions both in and on the present; and in this way too he continues to "live".

To insist, however, that Pasolini owes his lasting popularity to the persistent problems bedevilling post-war Italian society is without doubt excessive. Such an emphasis obscures the complexity and allure of the "myth". Thus it disregards the extent to which Pasolini, on account of the moral aura with which he has been endowed, as well as the perceived tragedy of his personal history, has succeeded in eliciting strong subjective reactions (for instance, several of those who have written on him openly identify themselves with the poet).[21] Pasolini's is a powerful "myth" precisely because it can speak both to the individual and to the community, thereby merging the social and the personal. Connected to this aspect, and once again casting light on the breadth and flexibility of the *mito*'s appeal, is what I would term Pasolini's "adaptability", that is, the way in which, because of the vagueness, imprecision and ambiguity of many of his declarations, especially in the 1960s and 1970s, it has not been difficult for others to "adapt" Pasolini to their own ends, and hence to make his moral authority their own.

All the ingredients—historical, biographical, artistic, social—necessary to bring the *mito pasoliniano* into being were in place at the moment of the poet's death. It is unlikely, however, that the "myth" would have made the lasting impact it has if it had not been given "official" sanction. To put it another way, not only did the *mito* have to be fabricated and disseminated and to appear relevant; it also had to be sustained in a valid manner. Even though it was principally the press that, in the days after Pasolini's murder, first redrew the writer's lineaments, decisive legitimacy was given to this revision when, between 1976 and 1982, thanks to what Robert Gordon not inappropriately calls "semi-hagiographical critical initiatives",[22] the *mito* became part of academic discourse. The transition was not difficult, since, time and again, the very intellectuals who had first propagated the "myth" in the newspapers were also the authors of scholarly studies. The alliance between academic publishing and the press, which, as we have seen, has never ceased its promotion of the poet, has had a determining effect on the development of Pasolini scholarship. Rather than examine what Pasolini actually wrote or filmed, too many, especially in Italy and France, have accepted the interpretative parameters established by the "semi-hagiographical critical initiatives". They have fallen prey, and continue to fall prey, to the temptation to subordinate Pasolini's *œuvre* to the "myth", or, at least, they have found it difficult to distinguish between the two; or they have even added new, often highly personal, layers to the *mito*—bad philology, as I have had occasion more than once to remark.[23] (Indeed, my fellow contributors, both in their studies collected in this volume and, in the main, in their other work on Pasolini, capably demonstrate how much actually separates the *œuvre* from the "myth".)[24] The lack of philological sensitivity has had other negative consequences. It has allowed criticism, historical reconstruction, personal musings and fiction to become confused;[25] it has encouraged scholars to make other questionably subjective and anachronistic claims about Pasolini (such as the recent North-American proposals which read *Empirismo eretico* as a work of Post-structuralist or Post-modernist theory);[26] and, most worryingly, it has led to an absence of rigour in the editing and publishing of his texts.[27]

Yet it is not the editorial deficiencies of individual works that constitute the most significant feature of the publishing history of Pasolini's texts since his death. This is to be sought rather in the key role which the publication of his works seems to have been made to play in sustaining and renewing the *mito*. As Gordon succinctly observes, "Canonization must depend on the availability of material above all."[28] Thus the suspicion arises that, rather than scholarly criteria, it has been primarily non-academic demands that have regulated how and when particular texts have been published.[29] As I indicate and document elsewhere in this volume, book-length editions of previously unknown works, of known yet unpublished texts, and of partially published and uncollected works have appeared with an almost mechanical recurrence since Pasolini's demise.[30] Not only has the way in which these have been carefully dosed ensured that Pasolini has been effectively kept in the public eye and an audience for his writings created and maintained: the regularity of their publication may also be said to have helped strengthen the impression, so crucial—in my view—for the success of the *mito*, that their author is still "alive". Like any living writer, Pasolini continues to write and publish.

It is, however, the choice of texts to print which, more than anything, points to the apparently programmed manner of their publication. Thus between 1976 and 1979 the majority of new texts released onto the market—*Lettere luterane* (1976), *Volgar' eloquio* (1976), *Le belle bandiere* (1977), *Il caos* (1979)—all tended to confirm the image, fashioned in the aftermath of his murder, of Pasolini as a major social commentator bravely expounding his uncompromised views.[31] The other works published during those years equally served to create and reinforce a positive idea of the poet. *Lettere agli amici* (1976) countered the impression that Pasolini was an isolated and cranky figure;[32] *Descrizioni di descrizioni* (1979) presented Pasolini as an honest reviewer who did not allow his judgements to be affected by sectional interests;[33] finally, the publication of a collection of pieces written before the fall of Fascism (1977), of his plays (1977 and 1979) and of a volume reproducing his drawings (1978) introduced areas of his intellectual and artistic activity which were largely unknown,[34] thereby highlighting the range of his interests and abilities—Pasolini truly was the Artist with a capital "A", whence the privileged nature of his insights. The correlation between the *mito pasoliniano* and this first phase of publication of new works by Pasolini is remarkable. All the texts present their author in a favourable light and provide a weighty counterbalance to the shocked reactions engendered by *Salò's* overt sado-masochism (even this possible blemish on the "myth", however, was quickly adapted to fit its requirements: the film was interpreted in an ethical key, while attempts to ban it were exposed as a new act of persecution).[35]

Yet an important group of Pasolini's *inediti* could be said to be "scandalous". Several works deal openly with homosexual themes, and hence needed to be handled with care. The way in which these texts have been published (or not) again appears to offer evidence of the careful control which Pasolini's literary executors have exerted over what has been made publicly available and thus over his posthumous reception. It was only once the *mito* had been firmly established and attitudes to sexual mores had visibly changed, in 1982, that *Amado mio* and *Atti impuri* were published.[36] By the early 1980s homosexuality had become much less of a taboo subject, while explicit depictions of sexual behaviour were widespread after the liberalization of Italian censorship laws. Nor does it seem just coincidence that the two Friulan novels were the texts chosen to introduce Pasolini's writing on homosexuality. With their lyricism and literariness, especially when compared to a work such as Tondelli's *Altri libertini,* which had appeared in 1980, *Amado mio* and *Atti impuri* had an old-fashioned *naïveté* and reticence about them which played down the potentially problematic nature of their subject-matter. If anything—and in sharp contrast to the stark representations of sex which had become increasingly part of Italian culture—Pasolini's rustic treatment of male homosexual desire had all the attributes of "art", and hence could be accommodated within the confines of the *mito.* Once Pasolini's credentials as a homosexual writer had been established, it was that much easier for other texts dealing with the same subject, most notably some of his letters, to be published, though it was not until 1992 that *Petrolio* finally appeared,[37] while there is still no news as to when the so-called *Quaderni rossi* will be made public, though excerpts from these may be found in Naldini's biography.

I should like to make one point absolutely clear at this juncture. My assessment so far of the history of Pasolini's posthumous publication is in no way intended to imply that I somehow subscribe to the opinion, expressed by some, that his *inediti,* or at least the more "problematic" among them, should not have been published. Such a position could not be further from my view of the matter. Not only do I firmly believe that all Pasolini's unpublished works should be, and should have been, made public as quickly as possible: I also believe that all his autographs should have been made easily and readily accessible to scholars—which is still far from the case.[38] What I do find troubling, nevertheless, is the effects on Pasolini's literary patrimony, and, by extension, on his reception, of the manner in which elements of the former have been introduced into the public domain. There is no doubt that the operation has been handled in a highly efficacious and skilful fashion as far as the needs of the *mito* are concerned. It is hard to say the same, however, as regards the claims of scholarship and—I would add, ultimately and more significantly—of Pasolini himself.

There are, I believe, two main ways in which academic work has been adversely affected. First, on account of the prolonged, and so far unabated, trickle of new works, as well as on account of the restrictions placed on consulting the bulk of the autograph material, it has been, and continues to be, difficult to arrive at satisfactory conclusions both about particular moments in Pasolini's life and about his career as a whole. In such circumstances it is perhaps not surprising that so much critical writing on Pasolini is marked by a lack of precision and a tendency towards subjective re-elaboration; or that it has been easy for the *mito* to fill the vacuum left by criticism. Pasolini is important, but the "myth" makes it arduous to recognize where exactly his importance might lie. Second, doubts cannot but surround the accuracy both of the texts published and of their supporting apparatus, since it is often not possible to check editorial decisions against the originals. Where this has been possible, there is no question that an unacceptable number of errors and imprecisions mars the work of editors.[39] The dominion which has been maintained over Pasolini's autographs, however, does not just influence the quality of new texts: it also affects the quality of texts which had been published during Pasolini's lifetime. As regards these, at present the only edition which might even begin to be termed "critical" is the 1985 Einaudi version of *Passione e ideologia*, whose constituent texts, according to the "Nota dell'editore", "sono stati controllati attentamente sugli originali. L'opera è stata cosí emendata da numerosi refusi e inesattezze" ["have been carefully checked against the originals. Many misprints and inaccuracies in the work have thus been corrected"].[40] There are, however, other texts which require similar verification, most notably *Ragazzi di vita*. We now know from Pasolini's own pen that the text of the novel published in 1955, which continues to be reprinted to this day, is not the version he intended to publish:

> Io sono precipitato in una serie di giorni atroci, con Garzanti: a un certo punto pareva che il romanzo non si dovesse pubblicare piú (per lo scandalo dei librai): ho dovuto fare correzioni, tagli

> [I have fallen into a series of terrible days, with Garzanti: at a certain moment it seemed that the novel was no longer going to be published (because of the shocked reaction of booksellers): I have had to make corrections, cuts]

—and all this at the proof stage.[41] The time has surely come for the original text to be reconstructed and made available, and for the 1955 published version to be recognized as the compromise that it undoubtedly is.[42]

Philology does not mix with "myth-making", any more than it sits comfortably with the commercial aspects of publishing. The former relies on openness and disinterest, while the latter depend on control and expediency. Of course one is grateful that Pasolini's texts have been made available and that publishing houses have been keen to print his works. The manner in which some of these posthumous books have been "packaged", however, leaves much to be desired. Thus the two-volume collection *Bestemmia: tutte le poesie* does not in fact bring together "all" Pasolini's poems: "Si pubblica qui l'intera opera in versi edita di Pier Paolo Pasolini, accresciuta da una scelta antologica di poesie inedite" ["All Pier Paolo Pasolini's previously published poems are printed here, as well as a selection of unpublished poems"].[43] Too often the advent of a new work by Pasolini, rather than an occasion for reflection, is transformed into a publishing and media event—an occasion to rehearse some of the now standard facets of the *mito* in order to boost sales. Naturally, it is a good thing that Pasolini's works should reach as wide an audience as possible; the ways in which this is done, however, are not neutral. They impinge—as I have tried to suggest—both on the letter of the texts and on their interpretation; they also tell us much—as we have seen—about the meanings and values which have accrued around Pasolini since his death.

The publication of one work, *Petrolio*, handily brings together the various points I have been attempting to make in the preceding paragraphs about the equivocal state in which Pasolini's texts and papers are now to be found. There is little doubt that the novel was aimed at as heterogeneous an audience as possible. On the one hand, the—both sexually and politically—uncompromising character of the work was loudly trumpeted in the press before and after its appearance;[44] while, on the other, the Einaudi edition presents itself as a model of philological sobriety. Both images are problematic. *Petrolio* is much more than a graphic account of sexual

activity and a violent polemic against post-war Italian political life; indeed Aurelio Roncaglia, in his "Nota filologica",[45] rightly warns against giving exaggerated weight to *Petrolio*'s "excessive" passages, and hence misreading the book (*P*, 575). As regards the editing of *Petrolio*, there is no doubt that considerable philological effort and acumen went into the preparation of its text.[46] What is of some concern, however, in textual critical terms, is the criteria employed to establish the text and the decisions taken to improve its "readability". Roncaglia underlines the "carattere frammentario e non rifinito dei materiali" ["fragmentary and unfinished character of the materials": *P*, 577] on which the published text is based, as well as the fact that "se Pasolini avesse finito il libro […] l'insieme dell'opera sarebbe risultato profondamente diverso da quello che abbiamo dinanzi" ["if Pasolini had finished the book (…) the overall appearance of the work would have been very different from the text that we have before us": *P*, 577]. He then goes on to stress, quite rightly, the difficulties created by the precarious state of the *Petrolio* autographs for the preparation of the published version—the difficulties, in particular, of arriving at what he terms elsewhere "la definizione delle procedure tecniche d'edizione" ["the definition of the technical editorial procedures": *P*, 576].

I am not persuaded, however, that the "correct" (*P*, 578) way of establishing editorial criteria and of solving the problem of "il singolarissimo stato di provvisorietà, frammentazione e sconnessione dei materiali" ["the quite singular condition of provisionality, fragmentation and disconnectedness of the materials": *P*, 578] was to rely, as Roncaglia and his collaborators did, on Pasolini's pseudo-philological notes appended to *La Divina Mimesis*. These notes form part of the *fictio* and overall structure of Pasolini's work,[47] and are highly specific to its particular poetics and ideology. In fact the more one considers in their entirety the three *note* appended to *La Divina Mimesis* (and not just the highly selective fragments from the first and third "notes" quoted by Roncaglia: *P*, 578) and then compares what these say about the character of their text both with the condition of the *Petrolio* papers as described by its editors and with the editing procedures they employed in establishing the text of the novel, the more the discrepancies between them become apparent. For instance, as "Per una 'Nota dell'editore'" explains, the fabricated reconstruction of *La Divina Mimesis* is rigidly structured according to

lo scrupolo dell'esattezza della successione cronologica [che] era l'unico scrupolo che io potessi avere. Mi sono dunque attaccato ad esso come a un'ancora di salvezza. Capisco naturalmente che la lettura di questi frammenti possa venir turbata da una successione cronologica che è quella della scrittura e non quella del senso. (*La Divina Mimesis*, p. 61)

[the scruple of the precision of the chronological succession (which) was the only scruple that I could have. I therefore attached myself to it as to a sheet-anchor. I understand, of course, that the reading of these fragments may be disturbed by a chronological succession which is that of the time of their composition rather than that of the meaning.]

Consequently, in the light of the invented history of *La Divina Mimesis*'s composition, the chronological order assigned to the published text is unlikely to have conformed to the anonymous and fictional murdered author's wishes. On the other hand, *Petrolio* is organized according to an artificial logic imposed by its dead historical author:

Pasolini [...] agli appunti della cartella [containing *Petrolio*] aveva dato un ordine non casuale (contraddicendo anche, in qualche caso, alla numerazione da lui stesso apposta in precedenza). Non c'è ora che da rispettare quest' ordine. (*P*, 580; and compare 570–71)

[Pasolini (...) had given to the notes in the folder a non-arbitrary order (contradicting, in some instances, the numbering which he himself had previously given). All that needs to be done now is respect this order.]

Another obvious discrepancy between the two works involves the fact that, as "Nota n. 1" underlines, *La Divina Mimesis* is a text "che non cancella nulla" ["which does not delete anything"], since it is based on the co-existence of its different "strati", "dove una nuova idea non cancelli la precedente, ma la corregga, oppure addirittura la lasci inalterata, conservandola formalmente come documento del passaggio del pensiero" ["where a new idea should not delete the previous one, but should correct it, or even leave it unaltered, formally preserving it as a document of the passing of thought": *La Divina Mimesis*, p. 57]. On the other hand, there is no suggestion

that *Petrolio* was supposed to have such an all-embracing con-
servationist remit; in fact, as the letter to Moravia, with which the
cartella and the printed text close, makes clear, *Petrolio* is a work
which accepts the rewriting and elimination of earlier versions (*P*,
545); indeed the editors have normally respected manuscript deletions.[48] The decision to draw on *La Divina Mimesis* is odd; and it
is odder still when it is remembered that Pasolini did leave annotations about the the nature of his *romanzo "in fieri"*, such as the letter
to Moravia, which could have been of use from an editorial point
of view. The most important such document is the untitled and
unnumbered "initial note" (*P*, 577) which explains the highly
complex ways in which "tutto PETROLIO (dalla seconda stesura)
dovrà presentarsi sotto forma di edizione critica di un testo inedito" ["the whole of PETROLIO (from its second version) will have to
present itself under the guise of a critical edition of an unpublished
text": *P*, 3]—a statement (and view of the novel) which is in stark
contrast with *La Divina Mimesis*'s express claim that it is not
"un'edizione critica" ["a critical edition": "Per una 'Nota dell'editore'", p. 61].

To be honest, I do not understand why, in textual critical terms,
it was necessary to involve *La Divina Mimesis*'s "notes" in defining
the editorial criteria for *Petrolio*. They are clearly not relevant; nor
is it easy to see how, in practice, they have been followed by
Petrolio's editors. In any case they are a literary invention and not
a contribution to textual scholarship by Pasolini. Fact and fiction,
as so often in the history of Pasolini's reception, have become
confused, so that their differences become irrelevant or forgotten.
The *mito* is indeed remarkably powerful: it even transpires in the
work of textual critics. Indeed, I suspect that the "myth" had a not
insignificant role to play in the preparation of *Petrolio* and especially in the drafting of the "Nota filologica". As Roncaglia insist-
ently acknowledges, the novel, because of its content (*P*, 575–78),
could have had a damaging effect on Pasolini's "image" (*P*, 576),
not least given the fact that "questo autore, a diciassette anni dalla
sua scomparsa, è considerato piú attuale che mai" ["this author,
seventeen years after his demise, is considered more relevant than
ever": *P*, 577]. One cannot but wonder what such "unscientific"
musings are doing in a "philological note", in particular since, as
Roncaglia himself declares, "nell'operazione ecdotica, il tecnico è
tenuto a non oltrepassare i confini professionali. In questa sede egli

deve inibirsi qualsiasi intrusione di gusto e di giudizio" ["in
editing a text, the technician is obliged not to go beyond professional limits. In this context he must forbid himself any intrusion of
taste and of judgement": *P*, 581]. Yet, in line with the workings of
the *mito*, a "personal" desire to protect Pasolini's "image" is clearly
discernible; and an important way in which such protection is
offered is by claiming that, by not publishing, Pasolini would
somehow be impoverished (*P*, 576–77, 579), and that the possibility
of doing something "autenticamente pasoliniano" ["authentically
Pasolinian": *P*, 578] would be lost. Not to publish would thus go
against that standard of absolute honesty which, according to the
mito, Pasolini embodied; it would also deprive the world of a work
of contemporary relevance—another facet, as we have seen, of the
"myth"—, and, most significantly, such a decision would go against
Pasolini's own wishes, as these apparently emerge from *La Divina
Mimesis*'s "notes" (*P*, 578–79). It is almost as if, still "alive" (once
more the *mito*'s key conceit peeps through), Pasolini himself were
directing the work of the editors:

> Chi oggi cura la pubblicazione si trova esattamente nella situazione
> che Pasolini aveva immaginato piú di vent' anni fa, e non può
> dunque che attenersi, con commossa e reverente docilità, al suo
> dettato. (*P*, 579)

> [Those who today prepare the text for publication find them-
> selves exactly in the situation that Pasolini had imagined more
> than twenty years ago, and therefore cannot but adhere, with
> sympathetic and reverent docility, to his prescription.]

As if to counter the "subjective" and emotional strains of the
edition's guiding principles, much is made of its fidelity to the
manuscript originals:

> Non si vede bisogno di manipolazione alcuna. [...] Nel nostro
> caso, non solo qualsiasi interpolazione, fosse pure per gettare il
> ponte d'una "transition quelconque" sui crepacci della provviso-
> ria stesura, ma anche qualsiasi espunzione di elementi (ce ne
> sono) che potessero risultare superflui o perturbanti, contraddi-
> rebbe inammissibilmente alla volontà dell'autore. Dalle premes-
> se discende che tutto in questo libro—anche le lacune e le incon-
> gruenze—debba essere considerato in un modo o nell'altro signi-
> ficativo, e dunque intangibile. (*P*, 579–80)

[There is no need for any kind of manipulation. (…) In our case, not just any interpolation, if only to throw the bridge of a "transition quelconque" over the crevasses of the provisional version, but also any excision of elements (and there are some) which might appear superfluous and disturbing, would inadmissibly contradict the author's wishes. It results from the premisses that everything in this book—even the lacunae and the incongruities—must needs be considered significant in one way or another, and thus untouchable.]

Yet, despite the steely rigour of this statement, the actual printed text, as we learn from the "Avvertenza" (*P*, v–vi), does make concessions to ensure "la possibilità d'una lettura scorrevole […] letterariamente godibile da tutti" ["the possibility of a smooth reading (…) which everyone can enjoy as literature": *P*, 580], by restoring any deletion "essenziale per la comprensione del contesto" ["essential for the understanding of the context": *P*, v], and thereby adding to the book's marketability. It thus cannot be said that "la trascrizione […] riflette fedelmente l'ultima redazione del romanzo" ["the transcription (…) faithfully reflects the novel's last redaction": *P*, v]; and until the folder containing the materials relating to *Petrolio* has been made widely available to scholars, doubts will certainly persist about the accuracy and criteria of the Einaudi text. What may be said with more confidence, however, is that the present version is a compromise between the demands of the *mito* and those of textual criticism. That a work of such philological effort as the 1992 edition of *Petrolio* should be so tarred, reveals, once and for all, the burden of the *mito pasoliniano*; it also highlights the desperate need for a truly critical edition of Pasolini's *opera omnia* to be undertaken by an independent group of scholars working with a coherent set of editorial conventions and outside the confines of commercial publishing.

Throughout his career Pasolini was deeply interested in the Italian literary tradition and keen to establish his own position within it. As John Welle and Patrick Rumble both show in their contributions to the present volume, Pasolini was careful to align his own work in relation to that of other eminent artists; equally, *Passione e ideologia*—the text which, in my view, shows Pasolini the essayist and literary critic at his best—stands as his major statement on the organic interrelationship between writers.[49] Pasolini not only wanted his own literary antecedents and influences to be recognized and appreciated: he also wanted to be a point of reference for other authors; he wanted his own works to live on in the writings of others.[50] Given Pasolini's high profile in the twenty or so years before his death and the impact of the *mito pasoliniano* since 1975, one might well imagine that Pasolini would be a major presence in contemporary Italian literature. Yet in general this is far from the case. Although it is impossible that any Italian writer since the 1950s could have been unaware of Pasolini,[51] the extent of his influence on the formal and artistic texture of Italian literature is surprisingly limited. With one major and important exception, there is no obvious Pasolinian line in modern Italian literature.

The one exception, of course, is the flourishing post-war tradition of dialect poetry which owes significant debts both to *Poesie a Casarsa* and to Pasolini's anthology, *Poesia dialettale del Novecento*, with its brilliant introductory assessment of the merits and uniqueness of dialect verse and its expressionist possibilities.[52] For the rest, signs of Pasolini's influence are rare: some echoes from *Le ceneri di Gramsci* in Amelia Rosselli's *Impromptu*,[53] and strongish traces of *Petrolio* in Walter Siti's *Scuola di nudo*—both Rosselli and Siti, interestingly, being writers on the margins (and personally close to Pasolini or to his family) drawing on another "marginal" writer. And it is Pasolini's "marginality", or more precisely his "subjectivity", of style, content and thought which makes him a difficult and alienating model to follow. For all his effort to associate his work with that of the great classic figures of literature, cinema and art, Pasolini's experimentation is highly personal and idiosyncratic; indeed, as I have argued elsewhere,[54] his *œuvre* is consistently self-referential—one might even say solipsistic. It constitutes a sort of "closed universe" into which it is often difficult to enter and from which it is far from easy to extract formal elements and a view of art which can be re-utilized in other contexts. In addition, and further limiting the appeal of his work for other writers, Pasolini's literary experimentation is frequently tied both to a specific historical moment and its aesthetic debates, and to his own theorizing. This is certainly the case with *Teorema* film and book and their complex links to *Empirismo eretico*, structuralism, semiotics, and the multi-media artistic concerns of the 1960s.[55] Similarly, as Lino Pertile has noted, "In the extremely mobile society of post-war Italy any attempt at mimicking the language of the people in any one of its ephemeral stages was bound to become quickly obsolescent. The language of Pasolini's Roman novels [...], precisely because it was modelled on that of the Roman *lumpenproletariat* of the 1950s, sounds now incredibly dated."[56] It is no coincidence that the most influential part of Pasolini's *œuvre* should have been his dialect verse. As Contini almost immediately noticed when *Poesie a Casarsa* appeared in 1942, the collection's importance resides in the fact that it opens up radically new possibilities for poetry in dialect:

> In questo fascicoletto si scorgerà la prima accessione della letteratura "dialettale" all'aura della poesia d'oggi, e pertanto una modificazione in profondità di quell'attributo. [...] L'esperienza di Pasolini si svolge [...] sopra un tendenzialmente pari livello linguistico [con la lingua letteraria].[57]
>
> [In this thin volume one will note the first accession of "dialect" literature to the atmosphere of today's poetry, and at the same time a profound change of that epithet. (...) Pasolini's experience takes place (...) on a level tending towards linguistic parity (with the literary language).]

And Pasolini himself must have felt the lasting allure and relevance of his youthful Friulan poetry when, in the 1970s, he decided to rewrite it (an operation whose complex significance is analysed with considerable sophistication elsewhere in this volume by Angela Meekins).

Pasolini's art is of limited practical appeal for other artists. It is not the stuff out of which new films, novels or poems are easily shaped. In saying this I am in no way suggesting that Pasolini's work is not, in itself, important; it is in fact its "self-centredness" which is both the source of its considerable originality and its "untranslatability"; in any case, importance and influence are far from synonymous. Yet judgements on Pasolini's position in Italian literature remain the preserve of specialists, of literary historians. They tell us little of his actual standing in Italian culture. Paradoxically, the less Pasolini has been present in the weave of the works of others (and, I suspect, the less he has been read), the more he has continued to "live" in the collective memory. The "myth" of the victimized *poeta-vate*, because of its stereotypical accessibility, has bridged the gap, created by the difficulties of much of Pasolini's art, between the poet and that mass audience which, when alive, he so wanted to reach. Not the least of the *mito*'s various allures is to be sought in the fact that it provides answers about Pasolini's import- ance without the need to read his books or see his films. To put it another way, the *mito* has been such a national and popular success precisely because Pasolini failed in his aim to embody through his work Gramsci's ideal of the "national-popular" artist. It is hard to see how, if his texts had been better known, the *mito pasoliniano* could have taken such a powerful hold.

The myth imprisons Pasolini and his work. It makes objective and informed judgement difficult; it discourages first-hand know- ledge of his *œuvre*, to the extent that even other artists prefer to engage with the *mito* rather than with the *opera*.[58] I suspect, too, that Pasolini's mask as "conscience" of Italy cannot fail to irritate all those artists who view what they do in less grandiose terms, and hence cannot but discourage direct contact with his texts. In particular, the image of Pasolini which many of the writers who have come to prominence since the 1980s—from Tondelli to the very recent Ammaniti, Brizzi and the writers of the *Gioventú cannibale* anthology—almost certainly must have is that of the quintessential establishment artist.[59] With his bourgeois morality, his sentimental commitment, his Romantic association with "great" art, Pasolini represents precisely that view of literature which they are so keen to rebut. Yet even though Pasolini did in part subscribe to such values during his lifetime, they are not so much his values as those of the *mito*. There is much more to Pasolini: for instance, he shares with Tondelli, Ammaniti and other young non-conformist writers an irritation with conventional behaviour and with the formal and thematic limits imposed on artists. Yet we find in their writings no evidence of an awareness of the links that bind them to Pasolini. The "myth" conceals and neutralizes all that is problem- atic in Pasolini; in particular, it ignores the terrible ambiguities, contradictions and doubts which are such a mark of his ideology and experimentation, and the fuel that propelled his unceasing and troubled search for new forms of expression. The *mito* thus ignores what is truly important in Pasolini: his linguistic and stylistic originality; his fusion of the lyrical and the political; his feverish attempts to deal with the discrepancies between life and art, which led him to formulate and reformulate theories of realism; his "mancanza di reticenza",[60] which challenged the idea that commitment and subjectivity were somehow at odds; his awareness of the complexity of Italian culture; his sense of the precariousness of art as evidenced by his obsessive reworking of his own texts and those of others; his willingness to "re-invent" himself. Where the "myth" sees stability and constancy, there is in fact flux and uncertainty. Ironically, a "myth" which presents its subject as "victim" can itself be accused of "victimization", of distorting and exploiting his achievements for its own ends. The time has surely come to leave Pasolini in peace and to see through the *mito*. Failure to do this can only continue to undermine efforts both to establish the corpus of his works and to evaluate his standing in Italian culture. Without the interference of the "myth", he may also find ways of speaking to other artists.

Pasolini—one is obliged to conclude—deserves a better reception than the one he has so far been accorded.[61]

NOTES

1   See G. Borgese, "Pasolini, l'archivio conteso", *Corriere della sera*, 1 July 1997, 3 (this article was summarized on the front page of the same issue of the *Corriere* under the title "Allarme per l'archivio Pasolini: rischia di finire all'estero"; the epigraph to this Introduction is taken from a statement by Laura Betti reproduced in "Pasolini, l'archivio conteso"); G. Borgese, "Pasolini bocciato dallo Stato, salvato dal Campidoglio", *Corriere della sera*, 2 July 1997, 23.

2   On the contribution made by the Fondo to Pasolini scholarship, see R. Gordon, "Recent Work on Pasolini in English", *Italian Studies*, 52 (1997), 180–88 (pp. 180–81); P. Rumble and B. Testa, "Introduction", in *Pier Paolo Pasolini: Contemporary Perspectives*, edited by P. Rumble and B. Testa (Toronto, University of Toronto Press, 1994), pp. 3–13 (p. 4).

3   See E. Golino, *Tra lucciole e Palazzo: il mito Pasolini dentro la realtà* (Palermo, Sellerio, 1995); R. Gordon, "Identity in Mourning: The Role of the Intellectual and the Death of Pasolini", *Italian Quarterly*, 32 (1995), 61–75, and "Recent Work on Pasolini in English"; R. Paris, "Viva Moravia, abbasso Pasolini", *L'espresso*, 3 May 1992, 84–86. See also C. Bordini, "Un coraggio a metà", in *Per Pasolini* by various authors (Milan, Gammalibri, 1982), pp. 29–36; G. Scalia, *La mania della verità* (Bologna, Cappelli, 1978), who, as early as 1976, had interesting things to say about how Pasolini "è diventato 'di consumo'" (pp. 31–33, 37); D. Ward, *A Poetics of Resistance: Narrative and the Writings of Pier Paolo Pasolini* (Madison, NJ, Fairleigh Dickinson University Press, 1995), pp. 13–23. For an excellent analysis of Pasolini's relationship with the press while he was still alive see T. De Mauro, "La stampa italiana e Pasolini", in *Pasolini:*

cronaca giudiziaria, persecuzione, morte, edited by L. Betti (Milan, Garzanti, 1977), pp. 246–75.

4   Robert Gordon too recognizes the impact of what he calls "Pasolini the phenomenon" on academic writing about the poet: "With a figure like Pasolini, given the extent to which he has been mythicized and instrumentalized beyond all recognition before and since his death, by others and by himself, the study of his reception swiftly and rightly acquires central significance in the secondary literature. [...] Pasolini the phenomenon—that is, all the auxiliary, subjectivizing, distorting appendages to his work—interferes with the texts or films" ("Recent Work on Pasolini in English", p. 183). I attempt to describe the constituent elements of the *mito*, as well as the context in which it was created, in the following section.

5   The "Critical Bibliography" at the end of this book gives a good preliminary idea of the wealth of criticism on Pasolini. I am not aware of a detailed bibliography of critical writing on the poet; see, however, *Tra continuità e diversità: Pasolini e la critica*, edited by P. Voza (Naples, Liguori, 1990).

6   On Italian intellectuals, see, at least, *Letteratura italiana: il letterato e le istituzioni*, edited by A. Asor Rosa (Turin, Einaudi, 1982); *Storia d'Italia: intellettuali e potere*, edited by C. Vivanti (Turin, Einaudi, 1981).

7   See R. Gordon, "Identity in Mourning".

8   See *Pasolini: cronaca giudiziaria*; R. Gordon, "Identity in Mourning", especially pp. 61–62; I. Moscati, *Pasolini e il teorema del sesso: 1968: dalla Mostra del cinema al sequestro: un anno vissuto nello scandalo* (Milan, Saggiatore, 1995).

9   See E. Siciliano, *Vita di Pasolini* (Milan, Rizzoli, 1981), pp. 441–61; though Siciliano also twice makes the unsubstantiated claim that just before his death Pasolini's popularity was increasing among the young (pp. 460–61) (I suspect that this claim, like so much of Siciliano's "life", is made in the service of the *mito pasoliniano*). See also, by Siciliano, "L'odiato Pasolini", *Il mondo*, 14 July 1972. On Pasolini's difficult relationship with other writers and intellectuals see E. Golino, *Tra lucciole*, pp. 74–81, 91–113; as well as De Mauro's contribution to the present book.

10   *Pasolini: Forms of Subjectivity* (Oxford, Oxford University Press, 1996). See also Gordon's essay in the present collection.

11   See R. Gordon, "Identity in Mourning", pp. 62–63, 71 n. 9. Angelo Romanò's assessment of Pasolini's killing is not atypical: "Parlare di Pasolini, rievocarlo, tenerlo vivo nella memoria è dunque anche un impegno civile, in questa Italia di misteri e di trame, di complotti impuniti, di tradimenti e di agguati. Non rassegnarsi a considerare fatale il disegno che presumibilmente la sua morte nasconde è un dovere per chi crede che il futuro del nostro paese non deve essere consegnato alle mani dei criminali e degli assassini" ("Introduzione", in E. Siciliano, *Vita*, pp. 5–13 [p. 6]). See also M. Bettarini, "Pasolini, le culture e noi", in *Perché Pasolini: ideologia e stile di un intellettuale militante*, edited by G. De Santi and others (Florence, Guaraldi, 1978), pp. 215–23 (p. 216).

12   See G. De Lutiis, *Storia dei servizi segreti in Italia* (Rome, Editori Riuniti, 1984); G. Galli, *L'Italia sotterranea* (Bari, Laterza, 1983), pp. 134–38.

13   See, most notably, A. Asor Rosa, *Scrittori e popolo* [1965], third edition (Rome, Samonà and Savelli, 1969), pp. 349–449; G. C. Ferretti, *Letteratura e ideologia* [1964], second edition (Rome, Editori Riuniti, 1974), pp. 163–356. See also F. Fortini, *Attraverso Pasolini* (Turin, Einaudi, 1993), pp. 3–51. Elsewhere in the present volume Sam Rohdie provides a clear explanation of the peculiarities

of Pasolini's notion of "realism", while Joseph Francese examines the idiosyncrasy of his political commitment.

14 See R. Gordon, "Identity in Mourning", especially pp. 62–67, 70, 71 n. 11. On the persistence of the "myth" see E. Golino, *Tra lucciole*, in particular pp. 15–72, 111–12.

15 The idea that Pasolini is still alive, that he continues to be "in contact with the whole world", is also a component of the *mito*: see, for instance, F. Camon, "PPP contro PPP", *Panorama*, 3 Oct. 1993, 135–36 (p. 135). See also n. 20 below.

16 The three films are: *Le ceneri di Pasolini* (1994; directed by Pasquale Misuraca); *Pasolini: un delitto italiano* (1995; directed by Marco Tullio Giordana); *Nerolio* (1996; directed by Aurelio Grimaldi). For written accounts and interpretations of Pasolini's death see, for instance, D. Bellezza, *Morte di Pasolini* (Milan, Mondadori, 1981), and *Il poeta assassinato: una riflessione, un'ipotesi, una sfida sulla morte di Pier Paolo Pasolini* (Venice, Marsilio, 1996); G. Contini, "Testimonianza per Pier Paolo Pasolini" [1980], in his *Ultimi esercizî ed elzeviri (1968–1987)* (Turin, Einaudi, 1988), pp. 389–95 (p. 395); D. Fernandez, *Dans la main de l'ange* (Paris, Grasset, 1982; Italian translation *Nelle mani dell'angelo* [Milan, Bompiani, 1983]); M. T. Giordana, *Pasolini: un delitto italiano* (Milan, Mondadori, 1994); E. Siciliano, *Vita*, pp. 19–40 (and see also E. Siciliano, "Non cercava la morte", *L'espresso*, 22 Oct. 1995, 34–35); S. Vassalli, "Avrebbe aperto un ristorante…", *Panorama*, 3 Oct. 1993, 139–41; G. Zigaina, *Hostia: trilogia della morte di Pasolini* (Venice, Marsilio, 1995). Even Giuseppe Pelosi, the youth convicted of Pasolini's murder, has written a book, with the help of a journalist, which recounts his fateful encounter with Pasolini and its impact on his life: *Io, Angelo Nero* (Rome, Sinnos, 1995). On recent efforts to re-open the Pasolini murder case, see E. Vinci, "Pasolini, si riparte: oggi la decisione", *Repubblica*, 4 Sept. 1995. See also E. Golino, *Tra lucciole*, pp. 47, 49, 57–59, 61, 135–48.

17 See, for instance, M. Bettarini, "Pasolini, le culture e noi", pp. 215–16; E. Siciliano, *Vita*, pp. 492–93.

18 See R. Gordon, "Identity in Mourning", especially p. 63.

19 On the left's appropriation of Pasolini see *Perché Pasolini*; M. Fortunato, "Pasolini, avanti gli eredi", *L'espresso*, 15 Sept. 1985, 30–31; on the Lega's recourse to Pasolini, see "Vostro Pier Paolo leghista", *L'espresso*, 3 Oct. 1993, 102–06; on Italy continuing to mistreat Pasolini by not funding the Fondo, see G. Borgese, "Pasolini, l'archivio conteso", p. 3. See also E. Golino, *Tra lucciole*, pp. 29, 34, 36, 45–46, 50, 54, 65; M. Serri, "Un governissimo per Pier Paolo: se lo contendono tutti, dal Msi al Pds", *L'espresso*, 3 May 1992, 88.

20 See, for instance, A. Asor Rosa, "Pasolini il veggente", *Rinascita*, 11 Nov. 1990, 60–61; S. Mauro, "Una vita futura che inizia adesso", *Il mattino di Padova*, 12 Oct. 1985; G. Raboni, "Poeta senza poesia", in *L'espresso*, 22 Oct. 1995, 25; A. Romanò, "Introduzione", p. 13; C. Segre, "Prefazione", in P. P. Pasolini, *Il portico della morte*, edited by C. Segre (Rome, Associazione Fondo Pier Paolo Pasolini, 1988), pp. ix–xxvii (p. xxiii). Robert Gordon documents how "prophetic" powers were ascribed to Pasolini in the days after his murder: "Identity in Mourning", p. 62; see also E. Golino, *Tra lucciole*, pp. 23, 32, 46. It is suggestive, therefore, that *L'espresso* of 22 October 1995 should have announced its commemoration of the twentieth anniversary of Pasolini's death with the front-page slogan "Un profeta e il suo paese: Pasolini che cosa vive ancora". Employing a variation on the same idea, *Panorama* of 3 October 1993 published a piece in which ten intellectuals were asked what Pasolini would

have made of Tangentopoli (M. Ajello, "Riscritti corsari", *Panorama*, 3 Oct. 1993, 134–43). Despite my reservations concerning the trend to ascribe "prophetic" powers to Pasolini, it is certainly true that he did occasionally demonstrate an uncanny prescience as regards broad general developments in modern life. It is enough to think of his assessments of the future of consumerism and of television. The significance of such assessments, however, should not be exaggerated: Pasolini was far from alone in the 1960s and 1970s in warning about the dangers inherent in advanced neo-capitalism. Most radical thinkers influenced by the Frankfurt School or by Althusser were expressing opinions not dissimilar to his.

21 See for instance S. Rohdie, The *Passion of Pier Paolo Pasolini* (London, BFI; Bloomington, Indiana University Press, 1995).

22 "Pasolini's Strategies of Self-construction" in this volume, p. 41.

23 See, most recently, my "Pier Paolo Pasolini: teoremi e teorie", in *Lezioni su Pasolini*, edited by T. De Mauro and F. Ferri (Ripatransone, Sestante, 1997), pp. 99–112. Cesare Segre has important things to say about the problems, especially in Italy, affecting the study of Pasolini: "Io faccio autocritica ma gli altri stanno zitti", *L'espresso*, 21 Feb. 1988, 102–03. See also E. Golino, *Tra lucciole*, p. 18.

24 I am not advocating that all writing on Pasolini follow the same "philological" approach. Important studies of the poet have been written applying a variety of methods (for an assessment of some of these see R. Gordon, "Recent Work on Pasolini in English" and D. Ward, *A Poetics*, pp. 13–21). Indeed, one of the contributors to this volume, Sam Rohdie, has written an excellent and idiosyncratic book (see n. 21 above) which is rich both in interpretative insight and in personal reflection. What I am underlining is the extent to which scholarly work on Pasolini, often—I suspect—unconsciously, has been affected by non-scholarly concerns. In such circumstances, I believe it is crucial that we learn to separate the man and his texts from the "myth". Not an easy task, I admit, given Pasolini's own penchant for mythicization.

25 See, for instance, the texts cited in notes 9, 11 and 16 above.

26 See, in particular, G. Bruno, "Heresises: The Body of Pasolini's Semiotics", *Cinema Journal*, 30, iii (1991), 29–42; T. de Lauretis, "Re-reading Pasolini's Essays on Cinema", *Italian Quarterly*, 21–22 (1980–81), 159–66; M. Viano, *A Certain Realism: Making Use of Pasolini's Film Theory and Practice* (Berkeley etc., University of California Press, 1993). For a thorough critique of these studies, as well as a clear exposition of Pasolini's theoretical writings, see Christopher Wagstaff's essay in the present volume.

27 For a presentation and analysis of several questionably edited texts, see "Pasolini, Friuli, Rome (1950–51): Historical and Philological Notes", in the present collection, pp. 268–69, 274–80. See also the discussion of *Petrolio* below.

28 R. Gordon, "Recent Work on Pasolini in English", p. 181.

29 The issue of the way in which Pasolini has been published since 1975 is a delicate one; and I am more than aware that, in trying to address the question, I am entering into difficult territory which others have studiously avoided. Nevertheless, it is the responsibility of scholarship to confront, in as balanced a manner as possible, even the most precariously tricky of problems, especially when these have a direct bearing on the manner in which a field of knowledge has been delimited. It is this that interests me: the relationship

between Pasolini's reception and his editorial history, and in particular the impact which the former has had on the quality of the latter. As regards the appearance of Pasolini's works since his murder, Gordon notes that "partly commercial considerations need to be made about the steady drip of newly published, newly collected or anthologized primary material by Pasolini" ("Recent Work on Pasolini in English", p. 181 n. 2).

30 "Pasolini, Friuli, Rome (1950–51)", p. 268.
31 *Lettere luterane* (Turin, Einaudi, 1976); *Volgar' eloquio*, edited by A. Piromalli and D. Scarfoglio (Naples, Athena, 1976); *Le belle bandiere: dialoghi 1960–1965*, edited by G. C. Ferretti (Rome, Editori Riuniti, 1977); *Il caos*, edited by G. C. Ferretti (Rome, Editori Riuniti, 1979).
32 *Lettere agli amici (1941–1945)*, edited by L. Serra (Milan, Guanda, 1976).
33 *Descrizioni di descrizioni*, edited by G. Chiarcossi (Turin, Einaudi, 1979). Revealingly, the blurb on the back cover describes Pasolini's approach as a reviewer thus: "Tra luce la passione del lettore disinteressato e si può misurare ad ogni passo l'indifferenza alle leggi di mercato e agli obblighi del recensore-amico."
34 *Pier Paolo Pasolini e "Il setaccio" (1942–1943)*, edited by M. Ricci (Bologna, Cappelli, 1977); *Affabulazione; Pilade* (Milan, Garzanti, 1977); *Porcile; Orgia; Bestia da stile* (Milan, Garzanti, 1979); *I disegni 1941–1975*, edited by G. Zigaina (Milan, Scheiwiller, 1978). The screenplay of an unmade film, *San Paolo*, was also published by Einaudi in 1977.
35 For a selection of early reactions to *Salò*, see *Da Accattone a Salò*, edited by V. Boarini and others (Bologna, Tipografia Compositori, 1982), pp. 125–40. See also *Pasolini: cronaca giudiziaria*, pp. 213–18.
36 *Amado mio preceduto da Atti impuri*, edited by C. D'Angeli (Milan, Garzanti, 1982).
37 *Petrolio*, edited by M. Careri and G. Chiarcossi under the supervision of A. Roncaglia (Turin, Einaudi, 1992).
38 See "Pasolini, Friuli, Rome (1950–51)", pp. 268–69.
39 See "Pasolini, Friuli, Rome (1950–51)", pp. 268–69, 274–80.
40 "Nota dell'editore", in P. P. Pasolini, *Passione e ideologia (1948–1958)*, with an introductory essay by Cesare Segre (Turin, Einaudi, 1985), p. xxii. The "Nota" is unsigned and there is no indication in the book as to the identity of the volume's editor.
41 Letter to the editors of *Officina* dated 19 May 1955, in *Lettere 1955–1975*, edited by N. Naldini (Turin, Einaudi, 1988), p. 67. For an account of the changes and cuts, see Pasolini's letter to Livio Garzanti dated 11 May 1955, in *Lettere 1955–1975*, pp. 65–66.
42 For information on the autograph material relating to *Ragazzi di vita* see L. de Nardis, "Sulla prima redazione di *Ragazzi di vita* e di *Una vita violenta*", *Revue des études italiennes*, 28, ii–iii (1981), 123–39; W. Siti, "Nota al testo", in P. P. Pasolini, *Storie della città di Dio* (Turin, Einaudi, 1995), pp. 171–73.
43 W. Siti, "Nota al testo", in *Bestemmia: tutte le poesie*, edited by G. Chiarcossi and W. Siti, 2 vols (Milan, Garzanti, 1993), xxv–xxx (p. xxv).
44 See, for instance, A. Arbasino, "Bruciare *Petrolio*?", *Repubblica*, 27 Oct. 1992, 27; D. Pasti, "L'inferno di Pier Paolo", *Repubblica*, 27 Oct. 1992, 27; C. Valentini, "Scandaloso Pier Paolo", *L'espresso*, 1 Nov. 1992, 74–77. For an interesting collection of critical analyses of the novel, written approximately a year after its publication, and hence still touched by the polemics surround-

ing its appearance, see *A partire da "Petrolio": Pasolini interroga la letteratura*, edited by C. Benedetti and M. A. Grignani (Ravenna, Longo, 1995).

45 A. Roncaglia, "Nota filologica", in *P*, 567–81.

46 See the critical apparatus to the novel as well as Roncaglia's "Note". On *Petrolio*'s (possible) form, see G. Patrizi, "*Petrolio* e la forma romanzo", and M. A. Grignani, "Questione di stile?", both in *A partire da "Petrolio"*, pp. 15–25 and 137–51, respectively.

47 P. P. Pasolini, *La Divina Mimesis* (Turin, Einaudi, 1975), pp. 57–62. Although I do not believe that *La Divina Mimesis* can help in establishing the text of *Petrolio*, this does not mean that, from a critical-exegetical perspective, one text cannot help to illuminate the other.

48 For a fuller discussion of the editorial problems relating to the deletions, see below.

49 For a brilliant assessment of *Passione e ideologia*, see C. Segre, "Prefazione", in P. P. Pasolini, *Passione e ideologia* (Turin, Einaudi, 1985), pp. v–xxii.

50 See E. Golino, *Pasolini: il sogno di una cosa* (Bologna, Mulino, 1985).

51 "Intorno alla metà degli anni cinquanta si ha la rivelazione di un poeta che mostra subito tutte le caratteristiche del protagonista: figura pubblica, attore culturale rapidamente al centro della scena, Pier Paolo Pasolini" (A. Berardinelli, "La poesia: l'area sperimentale", in *Manuale di letteratura italiana, IV: Dalla unità d'Italia alla fine del Novecento*, edited by F. Brioschi and C. Di Girolamo [Turin, Bollati Boringhieri, 1996], pp. 460–71 [p. 460]).

52 *Poesia dialettale del Novecento*, edited by M. Dell'Arco and P. P. Pasolini (Parma, Guanda, 1952). The introductory essay was subsequently used by Pasolini to open *Passione e ideologia*.

53 See E. Tandello, *La passione mai spenta: la poesia di Amelia Rosselli* (Pisa, Giardini, 1998).

54 "Pier Paolo Pasolini: teoremi e teorie".

55 See "Pier Paolo Pasolini: teoremi e teorie".

56 L. Pertile, "The Italian Novel Today: Politics, Language, Literature", in *The New Italian Novel*, edited by Z. G. Barański and L. Pertile (Edinburgh, Edinburgh University Press, 1993), pp. 1–19 (p. 12).

57 "Al limite della poesia dialettale" [1943], in G. Contini, *Pagine ticinesi*, edited by R. Broggini, second edition (n. p., Salvioni, 1986), pp. 116–21 (pp. 116, 118).

58 See, for instance, G. Raboni, "Poeta senza poesia". See also A. Codacci-Pisanelli, "Pasolini: giudicato dagli scrittori under 30: non chiamatelo Maestro", *L'espresso*, 22 Oct. 1995, 26–28.

59 See *Gioventú cannibale: la prima antologia italiana dell'orrore estremo*, edited by D. Brolli (Turin, Einaudi, 1996). See also A. Codacci-Pisanelli, "Pasolini: giudicato dagli scrittori under 30"; F. De Melis, "L'abiura del corsaro", *Il manifesto*, 24 Oct. 1993.

60 A. Berardinelli, "La poesia: l'area sperimentale", p. 461.

61 I should like to thank my friends Robert Gordon, Giulio Lepschy, Angela Meekins and David Ward for their excellent comments on an earlier version of this Introduction.

PASOLINI'S STRATEGIES
OF SELF-CONSTRUCTION

Robert Gordon

After his death in November 1975, Pasolini's reputation among literary and cultural critics underwent a radical, if perhaps predictable, transformation. From being widely discounted as an unoriginal and irritating *provocateur* in his polemical articles in the *Corriere della sera* and elsewhere (despite, or perhaps because of the popular chord they struck),[1] and from being heavily criticized for the thinly veiled, disingenuous pornography of the *Trilogia della vita* films,[2] for many observers he immediately took on a more or less explicit aura of moral authority and integrity. A survey of print-media reactions to his death reveals a remarkably consistent set of facets of Pasolini acknowledged by writers of very different political and cultural persuasions: these centre around a clearly Romantic vision of the artist as an isolated, persecuted figure, who is thereby a privileged source of truth or of an absolute—even mystic—insight into reality and art.[3] From such responses, the well-touted *mito pasoliniano* grew, promoted by a series of collective, semi-hagiographical critical initiatives.[4] In secondary reaction to these, a number of studies after 1980 mapped out the parameters for a return to a more rigorous and perhaps more traditionally based academic analysis of Pasolini's work; and the most successful of these remain the most convincing global accounts of Pasolini's *œuvre* so far produced.[5] The latter, however, despite their successes, are not entirely free of compromise with the terms and attitudes of the mythologizers. Both groups tend to treat either the life or the work or both as a coherent entity which may be decoded and thus read as symptomatic either of an external perspective brought by the critic, or of a unified idea of the "meaning" of "Pasolini".[6] Both present themselves as autonomous and in control of their object of analysis; I would argue, however, that in making such assumptions both groups are disingenuous to a significant degree. Both appropriate certain aspects of Pasolini without fully acknowledging the extent to which he refuses to serve as a receptacle for "innocent" or "authentic" sets of meanings. Pasolini himself, in his actions and in his texts,[7] always impinges upon, conditions and circumscribes the hermeneutic potential he creates. His own discursive practices emanate a complex, centripetal force of gravity which draws in and distorts dependent discourses, of which criticism is a major exemplar. He constructs himself in his own discourses and in those of others, autocratically and always ambiguously, both through cynical acts of *mauvaise foi* and through reflexive textual patterning. What follows is a preliminary investigation of the features of the practices which create such a gravitational force, and aims to serve as a corrective to earlier, more innocent intepretations of Pasolini.

Any discussion of the role of self-construction in Pasolini must start from the primary and absolute importance assigned in his value system to selfhood and to the potentially overwhelming expressivity of the self and its desires. This is clear from his earliest works, whether in the posthumously published autobiographical works, *Amado mio* and *Atti impuri*,[8] which both draw heavily on his own personal diary, the so-called *Quaderni rossi*,[9] or in the animistic idyll, written in Friulan dialect, of the first part of *La meglio gioventú* (*TLP*, 1–172),[10] where the figure of the "io" is at the centre of a fluid innocent world of ambiguous desire and precious song.[11] But it is in the Italian lyrics of *L'usignolo della Chiesa Cattolica* (*TLP*, 283–413) that the obsession with introversion is transformed and promoted into an ethical and aesthetic axiom. In "La Crocifissione" a vision of Christ on the cross is experienced as an epiphany of a particular kind:

> Bisogna esporsi (questo insegna
> il povero Cristo inchiodato?),
> la chiarezza del cuore è degna
> di ogni scherno, di ogni peccato
> di ogni piú nuda passione...
> (questo vuol dire il Crocifisso?
> sacrificare ogni giorno il dono
> rinunciare ogni giorno al perdono
> sporgersi ingenui sull'abisso).

> Noi staremo offerti sulla croce,
> [...]
> per testimoniare lo scandalo.
> (TLP, 376–77)

[We must expose ourselves/(is this what poor Christ nailed up teaches us?),/the clarity of the heart is worthy/of every derision, of every sin/of every barest passion.../(does the Crucifixion mean this?/sacrificing every day the gift/renouncing every day forgiveness/leaning out ingenuous over the abyss).//We shall be offered on the cross/(...)/to bear witness to the scandal.]

The matrix of images of display and openness ("esporsi" [see *EE*, 274], "chiarezza", "ogni piú nuda passione", "sporgersi ingenui", "offerti") creates a rhetoric around the self—the "si" being reinforced by elaborate alliteration of its phonemes—in which the private is assigned value and meaning by being made both innocent and authentic, and also by being projected into a public role ("testimoniare lo scandalo"). Elsewhere in *L'usignolo* this rhetorical dynamic is complemented by a confessional idiom through which the self is validated and purified, or rendered ambiguously innocent again by its articulation in a public, ritualized language:

> No, non ho madre, non ho sesso,
> ho ucciso il padre col silenzio,
> amo la mia pazzia di acqua e assenzio,
> amo il mio giallo viso di ragazzo,
> le innocenze che fingo e l'isterismo
> che celo nell'eresia o lo scisma
> del mio gergo, amo la mia colpa [...].
> ("Lingua", TLP, 353)

[No, I have no mother, I have no sex,/I have killed the father with silence,/I love my madness of water and absinth,/I love my yellow boy's face,/the innocences which I pretend and the hysteria/which I hide in the heresy and schism/of my slang, I love my guilt (...).]

In both cases the dynamic is based on a paradoxical combination of expression of the self's innermost, guilt-ridden being and an apparent inability to control or dictate the terms of expression. The full force of impersonal compulsion in the declaration "*Bisogna* esporsi" becomes apparent: the self is set against its own profound impulses, and thus the apparent authenticity of the expression/exposition is further reinforced—unable to control, "he" is incapable of deceit, he is innocent.

A large swathe of the *topoi* of Pasolini's later work may be traced back to this nexus of images and patterns. The sheer variety of genres, idioms and arenas in which he operated comes to suggest that the processes of expression/exposition are not conditioned by formal constraints. Indeed they are seen as the sole guarantors of specificity in the "magma" of formal plurality. Selfhood transcends its media. More specifically, the "buie viscere" ["dark entrails"] of "Le ceneri di Gramsci" (*TLP*, 223–35) are precisely the same locus of authentic innermost being, displayed as helplessly in conflict—"lo scandalo del contraddirmi" ["the scandal of contradicting myself"]—with a reasonable "coscienza". The bitter parody of confession and self-exposure in the mock-interview of "Una disperata vitalità" (*TLP*, 726–48); the naive, essentialist primitivism of his attitude towards the third world in films, poems and novels after 1960;[12] the violent poetry of desire in his verse tragedies;[13] his defence in *Officina* of Mario Luzi's poetry, despite its hermeticism, because of its "authenticity";[14] the loaded distinction between communication and expression which dominates the sociolinguistic polemic "Nuove questioni linguistiche":[15] all these, and many other possible examples, grow out of the rhetoric of authenticity, the poetics of expressivity and the expressivity of the poetic which govern the economy of selfhood in Pasolini's work.

Now that the central importance and nature of a vision of selfhood in Pasolini's work has been established, it is not difficult to undermine its reliability, to reclaim it as rhetoric. Franco Fortini, the subtlest early reader of Pasolini, dismissed the effect of authenticity in Pasolini's work as a product of its exact opposite: "Il proposito di un'autenticità attraverso l'inautentico [...] è la formula morale piú cara a Pasolini" ["The idea of an authenticity through the inauthentic (...) is the moral formula Pasolini holds dearest"]. He noted the nature of his work as performance, or masquerade—a pretence of expressivity, a delusion of exemplarity—, and later sharply reiterated this in his epigram "Per Pasolini":

> Ormai se ti dico buongiorno ho paura dell'eco,
> tu disperato teatro, sontuosa rovina.[16]

[These days if I greet you I'm afraid of the echo,/you desperate spectacle, sumptuous ruin.]

Pasolini's noisy and overbearing attempts to make his presence felt, under this schema, would thus indicate a centrifugal dynamic, a sublimation of the void at the centre of the self-in-language into a pathologically fantastic construct. Inauthenticity would account for the cynical manipulation of media and idioms for the falsification, in bad faith, of self-image. From this sort of reading derive compelling comparisons with d'Annunzio and the possibility of synthesizing life and art, imbricating one into the other, to attain meaning.[17] And indeed a significant degree of this sort of cynicism can be identified in Pasolini. His poetry is always mannered and dense, in constant manipulative tension with rhetorical and prosodic tropes largely abandoned by modern poets (for example, rhyme, *terzine*, popular song forms). His films pretend to a grandiose exemplarity by deploying mythical and Biblical narratives as vehicles for self-expression. He "cynically" positions himself as the *escluso* or the *poète maudit*, while apparently refusing such labels,[18] and while largely disavowing their origin in his homosexuality.[19] And despite such trumpeted isolation, he gradually acquires considerable cultural and political power, promoting young writers, actors and film-makers, and intervening to great effect in political debates. He himself makes much of the idea of cynicism in justifying his decision to write a column for the apolitical, neo-capitalist, consumerist magazine *Tempo illustrato*: "Io approffitto delle strutture capitalistiche per esprimermi: e lo faccio, perciò, *cinicamente*" ["I exploit capitalist structures to express myself: I therefore do so *cynically*": *Il caos*, p. 38]. This statement may be applied more broadly to his myriad activities in print, publishing and film media, which he pursued refusing to "avere paura della sede",[20] to be afraid of *where*, or in which arena, he spoke out.

It is again worth noting, however, the basis of the justification in the primacy of self-expression ("esprimermi"). Indeed, the acquiescence to cynicism or ideological inauthenticity for the sake of an overriding impulse to express the self in public points to the inadequacy of the Fortinian accusation, despite its initial corrective validity. For if the rhetoric of authenticity is not to be taken at face value, neither in turn is its reversal, the simple deception of the inauthentic. It is rather that these two rhetorics are both traces of an order which transcends their "true" or "false" visions of selfhood. This order may be termed subjectivity—a process which produces through signifying practices the dual effects of selfhood already outlined, and which subsumes both these and others, constructing a space populated by multiple images and traces of selfhood. It is by analysing the processes of such a subjectivity that the complex and plural strategies of self-construction in Pasolini may best be elucidated. In what follows, three strategies, each exemplified by a different order of signifying practice, will be examined in turn, in an attempt to set out some preliminary possibilities for understanding the operations of subjectivity in Pasolini. It is worth noting that the very dynamic under scrutiny dictates that each strategy could also be traced in other signifying practices, but an extreme degree of sampling is inevitable here. First, his poetry may be shown to illustrate textual strategies of self-construction; second, Pasolini's journalism shows the act or the pragmatics of public intervention as itself loaded with meaning for subjectivity; and, finally, elements of his work in cinema, and in particular the formal genesis of screenplay and film, demonstrate how subjectivity also operates between and across momentary formal stability, in a space constantly projected forward, "ancora da farsi".

THE LANGUAGE OF SUBJECTIVITY

Pasolini's poetic style is broadly characterized by a restless variation in register and form, underpinned by an insistent web of modulated iteration—of syntactic structures, lexicon and poetic object. The former provides contexts against which the modulation of the latter is set into relief as a significant operation. In *L'usignolo*, for example, the dominant linguistic register is Biblical, confessional or litanistic. In *Trasumanar e organizzar*, a less immediately apparent but powerful context is provided by the recourse to press-language pastiches ("Comunicati all'ANSA", *TLP*, 899–903, 972) or the pamphletistic rhetoric of the student movement ("Poesia della tradizione", *TLP*, 960–62). At the same time traditional poetic forms—"poesia civile" for "Poesia della tradizione", popular song for *La meglio gioventù*—interact with these adopted registers to enhance their lexical ambit. The latter work to reinforce the bind between subjectivity and language, as the repeated terms are transformed in meaning and association as a result of reflecting the processes of variation. Micro-narratives of the evolution of key terms may thus be followed through as part of the history of Pasolini's poetry. The recurrence of the term "scandalo" in two poems already mentioned—first as an articulation of a suffered image of sacrifice and moral purgation in "La Crocifissione", and then as a *topos* of the self split between desire and materialist conscience in "Le ceneri di Gramsci"—may be taken as an initial example of lexical iteration. To take a more articulated yet still minor example,[21] which relates intimately to the very problems of poetry and the expressivity of the self noted above, interlocking threads of aural imagery are present throughout Pasolini's work, from *La meglio gioventú* to *La nuova gioventú*. Imagery of crying, of song, of noise and of silence provides an elaborate cluster of associative language which forms a soundtrack for the trajectory of the "io". To take only the first of these—"il pianto" ["crying"]—a sequence may be traced from the mournful laments of "Corots" (*La meglio gioventú*, *TLP*, 1518) and the 1946 plaquette of poems for the death of his grandmother *I pianti* (*TLP*, 1281–309), to the refrain of bird song and tears in "Il lujar" (*TLP*, 94). Equally, in the section "Il pianto della rosa" in *L'usignolo* (*TLP*, 319–48), where the "io" brings together a self-destructive narcissism, a blasphemous defiance and a guilt-ridden sexual charge, "il pianto" of innocence is exhausted:

> è lontano
> (no, non piango, non rido)
> in questo cielo il Dio
> che io non so né amo.
> (*TLP*, 342)

[He is far away/(no, I'm not crying, I'm not laughing)/in this heaven the God/I neither know nor love.]

The entry into history is marked by the screeching "pianto della scavatrice" ["cry of the digger"] in *Le ceneri di Gramsci* (*TLP*, 243–63 [262–63]), echoing the "latrato" ["howl"] of "Récit" (*TLP*, 239), and both come together in the emblematic "urlo della Magnani" ["(Anna) Magnani's scream"] in "La ricchezza" (*La religione del mio tempo*, *TLP*, 465) and the poet's own "Avrei voluto urlare, e ero muto" ["I wanted to cry out, and I was silent", *TLP*, 494]. The mutation into a more violent cry of pain continues in "La rabbia" (*TLP*, 582) and in the "urlo" which is the climax of "La realtà" (*Poesia in forma di rosa*, *TLP*, 647), and collapses into the incoherent "ecolalia" of *Trasumanar* (*TLP*, 895). Finally, the closure and (self-)annihilation of *La nuova gioventú* is marked by a turn to silence: "Hic desinit cantus" (*TLP*, 1181).

Lexical patterning is not the only form in which the subjective function is bound in poetic language. A related process is that of the (re)figuration or identification of the self in secondary, fictional or indeed mythical subjects that are both objects of projective desire and of "misprision" which work to amplify the epistemological potential of selfhood.[22] The sense of amplification was noted by Pasolini himself:

> La nostra vita è un folle identificarsi
> con coloro che qualcosa di immensamente nostro
> ci mette accanto.
> ("Teoria dei due paradisi" [1966], *TLP*, 1821)

[Our life is an insane identification/with those whom something immensely ours/places beside us.]

The energy of the "folle identificarsi" is to be located in the unstable fluidity and uncertain validity of these figures, and their relation to the speaking subject of the poetry. The incessant recourse in both *La meglio gioventú* and *L'usignolo* to the figure of Narcissus, as an image which binds the bucolic landscape and the charged sexuality of the idyll to the "io", has been well documented, at least as a poetic device which reflects a psychological condition.[23] Later, in *Poesia in forma di rosa*, the exclusion and suffering of the self are figured in an extensive rhetorical identification with Jews, among other oppressed groups:

> E cerco alleanze che non hanno altra ragione
>
> d'essere, come rivalsa, o contropartita,
> che diversità, mitezza e impotente violenza:
> gli Ebrei... i Negri... ogni umanità bandita...
> ("La realtà", *TLP*, 639)

[And I search for alliances which have no other reason//to exist, as compensation, or reward,/than difference, meekness and impotent violence:/Jews... Blacks... every banished humanity...]

The weakness of the affinity set up here reflects a disintegration of the processes of figuration in Pasolini's later work into unreliable and ironic simulacra which only underline their own lack of specificity.

In between Narcissus and the Jew, "La Crocifissione" and "Le ceneri di Gramsci" introduce two of the most significant figures with whom Pasolini identified himself—Christ and Gramsci.[24] Both are appropriated as myth and deployed as emblems of patterns of being which clarify the self. But in both cases there is a tension with the respective Biblical and ideological (that is, textual) reality of the figures. Identification takes place on the level of profound impulse—another element of visceral authenticity. This tension is subtly transposed into the heuristic uncertainty that marks each case. Gramsci for example is tentatively assimilated into the poet's schema of himself by way of a series of plaintive questions which structure the poem:

> Non puoi,
> lo vedi?, che riposare in questo sito
> estraneo, ancora confinato.
>
> (*TLP*, 223)

[You cannot,/do you see?, but rest in this foreign/place, still imprisoned.]

> Mi chiederai tu, morto disadorno,
> d'abbandonare questa disperata
> passione di essere nel mondo?
>
> (*TLP*, 232)

[Will you ask me, dead and stripped bare,/to abandon this desperate/passion for being in the world?]

Another question, as the poet nervously approaches the tombstone—"tra speranza/e vecchia sfiducia" ["between hope/and old misgivings": *TLP*, 226]—hints at the still more radical misreading, or even betrayal, of Gramsci which is to follow, when he is all but dislodged by the figuration of the "disperata passione" of Shelley:

(O è qualcosa
di diverso, forse, di piú estasiato

e anche di piú umile, ebbra simbiosi
d'adolescente di sesso con morte...)
(*TLP*, 226)

[(Or it is something/different, perhaps, more enraptured//and also more humble, a heady adolescent symbiosis/of sex and death...)]

The "ebbra simbiosi" prefigures the "ebbro peccare" ["the heady sinning": *TLP*, 230] which will divert the poet's gaze from Gramsci's onto Shelley's grave.

As with the patterns of lexical evolution, these figurations may be read across the poetry as narratives of subjective inscription which come together dialogically to produce images of the self. Two supplementary types of figure are worth pointing out in this respect. First, as implied by the use above of the Bloomian term "misprision" to describe this strategy, there is clearly a whole range of poetic *maestri* against whom the self is defined, in a manner which goes beyond the niceties of literary history. Poetic precedents are deployed more as cyphers, or symbolic icons in a vision of the self, than as textually vibrant interlocutors. Intertextuality is a point of suture for a broader, looser interaction. This phenomenon encompasses Pasolini's elaborate poetic education, from the Hermetics and the European Symbolists to Machado and Lorca, to the Ottocento and Dantesque forms which subtend the *poemetti* of the 1950s. Perhaps the most telling examples, however, are cases where he appropriates for his own rhetorical purposes an image of a poet only partially understood: thus, Wordsworth ("And O ye fountains", *TLP*, 225) and Shelley in "Le ceneri di Gramsci"; Ezra Pound in "Versi prima fatici e poi enfatici" (*Trasumanar e organizzar*, *TLP*, 914);[25] Joyce in "La baia di Kingstown" (*TLP*, 1020–22). These are all "misprisions" in the strongest sense, and are significant because they echo a much wider characterstic of Pasolini—the wholesale, eclectic and emotive adherence to an intellectual line without a necessarily complete understanding of its substance. His readings of Croce, Gramsci, Longhi, Spitzer, Freud, and later Barthes, Metz, Lévi-Strauss, Marcuse and many others—in poetry and beyond—all betray signs of misconception which seems to matter less than the weight of significance which their names and their idioms can add to discourses around the construction of the self.[26]

The second supplementary type of figuration of the self could be labelled "pseudo-figuration". In this category identification is directed towards archetypes of reflexive discourse which reinforce the sense of internal multiplicity in subjectivity and establish channels of energy parallel to those associated with matrices of keywords and of "real" figurations. Most commonly, these archetypes are drawn from family or from generational strata, always shot through with more or less explicit Oedipal or broadly libidinal impulses. In *La meglio gioventú*, this is most apparent in the obsessive figuration of the young boy, variously reincarnated as "nini" (*TLP*, 14), "fantassút" (15), "donzel" (17), "biel fí" (18), "frut" (20), "zòvin" (21), "soranèl" (36), "zovinút" (1530). The fluidity and sexual indeterminacy of the landscape allows these terms to be then feminized with little loss of identificatory impulse and, in turn, the feminine figures are assimilated to the image of the child-mother, who is the poet's most intimate interlocutor. The first young girl appears in "Tornant al país" (22), while "Aleluja III" (30) introduces the figure of the child-mother:

> to mari tal soreli
> a tornava fruta.

[your mother in the sunlight/became a girl once more.]

"Romancerillo" (37–39) gives a voice to the mother-figure. "La domènia uliva" (41–50) splits her into the "madre" and the "madre-fanciulla", each in dialogue with the "figlio". The dialogue not only interweaves the two mother-figures, but also conflates the seasonal cycle of nature, embodied by the olive-selling girl, with the liturgical cycle which marks Easter Sunday. Precisely the same synthesis is to be found in "La messa", "L'annunciazione" and "Litania" (*L'usignolo*, *TLP*, 309, 313–18), where the "madre-fanciulla" slips into the iconography and litany of the Virgin Mary. In "La domènia uliva", however, the figure of the son, in his obsessive, iterative introversion, recalls the figure of Narcissus:

> FI   Jo i no sai di cròus!
>   Pierdút ta la me vòus

> i sint sòul la me vòus
> i cianti la me vòus.[27]
>
> (*TLP*, 47)

[SON I know nothing of crosses!/Lost in my voice/I hear only my voice/I sing my voice.]

The mother-figure also comes to the fore in two poems near the end of "Suite furlana", "Sera di estat" and "Suspir di me mari ta na rosa". Both draw the mother into a language of desire, and hence once more recall the shadow of self-desire in the son:

> Al àia bussàt doma...
> so mari? Epúr a disin
> i so vuj: bussàimi!
>
> (*TLP*, 1534)

[Did he kiss only.../his mother? And yet his eyes/say: kiss me!]

> Dutis dos dismintiadis,
> la mari e la rosa!
> Zint cui sa dulà
> al ni à dismintiadis.
>
> (*TLP*, 98)

[Both forgotten,/the mother and the rose!/Going who knows where/he has forgotten us.]

The figure of the father, on the other hand, is all but absent from *La meglio gioventú*, as it is from *L'usignolo*: "ho ucciso il padre col silenzio" ("I have killed the/my father with silence", *TLP*, 353).[28] Later poetry, however, picks up on the imagery of the boy and the body from this earlier work as a transubstantiating vehicle for sexual desire and for an ontological desire of the real, and conflates it with the growing terror of becoming the father—

> a ripetere a uno a uno gli atti del padre,
> anzi, a ricreare il padre in terra.
> ("Nuova poesia in forma di rosa", *Poesia in forma di rosa*, *TLP*, 753)

[to repeat one by one the acts of the father,/or rather, to recreate the father on earth.]

The Father becomes an archetype rather than a figure of autobiographical record and thus acts as a vessel for ideological articulation—of the confrontation with the "figli" of the 1968–69 student movements (see *Trasumanar e organizzar, passim*)—and for allegories of desire ("Teoria dei due paradisi", *TLP*, 1818–23). In the cycle of poems dedicated to Maria Callas in *Trasumanar e organizzar*,[29] the key recurrent image of the "vuoto" is consistently identified with the absence of "il padre":

> Chi c'è, in quel VUOTO DEL COSMO,
> che tu porti nei tuoi desideri e conosci?
> C'è il padre, sí, lui!
> ("Timor di me?", *TLP*, 1013)

[Who is there, in that COSMIC VOID,/that you carry in your desires and you know?/There is the father, yes, him!]

> ciò che conta è lui, il Padre, sí, lui:
> lo dice uno che non lo conosce
> non ne sa nulla, non lo ha mai visto,
> non gli ha mai parlato, non l'ha mai ascoltato,
> non l'ha mai amato, non sa chi è, non sa se c'è.
> ("Rifacimento", *TLP*, 1017)

[what matters is him, the Father, yes, him:/one who does not know him says so/who knows nothing of him, has never seen him,/has never spoken to him, has never listened to him,/has never loved him, does not know who he is, does not know whether he is.]

Callas is presented as nurtured by the presence of the Father, which she attempts to find in the poet. For him, the lack is a terrifying weak point, where all the imperfections of the self are concentrated. The absence of the father, in a manner which returns to the very earliest of his poetry, determines the search for a secondary Other, in himself or God, in the body or poetry. But the failure of each model—"al posto dell'Altro/per me c'è un vuoto nel cosmo" ["in the place of the Other/for me there is a cosmic void": *TLP*, 1015]—is laid bare by the desire of Maria, and the result is terror:

è lo sgomento, piú terribile, ben piú terribile
di avere un corpo separato, nei regni dell'essere;
(TLP, 1015)

[it is horror, more terrible, much more terrible/than having a
divided body, in the realms of being;]

e il mio corpo è attratto dal pieno
dove già ciò che regna è la morte.
(TLP, 1017)

[my body is drawn to the plenitude/where already what reigns
is death.]

Lack is written across the body of the subject, who can only
compensate with already compromised secondary plenitudes.

The forms of lexical patterning and of figurations of the subject
outlined thus far all rely on a dynamic of iteration and modulation
of discrete but related textual elements. It was suggested above that
the dynamic creates a series of "micro-narratives" which cut across
textual boundaries, and that these "micro-narratives" are largely
responsible for the capacity of Pasolini's language to embody its
own understanding of itself as a language of subjectivity. There are
inevitably, however, other, syntagmatic dynamics which also play
a part, and perhaps the most important of these is autobiography.[30]
Pasolini regularly writes and rewrites his own history in fragments
which are constructed on a number of different temporal levels.
Poetic memory and experience of time allow for a formal distortion
of experience into a lyricized narrative whose very distortions are
predicates of subjectivity. Perhaps the clearest illustration of this is
the long, explicitly autobiographical poem "Poeta delle Ceneri",
whose original title was "Who is me" (*TLP*, 2056–84).[31] There, the
expression and perception of experience informs the history of
experience to create a hybrid where the lyric overlays narrative.
The poem's account of the flight to Rome in 1950 acknowledges this
indirectly and justifies it by ironic recourse to psychopathology:

Ho vissuto <…> quella pagina di romanzo, l'unica della mia vita:
per il resto, <che volete,>
son vissuto dentro una lirica, come ogni ossesso.
(TLP, 2061)

[I lived <...> that page out of a novel, the only one of my life:/
otherwise, <what do you want,>/I have lived within a lyric, like
every man possessed.]

The structure of the poem is governed by implicit or explicit
questions from a journalist—thus leaving the text open and only
projected towards a definitive response—and by a chronological
sequence of sorts, but also by a progression along channels of the
founding motifs of Pasolini's work, where autobiography, metaphor and myth combine. It opens with an image of his birth in
Bologna, "una città piena di portici" ["a city full of porticoes"] and
moves swiftly over his mother, father and brother, his first poems
and Friuli, which then dilate to fill the first section of the poem.
Elsewhere other events are similarly dilated: the trial for armed
robbery in Circeo, the trial for *La ricotta*, his "opere future", from
Teorema to *Affabulazione*. There is also a striking contraction of
certain events which produces a lapidary tone of momentous
importance. His "conversion" to Marxism is a case in point. An
extended description of the Friulan peasants ends thus:

> Fu cosí che io seppi ch'erano braccianti,
> e che dunque c'erano padroni.
> Fui dalla parte dei braccianti, e lessi Marx.
> (*TLP*, 2062)

[It was thus I came to know they were day-labourers,/and that
therefore there were bosses./I took the side of the labourers, and
I read Marx.]

The incisive preterite verbs, which indicate stability, but also
become markers of loss and absence, are a recurrent feature of
Pasolini's self-creation in poetry.

Finally, the poem is marked by a fluid and organic relationship
between the autobiographical past, in its lyricized and provisional
form, and the consideration of the present and the future, as both
an extension of the project of self-definition and as a generalizing
expansion beyond the simple life of the individual:

> —in quanto poeta sarò poeta di cose.
> Le azioni della vita saranno solo comunicate,
> e saranno esse, la poesia.
> (*TLP*, 2083)

[—as a poet I shall be a poet of things./The actions of life will be simply communicated,/and they will be poetry.]

The unfinished patchwork of "Poeta delle Ceneri" is, like much of Pasolini's poetry after 1964, deliberately diffuse and unpoetic.[32] He repeats three times within three pages (*TLP*, 2070–72) variations on the refrain

>   ho raccontato queste cose
> in uno stile non poetico
> perché tu non mi leggessi come si legge un poeta.

[I have related these things/in an unpoetic style/so you do not read me as you read a poet.]

But the open combination of autobiobraphical effects works as a guide to the often latent and even involuntary lyric autobiography in the mainstream of his work, which comes to function as—to borrow Genette's term—an "architexte", a submerged, but immanent category upon which the surface discourse of the text positions itself, and through which the text contains and even controls its own interpretation.[33]

At strategic points within poems, within collections and within the span of his literary career, Pasolini deploys autobiographical techniques such as those in "Poeta delle Ceneri", and their development gives some indication of the varying prominence of the subject's concern to derive meaning from its own history.[34] What it is important to note here is the synthesis, made possible by their particular fragmented, tendentious and distorted temporal framework, between the lexical and figurative dynamics of subjectivity and the autobiographical. The textual subject is made into an allegory and/or an analogy of subjectivity, or of itself.

THE PRAGMATICS OF SUBJECTIVITY

The iterative strategy identified in Pasolini's poetry finds a more operational equivalent in his manipulation of role and position in his journalistic work. If the poetry, by cumulative effect, builds up a matrix of subject relations, Pasolini's cultural *interventi* in various arenas between 1942 and 1975 show him constantly redefining the image of the self, and thereby delimiting the potential reception of his message.[35] A brief examination of two pivotal moments in that trajectory, from the 1940s and 1960s respectively, will illustrate the manipulation of this cultural activism in the service of self-construction.

Pasolini's first active involvement of this kind was with two small journals *L'architrave* and *Il setaccio*, sponsored by the Fascist youth organizations—respectively GUF and GIL—in Bologna in 1942–43. His contributions to these organs, like his letters of the same period, reflect an undisguised ambition to achieve literary success and intellectual sophistication of a wholly traditional kind. The manner in which they also delineate a role for the intellectual, however, is indicative of an already formed idea of how public statements impinge upon the operations of subjectivity. In a number of essays, Pasolini confronts two of the major debates of the dying years of Fascism—on the role of youth and on the role of the intellectual. In "I giovani, l'attesa",[36] he programmatically declares a role for "noi giovani":

> È ora posta in noi giovani la nuda responsabilità di non tradire il nuovo senso della vita [...] anzi di approfondirlo, scavarlo, ridonarlo alla storia come purificato attraverso la completa attuazione. (*PS*, 50)

> [It is now the bald responsibility of us young people not to betray the new sense of life (...) but rather to deepen it, to plumb its depths, to return it to history as purified by complete realization in the present.]

The young are in a state of suspense ("attesa"), waiting to be called to their vocation for renewal, but also to a certain heroic suffering: "Il duro mestiere, di conoscerci, e conquistarci [...]. Fatica, estrema autoconoscenza, travaglio interiore individuale e collettivo, sofferta sensibilità critica, saranno gli attributi del nostro nuovo entusiasmo" ["The harsh profession, of knowing ourselves and conquering ourselves (...). Toil, extreme self-knowledge, inner turmoil, these will be the attributes of our new enthusiasm": *PS*, 50].

The obvious bombastic (even fascistic) rhetoric of these statements, with their confessed acquiescence to the (political) status quo—"Non abbiamo proprio niente contro cui batterci" ["We have absolutely nothing to fight against": *PS*, 52]—, will soon disappear, but some of the underlying rhetorical strategies will be retained and developed. First, the attempt to involve the reader and an intimate group of interlocutors in a collective consensus—"noi giovani"—will recur throughout Pasolini's work, whether in the "sodalizio" of *Officina* and of *Nuovi argomenti*, or in the traumatic response to hostile groups such as the Gruppo '63, or in a series of pedagogic initiatives from the "Academiuta" to "Gennariello" in the *Lettere luterane*.[37] In "I giovani, l'attesa", it represents an innocent synthesis of youth (always an absolute in his value system), the group and individual identity: "Noi non vogliamo avere un nome: o meglio, ciascuno di noi vuole avere il proprio nome" ["We do not wish to have a name: or rather, each of us wants his own name": *PS*, 51]. Second, the idea of "l'attesa" is the first formulation of Pasolini's complex positioning of his various discourses on a temporal level. As if to render an intellectual or ideological stance elusive and ungraspable—what he later calls "unrecognizable" (*LL*, 195)—, its terms are projected forward to an always unrealized potential moment of "attuazione". The forward-projected energy of such a strategy, and its mirror-image in the individual and mythical nostalgia of much of his aesthetic work, are primary markers of the transcendence of the immediate in all Pasolini's work. Among other effects, they also project the reader's response to a secondary level of interpretation channelled by the primary subjective voice. Finally, the studied ambiguity between suffering and desire for fulfilment which "l'attesa" implies introduces a bind and a contrast between the driven, visceral impulse to act, or to express, and the ironic impossibility of experiencing such an act teleologically: "Siamo, forse, come l'atleta [che, se] vince, non sa valutare la vittoria, che gli altri esaltano, e pensa quasi tremante, benché pieno d'orgoglio, all'avvenire" ["We are perhaps like the athlete (who, if) he wins, cannot assess his victory, which others exalt, and who thinks almost trembling, but full of pride, of the future": *PS*, 50].

Between May 1960 and September 1965, Pasolini wrote a column of "dialoghi con i lettori" in the popular PCI weekly *Vie nuove*, in which he responded to letters on any topic from existentialism to drugs or Brigitte Bardot. In contrast to the 1940s articles, these dialogues chart the disintegration and crisis of his cultural position established in the late 1950s: his films cause ever more hostility, he becomes ever more embroiled in sordid media and judicial scandal, and the horrors of neo-capitalism grow ever greater. As always, however, the apparently candid outpouring of traumatic confession always also masks a strategy for shoring up the construction of subjectivity.

The dialogue form represents a preservation of the intimate circle of communication and consensus—here an implicit "noi comunisti"—despite its location in a mass-circulation medium.[38] Pasolini disingenuously insists in several early articles that he does not wish to talk about himself: "Vorrei evitare di parlare troppo di me" ["I'd like to avoid talking too much about myself": *BB*, 60]; "Mi vergogno di parlare di me" ["I'm ashamed to talk about myself": *BB*, 87, and see also 257).[39] The negativity of such reluctance is echoed by his regular disparagement of his own activities: "So bene che le mie lettere su *Vie nuove* sono piene di difetti" ["I am well aware that my letters in *Vie nuove* are full of flaws": *BB*, 238); "L'egoismo che mi protegge nel mio vero lavoro [fa sí che] questa rubrica di *Vie nuove* è spesso una faticosa interruzione" ["The egoism that protects me in my true work (means that) this column in *Vie nuove* is often a tiresome interruption": *BB*, 342). Despite, then, the return to the pedagogical mode of interaction which characterized his earliest cultural ventures, Pasolini is clearly ambivalent about the authority that might be invested in him:

> È vero che noi abbiamo bisogno di "miti" e "autorità", e colui che, attraverso l'industria culturale o l'appoggio di una corrente di opinione o l'organizzazione di un partito o il caso, diventa un "mito", "un'autorità", acquisisce nuovi doveri verso se stesso e verso gli altri [his examples are Guttuso and C. Levi]. Forse un po' anch' io ormai: ma lasciatemi ancora qualche anno di lavoro e di studio per imparare a farlo meglio, a trovare meglio il punto di coincidenza tra autorità e sincerità. (*BB*, 250)

> [It's true that we need "myths" and "authorities", and that whoever becomes a "myth" or an "authority", through the culture industry or the support of a current of opinion, through a party organization, or by chance, takes on new duties both for himself and for others. Maybe even I fall into this category by now: but give me a few more years of work and study to learn to do it better and to search out with more success the point of contact between authority and sincerity.]

Concern over the status of the project spills over into concern over the status of the self in its textual incarnation ("autorità"), both in and beyond *Vie nuove*. His response to this perceived inadequacy is to promote incoherence and, as in *Officina*, eclecticism to a positive value or element of identity, akin to artistic licence: "In definitiva io sono protetto dalle mie contraddizioni" ["In point of fact I am protected by my contradictions": *BB*, 251]; "A un artista va lasciato il diritto all'errore almeno in quanto contraddizione o ipotesi precoce o ritardata" ["An artist should have the right to err, at least to be contradictory, premature or out-of-date in his ideas": *BB*, 269]. The poet, or artist, is furthermore bound to truth in familiar assertions of the visceral need to express:

> Egli [l'artista] non deve tacere nulla, perché in un artista il peccato piú grande è l'omissione—essendo la sua funzione l'esprimere, e dunque l'esprimere è tutto. (*BB*, 269)

> [He (the artist) must not keep silent about anything, because the greatest sin for an artist is the sin of omission—since his function is to express and hence to express is all.]

He has a quasi-contractual obligation to express himself and/as the truth: "Non pensa il giornalista borghese, nemmeno per un istante a servire la verità: a essere in qualche modo onesto: cioè personale" ["The bourgeois journalist never for a moment thinks of serving truth: of being in some fashion honest: that is, personal": *BB*, 77]. Hence he is able to defend himself when read over-literally, as in the controversy caused by his claim that Marxism had become a ritualistic church (*BB*, 210–15). He describes his struggle as "ideale" (not literal), to be "integrated" through his other works.[40] The incomplete text, in permanent transition ("in attesa"), is identified with the poetic and with the true. His own status within literary history is a simultaneous clash between and fusion of a politics of revolution (Marxist and prospective) and an aesthetics of decadence "per quanto modificata" (retrospective). Poetry is located beyond the present—in his misused terminology, it is "diacronica" (*BB*, 310). The writer, commodified by the culture industry (*BB*, 243), is no longer a sacred oracle, but is potentially still associated with the prophetic in his/her relationship with time.

By constructing a voice bound up with self-expression and humble self-effacement, with truth and with prophecy, the dominant tone of catastrophic disintegration in the articles is infused with a power which undermines the very crisis of subjective autonomy that it records. The keyword for the analysis of this crisis is "mistificazione": "la mistificazione della mia opera [è] una mistificazione totale, completa, irrimediabile" ["the mystification of my work (is) total, complete, irremediable": *BB*, 205]; "Mettiti un po' nei miei panni, e cerca di capire esistenzialmente l'esperienza di uno che viene sistematicamente, regolarmente, atrocemente mistificato" ["Put youself for a moment in my shoes, and try to understand existentially the experience of someone who is systematically, regularly and cruelly mystified": *BB*, 165]. The reader is drawn to identify with the self—"Mettiti nei miei panni"—, which is then depersonalized and rendered passive—"uno che viene" (see "I giovani, l'attesa"). The agent of that "mistificazione" is "industrial power and the subsequent state conformism" (*BB*, 203). The name given to the former by the latter is success:

> Ecco che cos' è il successo: una vita mistificata dagli altri, che torna mistificata a te, e finisce col trasformarti veramente [...]. So cosa significa essere guardati come bestie rare, essere dati in pasto senza discriminazione all'odio (e assai piú raramente alla simpatia), essere continuamente, sistematicamente falsificati; (*BB*, 77–78)

> [This is what success is: a life which is mystified by others, which comes back to you in its mystified form, and in the end actually changes you [...]. I know what it's like to be stared at like rare beasts, to be exposed indiscriminately to hatred (and somewhat less often, to sympathy), to be continually and systematically falisified;]

"Il successo è, per una vita morale e sentimentale, qualcosa di orrendo, e basta" ["For a moral and emotional life, success is appalling, and that's that": *BB*, 219].[41] The result is an apparent loss of control over his work (beyond *Vie nuove*), attacked not only by an invisible oligarchy but also by a (manipulated) public:

> Io non posso permettermi di sbagliare un'opera; sono ridotto a questo [...]. Le masse [...] sono come dei re. E io di fronte a questi re, ormai, sono un po' come un giullare che se sbaglia un motto viene condannato a morte. (*BB*, 208)

[I cannot allow myself to err with a single work of mine; I have come to this (…). The masses (…) are like kings. And I am now before these kings like a court jester who has only to err once to be condemned to death.]

More seriously still, the subject becomes alienated from its very self: "Io cerco di lottare, donchisciottescamente, contro questa fatalità che mi tolgie a me stesso" ["I endeavour to struggle, like Don Quixote, against this fatal force which deprives me of myself": *BB*, 219]. But the image of the "giullare" and the laboured adverb "donchisciottescamente" both create a heroic, tragicomic circle of sympathy for his struggle and work to preclude rational dissent from his position. The mock authority which is acquired and cultivated as it is denied in these articles actually enhances a rhetoric of condemnation of power.

Both the "dialoghi" and Pasolini's articles for *L'architrave* and *Il setaccio*, in common with most of his journalism, exploit the tensions between the operations of subjectivity and the constrictions of arenas of expression. Despite the increasing negativity of the governing ideology of the various *sedi*, and the consequent weakened autonomy of a subjective voice, the latter learns how to resist and undermine the former by rhetoricizing itself, its instability and its potential interlocutors. Such a strategy suggests how the actual opinions expressed by Pasolini—often contradictory, easily refutable, eccentric and objectionable—remain secondary to the possibility of a "pragmatic" response to the apparatuses of cultural subjection.

SUBJECTIVITY AND THE PRE-FILMIC

The very aspect of cinema which most attracts Pasolini as a language for aesthetic renewal—its apparent absolute affinity with the material presence of physical reality—also displaces the operations of subjectivity away from the primary processes of signification of the medium. The totality of cinematic "realtà" attentuates the plurality of signifying practices, dispersed along different temporal and hermeneutic axes, on which the language of subjectivity as explained above was built. The displacement moves towards the processes of genesis which precede and produce the film, and it is these processes which this section will examine.

One of the most fascinating and stimulating of Pasolini's essays on cinema is "La sceneggiatura come 'struttura che vuole essere altra struttura'" ["The screenplay as a 'structure which wishes to be another structure'": *EE*, 192–201], which reconsiders the relationship between cinema and literature by recasting the problem in terms of what might now be called intertextuality.[42] It analyses the structure of a sort of text which must needs be provisional and incomplete—the screenplay—and from the analysis fundamental elucidations of Pasolini's attitude to textuality, literary and filmic, and the role of a textual *dynamic* in the signifying structures of cinema may be deduced.

The screenplay, he writes, should be considered an autonomous form, beyond an original literary text which may or may not exist empirically, and in tension towards a film which is as yet unmade ("da farsi"). It has, in other words, "una volontà di forma […] un vuoto, una dinamica che non si concreta" ["a will/desire for form […] a void, a dynamic which is not realized": *EE*, 193]. A signifier splits into a written, actual signified, and a hypothetical signified of the film "da farsi", and this necessarily induces a visual, image-led reading. The screenplay's founding stylistic trope is its "roughness and incompleteness" (*EE*, 193),[43] and it is only completed by a sort of shadowy presence of a visual sign ("cinèma") latent within the written sign ("grafema"), as the oral ("fonema") is present in the written. In the case of the "cinèma", however, the screenplay contains within itself the sign of "un'altra *langue*", an entirely separate signifying system or form (*EE*, 194–95): "coglie 'la forma in movimento'" ["it captures 'the form in movement'"]; "[è] una struttura che vuole essere altra struttura" ["(it is) a structure which wishes to be another structure": *EE*, 198]. Split between two posited end-points, without departure or arrival, the "sceno-testo" ("screen-text") is pure process, "un processo che non procede" ["a process which does not proceed": *EE*, 199]. Furthermore, its formal status is so ambiguous as to lack any identifiable norms of its own, and thus its system is purely a "stylistic" one. The only access we have to norms is via analogy with the literary norms of the origin (*EE*, 193–94).

This summary of the essay contains several points of interest. First, in his insistence on the formal autonomy of the screenplay as a genre or a distinct "langue", he confirms his insistence on the primacy of the technical as a criterion for distinction and analysis, recalling his assertion that his move from literature to cinema was above all a change of technique.[44] From a biographical point of view, it comes as no surprise that his activity as a screenplay-writer after 1954 should be promoted to the status of autonomous art-form.[45] In itself, this smacks of the need for self-affirmation, but more interesting are the terms in which the promotion is cast. At first these seem denigratory, and militate against any apparent generic stability of the form; "rozzezza e incompiutezza", coupled with elusive movement and change, seem to denote an anti-text, as much of his later poetry, which projects itself into oblivion, or into another form, is destructive and studiedly anti-poetic. As in that case, however, here vocabulary of flux—"movimento", "processo", "un film da farsi"—sets up a dialectic between the dynamic and the static, in which the former is a privileged tenor of potential energy, but in which the latter is always already present—"il processo *che non procede*"; "*coglie* 'la forma in movimento'." The potential supersedes the actual, and the latter becomes associated with reification ("un vuoto che non *si concreta*") and ultimately death.

This is not to say that Pasolini simply prefers the screenplay as an artistic form. The emphasis on the visual here, and the audio-visual in other essays,[46] and his actual practice demonstrate the contrary. The possibility, however, of extending the notion of textual dynamism beyond the direct contrast screenplay–film and into areas connected to problems of subjectivity, is offered by another element in the essay, the description of the dual structural ambiguity of the screenplay as a "*volontà* di forma", "una struttura che *vuole* essere altra struttura".[47] This inscription of will or desire into a text may be taken as conterminous with the inscription of a subject into a text. Furthermore, the formulation strongly implies that textual desire, and thus subjectivity, are located only within the process of transition, within what Pasolini again misnames the "diacronia" (*EE*, 198) between the structures and languages which make up the ambiguous text. "Volontà di forma" differs from "forma" in that it lacks fulness of form, but also in that it is inscribed with will, or desire. A structure which does not desire to be another structure is a structure which does not desire. This truism may be mapped onto many other structures, or pairs of structures, even when the desired "altra struttura" is not defined by anything beyond its otherness. Hence Pasolini's poetics of pastiche may be reformulated as a variation on, or a reversal of, this model, wherein, for example, the filmic reconstruction of Pontormo's *Deposizione* in

La ricotta desires to be and cannot be the actual image or fresco, so that within the tension between the two images lies the space on which subjective discourse and interpretation centre. The comedy derives from just such (Mannerist) tensions: the inability of the actors to remain as still as a picture and also to express emotion, their forced laughter, the playing of the wrong music, the silent scream, "basta" ["enough"], of the diva (Laura Betti). An analogous dynamic is to be found in Pasolini's formulation of *Il Vangelo* as "the life of Christ plus two thousand years of story-telling about the life of Christ".[48] There too a space—between a fixed past and the present—is opened, and is filled by the plenitude of "storia": the specificity of the film's reading of the Gospel and its subjective impact are located within the filling.

More generally apparent is Pasolini's repeated desire to leave his films unfinished, or better, suspended in a Barthesian sense: "I always intend [my films] to remain suspended" (*Pasolini on Pasolini*, p. 57); "Le message 'politique' circule à travers tous mes films mais [il] reste toujours suspendu" ["The 'political' message circulates through all my films but (it) remains always suspended": J. Duflot, *Entretiens*, p. 57]. A critic reviewing *Uccellacci e uccellini* at its general release in 1966 describes its end as "volutamente sospeso" ["willfully in suspense"].[49] The same pattern recurs in Pasolini's self-portrait "Al lettore nuovo", in his (mis)quotation of Jakobson's citation of Valéry's view of poetry as "une hésitation prolongée entre le sens et le son" ["a prolonged hesitation between sense and sound"], which clearly presents an identical dynamic to that of a space held between a signifier and an uncertain signified, as described here.

The most direct manifestation of this trope is in the remarkable variety of processes of construction in the genesis of the films. Before 1964, the relationship between planning and production seems straightforward, largely dominated by the attempt to realize as faithfully as possible the vision of the former in the latter.[50] The screenplays of *Accattone*, *Mamma Roma* and *La ricotta* derive from the world of the Roman novels and of earlier screenplays.[51] The "film-saggio" *La rabbia* and the "film-inchiesta" *Comizi d'amore* are both somewhat muted attempts to make use of the film medium for directly socio-ideological purposes, and are if anything films which "desire to become" linguistic discourse ("saggio"/"inchiesta"), rather than the inverse. After 1964, textual status is more complex,

and the filmic product cedes in different ways parts of its autonomy to other forms or images. The *Sopralluoghi in Palestina* are
presented as complementary footage to *Il Vangelo*, and their mere
existence, organization and release demonstrate an interest in the
prospective, forward-projected status of such footage. Certain
techniques derive directly from *Comizi d'amore*, and will be reused
with resounding success in *Appunti per un'Orestiade africana*, where
the lack of a realized narrative film, and the sophisticated combination of narrative information for the proposed final product, pure
observation, speculation on how narrative and landscape might be
spliced together, and open discussion of the contemporary political relevance of the myth, powerfully promote the transitional
form. The autonomy of this improvised form challenges its assumed status as signifier by drawing instability into itself as
signified, and, in the case of a final product such as *Medea*, casting
the film as itself a signifier of a latent and unstable cluster of implicit
questioning discourses. *Le mura di Sana'a* repeats the combination
of history, observation and enquiry, and makes explicit and political an appeal implicit in the *Trilogia della vita*. The subtitle itself,
"Documentario in forma d'un appello all'UNESCO" ["Documentary
in the form of an appeal to UNESCO"] is of a type constantly
reinvented by Pasolini, from "Poesia in forma di rosa" to "sceneggiatura in forma di un poema" or "romanzo sotto forma di sceneggiatura" (*Lettere 1955–1975*, pp. 617, 624), which neatly formulates
the transitional nature of the text in each case. To return to *Il Vangelo*
and the *Sopralluoghi*, the former is the product of the latter's
provisionality or its failure to discover required locations in the
historical Biblical site. This moment of failure may be seen as a
founding trauma of the literal—what is present can no longer
faithfully or literally represent what is past—and leads to the
important discovery of the analogous method—what is present
can represent analogously what is past. It is no coincidence that this
point marks the end of the non-problematic, or naïve, transition
from "soggetto-sceneggiatura" to film.

Il Vangelo in itself is a special case with regard to the relationship between text and film, because of Pasolini's decision to remain
entirely faithful to the text of the Gospel: "Non ho aggiunto una
battuta e non ne ho tolto nessuna" ["I have neither added nor taken
away a single line"].[52] But for Pasolini textual fidelity was in fact a
vehicle for pastiche. Literalness liberated the visual and aural as

variegated interpretative discourses in their own right; hence his assertion that "la visualizzazione [è] la lettura migliore che si possa fare di un testo" ["visualization (is) the best reading one can have of a text": *V*, 14].

The experiment of textual fidelity was not repeated, but the underlying interplay between an original text and a filmic representation of it subtends the dominant group of adaptations in Pasolini's filmography after *Il Vangelo*: *Edipo, Medea, Il Decameron, I racconti di Canterbury, Il fiore delle "Mille e una notte"* and *Salò* are all readings of fundamental mythical texts, as would have been *San Paolo* and *Un'Orestiade africana*.[53] In a different sense, both *Teorema* and *Porcile* interact with written texts by Pasolini himself: the former with the "novel" of the same name (originally conceived as a play), and the latter with a play of the same name. It has already been noted how, in *Edipo*, the Sophoclean original is deployed strategically as a marker of authorial presence. Also, the occasional use of intertitles disturbs the audio-visual and therefore narrative fluidity of the film, recalling the textual source of the universalized, mythical world.

Il Decameron's textual adaptation operates on several different levels. The most notable deviation from the letter of Boccaccio's text is the abandonment of the "lieta brigata" in favour of a narrative frame closely bound up in the matter of the stories themselves. One story, of Ser Ciappelletto, itself becomes a frame; and the artist played by Pasolini begins as a protagonist of his own brief story, and then becomes the observer of the Neapolitan market-place, from which all the subsequent protagonists emerge. Further, the setting in Naples, and in Neapolitan, of large parts of the film allows Pasolini's interest in dialect as a token of genuine popularity and reality to resurface.

Salò marks an end-point in the exploration of the modes of visualization of text in film, as it marks an end-point in many other senses. De Sade's *Les cent-vingt jours de Sodome* is taken as a negative mirror-image of the founding moment of European bourgeois hegemony, the Enlightenment, and adopted as a cypher. Textual fidelity is irrelevant, as is narrative reconstruction. What matters is the immanence of the secondary symbolic impact of its qualities of exhaustive, repetitive, systematic, total perversion in the equally symbolic interpretation of the Repubblica Sociale Italiana (Salò), and the interaction or synthesis of the two.

A final, but significant level of intermediary textuality between idea and film is to be found in Pasolini's regular use of story-board pictures or *fumetti* as preparatory aids in filming. There is evidence of this as early as *Mamma Roma*,[54] and, given Pasolini's activity as an artist in his youth, and his reliance on the iconography of art for his early filmic technique, such a practice is far from surprising. At that time, however, when critics generally perceive his first substantial recourse to cinematographic, as opposed to literary or iconographic pastiche—that is to say, with *Uccellacci e uccellini*, and its clear homage to Rossellini's *Francesco, giullare di Dio* (1950) and the Fellini of *La strada* (1954)—, a different attitude emerges to the *disegni*. The opening photograph in *Mamma Roma* shows Pasolini transferring directly from "soggetto-sceneggiatura" to a shot-by-shot story-board. In *La terra vista dalla luna* he uses drawings as a substitute for the screenplay, adopting a new language:

> Non possedendo un linguaggio, uno stile per esprimere per iscritto, verbalmente, questo tipo di comicità, sono stato costretto a scrivere la sceneggiatura facendola a fumetti, cioè disegnando Totò e Ninetto nelle varie situazioni appunto come fumetti.[55]

> [As I have no language, no style to express in writing, in words, this type of comedy, I have been forced to write the screenplay in cartoon form, that is, drawing Totò and Ninetto in the various situations in cartoon form.]

The written screenplay, under the provisional title *Il buro e la bura*, is prefaced by advice that "queste righe vanno lette pensando alle 'comiche' di Charlot o Ridolini o ai fumetti di Paperino" ["these lines should be read thinking of Chaplin's or Ridolini's comedies or of Donald Duck cartoons"].[56]

In the introduction to the catalogue of Pasolini's collected drawings, De Micheli comments thus on the *fumetti* of *La terra*:

> Pasolini "vede" i suoi personaggi, li segue nei gesti, nei dialoghi, nelle scene. Il suo segno è rapido, vivace e rappresentativo [...]. L'occhio del disegnatore coincide con l'occhio del regista, che immagina sequenze, primi piani, ritmi e dissolvenze. Questo gruppo di fogli illumina come meglio non sarebbe possibile il suo meccanismo creativo che sa tradurre in una successione mobilissima d'immagini l'essenza poetica di un racconto.[57]

[Pasolini "sees" his characters, follows them in their gestures, dialogue and scenes. His mark is swift, lively and representative (...). The eye of the draughtsman coincides with the eye of the director, who imagines takes, close-ups, rhythms and dissolves. This group of papers shows us better than anything his creative mechanism which manages to translate the poetic essence of the story into a highly mobile sequence of images.]

De Micheli emphasizes the position of the drawings at the cusp of two visualizations ("l'occhio [...] coincide") and the rapidity of Pasolini's tranformations, and he thus intuits the search for "la forma in movimento" for which the *fumetti* amply allow.[58]

The fluidity of form allows Pasolini to adapt every aspect of his technique and choice of medium for the purposes he requires. *La terra* is pure fable, constructed around silence and mime and the miraculous resurrection of an image. A modern-day *convenentia* allows him to adopt the language of *fumetti* as the only possible language to intersect both that of fairy-tale and that of film magic. In general, the formal dynamic of the pre-filmic in Pasolini acts as a pretext or preconscious to the actual film. It works to introduce meaning and interpretation, in the movement from text to idea to image, and also to produce processes of subjectivity, through the interplay between desire for the other and stasis.

The affinity of cinematic processes of subjectivity to Pasolini's poetics of pastiche was noted above in passing. His commitment to pastiche is evident in his earliest writings:

La vera necessaria novità consisterebbe nella vera e propria tecnica musicale [...]. Apporterei delle nuove note "stonate" e per indicarle dovrei indicare nuovi segni. Improvvisamente, nell'attimo piú snervante e tenero della melodia, dovrebbero intervenire delle stonature scelte e dosate con estrema razionalità [...]. Farei un pastiche fantastico. (*Amado mio*, p. 105)

[The true, necessary novelty would consist in real musical technique [...]. I would bring new "dissonant" notes and to highlight them I would have to use new signs. Suddenly, at the most unnerving and tender moment of the melody, dissonant elements, chosen and distributed with extreme logic, should intervene [...]. I would produce a fantastic pastiche.]

The construction of an enveloping discourse of subjectivity which this essay has examined in Pasolini's poetry, journalism and film-work rests on the dissonance between such "note stonate" and "disaccordi" of the texture of expression. Other dominant aspects of his work may be drawn in to reinforce this assertion. His eclecticism, in choice both of genre and medium and of intellectual and artistic affinities, also betokens a displacement from the manifest meaning of any phenomenon towards the dynamic of exchange and movement between phenomena. And his theorization and practice of experimentalism are also built upon the overlap between constant and plural renewal of language and style,[59] and the profound subjective impact of such renewal:

> Il suo sperimentalismo non è altro che il suo attaccarsi alla vita: un solo gesto, cioè per valere deve essere sempre diverso. Inoltre appunto perché la vita lo esclude e lo isola, il "segnato" la ama di un amore più forte: e la ricerca di continuo, nella sua monotonia si rinnova incessantemente. (*PI*, 470)

> [His experimentalism is nothing other than his devotion to life: a single gesture must always be different to be of worth. Besides, precisely because life excludes and isolates him, the "marked" man loves it with an even greater passion: and the search, in its monotony, is continually and incessantly renewed.]

Stylistic experimentation is here denied any formalist or ludic connotation and is instead linked to that rhetoric of visceral subjective authenticity noted at the start of this essay. Pasolini is here describing the young poet Massimo Ferretti, but it is a cliché of Pasolini criticism to identify self-portraits in every portrait penned by him. It is, however, the cliché which here provides the fundamental qualification to the rhetoric. It implies once again that the overriding strategy for self-construction in Pasolini is for any discourse to contain and be contained by discourses which are not so much simply self-reflections—talking about himself—as hermeneutic markers, hidden controls on our reading and interpreting, pre-emptive assertions of the authority of the origin, by way of a construction of possible returns to the origin as an interpretative key. In this sense, the discourse is also autogenetic: it reproduces itself (and its self) by creating the conditions for and then executing discourses about itself. Hence it should be no surprise to find Pasolini's critics channelled along lines laid down by his own aesthetic practices. His work desires as much. But to appreciate and analyse the autogenesis which draws other discourses into the central construct is to readjust our overall understanding of Pasolini's work.

As a coda, the recently published sprawling fragment *Petrolio* provides a final epic confirmation of the desire of Pasolini's texts to control and contain their own meaning.[60] The completed novel was planned as a sort of Nabokovian construct which would present the narrative text under the guise of a critical edition of various manuscripts, with lacunae filled in by a scrupulous editor (*P*, 3–4). In part, the manuscripts would even have been transcribed in Greek (*P*, 139) and Japanese (*P*, 534). This form, constructed with its own univeral rules, more than the narrative, is envisaged as the force and function of the novel, and the desire for self-scrutiny reaffirms the strategies of subjectivity which subtend all Pasolini's work:

> Parlo della mia ambizione a costruire una forma con le sue leggi autopromuoventisi e autosufficienti, piuttosto che a scrivere una storia che si spieghi attraverso concordanze piú o meno "a chiave" con la pericolosissima realtà. [...] Ciò che io desideravo fare si attua proprio in *questo farsi e spiegarsi dell'opera con se stessa, anche letteralmente.*[61] (*P*, 534; my italics)

> [I'm talking about my ambition to construct a form with its own self-promoting and self-sufficient laws, rather than writing a story that is explained by way of more or less hidden concordances with a highly dangerous reality [...]. What I wanted to do is realized precisely in *this creation and explanation of the work with and through itself, even in a literal sense.*]

NOTES

1   See *Lettere luterane* [1976] (Turin, Einaudi, 1980) and *Scritti corsari* [1975] (Milan, Garzanti, 1990). Some of the most damning attacks were by U. Eco [Dedalus], "Le ceneri di Malthus", *Il manifesto*, 21 Jan. 1975; M. Ferrara, "I pasticci dell'esteta", *L'unità*, 12 June 1974, and "I connotati di un potere reale", *L'unità*, 27 June 1974; L. Firpo, "Quel reazionario di Pasolini", *La*

stampa, 31 Aug. 1975; G. Manganelli, "Risposta a Pasolini", *Corriere della sera*, 22 Jan. 1975. On Pasolini's journalism see Michael Caesar's essay in the present volume.

2   *Il Decameron* in particular spawned a series of pornographic imitations. See P. Bondanella, *Italian Cinema: From Neorealism to the Present* (New York, Continuum, 1990), p. 291; and also Pasolini's own "Abiura dalla *Trilogia della vita*" (*LL*, 71–76) and "Tetis", in *Erotismo, eversione, merce*, edited by V. Boarini (Bologna, Cappelli, 1974), pp. 95–103.

3   For a more detailed account of this survey, see R. Gordon, "Identity in Mourning: The Role of the Intellectual and the Death of Pasolini", *Italian Quarterly*, 32 (1995), 61–75. An important recent attempt to analyse Pasolini's continuing presence in Italian media and culture is to be found in E. Golino, *Tra lucciole e Palazzo: il mito Pasolini dentro la realtà* (Palermo, Sellerio, 1995).

4   Some examples are *Dedicato a Pasolini* by various authors (Milan, Gammalibri, 1976); *Pasolini nel dibattito culturale contemporaneo* by various authors (Pavia, Amministrazione Provinciale di Pavia; Alessandria, Comune di Alessandria, 1977); *Perché Pasolini: ideologia e stile di un intellettuale militante* by various authors (Florence, Guaraldi, 1978); *Per conoscere Pasolini* by various authors (Rome, Teatro Tenda/Bulzoni, 1978); *Pasolini: cronaca giudiziaria, persecuzione, morte*, edited by L. Betti (Milan, Garzanti, 1977); *Pier Paolo Pasolini: testimonianze*, edited by A. Panicali and S. Sestini (Florence, Nuova Salani, 1982).

5   See F. Brevini, *Per conoscere Pasolini* (Milan, Mondadori, 1981); R. Rinaldi, *Pier Paolo Pasolini* (Milan, Mursia, 1982), and *L'irriconoscibile Pasolini* (Rovito, Marra, 1990); G. Santato, *Pier Paolo Pasolini: l'opera* (Vicenza, Neri Pozza, 1980), and *Pier Paolo Pasolini: l'opera e il suo tempo*, edited by G. Santato (Padua, CLEUP, 1983).

6   P. Valesio, "Pasolini come sintomo", *Italian Quarterly*, 82–83 (1980–81), 29–42, sees Pasolini's contributions to literary, political and sociological debate as limited precisely because he functions as a "sintomo" and not a proactive "segno" of his context. But the relation can be reversed, so that his efficacy as a vessel for the ideas and projective fantasies of others becomes both part of the mechanics of mythologization and a facet of the ambiguous self-construction which this essay outlines.

7   The struggle to reconcile "il dire" and "il fare" was fundamental to Pasolini's work, particularly after 1966. See his *Empirismo eretico* (Milan, Garzanti, 1972), pp. 203–30, and "Fare e pensare", in his *Il caos*, edited by G. C. Ferretti (Rome, Editori Riuniti, 1979), pp. 229–31, where the governing metaphor of *Trasumanar e organizzar* is first sketched out.

8   *Amado mio preceduto da Atti impuri*, edited by C. D'Angeli (Milan, Garzanti, 1982).

9   These notebooks were used extensively by Naldini in his edition of Pasolini's letters and subsequent biography: *Lettere 1940–1954* (Turin, Einaudi, 1986) and *Lettere 1955–1975* (Turin, Einaudi, 1988); and N. Naldini, *Pasolini: una vita* (Turin, Einaudi, 1989). The diary form also played a central part in Pasolini's early poetry, as is indicated by a number of plaquette collections—*Diarii, Dal Diario (1945–47)* and *Roma 1950: diario* (all reprinted in P. P. Pasolini, *Bestemmia: tutte le poesie*, edited by G. Chiarcossi and W. Siti, 2 vols [Milan, Garzanti, 1993], pp. 1263–75, 1417–41, 1477–95).

10   *TLP*, 1–172 reprints the original text of *La meglio gioventú* (1954), which Pasolini later modified and included as the first part of *La nuova gioventú*

(Turin, Einaudi, 1975). Thus some poems from the latter are reproduced elsewhere in *TLP*, but are nevertheless cited here as part of *La meglio gioventú*.

11 See M. Sehrawy, "The Suffering Text: *Poesie a Casarsa* and the Agony of Writing", *The Italianist*, 5 (1985), 9–35.

12 See in particular his preface to *Letteratura negra*, edited by M. De Andrade (Rome, Editori Riuniti, 1961); *TLP*, 580, 602–10; *Il padre selvaggio* (Turin, Einaudi, 1975); *San Paolo* (Turin, Einaudi, 1975); and the film *Appunti per un'Orestiade africana*; and see C. Bongie, *Exotic Memories: Literature, Colonialism and the Fin de Siècle* (Stanford, Stanford University Press, 1991), pp. 188–228.

13 See his *Teatro*, edited by G. Davico Bonino (Milan, Garzanti, 1988). On Pasolini's theatre see G. Bàrberi Squarotti, "L'anima e la letteratura, il teatro di Pasolini", *Critica letteraria*, 8 (1980), 645–80; S. Casi, *Pasolini: un'idea di teatro* (Udine, Campanotto, 1990); J. Gatt-Rutter, "Pier Paolo Pasolini", in *Writers and Society in Contemporary Italy*, edited by M. Caesar and P. Hainsworth (Leamington Spa, Berg, 1984), pp. 143–65; E. Groppali, *L'ossessione e il fantasma: il teatro di Pasolini e Moravia* (Venice, Marsilio, 1979); W. Van Watson, *Pier Paolo Pasolini and the Theater of the Word* (Ann Arbor, UMI Research Press, 1989).

14 See "*Officina*": *cultura, letteratura, e politica negli anni cinquanta*, edited by G. C. Ferretti (Turin, Einaudi, 1975), pp. 36–37.

15 First in *Rinascita*, 26 Dec. 1964, then in *EE*, 9–28. For reaction to it, see C. Segre, "La nuova questione della lingua", *La battana*, 3, vii–viii (May 1966), 37–48; *Rinascita: dialogo con Pasolini; scritti 1957–1984*, edited by A. Cadioli as a supplement to *Rinascita*, 9 Nov. 1985.

16 References are to, respectively, F. Fortini, *Saggi italiani* (Bari, Laterza, 1974), p. 130; F. Fortini, *Nuovi saggi italiani* (Milan, Garzanti, 1987), p. 213; and F. Fortini, *L'ospite ingrato* (Bari, De Donato, 1966), p. 105. All Fortini's writings on Pasolini are now in F. Fortini, *Attraverso Pasolini* (Turin, Einaudi, 1993). See also G. Bàrberi Squarotti, "La poesia e il viaggio a ritroso nell'io", in *Pier Paolo Pasolini: l'opera e il tempo*, pp. 206–26 (p. 226).

17 On Pasolini and d'Annunzio, see for example F. Fortini, *I poeti del Novecento* (Rome–Bari, Laterza, 1977), p. 171.

18 See, for instance, *Le belle bandiere: dialoghi 1960–1965*, edited by G. C. Ferretti (Rome, Editori Riuniti, 1977), pp. 144, 182.

19 See *Desiderio di Pasolini: omosessualità, arte e impegno intellettuale*, edited by S. Casi (Turin, Sonda, 1990), pp. 149–82 and *passim*.

20 *Pasolini nel dibattito culturale contemporaneo*, p. 87.

21 The task of exploring the central founding terms of Pasolini's poetry would be a major one in each instance, and has not as yet been comprehensively attempted. See P. Larivaille, "Autobiografia e storia nella poesia di Pasolini", *Galleria*, 25, i–iv (1985), 106–45, on "storia"; and S. Vannucci, *Pier Paolo Pasolini: il colore della poesia* (Rome, Associazione Fondo Pier Paolo Pasolini, 1985) on colour.

22 On "misprision" see H. Bloom, *The Anxiety of Influence: A Theory of Poetry* (New York, Oxford University Press, 1973).

23 Most of Pasolini's major critics have discussed his narcissism; see A. Asor Rosa, "La crisi del populismo: Pasolini", in his *Scrittori e popolo: il populismo nella letteratura italiana contemporanea* [1965] (Rome, Samonà and Savelli, 1969), pp. 349–449 (pp. 365–70); M. David, *La psicanalisi nella cultura italiana*

(Turin, Boringhieri, 1970), pp. 556–62; G. Santato, *Pier Paolo Pasolini: l'opera*, pp. 11–13, 56; R. Rinaldi, *Pier Paolo Pasolini*, pp. 9, 35–41. For Rinaldi, the section of *La meglio gioventú* entitled "Suite furlana" is "il piú vasto manuale poetico del Novecento sui misteri di Narciso" (p. 36). See also Angela Meekins's essay in the present collection.

24 Gramsci appears only in the monumental encounter of the title poem of *Le ceneri di Gramsci*. For instances of the figure of Christ apart from in "La Crocifissione", see "La passione", "L'usignolo v", "La Chiesa viii", "L'ex-vita" (*TLP*, 291–95, 301, 307, 400).

25 On Pasolini and Pound see A. Lo Giudice, "Pound e Pasolini: viaggio verso il padre", *Letteratura italiana contemporanea*, 12 (Sept–Dec. 1991), 33–64; and V. Ronsisvalle, "Pasolini e Pound", *Galleria*, 35, i–iv (1985), 168–74.

26 See Z. G. Barański, "Pier Paolo Pasolini, Culture, Croce, Gramsci", in *Culture and Conflict in Postwar Italy*, edited by Z. G. Barański and R. Lumley (Basingstoke, Macmillan, 1990), pp. 139–59.

27 The dialogue continues with the son denying voice in turn to the sky, the years, bodies and women, and finally reiterating "sòul la me vous", thus setting out the determinants of the narcissistic voice as nature, time or memory, the body and desire.

28 On the figure of the father see G. C. Ferretti, "'Mio padre, quando sono nato...'", *Galleria*, 35, i–iv (1985), 85–105.

29 Contained in the last four sections of *Trasumanar*, *TLP*, 963–1044, and in the screenplay of *Medea*, edited by G. Gambetti (Milan, Garzanti, 1970), pp. 109–47 and then *TLP*, 1874–918, they intermingle and overlap with some of the most highly politicized poems. On Pasolini and Callas, see C. Clément, "La Cantatrice muette ou le maître chanteur démasqué", in *Pasolini: séminaire*, edited by M. A. Macciocchi (Paris, Grasset, 1980), pp. 265–68; E. Siciliano, *Vita di Pasolini* [1978] (Milan, Rizzoli, 1981), pp. 403–07. On this cycle see R. Rinaldi, *Pier Paolo Pasolini*, pp. 350–57; F. Cigni, "Né timor di me ti prenda...", in *Desiderio di Pasolini*, pp. 119–48.

30 See P. Larivaille, "Autobiografia e storia".

31 See also "Coccodrillo" (*TLP*, 2085–93). "Poeta delle Ceneri" was a product of Pasolini's first stay in New York in July 1966—hence references to America, the original English title and the couching of the poem in terms of an interview (see "La disperata vitalità"). It seems to be an early version of the prose introduction to the 1970 selection of Pasolini's poetry, "Al lettore nuovo", in *Poesie* (Milan, Garzanti, 1970), pp. 5–11.

32 I am grateful to Zygmunt Barański for pointing out the several Dantesque echoes in "Poeta delle Ceneri", from the label "poeta di cose" traditionally applied to Dante, to the poet's self-presentational style, which recalls that of the souls in Dante's afterlife.

33 For the term "involuntary autobiography" see P. Bellocchio, "L'autobiografia involontaria di Pasolini", in his *Dalla parte del torto* (Turin, Einaudi, 1989), pp. 145–66. See also G. Genette, *Introduction à l'architexte* (Paris, Seuil, 1979).

34 Rinaldi sees Pasolini's career as alternating between autobiographical and impersonal phases (*L'irriconoscibile Pasolini*, p. 100); this perspective correlates interestingly with the alternation of historical stasis and mobility described by Larivaille ("Autobiografia e storia").

35 E. Golino, *Pasolini: il sogno di una cosa* (Bologna, Mulino, 1985), concentrates on this area of Pasolini's work.

36 *L'architrave*, Nov. 1942; then in *Pasolini e "Il setaccio"*, edited by M. Ricci (Bologna, Cappelli, 1977), pp. 49–52.

37 On the Academiuta see P. P. Pasolini, *L'Academiuta friulana e le sue riviste*, edited by N. Naldini (Vicenza, Neri Pozza, 1994). On pedagogy see E. Golino, *Pasolini: il sogno di una cosa*; A. Zanzotto, "Pedagogia", in *Pasolini: cronaca giudiziaria*, pp. 361–72.

38 On *Vie nuove*, see S. Gundle, "Cultura di massa e modernizzazione: *Vie nuove* e *Famiglia cristiana* dalla guerra fredda alla società dei consumi", in *Nemici per la pelle, sogno americano e mito sovietico nell'Italia contemporanea*, edited by P. D'Attore (Milan, Angeli, 1991), pp. 235–68; M. Isnenghi, "Pasolini giornalista", in *Pier Paolo Pasolini: l'opera e il suo tempo*, pp. 153–67 (pp. 159–62).

39 In fact he constantly discussed his own work: see, for example, 1 July 1961 on *Accattone*; 18 Oct. 1962 on *Mamma Roma*; 29 Oct. and 19 Nov. 1964 on *Il Vangelo secondo Matteo*; 29 Apr. to 20 May 1965, *passim*, on the genesis of *Uccellacci e uccellini*.

40 See *SC*, 1–2; and the disingenuous denial, after much hostile response, that his 1975 proposals to abolish school and television were meant literally (*LL*, 165–78; and *Volgar' eloquio* [Naples, Athena, 1976]).

41 See Pasolini's earlier unproblematic ambition to achieve success, noted above.

42 See J. Kristeva, *La Révolution du langage poétique* (Paris, Seuil, 1974); *Intertextuality: Theories and Practices*, edited by M. Worton and J. Stil (Manchester, Manchester University Press, 1990), pp. 1–44 and *passim*.

43 The essay goes on (194–95) to a comparison with much modern poetry, which leaves the reader to "complete" the work, or to collaborate with the text.

44 See F. Duflot, *Entretiens avec Pier Paolo Pasolini* (Paris, Belfond, 1970), p. 16.

45 See *Il caos*, p. 207 (to Moravia): "E smettila anche di pensare che le parole nelle sceneggiature non abbiano un valore letterario ossia estetico. Perché ciò mi offende personalmente."

46 See, for example, *EE*, 204. Later this emphasis is corrected to take spatio-temporal factors into account (*EE*, 290). On the differences between his essays from 1965–67 and a second group from 1971, see R. Turigliatto, "La tecnica e il mito" in *Lo scandalo Pasolini*, edited by F. Di Giammatteo as a special issue of *Bianco e nero*, 37, i–iv (Jan–Apr. 1976), 113–55 (pp. 123–24).

47 A. Bertini, *Teoria e tecnica del film in Pasolini* (Rome, Bulzoni, 1979), p. 79, actually sees the "sceneggiatura" as a metaphor for Pasolini's self, which is "dimidiato, o, meglio, partecipe di due 'strutture'".

48 In O. Stack, *Pasolini on Pasolini* (London, Thames and Hudson, 1969), p. 83.

49 A. Savioli, *L'unità*, 14 May 1966. On the fly-leaf of *Teorema* the novel (Milan, Garzanti, 1968), Pasolini described the work as "questo manualetto laico, a canone sospeso". Compare "ogni sistema o struttura è in realtà un processo" (*Il caos*, p. 211). F. Gérard, *Pasolini ou le mythe de la barbarie* (Brussels, Editions de l'Université, 1981), p. 117, sees Pasolini's thought as "en perpétuel devenir".

50 See *Mamma Roma* (Milan, Rizzoli, 1962), p. 140: "Coordino in un montaggio che è esattamente quello che ho in mente prima di girare."

51 *La ricotta* is included in *Alí dagli occhi azzurri* [1965] (Milan, Garzanti, 1989), pp. 249–464, 467–87.

52 *Il Vangelo secondo Matteo*, edited by G. Gambetti (Milan, Garzanti, 1964), p. 298. The claim is disinguous: see *Pasolini on Pasolini*, p. 91, and Barański's "The Texts if *Il Vangelo secondo Matteo*", in the present volume.

53   Many of Pasolini's screenplays written between 1954 and 1960 were adaptations: *Il prigioniero della montagna* (L. Trenker, 1955; novel by G. Benek), *Il sole nel ventre* (1955, unproduced; from J. Hougron), *I promessi sposi* (1960, unproduced; from Manzoni—see G. P. Brunetta, "Il viaggio di Pasolini dentro i classici", in *Galleria*, 35, i–iv [1985], 67–75), *Il bell'Antonio* (M. Bolognini, 1960; from V. Brancati), *La giornata balorda* (M. Bolognini, 1960; from A. Moravia) and *La lunga notte del '43* (F. Vancini, 1960; from G. Bassani).

54   See the photographs of the director and his story-boards in *Mamma Roma*, pp. 160ff. See also *Pier Paolo Pasolini: A Future Life*, edited by L. Betti and L. Gambara Thovazzi (Rome, Associazione Fondo Pier Paolo Pasolini, 1989), pp. 25–33.

55   From "Per conoscere Pasolini", an interview with RAI-TV by Leonardo Lucchetti, later transcribed in *Pier Paolo Pasolini: il cinema di poesia*, edited by L. De Giusti (Rome, Gremese, 1983), p. 54. Thirty-four of the comic frames are to be found in his collected drawings, *I disegni 1941–1975*, edited by G. Zigaina with an introduction by M. De Micheli (Milan, Scheiwiller, 1978), plates 89–122.

56   First page of an undated, unpaginated typescript screenplay, now in the Fondo Pasolini, Rome.

57   M. De Micheli, in his introduction to *I disegni*, unpaginated but p. 15.

58   Compare De Micheli's term "tradurre" with *EE*, 207–08, 267–69, and with Pasolini's notion of "translatability" which is present in his work from "Dialet, lenga, stil", *Stroligút di cà da l'aga*, Apr. 1944, to *SC*, 1–2. See R. Gordon, "Tradizione e metafora: lingue e dialetto in Pasolini", in *Poesia dialettale e poesia in lingua*, edited by A. Dolfi (Milan, Scheiwiller, 1994), pp. 35–50. See also G. Scalia, *La mania della verità* (Bologna, Cappelli, 1978).

59   See *Passione e ideologia* [1960] (Milan, Garzanti, 1977), pp. 263–72, 466–79, 480–87.

60   *Petrolio*, edited by M. Careri and G. Chiarcossi (Turin, Einaudi, 1992).

61   See E. De Angelis, "Corpi simbolici", *L'indice dei libri del mese*, 2 (Feb. 1993), 6–7, for a rare positive review of the book; F. Fortini, "Petrolio [1992]", in his *Attraverso Pasolini* (Turin, Einaudi, 1993), pp. 238–48; *A partire da "Petrolio": Pasolini interroga la letteratura*, edited by C. Benedetti and M. A. Grignani (Ravenna, Longo, 1995); and D. Ward, *A Poetics of Resistance: Narrative and the Writings of Pier Paolo Pasolini* (Madison, NJ, Fairleigh Dickinson University Press, 1995), pp. 88–114.

PASOLINI'S LINGUISTICS

Tullio De Mauro

Gianfranco Contini described Pasolini's involvement with Marxist ideology as "intelligent dilettantism". The same could be said of his relationship to linguistics. His dilettantism may be discerned in his sometimes mistaken use of key linguistic terms and in the generality of his references to scholars and trends in the field.[1] A common result of this is that specialists have distanced themselves from Pasolini's linguistic ideas and theories, and it has taken a long time for these to be accorded understanding and respect.[2]

Nevertheless, Pasolini had an incredibly wide-ranging and intense experience of linguistic expression, which, as I have attempted to show elsewhere,[3] allowed him to develop important and original ideas around at least three thematic nuclei of major interest for scholars of historical descriptive linguistics and of linguistic theory. These are: the difficulties and limitations of using ordinary Italian and/or one of its dialects in literary texts and in the contemporary theatre; the sweeping linguistic and cultural changes which took place in Italian society during the 1950s and 1960s; the conflict between different languages regarded as the channels of expression for that tragic sense of reality which pervaded Pasolini's entire life.

Since ancient Greece, the European tradition has embraced many writers who have turned their hand to more than one form of art. The modern era has seen figurative artists who, like Michelangelo, were also notable poets, and talented writers who were also musicians, following the example of Schumann and Wagner. Over the past few decades, many European and American writers have been closely involved with cinema and, for their part, people in the film industry have made an important contribution to literature. In Italy many playwrights and novelists—Vitaliano Brancati, Diego

Fabbri, Giuseppe Berto, Corrado Alvaro, Alberto Moravia, Giuseppe Marotta, Vasco Pratolini, Cesare Giulio Viola—, as well as the poets Libero De Libero and Leonardo Sinisgalli, have worked in the film industry as scriptwriters, while the novelist and poet Alberto Bevilacqua moved on to directing. Various people have made the move from cinema to literature, the most significant case probably being that of Tonino Guerra.

The mingling of art forms, therefore, is not unusual. Again in Italy, we have the varied artistic experiences of Cesare Zavattini, who, despite his notable work as a watercolourist, humourist and dialect poet, is basically regarded as a man of the cinema. What makes Pasolini's artistic experience exceptional, however, is above all the way in which he employed, often as a matter of course and for long periods of time, a wide range of languages and forms of expression: lyric poetry in Friulan and Italian, didactic and epic poetry,[4] novels,[5] plays,[6] music,[7] film-making,[8] drawing,[9] while fusing all these activities with his continual work as a literary critic, journalist, pamphleteer and essayist.[10]

Pasolini was jealous of the autonomous dignity of his own aesthetic, linguistic and semiological observations and theorizations. To one of Jean Duflot's question, he replied forcefully:

> Voi siete matti. È molto spiacevole, sapete, per un autore, sentirsi sempre considerare come una "bestia da stile". E che tutto, per quel che lo riguarda, venga ridotto a pedina per comprendere la sua carriera stilistica. Ciò è disumano. È vero che studiando un autore bisognerà cercarne un'unità! Tuttavia ciò non va fatto in modo elementare [...]. Anzi, ve lo dico in faccia: mi offende molto che tutto quello che faccio venga ricondotto a spiegare il mio stile. È un modo di esorcizzarmi, e forse di darmi dello stupido. Uno stupido nella vita che magari è bravo nel suo lavoro. È quindi anche un modo di escludermi e di mettermi a tacere. (*Il sogno del centauro*, p. 118)

> [You're all mad. It is most disagreeable, you know, for an author to feel that he is always being judged as a "beast of style". And that everything he does is simply used to understand his stylistic career. This is inhuman. It's true that the study of an author invariably involves a search for unity! However, this cannot be done in an elementary fashion (...). In fact, I'll tell you straight: I'm extremely offended that everything I do is reduced to explaining my style. It's a way of exorcizing me, and perhaps of making

me out to be a fool. A fool in life who, at most, is good at his work. So it's also a way of excluding me and of shutting me up.]

Pasolini's human concern, however, is not contradicted by the fact that his observations on dialect and language, on literary style and on the relationship between different languages carry that particular weight which stems from a wide-ranging and intense experience, at once direct, living and productive. His unsystematic historical researches, theoretical essays and terminological and conceptual errors should not be allowed to reduce the significance of his thinking. I will attempt to give a sense of this by considering Pasolini principally as an observer and explorer of the Italian linguistic situation, and as an observer and theoretician of the relationship between different types of language and forms of expression.

Pasolini's decision to move from his early poetic attempts in Italian to writing verse in Friulan was immediately accompanied by critical reflection. In diary notes published after his death and in writings of the 1940s (which appeared later) he expressed a sense of unease with regard to the national language, which he considered sterile,[11] while, at the same time, feeling Friulan, his mother's dialect, to be a concrete and physical reality endowed with an authentic tradition as regards both life and culture.[12] As I have noted elsewhere, Pasolini was one of the first Italian writers, perhaps the first one of note, who lacked a native dialect and was brought up speaking an early form of that Italian which, in the 1940s, outside Tuscany and Rome, was spoken only in itinerant households drawn from different regions, as his was. In contrast to this kind of Italian, understandably felt to be an academic language always spoken according to formal registers, and marked by a lack of feeling, dialectal speech gave rise to those wondrous emotions which he recalled with affection even many years later.[13] Of course Pasolini was well aware that by using Friulan in his poems he was initiating a cultured and literary operation, and he stated that the Friulan words he wrote were often "looked up in Pirona's dictionary".[14] But what Friulan offered him was precisely what was lacked by other writers who had literary intentions when writing in Italian and were not native of certain parts of the country: namely, the possibility of using in a literary mode a linguistic heritage that was also used and experienced in the emotional and concrete life of every day. Pasolini believed he could find this continuity by choosing as the language of his poetry the Friulan spoken by his mother and by his friends from Casarsa.

During the 1950s, having moved, or rather fled, to Rome, Pasolini enriched his linguistic ideas by drawing on three new sources: Contini, Gadda and Gramsci.

As is well known, it was Contini who discovered and immediately praised the young poet's early attempts at writing, and had a determining influence on Pasolini. When Pasolini read Contini's essay on Petrarch's language (1951), it became clear to him that the issue of dialect in the Italian literary tradition was not necessarily one of languages in opposition. Indeed, since Dante's time, dialect had been and could be a component of the highest form of the nation's literature.[15] The four attributes which Contini recognized in Dante may be seen as a sort of prophetic mirror of Pasolini's progress. They are: plurilingualism, as the "poliglottia degli stili e [...] dei generi" ["polyglotism of style and genre"]; "pluralità di toni e pluralità di strati lessicali come compresenza" ["plurality of tones and plurality of lexical strata as co-presence"]; "l'interesse teoretico [...], l'ansia di giustificarsi linguisticamente" ["theoretical concerns (...), the anxiety to justify himself in linguistic terms"]; "la sperimentazione incessante" ["unceasing experimentation"].

Contini's suggestions cast light on Pasolini's relationship to Gadda, whose writings Pasolini took to be the embodiment of plurilingualism as the co-presence of several linguistic strata on a single page and who, at the same time, served as a model and a source of inspiration.[16]

Gramsci's writings, which were beginning to be published by Einaudi, played a decisive role in the development of Pasolini's historical research and theoretical thinking. Thanks to Gramsci, Pasolini understood that linguistic choices not only involve literary premises and consequences, but are also woven into the fabric of social relations and conflicts; that, whether consciously or not, they carry political weight; and that they are connected to the processes involved in the creation of hegemony in cultural and political life.[17] This interpretation of Gramsci was significant not only because it guided Pasolini's intellectual activity from then on, but also because of the originality which lay at its heart. It clearly highlighted the key importance of questions of language, and

therefore of culture, in Gramsci's political and social theory—
something which was only very gradually, and only in the 1970s,
properly understood.[18]

Inspired by Gramsci, Pasolini was led to emphasize the political importance of "communal democraticism", of Dante's and
Gadda's plurilingualism and of the "linguistic revolution" inherent in the lexical and stylistic choices of Pascoli (*PI*, 264–65, 269–
70). The great analytical frescos of *Poesia dialettale* (1952) and
Canzoniere italiano (1955) paint a historically sensitive picture. They
make reference to the concrete nature of local and regional affairs;
to the elective and minority status of the tradition of literary Italian;
to the renewed value placed on the contribution made by dialects
to the creation of a national literature; to the specific flavour, given
the Italian linguistic situation, acquired by examples of popular
poetry, often the link between literature written in the Italian
language and literature written in dialect—in a language which
(outside Tuscany) has no popular base, and in dialects with no
national range.

As had been the case with Dante, Pasolini's desire to justify
himself linguistically took on the appearance of a primarily historical justification, rather than a theoretical one. His research and
notes on the slang spoken in the Roman *borgate*, and the linguistic
choices made in *Le ceneri* and in his two most famous novels may
be seen as experimental verifications of the historical and cultural
hypotheses he developed during the early 1950s.[19]

The first-hand experience of literary creation in both Italian and
Friulan, the linguistic and literary experiments which went against
the tradition of bureaucratic and *petit bourgeois* Italian,[20] the histor-
ical-linguistic and political-cultural reflections suggested by the
Contini–Gadda–Gramsci triad, and the direct contact with several
quite different socio-cultural strata—the countryside and the city,
the urban underclass and avant-garde intellectual groups in different cities—endowed Pasolini with a highly refined sensibility to
any symptom, as soon as it appeared, of profound change in the
linguistic order of Italian society.

It may be conjectured that Pasolini's cinematic experiences during
the early 1960s—*Accattone* (1961), *La ricotta* (1963) and *Il Vangelo
secondo Matteo* (1964)—gave him the sense that an Italian imbued

with elements of Roman dialect or, more simply, with realistic and direct tones, could have its own national audience and serve as its means of expression. Undoubtedly the birth of the centre-left played its part in this, together with the hopes that arose at the prospect of no more overtly anti-socialist governments (*Il sogno del centauro*, pp. 59–60, 97–99). What is certain, however, is that at the end of 1964, in a series of lectures to the Associazione Culturale Italiana published in *Rinascita* (26 December 1964) and which had a widespread impact, Pasolini indicated that a new linguistic reality was dawning in Italy—a kind of Italian which was no longer confined to a particular class but extended over a wide social base and was at one with the socio-economic developments taking place at the time: "È nato l'italiano come lingua nazionale" ["This is the birth of Italian as a national language"].[21]

This claim, expressed in such terms, was quite correct and for many revealed what was really happening. Four factors, however, called it into doubt. In the first place, Pasolini was speaking in terms not of usage but of "language", and this led those with little knowledge of linguistics to imagine, on Pasolini's authority, that a new vocabulary, grammar, syntax, and so on, were coming into being (which in turn led professional linguists to deride Pasolini's ideas precisely because of their lack of linguistic foundations). Secondly, Pasolini pushed the relationship between linguistic and socio-economic developments too far by asserting that the new language was "technological" and derived its uniformity from this. In actual fact, the linguistic unity which was being created was due to the growing convergence of speakers towards Italian, towards the lexical, grammatical, syntactic (and so forth) heritage of traditional Italian, rather than towards the undeniable, though quantitatively negligible, unitary circulation of forms linked to the worlds of industry and new technology.[22] Thirdly, and connected with that, Pasolini asserted that this new, technological language had its roots in the "industrial triangle" of Turin, Genoa and Milan. Although it is undoubtedly true that this period saw the beginnings of the growing prestige of the Milanese variety of Italian,[23] the remaining two points of the triangle have enjoyed, and continue to enjoy, far less linguistic prestige than other cities and regions, especially Rome and Naples. Lastly, the lectures seemed to value in a positive and enthusiastic way what they were uncovering in the new Italian linguistic situation, so much so that it almost seemed that Pasolini wanted to give approbation to the literary and daily use of formulae derived from technological Italian, which he bizarrely exemplified in and with the style of Aldo Moro (a jurist educated in humanistic and historical studies, and whose background was Southern Italian and Roman).

Subsequently, Pasolini toned down his thesis. He repeatedly stressed the merely "incipient" nature of the process he had spoken about. He also indicated that it entailed paying the high price represented by many subproletarian groups and young people abandoning their traditional dialects without having the tools with which to master Italian properly, thereby ending up in a state of "aphasia".[24] Above all, he asserted the need, in such a complex situation as Italy's, of instruments with which to recognize current sociolinguistic changes in a systematic manner.[25] This idea of a linguistic observatory is certainly a valuable one and has often been reiterated, but so far without any concrete results.[26]

Pasolini's first-hand experience of theatre and cinema, and his consequent comparison of cinematic speech with the rather more stereotypical form to be found in the performance tradition of Italian theatre, led him to reflect on the relationship between oral execution, gesture and meaning.[27] Increasingly it was cinema that appeared to him to be the medium capable of transmitting that sense of reality which as an artist he was trying to capture. Pasolini spoke of cinema with enthusiasm for precisely this reason:

> Mi ci è voluto il cinema per capire una cosa enormemente semplice, ma che nessun letterato sa. Che la realtà si esprime da sola; e che la letteratura non è altro che un mezzo per mettere in condizione la realtà di esprimersi quando non è fisicamente presente. (*EE*, 141)

> [It was cinema that made me understand something extremely simple, but which no writer knows. That reality expresses itself, and that literature is nothing more than a means of providing the right conditions for reality to express itself when it is not physically present.]

This statement may appear stark; if it is taken in context, however, one may see what Pasolini was driving at in expressing himself so provocatively. Compared to all the other expressive media, cinema seems to be best at functioning as the "lingua della

realtà" ["language of reality"], because the complex interaction
between different languages, just as in reality, guarantees the
maximum continuity between reality and its representations (*EE*,
202ff, 243ff). He regards meaning as something vital which acts as
an escape-point where the signs of different languages converge,
and which only the interrelation of many languages (and therefore
principally cinema) is able to decipher (*EE*, 244–45; *Il sogno del
centauro*, pp. 108–16). Pasolini longed for a "general semiology" as
a theory of the meaning of reality; equally, the channels through
which this meaning is expressed need constantly to be challenged
(*EE*, 246–51; *Il sogno del centauro*, pp. 24–25). Alongside these
theoretical sketches stand the many observations which, in a fresh
and direct way, render explicit Pasolini's various experiences
stemming from his comparison of different languages, experiences
which often contradict or visibly correct his more general assertions. They rightly highlight the constructed and pastiche-like
character of the amalgam of heterogenous languages (music, song,
live dialogue and dubbed dialogue, images of static and moving
bodies, of objects, and so on) which cinema is (*Il sogno del centauro*,
pp. 24, 108–11). In a very humble manner, they tell, from the inside,
of Pasolini's apprenticeship in the film industry.[28] They testify to
the technical breadth, both autonomous and specific, of film technology:

> Nella mia concezione del cinema come lingua scritta del linguag-
> gio della realtà, la realtà esteriore ha però anch' essa la sua
> importanza. Ancora oggi il montaggio rimane un'operazione
> filmica pericolosa... Ho creduto per parecchio tempo che l'"azio-
> ne profilmica", quella che si svolge davanti alla cinepresa, avesse
> maggiore importanza. Dopo, mi sono messo a dosare il tempo, o
> piuttosto la "durata" delle immagini. È a questo livello che le
> immagini assumono il suo valore. Un secondo di piú o di meno
> cambia completamente il valore di un piano, di un'immagine. È
> durante il montaggio che si opera la stilizzazione. Addirittura,
> dirò, è lí che coesistono la convenzione e la libertà del cinema. (*Il
> sogno del centauro*, p. 115)

> [In my conception of cinema as the written form of the language
> of reality, external reality, too, still has its own specific import-
> ance. Even today editing remains a dangerous film-making
> process... For a long time I believed that "profilmic action", that
> which takes place in front of the camera, was of the greatest

importance. Later, I began to meter the time, or rather the "duration" of the images. It is at this level that images acquire their worth. A second more or a second less completely changes the value of a shot, of an image. Style comes into it at the editing stage. In fact, I would say that it is here that cinema's conventionality and freedom coexist.]

But this is not to deny that cinema is bound "[ad] esprim*ersi sempre mediante la realtà*" ["always to express itself by means of reality"], with its "*segni iconici viventi, che rimandano a se stessi*" ["living iconic signs that refer to themselves": *Il sogno del centauro*, pp. 94–95]. For Pasolini, it was this that made cinema the most effective instrument with which to delve into the things of real life:

> Io cerco di creare un linguaggio che metta in crisi l'uomo medio, lo spettatore medio, nei suoi rapporti con il linguaggio dei mass-media, per esempio... Nel momento in cui io odio le istituzioni e lotto contro di esse, provo un'immensa tenerezza per questa istituzione della lingua italiana in quanto *koinè*, per questa lingua italiana nel senso piú esteso del termine, perché è proprio all'interno di questo quadro che mi viene concesso di innovare, ed è tramite questo codice istituito che fraternizzo con gli altri; quel che piú m'importa nell'istituzione è il codice che rende possibile la fraternità [...]. Il codice, soprattutto il codice linguistico, è la forma esterna indispensabile a questa fraternità umana che provo sempre in me come qualche cosa che ho perduto. (*Il sogno del centauro*, p. 58)

> [I am trying to create a language which plunges into crisis the average person's, the average spectator's relationship with the language of the mass media, for example... While hating institutions and fighting against them, I have a deep fondness for this institution that is the Italian language insofar as it is a koine, for this Italian language in the broadest sense of the term, because it is precisely within this framework that I am able to innovate, and it is by means of this established code that I fraternize with others; for me the most important aspect of the institution is the code which makes brotherhood possible (...). Codes, especially the linguistic code, are the external forms indispensable for this human brotherhood, which I always feel is something I have lost.]

(*Translated from Italian by Henryk Barański*)

NOTES

1   For Pasolini, "diachrony" and "diachronic" seem intended to evoke something like "separation, detachment, belonging to the past". Thus in *Empirismo eretico* (Milan, Garzanti, 1972) he speaks of the "diacronia fra lingua scritta e parlata" (see G. Lepschy's critique, "Metalingua", *Delta*, 7 [1967], 1–4, [p. 2]); he asserts, albeit obscurely (p. 58), that "Gramsci [...] usava [...] contemporaneamente due lingue orali [...] in diacronia"; he states that "la cultura romanesco-napolitana si è rivelata improvvisamente diacronica" by the actions of the "città del Nord" (p. 25), etc. A real problem, that of the poverty of the Italian language's oral tradition, is identified and discussed by means of acute observations mingled with unacceptable assertions such as that (already noted by Lepschy) of "lingua orale" being "una categoria distinta da ogni 'langue' e da ogni 'parole', una specie di ipo o meta struttura di ogni struttura linguistica" (p. 63). The wave of discussions (between C. Metz, R. Barthes and others) on the form of language recognizable in cinema led Pasolini to look for minimal units in films, of secondary articulation, which he called *cinèmi* and which are supposed to be "gli oggetti, le forme e gli atti della realtà che noi cogliamo coi sensi" (*EE*, 206–08; these are rightly criticized by E. Garroni, *Semiotica ed estetica* [Bari, Laterza, 1968], pp. 14–17). In *EE*, 26, and elsewhere, "allocuzione" stands for "locuzione", etc. On the distorted use of slang glossaries, see M. Jacqmain, "Appunti sui glossari pasoliniani", *Linguistica Antwerpiensa*, 4 (1970), 109–54. Among authors mentioned, those used in a relatively direct and appropriate manner are G. I. Ascoli (*Passione e ideologia* [Milan, Garzanti, 1960], pp. 124ff; *EE*, 33; *Le belle bandiere*, edited by G. C. Ferretti [Rome, Editori Riuniti, 1978], p. 85), G. Contini (see nn. 15 and 17 below), G. Herczeg (*EE*, 85ff), R. Barthes (*EE*, 126ff, 236ff; *Il sogno del centauro*, edited by J. Duflot [Rome, Editori Riuniti, 1983], pp. 93ff, 123ff and *passim*). Not always as accurate are the references to (De) Saussure (*EE*, 74, *Il sogno del centauro*, pp. 93, 125; but see n. 15 below), Jakobson and the Prague School (*EE*, 60–61, 142; *Il sogno del centauro*, pp. 92–93).

2   Reservations and criticisms are expressed by: B. A. Terracini, "Lingua e dialetti", *Ce fastu?*, 39 (1963), 8–13 (p. 12: Pasolini ideologizes and takes to extremes the relationship between language and dialect), and his reply to the inquiry "Come parleremo domani", *Fiera letteraria*, 7 Mar. 1965, 6–7 (Pasolini has no sense of historical continuity); G. Devoto, *Profilo di storia linguistica italiana*, second edition (Florence, La Nuova Italia, 1964), p. 178; G. Lepschy, "Metalingua"; E. Garroni, *Semiotica*, where it is nevertheless stated that "nonostante la sua inaccettabilità e il suo carattere d'improvvisazione, crediamo che la posizione di Pasolini contenga una sua innegabile esigenza di verità" (p. 14). From the 1970s onwards, while criticisms and reservations did not disappear, they were accompanied by a growing interest in Pasolini's ideas: T. O'Neill, "*Il filologo come politico*: Linguistic Theory and its Sources in Pier Paolo Pasolini", *Italian Studies*, 25 (1970), 63–78; G. L. Beccaria, "Con Pier Paolo linguista", *La stampa*, 29 Sept. 1972 (on *Empirismo eretico*: "Sarebbe troppo chiedere a questo libro coerenza metodologica, salde costruzioni [...].

Tra tanto fluire furioso ed anarchico c'è [...] tutto un traboccare di osservazioni finissime"); G. and A. L. Lepschy, *The Italian Language Today* (London, Hutchinson, 1977), pp. 31–32; A. M. Mioni and L. Renzi, "Introduzione", in *Aspetti sociolinguistici dell'Italia contemporanea*, edited by R. Simone and G. Ruggiero, 2 vols (Rome, Bulzoni, 1977), I, 1–8 (p. 3); G. Folena, "La storia della lingua oggi", in *Lingua, sistemi letterari, comunicazione sociale* by various authors (Padua, CLEUP, 1977), pp. 109–36 (pp. 133–35); and see nn. 14, 19, 21, 23 below. A good student dissertation on the topic is R. Monti, *Pier Paolo Pasolini linguista e filologo*, unpublished, University of Rome "La Sapienza", 1982 (an extract has been published as "Lineamenti di una ricerca linguistica dal Friuli alle *Ceneri di Gramsci*", *Galleria*, 35, i–iv [1985]).

3   T. De Mauro, "La ricerca linguistica (di Pasolini)", *Nuova generazione*, 19 (1976), 23–24; "Pasolini critico dei linguaggi", *Galleria*, 35, i–iv (1985), 7–30. I also referred to Pasolini in my *Storia linguistica dell'Italia unita* (Bari, Laterza, 1963), pp. 126, 241, 275, 364.

4   *Poesie a Casarsa* (Bologna, Libreria Landi, 1942), reprinted in *Tal cour di un frut* (Tricesimo, Ed. Friuli, 1953) and in *La meglio gioventú* (Florence, Sansoni, 1954), which also includes poems in Italian, *poemetti*, etc.; *Le ceneri di Gramsci* (Milan, Garzanti, 1957); *L'usignolo della Chiesa Cattolica* (Milan, Longanesi, 1958; reprinted Turin, Einaudi, 1976); *La religione del mio tempo* (Milan, Garzanti, 1961); *Poesia in forma di rosa* (Milan, Garzanti, 1964); *Trasumanar e organizzar* (Milan, Garzanti, 1971); *La nuova gioventú* (includes *La meglio gioventú*; Turin, Einaudi, 1975); *Poesie* (includes *Le ceneri, La religione, Poesia in forma di rosa, Trasumanar* and others; Milan, Garzanti, 1975); *Poesie e pagine ritrovate*, edited by A. Zanzotto and N. Naldini (Rome, Lato Side, 1980). Now see also P. P. Pasolini, *Bestemmia: tutte le poesie*, edited by G. Chiarcossi and W. Siti, 2 vols (Milan, Garzanti, 1993).

5   Apart from his two best-known novels, see *Il sogno di una cosa* (Milan, Garzanti, 1962); *Alí dagli occhi azzurri* (Milan, Garzanti, 1965); the "pastiche" *La Divina Mimesis* (Turin, Einaudi, 1975); *Amado mio* (Milan, Garzanti, 1982); see also P. P. Pasolini, "*...Avec les armes...*", edited by L. Betti, G. Corapi and E. Pecora (Milan, Garzanti, 1984), p. 229.

6   *Orestiade di Eschilo*, translated by P. P. Pasolini (Urbino, STEU, 1960); *Il vantone* (Pasolini's translation of Plautus's *Miles Gloriosus*; Milan, Garzanti, 1963); *Calderon* (Milan, Garzanti, 1973); *Affabulazione; Pilade* (Milan, Garzanti, 1977); *Porcile; Orgia; Bestia da stile* (Milan, Garzanti, 1979).

7   Pasolini was the co-writer of songs for Laura Betti: see *Giro a vuoto: le canzoni di L. Betti* by various authors (Milan, Longanesi, 1965). As a film director, Pasolini always collaborated in the choice of music for his films, even though he was not listed in the soundtrack credits until *Edipo re*: see n. 8 below. This aspect of Pasolini's output is discussed in E. Micocci, "Musica, poesia, e aggregazione giovanile", in *L'industria della canzone*, edited by M. Gaspari (Rome, Editori Riuniti, 1981), pp. 138–44 (pp. 140–41).

8   For a full breakdown of Pasolini's varied work in the cinema, see *Pier Paolo Pasolini: corpi e luoghi*, edited by M. Mancini and G. Parrella (Rome, Theorema, 1981), pp. 525–37; and P. P. Pasolini, "*...Avec les armes...*", pp. 238, 242–45.

9   *I disegni, 1941–75*, edited by G. Zigaina (Milan, Scheiwiller, 1975); and P. P. Pasolini, *Zeichnungen and Gemälde* (Hamburg, Reimer, 1982); see also *Il sogno del centauro*, edited by J. Duflot, preface by G. C. Ferretti (Rome, Editori Riuniti, 1983), p. 22.

10   The best examples of Pasolini's study of dialect and popular poetry are *Poesia dialettale del Novecento*, edited by M. Dell'Arco and P. P. Pasolini, with an introduction by Pasolini (Parma, Guanda, 1952), and *Canzoniere italiano: antologia della poesia popolare italiana* (Bologna–Parma, Guanda, 1955; reprinted Milan, Garzanti, 1972), with two important introductory essays reprinted in *Passione e ideologia* (Milan, Garzanti, 1960), pp. 7–134, 137–259. Pasolini critically examines his own Friulan experience; he tackles head-on the complex historical-critical and folkloric tradition; he forcefully inserts himself into the (minority) line which places value on dialect literature and on the role of dialect in the Italian context (Ferrari, Croce, Sansone, Contini, Muscetta): see my study "Anonimo Romano e la nuova poesia dialettale italiana", in Anonimo Romano, *Er communismo co' la libbertà*, edited by M. Ferrara, with an introduction by T. De Mauro (Rome, Editori Riuniti, 1979), pp. xi–xl (pp. xiii–xv). The study of Pasolini cannot be reduced "alla [...] rivisitazione del dialetto in chiave solipsistica-nostalgica-decadente", as V. Coletti reduces it in "La letteratura dialettale e le preoccupazioni unitarie della storiografia e della critica letteraria", in *I dialetti e le lingue delle minoranze di fronte all'italiano* by various authors, 2 vols (Rome, Bulzoni, 1977), I, 655–66, which, overall, is a very good piece of work. Pasolini's essays on literary criticism, on language and language use, on film criticism and theory, on pedagogy and politics are brought together in the following collections, some published after his death: *Passione e ideologia*; *Uccellacci e uccellini* (Milan, Garzanti, 1966); *Empirismo eretico* (Milan, Garzanti, 1972), *Scritti corsari* (Milan, Garzanti, 1975); *Lettere luterane* (Turin, Einaudi, 1976); *Volgar' eloquio*, edited by A. Piromalli and D. Scarfoglio (Naples, Athena, 1976); *Le belle bandiere*, edited by G. C. Ferretti (Rome, Editori Riuniti, 1978); *Descrizioni di descrizioni*, edited by G. Chiarcossi (Turin, Einaudi, 1979); *Il caos*, edited by G. C. Ferretti (Rome, Editori Riuniti, 1979). Of importance for Pasolini, and for Italian life in general, are the as yet uncollected newspaper interviews and articles (an important collection of these may be found in the Fondo Pier Paolo Pasolini in Rome), some of which are cited and used in *Pasolini: cronaca giudiziaria, persecuzione, morte*, edited by L. Betti (Milan, Garzanti, 1977); and in E. Siciliano, *Vita di Pasolini* (Milan, Rizzoli, 1978); and see also *Pier Paolo Pasolini: corpi e luoghi*, pp. 541–65. The following books of interviews are also important: *Pasolini on Pasolini*, edited by O. Stack (London, Thames and Hudson, 1969); *Entretiens avec P. P. Pasolini*, edited by J. Duflot (Paris, Belfond, 1970), reprinted, with important additions by the author and with the title *Les Dernières Paroles d'un impie* (Paris, Belfond, 1975); *Il sogno del centauro* is an Italian translation of the latter, with further additions and manuscript variants by the author and by the French and Italian editors.

11   P. P. Pasolini, "Sulla poesia dialettale", *Poesia*, vol. VIII, edited by E. Falqui (Milan, Mondadori, 1947), pp. 105–16.

12   P. P. Pasolini, *Poesie e pagine ritrovate*, pp. 23, 28–29; and "I parlanti", *Botteghe oscure*, 8 (1951), 405–36.

13   "Al lettore nuovo", in *Poesie* (Milan, Garzanti, 1970), p. 6; *EE*, 62–64; *Il sogno del centauro*, pp. 23, 24, 27, 29.

14   Pasolini was referring to the "old" and the "new" *Vocabolario friulano*: the first was by Abbot Jacopo Pirona and was edited by G. A. Pirona (Venice, Antonelli, 1871); the second used as its point of departure work done by G. A. Pirona for the dialect dictionary competition launched by Boselli, the

Minister of Education (1890–93), which was then taken up by E. Carletti and G. B. Corgnali and published serially (Udine, Bosetti, 1928ff); it was republished in Udine by the Società Filologica Friulana in 1967. Pasolini insisted on the experimental, *felibrige* character (perhaps suggested by Contini?) of his Friulan experience: "Lettera dal Friuli", *Fiera letteraria*, 29 Aug. 1946; "Al lettore nuovo"; *Il sogno del centauro*. Certainly, his writings stretch the limits of the language of Casarsa, not just "with the help of Pirona", but with that of insertions not included in the Pirona of either 1871 or 1928, such as *rustic*, which may be found in E. Carletti's *Giunte* of 1967. What really fascinated him, however, was the continuous, unbroken contiguity of his relationship with the local speech, as he wrote in a letter to Andreina Ciceri in 1953 (which includes what is probably the first reference Pasolini made to Saussure). Some of these points are examined by T. De Mauro, "Pasolini critico dei linguaggi"; the major discussion, however, is A. Ciceri's complex study in *Antologia della letteratura friulana*, edited by B. Chiurlo (Udine, Libreria Editrice Udinese, 1927), with a sequentially numbered addition in a single volume by A. Ciceri, *I contemporanei* (Tolmezzo, Aquileia, 1975), pp. 576–607. See also G. Francescato, "Considerazioni per una storia del friulano letterario", *Atti dell'Accademia di Scienze, Lettere e Arti di Udine*, seventh series, 1 (1957–60), 1–23 (pp. 17–19 and notes); G. Francescato and F. Salimbeni, *Storia, lingua, società in Friuli* (Udine, Casamassima, 1976), pp. 211, 216–17; N. Naldini, *Nei campi del Friuli (la giovinezza di Pasolini) e una conversazione di Andrea Zanzotto* (Milan, All'Insegna del Pesce d'Oro, 1984).

15   G. Contini, "Preliminari sulla lingua del Petrarca" (originally published in *Paragone*, Apr. 1951), in *Il Trecento* by various authors (Florence, Sansoni, 1953), pp. 95–120, and in *Varianti e altra linguistica* (Turin, Einaudi, 1970), pp. 169–92 (pp. 171–72 for Dante's "attributes"). As regards Pasolini's relations with Contini, see A. Ciceri, *I contemporanei*, which includes an important letter from Contini to Pasolini; E. Siciliano, *Vita*, pp. 66, 67, 167; and n. 17 below.

16   P. P. Pasolini, "Il *Pasticciaccio* di Gadda", *Vie nuove*, 18 Jan. 1958, 16 (Belli represents regression into dialect, Verga the naturalistic mimesis of dialect speech, Gadda the assumption of dialect elements in free indirect speech which is "estro, ghirgoro, sberleffo"), and *PI*, 309–11. See also E. Siciliano, *Vita*, p. 167 and index.

17   Gramsci and Contini are referred to as "my teachers" in E. F. Accrocca, "Che cosa fanno gli scrittori italiani: dieci domande a PPP", *Fiera letteraria*, 30 June 1957; as regards Gramsci in particular, see *PI*, 309–11; *Il sogno del centauro*, p. 27. "Il solo critico italiano i cui problemi siano stati i problemi letterari di Gramsci è Contini," declares a note in *La Divina Mimesis*, pp. 91–92.

18   Pasolini was the first to realize the central importance of language in Gramsci's ideas on culture and political hegemony; see T. De Mauro, "La ricerca linguistica". On this area of Gramsci's thought see F. Lo Piparo, *Lingua, intellettuali, egemonia in Gramsci* (Bari, Laterza, 1979).

19   T. De Mauro, "La ricerca linguistica"; and *Il sogno del centauro*, pp. 27–30.

20   *PI*, 329–30. See also S. Gensini, *Elementi di storia linguistica italiana* (Bergamo, Minerva Italica, 1982), pp. 410–13.

21   *EE*, 9–28 (especially pp. 24ff); see also O. Parlangeli, *La "nuova" questione della lingua* (Bari, Facoltà di Lettere e Filosofia, 1969; reprinted Brescia, Paideia, 1971), which introduces (pp. v–lxii) and reprints Pasolini's most important

articles, as well as those for and against him; T. O'Neill, "*Il filologo come politico*"; M. Vitale, *La questione della lingua*, second edition (Palermo, Palumbo, 1978), pp. 616–21, 769–75; U. Vignuzzi, "Discussioni e polemiche novecentesche sulla lingua italiana", in *Letteratura italiana contemporanea*, edited by G. Mariani and M. Petrucciani (Rome, Lucarini, 1982), pp. 709–36.

22   The first references to this are in T. De Mauro, *Storia*, pp. 144–45.

23   T. De Mauro, *Storia*, p. 148; more analytically in subsequent editions. N. Galli de' Paratesi, *Lingua toscana in bocca ambrosiana* (Bologna, Mulino, 1984), particularly pp. 213ff, explicitly agrees with much of the substance of Pasolini's positions and provides data and analyses.

24   See *BB*, 299–302; and *LL*, 9, 27–30; "Vagisce appena il nuovo italiano nazionale", *Il giorno*, 24 Feb. 1965, reprinted in *EE*, 37–39; *Volgar' eloquio*. See also S. Martelli, "Dal 'linguaggio tecnologico' al 'volgar eloquio' (questioni e nuove questioni linguistiche di Pasolini)", *Misure critiche*, 7 (1977), 55–74.

25   "Sulla lingua: sette risposte a sette punti interrogativi", *Il giorno*, 3 Mar. 1965; and *EE*, 33–36.

26   On the linguistic observatory, see "Vagisce appena", and two of my articles: "Un osservatorio della lingua", *Paese sera*, 25 May 1973, reprinted in *Le parole e i fatti* (Rome, Editori Riuniti, 1977), pp. 72–75; "Per l'osservatorio linguistico e culturale: apologia di un ritardo", *Linguaggi*, 1 (1984), 7–13.

27   *BB*, 310–12; *EE*, 55ff; *Il sogno del centauro*, pp. 137ff (on the "theatre of the word"); the second page of *Il vantone*'s flyleaf is important as regards traditional theatrical diction.

28   *Il sogno del centauro*, pp. 39–40, 97. On Pasolini's apprenticeship in cinema there are interesting statements by E. De Concini and T. Guerra in P. P. Pasolini, "Lettere inedite dal 'confine' a De Concini", *Marka*, 4, viii (Apr–June 1983), 28–46.

PASOLINI TRADUTTORE:
TRANSLATION, TRADITION AND REWRITING

John P. Welle

> In translating, we change what we
> translate and above all that we change
> ourselves.
>
> (Octavio Paz)[1]

As is well known, Pier Paolo Pasolini was remarkably prolific. He was the author of poetry, novels, films, critical and theoretical essays, verse tragedies, screenplays, journalism, paintings, drawings and art criticism. He also edited two important anthologies of dialect and popular poetry, and produced a significant number of literary translations. Despite the vast critical literature on Pasolini, and despite the profoundly interdisciplinary nature of his work, few critics have sought to analyse the interconnections between his experimental forays in so many diverse media.[2] In fact the difficulty of dealing with Pasolini's multiform activities in a methodologically coherent and unitary fashion has itself become a kind of critical cliché. And necessarily so, for as Tullio De Mauro has succinctly noted:

> Pasolini [...] è il primo artista di grande livello internazionale che possa definirsi multimediale nel mondo di oggi. Pasolini è un infaticato sperimentatore di linguaggi profondamente diversi. E per ciascun linguaggio, cioè per ciascuna famiglia di codici, dal pittorico al musicale, al filmico, a quello verbale, è un infaticato sperimentatore di lingue, di idiomi diversi.[3]

> [Pasolini (...) is the first artist of high international standing who might be defined as multimedial in today's world. Pasolini is a

tireless experimenter with profoundly different languages. And
for each language, that is, for each family of codes, from the
pictorial to the musical, the filmic to the verbal, he is a tireless
experimenter with tongues, with different idioms.]

De Mauro reminds us not only of Pasolini's unrivalled capabilities
for experimentation, but also of his love of language, his passion for
idioms and the idiomatic, and his philological devotion to Italy's
plurilinguistic culture. Pasolini's singular determination to move
among and between various languages, cultures and modes of
expression constitutes the most salient defining characteristic of
his textual practice. At the same time, he combined his multimedial
artistic explorations with practical criticism, theoretical reflection
and political intervention. The present essay will focus on aspects
of literary translation in the development of Pasolini's career, in
order to demonstrate its continuing presence and influential role in
his multimedial experimentalism. Indeed, translation represents
one of the few unifying elements in Pasolini's experience and
beckons as a promising link between his linguistic, artistic, theoretical and political concerns.

Recent decades have witnessed a dramatic increase in translation studies.[4] Within the Italian context, Pier Vincenzo Mengaldo
has called attention to the importance of translation in the formation and development of the major Italian poets of the twentieth
century:

> Il diffondersi delle traduzioni poetiche d'autore è indiscindibile
> dal formarsi di una figura di poeta in cui il mestiere lirico si
> dirama in una piú complessa attività di intellettuale militante ed
> è quasi costituzionalmente accompagnato e doppiato dal conti-
> nuo esercizio della funzione "metapoetica" in tutte le sue forme.
> Non è in causa semplicemente, in breve, la contiguità di poeta e
> traduttore, ma l'affermarsi di un tipo d'operatore che è insieme
> poeta, traduttore e critico [...]. Occorre sempre riflettere sul fatto
> che nel numero dei critici letterari in assoluto maggiori del nostro
> Novecento siano senza dubbi poeti come Montale e Solmi, Fortini
> e Pasolini.[5]

[The diffusion of poetic translations by major authors is inseparable from the formation of a figure of the poet in which the
occupation "lyric poet" branches out into a more complex activity of militant intellectual and is almost constitutionally accompanied and doubled by the continual exercise of the "metapoetic"

function in all its forms. It is not simply a matter, in brief, of the contiguity of poet and translator, but the assertion of a type of operator that is at once poet, translator and critic (…). It is always necessary to reflect on the fact that among the unquestionably greatest literary critics of the Italian twentieth century there are poets like Montale and Solmi, Fortini and Pasolini.]

Whereas earlier criticism of the "traduzioni poetiche d'autore" had focused almost exclusively on questions of style, poetics and "influence" between the poet translated and the poet translator, Mengaldo rightly emphasizes the implications of translation not only for literary history, but also for our understanding of the careers of literary intellectuals who are poets, translators and critics.

Within this context, Pier Paolo Pasolini is a particularly significant example of "un tipo di operatore che è insieme poeta, traduttore e critico". Because he is, in Asor Rosa's phrase, "forse, l'ultimo grande letterato della tradizione italiana" ["perhaps, the last great man of letters in the Italian tradition"],[6] Pasolini's translation activities shed an important light on the role of translation in Italian poetry between the 1940s and 1970s. Thus, even though his translations are generally considered the least "original", and therefore the least prestigious element in his *curriculum vitae*, they most certainly merit study in their own right.[7] Rather than analysing the stylistic qualities of his numerous translations, however, I propose to retrace the familiar trajectory of Pasolini's career from an unfamiliar perspective. By exploring Pasolini's activities as a translator, it may be shown that translation, far from being a marginal element in his experience, made a profound impact on his development as a poet, dramatist, critic, film-maker and theorist.

Ranging from Friulan versions of such modern poets as Tommaseo, Rimbaud, Ungaretti and T. S. Eliot, made in the 1940s, to Italian (and in one case *romanesco*) renderings of ancient authors like Virgil, Sophocles, Aeschylus and Plautus, done in the 1950s and 1960s, Pasolini's work as a translator includes such diverse modes as verse translation, drama translation and the translation (in collaboration with Dacia Maraini) of film dialogue (see the Appendix for a list of his translations). From the 1940s through to the 1970s, translation represents a frequent option in Pasolini's artistic production. It exerts an important influence on his textual strategies, as well as constituting a central paradigm in his critical and theoretical discourse. Yet because of the translator's traditional invisibility, the critical marginalization of the study of literary translation, and the dominance of *contaminazione* as the critical paradigm for approaching Pasolini's complex intertextuality, translation has seldom received critical attention as an important element in Pasolini's *œuvre*.

REWRITING AND TRADITION: "SOLO NELLA TRADIZIONE È IL MIO AMORE"

Franco Fortini, in one of his seminal articles on Pasolini, originally published in 1960, described the poet's textual strategies in terms of "pastiche", "la traduzione immaginaria", "la copia". He gathered all these closely related but diverse techniques under the suggestive title "contaminazioni":

> Pasolini, nella esperienza biografico-psicologica dell'antitesi e della contraddizione, scopre le incommensurabili possibilità stilistiche ed espressive del "pastiche", della traduzione immaginaria, della "copia" e [...] crea una serie di opere, attraverso le quali, non nelle quali, egli riesce a dare delle concrete rappresentazioni poetiche. Sarebbe facile un elenco: le imitazioni e i calchi dai provenzali e dal *Romancero* ne *La meglio gioventú*, il Rimbaud dell'*Usignolo*, il Baudelaire di *Récit* [...]. In una parola, contaminazioni.[8]

> [Pasolini, in the biographical-psychological experience of antithesis and contradiction, discovers the incommensurable stylistic and expressive possibilities of the "pastiche", of the imaginary translation, of the "copy" and (...) creates a series of works through which, not in which, he succeeds in giving some concrete poetic representations. A list would be easy: the imitations and tracings from the Provençals and from *Romancero* in *La meglio gioventú*, the Rimbaud of *L'usignolo*, the Baudelaire of *Récit* (...). In a word, contaminations.]

Originating in his analysis of the poetic style of *Le ceneri di Gramsci*, Fortini's emphasis on "contamination" has become the most frequently adopted trope for describing Pasolini's textual strategies; and this choice is not without good reason. Indeed, according to Rinaldi, "contaminazione" represents one of the few critical paradigms that influenced Pasolini himself:

Alcuni contributi critici hanno stimolato una risposta da parte dello scrittore e perfino un aggiustamento o un adeguamento della sua pratica, come se egli obbedisse ad una sorta di consiglio (pensiamo al primo intervento di Contini oppure a quelli di Fortini).[9]

[Some critical contributions stimulated a response on the part of the writer and even an adjustment or an adaptation of his practice, as if he were obeying advice of some kind (we are thinking of Contini's first essay or of those by Fortini).]

In a 1964 interview originally published in *Bianco e nero* and translated into English the following year, Pasolini himself claimed to work "under the sign of contamination".[10] Moreover, in discussing the technique of "free indirect discourse", Pasolini uses the term "contaminazione" in a linguistic sense throughout the essays of *Empirismo eretico*.[11]

"Contamination", however, like all paradigms and theories, is not without its limits. Deriving from Erich Auerbach's magisterial studies of the stylistic interplay between *sermo sublimis* and *sermo humilis*, "contaminazione" suggests a vertical and hierarchical relationship between texts with connotations of high and low, superior and inferior, original and derivative. Under the sign of "contamination", Pasolini's works inevitably appear slightly inferior, tainted, "impure". Furthermore, as a critical commonplace, "contamination" has been transposed by Giuseppe Zigaina from a literary to an ontological plane.[12] In constructing his "fantasiosa ipotesi" ["fanciful hypothesis"] concerning the poet's tragic death (a carefully orchestrated suicide, according to the Friulan painter and Pasolini's former friend), Zigaina would have us consider

il carattere di totalità della contaminazione pasoliniana. Che non esclude, dalla commistione dei vari linguaggi, quello della sua vita fisica, del suo agire politico e sociale, insomma del suo generale comportamento: compresi gli attimi estremi della sua vita e cioè la sua morte.[13]

[the character of totality of Pasolinian contamination. Which does not exclude, from the mixture of various languages, that of his physical life, of his political and social action, in sum of his general behaviour: including the final moments of his life, that is, his death.]

When a single critical paradigm is applied in such a totalizing fashion it should make us pause and reflect. While it is not my intention to intervene here in the debate concerning the "meaning" of Pasolini's death, I would argue that "contamination" in Zigaina's theory of "total contamination" has reached (indeed, overreached) its limits as a critical paradigm. It is therefore necessary, as Rinaldi asserts, to "partire semmai da altri punti [...] magari concedendo piú spazio a testi considerati marginali, cambiando le carte in tavola" ["to set out from other points (...) perhaps allowing more space to texts considered marginal, changing the cards on the table"].[14] By shifting the metaphor from *contaminatio* to *translatio*, we may be able to visualize a horizontal rather than vertical axis sustaining the pluriform modes of Pasolini's restless experimentation. By focusing critical attention on translation rather than on "contamination", we can rethink the driving forces behind Pasolini's textual strategies and explore new paths linking his work in various modes, genres and media.

Pasolini's translations, like literary translations in general, may perhaps best be analysed in their relationship to the literary tradition, the literary canon, or what some critics call the literary "polysystem".[15] In order to discuss their relationship to the tradition, it is useful to see them as manifestations of what Susan Bassnett and André Lefevere have called "rewritings". These scholars have argued persuasively for the need to study translation within a wide context which would embrace "translations, histories, critical articles, commentaries, anthologies, anything that contributes to constructing the 'image' of a writer and/or a work of literature".[16] For Lefevere, one may contribute to the growth of literary knowledge in two ways: either by producing literary works (writing) or by translating, commenting on and/or editing literary works (rewriting). As Lefevere asserts: "The interaction of writing and rewriting is ultimately responsible, not just for the canonization of specific authors or specific works and the rejection of others, but also for the evolution of a given literature, since rewritings are often designed precisely to push a given literature in a certain direction."[17] Pasolini's translations in the 1940s, 1950s and 1960s, together with his poetry, novels, films, plays, journalism and criticism, constitute an important manifestation of what Lefevere calls "the interaction of writing and rewriting" intended to "push a given literature in a certain direction". As a translator Pasolini interacts with three fundamental elements in the literary tradition: dialect poetry, the ancient classics and modern European poetry.

Pasolini's "writings and rewritings" were singularly effective in pushing Italian dialect poetry in a new direction. The Friulan translations, for example, shed light on Pasolini's neo-Romantic and Symbolist roots, on the development of his regional cultural politics, and on his propensity towards a textual strategy of juxtaposing two texts. Literary translation, as we shall see, was an important factor in his innovative approach to the dialect tradition and contributed to his life-long penchant for rewriting authoritative source texts in a personal manner.

Gianfranco Contini, in his by now legendary review, "Al limite della poesia dialettale", originally published in 1943, intuited and succinctly articulated the significance of Pasolini's initial use of Friulan:

> Sembrerebbe un autore dialettale, a prima vista, questo Pier Paolo Pasolini, per queste sue *Poesie a Casarsa* [...], un librettino di neppur cinquanta pagine, compresa la non bella traduzione letterale che di quelle pagine occupa la metà inferiore. E tuttavia [...] in questo fascicoletto si scorgerà la prima accessione della letteratura "dialettale" all'aura della poesia di oggi, e pertanto una modificazione in profondità di quell' attributo.[18]

> [He would seem to be a dialect author, at first glance, this Pier Paolo Pasolini, on the evidence of these *Poesie a Casarsa* of his (...), a little book of not even fifty pages, including the ungraceful literal translation, which occupies the bottom half of those pages. And nevertheless (...) in this little edition one will discern the first adherence of "dialect" literature to the aura of the poetry of today, and even a deepening modification of that attribute.]

Having recognized the profound significance of Pasolini's innovative undertaking, and having commented in passing on the poor quality of the literal translations at the bottom of the page, Contini goes on to suggest that Pasolini's use of Friulan, rather than pointing to the untranslatability of the "dialect", emphasizes the internal translatability of the language: "Pasolini insiste sull'intraducibilità, tipico carattere dialettale, mentre non s'è fatto che sottolineare l'interna traducibilità della lingua. Altro che sfumature sottratte alla parlata corrente!" ["Pasolini insists on untranslatability, a typical dialectal characteristic, while all he has done is underline the internal translatability of the language. These are

anything but nuances derived from the current spoken idiom!"].[19]
Contini's insight into Pasolini's "non dialettale" use of "dialetto"
was to help inspire the poet to redefine and reposition the entire
modern Italian tradition of poetry in dialect. Contini's highly
intuitive remark concerning Pasolini's Friulan text as a kind of
"translation" or metaphor for Italian was to become the centre of
Pasolini's poetics of dialect poetry, and to have important ramifications concerning the role of translation in his career.

Three years after Contini's review, Pasolini referred to the great
philologist's sympathetic reading of *Poesie a Casarsa* in a newspaper article promoting the second volume of the literary review
Stroligût, published by the Academiuta di Lenga Furlana. Pasolini
wrote:

> Centro ideale del quaderno sono le esemplari pagine del Contini;
> pubblicate nel '43 sul *Corriere ticinese* per le mie *Poesie a Casarsa*,
> esse rappresentano tuttora, a piú di tre anni di distanza *l'ideale
> prefazione—e una sorgente inesauribile di idee—per il nostro lavoro
> poetico in friulano*. Con estremo nitore vi è indicato il limite tra
> dialetto e non dialetto.[20]

> [The ideal centre of the journal is the exemplary pages of Contini;
> published in '43 in the *Corriere ticinese* for my *Poesie a Casarsa*, they
> represent even today, at more than three years' distance, *the ideal
> preface—and an inexhaustible fount of ideas—for our poetic work in
> Friulan*. The limit between dialect and non-dialect is there indic-
> ated with extreme clarity.]

Throughout his career Pasolini would acknowledge Contini's
singular influence on his work. Thus, when tracing the early stages
in the genealogy of Pasolini *traduttore*, it is important to emphasize
the subtle implications of Contini's reading. He gave a critical seal
of approval to Pasolini's juxtaposition of two texts, a juxtaposition
which creates a tension between "traducibilità" and "intraducibilità", and between "dialetto e non dialetto". In noting that "sembre-
rebbe un autore dialettale [...] questo Pier Paolo Pasolini", Contini
hints at an aesthetic operation which is akin to translation. Pasolini
was not relying primarily on the spoken language that he heard
around him, Contini's remarks suggest, but was rather "translating" from an "internal" Italian text that he was composing
simultaneously. This important point may be made clearer by
briefly noting the salient characteristics of Pasolini's linguistic

biography and by reviewing his own remarks regarding the composition of his dialect poetry.

As is well known, the Italian poet most responsible for the postwar revitalization of dialect poetry was not a "native" speaker of any dialect. In fact De Mauro has argued that, among modern Italian writers, Pasolini stands out for his conspicuous lack of a dialect: "Pasolini è uno dei primi scrittori italiani, forse tra i maggiori il primo, che non abbia avuto un dialetto nativo" ["Pasolini was one of the first Italian writers, perhaps the first one of note, who lacked a native dialect"].[21] In another context, De Mauro observes that "il dialetto, per lui, è qualche cosa di altro biograficamente" ["dialect, for him, is something biographically other"].[22] Pasolini himself indicated that he learned Friulan only after he had begun to write poetry in it.[23] He claimed to have written his dialect verse with the Pirona dictionary close at hand and that he moved "da una lingua (l'italiano) ad un'altra lingua (il friulano) [from one language (Italian) to another language (Friulan)].[24] Furthermore, in a note to *La meglio gioventú* (1954) reproduced verbatim in *La nuova gioventú* (1974), Pasolini commented on the composition of his dialect poems and provided explicit authorial directions on how they were to be read:

> Se le versioni in italiano a pié di pagina sostituiscono un glossario [...] fanno parte insieme, e qualche volta parte integrante, del testo poetico: le ho perciò stese con cura e quasi, idealmente, contemporaneamente al friulano, pensando che piuttosto che non essere letto fosse preferibile essere letto soltanto in esse.[25]

> [If the versions in Italian at the bottom of the page take the place of a glossary (...) they form part, and sometimes an integral part, of the poetic text as a whole: I have therefore composed them with care and almost, ideally, contemporaneously with the Friulan, thinking that rather than not be read it was preferable to be read only in them.]

This note constitutes the poet's own *a posteriori* gloss on a literary operation whose translation-like qualities had been intuited by Contini. In sum, because the Italian "versions" form an integral part of the poetic text as a whole and were composed simultaneously with the Friulan "originals", Pasolini's dialect poetry may be gathered under the sign of translation and stands as an example of autotranslation.[26]

In addition to the experience of autotranslation shaping his dialect poetry, and the fascination with a textual format integrating two different languages, Pasolini also translated the work of other poets into Friulan. In this way, from the early stages of his career, translation emerges as an important coterminous activity that has distinct affiliations with his writing in other genres.[27] For example, in an article entitled "Dalla lingua al friulano", which appeared in December 1947, Pasolini argues that translation can help promote Friulan as a literary language:

> Il friulano ha bisogno di traduzioni essendo questo il passo piú probatorio per una sua promozione a lingua. È vero che per noi il friulano è aprioristicamente lingua, a parte le considerazioni glottologiche (un deliberato ritorno all'Ascoli) o a parte lo sforzo cosciente di usarlo in condizioni di parità se non di uguaglianza con le grandi lingue romanze; tuttavia una prova come quella del tradurre verrebbe a costituire un terzo fatto, se non molto profondo, almeno perentorio.[28]

> [Friulan has need of translations, this being the most probatory step for its promotion to the status of a language. It is true that for us Friulan is *a priori* a language, glottological considerations aside (a deliberate return to Ascoli) or apart from the conscious effort to use it in conditions of parity if not of equality with the great Romance languages; nevertheless an attempt like that of translation would come to constitute a third fact, which, if not very profound, is at least peremptory.]

In order to assert that Friulan was the equal of the other Romance languages, Pasolini and the members of the Academiuta di Lenga Furlana translated Catalan poets, the Spanish poets Machado and Lorca, French poets such as Verlaine and Rimbaud and Italian poets such as Tommaseo and Ungaretti, as well as T. S. Eliot. In this way they created a "new Friulan poetry", using a regional idiom to write poetry and to produce translations perfectly *à la page* with the most advanced European and American poetic movements. In this operation translation provided "una prova" that Friulan was capable of rendering the most exquisitely literary elements of the modern lyric.[29] Pasolini pursued this argument in a series of articles that promoted *Stroligút*. For example, in an article of May 1946 written for the Udinese daily *La libertà*, Pasolini links the dignity of Friulan to its ability to render the most difficult modern poets:

E cominciamo col presentare, qui, proprio quelle cose dello *Stroligút* che possono essere l'indice piú evidente di un friulano-lingua, cioè le traduzioni, che sono poi traduzioni di alcuni dei poeti piú difficili delle moderne lingue romanze. Essi rappresen-tano quella tradizione, che partendo da Baudelaire e da Mallar-mé, trova la propria caratteristica essenziale nella coscienza della poesia, o, in termini piú netti, nella poesia pura; e dove è quindi esasperata la ricerca linguistica.[30]

[And let us begin by presenting, here, precisely those things from *Stroligút* that can be the clearest index of Friulan as a language, namely the translations, which, moreover, are translations of some of the most difficult poets of the modern Romance lan-guages. They represent that tradition which, starting with Bau-delaire and Mallarmé, finds its own essential character in the consciousness of poetry, or, in clearer terms, in pure poetry; and where, therefore, the linguistic search is particularly acute.]

While there have been numerous translations and *rifacimenti* into dialect throughout Italian literary history, Pasolini was pro-posing a different kind of translation into Friulan. As he argues in "Dalla lingua al friulano",

Non si tratterebbe [...] di ridurre, ma di tradurre; cioè non si tratterebbe di trasferire la materia da un piano superiore (la lingua) a un piano inferiore (il friulano), ma di trasporla da un piano all'altro a parità di livello. ("Dalla lingua al friulano", p. 24)

[It would not be a question of reduction, but of translation; that is, it would not involve transferring the material from a higher plane (the Italian language) to a lower plane (Friulan), but trans-porting it from one plane to the other on an equal level.]

Refusing to view Friulan as an inferior linguistic instrument, Pasolini promoted it as a contemporary "volgare illustre", on an equal footing with the other Romance tongues. Through trans-lations, and through his own (re)writing in Friulan, Pasolini came to develop an innovative, modernizing approach to the use of dialect, an approach recognized and sanctioned by Contini, and which has been characterized by Santato as "una teoria del dialetto come *ideale traduzione* dell'italiano, metafora della lingua" ["a theory of dialect as an ideal translation of Italian, a metaphor of the language"].[31] Just as the screenplay in the 1960s will come to represent for Pasolini "il dato concreto del rapporto tra cinema e letteratura" ["the concrete datum of the relationship between cinema and literature"] and will become, in Pasolini's famous formulation, "una struttura che vuole essere altra struttura" ["a structure that wants to be another structure"], so too his Friulan translations of the 1940s may be seen as hybrid "structures" with important metapoetic and mediating functions.

According to Pasolini the Friulan translations represent "l'indice piú evidente di un friulano-lingua". Thus they function meta-poetically to create an "image" of Friulan intended to lend dignity to the linguistic and cultural identity of Friuli, a distinct region, "una piccola patria" with its own history, language and culture, and whose specific difference needed to be defended. Through poetry and through translations Pasolini wanted to project its diversity, its vital heterogeneity, into the future.[32] At the same time, for example, Pasolini's Friulan version of T. S. Eliot's "Death by Water" sequence from *The Wasteland*, his version of Ungaretti's "Peso", and his rendering of Rimbaud's "Enfance" establish import-ant affinities between the poet translator and the poets translated. These texts mediate between the young poet and the modern masters, and help the young poet establish his reputation.

Viewed within the chronological development of Pasolini's career, the Friulan translations represent the first stage in a series of rewritings destined to transform the Italian dialect tradition. Pasolini's verse translations into *friulano*, as well as his translation of Plautus into *romanesco*, together with his own Friulan poetry, his monumental anthologies of dialect and popular poetry, his Roman novels and films, and his essays in *Passione e ideologia*, all worked together through "the interaction of writing and rewriting" to revitalize the dialect tradition in the second half of this century, and to revalorize the plurilinguistic dimensions of Italian cultural identity. Beginning with Contini's highly intuitive review of *Poesie a Casarsa* in 1943, Pasolini's singular role in this operation has been widely acknowledged.[33] As Mengaldo has observed:

> Il nostro attuale interesse per la poesia dialettale moderna in Italia, la nostra coscienza della sua pari dignità (e insieme della sua potenziale diversità) rispetto a quella in lingua, devono allo scavo erudito e critico di Pasolini quanto a nessun altro.[34]
>
> [Our current interest in modern dialect poetry in Italy, our consciousness of its equal dignity (together with its potential

diversity) to poetry in Italian, owe more to the erudite and critical excavation of Pasolini than to anyone else.]

While Pasolini's youthful experiments in autotranslation and in literary translation *tout court* exemplify his innovative approach to poetry in dialect, his translation projects of the 1960s—the Italian version of the *Orestiade* of Aeschylus (1960) and his translation into *romanesco* of the *Miles Gloriosus* of Plautus, *Il vantone* (1963)—point to the role of translation in his engagement with the theatre and highlight his relationship with classical Greek and Latin literature.[35] Moreover, in the late 1950s he began, but soon abandoned, a version of Virgil's *Aeneid;*[36] and in 1960 he apparently translated Sophocles's *Antigone,* which also remains unpublished and for which little documentation exists.[37] In 1968 he proposed to coordinate a project of translations from the classics which would have involved such poet/writer/translators as Leonardo Sciascia, Francesco Leonetti, Enzo Siciliano, Attilio Bertolucci, Elsa Morante and Andrea Zanzotto. In a letter to Sciascia, Pasolini described the project as follows:

> Hai letto il mio *Manifesto per un nuovo teatro* sull'ultimo *Nuovi argomenti*? Se sei appena un po' d'accordo su quanto dico—un teatro di schema ateniese, senza azione scenica—perché non pensi a scrivere una tragedia? O a tradurne, almeno, una dal greco (Bertolucci Alcesti, Leonetti Prometeo, Siciliano Ippolito, Morante Filottete…). Infatti lo Stabile di Torino e di Roma mi finanziano insieme un teatro, che sarà anche un centro di incontri, un vero e proprio "foro".[38]

> [Have you read my *Manifesto for a New Theatre* in the latest *Nuovi argomenti*? If you agree with what I say, even just a little—a theatre with an Athenian bent, without scenic action—why don't you consider writing a tragedy? Or, at least translating one from the Greek (Bertolucci Alcestes, Leonetti Prometheus, Siciliano Hippolytus, Morante Philoctetes…). In fact the Teatro Stabile of Turin and that of Rome are together providing me with funds for a theatre, which will also be a meeting place, a real and true "forum".]

Just as the Friulan translations of the Academiuta were part of Pasolini's strategy for promoting Friulan and, by extension, modern poetry in dialect, so too these proposed classical "traduzioni d'autore" proposed in 1968 form an integral part of his "teatro della parola": an experimental alternative to bourgeois theatre and a project described by Casi as "un teatro di intellettuali per intellettuali" ["a theatre of intellectuals for intellectuals"].[39] While these proposed translations, like many of his film projects, remained unrealized, his translations of Aeschylus and Plautus completed in the early 1960s, as well as his incomplete translation of Virgil's *Aeneid*, constitute important moments in Pasolini's career as a translator. It is to these translations that we now turn.

For Pasolini, who by the late 1950s had become widely known as a poet, novelist and literary critic, Vittorio Gassman's request to translate the *Oresteia* in January 1960 provided a golden opportunity. In his "Nota del traduttore", a brief statement accompanying the translation, Pasolini offers the following gloss on Gassman's invitation: "La richiesta di Gassman mi è stata fatta in seguito alla notizia che io stavo traducendo Virgilio" ["Gassman's request was made to me following the news that I was translating Virgil"].[40] Stefano Casi, however, offers a more plausible explanation for Gassman's request:

> È piú credibile, nella commissione di una traduzione a Pasolini, che si sia voluto scegliere lo scrittore piú stimolante di quegli anni e l'intellettuale piú appariscente e chiacchierato della sinistra italiana. L'occasione che si presenta a Pasolini è particolarmente allettante: l'ingresso nel teatro ufficiale si spalanca [...] con la traduzione della trilogia eschilea su commissione di una compagnia di una certa risonanza come il TPI per il Teatro Greco di Siracusa nell'ambito del festival biennale del teatro classico e in occasione di un convegno internazionale di studi sulla tragedia greca.[41]

> [It is more credibile that in the commissioning of a translation from Pasolini the aim was to choose the most stimulating writer of those years and the most visible and talked-about intellectual of the Italian left. The opportunity presented to Pasolini is particularly alluring: entry into official theatre opens wide (...) with the translation of Aeschylus's trilogy commissioned by a company with a certain resonance such as the Teatro Popolare Italiano for the Teatro Greco of Siracusa in the context of the biennial festival of classical theatre and on the occasion of an international scholarly congress on Greek tragedy.]

While Pasolini played down his role as a translator, emphasizing "il poco tempo a disposizione" ["the little time available"] and acknowledging the existence of "altre buone traduzioni italia-ne" ["other good Italian translations"], he seized this opportunity to rewrite Aeschylus in the style and language of his own *Ceneri di Gramsci*:

> Come tradurre? Io possedevo già un "italiano": ed era natural-mente quello delle *Ceneri di Gramsci* (con qualche punta espressi-va sopravvissuta da *L'usignolo della Chiesa Cattolica*); sapevo (per istinto) che avrei potuto farne uso [...]. La tendenza lingui-stica generale è stata a modificare continuamente i toni sublimi in toni civili: una disperata correzione di ogni tentazione classicista. Da ciò un avvicinamento alla prosa, all'allocuzione bassa, ragio-nante. ("Nota del traduttore", p. 176)

> [How to translate? I already possessed an "Italian": and it was naturally that of the *Ashes of Gramsci* (with some expressive points carried over from *The Nightingale of the Catholic Church*); I knew (by instinct) that I would be able to use it (...). My general linguistic tendency has been continually to modify sublime tones into civil tones: a desperate correction of every classicist tempta-tion. Hence a drawing near to prose, to low, reasoning speech.]

Framing his translation as an attempt to reclaim the text from the academic specialists, Pasolini had to resist, as he puts it, "ogni tentazione classicista". He worked to deflate the abstract, ahistorical notion of the "classic" as a timeless literary masterpiece by avoid-ing what he called "degli aloni e degli echi che il classicismo romantico ci ha abituati a percepire, quale continua allusività del testo classico a una classicità paradigmatica, storicamente astratta" ["the haloes and echoes that Romantic classicism have accustomed us to perceiving, such as the constant allusivity of the classical text to a paradigmatic historically abstract classicalness": "Nota del traduttore", p. 176]. He sought to accomplish these aims by trans-lating the language of Aeschylus into the discursive, civil tones of the poetic language that he had previously developed. In fact according to Umberto Albini Pasolini's attempt to construct a depoeticized, prose-like translation that would lend itself to recita-tion served a democratic ideological function, and had a significant impact on the translators who followed in his wake:

> Nel campo delle versioni dal teatro antico, il secondo Novecento ha scoperto la dimensione della recitazione, del dialogo a viva

voce, della componente fonico-ritmica [...]. Pioniere, in questa direzione, è stato Pier Paolo Pasolini con l'*Orestiade* di Eschilo (Torino, 1960). Pasolini prospetta già nella pagina scritta la resa fonica e pone segni diacritici che la indirizzino [...]. Sulla strada di Pasolini, con diverso temperamento e diverso assunto (l'*Orestiade* curata da Pasolini, si sa, è in funzione di un'ideologia democratica) si sono mossi molti altri interpreti: persino il curiale Teatro di Siracusa ha avvertito a un certo punto la necessità di affiancare a traduttori esperti della lingua greca cotraduttori (o consiglieri) con pratica della scena.[42]

[In the field of versions from ancient theatre, the second half of the twentieth century has discovered the dimension of recitation, of spoken dialogue, of the phonic and rhythmical component (...). Pier Paolo Pasolini was a pioneer in this direction with his version of Aeschylus's *Oresteia* (Turin, 1960). Pasolini already shows the phonic delivery on the written page and sets out diacritical marks to direct it (...). On Pasolini's road, with different temperament and different assumptions (the *Oresteia* prepared by Pasolini, as is well known, serves a democratic ideological function) many other interpreters have set forth: even the curial Teatro di Siracusa at a certain point felt the need to flank translators expert in the Greek language with co-translators (or advisers) with expertise in the theatre.]

Pasolini's *Orestiade* made a significant contribution to the translation and reception of the Greek classics in the Italian theatre. Furthermore, this translation provided the poet/novelist/critic/translator with a point of entry into yet another arena of cultural activity. Stefano Casi sheds light on the role of this translation in Pasolini's move into the theatre:

> Con l'*Orestiade*, cioè con la traduzione di un'opera classica, Pasolini chiarisce la possibilità di una propria strada autonoma nella drammaturgia contemporanea, tracciata con i suggerimenti del teatro greco: dalla struttura lineare dell'esposizione del processo storico e politico, alla forma linguistica "verso un ragionamento tutt' altro che mitico e per definizione poetico". Pasolini *diventa* Eschilo [...]. Riferendosi piú volte alle *Ceneri di Gramsci* per spiegare la lingua usata nella traduzione dal greco, egli presenta la sua *Orestiade* non come tragedia dell'Atene del v secolo avanti Cristo, ma come tappa di un proprio percorso linguistico e intellettuale nell'anno 1960.[43]

[With the *Oresteia*, that is, with the translation of a classical work, Pasolini clarifies the possibility of his own autonomous road in contemporary dramaturgy, traced with the suggestions of Greek theatre: from the linear structure of the exposition of the historical and political process, to the linguistic form "towards a reasoning which is anything but mythical and by definition poetic". Pasolini *becomes* Aeschylus (...). Referring again and again to the *Ashes of Gramsci* to explain the language used in the translation from the Greek, he presents his *Oresteia* not as an Athenian tragedy of the fifth century BC but as a stage of his own linguistic and intellectual journey in the year 1960.]

Following the success of the *Orestiade*, Pasolini accepted another invitation from Gassman to translate a classical author: in 1963 his translation of Plautus's *Miles Gloriosus*, with the title *Il vantone*, once again highlighted his deep engagement with the classical tradition. On this occasion, however, according to Casi, Pasolini's translation "si presenta quasi 'manieristicamente' rispetto all'*Orestiade* e non propone elementi di particolare interesse per l'evoluzione della drammaturgia pasoliniana o della sua idea di teatro" ["presents itself almost 'manneristically' compared to the *Oresteia* and does not offer elements of particular interest for the evolution of Pasolini's dramaturgy or his idea of theatre"].[44] Nevertheless, even if this work does not contribute significantly to Pasolini's theatre, it does constitute an important point of reference in his experience as a translator. Just as the Friulan translations were contiguous with Pasolini's own dialect poetry, and his translation of the *Orestiade* relied on the language of *Le ceneri di Gramsci*, *Il vantone* may be related to his previous experiments in *romanesco*. Akin to his novels in *romanesco* from the previous decade, *Ragazzi di vita* (1955) and *Una vita violenta* (1959), and his Roman films *Accattone* (1960) and *Mamma Roma* (1962), Pasolini's *Il vantone* stimulated debate and controversy.[45] For example, the drama critic Aggeo Savioli took issue with the language of the translation:

La lingua adoperata da Pasolini è quella, grosso modo, che i lettori e gli spettatori di cinema conoscevano già: un impasto di italiano, di romanesco e di dialetti "burini", con locuzioni di gergo e di parlar corrente periferico. L'operazione è però assai meno riuscita che altrove [...]. Il romanesco maccheronico e annacquato del *Vantone* [...] non richiama alla mente né Pascarella né Trilussa (lasciamo perdere Belli), ma semmai il "sor Capanna" […]. Da Pasolini, in conclusione, c'era da attendersi qualcosa di maggior peso.[46]

[The language adopted by Pasolini is more or less the language with which readers and film audiences were already acquainted: a mixture of Italian, *romanesco* and 'peasant' dialects, with phrases of jargon and of current speech of the suburbs. The operation however is much less successful than elsewhere (…). The macaronic and watered-down *romanesco* of *Il vantone* (…) does not call to mind either Pascarella or Trilussa (not to mention Belli), but if anyone "Sor Capanna" (…). From Pasolini, in conclusion, one would have expected something of greater weight.]

Pasolini's *Il vantone* met with mixed reviews and Savioli's demolition of it was one of several.[47] Nevertheless, Savioli's remarks are useful for the attention they pay to the language of the translation. In characterizing this language as "un impasto di italiano, di romanesco e di dialetti 'burini'", Savioli highlights an experimental literary operation based on a creative mixture of various idioms. Because he denigrates the results of this experiment, however, he seems to have misunderstood Pasolini's overall intentions as well as the very nature of the undertaking. Pasolini made no claim that his work should be seen in the rich tradition of literature in *romanesco*, a tradition evoked by Savioli with references to Belli, Trilussa and Pascarella. On the contrary, Pasolini dubbed this work a "traslazione da Plauto" and emphasized repeatedly that it was more a "rifacimento" ["rewriting"] than a translation in the strict sense: "Posso dire proprio solo due parole su questa traslazione da Plauto. Essa è nata casualmente […] nel caso di una rappresentazione reale: su ordinazione, insomma" ["Really I can say only one thing about this rewriting of Plautus. It was born by chance (…), occasioned by an actual performance: in short, on commission"]. Distancing himself from the translator's "duty" to literal fidelity, Pasolini underlined the perplexing historical circumstances of the language of the source text: "Non sapevo decidermi: era Plauto un sobrio aristocratico? o uno sbrigativo plebeo […]? Non ho risolto la questione" ["I couldn't decide: was Plautus a sober aristocrat? or a hasty plebeian? [...] I haven't solved the problem"]. Furthermore, in trying to find a contemporary equivalent to the ancient theatre of Plautus's comedies, Pasolini looked towards the *avanspettacolo* or variety theatre of his own day.

He freely admitted that this choice contained more than a little ambiguity:

> Che in Italia ora esista un "teatro" analogo a quello in cui affondava le sue prepotenti radici il lavoro di Plauto è cosa da mettere senza esitazione in dubbio. Per che palcoscenico, dunque, per che spettatori traducevo io? [...] Beh, qualcosa di vagamente analogo al teatro di Plauto [...] mi pareva di poterlo individuare forse soltanto nell'avanspettacolo... È a questo, è alla lingua di questo, che, dunque, pensavo.[48]

> [It must be unhesitatingly doubted whether in Italy today there exists a "theatre" analogous to the one into which Plautus's work thrust its imposing roots. For what stage, then, for what spectators was I translating? (...) Well, something vaguely analogous to Plautus's theatre (...) I seemed able to recognize perhaps only in variety theatre... I was thinking of this, therefore, and of its language.]

Furthermore, Pasolini described the linguistic results of his experimental rewriting in the following terms: "Sa piú di palcoscenico che di trivio [...]. Il nobilissimo 'volgare', insomma, contagiato dalla volgarità direi fisiologica del capocomico" ["It has more of the stage about it than the street (...). The most noble 'vulgar tongue', in sum, infected by what I'd call the physiological vulgarity of the actor-manager": dust-jacket of *Il vantone di Plauto*]. Pasolini's description of the language of *Il vantone* brings to mind his earlier characterization of the language of his Friulan poetry. In both instances he arrives at a highly literary use of dialect, a "volgare illustre".

As we have seen, Pasolini's translations and "rewritings" of classical authors form one of the fundamental elements of his artistic identity. Franco Fortini argued that literary translation represents "un modo economico per assumere un'identità diversa dalla propria" ["an economical way of assuming an identity different from one's own"].[49] The classical inheritance is particularly strong in Italy, and Pasolini's lifelong engagement with this tradition reflects the humanistic intertext of his *forma mentis*. More importantly, his rewriting of classical authors may be seen as part of his "struggle with the Father", to use Contini's phrase,[50] which was also quite literally a "struggle with the fathers"; that is, an obsessive psychological need to recast classical authors within a contemporary context reflecting historical, political and ideological realities but also coloured by his own subjective concerns. For example, Pasolini's manipulation of classical authors in a cinematic vein has been described by Gian Piero Brunetta as "un viaggio dentro i classici" ["a journey inside the classics"]. Brunetta emphasizes Pasolini's need to use the classics as a kind of free space "entro cui muoversi, mimetizzarsi, proiettarsi, riconoscersi e rivelarsi a seconda delle esigenze e delle tappe di un itinerario che altre volte ha tentato di percorrere" ["within which to move, to camouflage himself, to project himself, to recognize himself and to reveal himself according to the exigencies and the stages of an itinerary which he sought to traverse on other occasions"].[51] Brunetta's interpretation of Pasolini's film adaptations of the classics may be extended to include his literary translations as well.

Pasolini's unfinished and unpublished translation of the *Aeneid*, undertaken and abandoned during the late 1950s, provides an interesting case in point. A fragment of that translation follows:[52]

> Canto la lotta di un uomo che, profugo da Troia
> la storia spinse per primo alle sponde del Lazio;
> la violenza celeste, e il rancore di una dea nemica
> lo trascinarono da un mare all'altro, da una terra
> all'altra, di guerra in guerra, prima di fondare la sua città
> e di portare nel Lazio la sua religione: origine
> del popolo latino, e albano, e della suprema Roma.
> Tu, spirito, esponi le intime cause: per quale offesa,
> o per quale dolore, la regina degli dèi obligò quell' uomo
> cosí religioso, a dover affrontare tanti casi, tante
> fatiche: miseria di passioni nei cuori celesti![53]

[I sing the struggle of a man, a refugee from Troy,/whom first history pushed to the shores of Latium;/celestial violence, and the rancour of an enemy goddess,/carried him from one sea to another, from one land/to another, from war to war, before founding his city/and bringing his religion to Latium: origin/of the Latin and Alban people, and of supreme Rome./You, Spirit, make known the intimate causes: for what offence,/or for what affliction, did the queen of the gods force that man/so pious, to face so many trials, so many/labours: lack of feeling in celestial hearts!]

These lines, viewed subjectively, can suggest Pasolini's own flight from Casarsa and arrival in Rome in 1950. It is not difficult to imagine Pasolini projecting himself as a "profugo da *Casarsa* [che] la storia spinse [...] alle sponde del Lazio". While Pasolini was translating Virgil he was also working with Ennio De Concini on a screenplay of Manzoni's *I promessi sposi*. Although Manzoni's novel is obviously not an *ancient* classic, Brunetta has interpreted this unpublished screenplay in a biographical vein similar to my reading of Pasolini's work on the *Aeneid*:

> Attraverso la storia di Renzo e Lucia perseguitati dalle chiacchie-re di paese e, in un certo senso, alla ricerca di una dimora stabile, Pasolini intende raccontare, agli inizi degli anni sessanta, la storia del proprio viaggio dal Friuli verso Roma.[54]

> [Through the story of Renzo and Lucia persecuted by the gossip of the village, and, in a certain sense, in search of a fixed abode, Pasolini intends to recount, at the beginning of the 1960s, the story of his own flight from Friuli towards Rome.]

As is well known, throughout his film career Pasolini rewrote ancient, medieval and modern canonical texts, including *Oedipus Rex*, St Matthew's Gospel, the *Divine Comedy*, the *Decameron*, the *Canterbury Tales* and numerous others, in a highly personal manner. Running the gamut from the "faithful" adaptation (*Il Vangelo secondo Matteo*, 1964) and clearly autobiographical rewriting (*Edipo re*, 1967) to explicitly transgressive intrepretations (*Il Decameron*, 1971 and *I racconti di Canterbury*, 1972), Pasolini assumed the identities of some of the most prestigious literary *auctores* of Western civilization. For example, in his film adaptations Pasolini's cameo appearances as Giotto's disciple in the *Decameron*, as Chaucer in *I racconti di Canterbury*, and as a character in *Edipo re* provide visual proof of how Pasolini sought to assume an identity different from his own. His interview with Ezra Pound on Italian television in 1968 may similarly be related to the younger poet's desire to be associated with authoritative, canonical figures.

Through translation and rewriting of poetry, theatre and film, Pasolini became remarkably adept at refashioning, manipulating and appropriating authoritative source texts. Rather than simply representing one of the many literary genres through which he expressed himself, translation and rewriting are the best terms with which to describe the creative manifestations of his "struggle with the fathers". I submit that translation and rewriting, with their interplay between two languages and two texts, helped to propel

Pasolini from one channel of communication to the next, from one composition to the next, from one "work in progress" to the next. In order to appreciate more fully the influence of translation on Pasolini's restless experimentation, to understand how it gave him what Barnstone has called "an arsenal of possibilities",[55] and to follow the thread of translation woven within the fabric of his own artistic creativity, let us now turn to his poetics of translation. Although translation served different purposes at different moments in Pasolini's itinerary, his basic approach to literary translation—as we shall see—remained constant throughout his career and provided him with a strategy of rewriting that served him well in his multimedial experimentation.

PASOLINI'S POETICS OF TRANSLATION: "AFFINITÀ ELETTIVE"

In an article entitled "Arte e divulgazione" and published in 1956, Pasolini distinguishes between two types of translation:

> L'idea piú corrente che si ha della traduzione è che si tratti di un atto assolutamente approssimativo: che si tratti, piuttosto, di una riduzione [...]. In genere ciò che giustifica una traduzione è il fine informativo [...]. Ma esiste un secondo modo di tradurrre: in cui, alla funzione del divulgare [...] si aggiunge l'intenzione di fare, o, meglio, di rifare, poesia. Al limite alto tale intenzione si concreta tout court in una assunzione del testo tradotto al linguaggio del traduttore in quanto egli stesso poeta: una specie di rigenerazione (esempi tipici: l'Omero di Monti, i romantici di Carducci, i greci di Quasimodo).[56]

> [The most widespread idea regarding translation is that it is a completely approximate act: that it involves, rather, an adaptation (...). In general what justifies a translation is its informative end (...). But there exists a second mode of translating: in which, to the function of spreading information (...) is added the aim of making, or, more precisely, of remaking, poetry. At the upper limit such an aim becomes concrete *tout court* when the translated text is assumed into the language of the translator in as much as he is a poet himself: a kind of regeneration (typical examples: Monti's Homer, Carducci's Romantics, Quasimodo's Greeks).]

Pasolini here expresses the familiar distinction between "literary" and "non-literary" translation. Whereas the scholar who translates might succeed in rendering a poetic text more familiar to a wide audience, only the poet can revitalize, regenerate and recreate poetry through translation. In addition, according to Pasolini, the poet/translator brings the source text over into the system of his or her own target language and style, both of which s/he has previously developed. As we have seen, these were clearly the criteria which Pasolini applied when translating.[57] He also went on to argue that successful literary translation depends on "affinità elettive" and "misteriose correspondenze storiche" not only between poets and translators, but also between cultures, languages and historical periods:

> Di qui la necessità di affinità elettive, di misteriose corrispondenze storiche, non solo tra poeta tradotto e poeta traduttore, ma tra epoca letteraria ed epoca letteraria [...]. Tutto questo mette in evidenza il fatto che la traduzione è soprattutto, esplicitamente o implicitamente, un atto storiografico. ("Arte e divulgazione", p. 21)

> [Hence the necessity of elective affinities, of mysterious historical correspondences, not only between poet translated and poet translator, but between literary epoch and literary epoch (...). All this shows that, explicitly or implicitly, translation is primarily an act of historiography.]

Like many of the poet's theoretical pronouncements on other cultural subjects, this statement grows out of his previous artistic practice. Pasolini's versions from Catalan, for example, provide an illuminating illustration of this fact.

In 1947, Pasolini translated nine Catalan poets into Italian and presented them with the title "Fiore di poeti catalani".[58] In connection with these translations Giuseppe Zigaina has observed:

> Non solo li traduce, ma li presenta nella scrittura originaria, proprio per sottolineare ai suoi lettori la assoluta affinità con la poesia friulano-casarsese, affinità della grafia, dei dittonghi, delle finali in 's'.[59]

> [Not only does he translate them, but he presents them in the original, in order to underline to his readers the absolute affinity with the poetry of Friuli–Casarsa, affinities of spelling, of diphthongs, of endings in 's'.]

The linguistic similarities between Catalan and Friulan, as made evident by Pasolini's inclusion of the original Catalan text, underline common neo-Latin roots in the past. By extension, they also suggest an alliance of subaltern Romance languages and cultures in the present. In fact these translations provided the young Pasolini with an opportunity to denounce Franco's repression of the Catalan language. In a statement published together with the translations in the *Quaderno romanzo* of 1947, Pasolini declared:

> La dittatura fascista di Franco ha condannato la lingua catalana al piú duro ostracismo, espungendola non solo dalla scuola e dai tribunali, ma dalla tribuna, dalla radio, dalla stampa, dal libro, e perfino dalla Chiesa. Ciò nonostante, gli scrittori catalani seguitano a lavorare nelle catacombe in attesa del giorno, forse non lontano, in cui il sole della libertà splenderà di nuovo su questa lingua.[60]

> [The Fascist dictatorship of Franco has condemned the Catalan language to the harshest ostracism, expunging it not only from the school and from the tribunals, but from the radio, the press, books, and even from the Church. Despite this, Catalan writers continue to work in the catacombs in expectation of the day, perhaps not distant, when the sun of freedom will shine again on this language.]

Through the translations of the Catalan poets, Pasolini wished to align himself, and the movement for Friulan autonomy, with a subaltern Romance language and an oppressed minority culture that also needed to be defended in the present. Two of the Catalans translated by Pasolini, Jacint Verdaguer and Miquel Costa i Llobera, were nineteenth-century Romantic poets who spearheaded a revival of Catalan poetry and culture. What they had done for Catalan Pasolini sought to do for Friulan.[61] His translations from Catalan allowed Pasolini to conjure forth "corrispondenze storiche" between medieval Italy and Spain, Friuli and Catalonia, the movement for Friulan autonomy and Franco's oppression of the Catalan language.

While seeking to intervene in a contemporary situation, translation allows Pasolini to keep faith with the past. In his prose commentary on the Catalan translations, he calls attention to the "corrispondenze storiche" linking Catalan to Italian culture, ties that were particularly strong in the Middle Ages. In fact Pasolini argues that the contact between these cultures was so deep that

> i migliori scrittori catalani imitarono i sommi poeti e prosatori italiani di quel tempo: Ramon Lull fu figlio di San Francesco come poeta e di San Bonaventura come filosofo, Bernard Metge imitò il Boccaccio, Jordi de Sant Jordi ed il grande Auzias March furono seguaci del Petrarca, e catalana fu la prima traduzione, dovuta a Andreu Febrer, della *Divina commedia*.[62]

> [the best Catalan writers imitated the greatest Italian poets and prose writers of that age: Ramon Lull was a son of Saint Francis as a poet and of Saint Bonaventure as a philosopher, Bernard Metge imitated Boccaccio, Jordi de Saint Jordi and the great Auzias March were followers of Petrarch, and the first translation of the *Divine Comedy*, produced by Andreu Febrer, was in Catalan.]

Pasolini's reference to the first translation of the *Commedia* and to the first translator of Dante further illustrates his poetics of "affinità elettive". Dante was a constant presence and guiding star throughout his career. Pasolini's recognition in 1947 that "catalana fu la prima traduzione, dovuta a Andreu Febrer, della *Divina commedia*" constitutes one of the first in what will become a long list of references by Pasolini to Dante.[63] Following the example of the medieval Catalan writers, Pasolini imitated, appropriated and rewrote Dante in numerous ways. In short, he established "affinità elettive" with Dante through rewritings that, whether implicitly or explicitly, are intended, like his literary translations, as "historiographical acts".

Pasolini's Friulan translation of Ungaretti's "Peso" merits a brief comment in the light of his poetics of "affinità elettive". It appears together with translations of T. S. Eliot and Rimbaud in the article entitled "Dalla lingua al friulano" cited earlier. Pasolini's attraction to Ungaretti's text, which presents a brief narrative involving a peasant and his religious medallion, could be seen as an early manifestation of Pasolini's "Catholic" strain: his interest in the sacred, the irrational, and the peasant experience of popular religion. Secondly, this poem by Ungaretti reappears in Pasolini's critical analysis of the poet written between 1948 and 1951, entitled "Un poeta e Dio" and published in *Passione e ideologia*.[64] Here "Peso" is one of a number of texts that Pasolini refers to in reflecting on the linguistic effects of Ungaretti's religiosity. This connection between translation and critical essay marks an interesting trend in Pasolini's career: texts that he translates tend to reappear in his later writings. Because his translations frequently gave birth to critical intuitions and interpretations that manifested themselves at a later stage, it appears that Pasolini *traduttore* influenced Pasolini *critico letterario*, as well as Pasolini *scrittore* and Pasolini *regista*. Pasolini's translation of Aeschylus's *Oresteia* provides another example of this tendency. His initial contact with the text occurred through the translation of 1960.[65] In that same year, Maria Luisa Astaldi, director of the literary review *Ulisse*, invited Pasolini to reply to the question "Dove va la poesia?" Pasolini framed his response in terms of his current translation project:

> Sto traducendo in questi giorni l'*Orestiade* di Eschilo: e sa quale è, gentile direttrice, il momento che mi ha dato piú profonda e totale emozione? la parte finale delle *Eumenidi*, quando Atena trasforma le Maledizioni in Benedizioni, lasciandole tali e quali, ossia forze irrazionali. Ci occorre, evidentemente, una Atena […]. Trasformare gli elementi irrazionalistici della critica stilistica in strumenti adatti all'esame razionale della critica marxista […]. Problemuccio minore: ma estremamente significante.[66]

> [I am at the moment translating Aeschylus's *Oresteia:* and do you know, dear director, which moment has given me the most profound and total emotion? The final part of *Eumenides*, where Athena transforms the Maledictions into Benedictions, leaving them exactly as they are, that is, irrational forces. Evidently, an Athena is called for (…). To transform the irrationalist elements of stylistic criticism into tools fit for the rational examination of Marxist criticism (…). A minor problem: but extremely important.]

He subsequently multiplied his encounters with the *Oresteia* by adapting it in various media. For example, in 1962 he began work on the treatment for a film which was never produced, *Il padre selvaggio*, eventually published in 1975. This text transfers Aeschylus's plot to post-colonial Africa. As Pasolini declared in his postface to the translation of the *Oresteia*:

> La trama delle tre tragedie di Eschilo è questa: in una società primitiva dominano dei sentimenti che sono primordiali, istintivi, oscuri (le Erinni), sempre pronte a travolgere le rozze istituzioni […]. Ma contro tali sentimenti arcaici, si erge la ragione […].

Tuttavia certi elementi del mondo antico, appena superato, non andranno del tutto repressi, ignorati. ("Nota del traduttore", p. 177)

[The plot of Aeschylus's three tragedies is this: in a primitive society feelings (the Furies) that are primordial, instinctive, obscure, dominate, always ready to overturn the crude institutions (...). But against such archaic feelings, reason rises up (...). Nevertheless certain elements of the ancient world, barely overcome, will not be completely repressed, ignored.]

This is the plot of the *Oresteia*, according to Pasolini. His *Padre selvaggio* explores a similar relationship between an irrational archaic substratum and the influence of modern rationality in a post-colonial African society.[67]

In 1967 he (re)wrote a verse tragedy, *Pilade*, based on the classical text, while in 1970 he produced a brief experimental film entitled *Appunti per un'Orestiade africana*.[68] Given Pasolini's tendency to return to texts with which he felt an "affinity", his translations constitute valuable intertextual links that point to capillary connections in his experimentation between various genres and media. Pasolini's incomplete translation of the *Aeneid* provides a further example. After forsaking this project in the late 1950s, he resuscitated Virgil in his Dantean rewriting, *La Divina Mimesis*, where he functions as a Pasolinian alter ego. In this way *La Divina Mimesis* is genealogically connected to the abandoned *Aeneid* of the late 1950s. It should be added, of course, that the capillary connections in Pasolini's work are not simply a matter of formal intertextuality and literary experimentation. Rather, the textual interconnections point to deep-seated psychological needs as well as persistent ideological concerns: in short, the interplay between translation, rewriting and tradition in Pasolini's work stems from and gives expression to his on-going "struggle with the Father".

Translation also constitutes a central paradigm in his critical and theoretical work. From his two major essays of the 1950s, "La poesia dialettale del Novecento" (1952) and "La poesia popolare italiana" (1955), to his essays on film theory written in the 1960s, as well as in his literary criticism from the 1940s to the 1970s, translation figures again and again as a critical point of reference. For example, his remarks on the great nineteenth-century (re)writer, Niccolò Tommaseo, whom he translated into *friulano* in the 1940s, shed light on Pasolini's attitude towards translation:

La complessità del Tommaseo [...] può essere analizzata [...] in
quel suo paradigma strutturale che è il rapporto periferia–centro,
Dalmazia–Firenze, che permette di veder risolta in lui ogni
contraddizione attraverso il piú semplice processo dialettico [...].
Ed è da notarsi come tutto questo che abbiamo detto, non sia stato
espresso dal Tommaseo sistematicamente, in scritti teorici: ma si
sia lasciato dedurrre [...] dalle sue *riproduzioni*, o per cosí dire,
trascrizioni, dei canti toscani uditi oralmente, e soprattutto dallo
stile delle sue *traduzioni* dei canti illirici e greci.[69]

[The complexity of Tommaseo (...) may be analysed in that
structural paradigm of his which is the periphery–centre relationship, Dalmatia–Florence, which shows every contradiction to be
resolved in him through the simplest dialectical process (...). And
it should be noted that all that we have said was not expressed by
Tommaseo systematically, in theoretical writings: he left it to be
deduced (...) from his *reproductions*, or, we might say, *tran-
scriptions*, of Tuscan songs heard orally, and above all from the
style of his *translations* of Illyrian and Greek songs.]

By directing readers to consider the style of Tommaseo's versions,
Pasolini suggests that translations can reveal a great deal about
poetic style, poetic language and the evolution of literary history,
as well as offering insights into the translator's own cultural
activities.[70] Pasolini's film criticism also focuses on the implications
of translation and rewriting. In an article entitled "Gli stranieri non
ridono: la comicità di Sordi", he comments on the international
reception in the early 1960s of two Italian film actors, Alberto Sordi
and Anna Magnani, who embody particularly local, popular
characteristics:

In questo momento la comicità nazionale coincide in gran parte
con quella di Sordi [...]. Ma all'estero non fa ridere. Bisognerà pur
chiederci il perché. Vediamo un po': in fondo il mondo della
Magnani è, se non identico, simile a quello di Sordi: tutti due
romani, tutti due popolani, tutti due dialettali, profondamente
tinti di un modo di essere estremamente particolaristico, il modo
di essere della Roma plebea ecc. Eppure la Magnani ha avuto
tanto successo, anche fuori d'Italia: il suo "particolarismo" è stato
subito compreso, è diventato subito, come si usa dire, universale,
patrimonio comune di infiniti pubblici [...]. Alberto Sordi, no.
Parrebbe *intraducibile*. Lo si direbbe un canto popolare che non si
può trascrivere.[71]

[At present national comicality coincides to a large extent with that of Sordi (…). But abroad he is not considered funny. Why might this be so? Let's see: basically Magnani's world is similar, if not identical, to Sordi's: they are both Roman, both commoners, both dialectal, deeply coloured by a way of being which is extremely particular, the mode of being of the Roman populace etc. And yet Magnani has had so much success, even beyond Italy: her "particularism" was understood immediately, and quickly became, as they say, universal, the common patrimony of infinite audiences […]. The same is not true of Alberto Sordi. He would seem *untranslatable*. He might be seen as a popular song that cannot be transcribed.]

In comparing Alberto Sordi, one of the most successful Italian comic actors of the post-war period, to a popular song—"che non si può trascrivere"—Pasolini brings his experience as a translator, a philologist and a cultural theorist into the realm of film criticism. "Gli stranieri non ridono" represents one of Pasolini's first incursions into this area. Not surprisingly, in moving into a new field he relied on what was familiar to him. Consequently he places Sordi, known affectionately in Italy as "il nostro Albertone nazionale" ["our great national Alberto"], within a framework informed by questions of literary translation: questions that involve the interrelationship of regional, national and transnational cultures.

Finally, translation plays an important role in Pasolini's theoretical reflections, as is evident in one of his major essays on film theory, "La sceneggiatura come 'struttura che vuole essere altra struttura'". In theorizing the relationship of the written screenplay to its subsequent visual and oral realization as a film, Pasolini returns to his previous experience as a translator, and, more precisely, to his experience as a writer and reader of bilingual texts:

Anche la traduzione implica un'operazione analoga a quella che abbiamo visto per lo sceno-testo (e per certe scritture come la poesia simbolista): richiede cioè una collaborazione speciale del lettore e i suoi segni hanno due canali di riferimento al significato. *Si tratta del momento della traduzione letterale con testo a fronte* [my italics]. Se su una pagina vediamo il testo bantu, e sull'altra il testo italiano, i segni da noi percepiti (letti) del testo italiano eseguono quella doppia carambola che solo delle raffinatissime macchine per pensare, come sono i nostri cervelli, possono seguire. Essi cioè rendono il significato *direttamente* […] e *indirettamente*, rimandando al segno bantu che indica la stessa palma in un mondo psico-fisico o culturale diverso. Il lettore, naturalmente, non comprende il segno bantu, che è per lui lettera morta: tuttavia si rende conto almeno che il significato reso dal segno "palma" va integrato, modificato... come? magari senza sapere come, da quel misterioso segno bantu: comunque il sentimento che esso va modificato in qualche modo lo modifica. L'operazione di collaborazione tra traduttore e lettore è quindi doppia: *segno-significato*, e *segno-segno di un'altra lingua (primitiva)-significato*.[72]

[*Translation also* implies an analogous operation to what we have seen in the case of the screenplay-text (and of certain writings like Symbolist poetry): it requires, therefore, the reader's special collaboration, and its signs have two channels of reference to the meaning. *I'm thinking of the instance of literal translation facing the original text.* If on one page we see the Bantu text, and on the other the Italian text, the signs of the Italian text perceived (read) by us require that double carom which only the most refined machines for thinking, such as our brains, can perform. They (the signs) render the meaning *directly* (...) and *indirectly*, pointing to the Bantu sign that indicates the same palm tree in a different psycho-physical or cultural world. The reader, naturally, does not understand the Bantu sign, which is for him a dead letter; nevertheless, he notices at least that the meaning rendered by the sign "palm tree" must be integrated, modified... how? perhaps without knowing how, by that mysterious Bantu sign: in any case, the feeling that it must be modified in some way does modify it. The operation of collaboration between the translator and reader is therefore double: *sign-meaning*, and *sign-sign of another (primitive) language-meaning*.]

Although Pasolini here reflects on the literal translation with *testo a fronte* with reference to the screenplay, the image on which it rests, that of the "doppia carambola", could refer equally well to his own dialect poetry. In fact Pasolini's innovative, theoretical approach to the screenplay has its origins in the translation-like qualities of that poetry and in his own experience as a literary translator. Here again we witness the importance of Contini's initial insights into the dynamic tension between Pasolini's Friulan "originals" and his Italian "translations". In translating, creating film adaptations and screenwriting, Pasolini discovered and mined the aesthetic power of the "double carom". He exploited this power and explored this

technique over and over again throughout his career in juxtaposing one text with another.[73]

While other poet/translators of Pasolini's generation such as
Franco Fortini, Vittorio Sereni and Giovanni Giudici remained and
remain productive translators throughout their careers, Pasolini
published no literary translations after 1963. If, however, he had
failed to obtain the financial backing to produce *Il Vangelo secondo
Matteo*, he wrote in a letter to Guido Davico Bonino, he would have
had "molto tempo libero" ["a great deal of free time"] and, given
the success of *Il vantone*, would have considered translating Molière's
Tartuffe (*Lettere 1955–1975*, p. 540). As Pasolini's film career became
more demanding, his urge to translate was no doubt transferred to
other, parallel activities. In fact from the early 1960s until his tragic
murder, the majority of Pasolini's "original" works, including
films, poetry, screenplays and verse tragedies, are thinly disguised
or explicit "remakes", "refractions", "manipulations", "adaptations": in short, *rewritings* (in the literal sense of the word) of other
texts—most of them classical and canonical, some of them his own.
From St Paul to Allen Ginsberg, from Shakespeare to De Sade,
Pasolini, primarily in the later stages of his career, rewrote in a
highly personal vein a vast array of authors and texts. He also
injected elements from various literary traditions into the cinema.
For example, his verse tragedy *Calderon* (1967) reworked Calderón
de la Barca's *La Vida es sueño*. Pasolini's *La Divina Mimesis* is a
fragmented rewriting of Dante's *Inferno* according to Pasolini's
apocalyptic vision of neo-capitalist Italy in the early 1960s. His
published screenplay of an unproduced film, *San Paolo* (1977),
rewrites the life of the Apostle, who travels between New York,
Paris and Washington rather than Athens, Jerusalem and Rome.
Finally, Pasolini's last book of poetry, *La nuova gioventú* (1975)
rewrites his own volume *La meglio gioventú* of 1954.

CONCLUSION: "NO SAVÍNT/SE CH'I AMI IL LATÍN, IL GREC"

Pasolini's last poem in Friulan, "Saluto e augurio", published as the
concluding text of *La nuova gioventú*, dramatizes the interdependence
of translation, tradition and rewriting that we have been exploring
in this essay. Establishing an imaginary dialogue with a young neo-
fascist, Pasolini writes:

i crot ch'a no'l savedi nuja di politica

e ch'al serci doma di difindi il latín
e il grec, cuntra di me; no savínt
se ch'i ami il latin, il grec

(*TLP*, 1177)

[I think he knows nothing of politics/and that he is merely trying
to defend Latin/and Greek against me; not knowing/how much
I love Latin, Greek]

Here Pasolini professes his love for Latin and Greek in a Friulan
text *à la page* with contemporary European poetry. As its insistent
imperatives suggest in another section of the text—"Difínt, conserva,
prea!" ["Defend, conserve, pray!": p. 1178]—, this poem represents
one of Pasolini's rewritings of Ezra Pound and includes, among
other Poundian references, the famous line "Hic desinit cantus"
["Here the song ends": p. 1181]. Ironically, as Pasolini takes leave
of his readers, his song ends where his career as a poet began thirty
years earlier; by rewriting Pound in the Friulan of his "tetro
entusiasmo", Pasolini *traduttore* comes full circle. "Saluto e augurio"
completes the move towards translating and rewriting in *friulano*
that Pasolini had begun in the 1940s with his versions of Rimbaud,
Ungaretti and T. S. Eliot. While "Saluto e augurio" is an imitative
rewriting of Pound rather than a literary translation in the strict
sense, it is altogether fitting that in his final poem Pasolini should
render an ideologically transgressive homage to the modern poet
who did most to valorize translation as a form of rewriting, and
who, in the process, reinvented the spirit of Romance for Pasolini's
generation while revitalizing the tradition of classical antiquity.[74]

NOTES

1   O. Paz, "Introduction", in O. Paz et al., *Renga: A Chain of Poems* (New York,
      Braziller, 1971), pp. 17–27 (p. 18). An earlier version of this essay was
      presented at a symposium on "Lingua, dialetto e stile in Pasolini" organized
      by Professor Hermann W. Haller at Queens College, City University of New
      York on 7 May 1990.

2   Among the most interesting recent attempts to provide fresh insights into Pasolini's experimental use of different genres and media are R. Rinaldi, *L'irriconoscibile Pasolini* (Rovito, Marra, 1990), and R. Gordon, *Pasolini: Forms of Subjectivity* (Oxford, Oxford University Press, 1996).

3   T. De Mauro, "Pasolini critico dei linguaggi", *Galleria*, 35, i–iv (1985), 7–20 (p. 8).

4   The increasing interest in translation studies, particularly in Italy, may be traced through N. Briamonte's *Saggio di bibliografia sui problemi storici, teorici e pratici della traduzione* (Naples, Edizioni Libreria Sapere, 1984). See the articles on translation by F. Fortini, "Cinque paragrafi sul tradurre", and "Traduzione e rifacimento", in his *Saggi italiani* (Bari, De Donato, 1974), pp. 332–50, 351–56; Fortini's *Nuovi saggi italiani* (Milan, Garzanti, 1987), which contain numerous articles on translation (pp. 142–149, 345–91); P. V. Mengaldo, *La tradizione del Novecento: nuova serie* (Florence, Vallecchi, 1987); *Tradizione traduzione società*, edited by R. Luperini (Rome, Editori Riuniti, 1989). See also L. Borghese, "Tia Alene in bicicletta: Gramsci traduttore dal tedesco e teorico della traduzione", *Belfagor*, 36 (1981), 635–65.

5   P. V. Mengaldo, *La tradizione del Novecento*, p. 41.

6   A. Asor Rosa, *Scrittori e popolo*, second edition (Turin, Einaudi, 1988), p. 417.

7   Reflecting a new attitude towards the study of translation, Willis Barnstone writes: "Because translation comprises the transforming principle at the heart of all literary activity, any diffidence with regard to it is out of place for either its formal study or its creations": *The Poetics of Translation* (New Haven–London, Yale University Press, 1993), p. 8.

8   F. Fortini, "Le poesie italiane di questi anni", in *Tra continuità e diversità: Pasolini e la critica*, edited by P. Voza (Naples, Liguori, 1990), pp. 98–103 (pp. 99–100).

9   R. Rinaldi, *L'irriconoscibile Pasolini*, p. 11. Giuseppe Zigaina argues that "contaminazione" constitutes Pasolini's chief *ars poetica* and that a declaration of his poetics of pastiche may be found as early as 1946. See his *Pasolini e la morte* (Venice, Marsilio, 1987), p. 23.

10 P. P. Pasolini, "Una visione del mondo epico-religioso", *Bianco e nero*, 25 (June 1964), translated as "An Epical-Religious View of the World", *Film Quarterly*, 18 (Summer 1965), 31–45.

11 L. K. Barnett and B. Lawton distinguish between "contaminazione" in its modern, specialized linguistic usage and *contaminatio* as a term in literary criticism deriving from classical antiquity. "In its specialized linguistic usage 'contamination' lacks the pejorative connotation inescapable in translation; it refers to 'the action of one element on another with which it finds itself associated'" ("Introduction", in P. P. Pasolini, *Heretical Empiricism*, translated by L. K. Barnett and B. Lawton [Bloomington–London, Indiana University Press, 1988], pp. xiii–xxviii [p. xviii]). *Contaminatio*, on the other hand, can be pejorative and was "originally applied by critics of Terence's practice of incorporating parts of one Greek play into his translation of another" (p. xxvi).

12 I do not mean to suggest that "contaminazione" is no longer a valid critical term. Keala Jewell, for example, puts it to good use in describing Pasolini's poems as palimpsests. See her *The Poesis of History: Experimenting with Genre in Post-war Italy* (Ithaca–London, Cornell University Press, 1992). See also

P. Rumble, *Allegories of Contamination: Pier Paolo Pasolini's "Trilogy of Life"* (Toronto, Toronto University Press, 1996), where Pasolini's style is characterized as one "of contamination and of excess" (p. 13). See also Patrick Rumble's contribution to the present collection.

13 G. Zigaina, *Pasolini e la morte*, p. 27.

14 R. Rinaldi, *L'irriconoscibile Pasolini*, p. 26.

15 Recent decades have seen a growing interest in the study of literary translation with a concurrent increased awareness of the fundamental role of translation in the formation of literary canons. As Susan Bassnett-McGuire observes: "It cannot be emphasized too strongly that the study of translation, especially in its diachronic aspect, is a vital part of literary and cultural history": *Translation Studies* (London, Methuen, 1980), p. 40. See also I. Even-Zohar, *Polysystem Studies*, published as a special issue of *Poetics Today*, 11, i (Spring 1990).

16 "Introduction", in *Translation, History and Culture*, edited by S. Bassnett and A. Lefevere (London–New York, Pinter, 1990), pp. 1–13 (p. 10). See also *Translation/History/Culture: A Sourcebook*, edited by A. Lefevere (London–New York, Routledge, 1992).

17 A. Lefevere, "Why Waste Our Time on Rewrites?", in *The Manipulation of Literature*, edited by T. Hermans (New York, St Martin's Press, 1985), pp. 215–43 (p. 219).

18 G. Contini, "Al limite della poesia dialettale", *Corriere del Ticino*, 24 Apr. 1943, then in *Tra continuità e diversità*, pp. 49–52 (p. 49).

19 G. Contini, "Al limite", *Tra continuità e diversità*, p. 51.

20 P. P. Pasolini, "Presentazione dell'ultimo *Stroligút*", *Libertà* [Udine], 26 May 1946 (my italics).

21 T. De Mauro, "Pasolini linguista", *The Italianist*, 5 (1985), 66–76 (p. 67). An English version appears in the present volume, where the passage in question is on p. 79.

22 T. De Mauro, "Pasolini critico dei linguaggi", p. 10.

23 In an interview with Oswald Stack, Pasolini described his initial relationship with Friulan as follows: "I heard Friulan spoken by the peasants, who were absolutely authentic peasants; but I never spoke it myself, I only learnt it after I'd begun to write poetry in it. I learnt it as a sort of mystic act of love, a kind of *félibrisme*, like the Provençal poets [...]. The central idea of hermetic poetry was the idea of the language of poetry as an absolute language [...]. I took up Friulan as a special language for poetry—i.e. the complete opposite of any tendency towards realism": *Pasolini on Pasolini: Interviews with Oswald Stack* (Bloomington, Indiana University Press, 1969), pp. 15–16. For a detailed analysis of Pasolini's rapid evolution from Hermeticism to realism, from the use of a Friulian *koinè* to various Friulian dialects, see P. Rizzolati, "Pasolini e i dialetti del Friuli occidentale", *Diverse lingue*, 6 (Feb. 1986), 27–38; see also T. O'Neill, "Pier Paolo Pasolini's Dialect Poetry", *Forum Italicum*, 9 (1975), 343–67; F. Brevini, "La lingua che piú non si sa: Pasolini e il friulano", *Belfagor*, 34, iv (1979), 397–409; R. Rinaldi, *Pier Paolo Pasolini* (Milan, Mursia, 1982), pp. 5–91.

24 Pasolini as cited by F. Fido, "Pasolini e il dialetto", *Italian Quarterly*, 21–22 (1980–81), 69–78 (p. 69). Fido describes Pasolini's use of dialect as the "fine di un'operazione letteraria" (p. 69). My own reading underlines the view that,

through this "literary operation", Pasolini was essentially translating into Friulan.

25 *La nuova gioventú* (Turin, Einaudi, 1975), p. 157.

26 On autotranslation, see G. Meo Zilio, "Andrea Zanzotto: come un poeta veneto traduce se stesso (per una critica stilistica della traduzione)", *Quaderni veneti*, 14 (1991), 95–107.

27 According to Robert Gordon, Pasolini's interest in translation, translatability and *equivalenza* not only sheds light on his stylistic experimentation, but also provides the key to understanding the work of subjectivity in his *œuvre* as a whole: "For Pasolini, [*equivalenza*] suggests a dual dynamic, in which the subjectivity of poetry creates languages and collapses difference, but in which, conversely, the constant residual interplay between languages and dialects (and any medium of expression, as Pasolini's entire career will demonstrate) creates a style, and thus embodies and emblazons the subject. The movement of forms creates the phantasm of unitary, originary subject" (R. Gordon, *Pasolini*, p. 36).

28 P. P. Pasolini, "Dalla lingua al friulano", *Ce fastu? Rivista della Società filologica friulana*, 23, v–vi (Dec. 1947), 24–26 (p. 24).

29 G. Santato writes in "La poetica dialettale di Pasolini", *Sigma*, 14, ii–iii (May–Dec. 1981), 3–24: "Negli anni 1944–1947 Pasolini viene elaborando in momenti successivi una poetica radicalmente nuova nel panorama della poesia dialettale italiana: una poetica caratterizzata dal programmatico rifiuto d'ogni concezione regionalistica, d'ogni pratica riduttivamente vernacolare e, al contrario, dalla dichiarata apertura, dall'intensa osmosi con la grande tradizione del simbolismo e del decadentismo europei" (p. 3).

30 "Presentazione dell'ultimo *Stroligút*".

31 G. Santato, "La poetica dialettale di Pasolini", p. 3.

32 In describing the fundamental importance of the Academiuta for Pasolini's future development, Andrea Zanzotto sees a common thread running through the wide-ranging forms of Pasolini's communicative experience: "Bisognava trovare un punto in cui ricomporsi e ricomporre, senza che peraltro questo punto diventasse una nuova truffa camuffata da logos monocentrico, terrificante, capace di annichilire ogni zona di marginalità. Anzi, il piú importante sogno-mito di Pasolini era di far sí che la marginalità entrasse nella centralità per poi uscirne lasciandovi il suo segno e la sua traccia" (A. Zanzotto, "Pasolini nel nostro tempo", in *Pier Paolo Pasolini: l'opera e il suo tempo*, edited by G. Santato [Padua, CLEUP, 1983], pp. 235–39 [p. 237]). Other important remarks by Zanzotto concerning the Academiuta may be found in N. Naldini, *Nei campi del Friuli (la giovinezza di Pasolini) ed una conversazione di Andrea Zanzotto* (Milan, Scheiwiller, 1984).

33 Italo Calvino, for example, remarked on the influence of Pasolini's anthology of popular poetry on his own work in collecting and transcribing Italian folktales. In a letter to Pasolini (1 March 1956), Calvino wrote: "Da tempo volevo scriverti quanto il *Canzoniere italiano* mi sia piaciuto, quanto lo stimi un libro bello e importante. La scelta è di una bellezza davvero che supera ogni aspettativa e speranza. Me lo sono letto tutto a poco a poco, e ogni tanto restavo a bocca aperta [...]. La tua scelta è di una grande intelligenza poetica [...]. Ci sono quelle specie di ritrattini delle varie regioni attraverso i loro canti, che sono bellisimi (e offrono un interessantissimo spunto di confronto

a me per le fiabe) [...]. Dunque, io ti volevo dire questo, che il tuo non è soltanto un importante libro sulla poesia popolare italiana, ma è un importante libro sull'Italia e un importante libro sulla poesia" (P. P. Pasolini, *Lettere 1955–1975*, edited by N. Naldini [Turin, Einaudi, 1988], pp. 175–76).

34 P. V. Mengaldo, *La tradizione*, p. 440.

35 On Pasolini's translations from Greek and Latin, see I. Gallo, "Pasolini traduttore di Eschilo", M. G. Bonanno, "Pasolini e l'*Orestea*: dal 'teatro di parola' al 'cinema di poesia'", V. Russo, "Riappropriazione e rifacimento: le traduzioni" and U. Todini, "Sotto il segno di Molière: il latino di Pasolini", all in *Pasolini e l'antico: i doni della ragione*, edited by U. Todini (Naples, ESI, 1995), pp. 33–43, 45–66, 117–43 and 145–63, respectively.

36 Umberto Todini includes a fragment of this incomplete and unpublished translation in his article "Pasolini e Plauto", *Galleria*, 35, i–iv (1985), 52–63 (pp. 62–63); Todini's "Sotto il segno di Molière" is a reprint of that article. Pasolini mentions the same translation in an interview of the late 1950s: see *Ritratti su misura di scrittori italiani*, edited by E. F. Accrocca (Venice, Sodalizio del Libro, 1960), p. 321.

37 I have found no reference to this translation in any of the current Pasolini bibliographies. In his *Cronologia* of Pasolini's correspondence, Naldini indicates that Pasolini finished it in 1960: "Alla fine dell'anno termina la traduzione dell'*Antigone* e riordina i versi de *La religione del mio tempo*" (*Lettere 1955–1975*, p. lxiv). Pasolini's translation of *Antigone* is not only of interest *per se* but may shed light on the genesis of his subsequent film adaptation, *Edipo re*, which reworks elements from Sophocles's *Oedipus the King* and *Oedipus at Colonus*. The lack of information about *Antigone* points to the need for a systematic editing of Pasolini's unpublished works. In a letter of 4 October 1991 to the present author, Naldini provided the following information regarding Pasolini's translations: "Non so dirti niente delle traduzioni che ti interessano. Sono cose molto marginali ed episodiche. Ho soltanto il ricordo delle traduzioni per l'antologia di Bertolucci il quale ha scelto per Pasolini le poesie da fargli tradurre." In a private interview which took place in Rome on 21 October 1991, Professor Portia Prebys asked Attilio Bertolucci for detailed information about Pasolini's contributions to his anthology *Poesia straniera del Novecento* (Milan, Garzanti, 1958). According to Bertolucci "quelle poesie si prestavano alle qualità di Pasolini come poeta e davano a Pasolini la possibilità di mostrare doti come poeta." I am grateful to Professor Prebys for this information. For interesting comments regarding the genre of the poems chosen by Bertolucci and their relationship to Bertolucci's own work see K. Jewell, *The Poesis of History*, pp. 120–45.

38 *Lettere 1955–1975*, p. 644. For references to Pasolini's suggestion that Zanzotto translate Seneca, see *Lettere 1955–1975*, p. 649.

39 S. Casi, *Pasolini: un'idea di teatro* (Udine, Campanotto, 1990), p. 156.

40 P. P. Pasolini, "Nota del traduttore", in Eschilo, *L'Orestiade*, second edition (Turin, Einaudi, 1985), pp. 175–78 (p. 175).

41 S. Casi, *Pasolini: un'idea di teatro*, p. 70.

42 U. Albini, "Tradurre i greci", in *La traduzione dei classici greci e latini in Italia oggi: problemi, prospettive, iniziative editoriali*, edited by P. Janni and I. Mazzini (Macerata, Pubblicazioni della Facoltà di Lettere e Filosofia, 1991), pp. 11–16 (p. 14).

43 S. Casi, *Pasolini: un'idea di teatro*, p. 72.

44 S. Casi, *Pasolini: un'idea di teatro*, p. 81.
45 For remarks by Pasolini on this project, see his letter to Ennio Flaiano, *Lettere 1955–1975*, p. 516. See also Todini's "Pasolini e Plauto".
46 A. Savioli, "*Il vantone*: da Plauto al Sor Capanna", *L'unità*, 13 Nov. 1963.
47 S. Casi writes: "Nonostante tutto la traduzione risulta 'pertinente e viva', come si può leggere in una recensione dell'epoca. Non mancano però alcune 'stroncature', alle quali Pasolini risponde ribaltando il concetto di chiarezza dell'opera e accusando il critico di non sforzarsi per comprendere i significati dello spettacolo" (*Pasolini: un'idea di teatro*, p. 83). For a more thorough treatment of *Il vantone* see U. Todini, "Pasolini e Plauto".
48 All these quotations are taken from the dust-jacket of P. P. Pasolini, *Il vantone di Plauto* (Milan, Garzanti, 1963).
49 F. Fortini, "Cinque paragrafi sul tradurre", p. 351.
50 Gianfranco Contini's eloquent remarks on Pasolini's death urge respect for the ambiguity of his tragic end: "Rispettiamo il nostro amico nella sua solitudine di sfidatore e lottatore col Padre, pagando, lui l'autore del *Vangelo* e della *Ricotta*, il prezzo piú alto" ("Testimonianza per Pier Paolo Pasolini", in *Pier Paolo Pasolini: testimonianze*, edited by A. Panicali and P. Sestini [Florence, Nuova Salani, 1982], pp. 13–15 [p. 15]).
51 G. P. Brunetta, "Il viaggio di Pasolini dentro i classici", *Galleria* 35, i–iv (1985), 67–75 (p. 69).
52 In his discussion of this incomplete translation, A. Todini notes that "Pasolini [...] anche per i classici mette in movimento [...] una pratica costante dei linguaggi settoriali e una sapiente filologia, un laboratorio *sui generis*, un'officina nella quale presente e passato si affrontano sempre sul tema di una scrittura piú vitale di entrambi" ("Pasolini e Plauto", p. 62).
53 Quoted by A. Todini, "Pasolini e Plauto", pp. 62–63.
54 G. P. Brunetta, "Il viaggio di Pasolini dentro i classici", p. 67.
55 Willis Barnstone points to the influence that literary translation exerts on the poet translator: "The act of creating the translated poem and reading that creation, of having the experience and confidence of the new creation, gives the poet translator a work model in her or his own hand, a work unthinkable except through the activity of translation. This leads us to a new formula: *Poets are influenced by themselves, by their own inventions* [...]. The poet translator owns the new text through the experience of having created it, and, as a poem re-created by the poet, it supplies him or her with an arsenal of possibilities" (*The Poetics of Translation*, p. 109).
56 P. P. Pasolini, "Arte e divulgazione", *Il punto*, 8 Dec. 1956, 21.
57 As we noted earlier, Pasolini translated the *Oresteia* into the poetic language he had previously developed ("Nota del traduttore", in *L'Orestiade di Eschilo*, p. 176).
58 *Quaderno romanzo*, 3 (1947), 10–30.
59 G. Zigaina, "Pier Paolo Pasolini e il dialetto", *Italian Quarterly*, 21–22 (1980–81), 79–84 (p. 82).
60 Quoted by G. Zigaina, "Pier Paolo Pasolini e il dialetto", pp. 82–83.
61 In a letter to G. Contini dated 5 February 1947, Pasolini makes explicit his intention to compare the Friulan situation with that of Catalonia: "La prego di informare il Cardò, che lo *Stroligút*, col nuovo nome di *Quaderno romanzo*, uscirà fra circa un mese e mezzo o due; che ci sarà tutta la sua antologia catalana. Se poi egli mi inviasse qualche dato potrei scrivere un articolo sulla

Catalogna, inserendo l'argomento nel problema dell'autonomia friulana" (*Lettere 1940–1954*, edited by N. Naldini [Turin, Einaudi, 1988], p. 285).

62   Quoted by G. Zigaina "Pier Paolo Pasolini e il dialetto", p. 84.

63   Following Contini's famous distinction between Dantean plurilingualism and Petrarchan monolingualism in the Italian tradition, Pasolini came to see himself as a contributor to and a champion of the Dantean line: G. Contini, "Preliminari sulla lingua del Petrarca" [1951], in *Varianti e altra linguistica* (Turin, Einaudi, 1970), pp. 169–92. For a discussion of Dantean imitation in modern Italy, see Z. G. Barański, "The Power of Influence: Aspects of Dante's Presence in Twentieth-century Italian Culture", *Strumenti critici*, new series, 1 (1986), 343–76.

64   Tom O'Neill describes the genesis of this article and characterizes it as "one of the most balanced and penetrating essays ever written by Pasolini": "*Passione e ideologia*: The Critical Essays of Pier Paolo Pasolini within the Context of Post-war Italian Criticism", *Forum for Modern Language Studies*, 9, iv (1973), 346–62 (p. 360). See also T. O'Neill, "*Il filologo come politico*: Linguistic Theory and its Sources in Pier Paolo Pasolini", *Italian Studies*, 25 (1970), 63–78.

65   For criticism of Pasolini's translation of the *Oresteia*, see the anonymous review "Un poeta traduttore", *Il mulino* (Dec. 1961), 961–64. With regard to this text, G. Bàrberi Squarotti notes that Pasolini "è stato anche traduttore fra i piú sensibili ed efficaci [...] tra i contemporanei" (*Le maschere dell'eroe: dall'Alfieri a Pasolini* [Lecce, Milella, 1990], p. 339). See also I. Gallo, "Pasolini traduttore di Eschilo"; M. G. Bonanno, "Pasolini e l'*Oresteia*".

66   P. P. Pasolini, *Il portico della morte*, edited by C. Segre (Rome, Associazione Fondo Pier Paolo Pasolini, 1988), pp. 177–79.

67   Chris Bongie reads *Il padre selvaggio* differently, using it, convincingly, to analyse Pasolini's "exotic legacy": *Exotic Memories: Literature, Colonialism, and the Fin de Siècle* (Stanford, Stanford University Press, 1991).

68   See P. P. Pasolini, *Appunti per un'Orestiade africana*, edited by A. Costa (Copparo, Quaderni del Centro Culturale di Copparo, 1983).

69   *Passione e ideologia*, second edition (Milan, Garzanti, 1977), pp. 139–40.

70   In a book review, Pasolini expresses the high esteem in which he held Tommaseo as a translator: "La sua traduzione dei *Canti popolari greci* è la piú bella opera della letteratura italiana del pieno Ottocento, dopo il Porta, il Belli, i *Canti* del Leopardi e *I promessi sposi*. Gli è pari solo qualche pagina del suo nemico Cattaneo" (*Descrizioni di descrizioni*, edited by G. Chiarcossi [Turin, Einaudi, 1979], p. 92).

71   "Gli stranieri non ridono: la comicità di Alberto Sordi", *Il reporter*, 19 Jan. 1960.

72   *Empirismo eretico*, second edition (Milan, Garzanti, 1981), p. 193.

73   For example, in *Descrizioni di descrizioni*, Pasolini describes the "double carom" of juxtaposing two texts as follows: "Leggendo l'*Historia calamitatum*, cioè la *Storia delle mie disgrazie* di Abelardo, con l'annesso epistolario tra lui e Eloisa, non son sfuggito neanche un istante alla tentazione di confrontare incessantemente il testo che leggevo con un possibile film tratto da esso" (p. 436). See also Robert Gordon's comments on translation, experimentation and subjectivity cited in n. 27 above.

74   In a meeting with students in Lecce on 21 October 1975, only two weeks before his tragic murder, Pasolini read the final monologue from *Bestia da stile*, which resembles "Saluto e augurio" in its Poundian references. Accord-

ing to the poet, "È una poesia che cita e, in un certo senso, rifà e mima i *Cantos* di Pound; quindi ci sono anche citazioni di Pound dentro e altre citazioni [...] quasi prese alla lettera, a cui ho aggiunto delle spiritosaggini, cosí, tanto per portare l'argomento ad una maggiore attualità" (*Volgar' eloquio*, edited by G. C. Ferretti [Rome, Editori Riuniti, 1987], pp. 23–26). Anna Lo Giudice asserts that "Pasolini non assimila Pound al Fascismo" and that "il nostro poeta vedeva Pound un po' come vedeva se stesso: una coraggiosa, scandalosa e certamente abnorme vittima sacrificale" ("Pasolini e Pound: il viaggio verso il padre", *Letteratura italiana contemporanea*, 12, xxxiv [1991], 33–64 [p. 38]).

APPENDIX
Pasolini's Translations

"A la so pissula patria", by N. Tommaseo, *Il stroligút*, 1 (1945), 19

"Luna", by G. Ungaretti, *Il stroligút*, 2 (1946), 19

"Peso", by G. Ungaretti, *Ce fastu?* 5/6 Dec. 1947, 25

"Muart ta l'aga", by T. S. Eliot, *Ce fastu?* 5/6 (Dec. 1947), 25

"Enfance IV", by A. Rimbaud, *Ce fastu?* 5/6 (Dec. 1947), 26

"Fiore di poeti catalani", *Quaderno romanzo*, 3 (1947), 10–30

"Tre framens da Safo", in M. Fusillo, *La Grecia secondo Pasolini: mito e cinema* (Scandicci, La Nuova Italia, 1996), pp. 243–45

Poesia dialettale del Novecento, in collaboration with M. Dell'Arco (Parma, Guanda, 1952)

Canzoniere italiano (Milan, Garzanti, 1955)

"Storia di Yvonne", in *Poesia straniera del Novecento*, edited by A. Bertolucci (Milan, Garzanti, 1958), pp. 82–87

"La romanza del ritorno", by J. Pellerin, in *Poesia straniera del Novecento*, edited by A. Bertolucci (Milan, Garzanti, 1958), pp. 88–93

Eneide, by Virgil, incomplete and unpublished translation, partially published in A. Todini, "Pasolini e Plauto", *Galleria*, 35, i–iv (1985), 52–63

Orestiade, by Aeschylus (Turin, Einaudi, 1960)

"Esortazione ai poveri", by A. Frénaud, *L'Europa letteraria*, 5–6 (Dec. 1960), 87

La poesia popolare italiana (Milan, Garzanti, 1960); second, revised edition of *Canzoniere italiano*

Il vantone, by Plautus (Milan, Garzanti, 1963)

Italian dialogues of *Trash*, by P. Morissey, in collaboration with D. Maraini, *Filmcritica* (Oct–Dec. 1973), 325–60

THE LATENT PRESENCE
OF CROCEAN AESTHETICS
IN PASOLINI'S "CRITICAL MARXISM"

Joseph Francese

> I poeti appartengono sempre a un'*altra civiltà*.
> [Poets always belong to *another civilization*.]
>
> (*Bestia da stile*)

CROCE'S LEGACY

In "La posizione", an essay first published in *Officina* in 1956, Pasolini stated, "Una formazione intellettuale ipoteca un'intera esistenza letteraria: e chi meno se ne vuole ricordare piú ne è determinato" ["An intellectual formation mortgages an entire literary existence: and those who least wish to remember this are those who are most determined by it"].[1] Pasolini's training, much like that of other intellectuals of his generation, was informed by Crocean aesthetics; his (and their) "conversion" to leftist politics was motivated less by political or theoretical criteria than by moral and cultural considerations.[2] In the decade immediately following the Second World War, attempts by many progressive Italian intellectuals to appropriate what was to be learned from Gramsci's notebooks were hampered by their inability to appraise objectively the elements of Crocean Idealism in their work (part and parcel of which was the firm belief in the intrinsic value of culture and of intellectual labour).[3] The provincialism of Italian culture in the late 1940s and early 1950s was not only a result of Fascism's *de jure* censorship, but also due to a more subtle type of censorship effected by Croce over those schools of thought to which he was averse.[4] During this period, particularly the years between his move from Friuli to Rome and the mid-1950s, Pasolini attempted to give his literary production and criticism a Gramscian patina in order to conceal its underlying Crocean Idealism.[5] By repressing Croce's influence on his intellectual training he precluded its overcoming, notwithstanding his frequent evocation of what he called the determining influence of Gramsci.

When Pasolini, at the end of *Passione e ideologia*, wrote of irrational passions in search of a rational systematization in Marxism (*PI*, 484, 489)—in his own idiosyncratic verbal shorthand, "ideology"—he borrowed from Croce the idea of a passage within art from the singular and irrational to the universal and rational. Using his own characteristic empiricism—a tendency especially evident in the 1960s—he would project and objectify what was subjectively perceived. Self-expression for Pasolini in the 1960s did not connote a dialectical relationship with reality, but rather the objectification of his own interior world. As he wrote in "Una disperata vitalità":

> La morte non è
> nel non poter comunicare
> ma nel non poter più essere compresi.[6]

[Death is not/the inability to communicate/but the inability to make oneself understood.]

As a consequence, arguably, of his superficial recourse to Gramsci in the 1950s, Pasolini never fully appropriated the more innovative elements of the Sardinian's thought, particularly the recognition of the dialectical relationship, the "necessary reciprocity", between literature and society. In the 1960s Pasolini considered the proposals of the late revolutionary anachronistic owing to the social changes brought about in Italy by the post-war economic "boom". The so-called Economic Miracle had "corrupted" the workers, provoking in turn the "resa operaia" ["workers' surrender"] lamented in *La religione del mio tempo*.[7] Whether or not this was the case, Pasolini then envisaged himself surrounded by an "entropia borghese" ["bourgeois entropy"], an atemporal continuum devoid of class conflict. The empiricism that led him to redimension the importance of historical dialectic as an instrument for interpreting reality also reinforced the propensity to project his interior reality outside the self. Because of this extreme subjectivism, he was unable to historicize himself, to isolate and analyse the forces that determined and conditioned his poetic research. As a result of his penchant for elevating himself as synecdoche of a general human condition, Pasolini postulated a meta-historical human essence or "physicality", a pseudo-materialistic construct that ignored the inherent historicity of human biology.[8]

Gramsci recognized the dialectical relationship between economic base and ideological superstructure and between thought and praxis. For Croce, however, history was mere content, raw material for the Spirit, a stimulus for artistic intuition. In Croce's system the Spirit was realized in the "fatto estetico", equivalent in his definition with intuition, a purely intellectual, meta-historical activity that existed independently of the "fatto artistico". What Croce called the "fatto artistico" was the extrinsic expression, the concrete and therefore historical manifestation of artistic intuition, the "fatto estetico". The "fatto artistico" was merely the practical act infused with artistic intuition; it was an externalization of the "fatto estetico" which was of primary concern. For Croce the "fatto artistico" would be expended by critical reflection: art was not to be necessarily subjected to contemplation, but was to stimulate the intuitive understanding of the beholder/reader.

A fundamental part of Crocean aesthetics was the distinction between meta-historical "poesia" and structural elements within and outside the text, what Croce called "non poesia". Pasolini, during the final years of his life (the period characterized by his poetics of "unpopular realism"),[9] felt that social progress was to be carried forward by an intellectual élite acting under the hegemony of avant-garde artists. Following Croce, he minimized the importance of the dialectical relationship between artist and public, and reaffirmed the primacy of the writer-artist. At the same time, Pasolini postponed interaction with the masses. His hope was to effect changes in the ideological superstructure by dealing exclusively with representatives of the more educated social strata. Thus he not only remained faithful to Croce's philosophical system, but, by subordinating politics (to use Croce's phrasing "la volontà economico-utile" ["the economic-practical will"]) to intellectual work ("la volontà etico-morale" ["the ethical-moral will"]), Pasolini followed in Vittorini's footsteps. In the years immediately follow-

ing the Second World War (but prior to his "rediscovery" of Croce),
Vittorini had distanced himself from the official cultural politics of
the Italian Communist Party (which was often conditioned by
political rather than cultural considerations, particularly after 1947)
and gave impetus in Italy to a brand of Marxism that was critical of
official Communist political strategy and of the methods of philosophical and literary analysis common to those intellectuals in or
near the Party.[10] In the late 1950s and early 1960s Pasolini wavered
between this "critical" Marxism (whose exponents supported the
use of methods of inquiry extraneous to the Marxist tradition) and
openness to a *rapprochement* with intellectuals close to the Communist Party and more inclined to use a critical method grounded in
historiography. Pasolini, however, lacked the theoretical foundation that would have allowed him to mediate the differences
separating the two tendencies (had he been inclined to serve in this
capacity). In the aftermath of 1968, with the waning of "critical"
Marxism in Italy and the rise of a neo-Marxist current,[11] Pasolini's
scomodo return towards the Communist Party took place. At this
same time, he claimed for the artist a privileged social condition
while moving artistically towards a poetics of "unpopular realism". He also emphasized self-expression at the expense of dialogic
exchange, thus reaffirming the importance of the "fatto estetico"
and thereby precluding the recognition and surpassing of the
irrational and subjective foundations of his thought.

In this essay I shall attempt to contrast Pasolini's idiosyncratic
position, determined by his predominately Crocean intellectual
training, with the backdrop of the two divergent interpretations of
Marx prevalent in Italy during the 1950s. I shall then examine the
return towards Crocean aesthetics in Pasolini's later work. This
will be done primarily through an analysis of the presence of
Croce's concept of intuition and of the philosopher's opposition of
poetry and non-poetry in Pasolini's ideas on the "cinema of poetry" and in several of his later autobiographical works.[12]

Pasolini's Gramsci

Pasolini's initial support for the workers' movement was inspired
first by emotional, then by linguistic and literary concerns; his so-
called Marxism was a consequence of this involvement. Pasolini's

early political activism and his enrolment in the Italian Communist Party in 1947 were largely consequences of his attempt to give literary validity to the Friulan dialect. As has recently been indicated, Pasolini's linguistic concerns contributed to a heightened social awareness which led to Pasolini's involvement with a group devoted to Friulan autonomy. This was followed by Pasolini's attendance at meetings of the local Party office and his enrolment in the Communist Party.[13] As he was to say years later, the use of the language of his maternal ancestors was for him an act of pure expressionism, "il massimo dell'ermetismo, dell'oscurità, del rifiuto di comunicare" ["the utmost hermeticism, obscurity, refusal to communicate"].[14] Pasolini's subsequent use of an "incomprehensible" poetic language as part of a proselytizing campaign for a workers' party is not perplexing if we keep in mind that—as we shall see—Pasolini subordinated his political activism to what he called the "missione didattica" of the intellectual class.

As Barański has convincingly argued, neither Marx nor Gramsci figured prominently in Pasolini's initial involvement with leftist politics.[15] In fact, prior to 1955 Pasolini had acquired little more than an exceedingly superficial knowledge of the more popularized aspects of Gramsci's thought. In that year he probably gained direct knowledge of Gramsci's work, but his reading was limited to *Letteratura e vita nazionale*. What Barański has called Pasolini's "carefully fostered image as a radical",[16] was the result of the intentional dissembling in the 1950s by Pasolini of a Gramscian influence on his intellectual formation. Barański has shown that Pasolini's critical perspective did not change dramatically after 1949, following his presumed reading of Gramsci. During the last fifteen years of his life Pasolini would refer to the influence of the Sardinian revolutionary on his intellectual roots as part of an attempt to reinforce the culturally fabricated self-image so painstakingly created during the 1950s.

Along with the purposeful concoction of a self-image, Pasolini's auto-validation of his empirical perceptions often led him to reify his subjective observations through projection. Hence his Gramsci did not correspond to the one typically associated with the *Quaderni*, but rather more closely resembled Pasolini's *alter ego*. As Barański has written, "As well as an intellectual influence, Gramsci exerted an aesthetic-sentimental one, whereby Pasolini came to identify himself with his mentor." Moreover, Pasolini's belated and "poorly assimilated" acquaintance with Gramsci was determined by an insistent irrationality augmented by the lack of further reading that conditioned his highly subjective view of the Sardinian revolutionary.[17] As Pasolini said in 1960:

> Il marxismo non ha mai affrontato in modo soddisfacente il problema dell'irrazionalità. Tutto esso potrà spiegarmi del pensiero e dell'azione di Gramsci, per esempio, ma non quel "sentimento", quella "fede", che gli ha fatto sopportare la prigione e la morte piuttosto che piegarsi al fascismo: o, se me lo spiega, me lo spiega in termini genericamente stoici, edificanti meramente umani.[18]

> [Marxism has never dealt satisfactorily with the question of irrationality. Marxism can explain to my satisfaction all Gramsci's thought and action, for example, but not that "sentiment", that "faith", which allowed him to withstand incarceration and death rather than submit to Fascism. Or if Marxism explains this to me, it explains it in generally stoic, edifying terms, as a mere fact of his humanity.]

Because of his proclivity for the irrational, Pasolini would ascribe a religious dimension to his Marxism, describing it as a form of mystical ascesis. Moreover, the "response" quoted above substantially reaffirms what was stated in *Passione e ideologia*, in an essay dedicated to the poetry of Eugenio Cirese, where Pasolini had specified what in his view Gramscian realistic literature was. In this context Gramsci was used as an example of a meta-historical aesthetic category:

> Esiste in Cirese un interesse diretto per la realtà intesa come la intenderebbe oggi all'incirca un realista di formazione gramsciana: assume per esempio ad argomento dei suoi versi la popolazione del suo paese [...] ma in aperta sfiducia, però, in quei dati attuali, spostandosi la sua simpatia verso il dolore inattuale ma eterno della madre che piange i figli. E dunque, da una realtà naturale e sociale a una realtà religiosa. (*PI*, 305)

> [There is in Cirese's work a direct interest in reality—reality understood more or less as a contemporary Gramscian realist would understand it: for example, he takes as a topic of his verse the population of his home town (...) but in open distrust of such time-bound elements, moving his sympathy towards the timeless yet eternal pain of the mother who laments the loss of her

children. And, therefore, from a natural and social reality to a religious one.]

The image of Gramsci put forward here does not contradict the one used at the conclusion of *Passione e ideologia*. There, Pasolini evoked the "incarcerated" Gramsci, paradoxically free despite and because of his confinement. Comparing Gramsci to Leopardi, Pasolini extolled his own idiosyncratic Gramsci, whom he condensed to nothing more than "pure and heroic thought".[19]

The elevation of Gramsci by Pasolini to a meta-historical aesthetic category is in keeping with his utilization of the Communist leader to justify what for Pasolini was the intellectual's social function. In both instances the Gramsci to be deduced from Pasolini's writings conforms less to the historical figure than to a projection of Pasolini's own self-image. In the essay "Marxisants" (1959), Pasolini wrote of the "riscoperta—cosciente e elaborata—da parte dello scrittore, di una sua condizione 'eletta', di una sua sostanziale 'aristocraticità'" ["consciously elaborated rediscovery by the writer of his 'chosen' condition, of his essentially 'aristocratic' social role"]. This aristocratic condition imbricated with the group's "funzione sacerdotale" ["priestly function"],[20] and was reminiscent of a traditional view of the intellectual caste, shared by others of Pasolini's generation and training who considered themselves "il sale della terra" ["the salt of the earth"].[21]

Pasolini's Gramsci was at once a projection of an *alter ego* and an affirmation of Pasolini's self-image, each reinforcing and corroborating the validity of the other throughout the last twenty-five years of Pasolini's life. Once Pasolini had established his self-image, he utilized it to lend theoretical support to his ideas regarding intellectuals' "missione didattica" ["didactic mission"] and "separatezza" ["separateness"] from the rest of society. As he said in 1969:

> In quegli anni '48–49, scoprivo Gramsci. Il quale mi offriva la possibilità di fare un bilancio della mia situazione personale. Attraverso Gramsci, la posizione dell'intellettuale—piccolo-borghese di origine o di adozione—la situavo ormai tra il partito e le masse, vero e proprio perno di mediazione tra le classi, e soprattutto verificavo sul piano teorico l'importanza del mondo contadino nella prospettiva rivoluzionaria. La risonanza dell'opera di Gramsci fu per me determinante.[22]

[In the years 1948–49, I discovered Gramsci. He offered me the chance to take stock of my personal situation. Through Gramsci I came to locate the *petit bourgeois*—by birth or by choice—intellectual between the Party and the masses, a true pivot of class mediation, and above all I ascertained theoretically the import-ance of peasant society within a revolutionary perspective. The resonance of Gramsci's work was decisive for me.]

It is important to note that in this interview Pasolini mentions the "discovery" and "resonance" of Gramsci and not a direct reading. This is indicative of Pasolini's recuperation of Gramsci, brought about, first, by Pasolini's culling of the Communist and popular press during the post-war years and, then, by a limited reading of Gramsci's writings. This highly subjective representation would facilitate Pasolini's efforts to present himself as "true heir to the Gramscian heritage".[23] Pasolini would use his idiosyncratic ver-sion of Gramsci to support his attribution of a "pedagogical function" to intellectuals—an idea that informed his thought from at least the early 1940s onwards,[24] and was reiterated periodically during the last fifteen years of his life.

PASOLINI'S "CRITICAL" MARXISM

In the years following the Second World War many intellectuals remained faithful to Croce's teachings on the intrinsic value of culture and to what Luperini has called their "caste mentality". Thus Italian intellectuals' "aristocratic way of living literature", in Pasolini's view, remained substantially unchanged, and a "social mission that would have otherwise been thrown into crisis by the new historical situation" was preserved.[25] Together with his youth-ful vision of the traditional pedagogical social function of the intellectual, this aristocratic view of literature was, in his non-fiction, to expand the anti-institutional polemic that had previ-ously characterized Vittorini's criticisms of the Italian Communist Party's cultural politics.[26] Inherent in Vittorini's refusal to "sound the fife for the revolution" was a conception of cultural activity related to but distinct from politics. For Vittorini culture satisfied internal exigencies while politics met external, economic needs.[27] As we have seen, this separation of theory from praxis closely followed Croce's thought.

It is not possible to ascertain any direct influence of *Il politecnico* on Pasolini. According to the latter's biographer, Naldini, Vittorini's periodical publication did not figure in Pasolini's reading during his stay in the Friuli region. In fact, in the immense legacy of essays and interviews there are few and perfunctory references to *Il politecnico*. This may be due to the personal antipathy felt by Pasolini for Vittorini;[28] in any case, we must underline the manner in which Pasolini evoked *Il politecnico* when it suited his polemical needs. For example, in 1960 he declared: "La critica marxista in Italia ha avuto un periodo glorioso nell'immediato dopoguerra (Politecnico ecc.) benché non fosse marxista se non nelle intenzioni, nella passione" ["Marxist criticism in Italy enjoyed a glorious flowering in the post-war years (*Politecnico* etc.) even though it was Marxist only in its intentions, in its passion"].[29] In other words, Pasolini avoided an analysis of Vittorini's work, preferring to use *Il politecnico* to depict an "atmosphere" that would have been conducive to his own presumed "radical" intellectual formation. Within the context of this representation, Vittorini's periodical served as an ideal and as a beacon of morality for Pasolini's own "discovery of Marx", and as a point of reference for that "unresolved drama" common to an entire generation of intellectuals.

A more mature Pasolini was to propose Vittorini's *Il politecnico* as a "typical" example of Marxist research in Italy during the immediate post-war period.[30] While in Friuli, however, Pasolini subordinated politics to literature. According to Naldini, in those years Pasolini read "*Il ponte* di Calamandrei e appart*eneva* idealmente al Partito d'Azione, professando molta ammirazione per Saragat perché cita*va* brillantemente Dante" ["Calamandrei's *Il ponte* and belonged ideally to the Action Party, declaring great admiration for Saragat because he could quote Dante with brilliance"].[31] In the *Scritti corsari* Pasolini maintained that he had read Marx and Gramsci during his period in Friuli.[32] Naldini, however, notes that "si accostò al pensiero marxiano leggendo una sintesi semplificata de *Il capitale*" ["he was drawn to Marxian thought on reading a simplified synthesis of *Capital*"].[33] In a 1961 column for *Vie nuove*, Pasolini described his turn to Marxism as a "mystical or ascetic act" and held it up as a model for Italy's youth. In his words, it was a "'moto della coscienza' che porta al tradimento della propria classe sociale" ["an 'impulse of the conscience' that leads to the betrayal of one's own social class"].[34] This suggestion was to be reiterated in the *Lettere luterane* and in the poems of "Tetro

entusiasmo" included in *La nuova gioventú*, where he began to
move beyond the élitism of his "unpopular realism". The re-
invigoration of a didactic monologue directed at the "young a-
ideological Fascists" of "consumeristic" Italy was predicated once
again on the utilization of his own autobiography as an *exemplum*
of the intellectual's condition. It therefore comes as no surprise that
when Pasolini approached the Communist fold again in the 1970s,
Marxism became for him once more a means of mystical ascesis
and not demystificatory praxis.[35] Pasolini's *rapprochement* to the
Party in the 1970s was conditioned by his desire to "trasumanare"
(that is, like Dante's Glaucus in *Paradiso* I, to become more than, or
quintessentially, human).

In the light of Pasolini's "critical" Marxism during the latter
half of the 1950s, it must be noted that Pasolini did not assume a
polemical stance, more in line with that of the "critical" Marxists,
regarding the cultural politics of the Italian Communist Party in
the years immediately following his expulsion from the Party. This
occurred only after he had established himself professionally,
specifically after *Ragazzi di vita* had failed to win the approval of the
Communist press.[36] When Pasolini became more vociferous in his
criticism of the Communists' cultural politics his views on the
relationship between politics and culture largely resembled those
put forward by Vittorini a decade earlier: political activity *tout
court* was subsumed into methodological and stylistic investigation. As he wrote in 1958:

> Nell'immergermi nel mondo dialettale e gergale della "borgata"
> io porto con me una coscienza che giustifica la mia operazione né
> piú né meno di quanto giustifichi, ad esempio, l'operazione di un
> dirigente di partito: il quale, come me, appartiene alla classe
> borghese, e da questa si allontana, ripudiandone momentanea-
> mente le necessità, per capire e fare proprie le necessità della
> classe proletaria o comunque popolare. La differenza è che
> questa operazione coscientemente politica, nell'uomo di partito
> prevede o prepara l'azione: in me, scrittore, non può che farsi
> mimesis linguistica, testimonianza, denuncia, organizzazione
> interna della struttura narrativa secondo un'ideologia marxista,
> luce interna.[37]

> [When I immerse myself in the slang and dialect of the *borgata*, I
> have an awareness that justifies what I am doing, very similar to
> that of a politician who, like me, belongs to the bourgeoisie, and

distances himself from that class, temporarily rejecting that class's priorities, in order to understand and appropriate the needs of the proletariat or at least of the popular classes. What distinguishes me from the politician is that this consciously political operation for the politician precedes or prepares for action, while for me, as a writer, it can only be transformed into linguistic mimesis, bearing of witness, denunciation, internal organization of the narrative structure according to a Marxist ideology, an interior light.]

Beginning in the immediate post-war period, those critics who were closely associated with the Communist Party attempted to introduce a historical component into the study of literature, as well as those structural elements that Croce had deemed "non poesia".[38] Specifically, they began to re-read literary history in order to reappraise the factors external to the text that determined and conditioned the historical genesis of the various poetics and individual works. At the same time they attempted to preserve the necessary specificity of art while denying the autonomy attributed to art by Croce.[39]

Pasolini's critical method differed from that of the intellectuals belonging or close to the Italian Communist Party who, according to the "critical" Marxists, employed a prevalently sociological approach. On the other hand, the "critical" Marxists claimed to be motivated by a spirit of openness towards non-Marxist schools of thought.[40] Many of these "critical" Marxists, Pasolini included, as a result of their refusal to politicize culture, emphasized the unique nature of their "intellectual condition": their prescription of intellectual freedom led them to demand the autonomy of cultural labour in respect of politics. As a critic Pasolini was interested primarily in stylistic questions and in the internal mechanisms of a text, not in the social context. In the late 1950s he contributed to the debate on literary Neo-realism proposing as a model for his creative work and that of others his own "unresolved drama" of the intellectual who "betrays", as he had, his own social class to advocate the welfare of the working classes. As a consequence, his criticism of "official" Neo-realism was substantially linguistic: he believed that form, not content, should have been of primary importance. In his opinion, the writers and critics who championed Neo-realism had been excessively concerned with the collectivity at the expense of the individual. While inherent in Pasolini's proposal is an attempt to move against the "calligraphism" Gramsci had disparaged in favour of a "genuinely innovative subject-matter",[41] we must be wary of a project that evokes Gramsci but places the poet squarely at the centre of investigation. If for Gramsci the concept of "national-popular" was "a means of drawing people's attention to the nature of their own lives as inseparable from the socio-economic system in which they live",[42] we must note the manner in which Pasolini's life is once again filtered through his creative work to become a model for his general, theoretical proposals.

THE CINEMA OF POETRY

After Pasolini had created for himself the image of a dyed-in-the-wool Gramscian, and after the personal "crisis" catalysed by his observation of a "workers' surrender", he began to investigate what he called "cinema di poesia" ["cinema of poetry"]. A fundamental element of his ideas on this subject was the recuperation of a Jungian collective unconscious. He posited a pre-linguistic code composed of images stored in a collective unconscious; these images were to be the means of communication between the director's and the public's "intuition". He hoped to use them to realize in the cinema, as he had in literature, a mode of expression that he described as "raccontare poeticamente per immagini" ["to narrate poetically through images"].

As Pasolini was to say in 1969, the film-going public, because of what he labelled the "anthropological change" of Italians from peasant to consumer society, had become a homologous, sociologically indistinct abstraction. As Pasolini often stated, *Uccellacci e uccellini* marked the beginning of a new phase of his cinema in which he consciously reacted against what he saw as the "homologation" of Italian society. Unlike that of theatre, the cinematic public was not a "folla" or "crowd"—"un grande numero di singoli, in quanto presenti in carne e ossa" ["a large gathering of individuals, present in the flesh"]—but a "mass".[43] Film was capable of "massifying" its audience and Pasolini hoped to exploit the medium in order to direct a "univocal" message to that "mass". Hence, when Pasolini stated in the essay "Il cinema di poesia" that "la lingua [del cinema] è per forza interdialettale e internazionale:

perché gli occhi sono uguali in tutto il mondo" ["cinematic language is ineluctably interdialectal and international because people's eyes are the same the world over": *EE*, 178], he levelled ideologically what was other, that is, he implied that his own interpretation of material reality coincided with that of the rest of humanity. This assumption was based on his belief in the existence of a common repertory of pre-linguistic images that defied interpretation and was able to "speak" directly to his and his audience's intuition, and provoke universal, instinctive reactions.

In her recent analysis of Pasolini's "cinema of poetry", Naomi Greene has emphasized the manner in which Pasolini linked the cinematic image to a pre-linguistic, "primal, non-conceptual, world of matter and presence".[44] Citing Pasolini's indebtedness to the *poètes maudits*, she notes that for Pasolini the images utilized in the cinema of poetry were to convey meaning through analogy. Communication through analogy was to circumvent language and reason, thereby linking the intuition of the artist and that of his public in a manner reminiscent of Croce's "fatto estetico". On account of its link to the images stored in the collective unconscious, a poetics of "physical reality or presence" would ultimately provide a glimpse of humanity's meta-historical essence. Thus Pasolini did not discard proposals made in the 1950s and early 1960s but continued with his attempt to embrace what he had called "un'attualità non posseduta ideologicamente" ["a reality not mastered ideologically": *PI*, 484]. In the 1950s Pasolini (and many other leftist intellectuals) thought it possible to use Marxism as a means of explaining a complete system. To that end, he hoped to direct his "passions" into an ideology informed by Marxism (understood as an ordered set of doctrines) and thereby adapt his perception of reality to a determinate world view, namely to a different form of false (albeit more progressive) consciousness. This manner of perceiving reality was already "ideological" because it inverted the relationship between material reality and consciousness, and could only lead him to a different form of objectified self-knowledge.

I should like to add parenthetically that, as J. Larrain has indicated, Marxists of the generation of Lenin, Lukács and Gramsci used the 1859 "Introduction" to the *Critique of Political Economy* as the basis of their interpretation of the concept of ideology. They accepted the existence of a proletarian ideology, but were not aware of the existence of the negative concept mentioned in *The German Ideology*.[45] Ideology, as Pasolini understood the term, followed these general lines: he borrowed the positive concept in order to postulate a possible alternative proletarian ideology. Moreover, Pasolini's definition of the concept of ideology allowed him to propose himself as a universal norm: presumably the rational ordering of his "passions" would provide access to a unifying view of reality. Therefore, after his disenchantment with the working masses, he sought within his own empirical, intrinsic reality the "sense" of human existence. Although the "crisis" of *La religione del mio tempo* seems to signal a change of direction (the repudiation of a method of research informed by Marxism),[46] it was merely a different, not contradictory, perspective on history. The "centre of gravity" had not changed: it was still Pasolini.

During the 1950s Pasolini claimed to search "Marxistically" to find in class conflict the driving force behind human events. His enquiry in the years between the publication of *La religione del mio tempo* and 1968, culminating to a large extent in his ideas on the "cinema of poetry", seemed to signal an abrupt reversal or break with what had preoccupied him in the previous decade. On closer examination, however, we see that this is not the case. Like Croce, Pasolini saw the individual's life as independent of surrounding historical forces.[47] As he wrote in 1966:

> È chiaro che un autore non desidera in nessun caso sentirsi determinato, neanche nel caso che la determinazione sia eufemisticamente chiamata omologia. Inoltre egli sente di non trovare la libertà nemmeno attraverso la vita e l'opera di un "individuo problematico", poiché non sa, tutto sommato, rinvenire autenticità neanche nei "valori d'uso": l'unica autenticità, e quindi libertà, che egli concepisce è nel sapere quello che fa.[48]

> [It is clear that no writer wishes to feel determined, even when it is euphemistically called homology. Also he feels incapable of finding freedom in the life and work of a "problematic individual", because he does not know, after all, how to find authenticity in "use value": the only authenticity, and hence freedom, of which he can conceive is in knowing what he is doing.]

Greene's reading of this passage leads her to affirm that here Pasolini "is virtually asserting that the only way an author can avoid being conditioned by capitalistic society [...] is to take as the subject of a work the problem of its own creation".[49] I would go one step further and state that the "operazione liberatoria" to which Pasolini made reference connoted a liberation from the determining forces of history. This was to be accomplished by the shifting of critical focus from the work to its genesis within the artist's intuition.

Pasolini's belief in the suprahistorical essence of art led him to state, in 1967, that only after death could the most significant events of an individual's life be abstracted, or to use his term, "synthesized", thereby giving that particular existence a "sense": "Una vita, con tutte le sue azioni," he wrote, "è decifrabile interamente veramente solo dopo la morte" ["A life, including all its actions, is truly and completely decipherable only after death": *EE*, 246]. In his opinion the naturalistic representation of the sequence shot did not abstract life's meaning from the flow of events; therefore, montage was better suited to represent life realistically. When he stated in "Il 'cinema di poesia'" that "gli autori del nuovo cinema non muoiono abbastanza dentro le loro opere" ["the authors of new cinema do not die enough in their works": *EE*, 246], he directed a ciphered criticism at *cinema verité*'s inability to express "synthetically", and therefore "realistically", the artist's intentions. Thus, because death permitted that process of abstraction, it became for Pasolini a metaphor of self-expression; and, as we have seen, self-expression connoted for Pasolini the Crocean concept of intuition, and not dialogic externalization. After visiting one of Pasolini's sets, Gideon Bachmann noted that while other directors might shoot ten scenes in a day, Pasolini shot forty. This was possible because under Pasolini's direction the takes did not evolve on the set through the exchange of interpretations between cast and director, but merely entailed the transfer of what was in Pasolini's mind onto film. In Bachmann's opinion the transcoding of the scene from mind to film was something of a nuisance for Pasolini, an obstacle between his imagination and the spectator.[50] That is, the realization of a work was subordinated to its conception. At the same time, montage was better suited to the "synthetic" representation of reality; it was an expressive means well fitted to that "raccontare per immagini", or "telling through images", that was fundamental to the "language" and to the "cinema of poetry".

Poesia

To understand better what Pasolini meant by "poetic language", we must return to a 1956 essay, "La lingua della poesia", subsequently collected in *Passione e ideologia*. According to Pasolini, an excellent example of this language was to be found in the work of Giotti, who was able to transfer the techniques of impressionistic painting into his poetry (*PI*, 274). In his reading, Pasolini discerned a poet who was able to go beyond an extreme "limit of pain" and evoke "the complete sense of existence".[51] The poetic language of which Pasolini spoke was "absolute" (*PI*, 276), capable of representing "un sentimento globale dell'esistenza, una 'sintesi' tenuta continuamente presente, con lo sguardo del vecchio cosí pieno di vita da essere fuori della vita" ["a global feeling of existence, a 'synthesis' continuously kept in mind, through the eyes of an elderly man so full of life as to be outside life": *PI*, 288]. To use his own phrasing, poetic language was "visual, irrational, impressionistic and then expressionistic". Since poetic language used imagery more concisely and effectively than prose (for him "rational, objective and informative"), and these images corresponded at an unconscious level to reality, poetry was, in his opinion, a more efficacious means of realistic representation, and therefore a superior model and tool for what he intended to accomplish in his cinema. Pasolini had hoped that the object of his meditation on the "cinema of poetry" would enable him to "narrate poetically through images". The synthesis of what was subjectively and "impressionistically" perceived was to catalyse an expressionistic poetic discourse whose "sense" was to be intuited by the user.

In the autobiographical "Poeta delle Ceneri" (1966–67) Pasolini affirmed:

> [...] io vorrei soltanto vivere
> pur essendo poeta
> perché la vita si esprime anche solo con se stessa.
> Vorrei esprimermi con gli esempi.
> Gettare il mio corpo nella lotta.
> Ma se le azioni della vita sono espressive,
> anche l'espressione è azione.[52]

[I would simply like to live/even though I'm a poet/because life expresses itself even just with itself./I would like to express myself through examples./Throw my body into the fray./But if life's actions are expressive,/expression is also action.]

By suggesting that we express ourselves through our actions, Pasolini hinted in this poem that he believed an interpersonal dynamic catalysed by poetry to be possible. As we have seen, however, for Pasolini *ex*pression was not directed at the *ex*ternal, as the prefix would have us believe. Expression and action were equivalent, but it became increasingly clear as time passed that action, too, was there to satisfy intrinsic needs corresponding to the artist's intuition. In a similar fashion the "oneiric physicality" (*EE*, 172) of cinema became for him a means of representing action—"il primo e principale linguaggio degli uomini" ["the first and primary language of humanity": *EE*, 199]—while written language was reduced to a mere "convention". Spoken language was closely linked "senza soluzione di continuità storica" ["without historical interruption"] to the origins of the human race, and, in his view, was also action.[53] Pasolini identified spoken language with action, considering both of them manifestations of a primary human language. He then found in poetry the written complement of that primary oral tradition: a purely expressive linguistic means capable of evoking images stored in a collective unconscious. Thus poetry too was a form of action:

Il primo linguaggio degli uomini mi sembra dunque il loro agire. La lingua scritto-parlata non è che un'integrazione e un mezzo di tale agire. Anche il massimo di distacco della lingua da tale agire umano—ossia il momento puramente espressivo della lingua— la poesia—non è a sua volta che una nuova forma di azione: se, nel momento in cui il lettore l'ascolta o la legge, insomma la percepisce, la libera di nuovo dalla convenzione linguistica e la ricrea come dinamica di sentimenti, di affetti, di passioni, di idee: la riduce a entità audiovisiva, cioè riproduzione della realtà, azione—e così il cerchio si chiude. (*EE*, 205–06)

[Humanity's first language, I would say, is its actions. Written and spoken language are merely a completion of and a means for those actions. Even the maximum detachment of language from such human action—which occurs in the most purely expressive use of language, poetry—is nothing more in its turn than another

form of action. This is the case if, in the moment when the reader
hears or reads the poetic word, s/he frees it from linguistic
convention and recreates it as a dynamic of feelings, affections,
passions, ideas: s/he reduces it to an audio-visual entity, namely
a reproduction of reality, action—in this way the circle is closed.]

We see here how Pasolini remained faithful to Croce's *Estetica*,
particularly the effects of the "fatto estetico" in the reader. In fact,
as Wagstaff has argued, the tension in *Empirismo eretico* towards
"reality" or seemingly "realistic" stances is justified by Pasolini on
the basis of Crocean aesthetics wherein *poesia* denotes immediate
expression.[54] In fact Pasolini's equation of poetry, action and intuition is further underlined not only by the presumed "univocity"
of his message, but also by the anticipated intuitive response of the
audience that would exempt the work from critical reflection. As
he wrote in "La lingua scritta della realtà" (1966):

> Ogni poesia è translinguistica. È un'*azione* "deposta" in un siste-
> ma di simboli, come in un veicolo, che ridiviene *azione* nel
> destinatario, non essendo quei simboli che dei campanelli di
> Pavlov. (*EE*, 199).

> [Every poem is translinguistic. It is an *action* "deposed" in a
> system of symbols, as in a vehicle, that becomes once again *action*
> in the addressee, since those symbols are nothing more than so
> many Pavlovian bells.]

Poetry, refractory to history, was both cognitive tool and action.
     The elevation of poetry to a sphere above human time and
space was a source of continuity in Pasolini's artistic research
through the 1950s and 1960s. In fact, even at the apex of his "Neo-
realist" period he saw poetry as something fundamentally opposed to history.[55] This is particularly evident in the essay "La
volontà di Dante a essere poeta". The eccentric use of the preposi-
tion "a" in the title underlines Pasolini's belief that true poetic
expression is a goal almost beyond our grasp. Although Pasolini
does not specifically cite Croce here, the fundamental dichotomy
between the historical time of the reader and that of the pilgrim
Dante on the one hand, and, on the other, the meta-historical time
of true poetry, is strikingly Crocean (*EE*, 107). This comparison is
reinforced by Pasolini's description of two opposing stylistic registers in the *Comedy*: the first the "non poesia", the "prosastic" story

of the pilgrim; the second is a poetic allegory wherein the poet becomes a synecdoche of human spirituality. To use Pasolini's words, Dante "riesprime autenticamente la metastoricità religiosa attraverso la storicizzazione di una 'irrazionalità poetica'" ["authentically re-expresses religious meta-historicity through the historicization of 'poetic irrationality'": *EE*, 112]. As Pasolini, following Croce, understood the term, poetry required the ability to *trasumanare*, to become more than human or quintessentially human. The words just quoted underline the identification of poetry with religion, and the separation of this metaphysical dimension from the textual historicization of "non poesia".

In 1968 Pasolini once again explicitly assigned to poetry a meta-historical function. He claimed that poetry "non è merce perché non è consumabile" ["is not a commodity because it cannot be consumed"]. Poetry was not "mass produced", and "la sua carica di ambiguità non si esaurisce in alcun momento storico concreto" ["its charge of ambiguity is not exhausted in any specific historical moment"].[56] Poetry, in fact, was "hyper-historical". This was substantially concordant with what he had stated in an interview of 1965:

> Nella mia cultura c'è un enorme rispetto per la poesia: non per niente mi sono formato in un'epoca in cui la poesia era un mito: il decadentismo, l'ermetismo, la poesia in senso assoluto, la poesia pura, la Poesia con la P maiuscola. Io "non posso" non avere un senso altissimo della poesia. Ma ho dovuto contraddir-mi proprio perché a livello storico la poesia era diventata un mito. Che andava demistificato. Perciò, con uno sforzo di volontà, ho reagito a me stesso, riconducendo la poesia a forme strumentali. Che, ripeto, son dovute a un mio sforzo di volontà, a una mia lotta storica, quotidiana: ma nel fondo di me resta, solido come quarzo, un senso di venerazione per la poesia.[57]

> [I have an enormous respect for poetry. Not for nothing did I come of age in a period in which poetry had achieved a mythic stature: Decadence, Hermeticism, poetry in an absolute sense, pure poetry, Poetry with a capital P. I "cannot" but have an extremely high regard for poetry. But I had to contradict myself precisely because historically poetry had become a myth. That needed to be demystified. Therefore, with an effort of will, I reacted against myself, and returned poetry to instrumental forms. This, I repeat, was accomplished thanks to an effort of will, to a historical and daily struggle on my part. But, after all is said

and done, in my heart of hearts, there remains, as hard as quartz,
a sense of veneration for poetry.]

His respect for myth, however, eventually prevailed over his
desire to demystify it. What is often called Pasolini's religiosity
belied his belief in the force of certain atavistic tendencies to
condition contemporary human behaviour. Following the personal "crisis" brought about by the student uprisings of 1968, he
began to search for the essence of the human condition in what was
for him the "immutable" mother–son relationship. Against this
background, history was articulated in the repetition of the Oedipal conflict within the generational cycle,[58] and was subsumed
into this atemporal continuum. Within this mythic dimension the
essence of humanity was preserved. Therefore the mythic, as it was
revealed through the poet who *trasumanava*, was to become for
Pasolini ever more clearly synonymous with his desire for "realistic" representation in his creative work.[59]

AUTOBIOGRAPHY

In *Passione e ideologia*, Pasolini, speaking of himself in the third
person, had commented on his own poetic production in the
following manner:

> Non potendo impadronirsene per le vie psicologicamente normali
> del razionale, non poteva che reimmergersi in esso: tornare
> indietro: rifare quel cammino in un punto del quale la sua fase di
> felicità coincideva con l'incantevole paesaggio carsarsese, con
> una vita rustica, resa epica da una carica accorante di nostalgia.
> Conoscere equivaleva a esprimere. (*PI*, 133)

> [Unable to master it through the normal psychological, rational
> channels, he could only reimmerse himself in it; go back in time
> to a point at which his personal happiness coincided with the
> enchanting countryside around Casarsa, with a rustic life which
> had attained epic proportions thanks to a heartfelt charge of
> nostalgia. To know meant to express himself.]

As we can see from this quotation taken from "La poesia dialettale
del Novecento", in 1952 to express oneself meant accentuating the
use value of the work, at the expense of its potential exchange

value. Thus the importance of Crocean intuition as both means and end of artistic production was reasserted in spite of Pasolini's appeal to his presumed Gramscian intellectual roots. A logical consequence of this stance was to reaffirm the social primacy of the artist, who for Pasolini was an exponent of a separate class blessed with privileged insight. Seen from this perspective, the artist was custodian of an extremely subjective, intuitive truth, to be reached without the objectifying dialectical contribution of dialogue. Following this line of reasoning, in order to gain a view of reality that was in any way "objective", it was necessary to combine many equally subjective artistic visions. As a consequence, a form of "objective" truth, if such a thing existed, was to be found only in the "chorus" of truths, that is, in the ensemble of externalized intuitions offered by the artistic class. Therefore the quotation from *One Thousand and One Nights* used by Pasolini as the epigraph to his homonymous film—"La verità non sta in un solo sogno, ma in molti sogni" ["The truth is not found in a single dream, but in many dreams"]—may be considered emblematic of Pasolini's quest for his particular brand of artistic "realism".[60] The "dream" evoked here by Pasolini refers to that "sogno innocente" ["innocent dream"] characteristic of a time when—according to Pasolini—life was a "natural" and "authentic whole", and not a "sogno orribile", a void mankind seeks to fill with "pretexts" and sundry interpretations of reality.[61] It is important to note here that in his essay "I sogni ideologici" (1971) Pasolini associated literature and religion, the only two "pretexts" still at humanity's disposal capable of permitting us to envisage what life was like when it was "whole".

If Pasolini is to be taken at his word, the quest for "realism" is a constant in his work. Realism, however, as Pasolini understood it, was a highly subjective notion in which the autobiographical subject was elevated by analogy to represent society as a whole. Intuition, that is, the impressionistic reification of what is other, was more "real" than what existed outside it. From this perspective, the following lines from *Trasumanar e organizzar* are indicative of the tremendous influence Croce's "fatto estetico" continued to exert over Pasolini well into the 1970s:

> Beh,
> non ho intenzione di scrivere l'intero Apocalisse:
> ormai basta solo progettarlo;
> e cosí le idee, basta enunciarle: realizzarle è superfluo.[62]

[Well,/I have no intention of writing the entire Apocalypse:/it's now enough just to plan it;/the same with ideas, it's enough to enunciate them: to carry them out is superfluous.]

What at times may appear to be a search for artistic realism, at a deeper level is a privileging of intuition or invention over production, the realization of the work. For this reason, Pasolini demanded direct contact between himself and his public; he refused to accept any interpretative mediation. He was the director of his screenplays and theatre; as he repeatedly stated, he did not allow his actors to "act" or interpret what he had written, but availed himself instead of their physical presence. Moreover, by insisting on "physicality", he postulated a human essence that would preclude any interpretative polyvalence in his audience. Pasolini's didactic monologue aimed to prevent readings that differed from authorial intentions. The tension toward self-expression was intended to funnel all readings towards the one proposed by Pasolini's persona, a reading that frequently coincided with that of the autobiographical subject.

The "examples of an at times excessively exasperated poetic autobiography" noted by Manacorda in Pasolini's youthful Friulan verse reappear frequently and throughout Pasolini's work.[63] In the autobiographical *Bestia da stile*, one of his concerns is to explain the motivation of his poetic research in the 1970s—"unpopular realism", whose cornerstone was his observation of the intellectual's inability to find a common ground for dialogue with the masses:

> Cosa diciamo, noi, al nostro poeta,
> noi, da contadini e piccoli borghesi divenuti tutti
> aristocrazia operaia? Al nostro poeta
> divenuto ora, da futurista, realista?
> Niente: non diciamo proprio niente.
> E questo atto della tragedia, dunque,
> non può consistere in altro che in due monologhi:
> il monologo degli operai,
> e il monologo del poeta
> —uno dopo l'altro.[64]

[What shall we say to our poet,/we, peasants and *petit bourgeois* who have all become/workers' aristocracy? To our poet/who, from being a Futurist, has become a realist?/Nothing: let's not say anything at all./And this act of our tragedy, then,/cannot consist of anything but of two monologues:/the monologue of the workers,/and the monologue of the poet/—one after the other.]

To this, Jan, Pasolini's *alter ego*, responds:

> [...] la coscienza di questo dramma è la mia poesia!
> Ciò che avviene qui
> in quest' anima, al centro di Praga,
> è indice di ciò che avviene nel mondo.
>
> (*Porcile*, p. 244)

[(...) the consciousness of this drama is my poetry!/What happens here/in my soul, in the centre of Prague,/is indicative of what happens in the world.]

Thus Pasolini elevated himself, as a poet, to the level of symbol of a general human condition, a microcosm that not only reflected reality but more importantly was also the critical consciousness of that reality. As a poet, his duty was not so much to *make* history as to *be* history. As an artist, he believed he was part of an autonomous class, endowed with the ability to perceive the "sense" of phenomena, synthesize them artistically and then project expressionistically what was "known" intuitively.

In the *Trilogia della vita*, autobiographical references inhere in Pasolini's decision to cast himself in two of the films, thereby highlighting his artistic preoccupations. While Pasolini's interpretation of Chaucer is not of particular relevance to our discussion, the same is not true of his decision to play Giotto's pupil. *The Decameron* goes beyond the facile autobiographical reference of *The Canterbury Tales*; in *The Decameron* Pasolini's presence, pervasive in the second half of the film, allows him to make a statement on the artist's condition and function in society.[65] His physical presence in the second narrative "frame" makes explicit the reference to his condition as an artist. The scenes involving Giotto permit the narrative to concentrate in a more explicit manner on Pasolini's autobiography. The director, in the guise of the Florentine painter, presents himself as engaged in a creative enterprise that is at once a collective effort in need of external financing, as is the film industry, and an individual effort similar to writing. Moreover, for Pasolini the decision to cast himself in the film meant, to use his own words, aver ideologizzato l'opera attraverso la coscienza di essa: coscienza non puramente estetica, ma, attraverso il veicolo della fisicità, cioè di tutto il mio modo di esserci, totale.[66]

[to have put the work in an ideological frame through my own awareness of it; an awareness that is not purely aesthetic, but physical, that is to say, my absolute way of being within the work.]

When Pasolini, as Giotto, "frames" in the marketplace the individuals who are to be the protagonists of the episodes "framed" in their turn by the tale of Giotto,[67] he underlines the physical presence of those who were to be figures in his poetic and filmic "word-painting". When Pasolini-Giotto asks himself at the work's conclusion "...perché realizzare un'opera, quando è cosí bello sognarla soltanto..." ["...why execute a work, when it is so beautiful simply to dream it..."],[68] the suspension marks do not serve to isolate Pasolini's comment from the rest of the text; rather they help to emphasize his desire as a writer to direct these words outside the film at the audience. At the same time, this form of punctuation leads us to believe that the reader has been given a glimpse of the writer's private thoughts. In this way Pasolini appears to circumvent the material realization of the film to establish a bond between his own intuition and that of the spectator. The "fatto estetico" would thus be preserved from the dialectical and historicizing influence of critical reflection.

CONCLUSION

Pasolini's conversion to leftist politics was catalysed by emotive experiences that were not really consolidated by the study of the works of Marx and Gramsci. Therefore Pasolini's politics was susceptible to modifications and "renunciations" dictated by changes in his humour and by contingent factors. Towards the end of the 1950s, Pasolini's belief in the ability and will of the Italian workers to effect radical change in society wavered. At the same time, he unwittingly confirmed the latent presence of Crocean aesthetics still conditioning his own artistic musings. In "Marxisants" he stated that, in the second series of *Officina*, the *équipe* intended to continue its methodological eclecticism, a fundamental element of which was "la storicizzazione crociana" (p. 72). Hence his utilization of the work of Gramsci (and Lukács, and non-Marxists for that matter) within the context of his "critical" Marxism in the 1950s did not signify a "break" with Crocean aesthetics, but at most a methodological rectification. In the 1960s he renounced Marx and redimensioned the presumed importance of Gramsci in his thought. Although Pasolini intentionally diminished the continuing importance of Croce during his "Neo-realist" period, he never explicitly denied it. Rather, it was set aside and then recuperated, when his youthful infatuation with the masses waned:

> Io non so cosa sia
> questa non-ragione, questa poca-ragione:
> Vico, o Croce, o Freud, mi soccorrono,
> ma con la sola suggestione
> del mito, della scienza, nella mia abulia.
> Non Marx [...].[69]

[I have no idea what/this non-reason, this little-reason is:/Vico, or Croce, or Freud assist me,/but only with the suggestion/of myth, of science, in my state of abulia./Not Marx (...).]

Following the reflux towards irrational thought during the 1960s, Pasolini published, in *Trasumanar e organizzar*, revisions of certain poems and, in *La nuova gioventú*, variations. Thus, what existed on the page was not to be considered a *factum*; instead, its exchange value was minimized in order to highlight both a vision of the work as something *in fieri* and its use value for the poet. In effect, he privileged the intuitive-creative process at the expense of the potential use value of the poems for the reading public. His insistence on the value of expression at the expense of communication removed his work from any dialectical process that might have modified its "meaning", thereby perpetuating a cardinal point of Crocean Idealism.

The contribution of Pasolini, "letterato tradizionale", to Marxist literary enquiry was limited by his inability to define his social role as intellectual and artist. Pasolini did not give sufficient importance to the passage from the first to the third person that inheres in the act of writing. Thus, he was never able to see himself as other and as part of a broader social context; hence he ideologically levelled what was other. He ignored the social nature of the intellectual condition. He considered himself isolated: having "betrayed" his class of origin, he did not believe he could become "organic", in the Gramscian sense, to the working classes, attributing to the Gramscian concept of "organicità" an absolute value, not a heuristic one. Pasolini returned to this question periodically throughout his life, and never succeeded in resolving the dilemma. He assigned to the intellectual a didactic or "priestly" function (while failing to see intellectuals as a class within a hegemonic apparatus). Consequently, when that idealized function proved unattainable, his frustration caused him to abandon his goal. Ironically, this is where Gramsci, had Pasolini read him more attentively, would have been of great assistance—in helping him overcome his "dramma irrisolto". For Gramsci the "cathartic" moment was the point of departure for the "philosophy of praxis": changes in the economic base (catalysed by a "catharsis" within individuals, that is, the rejection of dominant ideologies in favour of a clearer understanding of one's own place within class divisions and conflicts) would cause modifications in the superstructure, which would then contribute to the creation of new and diverse hegemonic relationships within society. This process would initiate another, through which individual and collective consciousness would be "reformed", thereby preparing the way for ulterior changes in the base. The intellectual would act as catalyst for collective intellectual progress.[70] Theory and praxis, united by and in the collective intellectual, would undermine the ideological constructs on which bourgeois domination is founded and, at the same time, change the manner in which reality is perceived. Pasolini, however, was unable or unwilling to overcome a traditional view of the intellectual's social function, but instead remained faithful to his Crocean intellectual training.

NOTES

1   P. P. Pasolini, "La posizione", in *"Officina": cultura, letteratura e politica negli anni Cinquanta*, edited by G. C. Ferretti (Turin, Einaudi, 1975), pp. 242–48 (p. 246).

2   R. Luperini, *Il Novecento* (Turin, Loescher, 1981), p. 375.

3   R. Luperini, *Il Novecento*, p. 374.

4   According to E. Jacobitti, Croce's hegemony over Italian culture during the first half of this century was achieved through "access to and diligent use of

scholarly journals and the scholarly press" in order "to saturate the intellectual life of Italy with a single point of view" ("Hegemony before Gramsci: The Case of Benedetto Croce", *Journal of Modern History*, 52 [1980], 66–84 [p. 69]). Jacobitti (p. 74) cites Garin, who affirmed that "the resonance of Croce's view was decisive" in Italian culture during this time. Only those works that were in agreement with Croce's "determinate point of view", were published by Laterza or in Croce's journal, *La critica*. Moreover, since Croce held sway over the vast majority of Italian intellectuals, those foreign works he chose to ignore were neither translated into Italian nor discussed. Jacobitti mentions in support of his thesis the "singular perspective" of the series Classici di Filosofia Moderna, directed by Croce for Laterza, from which works whose theses were contrary to Croce's thought were excluded.

5   Z. G. Barański, "Pier Paolo Pasolini: Culture, Croce, Gramsci", in *Culture and Conflict in Postwar Italy: Essays on Mass and Popular Culture*, edited by Z. G. Barański and R. Lumley (London–Basingstoke, Macmillan, 1990), pp. 139–59 (p. 153).

6   P. P. Pasolini, *Poesia in forma di rosa* (Milan, Garzanti, 1976 [1964]), pp. 127–28.

7   See P. P. Pasolini, *Le belle bandiere*, edited by G. C. Ferretti (Rome, Editori Riuniti, 1977), p. 164.

8   See F. Rossi-Landi, *Marxism and Ideology*, translated by R. Griffin (Oxford, Clarendon Press, 1990), particularly the section on "purely natural properties" (pp. 104–12). According to Rossi-Landi, we "operate on a world already objectivized and hence received passively as objective in itself" (p. 104). That is to say, "the procedure which [...] manages to piece together an external world existing objectively for us in the form of nature as opposed to society [is] therefore also the procedure by which, within this objective world, properties are attributed to things and then recognized as belonging to them. It is, moreover, a historical procedure, from which follows that *a human nature divorced from history does not even exist with regard to the constitution of the objective world*. [...] The way in which the objective world is constructed varies in line with variation in socio-historical conditions. It is only with the institution of an international science of the physical world that *some sectors* of objectivity have been *constructed* on a world-wide scale so as to embrace all humanity. In this context, certain pages written by Gramsci, especially in the eleventh of the *Prison Notebooks*, are seminal: it is the *historical* emergence of the human race which promotes the emergence of 'objective' consciousness. It is a historical development which, considered in terms of the evolutionary scale, has taken place within an incredibly brief and recent period of time" (pp. 107–08).

9   See J. Francese, *Il realismo impopolare di Pier Paolo Pasolini* (Foggia, Bastogi, 1991).

10   R. Luperini, *Il Novecento*, pp. 390ff.

11   R. Luperini, *Il Novecento*, p. 892.

12   It is not my intention to contradict here what I have said elsewhere about Pasolini's sincere commitment and contributions to social and artistic progress. Nonetheless, it is necessary to reconsider certain aspects of Pasolini's intellectual formation *vis-à-vis* his later production. While reading Pasolini several years ago, I suspected that his frequent "disclaimers" of proposals made in *Passione e ideologia*, in *Empirismo eretico* [1972] (Milan, Garzanti, 1981) and in his correspondence (his remarks were often presented as "chaotic" or

"dilettantisms"), were indicative of an unwillingness to investigate ingenious but often superficial notions further. Despite the varying degrees of scholarly façade given to these proposals by their author, they were in dire need of further examination; this task was delegated "frettolosamente" to experts and scholars. I felt that the facility with which Pasolini confessed the limits of his individual contributions was a clever rhetorical strategy whose intended effect was to camouflage the *lacunae* in his theoretical preparation as he pursued what truly mattered to him, his artistic interests. Z. G. Barański's well-documented essay (cited above), because it undermines what have traditionally been considered the foundations of Pasolini's intellectual formation, necessitates the re-examination of the epistemological underpinnings of all Pasolini's political stances and artistic results.

13   See N. Greene, *Pier Paolo Pasolini: Cinema as Heresy* (Princeton, Princeton University Press, 1990), p. 11. What Naomi Greene states here is substantially in agreement with Barański's assertion that during 1940–54 "Pasolini considered his Friulan verse simply as a highly *recherché* experiment in 'pure poetry', and not, as subsequently has been widely claimed, as literary exercises in political commitment" ("Pasolini: Culture, Croce, Gramsci", p. 143). In Barański's view, "Pasolini came to Friulan for refined aesthetic reasons […]; for many years he openly continued to perceive it in terms which belonged to the rarified self-reflective canons of high culture. Particularly influential on his thinking were the canons of neo-romantic poetics, with Rimbaud as his ideal point of reference" (p. 144–45).

14   P. P. Pasolini, *Il sogno del centauro*, edited by J. Duflot (Rome, Editori Riuniti, 1983), p. 23.

15   In Barański's opinion, Pasolini's reaction in the post-war years to what Fascism had previously repressed was typical of the liberal intellectual: "Lacking as he did the adequate analytical tools to deal with the new realities, he inevitably turned to the oppositional discourses of his youth"—those neo-Decadent traditions with which the youthful Pasolini had been infatuated, whose "aestheticizing élitism ultimately had to come into conflict with the more egalitarian and more 'scientific' ideologies of the post-war period". "In practice," Barański concludes, "Pasolini represents an extreme example of this situation, hence the frequent violence of his reactions, whether intellectual or artistic. He needed to mythicize his origins and his ideological positions to counter his sense of crisis and bewilderment, and to give himself political credibility" (p. 155)—and, if I might be allowed a conjecture, to compensate (in a manner both reminiscent of, yet also very different from, Pavese) for his relatively limited participation in the Resistance, particularly when contrasted to his brother Guido, who died as a partisan (an event which remained of fundamental importance for Pasolini).

16   Z. G. Barański, "Pasolini: Culture, Croce, Gramsci", p. 144.

17   Z. G. Barański, "Pasolini: Culture, Croce, Gramsci", pp. 148, 150. Pasolini, in an essay of 1965, underlined the "pathos" of the *Prison Letters* (*EE*, 53), reiterating what in 1955 he had described as Gramsci's "Shelleyism": *Lettere 1955–1975*, edited by N. Naldini (Turin, Einaudi, 1988), p. 174. In this letter to Calvino, Pasolini had written: "Certi traumi della propria formazione letteraria sono difficilmente sanabili: quel che di 'allusivamente ermetico' che tu senti sussistere nella mia critica credo che sia una caratteristica, per ora, fatale, che andrà solo lentamente estinguendosi" (pp. 173–74). Hence it would

appear that the "Shelleyism" to which Pasolini refers is more his own than Gramsci's. W. P. Sillanpoa, in his analysis of Pasolini's "highly personal interpretation of Gramsci"—"Pasolini's Gramsci", *Modern Language Notes*, 96 (1981), 120–37 (p. 120)—, has in fact proposed that "the Gramsci of Pasolini remained first and foremost the pathetic hero of the prison letters" (p. 137).

18   Reply to "8 domande sulla critica letteraria in Italia", *Nuovi argomenti*, May–Aug. 1960, 63–69 (p. 66).

19   *PI*, 487. This image of Gramsci is similar to the "eterno Gramsci" evoked in 1968 in the autobiographical poem *Coccodrillo* (*Il sogno del centauro*, p. 180).

20   P. P. Pasolini, "Marxisants", *Officina*, May–June 1959, 69–73 (pp. 71, 73). In "Contro le sopravvivenze del materialismo storico" [1927], Croce, addressing the question of "idealità etica e l'arte politica", wrote: "Di quelle cose il genere umano ha sempre affidato cura alla 'gente spirituale', ai fondatori e riformatori di religioni, agli apostoli, ai sacerdoti, e poi agli uomini d'intelletto e di sapere, e a quelli che, spinti da profonda passione politica, si fanno braccio e spada d'idee, re, capitani, ministri, rivoluzionari, uomini dell'azione" (B. Croce, *Orientamenti: piccoli saggi di filosofia politica* [Milan, Gilardi and Noto, 1934], p. 42).

21   See R. Luperini, *Il Novecento*, p. 374.

22   *Il sogno del centauro*, p. 27.

23   Z. G. Barański, "Pasolini: Culture, Croce, Gramsci", p. 147.

24   See Pasolini's letter of July–August 1943 to Luciano Serra: "Noi abbiamo una vera missione, in questa spaventosa miseria italiana, una missione non di potenza o di ricchezza, ma di educazione, di *civiltà*": *Lettere agli amici (1941–1945)*, edited by L. Serra (Lodi, Guanda, 1976), pp. 33–34. See also "Filologia e morale", in *Pier Paolo Pasolini e il "Setaccio" (1942–43)*, edited by M. Ricci (Bologna, Cappelli, 1977), pp. 168–71: "*Educare*; sarà questo forse il piú alto— e umile—compito affidato alla nostra generazione."

25   R. Luperini, *Il Novecento*, pp. 373, 377.

26   E. Garin, "Quindici anni dopo", in his *Cronache di filosofia italiana 1900/1943* (Bari, Laterza, 1966), p. 523, labelled Vittorini's position "liberalism without capitalism". According to Giuseppe Vacca, "Alcuni temi della politica culturale di Togliatti", in P. Togliatti, *I corsivi di Roderigo* (Bari, De Donato, 1976), p. 28, Vittorini was "ispirato da una teoria aclassista dell'intellettuale e da una visione spontaneistica del processo storico".

27   In the view of R. Luperini, "veramente non resta*va* ormai piú alcun respiro marxista nella scissione che Vittorini vede*va* tra 'uomo politico' e 'uomo di cultura' […] ove evidentemente non si tiene affatto conto che il marxismo, impostando in modo nuovo il rapporto fra teoria e prassi, ha posto in crisi proprio la tradizionale distinzione […] tranquillamente accettata" (*Gli intellettuali di sinistra e l'ideologia della ricostruzione nel dopoguerra* [Rome, Edizioni di Ideologie, 1971], p. 80). Vacca has emphasized "il piano del tutto idealistico sotteso alla interpretazione vittoriniana della storia, intesa come storia degli intellettuali; nonché la svalutazione spiritualistica delle mediazioni e strumentazioni istituzionali della pratica politica, non meno che della azione culturale" ("I corsivi di Roderigo", pp. 27–28).

28   G. C. Ferretti "Saggio introduttivo", in *"Officina": cultura, letteratura e politica*, p. 119.

29   "8 domande sulla critica letteraria in Italia", p. 64.

30   See *Il sogno del centauro*, p. 27: "Per capire tale disincanto [con il PCI],

bisognerebbe forse essere stato un italiano all'indomani del 1945... Erano i tempi in cui intellettuali come Vittorini potevano ancora stabilire il dialogo con lo stato maggiore del partito, i tempi in cui a Milano e a Firenze si pubblicava la rivista marxista *Il politecnico*... in cui sia l'ortodossia comunista sia i marxisti erano intenti a raggiungere uno scopo comune, ritenuto quasi imminente." See also *PI*, 457.

31   N. Naldini, *Vita di Pasolini*, p. 112.

32   P. P. Pasolini, *Scritti corsari* [1975] (Milan, Garzanti, 1981), p. 144.

33   N. Naldini, *Vita di Pasolini*, p. 131. This event has in fact been confirmed by Pasolini's friend, the poet Paolo Volponi. According to Volponi, his last conversation with Pasolini took place at the end of October 1975. At that time, Pasolini told him: "Sono un marxista che ha letto poco Marx. Ho letto di più Gramsci" ("Vita e morte di Pasolini", in *Perché Pasolini*, edited by G. De Santi et al. [Florence, Guaraldi, 1978], pp. 15–28 [p. 27]).

34   P. P. Pasolini, *Le belle bandiere*, edited by G. C. Ferretti (Rome, Editori Riuniti, 1977), p. 169.

35   See J. Francese, *Il realismo impopolare*, pp. 83–97.

36   Pasolini did not use the events in Eastern Europe in 1956 as a pretext for burning his bridges with the PCI; intellectuals within or close to the Communist Party continued to figure among his preferred interlocutors. His bitterness was directed against those Communists who, because of their belief in the unsuitability of dialect and of the sub-proletariat in Neo-realist prose, wrote negative reviews of *Ragazzi di vita*. Some also took issue with what was perceived as Pasolini's infatuation with the more "morbid" aspects of Roman life. For an analysis of Pasolini's relationship with Communist intellectuals in the late 1950s I invite the reader to consult my "Pasolini's 'Roman Novels', the Italian Communist Party, and the Events of 1956", in *Pier Paolo Pasolini*, edited by P. Rumble and B. Testa (Toronto, University of Toronto Press, 1993), pp. 22–39.

37   P. P. Pasolini, "Il metodo di lavoro" [1958], in his *Ragazzi di vita* (Turin, Einaudi, 1979), p. 213.

38   As Vacca has indicated ("I corsivi di Roderigo", p. 112), during the post-war period "historiographic revision became the mainstay of the PCI's cultural politics." In his opinion, the Communists' programme for the renewal of Italian culture was limited to changing the orientation of the ideals of the intellectual class. Communist intellectuals wanted to revise the historiographic tradition, particularly its Crocean version, while preserving the fundamental importance of historiography in the PCI's cultural revision.

39   See R. Paternostro, *Critica, marxismo, storicismo dialettico: due note gramsciane* (Rome, Bulzoni, 1977), p. 111.

40   R. Luperini, *Il Novecento*, p. 698. Luperini has argued that "critical" Marxism took on various guises in the literary criticism of this period. While some made use of the work of Lukács, others, such as Armanda Guiducci, Leonetti and Scalia considered Gramsci's writings from a "Neo-positivist" perspective and emphasized the democratic and sociological elements to be found in them. Pasolini, according to Luperini, used a "Gramscian humanism" as a point of departure open to suggestions from stylistic criticism; Sebastiano Timpanaro stressed the importance of avoiding any "dilution" of materialism by Idealism or Historicism (p. 698).

41   R. S. Dombroski, *Antonio Gramsci* (Boston, Twayne, 1989), p. 84.

42 R. S. Dombroski, *Antonio Gramsci*, p. 91.

43 P. P. Pasolini, *Il caos* [1979], edited by G. C. Ferretti (Rome, Editori Riuniti, 1981), p. 218: "Il pubblico di cinema è 'massa'; infatti esso è irrappresentabile se non nelle statistiche o nei rendiconti, e obbedisce a regole reattive medie, identificate per astrazione. Al contrario, il pubblico del teatro è 'folla', perché cade sotto il dominio della percezione dei sensi, obbedisce a regole reattive concrete, direi fisiche. Perciò il cinema può essere medium di massa; il teatro no, mai, anche se si rivolgesse a 'folle' enormi."

44 N. Greene, *Pier Paolo Pasolini*, p. 109. Greene writes: "If Pasolini's defence of a meta-cinematic, essentially formalist, art reflected his belief that it was the only form of resistance still open to committed writers and directors, it was also deeply rooted in his lifelong attraction to symbolist poetics, which is the very incarnation of literary hermeticism and self-reflexivity" (p. 95).

45 The first chapter of *The German Ideology*, "Feuerbach", was published in Russian in 1924 and in German in 1926 (J. Larrain, *Marxism and Ideology*, p. 54). According to Larrain, Gramsci dismissed a conception of ideology interpretable as "arbitrary individual speculation which Marx would have rejected too" (p. 79). Because Gramsci lacked knowledge of *The German Ideology*, however, he could not have been aware of the alternative negative concept. In Larrain's words: "Gramsci did not realize that it is [...] possible to oppose to the conception of ideology as arbitrary appearance, ideology as a necessary *distorted* superstructure of a particular structure" (p. 79). To Gramsci's credit, however, he saw that ideology was to be considered an entity independent of the economic base. He also identified the reciprocal influence linking the base and the ideological superstructure. Gramsci dismissed the negative concept of ideology as he understood it, because in his view it was a form of economic reductionism.

46 P. P. Pasolini, *La religione del mio tempo* [1961] (Milan, Garzanti, 1976).

47 According to R. Paternostro (*Critica, marxismo, storicismo dialettico*, p. 119), Croce, in his literary criticism, considered only the aesthetic dimension of a work of art, at the expense of its function in society. As a result, Croce examined exclusively individual artistic expressions, with the inevitable consequence of isolating the poetry in question in a socio-economic and cultural vacuum.

48 P. P. Pasolini, "Confessioni tecniche" [1966], in his *Uccellacci e uccellini* (Milan, Garzanti, 1975), pp. 44–56 (p. 54).

49 N. Greene, *Pier Paolo Pasolini*, p. 95.

50 Quoted by N. Naldini, *Vita di Pasolini*, pp. 374–75.

51 *PI*, 287. In Pasolini's screenplay *Il padre selvaggio* (Turin, Einaudi, 1975) the African re-incarnation of Pasolini's sub-proletariat gives renewed vigour to his didactic spirit, while the use of an African *félibrige* connotes an anti-colonial, intellectual liberation. But if the lesson to be imparted by the teacher concerned the social awakening of the African youths, the means for their vindication was to be poetry, considered once again an expressionistic "raccontare per immagini".

52 P. P. Pasolini, "Poeta delle Ceneri", *Nuovi argomenti*, July–Dec. 1980, 3–26 (p. 25); reprinted in *TLP*, II, 2056–84 (p. 2982).

53 "È ben noto che quella che noi chiamiamo lingua, in genere, è composta da una lingua orale e da una lingua scritta. Sono due fatti ben diversi: la prima è naturale, e, vorrei dire, esistenziale. [...] Al contrario della lingua scritta, la

lingua orale ci riconduce senza soluzione di continuità storica alle origini, al momento in cui tale lingua orale non era che 'grido', o lingua delle necessità biologiche, o meglio ancora, dei riflessi condizionati. C'è un momento, permanente, della lingua orale che resta tale. *La lingua orale è cosí un 'continuo statico', come la natura—al di fuori dell'evoluzione storica.* C'è dunque un momento della nostra comunicazione orale che è dunque puramente naturale" (*EE*, 205; italics mine).

54 C. Wagstaff, "Reality into Poetry: Pasolini's Film Theory", *The Italianist*, 5 (1985), 107–32 (p. 109).

55 See "Fine dell'engagement" (1957): "La Resistenza ha soprattutto insegnato a credere nuovamente nella storia, dopo le introversioni evasive ed estetizzanti di un ventennio di poesia" (*PI*, 458). In the same essay Pasolini argues against the lyrical, "poetic" mystification of the Resistance movement in favour of its historical analysis.

56 P. P. Pasolini, *Il caos*, p. 100.

57 F. Camon, *Il mestiere di poeta* (Milan, Lerici, 1965), p. 197.

58 O. Stack, *Pasolini on Pasolini: Interviews with Oswald Stack* (Bloomington, Indiana University Press, 1969), p. 120.

59 *Il sogno del centauro*, p. 66.

60 The epigraph may be found in P. P. Pasolini, *Trilogia della vita*, edited by G. Gattei (Bologna, Cappelli, 1975), p. 96.

61 P. P. Pasolini, "I sogni ideologici", *Nuovi argomenti*, new series, 22, Apr–June 1971, pp. 20, 22. Within this context, Pasolini uses the term "pretesto" to signify "una specie di gioco che distrae da quella vita che non è scissa mai, in alcun modo, dalla morte".

62 P. P. Pasolini, *Trasumanar e organizzar* [1971] (Milan, Garzanti, 1976), p. 113.

63 G. Manacorda, *Storia della letteratura italiana contemporanea (1940–1975)* (Rome, Editori Riuniti, 1977), p. 276.

64 P. P. Pasolini, *Porcile; Orgia; Bestia da stile* (Milan, Garzanti, 1979), p. 241.

65 I hesitate to attribute to Pasolini intentions that he did not make explicit. Nonetheless, Ser Ciappelletto's confession and his subsequent sanctification seem to evince the process by which those who possess the means to disseminate ideologies are able to textualize and thus reify lived experience.

66 Quoted in N. Naldini, *Vita di Pasolini*, p. 351.

67 See B. Lawton, "Boccaccio and Pasolini: A Contemporary Reinterpretation of *The Decameron*", in *The Decameron*, selected, translated and edited by M. Musa and P. Bondanella (New York, Norton, 1977).

68 P. P. Pasolini, *Trilogia della vita*, p. 48.

69 "Il glicine", in *La religione del mio tempo*, p. 166.

70 R. Paternostro, *Critica, marxismo, storicismo dialettico*, p. 112.

NEO-REALISM AND PASOLINI:
THE DESIRE FOR REALITY[1]

Sam Rohdie

Among the terms used by film semiotics in the 1960s and 1970s
were "pro-filmic" (events and objects placed before the camera)
and "filmic" (events and objects transferred via film to the screen).
If it could be argued that the pro-filmic corresponded to the real,
then the filmic was its reproduction and its distortion. In so-called
realist films the distance between the pro-filmic and the filmic was
reduced, often to a minimum. For example, the duration and space
of events in reality might be presented unchanged on the screen.
What occurred in reality before the camera equally occurred on the
screen. Time, of course, was elided, but more frequently between
sequences than within them. Space too tended to be left unfrag-
mented. Actions were followed as they unfolded: they were observed, as a detective might observe things, not intruded upon, or
reshaped, or known in advance of their unfolding.

The duration of the reality of scenes in Rossellini's *Roma, città
aperta*, despite elisions between scenes, is equal to the duration of
the scenes on the screen. Similarly, for example, in De Sica's
Umberto D, and particularly in the scene (made famous by Bazin's
comments on it) of the maid getting up in the morning, killing the
ants and making the coffee, not only is the time of the event retained
in its representation, but so too is the real space left intact; the scene
is only marginally edited, and is virtually a shot-sequence.

This contrasted with Hollywood films, certainly in their classical phase, where dramatic moments and objects were highlighted, then edited together for maximum dramatic effect. In the
Hollywood film, the duration and space of the pro-filmic were
manipulated and fragmented to present an illusion of continuity
and wholeness on the screen, even though the fact of such whole-

ness was negated while its appearance was affirmed. Editing was invisible, covered by the drama of events and the course of the narrative.

This aesthetic has also been called realistic. But it is a manufactured realism, an illusion of the real. A documentary and naturalist aesthetic—in its way no less illusory than the aesthetic of Hollywood—maintained the fiction that it was true to the real, in the sense that the pro-filmic and the filmic were brought so close as to seem indistinguishable, with respect to time and space. This naturalism was thought to be characteristic of the films of Italian Neo-realism in its classical period, the years 1943–49. Bazin's argument was that Neo-realism had displaced the illusionistic, manipulated realism of Hollywood. In its stead, Neo-realism introduced a realism in which, simultaneously, one was aware of the reality of the world and the reality of its transposition to film.[2] It was an aesthetic that had more of the world in it than did the aesthetic of Hollywood, and more art as well. The Hollywood world was wholly manufactured, but the techniques of its manufacture were lost beneath the dramatic illusion produced, which made the illusion seem real.

The reason Neo-realism was thought of as a new realism was that it seemed to have rejected narrative conventions, and even stylistic ones, and to have used the camera directly to apprehend external, pro-filmic reality. In some comments on Neo-realism (especially by Bazin, but also by Pasolini), the shot-sequence was taken to be its principal technical device. The shot-sequence not only presented the pro-filmic real as it occurred, but refused to add a dramatic sense to it. The drama of reality, it was believed, would assert itself while it was being witnessed and awaited by filmmaker and audience alike. It was the sense, in a Rossellini film for example, that the miraculous revelation of a truth came to filmmaker and audience at precisely the moment it came to the character. Thus, the miracle was not only a fact within the fiction, but also between fiction and spectator. In the monastery sequence in *Paisà*, the audience only knows when the American chaplains know; and it was that moment, too, that Rossellini himself seemed to have awaited rather than plotted in advance. De-dramatized narratives were thought to be characteristic of Neo-realist films. Nothing, it seemed, was particularly highlighted, nothing unduly stressed, no precise connections were made. "Things are," Rossellini said. "Why manipulate them?"—a sentiment Christian Metz was to echo a generation later.[3] Rather than impose an order on the world, the film-maker simply reflected an order already there.

There are problems in these formulations. They represent more a critical ideal than an aesthetic fact. The narrative films of De Sica and Rossellini (certainly of De Santis, Germi, Lattuada) are evidently engineered, even if they are engineered not to appear so. Nevertheless, the practices of Neo-realist films did sometimes approach the ideal: the tuna-fishing sequence in *Stromboli*; the maid getting up and making coffee in the morning in *Umberto D*; the desperate walk through Rome by Antonio and Bruno in search of their lost bicycle in *Ladri di biciclette*; Zavattini's "La storia di Caterina" in *L'amore in città*.

Roughly speaking, the commitment to pro-filmic reality—wanting to reproduce reality in its entirety on the screen—exhibited a faith in the power of reality before which narrative forms, film language and style had to yield. The period of Neo-realism is the period of Italian Resistance culture. With the Resistance it seemed that a new, popular, democratic, anti-Fascist Italy was taking shape. The representation of that reality was thought of as a progressive political act. Because the reality was so positive, there was no particular need, it was felt, to reshape it. Reality spoke for itself. In that sense, Neo-realism's commitment to reality was, in the Italian context, also, and perhaps primarily, a political commitment.

It needs to be repeated that these positions were more coherent as arguments than as film practices, and not only for those who sought to practice something of what was preached, but also because there were other, different Neo-realisms in Italy, which, while accepting the need for commitment and the need for "reality", more openly adopted conventional and literary styles and genres—for example, in the films of De Santis and Germi, where the presence of Hollywood conventions was particularly noticeable.

NEO-REALISM AND ITALIAN POPULISM

Neo-realism, in theory, dealt with a central problem of cinema: cinema's vocation to duplicate reality and the pressing desire of film-makers (and audiences) for a fusion of art and story. The assertion that cinema was art, when stated strongly, was often linked to a position at the opposite extreme, of cinema as duplication. The problem was restated and formalized by semiotics in the 1960s. In part it involved the relation of the pro-filmic to the filmic; in part it involved the relation of the cinematic (what was specific to cinema) to the filmic (what was in films, but not specific to cinema). For example, the cinematic involved a notion of cinematic specificity which tended to centre on cinema's transparency in its relation to reality; the filmic, on the other hand, was what was added, and to some extent deemed artificial: story, narrative, characters—in effect, the entire artifice of fiction.

This area of debate concerning the filmic and the cinematic became political in Italy, beyond issues of cinema and aesthetics, or matters of technique. The manipulation and falsification of reality in narrative artifice was associated with the cinema under Fascism, a cinema of genres modelled on Hollywood. Manipulation and falsification were also associated with the culture of the Italian bourgeoisie, whose highly wrought literary literature spoke to a narrow class, not to the people or to the nation.[4] Italy did not have, as France did, a national literature or a national bourgeoisie which might claim that its voice was the voice of the nation. Nearly sixty per cent of the Italian population was illiterate in the immediate post-war period; Italy was predominantly rural; most Italians did not speak Italian as their first language. After 1943, in the populist-nationalist environment of the Resistance, there was a negative political-social sign above literature which the actual circumstances of cultural backwardness and a non-national bourgeoisie seemed to confirm. Because cinema was necessarily more popular than literature, it became a more political instrument. The realism of Neo-realism was an attempt, in part, to move away from the literary and hence away from the bourgeois, and also away from convention and style, which bore the stigma of falsity; the goal was to move towards a reality that was popular, true and hence national. It was as if, with the Resistance, not only were democratic institutions being set in place, but so too was a truly democratic culture... and for the first time. Neo-realism, like the Resistance, seemed to mark the beginning of the democratization of Italy and its "national-popular" unification. For many, a Gramscian dream was about to come true.

NATURALISM AND QUOTATION

Pasolini distinguished his own film-making from that of the Neo-realists. His, he said, had nothing to do with any form of naturalism; theirs had everything to do with a form of naturalism. They were wedded to the shot-sequence, to a durational and spatial wholeness; his films were wedded to the shot, to artificial time, to discontinuity, to fragments of space. Their impulse was documentary; his was artifice. They relied on spontaneity, intuition, contingencies; he relied on the script, on meticulously planning everything in advance.[5] Their approach seemed casual; his seemed overwrought.

Not only did Pasolini disjoin the pro-filmic and the filmic, which the Neo-realists had tried to bring closer together: he also had a different idea from them of the pro-filmic itself. It was not that the Neo-realists did not stage their reality, rather that, as part of the structure of that staging, they allowed an element of chance to shape the event to be filmed. It was a staging organized in such a way as to permit reality to make its appearance in the film, tempting it in from beyond the wings. Renoir, to whom Italian Neo-realism had an enormous debt, allowed reality to enter his films in this way, while reflecting on the process within his films. The fatal shooting at the end of *La Règle du jeu* is an example, or the shock of the transvestite cabaret in *La Grande Illusion*. Renoir commented that this "open door" to reality was cinema itself. "C'est le cinéma!" he commented in an interview with Bertolucci just before he died.[6]

If Bazin was correct in believing that the narrative sense of Neo-realist films always came *a posteriori*, in Pasolini's films the sense existed *a priori*. In Pasolini's films reality was not found or encountered or revealed, as in a Rossellini miracle, but created. Since little was left to chance, or to contingency, the impress of reality could not easily be felt. Pimps in *Accattone* looking like saints from a Caravaggio canvas or resembling Bernini angels were not analogies found in nature, but analogies formed in art. Quotations from the arts—from painting, music, literature—abound in Pasolini's films. This presence of art in his films is insistent and overwhelming.

For the Neo-realists the literary and the artistic were élitist and false. Rossellini's Neapolitan *scugnizzi* came from the streets, not from a Rosso Fiorentino or Pontormo painting. Franco Citti as Accattone may have come from the Rome *borgate*, but he always seems to be a textual quotation, either because he is modelled on a painting or a piece of music (as happens to d'Annunzio's characters who are made to imitate art), or because the *borgate* and its sub-proletarians were already mythical. For the Neo-realists, "art" worked into the texture of their films would have been alien, something non-specific to cinema. Because, for them, the vocation of cinema was to render reality, such a textual presence would have seemed false. The National Museum sequence of Bergman looking at the fleshy statues from Pompei in *Viaggio in Italia* is not a textual quotation, as it would have been in a Pasolini film, but an occurrence within reality and an encounter with it. The statues have the same concreteness as the bones in the catacombs or the dead lovers coming alive in their plaster mould; they are not quotations but facts. In Pasolini's films reality is quoted; it appears as something textual. If Neo-realist films contained concrete real instances, Pasolini's contained a highly organized pastiche of cultural quotations. What was stressed was the falsity, or at least the artistry. Pasolini's real was not only textual by being within a film, but textual in the manner of its formation, always removed from the thing or the event, always a quotation of them, not so much the object as its consciousness.

WRITING AND FILM

Pasolini was pre-eminently a writer. He made films related to literary texts, directly engaging with literature (and art). And through the script, half-way between literature and film, Pasolini the film-maker directly engaged with written language and the word. It was with language and through literature that Pasolini sought out the real, and manufactured it. The entire bias of Neo-realism was, on the contrary, anti-literary. It sought the specificity of cinema as against literature, and even—it could be argued— against language, since the presentation of the real often appeared as the effacement of all writing. It was as if, ideally, cinema would disappear. (Bazin, more incisively than anyone else, confronted and argued this paradox.) Pasolini was right: his films and those of the Neo-realists were a world apart.

THE DISAPPOINTMENT OF REALITY

Although Pasolini rejected the aesthetic of Neo-realism, and only began to make films in 1959, a decade after the classic period of Neo-realism, he was, of all Italian directors, the most dutiful heir of the Neo-realists, while at the same time their most disobedient son.

Like the Neo-realists, he asserted that the vocation of cinema was the reproduction of reality. Like them, he associated that vocation with political commitment. And he shared with them a community of themes and ideology.

In De Sica's and Rossellini's films there is an ideal reality and a real reality. The ideal is that you will find, if not the bicycle, your humanity, and that in seeking the material object you will encounter your soul. Your soul is the soul that hopes and loves. It is put rather differently by Rossellini, but in his films there are miracles of comprehension beneath and beyond all material appearances. Each incident of *Paisà*, for example, ends with a reversal of the course of the narrative as it has enfolded; there is a revelation of other relations, other understandings, which displaces the more obvious sense of things, and does so miraculously, that is, without apparent narrative preparation. The miracle is a reversal of narrative sense. It is the miracle of the conversion of Karin in *Stromboli*, of the American chaplains in *Paisà*, of the couple in *Viaggio in Italia* who cling to one another after being so distant. It is also a miracle of reality against design (the narrative).

The division between ideal and real was muted by historical realities immediately after 1943. It seemed then that ideals might come true. Ideology and reality just after the war appeared more aligned than they had before the war or would in the future. As the gap between hopes and the real seemed to be closing in social-political reality, Neo-realists duplicated a historical moment in bringing together the pro-filmic and the filmic, the real and its duplication. They did so with considerable faith in reality and in their ability to render it.

After 1950 it was clear that the actual world and a hoped-for reality were at odds; for some, especially the Neo-realists, hope itself became the victim. The society that was being formed, after 1948, was not the one the Neo-realists had envisaged. Bourgeois forces reasserted themselves against the popular and Socialist dreams of the Resistance. To go on hoping in the context of the economic boom, the political conservatism of Christian Democrat rule, social reaction, the American alliance, the Cold War, would have been foolish. As Asor Rosa has commented, "If you know, you don't hope."[7]

The actual state of things could no longer simply be reproduced; it needed to be criticized. That criticism, always present in Neo-realism, was a criticism that presumed it could be effective and trusted that social ills would be put right, that reform was possible, that ideals would come true, that heaven would come to earth. After 1948, certainly, such criticism was more open, more trenchant, but also more hopeless. It became nostalgic for something apparently lost for ever.

The idea of the real changed. It became associated with desires and fantasies, whose strengths as fantasies were in direct proportion to the impossibility of their realization. The more awful the world seemed, the more fabulous and desperate were the renunciations of it and the desire to escape from it. This became a dominant theme in the films of Rossellini and De Sica, and also of Visconti and Fellini. The real, increasingly fictionalized and fantasized, expressed a disappointment with actuality. It assumed a spiritual dimension (*Francesco, giullare di Dio*), or a fairy-tale one (*Miracolo a Milano*), or was purely private (*Europa '51, Viaggio in Italia*). The place for reality shifted towards fiction, away from the contemporary world. The gap that opened up between dreams and reality became a gap in the cinema between fiction and the representation of reality. Actuality was seen as ugly, vulgar, unacceptable, intolerable. The *commedia all'italiana* of Risi, Monicelli, Steno, Comencini, of the films of Totò, of those scripted by Age and Scarpelli, is bitter and vicious. The world—and this was particularly true of Risi— had become squalid and mad. Risi's protagonists were hysterical and crazy. Reality as it had been hoped for, and seemed for a moment to have existed, had disappeared. Certainly, the humanist, popular, progressive reality of the 1940s no longer existed. Reality had become a nightmare or a tawdry joke. Only Antonioni, I think, among the Italian film-makers who had grown up during

Fascism, unreservedly welcomed the new world, finding it not only interesting but productive. In any case he did not adopt—as did almost everyone else, including and even especially Pasolini—an attitude of moral indignation at what now existed in comparison to the better world that had preceded it. Antonioni looked forward, not back; and not a single one of his films has the nostalgia characteristic of much Italian post-war cinema.

Pasolini understood the gap in Neo-realism between the ideal and the real. By the time he entered cinema as a scriptwriter in the 1950s, Italy had changed. Ideals had been pushed further back. Naturalism was no longer an adequate instrument for discovering reality. The real, as it had been dreamed of, was no longer out there: it had to be created. In 1975, a few months before Pelosi, a thug from the *borgate*, murdered Pasolini in the squalor of an empty plot in Ostia, surrounded by filth and rubbish, Pasolini reflected that the gritty *borgate* he had depicted in *Accattone* and *Mamma Roma*, in which so many critics had found a sense of realism which reminded them of the Neo-realists, were in fact already sliding into myth. Pelosi was already present in the *borgate* of *Accattone*. It was as if reality had taken its revenge on Pasolini and his fantasy of it.

A LANGUAGE OF REALITY/A REALITY BEYOND LANGUAGE

Pasolini responded to the changed situation of Italy in the 1950s in a variety of ways: in his theory and writings, and later in the practice of his films, in their themes and in his political gestures.

All Pasolini's films, without exception, have a literary bias. They are based on classic literature, such as the works of Chaucer, Boccaccio and De Sade, or on novels and other writings by Pasolini himself, such as the novel *Teorema* and plays like *Orgia* (for *Porcile*), or on original Pasolini scripts/treatments (*Accattone, Mamma Roma, La ricotta, Uccellacci e uccellini*). The anti-literary bias characteristic of Neo-realism was absent from Pasolini's work. His cinema is a cinema concerned with the relations of words to images, language to film, art to reality. These were its principal relations, the real subject of his works. His best films are explicit about that. In *Accattone*, Accattone, at the moment of his death, gives birth to language: "Ahaa... Mo sto bene" ["Ahaa... Now I'm OK"]. In

Porcile, which is a parable about language, as are *Edipo re*, *Medea*, *La ricotta* and *Teorema*, the parable concerns the (painful) entry into the symbolic.

Nevertheless, despite Pasolini's film practice, in theory he saw his move to cinema as a move away from literature, away from language and the symbolic, away from artifice, towards reality. The terms in which he recounted that move were different from the interest in cinema expressed by the Neo-realists. There is, nevertheless, the same sense in Pasolini, as in them, that cinema belonged to reality, and that language was distant from it; and the same sense, too, of a bourgeois coming out of the narrowness of his culture towards the reality of ordinary people and events. "The people" were presented by an entire post-war generation of Italian intellectuals as the true and the good. The people stood outside established bourgeois culture, and even outside established language, speaking as they did predominantly dialect rather than Italian. The good and the true were associated not only with reality and the people, but also with something Edenic, primitive and natural.

Insofar as, within Neo-realism, cinema itself was associated with reality, it came to be viewed as an original language, outside cultural conventions and directly in touch with the real. Some Neo-realists, like Rossellini, maintained that their cinema was not a cinema of convention but of direct apprehension of the world, beyond convention and in that sense original. Pasolini took this position to an extreme, but it was shared by others. Even as Pasolini made his highly wrought cultural artefacts, quoting from Baudelaire and Vivaldi and Masaccio, the quotations were all designed to emphasize the primitive reality which for him, by definition, lay outside history and culture, certainly bourgeois history and culture. For Pasolini, the function of that history and culture as he manipulated them was to make one conscious of the real, that is, conscious of what history and culture were not. The function of Pasolinian language then, and of culture, was to lead one through consciousness to a self-effacement of consciousness, towards a pre-consciousness, a pre-symbolic, a pre-history, towards an irrationality and non-language, to dream and myth, which for Pasolini cinema perfectly embodied. Culture, for Pasolini, was an instrument for its own erasure, as if one tried to write or read until the very text disappeared and the reader and writer disappeared, hypnotized by language (or images). Cinema embodied a similar tendency and shared a similar paradox. For while it could be argued, as it was by Pasolini, that cinema was real because it had an analogical relation to reality, directly reproducing it without the intervention of cultural signs, it was also undeniably part of a cultural discourse which one had to enter in order to find that place of reality which existed before all discourse. Language was a necessity even in the attempt to cancel it out, or to seek its demise.

For Pasolini, and for the Neo-realists, cinema was a phenomenon outside language, outside a symbolic continuum, whose images could speak directly, as if cinema were almost made of flesh. This accounts for the rationale within Neo-realism of the effacement of language (of conventions, of style, of narrative artifice) before the beauty of reality, and the similar attempt by Pasolini to distance himself from language and culture. But Pasolini sought the distance through closeness, by acting upon language from within it, not by renouncing it but by using it.

BEYOND THE SYMBOLIC

The idea of cinema as being outside language was an old one which Pasolini refashioned. It had been central to debates on the specificity of cinema and on the nature of the cinematic from the beginnings of cinema, and even before that. Certainly, it was part of the theoretical capital of cinema. It had been an issue of crucial importance in Italy during the Fascist period, especially in the late 1930s, again in the 1940s during Neo-realism, and once more in the mid-1950s, signalled by the debate on *Senso* between those defending a direct realism (Neo-realism) and those arguing for a "critical" realism, exemplified by Visconti.[8] The debate was resumed in the 1960s within semiotics.

Pasolini entered those debates. At Pesaro in 1964, in the company of Roland Barthes and Umberto Eco, Pasolini gave his "heretical" semiotics paper, "Il 'cinema di poesia'".[9] Part of that paper is concerned with defining what is specific to cinema and what is specific to poetry. The paper ended with a criticism of the avant-garde. Pasolini was holier than the avant-gardists, using a notion of the real against their immersion in language; but it was dressed-up radicalism. At its heart, the paper was pure Croce.[10] It was subject to the same Idealism as characterized other Italian defenders of the specificity of cinema, where specificity, reality, poetry and art were interchangeable terms. These are Crocean notions. It is Croce, I think, who was the real link between Neorealism and Pasolini. (Similarly, d'Annunzian Decadence was another unacknowledged force in Pasolini's work which helped to place it within the literary tradition that Neo-realist populism had so vehemently rejected.)

Here is Pasolini recalling his entry into cinema. It is an entry into the real away from the symbolic, into a blissful state outside language:

> Queste mediazioni poetiche o romanzesche frapponevano tra la vita e me una sorta di parete simbolica, uno schermo di parole. Ed è lí forse la vera tragedia di ogni poeta, di non raggiungere il mondo se non metaforicamente, secondo le regole di una magia in definitiva limitata nel suo modo di impossessarsi del mondo. Già il dialetto era per me il mezzo di un approccio piú fisico ai contadini, alla terra, e nei romanzi "romani" il dialetto popolare mi offriva lo stesso approccio concreto, e per cosí dire materiale. Ora, ho scoperto molto presto che l'espressione cinematografica mi offriva grazie alla sua analogia sul piano semologico [...] con la realtà stessa, la possibilità di raggiungere la vita in modo piú completo. Di impossessarmene, di viverla mentre la ricreavo. Il cinema mi consente di mantenere il contatto con la realtà, un contatto fisico, carnale, direi addirittura sensuale.[11]

[Poetry and the novel placed between life and myself a kind of symbolic wall, a screen of words. And that perhaps is the real tragedy of every poet, to be kept from the world except metaphorically, according to the rules of a magic which in point of fact is limited in its ability to possess the world. Formerly dialect was the way for me to have a more physical contact with the peasantry, with the soil, and in my "Roman" novels popular dialect afforded me the same concrete approach, which was almost material. Now, I very quickly discovered that cinematic expression, thanks to its analogical relation on a semiological plane with reality itself (...), gave me the possibility of entering into life more completely—of taking possession of it, of living it at the same time as I was recreating it. Cinema permits me to maintain my contact with reality, a physical, fleshy—even sensual—contact.]

In Pasolini's poetry, in dialect and in Italian, and in his novels, there was a tension which revolved around a paradox. Pasolini sought reality as something prior to language, but could only approach that reality by means of language. The paradox was not resolved in the move to cinema. Rather it was reduplicated. Cinema may have offered him a more direct contact with reality than writing, but it equally required that he take a discursive path to arrive at it.

His theories of film turn on this problem: the script as a writing which tended towards its own erasure. Rather than encountering reality by such means, he encountered cinema and the image, both part of discursive and socially coded systems. Reality remained, for Pasolini, just beyond the horizon of language. It could never be possessed except through language, yet the means of possession effectively barred him from the possession he sought. He could console himself with the consciousness of what he had lost, all the while knowing that he had lost it in the attempt to get hold of it. Reality beckoned to him, but he was excluded from it. Here was a perfect machine for the perpetuation of desire.

Pasolini had an idea of cinema as ideal or in potential. Cinema corresponded to reality. He said that cinema was the analogue of reality—its mirror. Reality was, he said, like an infinite shot-sequence in cinema. But the infinite shot-sequence, of course, was an ideal, a never-ending cinema, and not at all like the actuality of films, which was necessarily finite. Film took something of this ideal of cinema, but it could never match it. Perhaps Neo-realist cinema was about as close as one could get.

Even as Pasolini made this formulation of an ideal cinema, he admitted the subjectivity and partiality of the idea. The shot-sequence, even if infinite, would always be seen from a particular perspective. Reality therefore could not be something firm, but was necessarily shifting and uncertain. And, more important, his ideal cinema, never realized in practice, could only be known in concrete films, where wholeness was necessarily disrupted. If the ideal cinema corresponded to reality, it was the fate of reality never to be actually possessed; it could only be recalled, or remembered, in its fragmentary traces in film. Here was an odd combination of reactionary nostalgia for a lost past and of Modernist methods for retrieving it. Reality, ultimately, was an idea and thus textual. It presupposed a writing.

Reality beyond the Edge of Fiction

Accattone, Mamma Roma, La ricotta and *Il Vangelo secondo Matteo*, works which Pasolini saw as belonging to his "national-popular Gramscian phase" (and thus most closely related to the political intentions of Neo-realism, though different from Neo-realism's aesthetic), depicted reality, or more precisely starred it, as something beyond the edge of fiction. In the case of Rossellini, or De Sica, or for that matter Renoir, while the films left the door open to the impress of reality, once reality appeared from outside the fiction it became integrated within it. The Rossellini miracle may involve the assertion of a miraculous in the real, but the miracle and the real were always domesticated and rationalized by the narrative fiction, which provided them with motives in action and in character. Pasolini's real, on the other hand, is real insofar as it remains unintegrated and unarticulated fictionally. A character grimaces, but to no one, to nowhere, without motive. A character moves out of character towards the reality of the actual actor and person in a sudden burst of laughter, or an unaccountable tumescence. And equally, shots in his films often have this characteristic of disarticulation, as if they were not part of narrative, and above all not articulated in a signifying narrative stream. This disarticulation and disconnection of sign and object were preconditions of being real for Pasolini. If gesture had no symbolic weight or narrative connection, it was by that token irrational; it was also pure undiluted reality by being non-functional to discourse.

This was only another fictional ruse, but what is important about it is that it evokes a reality while simultaneously asserting its loss. What remains in Pasolini's films is the shards and broken remains of a lost wholeness.

Neo-realism, on the contrary, recreated a wholeness in film by integrating everything within the fictional universe of film, and precisely for that reason only the slightest gap was perceptible between a pro-filmic real and its filmic representation. For Pasolini, that gap was unbridgeable. Film was the mechanism for declaring it. It is part of his modernism that he reasserted the separateness of the filmic and pro-filmic and bent his films, unashamedly, away from reality towards extremes of artifice and manipulation. But the cause in which such techniques were enlisted was retrograde.

INFINITE DESIRE

The tension of contraries in Pasolini's works is what makes the works so productive. His works were like self-perpetuating machines. Reality, for him, had all the intensity of a desire, but it was constructed in such a way as to maintain the desire infinitely. Desire was tempted but never satisfied. It was always turned away at the gates of reality by the discursive formations that had brought it there. His films were instruments for the production of the desire for reality, but his reality was produced in such a way as to make the desire insatiable. The insatiability of desire produced more and more texts, more and more films, more and more writing to achieve the impossible. Pasolini, of necessity, could never satisfy his desire for reality. But he could always satisfy his desire for writing. His desire for reality happily maintained the writing, which was always a writing about that desire. Pasolini's life was spent writing: his productivity was phenomenal. The direction of the writing was perhaps not exactly towards reality as it was towards death. Death was the place where writing necessarily stopped and where one achieved, simultaneously, in an eternal instant, an entry into reality and the finality of desire and writing.

THE BIRTH OF MEANING

Porcile is one of the most delicious instances of Pasolini's interest in the boundaries and irresolvable paradoxes of art, particularly literature and writing, in their relation to reality. *Porcile* is composed of two stories. One story, of primitive cannibalism, which is silent, or at least where articulated speech is absent, is juxtaposed with another story, of advanced culture in contemporary Germany, where language is excessively present. Words are incessant in the modern story and are theatricalized as poetry. The one section of the film is a poem in images, the other represents the poetry of language. The film as a whole is a dialogue between these two positions, these two languages, a natural, cinematic one of analogical images, and an unnatural one of symbolic words. At the end of the film, in the silent cannibal segment, the cannibal bursts into glorious speech to announce the destruction and dismemberment of the father; he is staked to the ground and eaten by dogs. The other segment, of Nazism and neo-capitalism, so rich in language, ends in silence, and with the death of the disobedient son at the hands of his father, symbolized in a herd of pigs. The pigs eat the son.

There is no film of Pasolini's, save perhaps *Teorema*, where the idea and the art which evokes it are so crystalline yet obscure, where the edge between image and language, reality and consciousness, primitivism and history, can literally be seen. In *Porcile*, one can almost touch time, feel it, as it enters the world, and as language, history and the symbolic of culture accompany it. As history enters through language in the cannibal segment, the primitive world disintegrates before a bourgeois world of order, law and retribution; what remains is the writing on film of that lost reality as the consciousness of it, or more exactly as the myth of it.

What was the point of Pasolini's regressive movement towards a pre-history and a pre-symbolic real, perhaps even towards a pre-birth at the edge of the womb? It was to encounter a contradictory place, "contaminated", as he said, by the contraries of history, writing and culture.

Pasolini tried to re-invent and re-experience the moment when meaning was born out of the indifference of reality as it was for the cannibal in *Porcile*, or for Accattone at the threshold of death. It was as if Pasolini sought to relive in that moment his own birth and with it, since he was a poet, the birth of poetry. This is part of the great neo-Romantic myth of a prelapsarian language or Mallarmé's blank page. Poetry had a double Oedipal edge for Pasolini. It had all the purity and innocence of sound and metre, but was composed in the structures and within the laws of language. Poetry was mother and father to Pasolini, up in the clouds and down to earth. He sought to escape the linguistic confines of language in the irrational, aesthetic beauty of poetry, only to be more bound by the language which afforded him the luxury and pain of comprehending the irrational and the ecstasy of beauty. In poetry, he regretted a lost innocence—the theme of so much of his poetry—, for whose loss language was responsible; yet only language, in this hybrid of poetry, could fully register the loss; and only poetry could resolve that loss by its own "senseless" beauty.

THE JOURNEY TO THE IRRATIONAL

Pasolini's interest in going back to the boundaries between language and reality had the purpose of reforming the relations between them, in the direction of consciousness and knowledge. It was an interest directly opposed to what he regarded as the Neo-realist assumption of an absolute transparency between reality and its representation, and which for him implied an acceptance of the world, not an understanding of it. Pasolini sought to find the place not where meaning was dissolved, which he said the avant-garde sought, but where it was formed, at a primitive, largely mythical stage, when the social entered, and when society and the symbolic were born from reality. Pasolini wanted to witness that birth, and, in every sense of the word, attend it. *Porcile* is a mark of this being-in-attendance when history is born. His poetry centred on the moment of this birth, the line where sense was compromised by rhythm and sound, and simultaneously where sense was formed out of rhythm's and sound's sensuality and reality.

Like other post-war Italian writers and intellectuals, Pasolini wanted to find the real, and like them found natural language an inadequate, impossible instrument. Cinema, happily, did not seem to be a language like natural language, but a more primitive language, more real because less cultured, and because less cultured less bourgeois, and because less bourgeois less literary. At last, in cinema—it seemed to him, and to many others—reality could be written with itself, finally freed from the symbolic substitutes of words. This dream was not fundamentally, in its intention at least, all that different from the Neo-realist dream. Was it not in fact the dream of Zavattini?

The uniqueness of Resistance culture for Pasolini, its realism, was due to a blending of voices, of the ordinary with the bourgeois, the vulgar with the literary, dialect with Italian, reality with art:

> La concomitanza di due punti di vista nel guardare il mondo, quello dell'intellettuale marxista e quello dell'uomo semplice, uniti in una "contaminatio" di "stile sublime" e di "stile umile".[12]
> (*EE*, 44)

[The overlap of two perspectives for seeing the world, that of the
Marxist intellectual and that of the ordinary person, united in a
"contamination" of the "sublime style" and the "humble" one.]

This was what Pasolini meant by his *discorso libero indiretto* referring to the literature of the Resistance. It was the displacement of
the voice of the bourgeois by the voice of the popular "other". It was
fictive, since the bourgeois was not the peasant, but real, because
the bourgeois was seeking truly to enter that other world. The
impulse was primarily political. In social and literary terms this
represented a considerable change. Before the Resistance, the
imitation of the other in literature was purely literary and, in the
end, despite the masquerade, nothing changed. In the Resistance,
on the other hand—Pasolini claimed—, the blend and shift of
voices represented a political intention, and, in part (or so it seemed
at first) a political reality. It was at the very heart of Italian
populism, of the notion of "commitment", and of the idea of the
"organic" Communist Party intellectual. This conjunction of cultures, and of party and people, bourgeois and peasant, not only
seemed a reality during the Resistance, but *was* a reality, if only for
a moment.

Bourgeois Italian writers began to shift towards popular ca-
dences in their writings and often towards the extreme realities of
dialect and slang. As the real became literary, literature in turn
became more real. That real—it could be argued—invigorated and
transformed a bourgeois literature that had been excessively, even
triumphantly artificial.

But something else was involved. There was a general sense,
expressed by many, that within the peasant, non-bourgeois
"other"—the people—there was a core of irrationality, of something primitive, close to nature and hence to truth, not like the
falsities inherent in bourgeois culture, or in culture *tout court*. Thus,
within the peasant, non-bourgeois world, it was believed, there
was something purer and more innocent than in the bourgeois
world. By going beyond the bourgeois, therefore, one went beyond
the social and beyond history since there was only ever bourgeois
history and bourgeois society. Thus, truly to find this other language was also for some, including Pasolini, a means of finding
another self, a self before culture, hence a non-bourgeois self, and
by that token a truer, better, more real self.

Pasolini's journey backwards in historical-social time was a personal-emotional journey back to his own biographical time and to his birth and infancy. It was an Oedipal journey where his infant reality confronted the adult reality of the symbolic of language and the father who had imposed it. Language literally took him from his mother. But it provided him with the means of re-embracing her with his work—with his poetry—and mourning the loss of her as he assumed his own, separate identity, as he entered society, language and history.

What thus began as an attempt to find a politically objective reality in Neo-realism in the 1940s moved, in the 1950s and 1960s, towards extremes of subjective, personal feeling, bordering on the Decadent. It was the way to bring culture once more to reality, but by personalizing the one and mythologizing the other. Art became the one true value in a world of falsity, because it touched a genuine primitivism and eroticism—a truth—against the functionalism of the modern world, which Pasolini saw as repressing that truth—a truth he sought to liberate by his work.

The problems the Neo-realists dealt with were not self-contained within the space of a few years, from 1943 to 1950. Those problems had emerged before Neo-realism and would continue after it, certainly well into the period when Pasolini began making his films. Pasolini cannot be understood outside this background; nor can he be understood, despite recent attempts, from a primarily biographical perspective, in which every move is a personal move, every reason an individual reason.[13]

Pasolini's quest for a primitivism and irrationalism outside the boundaries of the social was a social and Italian response to specific historical changes in Italian society. Pasolini was not an isolated "genius" whose "masterpieces" and ideas could be unbound from history, no matter how intensely he tried to escape such bonds, or outrageously to challenge them, and no matter how dutifully some have accepted Pasolini's quest as if he had made good his escape. His work is a testament to the impossibility of that escape, and to the necessity of language, whence the necessity of all that is social. Oedipus's journey was a social journey, and Pasolini's journey, in linking itself to it, not only took him through what all of us experience in trying to become ourselves, but took him through it along specific historical paths.

Despite Pasolini's celebration of the flesh and the irrational, he was a rationalist and a humanist. His political-social commitments were genuine and passionate. His regressions towards innocence, towards primitive reality, towards an asocial private world, even, perhaps, his regression into poetry, were aimed at knowing, and thus ways to confront these truths, to recognize them, to make them conscious, to be aware of their presence and their creative force. In his constant regressions to the other, to poetry, to those on the periphery of history and society—the pimps, the prostitutes, Jews, blacks, the poor—he found his own otherness, which was a way of finding his truth.

As a direct political position, his was too tied to the mythical and to the socially peripheral to be effective; and it was too filled with a reactionary and nostalgic populist Romanticism to be acceptable. On the other hand, as an artistic position it was enormously productive. And it approached a truth and a reality alien to politics. It is in that essentially aesthetic realism that Pasolini's politics resides. Because it was poetic and aesthetic, because it realized itself in fiction, in poetry, in film and in writing, it had the strength and the possibility never to compromise its truth. It contested the real world with a reality and truth only to be found in journeys of desire and fantasy. All Pasolini's films are road movies.

The journeys are taken not only by the characters in the films but by the films and thus by the spectator. They are journeys into the truths of fiction and desire; and, by that token, journeys into the irrational.

NOTES

1   This essay attempts to situate Pasolini in relation to Italian Neo-realism, a relation he vigorously denied. It represents a rewriting of a paper delivered at the University of Pescara in March 1993 entitled "Pasolini's *Mise-en-scène*", which concentrated on theoretical problems involving the shot-sequence, Pasolini's idea of reality and his political positions connected to this notion. Although this essay retraces thoughts in the earlier paper, it comes to different conclusions. I wish to thank Zygmunt Barański for his kind and helpful comments.

2   See A. Bazin, *What is Cinema?*, vol. II, edited and translated by H. Gray (Berkeley, University of California Press 1971), pp. 16–93. See in particular in that volume "Cinematic Realism and the Italian School of Liberation" (pp. 16–40). These essays in English exclusively concern Italian Neo-realism. They were selected and translated from A. Bazin, *Qu'est-ce que le cinéma?*, vol. IV: *Une Esthétique de la réalité: le néo-réalisme* (Paris, Cerf, 1962).

3   C. Metz, "The Cinema: Language or Language System?", in his *Film Language* (New York, Oxford University Press, 1974), pp. 31–91 (pp. 36–37). Metz was comparing Rossellini's aesthetic to Eisenstein's: "To Rossellini, who said 'Things are. Why manipulate them?' the Soviet film-maker might have replied, 'Things are. They must be manipulated.' Eisenstein never shows us the course of real events, but always, as he says, the course of real events refracted through an ideological point of view, entirely thought out, signifying from beginning to end. Meaning is not sufficient; there must also be signification."

4   See in particular G. Tinazzi, "Un rapporto complesso", A. Asor Rosa, "Il neorealismo o il trionfo del narrativo" and A. Abruzzese, "Scrittura, cinema, territorio", in *Cinema e letteratura del neorealismo*, edited by G. Tinazzi and M. Zancan (Venice, Marsilio, 1990).

5   *Il sogno del centauro*, edited by J. Duflot (Rome, Editori Riuniti, 1983), p. 114.

6   Renoir said to him: "Il faut toujours laisser une porte ouverte sur le plateau car c'est à travers elle que l'inattendu entrera"—quoted by P. Pitiot, "Bernardo Bertolucci s'explique", *Cinéma* [Paris], 472 (Dec. 1990), 9.

7   In its complete form Asor Rosa's remark is: "L'invito a sperare è sempre invito a ignorare. Non spera chi conosce" (*Scrittori e popolo* [Turin, Einaudi, 1988], p. 226).

8   See F. Carpi, "Finita l'inchiesta si trova il romanzo", *Cinema nuovo*, 3, xxxiv, 1 May 1954; G. Aristarco, "Senso", *Cinema nuovo*, 4, lii, 10 Feb. 1955; G. Aristarco, "Dal neorealismo al realismo", *Cinema nuovo*, 4, liii, 25 Feb. 1955; C. Zavattini, "Diario", *Cinema nuovo*, 4, liv, 10 Mar. 1955; G. Aristarco, "E realismo", *Cinema nuovo*, 4, lv, 24 Mar. 1955; L. Chiarini, "Tradisce il neorealismo", *Cinema nuovo*, 3, lv, 25 Mar. 1955; A. Bazin, "Parlatorio", *Cinema nuovo*, 5, lxxxix, 10 Sept. 1956. See also C. Metz, *Film Language*, pp. 3–30, 108–48, 185–227; P. P. Pasolini, "La lingua scritta della realtà", in *Empirismo eretico* (Milan, Garzanti, 1977), pp. 198–226.

9   P. P. Pasolini, "Il 'cinema di poesia'" (*EE*, 167–87).

10   On Pasolini and Croce see the essays by Joseph Francese and Christopher Wagstaff in the present collection.

11   *Il sogno del centauro*, pp. 24–25.

12   Professor Barański remarked in a note to me that Pasolini's distinctions derive from classical and medieval rhetoric (especially as it applied to Dante's stylistic hybridism in the *Commedia*).

13   N. Greene, *Pier Paolo Pasolini: Cinema as Heresy* (Princeton, Princeton University Press, 1990).

REALITY INTO POETRY:
PASOLINI'S FILM THEORY

Christopher Wagstaff

Empirismo eretico is Pasolini's selection from among his essays written between the years 1964 and 1971 and, notwithstanding his partial disclaimers,[1] must be seen as a "collection" formed around certain themes and issues, the main theme being what Pasolini would call—using the term very broadly—"linguistics" (see De Mauro's essay in this volume). The collection is ordered nearly chronologically, with a clear shift, around 1965, from literature to cinema.[2] Weaknesses in the theorizing and the often occasional nature of the essays have tempted critics to treat *Empirismo eretico* more as an expression of a personal poetics than as an attempt at objective theorizing. Pasolini has always protested:

> Con ciò che ho scritto sul cinema, e mi riferisco ai saggi che ho letto alla mostra di Pesaro, e che ho scritto per *Filmcritica*, non ho fatto dell'estetica, non ho espresso una poetica, ma ho fatto semplicemente un esame, o meglio dei tentativi di esami linguistici che riguardano appunto la semiologia o la grammatica della lingua cinematografica.[3]

> [In what I have written about the cinema, and I am referring to the papers I read at the Pesaro Film Festival and the essays I wrote for *Filmcritica*, I have not been dealing with aesthetics, nor have I been expressing a poetics, rather I have been carrying out—or trying to—a linguistic investigation concerning nothing other than the semiology or the grammar of cinematographic language.]

The first systematic analysis of *Empirismo eretico* was published in 1976 by Roberto Turigliatto, who chose to study the essays neither as theory alone nor as poetics alone, but as a "contaminazione tra teoria e poetica".[4] The present essay was first published nine years later, in 1985,[5] but in the meantime, in 1980, a brief but influential discussion of Pasolini's ideas concerning cinema had been published by Teresa de Lauretis.[6] Discussion in the 1990s has been intense in North America, and has followed the path laid down by de Lauretis, leading to an approach which starts from Post-structuralist and Post-modernist positions, and seeks intimations of those positions in the writings of Pasolini. This approach sees little point in attempting a systematic assessment of Pasolini's theorizing, partly because no one is interested in the semiology of cinema any more, and prefers to seek in the very ambiguity of Pasolini's positions their fertility for a completely different approach to theorizing about film, about culture and about reality.[7]

This essay attempts to expound those of Pasolini's "semiological" theories that bear directly on the language of cinema, and to examine the way Pasolini elaborates these theories by seeking to understand their logic, to translate them into more acceptable terminology, and to explain the gaps and contradictions in them. Where Pasolini's theories or terminology are criticized, the purpose is not to rap him over the knuckles for his defects, but rather to arrive at an understanding of the implications of those defects, and to try to tease from the theoretical tangle the main threads of his argument. Of these main threads there are two: the first is that of "poesia" ["poetry"] (which carries Crocean overtones, and is related in ways that are never explicitly detailed to the concept of "espressione" ["expression"], in which the artist imposes his own vision on his material through the use of "stylistic" devices); the second is that of "reality".[8] Is the essential artistic value of cinema to be found in its expressive potential, or in its potential for "realism"? *Empirismo eretico* revives the debate in a number of stimulating ways, and contains, in implication, an attempt to reconcile the two positions.

In "Dal laboratorio" we find this revealing, coy sentence:

> Mi piacerebbe offrire qui timidamente ai linguisti che si sono interessati a questo problema una suggestione, un'ipotesi... poetica: il terzo termine tra "langue" e "parole" (la cui radicale dicotomia sembra insostenibile), potrebbe essere il "momento puramente orale della lingua". (*EE*, 74)

[I should here like timidly to offer to those linguists who have concerned themselves with this problem a suggestion, a hypothesis that is… poetic: the third term, standing between *langue* and *parole* (a radical opposition which I find untenable), could be the "purely oral stage of language".][9]

Pasolini will become less timid with time; and those three dots are in the text: we have a hypothesis that is about theoretical linguistics and that can be qualified as "poetic". He is suggesting that verbal language was not, originally, arbitrary, but that its genesis was in "necessary", physical, conditioned reflexes—"il grido della bestia e delle necessità fisiche, degli istinti" ["the cry of the beast and of physical needs, of instincts"; see also "Lingua", p. 209].

Whatever the semiological validity of this "suggestion", it does bring together many of Pasolini's preoccupations. "I miei saggi nascono da una ideologia profonda […], questo mio amore, irrazionalistico, in qualche modo, per la realtà" ["My essays grow out of a profound ideology (…), this love of mine, irrational in a way, for reality: "Razionalità e metafora", pp. 79–80]. He saw verbal language as a barrier between himself and reality, and cinema as a way of breaking through the barrier of conventional symbols to a complete contact with reality. He was therefore fascinated by any possibility of pushing away the elements of conventionality and arbitrariness in the Saussurean notion of language (and eagerly quoted Metz, Barthes and Jakobson when he found them making suggestions in this direction). Yet he felt the contradictory pull of two desires: one to push aside the barrier of conventional language and make contact with reality, and the other to transform reality and language into poetry and make "poetry" his form of direct, active participation in the "pragma" of reality. Hence his hypothesis of an "expressive" stage of verbal language, placed in a past that is privileged with some kind of authenticity which he looks upon with nostalgia (and in this context belong his ideas about myth). It would be clearer if we gave to Pasolini's example the label of "index", according to the typology of signs of C. S. Peirce, for the "grido della bestia" does not "refer" to the "necessità fisiche", but is rather a symptom of them.[10] Contini and Gramsci are also, elsewhere, pulled into the struggle for a language that is rooted in a reality less alienated than that of the *petite bourgeoisie* of the neo-capitalist age.

In order to follow Pasolini's reasoning, it is necessary to bear in mind from the outset that he draws a sharp distinction between "comunicazione" ["communication"] and "espressione" ["expression"]: to understand "comunicazione" one needs "linguistic" notions, while to understand "espressione" one needs "stylistic" notions. While one can point to probable sources for this distinction, and while one may see it in operation in Pasolini's theorizing, it is not possible to define with any precision the exact terms of the oppositions involved. Whether Pasolini will slot some item of human communication into the category of "comunicazione" or into that of "espressione" is at times very nearly arbitrary.

In "Nuove questioni linguistiche" he begins his analysis of the Italian language with a denigration of *italiano medio* ["standard Italian"], a modern national language that is the product of *omologazione* ["homologation"—but meaning "making the same", which is not quite what the word usually means in English], dominated (according to Pasolini) by the requirements of technology and commerce. The positive pole corresponding to this negation is dialect, and poetry. Dialect is closer to the "original" language we have referred to above. Curiously, however, Pasolini notes above all, here and in "Intervento sul Discorso Libero Indiretto", the way that writers in the "high" style plunge downwards into a lower level of language, that of dialect, for instance, but only in order to carry it up with them like prey into the high level. Again, where one keeps expecting a purely linguistic analysis, one finds instead a preoccupation with poetry. What "Nuove questioni linguistiche" sets up is an opposition between language that is merely "strumentale" ["instrumental"—a tool] and for "comunicazione", and language that has a "funzione espressiva o espressionistica" ["expressive or expressionistic function": p. 14]. In a world where we witness "il prevalere del fine comunicativo sul fine espressivo" ["the communicative function prevailing over the expressive one": p. 26], "il fine della lotta del letterato sarà l'espressività linguistica, che viene radicalmente a coincidere con la libertà dell'uomo rispetto alla sua meccanizzazione" ["the goal for which the man of letters strives will be linguistic expressiveness, which comes to coincide with man's freedom in the face of the mechanization that threatens him": p. 27].

This will remain a constant theme in *Empirismo eretico*: the movement towards "reality", or towards what might seem to be "realist" linguistic positions, is in fact justified on the basis of a Crocean aesthetic of *poesia*, as immediate expression. It is poetry that stands between neo-capitalism and individual freedom, and it is precisely the Neo-avant-garde's rejection of this Crocean, lyrical aesthetic that provokes Pasolini's contempt, both in the essay under discussion (e.g. p. 18) and in "La fine dell'avanguardia". The same line of thought applied to the cinema gives us "Il 'cinema di poesia'", perhaps his most famous essay,[11] which follows rather more the teachings of men like Gadda, Contini, Spitzer, Croce and Gramsci than those of Saussure. Turigliatto thinks Pasolini did not know Metz's writings when he wrote "Il 'cinema di poesia'", and certainly it is in the essay written a year later, "La lingua scritta della realtà", that Pasolini first mentions having read Metz's essay "Le cinéma: langue ou langage?"[12] Similarities between "Il 'cinema di poesia'" and Metz's essay (published in 1964), however, make it hard for me to believe that Pasolini did not know some of it in 1965.

The distinction between "communication" and "expression" is fundamental to the argument of "Il 'cinema di poesia'" (pp. 171–91). Under the heading "expression" he puts "linguaggi letterari" ["literary languages"] and "il cinema come lingua espressiva" ["cinema as an expressive language"]. "Literary languages" are made possible by the existence of a purely communicative instrument, which is verbal language, on which they are based. Pasolini asks whether there are any such instrumental bases for cinema. He decides that there must be "una serie di archetipi comunicativi naturali" ["a series of natural communicative archetypes"] (in which may perhaps be discerned elements of his nostalgia for an aboriginal world of authenticity).

Firstly, Pasolini points to the way we carry on a "colloquio strumentale" ["instrumental dialogue"] with reality: reality "si esprime [...] con la pura e semplice presenza ottica" ["expresses itself (...) with its pure and simple optical presence"]; "oggetti e cose [...] si presentano cariche di significato e quindi 'parlano' brutalmente con la loro stessa presenza" ["objects and things (...) appear loaded with meaning and so "speak" brutally with their very presence"]. The addressee of the cinematic communication is used to "reading" reality. Secondly, in our experience, says Pasolini, a whole world is expressed through images, signs which he calls "im-segni" ["im-signs"] (as opposed to the "lin-segni" ["lang-signs"] of language): the world of memory and dreams. He even says that dreams and memories are organized into sequences of close-ups, long shots and so on. This world of meaningful images "prefigura e si propone come fondamento 'strumentale' della comunicazione cinematografica" ["prefigures and offers itself as the basic tool of cinematographic communication"]. This leads Pasolini to contrast poetry with cinema: the tool at the base of poetry is highly elaborated (verbal language); the tool at the base of cinema (the "im-signs" of reality, mime, dreams and memories) is "estremamente rozzo, quasi animale" ["extremely crude, almost animal-like"] and has a "profonda qualità onirica" ["profound dream-like quality"] and an "assoluta e imprescindibile concretezza, diciamo, oggettuale" ["the absolute and inalienable concreteness, as it were, of an object"]. Moreover, and he underlines this: "Lo strumento linguistico su cui si impianta il cinema è [...] di tipo irrazionalistico" ["The linguistic tool underlying cinema has (...) an irrational form"].

The contradictions contained in the essay so far will be remarkably fertile. On the one hand, the cinema relies for its meaning on the world of "reality" (what might properly be called its "referent"), because it has no "fondamento strumentale" ["instrumental foundation"—i.e. basic tool] on which to base itself; and on the other, the cinema bases itself on an essentially "irrational", "oneiric" "fondamento strumentale", the world of dreams and memories. It is not made clear what theoretical basis he has in mind for the meaning of dreams and memories, in the latter case.[13] Moreover, "meaning" and "referent" are not clearly separated categories in Pasolini's writings, and he confuses the two. In the parallel between literary languages and the cinema, for example, it is not clear why referents are excluded in the case of verbal language, and supply the answer to the whole problem in one (the language of reality), but not the other (the "oneiric"), hypothesis concerning cinematic communication. These contradictions will never exactly be cleared up in *Empirismo eretico*, but they will become less apparent as Pasolini drops parts of his argument. After "Il 'cinema di poesia'", the concept of the language of dreams being the instrumental basis for a cinematic language will subside into the background, and will be eclipsed by a search for a "Semiologia Generale della Realtà" ["General Semiology of Reality"].

Another contradiction looms immediately, as Pasolini goes on to say that the film-maker, not possessing a "dictionary" of words from which to construct his communication, has to take his "im-signs" "dal caos, dove non sono che mere possibilità o ombre di comunicazione meccanica e onirica" ["from chaos, where they are but mere possibilities or shadows of mechanical or oneiric communication"]. This "chaos", however, is, surely, that very reality which we have been told we "read". In any case, the film-maker has to carry out a double task: to take an "im-sign" and make it into a sign—"presupporlo come sistemato in un dizionario degli im-segni significativi (mimica, ambiente, sogno, memoria)" ["imagine it as being located in a dictionary of all the meaningful im-signs (mimicry, the environment, dream, memory)"]; and then to "aggiungere a tale im-segno puramente morfologico la qualità espressiva individuale" ["add to that purely morphological im-sign an individual expressive quality"]; his task is "prima linguistica poi estetica" ["first linguistic and then aesthetic"].

Pasolini admits that a sort of inventory of "stilemi" ["stylemes"] has been built up in fifty years of cinema, though from a convention that is "stilistica prima di essere grammaticale" ["stylistic before being grammatical"] (I think he means that the "stilemi" are like literary tropes, rather than like vocabulary items in a language that is a "strumento comunicativo" ["communicative tool"]). All this is complicated, however, by Pasolini's now returning to an earlier point, that of our "reading" of reality. "Ma devo insistere: se le immagini o im-segni non sono organizzate in un dizionario e non possiedono una grammatica, sono però patrimonio comune" ["But I must insist: even if the images or im-signs are not organized in a dictionary and do not possess a grammar, they are nevertheless common property"]. He has said that "l'immagine delle ruote del treno che corrono tra sbuffi di vapore [...] è uno stilema" ["the image of the wheels of a train racing along in the midst of puffs of steam (...) is a styleme"]. However, "la vaporiera [...] nella realtà [...] 'ci dice qualcosa'" ["the real steam engine (...) 'tells us something'"] (for example "quanto sia commovente l'operosità dell'uomo e quanto sia enorme la capacità della società industriale, e quindi del capitalista, ad annettersi nuovi territori di utenti" ["how moving is man's industry and how vast is the capacity of industrial society and hence of the capitalist to annex new territories of users"]). He concludes: "Non esistono dunque, in realtà degli 'oggetti bruti': tutti sono abbastanza significativi in natura per diventare segni simbolici" ["So the 'raw object' does not exist in reality: everything has enough meaning in nature to become a symbolic sign"]. Pasolini's formulation implies, I think, more than he intends. He seems to be implying that it is enough for a man to have a series of reactions and reflections upon contemplating an object for that object to become the "signifier" of a sign that has as its referent the man's emotional response ("commozione") and his reflections, and for that object then to be used as a conventional, symbolic sign for that referent. This implication may have run away with Pasolini, and had a lot to do with his dismissal as a serious theorist in this field—while this line of thinking is not developed any further in "Il 'cinema di poesia'", its attraction for Pasolini led to his reflections the following year in the essay "La lingua scritta della realtà". All I think he really needed to say is that since things in the world mean things to us, the cinematographer takes on board those meanings when he photographs the things, since he does not really have much other source of meaning. But this is a very banal statement: it does nothing to explain where agreement on meaning comes from, and why a steam engine in a film should not mean the same as a steam engine at the end of your street at three o'clock in the morning when you were trying to sleep off a hangover. What the cinematographer does, according to Pasolini, is this:

> Egli sceglie una serie di oggetti o cose o paesaggi o persone come sintagmi (segni di un linguaggio simbolico) che, se hanno una storia grammaticale storica inventata in quel momento—come in una specie di happening dominato dall'idea della scelta e del montaggio—hanno però una storia pre-grammaticale già lunga e intensa.

> [He chooses a series of objects, things, landscapes or people to use as syntagms (signs in a symbolic language) which, if their grammatical history has been invented in that moment—as though in a sort of happening ruled by the notion of choice and montage—already have a long and intense pre-grammatical history.]

I cannot relate this use of "pre-grammatical" to any conventional technical use of the term, and it is not compatible with the use made of the notion by Devoto, who is probably the source for Pasolini's use of it.[14] He goes on to say that poets legitimately use in their style "la pre-grammaticalità dei segni parlati" ["the pre-grammaticality of spoken signs"], and the cinematographer may similarly use in his style "la pre-grammaticalità degli oggetti" ["the pre-grammaticality of objects"]. He must mean that both "spoken signs" and "objects" can have "meaning" even before they become incorporated into a linguistic "system", with *grammaticale* meaning something like "part of a linguistic system". So, he concludes, "Il cinema è fondamentalmente onirico per la elementarità dei suoi archetipi [...] e per la fondamentale prevalenza della pre-grammaticalità degli oggetti in quanto simboli del linguaggio visivo" ["Cinema is dream-like because its archetypes are elementary, and because of the prevalence of the pre-grammaticality of objects inasmuch as they are symbols in a visual language"].

The inability of the cinema to be "espressione concettuale diretta" ["direct expression of concepts"] necessitates its "prevalente artisticità, [...] la sua violenza espressiva, la sua fisicità onirica" ["basic artisticness, (...) its expressive violence, its dream-like physicality"] (note how the argument is rhetorically buttressed by the use of the pattern of three, the delight in rhythmic effect, and the oxymoron in the last term).

If, as he has asserted up to this point, "la lingua del cinema [è] fondamentalmente una 'lingua di poesia'" ["the language of cinema [is] basically a 'poetic' language"], then Pasolini has to construct a Freudian explanation for why in practice the cinema has been prosaic:

> Tutti i suoi elementi irrazionalistici, onirici, elementari e barbarici, sono stati tenuti sotto il livello della coscienza: sono stati cioè sfruttati come elemento inconscio di urto e di persuasione: e sopra questo "monstrum" ipnotico che è sempre un film, è stata costruita rapidamente quella convenzione narrativa che ha fornito materia di inutili e pseudo-critici paragoni col teatro e il romanzo.

> [All its irrationalistic, dream-like, primitive and barbaric elements have been kept beneath the threshold of consciousness; that is to say, they have been used as an unconscious element for shocking and persuading the viewer; and on top of this hypnotic "monster" which a film still remains, has rapidly been built the narrative convention which has prompted useless and pseudo-critical comparisons with theatre and the novel.]

The argument becomes rather hard to summarize at this point because Pasolini finds himself like a juggler trying to hold two balls in the air: one is the concept of the language of cinema as oneiric, irrational, poetic and subjective, and the other is the observation that "anche film d'arte hanno adottato come loro lingua specifica questa 'lingua della prosa': questa convenzione narrativa priva di punte espressive, impressionistiche, espressionistiche ecc." ["art films have also adopted as their particular language this 'language of prose': this narrative convention devoid of features that are expressive, impressionistic, expressionistic, etc."], and that therefore the language of cinema has historically been objective. Potentially, the language of cinema has a "doppia natura" ["double nature"], "è insieme estremamente soggettivo e estremamente oggettivo" ["is both extremely subjective and extremely objective"], and shares this characteristic with literature, which has its "linguaggio della poesia" ["language of poetry"] and its "linguaggio della prosa" ["language of prose"]. Whereas in literature, however, the two "languages" are "talmente differenziati fra loro da essere in realtà diacronici, da seguire due diverse storie" ["so completely different from each other as to be in fact diachronic, having two separate histories"] (Pasolini uses the term *diacronico* in an unorthodox way), in the cinema "una sola convenzione linguistica" ["the same linguistic convention"] embraces "i film d'arte e i film d'evasione, i capolavori e i feuilletons" ["art films and escapist films, masterpieces and pulp fiction"]. The way Pasolini phrases this observation reveals that he is looking in vain for "expressive" language in "art films". He might, however, have found it had he looked more closely at "escapist films" like horror films. But Pasolini remains anchored to Crocean aesthetic judgements, linking the concept of "expression" with notions of value and of high art.

He proceeds to ask: "Come è teoricamente spiegabile e praticamente possibile, nel cinema, la 'lingua della poesia'?" ["How can we explain in theory and put into practice in the cinema the 'language of poetry'?"] The reader may be excused for feeling confused, because one of the major hypotheses of the discussion so far in the essay has been that the language of the cinema is fundamentally poetic. What appears to be happening is that Pasolini is opening a new chapter in his discussion, with a new definition of the way "expression" in the cinema can be poetic. The new definition will turn on notions of authorial voice, of the director imposing his vision of the world, and his feelings about reality, on the narrative of a film. Hence there is both continuity and discontinuity with the earlier part of the essay: continuity in the way that Pasolini tries to show how self-expression can be achieved by the artist in what has been defined (by Pasolini) as an essentially narrative medium; discontinuity in the way that "poetry" will no longer be sought so much in "language" as in questions of "style".

The gist of the argument Pasolini now develops may be summarized as follows. Just as in literature, says Pasolini, an author can immerse himself in the words and thoughts of his protagonist, by means of the device of free indirect discourse, so in the cinema a director can present images of reality as though seen by one of the characters in the narrative. And just as in literature this can be a pretext for the author to impose his own vision on reality, and so to express himself (thus conferring strong elements of "poetry" on the written narrative), so the film-maker can use the pretext of a character's point of view to express his own vision and feelings (thus conferring elements of "poetry" on the film narrative). Whereas in literature, however, the author can put to one side his own language (idiolect, dialect, social-class characteristics, and so forth) and adopt that of his character (indeed, Pasolini considers this *linguistic* aspect to be more important as a distinctive feature of free indirect discourse than matters of syntax, narrative perspective and point of view), in the cinema this is not possible, because there is only one, universal language of cinema, and this means that the "expressiveness" of the film must come from questions of *style*, such as the length of time that a shot is held, focusing, and so on. The goal of this section of the essay belongs more in the realm of aesthetics than in linguistics or semiology. Pasolini is trying to affirm to the reader and to himself that film-making is, or can be, a poetic activity, and of a similar order to that of literary creation.

He enters the topic via a discussion of free indirect discourse: "Trasformerò dunque momentaneamente la domanda: 'È possibile nel cinema una "lingua della poesia"?', nella domanda: 'È possibile nel cinema la tecnica del discorso libero indiretto?'" ["I shall for a moment transform the question 'Is a "language of poetry" possible in the cinema?' into the question 'Is the technique of free indirect discourse possible in the cinema?'"]. There may be purely casual reasons for his doing this; he was at the time reading and reviewing a book called *Lo stile indiretto libero in italiano.*[15] The proposed review became "Intervento sul Discorso Libero Indiretto" (pp. 85–107). This essay distinguishes between two types of free indirect discourse: in one type, the author adopts the language of his character, which is different from his own, "e la poesia, in quanto lirismo o espressività, nasce dalla contaminazione, nell'urto tra due anime, talvolta profondamente diverse" ["and the poetry, as lyricism or expressiveness, arises from the contamination, in the collision of two sometimes very different minds"]; this he calls "discorso libero indiretto" ["free indirect discourse"]. The other type is where the author either gives the character his own language, or chooses a character whose language is the same as his own; this he calls "monologo interiore" ["interior monologue"].[16] Certainly Pasolini sees free indirect discourse in terms not so much of narrative technique or perspective as of language: it is "lessicale piú che grammaticale" ["lexical rather than grammatical"]. The style may be used as a pretext in which

> i personaggi siano una pseudo-oggettivazione dell'autore, o i personaggi siano dei meccanismi per esprimere, in linguaggio sostanzialmente paritetico, le tesi dell'autore, o infine, inconsciamente, i personaggi vivano perfettamente allo stesso modo il mondo sociale e ideologico dell'autore.

> [the characters are a pseudo-objectification of the author, or the characters are devices for expressing the ideas of the author, in a language similar to his own, or finally the characters live out exactly the same social and ideological world as the author's.]

When this is all transferred to "Il 'cinema di poesia'", there is the slight alteration that in "Intervento" "poesia" is assigned to "discorso indiretto libero", while in "Il 'cinema di poesia'" it is assigned to the "monologo interiore".

Pasolini then applies this theory to cinema, and in doing so he makes, I think, a mistake that needs to be cleared up. He says that "il discorso diretto" (and he means in written narrative) "corrisponde, nel cinema, alla 'soggettiva'" (a shot in a film that is taken from the point of view of one of the characters in the film) ["direct speech corresponds, in the cinema, to a 'subjective shot'"]. Here I think he is wrong, for when the camera (as "objective" narrator) films a character speaking, this is best understood as being analogous to those moments in a novel when an "objective" third-person narrator relates, in direct speech, what a character says. But when, in a film, the viewpoint for the narrative becomes that of one of the characters in the narrative (in other words, in an "inquadratura soggettiva"), *then* we might say that this is analogous to the use of free indirect discourse in a written narrative. The whole question is rather more complicated than it might at first appear, but it seems safe to say that Pasolini's identification of "direct speech" and "subjective shot" is hasty and erroneous.[17]

He next asserts: "Che [...] anche al cinema sia possibile un discorso libero indiretto è certo: chiamiamola 'soggettiva libera indiretta'" [That (...) it is possible to have free indirect discourse in the cinema too is certain: let us call it the 'free indirect subjective shot'"]. It is not clear exactly what he means by this. Since, as I have said, "discorso indiretto libero" is closest to "soggettiva", the parallel being set up by Pasolini will not work as straightforwardly as he is asserting. It is probably necessary to understand Pasolini as using the terms "discorso indiretto libero" and "soggettiva libera indiretta" very loosely, to cover two quite different things: on the one hand, cases where authors (in film and prose) blend the point of view of the narration with that of one of the characters in the narrative, and, on the other hand, cases where authors use some stylistic device to express, through the narration, the feelings, the vision, the perspective, the modes of perception of one of the characters in the narrative. It is hard to find Pasolini explicitly pointing to examples of the first kind.

Perhaps an example, which he suggests himself, in passing, and not as part of his argument, can be found in *Il deserto rosso*:

> La sequenza del sogno: che, dopo tanta squisitezza coloristica, è improvvisamente concepita quasi in un ovvio technicolor (a imitare, o meglio, a rivivere, attraverso una "soggettiva libera indiretta" l'idea fumettistica che ha un bambino delle spiagge dei tropici).

> [The dream sequence: which, after so much subtlety of colour, is suddenly conceived in an almost obvious technicolor (to imitate, or rather to relive, by means of "free indirect subjective shooting", the comic-book idea that a child has of tropical beaches).]

Pasolini, however, chooses examples of the second kind: shots in *Il deserto rosso* where we see the world in a way that suggests the neuroticism of Giuliana, and that are, Pasolini maintains, a pretext for artistic self-expression on the part of Antonioni; similar shots where Bertolucci disguises his own vision behind the neurotic point of view of Gina in *Prima della rivoluzione*, and aspects of

Godard's style. Moreover, Pasolini denies the existence of truly "subjective" cinematography:

> Casi di sparizioni totali dell'autore in un personaggio, del resto, nella storia del cinema, io non sarei in grado—fino ai primi anni sessanta—di citarne: un film cioè che sia una intera "soggettiva libera indiretta" in quanto tutta la vicenda venga narrata attraverso il personaggio, in una assoluta interiorizzazione del suo sistema interno di allusioni, non mi pare esista.

> [Besides, I don't think I could come up with any cases of the total disappearance of the author in his character, up to the early 1960s: that is to say, I don't think there exists a film shot entirely in the "free indirect subjective", with the whole story being narrated through that character, in a complete interiorization of his internal system of allusions.]

It is not easy to be sure what qualifications he requires ("assoluta interiorizzazione", and so on), but the description would fit a film that was shot as a "soggettiva", rather than as a "soggettiva libera indiretta", and very famous examples do exist: *The Lady in the Lake* by Robert Montgomery, and the first part of *Dark Passage* by Delmer Daves.

Perhaps the main reason why many of these considerations are not taken into account in Pasolini's essay is that he is mainly interested in deciding whether the "soggettiva libera indiretta" (in the second, the looser, of my definitions) is a linguistic or a stylistic device, and how far it parallels the essentially linguistic emphasis he gives to "discorso indiretto libero". First of all, he says, the "soggettiva libera indiretta" cannot be a "monologo interiore" "in quanto il cinema non ha le possibilità d'interiorizzazione e d'astrazione che ha la parola" ["because the cinema does not offer the possibilities for interiorization and abstraction that words have"] (earlier, he gave this as the reason for the "expressive" quality of cinematic language). For reasons more germane to his discussion of "discorso indiretto libero", however, Pasolini finds that there is no dialect or idiolect for the "author" to adopt in a film, whose language is "per forza interdialettale e internazionale: perché gli occhi sono uguali in tutto il mondo" ["necessarily interdialectal and international, because eyes are the same all over the world"]. Although he says that "lo 'sguardo' di un contadino" ["the 'look' of a peasant"] and that of a "borghese colto" ["cultivated member of the middle classes"] are distinguishable, he maintains that "tutto ciò non è istituzionalizzabile, è puramente induttivo" ["all that cannot be institutionalized, it is purely inductive"], and that there may be social and psychological differences but not a linguistic one: the film-maker's activity "non può essere linguistica ma stilistica" ["cannot be linguistic, only stylistic"]. The arguments are less important than the point of arrival, which is that these stylistic procedures constitute "certi modi tipici del 'linguaggio della poesia'" ["certain modes typical of the 'language of poetry'"]. The "soggettiva libera indiretta" liberates

> le possibilità espressive compresse dalla tradizionale convenzione narrativa, in una specie di ritorno alle origini: fino a ritrovare nei mezzi tecnici del cinema l'originaria qualità onirica, barbarica, irregolare, aggressiva, visionaria.
>
> [The free indirect subjective technique (liberates) the expressive possibilities suppressed by the traditional narrative convention, in a sort of return to origins: to the extent of rediscovering in the technical devices of cinema its archaic dream-like, barbaric, irregular, aggressive and visionary quality.]

Pasolini's point of arrival is in essence identical to the aesthetic and ideological position with which he identifies in "Nuove questioni linguistiche" and to which I referred earlier in this essay. The linguistic and semiological parts of his discourse appear to be inessential decorations on a main theme. "Il 'cinema di poesia'", however, carries this theme into a further stage of development. The rest of the essay works towards a definition of this stylistic language of "poesia" as neo-capitalist bourgeois formalism.

In order to demonstrate that "il fondamento del film [*Il deserto rosso*] sia sostanzialmente questo formalismo" ["the basis of the film is really this formalism"], he examines "una particolare operazione ["a particular stylistic device"]. This stylistic device is one of devoting so much attention to shots of objects or figures that these become obsessively insistent, in a "mito della sostanziale e angosciosa bellezza autonoma delle cose" ["myth of the anguished autonomous beauty of things"]. "La legge interna al film delle 'inquadrature ossessive' dimostra dunque chiaramente la prevalenza di un formalismo come mito finalmente liberato, e quindi poetico" ["So the law of 'obsessive shots' operating in the film clearly shows the prevalence of a formalism that is a myth finally liberated, and therefore poetic"]. Antonioni achieves this "liberazione" through the use of "soggettiva libera indiretta" "perché ha sostituito, in blocco, la visione del mondo di una nevrotica, con la sua propria visione delirante di estetismo: sostituzione in blocco giustificata dalla possibile analogia delle due visioni" ["because he has replaced *en bloc* a neurotic woman's vision of the world with his own deliriously aestheticizing vision, a replacement justified by the possible analogy between the two visions"]. The concept of "inquadrature ossessive" will be frequently invoked by Pasolini, and also the concept of analogy between the stylistic devices of a director and the psychological state of one of the characters. Both are critical interpretations on the part of Pasolini: their validity is not self-evident,[18] and it is hard to see what is particularly new in a formalism that has often been a characteristic of the Italian cinema. Moreover, on the theoretical level the judgement that a shot is held for an obsessively long time is perhaps arbitrary, and only seems so self-evident to Pasolini because he is using as a norm the realist "codes" of Hollywood, and of Italian Neo-realism as enshrined in the self-effacing styles of Rossellini and De Sica, and on a more popular level in Italian film-making in the Fifties. This would partly explain the use of the concept of "liberation", as being a liberation from an implied norm of what he calls prose narrative in the cinema. The assertion that these stylistic effects are derived from a use of the "soggettiva libera indiretta" would carry real theoretical validity only if the concept of the "indiretto libero" were rigorously defined. However, both in the case of *Il deserto rosso*, and in the analysis of *Prima della rivoluzione* (which follows, and is on similar lines), Pasolini says that the use of "soggettiva libera indiretta" is "pretestuale", a pretext for poetic self-expression on the part of the director, and that what is being expressed is a delight in artistic form. If the theoretical machinery of Pasolini's argument is defective, then all one is left with is a series of apt critical interpretations: that the directors are using stylistic cinematic devices to express the psychological turmoil of their characters, and drawing analogies between such a vision and their own interests in form and beauty—all of which, it seems to me, amounts to things that critics have been saying about film-makers throughout the history of the cinema.

Pasolini, however, does take the argument an interesting stage further, without, unfortunately, giving detailed references. Beneath such a film as has been attributed to Antonioni and Bertolucci scorre l'altro film—quello che l'autore avrebbe fatto anche senza il pretesto della *mimesis visiva* del suo protagonista: un film totalmente e liberamente di carattere espressivo-espressionistico.

[runs the other film—the one the author would have made even without resorting to the pretext of imitating the point of view of its protagonist: a film totally and freely expressive-expressionist.]

In these films, their

ossessività contraddice non solo la norma del linguaggio cinematografico comune, ma la stessa regolamentazione interna del film in quanto "soggettiva libera indiretta". È il momento, cioè, in cui il linguaggio, seguendo un'ispirazione diversa e magari piú autentica, si libera dalla funzione, e si presenta come "linguaggio in se stesso", stile.

[obsessiveness contradicts not only normal cinematographic language, but the whole internal ordering of the film as a "free indirect subjective". This is where the language, following a different and possibly more authentic inspiration, frees itself from its function, and offers itself as "language for itself", style.]

Here Pasolini is laying a theoretical foundation for the existence of something like *poésie pure* in cinema, linking it, therefore, with a whole literary tradition that goes back through the twentieth-century Italian poetry he inherited to his early idol, Rimbaud.

Moreover, the conclusions he draws from this follow coherently from the premisses: that the kind of "tradizione tecnico-stilistica" ["technical-stylistic tradition"] that he has identified in Antonioni, Bertolucci and Godard forms a "lingua [...] del cinema di poesia" ["language of the cinema of poetry"] that is separate and distinct (he uses the word "diacronica") from the "lingua della narrativa cinematografica" ["language of film narrative"], and that the two "lingue" will necessarily continue to diverge further and further, as has happened, he maintains, in literature. The "stilemi cinematografici" ["cinematic stylemes"] that go to make up the poetic language of the cinema could be catalogued in linguistic terms forming a "'prosodia' non ancora codificata e funzionante, ma la cui normatività è già potenziale" ["still to be codified and applied 'prosody', which already has normative potential"]. One such "stilema" could be encapsulated in the notion "fare sentire la macchina" ["draw attention to the camera"]; poetic film-makers do, prose "narrators" do not. Unfortunately, in a series of about-turns that are a characteristic of this essay, Pasolini notices that in the great

> poemi cinematografici da Charlot, a Mizoguchi, a Bergman, la caratteristica generale e comune era che "non si sentiva la macchina": non erano girati, cioè, secondo un canone di "lingua del cinema di poesia".

> [film poems from Chaplin to Mizoguchi or Bergman, the common feature was that "you didn't notice the camera"; that is to say, they were not shot according to the rules of the "language of the cinema of poetry".]

"Questo significa che non erano poesie, ma racconti: il cinema classico è stato ed è narrativo" ["This means they were not poems but stories; classic cinema was and still is narrative"]. One detects here the influence of current Parisian debates in *Cinéthique*. Pasolini describes a "code" (that of "fare sentire la macchina" ["making one notice the camera"]), but, in doing so, defines its characteristics against a "norm" that is not made explicit—and I shall italicize those parts of his sentence that illustrate this:

> La macchina, dunque, si sente, per delle buone ragioni: l'alternarsi di obiettivi diversi, un 25 o un 300 sulla *stessa* faccia, lo *sperpero* dello zum, coi suoi obbiettivi *altissimi*, che stanno *addosso* alle cose *dilatandole come pani troppo levigati*, i controluce *continui e fintamente casuali* con i loro barbagli in macchina, i movimenti di macchina in mano, le carrellate *esasperate*, i montaggi *sbagliati* per ragioni espressive, gli attacchi *irritanti*, le immobilità *interminabili su una stessa* immagine ecc. ecc., tutto questo codice tecnico è nato quasi per *insofferenza* alle *regole*, per un *bisogno di libertà irregolare e provocatoria*, per un diversamente *autentico* o delizioso gusto dell'anarchia: ma è divenuto subito canone, patrimonio linguistico e prosodico, che interessa contemporaneamente tutte le cinematografie mondiali.

> [You notice the camera for good reasons: the changing from one lens to another, a wide-angle or a telephoto on the *same* face, *excessive use* of the zoom, with its *very high telephoto* settings, standing *right up against* things, *blowing them up like over-leavened loaves of bread, endless and not altogether casual* backlighting with its

dazzling flashes in the camera, hand-held shots, *overdone* track-
ing shots, *wrong* editing for expressive purposes, *irritatingly
abrupt* openings to shots, holding the *same image interminably*, etc.,
etc. This whole technical code grew almost out of an *impatience*
with the *rules*, a *need for an unregulated and provocative freedom*, a
newly *authentic* taste for or delight in anarchy. But it straightaway
became the new rule, a linguistic and stylistic property for
everybody in the cinema the world over to use nowadays.]

The norm is obviously Neo-realism, and what is sometimes
referred to nowadays as "classic realist cinema".[19] In asserting that
the new style of film-making is "formalist", Pasolini is assuming
that a concern for "form" was not part of the previous "norm". In
other words, he is expressing an interpretation of the procedures of
Neo-realism and "realist" cinema, and an interpretation that comes
as a surprise from someone purportedly analysing the "language"
of cinema and its "stylistic codes". Pasolini never really, in the rest
of his theorizing about cinema as the language of reality, returns to
the potential implications of the notion of "narrative language" or
narrative codes that, in "Il 'cinema di poesia'", he applies to
"prose" cinema.

The next stage in the argument is to assert that the cinema has
always been in advance of literature, and so "i film neo-decadenti
e neo-formalistici di Fellini o Antonioni hanno prefigurato il revival neo-avanguardistico italiano o lo stingimento del neo-reali-
smo" ["the neo-decadent and neo-formalist films of Fellini or
Antonioni heralded the Italian Neo-avant-garde revival and the
waning of Neo-realism"].

> Insomma, in un quadro generale, la formazione di una tradizione
> di "lingua della poesia del cinema", si pone come spia di una forte
> e generale ripresa del formalismo, quale produzione media e
> tipica dello sviluppo culturale del neocapitalismo.

> [All in all, the creation of a tradition of "a language of poetry of
> cinema" is a foretaste of a vigorous general renewal of formalism
> as the typical average product of the cultural development of
> neo-capitalism.]

The essay, therefore, concludes on a Lukácsian note, and one that
is to be taken up in Pasolini's polemic with the avant-garde, "La
fine dell'avanguardia":

Tutto ciò fa parte di quel movimento generale del recupero, da parte della cultura borghese, del terreno perduto nella battaglia col marxismo e con la sua possibile rivoluzione. E si inserisce in quel movimento, in qualche modo grandioso, dell'evoluzione, possiamo dire antropologica, della borghesia, secondo le linee di una "rivoluzione interna" del capitalismo: cioè il neocapitalismo che mette in discussione e modifica le proprie strutture, e che, nella fattispecie, riattribuisce ai poeti una funzione tardo-umanistica: il mito e la coscienza tecnica della forma.

[All that belongs to the general movement in which bourgeois culture recouped the territory lost in the battle with Marxism and its proffered revolution. And it fits into the bourgoisie's rather grandiose movement of what we might call anthropological evolution, along the lines of an "internal revolution" within capitalism: that is to say, neo-capitalism questioning and modifying its own structures and, in this case, re-attributing to poets a late humanistic function, that of the myth and technical self-consciousness of form.]

"Il 'cinema di poesia'" stands apart from the rest of Pasolini's theoretical writings on the cinema, for although it introduces itself as an attempt to apply the disciplines of semiology to the cinema, in actual fact it deals with aesthetic and ultimately ideological questions. But Pasolini's presence at the Pesaro round-table, where he delivered his paper in the summer of 1965, put him in contact with those who really were concerning themselves with semiology, and with the semiology of cinema in particular. His next major theoretical essay, "La lingua scritta della realtà" (pp. 202–30), addresses a number of semiological questions directly, and forms part of a debate with other researchers, particularly Metz, Garroni and Eco.

Pasolini asserts that the cinema is an audio-visual technique for reproducing reality. Hence he fastens onto the notion of a technical means of reproduction, and compares it with symbolic, conventional language. Briefly summarizing, we may say that: cinema communicates because the reality it reproduces is meaningful, and is therefore a language; and expression, in the cinema, hence poetry, comes from the adoption of stylistic devices during the process of reproduction.

If I were to continue, at this point, to outline Pasolini's theories without comment, a lot of confusion might arise. So I shall here make some distinctions that Pasolini does not make, and which will supply a terminology with which to describe Pasolini's theories.

Pasolini notices that the signs of the cinema are not arbitrary, and that they reproduce, or seem to, a large number of the qualities of the objects filmed. I should like to call the object filmed the "referent". Pasolini's awareness of a more than arbitrary link between sign and referent (even though he does not use the term or concept of referent) is never fully developed into a rejection of a strictly Saussurian paradigm, in which only the relationship of signifier to signified is dealt with. C. S. Peirce offers a typology of signs in which non-arbitrary relations between sign and referent are accounted for. The type that most closely fits the cinema is that of the index. The shadow thrown onto the screen in a cinema is mechanically and chemically *caused* by whatever was placed in front of the camera lens. The film is a record, and its relation to its referent is indexical, and the fact that this is the case means that the addressee has a special relationship to the referent, which he would not have through the mediation of a symbolic or iconic sign. Perhaps, indeed, indexicality strongly determines the signified of a sign, since the addressee has to take cognizance not only of what the sign signifies, but also of the ontology of the referent (in "Tabella" Pasolini refers to all this in connection with Mishima's suicide on "live" television). But a question is raised that Pasolini never attempts to answer. If I were to point a film camera at a bank robber shooting a security guard, I could claim to be carrying out the first steps towards "reproducing reality", or recording it. But if I went to a casting agency, hired two actors, and paid one of them to *pretend* to shoot the other, then would I be reproducing the referent, "reality", or rather a *performance*? The referent in the whole semiological endeavour might still be: "a bank robbery gone awry...", but the semiosis would not be so direct—my "sign" would be the image projected on the screen, meaning whatever the context made it mean, having as its referent, to which it was related *indexically*, the actions of men employed to pretend to be robber and guard, which in turn would be related *iconically* to a referent, which in this case would be robber and guard (either ones who really did exist, or imaginary ones), one shooting and the other dying. Hence, "meanings" (the axis of signified in the sign) are not simply "reproduced" in feature films, and referents are not necessarily linked in indexical chains with each other. The "reproduction of reality" passes through processes of mimesis, of conventionality and of complex mediation that are not accounted for in Pasolini's semiology, and which bring into play systems for generating "meaning" that are not reducible to inference from indexical signs.

Everybody knows this, surely, but Pasolini can still say:

> Il cinema non evoca la realtà, come la lingua letteraria; non copia la realtà, come la pittura; non mima la realtà, come il teatro. Il cinema *riproduce* la realtà: immagine e suono! Riproducendo la realtà, che cosa fa il cinema? Il cinema esprime la realtà con la realtà. Se io voglio rappresentare Sanguineti, non ricorro a evocazioni da stregone (la poesia) ma uso lo stesso Sanguineti. O, se Sanguineti non vuole, prendo un seminarista col naso lungo, o un ombrellaio coi panni della domenica: prendo, cioè, un altro Sanguineti. Non esco comunque dal cerchio della realtà. Esprimo la realtà—e cioè mi distacco da lei—ma la esprimo con la realtà stessa. ("Avanguardia", p. 139)

> [Cinema does not evoke reality, like literary language; it does not copy reality, like painting; it does not mime reality, like the theatre. Cinema *reproduces* reality: image and sound! In reproducing reality, what does cinema do? Cinema expresses reality with reality. If I want to represent Sanguineti, I don't reach for magical evocations (poetry) but I use Sanguineti himself. Or, if Sanguineti refuses, I take a student priest with a long nose, or an umbrella-seller in his Sunday best; I take, in other words, another Sanguineti. However, I don't step out of the circle of reality. I express reality—and that is, I detach myself from it—but I express it with reality itself.]

Perhaps, therefore, one may best formulate one of the principal pillars of Pasolini's theory of the "lingua della realtà" ["language of reality"] thus: the indexical reproduction of an iconically faithful representation of objects, persons and events guarantees that the signs so produced convey the same signified as those objects, persons and events carry in our non-cinematic experience of them.[20] In this guise, Pasolini's position would be close to that of a phenomenological "realist" like André Bazin. Human beings "decipher" reality, says Pasolini, though without it being clear exactly what he means by this.[21] Where human action is concerned, we can have a clear idea of what he wants to say: "Le prime informazioni di un uomo io le ho dal linguaggio della sua fisionomia, del suo

comportamento, [...] della sua azione" ["My first source of information about a man is the language of his physiognomy, of his
behaviour, (...) of his action"]. Human action in reality, he says,
forms a language, and so:

> La semiologia del linguaggio dell'azione umana [...] verrebbe
> poi a essere la più concreta delle filosofie possibili. [...] E non è chi
> non veda [...] quanto di comune avrebbe una simile filosofia [...]
> con la fenomenologia: con il metodo di Husserl, magari lungo la
> linea esistenzialista sartriana.

> [The semiology of the language of human action would turn out
> to be the most concrete philosophy possible. (...) And no one can
> fail to see (...) how much such a philosophy would have in
> common with phenomenology, with Husserl's method, possibly
> along Sartre's existentialist lines.]

But Pasolini goes further, as is demonstrated by the title of one of
his essays, "Res sunt nomina", in which he says: "La realtà è un
'insieme' la cui struttura è la struttura di un linguaggio" ["Reality
is a 'totality' whose structure is the structure of a language"]; "la
realtà come linguaggio le cui parole sono le cose" ["reality as a
language whose words are things"]. In the same essay he gives an
example of what he means:

> Prendiamo questo Joaquim: egli si presenta ai miei occhi, in un
> ambiente (la spiaggia di Barra, sotto il Corcovado), e si esprime,
> prima con la pura e semplice presenza fisica, il suo corpo; poi con
> la mimica (il modo di camminare non solo espressivo in sé, ma
> reso appositamente tale per comunicare certe cose e in un certo
> modo all'osservatore), infine con la lingua orale. Ma questi tre
> mezzi del suo esprimersi non sono che tre momenti di un solo
> linguaggio: il linguaggio di Joaquim vivente. [...] Joaquim è una
> parola o un insieme di parole (nomen), di cui io sono decifratore.
> Ora trasportiamo il corpo di Joaquim [...] dalla realtà della
> spiaggia di Barra allo schermo. Ammettiamo che questo schermo
> sia quello del cinema e non quello di un film: e che quindi si tratti
> di un piano-sequenza infinito come soggettiva dell'osservatore.
> Ammesso questo, c'è forse qualche differenza nel mio modo di
> decifrare Joaquim nella realtà e nello schermo? [...] Joaquim
> vivente è segno di se stesso. (pp. 262–63)

> [Let us take this Joaquim: he stands before my eyes in a setting
> (the beach of Barra, beneath the Corcovado), and he expresses

himself, first of all with his pure and simple physical presence, his
body; then with his gestures (his way of walking, not just expressive in itself, but deliberately made so in order to communicate
certain things and in a certain way to the observer), finally with
his oral language. But these three means of his self-expression are
but three facets of a single language: the language of Joaquim
living. (...) Joaquim is a word or a collection of words (nomen),
which I decipher. Now let us transport the body of Joaquim (...)
from the reality of the beach of Barra to the screen. Let us make
this screen that of the cinema, not that of a film, so that we are
talking about an infinite subjective sequence-shot from the point
of view of the observer. Granted this, is there perhaps any
difference between the way I decipher Joaquim in reality and on
the screen? (...) Joaquim living is a sign of himself.]

The notion of Joaquim as a sign in which signifier, signified and
referent (though the last is a category Pasolini does not use) are
identical raises ontological questions, as we shall see. But the
problem he is attempting to elucidate is this: can one hypothesize
an identical system of attributing meaning to reality as it is in
everyday experience and to reality as it is represented in the
cinema? There are enormous deficiencies in the way the question
is posed, but given Pasolini's affirmative answer to it, then the
theory of reality as a language can be built upon it. Cinema, by
recording the language of reality, carries out an operation similar
to "writing", which records the spoken language. Hence we have
a further parallel: the written word is to speech what the cinema is
to the language of reality. Cinema is, therefore, "la lingua scritta
della realtà" ["the written language of reality"]. And, even more
audaciously: "L'intera vita [...] è un cinema naturale e vivente: in
ciò, è linguisticamente l'equivalente della lingua orale nel suo
momento naturale e biologico" ["The whole of life is a natural,
living cinema, and for that reason it is the linguistic equivalent of
the oral language in its natural and biological stage"].

It is a small step from this to the affirmation, in "La fine
dell'avanguardia", that "in qualsiasi momento, la realtà è 'cinema
in natura': manca soltanto una macchina da presa per riprodurla,
cioè scriverla attraverso la riproduzione di ciò che essa è" ["at any
given moment, reality is 'cinema in nature'; it just lacks a camera to
reproduce it, that is to say, to write it down by reproducing what
it is"]. And from that to: "Il cinema è dunque virtualmente un

infinito 'piano-sequenza': infinito come la realtà che può essere riprodotta da una invisibile macchina da presa" ["Cinema is thus virtually an infinite sequence-shot: infinite like reality, which is capable of being reproduced by an invisible camera"]. In "Osservazioni sul piano-sequenza" he refers to the eight-millimetre film shot by a bystander of John Kennedy's assassination: it is a "piano-sequenza", from one point of view, and is in the present. If you had a number of similar films, shot from different points of view, and you made a montage from them, you would have created a narrative, which would have thrown everything into the past, and destroyed the presentness of the simple "piano-sequenza". (One could also express this in terms of montage interfering with the total indexicality of a filmed record.) Life, as experienced, in the present, is a "piano-sequenza" which only achieves "senso" ["sense"] when it is completed by death. This latter thought may be a *préciosité*, but it has a bearing on something that Pasolini says in "La fine dell'avanguardia" (pp. 142–43). He refers approvingly to an interview Barthes gave, in which he suggested that the cinema may belong to a category of communication dealing with larger signifying entities than the isolated and discontinuous signifieds of articulated language. This leads Pasolini to reflect that montage puts cinema into the rhetorical category of a metonymic art, and to follow Barthes in asserting:

> Il segno dominante di ogni arte metonimica—e quindi sintagma-tica—è la volontà dell'autore a esprimere un "senso", piuttosto che dei significati. [...] Quindi a evocare sempre direttamente la realtà, che è la sede del *senso* trascendente i significati.

> [The dominant characteristic of any metonymic—and hence syntagmatic—art is the desire of the author to express a "sense", rather than a number of meanings. (...) Hence always directly to evoke reality, which is what bears the *sense* transcending the meanings.]

He then quotes Barthes:

> Il senso [...] non è racchiuso nel significato. Il rapporto tra significante e significato (cioè il segno) sembra da principio il fondamento stesso di ogni riflessione "semiologica": ma in seguito si è portati ad avere del "senso" una visione molto più ampia...

[The sense is not contained in the meaning. The relation between signifier and signified (that is to say, the sign) seems at first the very basis for any "semiological" reflection; but one is subsequently led to have a much broader view of "sense"...]

Pasolini finds the ultimate source of this "senso" in reality, just as, in "Battute sul cinema", he transforms Barthes's statement: "Se io volessi ricondurre questa geniale intuizione di Barthes alla mia teoria [...], direi: 'Non è il cinema un'arte metonimica, ma è la realtà che è metonimica'" ["If I wanted to reconcile this brilliant intuition of Barthes with my theory (...), I would say: 'It is not cinema that is a metonymic art, but reality which is metonymic'": p. 233]. Returning to the question of cinema as the "lingua scritta della realtà", we find in "Battute sul cinema" the following reflection:

Il linguaggio della realtà, fin che era naturale, era fuori della nostra coscienza; ora che ci appare "scritto" attraverso il cinema, non può non richiedere una coscienza. Il linguaggio scritto della realtà, ci farà sapere prima di tutto che cos' è il linguaggio della realtà; e finirà infine col modificare il nostro pensiero su di essa, facendo dei nostri rapporti fisici, almeno, con la realtà, dei rapporti culturali. (p. 235)

[The language of reality, as long as it was natural, was outside our consciousness; now that we see it "written" in the cinema, it cannot help requiring a consciousness. The written language of reality will teach us first of all what is the language of reality, and it will end up by modifying our way of thinking about it, turning our physical, at least, relations with reality into cultural ones.]

Pasolini's tendency to locate all the sources of meaning for the cinema (except those prosodic devices that lead to "expression") in reality led Umberto Eco to accuse him of ignoring the fundamental goal of semiology, "che è di ridurre eventualmente i fatti di natura a fenomeni di cultura, e non di ricondurre i fatti di cultura a fenomeni di natura" ["which is to reduce the facts of nature to cultural phenomena, not to turn cultural facts into natural phenomena: *La struttura assente*, p. 152]. But it is easy to see how Pasolini might reply that he was doing quite the opposite, making reality a purely cultural entity: "Perché tutte le mie caotiche pagine su questo argomento [...] tendono a portare la Semiologia alla definitiva culturizzazione della natura" ["Because all my chaotic pages on this topic (...) tend to direct Semiology towards the definitive culturalization of nature": "Codice", p. 283]. For Pasolini, however, the culturalization of nature means more the fact that we perceive reality as speaking to us than that reality itself is a cultural construct.

This process of turning reality itself into a cultural, linguistic phenomenon acquires impetus from the concept of a "struttura che vuole essere altra struttura" ["one structure that wants to be another structure"], which is part of the title of an essay Pasolini wrote about screenplays, "La sceneggiatura come 'struttura che vuol essere altra struttura'":

> La caratteristica principale del "segno" della tecnica della sceneg-giatura, è quella di alludere al significato attraverso due strade diverse, concomitanti e riconfluenti. Ossia: il segno della sceneg-giatura allude al significato secondo la strada normale di tutte le lingue scritte e specificamente dei gerghi letterari, ma, nel tempo stesso, esso allude a quel medesimo significato, rimandando il destinatario a un altro segno, quello del film da farsi. (p. 194)

> [The main characteristic of the "sign" in screenplay-writing is that it alludes to its meaning by two different paths which run alongside and into each other. In other words: the sign of the screenplay alludes to its meaning in the normal manner of all written languages, and specifically literary jargons, but at the same time it alludes to the same meaning by referring the ad-dressee to another sign, that of the film to be made.]

Again, Pasolini prefers not to include in his analysis the con-cept of what the viewer sees as being a *performance*, for which the screenplay would be instructions to a performer (or cameraman), from which the reader would deduce things which would allow her or him to construct images in her or his mind, and mentally to "hear" the written dialogue spoken. Instead, he pursues the con-cept of the screenplay as "wanting" to move from the verbal to the language of reality. This concept was so attractive to Pasolini that he reprinted part of a written interview with Sergio Arecco in *Empirismo eretico*, calling it "Il non verbale come altra verbalità" ["The non-verbal as another verbality"], where he reformulates his theory of the language of reality in terms of a comparison with written language:

> Sicché, in sostanza, i "segni" delle lingue verbali non fanno altro che *tradurre* i "segni" delle lingue non verbali: o, nella fattispecie, i segni delle lingue scritto-parlate non fanno altro che *tradurre* i segni del Linguaggio della Realtà.

> [So that basically the "signs" of verbal languages do no more than *translate* the "signs" of the non-verbal languages; or, in this particular case, the signs of the written-spoken languages do no more than *translate* the signs of the Language of Reality.]

This concept of "translation" leads to the formulation: "Le lingue scritto-parlate sono *traduzioni per evocazione*; le lingue audio-visive (cinema) sono *traduzioni per riproduzione*" ["The written-spoken languages are *translations by evocation*; the audio-visual languages (cinema) are *translations by reproduction*"]. And for one moment reality seems about to be reduced to a process of semiosis:

> Che cosa fa il "segno" del "significato": lo "significa"? È una tautologia. Lo indica? non è scientifico. Vi si identifica? È vecchia bega tra "nomen" e "res" ecc. ecc. In realtà non c'è "significato": *perché anche il significato è un segno*. Mi si consenta la libertà del poeta che dice liberamente cose libere! Sí, questa quercia che ho davanti a me, non è il "significato" del segno scritto-parlato "quercia": no, questa quercia fisica qui davanti ai miei sensi, è essa stessa un segno: un segno non certo scritto-parlato, ma iconico-vivente o come altro si voglia definirlo.

> [What does the "sign" do with the "signified": does it "signify" it? It's tautological. Does it indicate it? that's not scientific. Does it identify itself with it? That's an old squabble between "nomen" and "res", etc. In fact there is no "signified", *because the signified too is a sign*. Allow me the freedom of the poet to say free things freely! Yes, this oak tree in front of me is not the "signified" of the written-spoken sign "oak tree"; no, this physical oak tree here before my senses is itself a sign: not, certainly, a written-spoken one, but an iconic-living one, or however you want to define it.]

Pasolini is right in saying that the real "quercia" is not the "significato" of the word "quercia". I, in this case, would say that the real oak tree is the *referent* of the verbal sign. But Pasolini's signs do not have referents, and can only denote other signs. I suspect that this is merely a theoretical oversight in his system, and that he failed to notice that the notion of signs only denoting other signs is incompatible with a statement like that quoted earlier, where he explained that "Joaquim vivente è segno di se stesso." The use of "vivente" for Joaquim, and for the "quercia", Pasolini's frequently expressed love of "reality", and the definition given in "La paura del naturalismo" ("Per realtà intendo dire il mondo fisico e sociale in cui si vive" ["By reality I mean the physical and social world we live in"]), lead one to doubt whether he really intends the total abolition of the ontological status of referents. What most concerns him is on the one hand that referents in their turn "speak" (by which he means that you can deduce things about a man by looking at him), and so may be used as signs, and on the other hand that you could say that a real object, taken as a sign, has as its referent itself: "Ora, che cos' è la presenza? È... è qualcosa che parla da se stessa... È un linguaggio" ["Now, what is presence? It is... it is something which speaks by itself... It is a language: "Avanguardia", p. 139]. If I am correct, then the notion of "traduzione per riproduzione" rests on an equivocation. The general drift of Pasolini's theories leads one to interpret him as implying that the cinema "reproduces" the referents of the language of reality (which are also its signs), and that these carry with them into the cinema all the possibilities for "signification" that they had "before" they were "reproduced". Nevertheless, this quibble apart, the concept of "traduzione per riproduzione" focuses attention on Pasolini's hypothesis of one language (that of cinema) being isomorphic with another (that of reality).

A large section of the essay "La lingua scritta della realtà" begins a public dialogue with Christian Metz, whose essay "Le Cinéma: langue ou langage?" led Pasolini to rethink some of his ideas. Metz says that the cinema is a manifestation of "langage sans langue"; that it lacks the "double articulation" that Martinet says is essential for language;[22] and furthermore that it is articulated syntactically, but not paradigmatically (it puts together items in sequence which have meaning, but it has no "vocabulary" from which to select items which derive their meaning from their difference from other items). Pasolini's main interest lay in the concept of double articulation, where he took issue with Metz, saying that the first level of articulation of cinematic language was that of the "shot", while the second level was that of the objects in reality that made up the content of the shot: hence the shot was the moneme,[23] and the objects photographed were the phonemes, which Pasolini called "cinèmi". This led to detailed rebuttals from Umberto Eco (*La struttura assente*, pp. 154–55) and Emilio Garroni,[24] both of whom pointed out that Pasolini's *cinèmi* could not be the "unità minime" ["minimal units"] of the language because they were infinite, or nearly, in number, and already endowed with meaning. As far as the whole theory of the language of reality was concerned, Eco criticized it because it failed to deal with the "iconic codes" according to which we give meaning to reality in conventionally agreed ways; Garroni denied that reality could be a code, and went further, complaining that Pasolini's position implied a "rinuncia alla concretezza ideologica [...] in favore di una sorta di diseredato e candido sottolinguaggio cosale, 'poetico', proprio perché sottolinguaggio e quindi pericolosamente incline al 'lirismo'" ["abandonment of ideological concreteness (...) in favour of a sort of disinherited and innocent sub-language of things, 'poetic' precisely because it is a sub-language, and hence dangerously close to 'lyricism'"].

"La lingua scritta della realtà" then proceeds to a "schema grammaticale della lingua del cinema" ["grammatical scheme of the language of cinema"], which I shall briefly summarize. The grammar has four "momenti" or "modi" [moments or modes]: (1) "Modi della riproduzione (o ortografici)" ["Modes of reproduction (or orthographic modes)"], which refers to the basic techniques of cinematography such as lighting and sound; (2) "Modi della sostantivazione" ["Noun modes"], the shot, or the moneme as an "insieme di cinèmi" ["collection of cinemes"]—it generally corresponds to what in verbal language would be called a "proposizione relativa" ["relative proposition"], for example: a schoolteacher who is teaching, or a number of pupils who are listening (Pasolini points out that moneme and shot do not necessarily coincide, for a sequence-shot might be an accumulation of monemes); (3) "Modi della qualificazione" ["Modes of qualification"], subdivided: (*a*) "profilmica" ["pro-filmic"], such as the "'trucco' degli oggetti e delle persone" ["make-up or the alteration of objects or people"], and (*b*) "filmica" ["filmic"], the choice of lens, distance from which to film—and this in turn leads to two categories of "qualificazione filmica" [filmic qualification]: (i) "passiva" ["passive"], where the camera moves and what is filmed does not (he calls this authorial action that is "lirico-soggettivo" ["lyrico-subjective"]), and (ii) "attiva" ["active"], where the

camera is still and what is filmed moves (he uses the term "realisti-co" ["realistic"] for this)—the words "active" and "passive" here referring to what is filmed, rather than to the filming process; (4) "Modi della verbalizzazione (o sintattici)" ["Verbal or syn-tactical modes"], which refers to the syntax of montage, and is subdivided into (*a*) "Montaggio denotativo" ["denotative mont-age"] where the result of the "aggiunzione" ["adding together"] of a shot of a teacher teaching and a shot of pupils listening would be "la frase 'il maestro insegna agli scolari'" ["the sentence 'the teacher teaches the pupils'"], and (*b*) "Il montaggio ritmico (o connotativo)" ["Rhythmic or connotative montage"], where the length of a shot might have connotations: if a shot is held much longer than necessary it carries "expressive" connotations, and the length of a shot taken in relation to the other shots in the film constitutes the "vero e proprio campo del montaggio ritmico" ["real field of rhythmic montage"]. Pasolini analyses, in turn, a passage from Olmi's *Il tempo si è fermato*, and Bertolucci's *Prima della rivoluzione*. Of the former, he concludes, after analysing eleven shots:

> La qualificazione profilmica, infatti, non esiste: che cosa significa questo? Che siamo davanti a un documentario, e che quindi l'autore non ha truccato in nessun modo la realtà [...]: l'ha lasciata intatta. La qualificazione filmica, poi, è tutta attiva o deponente (c'è un solo caso, ma leggerissimo, e forse discutibile, di passivi-tà). Il che significa che la macchina da presa non si sente, e che ciò che conta è l'azione reale. [...] Mai [...] una espressività ritmica predomina sul ritmo che nasce necessariamente dal montaggio denotativo.
>
> [There is in fact no pro-filmic qualification. What does this mean? That we are looking at a documentary, and that therefore the author has in no way altered reality (...): he has left it intact. The filmic qualification moreover is all active or deponent (there is just one example, but fleeting and perhaps questionable, of passivity). Which means that we do not notice the camera, and that what counts is the real action. (...) Never (...) does a rhythmic expressiveness predominate over the rhythm that arises neces-sarily from the denotative montage.]

The comparison with an analysis of thirteen shots from *Prima della rivoluzione* shows up in the latter the use of montage to render the reality filmed

passiva, cioè a far sentire l'attività della macchina da presa: cosí che la presenza del soggetto autore è assai prevalente sull'oggettività della realtà. Ad accentuare ancora di piú la soggettività del racconto, si ha una prevaricazione del montaggio espressivo, coi suoi ritmi non funzionali, sul montaggio denotativo, i cui ritmi sono per definizione funzionali.

[passive, that is to say, to make us notice the activity of the camera, so that the presence of the authorial subject prevails heavily over the objectivity of reality. The subjectivity of the narrative is further accentuated by the predominance of expressive montage, with its non-functional rhythms, over the denotative montage, whose rhythms are by definition functional.]

Olmi's film is prose, Bertolucci's *poesia*.

The importance of rhythm in montage is then taken up by Pasolini in another essay, "Teoria delle giunte", where he suggests that for the poetic and expressive purposes of film, what counts is the formal relations between spatial relationships in one shot and in another shot, and the temporal relationships between the length of one shot and the length of another. Spatially, it might be the relationship between "pieni e vuoti" ["filled in and blanks"] in one shot, and the "pieni e vuoti" in the next. These considerations lead to the theory of a "lingua spazio-temporale" ["spatio-temporal language"], an abstract artistic language running beneath the denotative language of reproduced reality, a return to a *poésie pure* of the cinema, to which I have already referred. This "code" of spatio-temporal relationships would bear comparison with Eisenstein's theories of montage, though Pasolini does not mention Eisenstein's name in this context.[25] The basis of Pasolini's spatio-temporal code is the "ritmema" ["rhythmeme"], the basic unit in the process of "successività spazio-temporale" ["spatio-temporal succession"], and he says in "La lingua scritta della realtà" (p. 218):

Il "ritmema" assume dunque nella lingua del cinema un valore particolare, sia nel montaggio comunicativo, che nel montaggio ritmico portato al limite dell'espressione. In quest' ultimo caso esso diventa la figura retorica principe del cinema, laddove in letteratura esso appare secondario o almeno in second' ordine.

[The "rhythmeme" therefore carries a particular value in the language of cinema, both in communicative montage and in rhythmic montage pushed to the limits of expression. In the latter case it becomes the cinema's principal rhetorical figure, whereas in literature it appears secondary or at least of a second order.]

Not only does this supply Pasolini with part of his theorization of a "linguaggio d'arte" ["language of art"], but it fuses with his whole theory of reality as a language which the cinema makes available to our consciousness through contemplation (as opposed to our active participation in life as we "live" it), producing an ideological interpretation of our relationship to this contemplated reality:

> Il barbaro non ha bisogno di illusioni per vivere, ossia per esprimersi. Ma dal momento in cui comincia a vivere la realtà come contemplazione (fin dal primo barlume di questa) e quindi ne inventa la successività e la spazio-temporalità, egli scopre la storia, cioè l'illusione. Di cui da quel momento in poi avrà sempre bisogno, e fonderà quindi su questo, e solo su questo l'inautenticità: l'alienazione prima contadina e poi piccolo-borghese. ("Tabella", p. 301)

> [The barbarian has no need of illusions to live, or to express himself. But as soon as he begins to live reality as contemplation (from the very first glimmerings), and hence to conceive of it as having progression and spatio-temporality, he discovers history, that is, illusion. Which from then on he will always need, and he will therefore build on this and on this alone his inauthenticity: first the alienation of the peasant, and then of the *petit bourgeois*.]

I detect here the influence of Mircea Eliade's theories, with which Pasolini was familiar, and for a development of Pasolini's theories concerning myth I refer the reader to *Il sogno del centauro* and to Turigliatto's essay.[26]

Related to the role of montage in the cinema is the distinction that Pasolini makes between "cinema" and "film", which he sees as closely paralleling the distinction Saussure made between "langue" and "parole". In the cinema:

> Noi conosciamo solo le varie "paroles", non conosciamo la "langue" o meglio, conosciamo la "langue" attraverso l'esperienza reale delle varie "paroles", ossia per deduzione. La "langue" perciò è un'astrazione: ma un'astrazione... concreta, dal momento che essa è divenuta la realtà di un codice e di una grammatica;

ossia un oggetto di studio, costituito con lo studio. [...] Ed è curioso, perché, se, per es., attraverso gli uomini sappiamo molto male costituire l'oggetto "umanità", oppure attraverso i poemi veniamo molto male a sapere cos' è la poesia—in linguistica succede il contrario: sappiamo assai meglio cos' è la "langue" che le "paroles" concrete! [...] Nel campo filmlinguistico, la ragione non ha ancora compiuto questo lavoro che le riesce di solito cosí sollecitante e piacevole: non ha "astratto" ancora il "cinema" dai vari "films". Conosciamo i "films" (come conosciamo gli uomini o le poesie), ma non conosciamo il "cinema" (come non conosciamo l'umanità o la poesia). ("Battute", p. 231)

[We only know the various "paroles", we do not know the "langue", or rather, we know the "langue" through our real experience of the various "paroles", or by deduction. The "langue" is therefore an abstraction, but an abstraction that is... concrete, once it has become the reality of a code and of a grammar, or an object of study, constituted by that study. (...) And it is curious because whereas, for example, studying men teaches us little about how to constitute the object "humanity", or studying poems teaches us little about what poetry is—in linguistics it is the other way round: we know much better what the "langue" is than the concrete "paroles"! (...) In the field of filmlinguistics, the human mind has not yet carried out that work which it usually finds so attractive and enjoyable: it has not yet "abstracted" "cinema" from the various "films". We know "films" (just as we know men and poems), but we do not know "cinema" (just as we do not know humanity or poetry.]

"Cinema" is a hypothetical infinite sequence-shot: "una ripro-duzione, ininterrotta e fluente come la realtà, della realtà" ["a reproduction, uninterrupted and flowing like reality, of reality: p. 234]. As we have seen, this is merely the corollary of the assertion that reality is an uninterrupted sequence-shot. "Films", therefore, are an author's selection of the most significant moments of this sequence-shot, joined together in a montage whose expressive powers are partly derived from the "lingua spazio-temporale" to which we have just referred.

Ora, la differenza fra il cinema e il film, tutti i films, consiste proprio in questo: che il cinema ha la linearità di un piano-sequenza infinito e continuo—*analitica*—mentre i films hanno una linearità, potenzialmente infinita e continua, ma *sintetica*. (p. 235)

[Now, the difference between cinema and film, all films, lies precisely in this: that cinema has the linearity of an infinite and continuous sequence-shot—an *analytical* linearity—while films do have a linearity, potentially infinite and continuous, but a *synthetic* one.]

This is developed in "La paura del naturalismo":

> Per realtà intendo dire il mondo fisico e sociale in cui si vive, qualunque questo sia. [...] Il facchino del *cinema* è lo stesso facchino della realtà, dunque: e poiché il cinema è una tecnica audiovisiva, il facchino del cinema si presenta e parla come nella realtà. Ma il facchino di *un* film? Il cinema è un piano-sequenza infinito— [...] è l'ideale e virtuale riproduzione infinita dovuta a una macchina invisibile che riproduce tali e quali tutti i gesti, gli atti, le parole di un uomo da quando nasce a quando muore. Il facchino di *un* film—a differenza del facchino del *cinema* che è un facchino vivo—è un facchino morto. ("Paura", p. 253).

> [By reality I mean the physical and social world we live in, whatever this is. (...) The porter in *cinema* is the same porter as in reality, therefore, and since the cinema is an audiovisual technology, the porter in cinema looks and speaks as he does in reality. But the porter in a particular film? Cinema is an infinite sequence-shot— (...) it is the ideal and essential infinite reproduction produced by an invisible machine which reproduces exactly all the gestures, the actions and the words of a man from when he is born to when he dies. The porter in *a* film—unlike the porter in *cinema*, who is a real live porter—is a dead porter.]

Interestingly, here "cinema" is defined in ideal terms, rather than in terms of an abstraction deduced from a body of concrete "paroles". Reality, as it happens, tends to be referred to in terms of "linguaggio" or "lingua"—"Il linguaggio piú puro che esista al mondo, anzi l'unico che potrebbe essere chiamato LINGUAGGIO e basta, è il linguaggio della realtà naturale" ["The purest language there is in the world, indeed, the only one which could be called LANGUAGE and that's all, is the language of natural reality"]— whereas both its "langue" and its "paroles" are consigned to the realm of the cinema/film. (The quotation comes from "I segni viventi e i poeti morti" ["Living signs and dead poets": p. 246], where he uses the expression "Codice della Realtà" ["Code of Reality"], but also where the purity of the "linguaggio" of reality is compared to the contamination of a "lingua".) All this serves to reinforce the idea of reality being "linguaggio", cinema its "langue" and films its "parole". We may complete the scheme with a quotation from "Res sunt nomina" (pp. 265–66):

> Insomma la caratteristica del cinema come si concreta nei films è quella di avere un "tempo" e uno "spazio" diversi che nella realtà: questo è soprattutto garanzia di "artisticità" nel cinema come "metalinguaggio": è l'autore che sceglie i passaggi di tempo.

> [So the characteristic of cinema, as realized in films, is to have a "time" and "space" different from those of reality. This is above all a guarantee of "artisticness" in cinema as "metalanguage"; it is the author who regulates the passing of time.]

We now have a scheme including "linguaggio", the attribute of what can be "deciphered", which can be the instrument of the cinema, and a "langue" which is yet to be defined by a process of deduction from films which are its "paroles", and which are the product of "choices" (the paradigmatic axis) made by the director who synthesizes these items (in a syntactical operation) into his film, which is an "artistic" discourse, and therefore "metalinguaggio". The trouble with Pasolini's exposition is that there is a little logical gap, which he is always leaping over, but which he wants to keep open, and it is the gap between narrative, prose, commercial, communicative film and "poesia" or "expression". As soon as he finds himself talking about the way in which montage, selection, rhythm, metonymy, and so forth, work in cinema, he labels it "style", and separates it off from the semiological analysis of cinematic communication, all of whose problems are solved with reference to "reality". Pasolini's argument that films offer their signs for reception according to exactly the same "langue" as the receiver uses to "decipher" the referents of those signs could be analysed as demonstrating no more than that *one of many possible cinematic styles* is so to organize a film that it invites such an interpretation. The only example Pasolini gives of a film whose "parole" is predominantly formed out of the "lingua della realtà" is the one by Olmi that he analyses in "La lingua scritta della realtà", where he acknowledges that Olmi's is a highly identifiable stylistic choice, that of the "documentario". Even here, Pasolini's analysis of the "spatio-temporal code" is so skimpy that one cannot be sure what "messaggi" might not be uncovered by a closer analysis of the "pieni e vuoti" and the "inclusioni e esclusioni" of Olmi's film. The way he arrives at a sharp distinction between Olmi's film and Bertolucci's is, in fact, by paying attention to formal characteristics in Bertolucci's film, and denying their existence in Olmi's. Hence the theory of the language of reality applied to cinema may not be much more than one possible formulation of a realist aesthetic. The theory of "reproduction" serves as a means to say that both "signs" and "reality" are organized according to the same code. Hence the repeated injunction, throughout *Empirismo eretico*, that what we need is a "Semiologia Generale della Realtà" ["General Semiology of Reality"], which would be a "Filosofia in quanto descrizione della Realtà come linguaggio"["Philosophy in the form of a description of Reality as a language"].

There are really only two essays in which the implications of the concept of "code" are treated at all systematically, and they are "Tabella" and "Il rema", where Pasolini talks about the viewer's awareness of drawing an analogy, as s/he views a film, between the images and sounds s/he perceives in the cinema and those same sounds and images in reality:

> In pratica la fusione o confusione tra il codice della realtà e il codice del cinema, non è mai totale o totalmente realizzata. Perché? Perché il cinema in concreto non esiste: esiste in concreto il "film" che sto guardando: e quindi non dimentico mai completamente di essere di fronte a una finzione della realtà, in quanto "riproduzione".

> [In practice the fusion or confusion between the code of reality and the code of cinema is never total or fully realized. Why? Because cinema does not exist concretely. What exists concretely is the "film" that I am watching. So I never forget that I am in front of a fiction of reality, in the form of a "reproduction".]

This leads to a brief list of the different "codes" that can apply to the "linguaggi 'sottostanti' l'Ur-codice" ["languages 'subordinate to' the Ur-code"], the latter being the "Codice della realtà vissuta" ["Code of lived reality"] or the "Codice dei codici" ["Code of codes"]. The codes are: (1) "Codice della realtà osservata (o contemplata)" ["Code of reality observed (or contemplated)"]; (2) "Codice della realtà immaginata (o interiorizzata)" ["Code of reality imagined (or internalized)"]; (3) "Codice della realtà rappresentata" (such as "il teatro o la finzione scenica") ["Code of reality represented" (such as "the theatre or stage fiction")]; (4) "Codice della realtà evocata (o verbale)" ["Code of reality evoked (or verbal)"]; (5) "Codice della Realtà raffigurata" (such as "una persona o un paesaggio dipinti o scolpiti") ["Code of reality depicted" (such as "a person or landscape painted or sculpted")]; (6) "Codice della realtà fotografata" ["Code of reality photographed"]; (7) "Codice della realtà trasmessa (audio-visiva)" ["Code of reality transmitted (audiovisual)"] ("live" television, for example); (8) "Codice della realtà riprodotta (audio-visiva)" ["Code of reality reproduced (audiovisual)"]. Where one might expect an analysis of the bases on which these different codes permit communication, however, there are instead *ad hoc* observations about stylistic implications, and variously elaborated versions of ideas expressed earlier (for instance in "Il 'cinema di poesia'") under the various headings ("Tabella", pp. 297–301). For example, under the heading "Codice della realtà trasmessa", Pasolini concludes: "Insomma il suo codice è sostanzialmente l'Ur-codice (lo scrittore giapponese [Mishima, who committed suicide on "live" television] si è ucciso veramente)" ["So its code is basically the Ur-code (the writer Mishima really killed himself)"]. The implications of this observation for his theory of the "Codice della realtà riprodotta", where the people killed may *not* be "uccisi veramente", and where part of our delight in seeing the film comes from knowing this, are not pursued. Nevertheless, even though Pasolini fails to develop the implications of what he is saying, he does raise issues in "Il rema" and "Tabella", such as the viewer's identification with the image, the relationship of the film image to fantasy images, and the status of the referent in "live" transmission. The tabulation of the various "codici" confirms once again the thrust of Pasolini's thinking, which is to seek to bring the relation between sign and referent to one of identity.

It is hard to resist the conclusion that Pasolini is attempting to elaborate a semiology of realist cinema, and it is hard to resist the suspicion that semiology and realism are never going to be entirely compatible. As a result, we are presented with a special semiology and a special realism. For Pasolini, semiology is ultimately to do with things "speaking", having meaning, and he calls anything that "speaks" a sign. Real things "speak" and so are signs. Some signs (cinematic ones) "speak" of real things by "reproducing" them, and he compares that to "writing down" speech. The cinema "writes down" the "signs" of reality. This makes us more aware of how reality is a "language". This concern with semiologically theorizing a realist cinema, however, is accompanied by an equally intense concern that cinema should be expressive or expressionist. The reason for this is the presence of Benedetto Croce's thinking in Italian culture of the time, and in particular the theory that art is the hypostatic union of an intuition and its expression. Pasolini appears to be wrestling with problems of value: in "Il 'cinema di poesia'", with artistic, poetic cinema, as opposed to the commercial cinema; in "La lingua scritta della realtà", with how the cinema is a means for arriving at a consciousness of reality as a language, so that the poetry that Pasolini is creating in his films may be said to be in contact with reality (in the same way that dialect so anchored some of his Friulan poetry and his Roman novels), rather than gratuitous "literature", which he attacked in the Neo-avant-garde. The reasons for Pasolini's concern with reality, and the ideological framework in which this justified his activity from a political-cultural point of view, are beyond the scope of this essay. So, really, are the reasons for his concern with what, in "Il 'cinema di poesia'", he admitted was basically a matter of terminology: "poesia" and its implications lead us in the direction of a Crocean inheritance.[27] What has concerned us is how Pasolini built out of this a film theory, much of which makes most sense when seen in the light of an attempt to bring together these two entities in a forced marriage: a realist-expressionist aesthetic.

NOTES

1   P. P. Pasolini, "Al lettore", in *Empirismo eretico* (Milan, Garzanti, 1972), pp. 53–54 (p. 53). I should like to thank Giulio Lepschy for a great deal of help and advice, though I take full responsibility for my errors.

2   The texts mentioned in the present essay are the following (after the title comes my abbreviation): "Nuove questioni linguistiche" ("Questioni"), first published in *Rinascita*, 26 Dec. 1964; "Al lettore"; "Dal laboratorio" ("Lab"), first published as "Laboratorio", in *Nuovi argomenti*, 1 (Jan–Mar. 1966); "Intervento sul Discorso Libero Indiretto" ("Int"), first published in *Paragone*, 184 (June 1965); "La fine dell'avanguardia" ("Avanguardia"), first published in *Nuovi argomenti*, 3–4 (July–Dec. 1966); "Il 'cinema di poesia'" ("Cin"), delivered at the Pesaro Festival in June 1965; "La sceneggiatura come 'struttura che vuol essere altra struttura'" ("Sceneggiatura"), written in 1965, the French translation, "Le Scénario comme structure tendant vers une autre structure", in *Cahiers du cinéma*, 185 (Dec. 1966); "La lingua scritta della realtà" ("Lingua"), delivered at the second Pesaro Festival, June 1966, and published

in *Nuovi argomenti*, 2 (Apr–June 1966); "Battute sul cinema" ("Battute"), first published as "Dialogo 1" in *Cinema e film*, 1 (1966–67); "Osservazioni sul piano-sequenza" ("Piano-sequenza"), dated in *EE* as 1967; "La paura del naturalismo" ("Paura"), dated in *EE* as 1967; "I segni viventi e i poeti morti" ("Segni"), first published as "I sintagmi viventi e i poeti morti" in *Rinascita*, 25 Aug. 1967; "Res sunt nomina" ("Res"), first published in *Bianco e nero*, 3–4 (Mar.–Apr. 1971); "Il non verbale come altra verbalità" ("Verbalità"), part of a written interview with S. Arecco, "Ancora il linguaggio della realtà", *Filmcritica*, 214 (Mar. 1971); "Il codice dei codici" ("Codice"), dated in *EE* as 1967, with a final note dated 15 January 1971; "Teoria delle giunte" ("Giunte"); "Il rema" ("Rema"); "Tabella"—these last three all dated 1971 in *EE*. To make the essay easier to read, I shall not continually give page references when I am progressively expounding the ideas of a particular essay (e.g. "Cin" and "Lingua").

3   Interview with Pasolini, "Razionalità e metafora", edited by P. Castaldini, *Filmcritica*, 174 (Feb. 1967), reprinted in *Con Pier Paolo Pasolini*, edited by E. Magrelli (Rome, Bulzoni, 1977), pp. 75–82; see also, in "Battute" (p. 232), a tirade against the tendency to interpret his theories as expressions of stylistic choices.

4   R. Turigliatto, "La tecnica e il mito", *Bianco e nero*, 37, i–iv (1976), most of the issue reprinted as an *estratto* in the series *Studi monografici Bianco e nero*, 23, with the title *Lo scandalo Pasolini*, edited by F. Di Giammatteo (Rome, Edizioni dell'Ateneo/Bizzarri, 1976), pp. 113–55 (p. 116).

5   This essay was first published in *The Italianist*, 5 (1985).

6   T. de Lauretis, "Re-Reading Pasolini's Essays on Cinema", *Italian Quarterly*, 21–22 (1980–81), 159–66.

7   De Lauretis calls a scientific semiology of the cinema a "moot case", and relates Pasolini's ideas to Post-structuralist concerns ("Re-Reading", p. 159). Giuliana Bruno takes the argument perhaps a little further than it will stretch—for example (with my comment in square brackets): "For Pasolini, it is not a question of positing a realistic cinema or viewing cinema as the reproduction of reality [It is very hard to read Pasolini as saying anything different], but rather reversing the terms of classic realism. Pasolini conceives of reality as the 'discourse of things' that cinema renarrates": G. Bruno, "The Body of Pasolini's Semiotics: A Sequel Twenty Years Later", in *Pier Paolo Pasolini: Contemporary Perspectives*, edited by P. Rumble and B. Testa (Toronto, University of Toronto Press, 1994), pp 88–105 (p. 93). Sam Rohdie's (in his *The Passion of Pier Paolo Pasolini* [London, BFI; Bloomington, Indiana University Press, 1995]) is an interesting position which does not take sides and which, despite the passion with which it is put forward, does not have any axe to grind. Rather than try to assimilate Pasolini's thinking to another kind of thinking, Rohdie stubbornly holds on to the particular characteristics of Pasolini's discourse: "The contrast in the 'Cinema of Poetry' essay between reason and unreason, the objective and the subjective, communication and expression, the real and the ideal, formed a familiar Pasolini structure which he played out on a variety of registers and in varied substances" (p. 52). "In his melodramatic and reductive association of knowledge and death, significance and loss, the disruption of reality by its symbolic transfer to language, he simultaneously expressed the (sad) loss of reality to language and its (joyous) restoration to consciousness, that is, to text, to writing" (p. 53). "His

cinema was not a poem to reason. It was, on the contrary, an attempt to recover a lost reality and irrational subjectivity in the concreteness of an art which was essentially poetic and expressive and whose expressiveness was constituted by artistic analogies of realities he felt reason had lost. It was a reasonable approach, but not one rationally argued. Pasolini's metalanguage is demonstrative not explicative, analogical not discursive. What makes writing about Pasolini so difficult is that the only effective way to grasp his thought is to find in one's own writing an analogy of it" (p. 53).

8   Pasolini manages to hold a mixture of philosophical attitudes towards "reality" in which elements of religious, phenomenological, realist, materialist and conventionalist positions sit side by side. Pasolini is less interested, as far as his theorizing about the cinema is concerned, in what reality "is" than in what it "means". I suspect that Pasolini's willingness to talk about reality without explicitly discussing his own epistemological or ontological position has tempted some readers into unexamined assumptions, e.g. M. Viano, *A Certain Realism: Making Use of Pasolini's Film Theory and Practice* (Berkeley etc., University of California Press, 1993): "Most of us would agree that there is no fixed reality 'out there'. Much post-modern theory claims that all we see are the simulacra of what once was 'the real'. Baudrillard and Eco have announced the advent of 'hyperreality', the feeling that something is real only if it is validated as a media image. The Italian philosopher Gianni Vattimo, too, argues that the end of modernity entails the disappearance of reality and its replacement with a series of images in competition with one another. My contention is that such an epochal change was illustrated in a considerably less specialized, and therefore more accessible, way by Pasolini's analogy of cinema as the written language of reality" (p. ix). "Cinema, then, helps our realization that we are nothing but images. As such, it ought to prompt us to seek out who and what is directing our roles, our performance. Hence, no more ontology but only ideology" (p. 319 n. 20). Viano then quotes Pasolini's "Bisogna ideologizzare, bisogna deontologizzare" ("Lingua", p. 222). The trouble is, here Pasolini means to analyse the techniques of audio-visual communication and unmask their seeming innocence, *not* to question the ontological status of real people.

9   All translations from Italian are my own, unless otherwise indicated. Pasolini has verbal ticks for creating emphasis, of which "radicale", with "radicalmente", is one (others are "fondamentale", "sostanziale" and "prevalente", for example). I have given myself a lot of freedom to do as I see fit with these ticks; my translations are offered merely as tools for comprehension for the reader who may at times have difficulty with the original Italian. On the matter of translations, see n. 11 below.

10 C. S. Peirce, *Collected Papers*, vol. 2 (Cambridge, Mass., Harvard University Press, 1932), pp. 134–73.

11 In 1985 (when this study was first published) "Il 'cinema di poesia'" was certainly the only essay widely known in the English-speaking world. Unfortunately it was poorly known, because the translation into English so wretchedly failed to construe the original. *Movies and Methods*, edited by B. Nichols (Berkeley etc., University of California Press, 1976), pp. 542–58, was perhaps the most accessible source for this translation, originally printed in *Cahiers du cinéma in English*, 6, and apparently a translation from the French text in *Cahiers du cinéma*, 171 (1965). Enormous progress has been made with

the Indiana University Press translation of *Empirismo eretico*, which may safely be recommended to an English speaker who needs help, though it will not solve all problems of comprehension, nor is it free of error: P. P. Pasolini, *Heretical Empiricism*, edited by L. K. Barnett, translated by B. Lawton and L. K. Barnett (Bloomington, Indiana University Press, 1988). Below I give (*a*) the Italian of the first paragraph of "Il 'cinema di poesia'", (*b*) the Indiana University Press English translation, and, (*c*) while far from perfect, an attempt at a translation that avoids crucial omissions, and makes the meaning of the original accessible. (*a*) "Credo che un discorso sul cinema come lingua espressiva non possa ormai cominciare senza tener presente almeno la terminologia della semiotica. Perché il problema, in parole molto semplici, è questo: mentre i linguaggi letterari fondano le loro invenzioni poetiche su una base istituzionale di lingua strumentale, possesso comune di tutti i parlanti, i linguaggi cinematografici sembrano non fondarsi su nulla: non hanno, come base reale, nessuna lingua comunicativa. Quindi, i linguaggi letterari si presentano subito come leciti in quanto attuazione al sommo livello civile di uno strumento (un puro e semplice strumento) che serve effettivamente per comunicare. Invece la comunicazione cinematografica sarebbe arbitraria e aberrante, senza precedenti strumentali effettivi, di cui tutti siano normalmente utenti." (*b*) "I believe that it is no longer possible to begin to discuss cinema as an expressive language without at least taking into consideration the terminology of semiotics. Quite simply, the problem is this: while literary languages base their poetry on the institutionalized premise of usable instrumentalized languages, the common possession of all speakers, cinematographic languages seem to be founded on nothing at all: they do not have as a real premise any communicative language. Literary languages thus have an immediate legitimacy as instruments (pure and simple instruments), which do, in fact, serve to communicate. Cinematographic communication would instead seem to be arbitrary and aberrant, without the concrete instrumental precedents which are normally used by all." (*c*) "I don't think a discussion of the cinema as an expressive language can begin now without an acknowledgement of at least the terminology of semiotics. Put simply, the problem is this: whereas literary languages use as a foundation on which to base their poetic inventions the institution of language as a tool, which is the common property of all who speak, cinematographic languages seem to be based on nothing at all: they do not have as their real foundation any communicative language. And so literary languages appear legitimate inasmuch as they are the deployment at the highest level of civilization of a tool (a tool, pure and simple) whose purpose is to communicate. In contrast, cinematographic communication would appear, in this line of argument, arbitrary and aberrant, lacking any of the basic elements of tools that everyone normally uses."

12   C. Metz, "Le Cinéma: langue ou langage?", *Communications*, 4 (1964), reprinted in C. Metz, *Essais sur la signification au cinéma*, vol. 1 (Paris, Éditions Klincksieck, 1968).

13   Recent North American approaches to *Empirismo eretico* make much of Pasolini's reference to dreams, and hence his possible affinity with psychoanalytical and feminist approaches to film theory (especially spectatorship). The absence in Pasolini of a clear articulation of what dreams might mean and how they might mean what they mean, and his emphasis on the production

(or to be more precise, reproduction) of meaning in cinema, rather than on what the viewer might want, need or receive from the cinema, make it difficult to know how seriously to take the suggestion that *Empirismo eretico* is a forerunner of Metz's *Le Signifiant imaginaire* (e.g. G. Bruno, "The Body of Pasolini's Semiotics"; see n. 7 above).

14 G. Devoto, *Fondamenti della storia linguistica* (Florence, Sansoni, 1951), pp. 7–11. Devoto discusses the notion of *pre-grammaticalità* in connection with the use made of it by A. Sechehaye, in an article in *Vox romanica*, 5 (1940), 7ff., on Saussure's "three linguistics".

15 G. Herczeg, *Lo stile indiretto libero in italiano* (Florence, Sansoni, 1964).

16 G. Genette, in *Figures III* (Paris, Seuil, 1972) uses the terms with the meanings the other way around to the way in which Pasolini uses them.

17 The question of point of view in the cinema is a vast one, and two places to begin looking for systematic discussion of it are: *Film Reader 5* (Evanston, Ill., Northwestern University Press, 1979); E. Branigan, *Point of View in the Cinema* (Berlin etc., Mouton, 1984). See also the discussion of Pasolini's views on this matter by Gilles Deleuze, *Cinéma 1: L'Image-mouvement* (Paris, Minuit, 1983), Ch. 5. Incidentally, the text of "Cin" is defective on p. 181: after the word "movimento" at the end of the first paragraph should come the words "nel *Vampyr* di Dreyer".

18 See Pio Baldelli's criticisms in "L'elegia dissimulata di Pasolini", *Problemi*, 15–16 (May–Aug. 1966), reprinted in *Pier Paolo Pasolini: materiali critici*, edited by A. Luzi and L. Martellini (n.p., Argalia, 1972–73), pp. 361–77.

19 C. MacCabe, "Realism and the Cinema", *Screen*, 15 (1974), 7–27.

20 This reformulation allows room for the cogent objections of Eco that iconic representation can involve "iconic codes" which are highly conventionalized: see U. Eco, *La struttura assente* (Milan, Bompiani, 1968), pp. 105ff. As may be seen, I do not share Eco's rejection of the category of the "index": see U. Eco, *A Theory of Semiotics* (Bloomington, Indiana University Press, 1979), pp. 151ff.

21 In an interview Pasolini said: "But who talks through a tree? God, or reality itself. Therefore a tree as a sign puts us in communication with a mysterious speaker": O. Stack, *Pasolini on Pasolini* (London, Thames and Hudson/BFI, 1969), p. 153. There seem to be echoes here of time-worn notions of the world as a "book" that extend from Plato to Galileo, and Eco places Pasolini's theories into the category of "le metafisiche pansemiotiche": U. Eco, *Segno* (Milan, ISEDI, 1973), pp. 94–96.

22 A. Martinet, *Éléments de linguistique générale* (Paris, Colin, 1960).

23 "Monemes" are the smallest units to contain expression and content: e.g. the word *cats* contains the monemes *cat* and *s*.

24 E. Garroni, "Popolarità e comunicazione nel cinema", *Filmcritica*, 175 (1967), reprinted in *Film segno*, edited by E. Bruno (Rome, Bulzoni, 1983), pp. 27–56.

25 There is a reference to Eisenstein in "Battute", p. 235: "Il cinema-verità può dare dei films sintetici o di montaggio né più né meno che *Ottobre* (quello sgradevole film di Ejzenstejn)." Pasolini's own films are made of a montage of short shots.

26 See M. Eliade, *Le Mythe de l'éternel retour* (Paris, Gallimard, 1949). Pasolini refers to Eliade's *Storia delle religioni*, with which I am not familiar, in *Il sogno del centauro* (interviews with J. Duflot) (Rome, Editori Riuniti, 1983), p. 83.

27 On Pasolini and Croce see Joseph Francese's contribution to the present volume.

PIER PAOLO PASOLINI: *NARCÍS TAL FRIÚL*[1]

Angela G. Meekins

The myth of Narcissus is a fundamental leitmotif of Pasolini's early Friulan poetry. Extensive use is made in this verse of many of the myth's key themes, which also recur—though less overtly—in his later work.[2] The myth has close contacts with the author's own life, as at various times Pasolini identified himself with the Narcissus of his early poetry and interpreted experiences in his life in the light of classical myth.[3] His exploitation of the myth of Narcissus in his early Friulan poetry has been widely commented on ever since the first review of *Poesie a Casarsa* by Gianfranco Contini in 1943.[4] In choosing the myth of Narcissus as the principal theme for his Friulan poetry, Pasolini was not only following tradition but, in particular, deliberately associating himself with the Decadents and Symbolists of the late nineteenth and early twentieth centuries, who had adopted the same myth as a basic component of their art.[5] Pasolini did not abandon the myth as his career progressed: it continued to be a constant presence both in his work and in his personal life, and he was to return to a more obsessive exploitation of its themes in the rewriting of his early poetry in the last years before his death in 1975.

In this study I intend to show how Pasolini's development of the theme of Narcissus in his early Friulan poetry, written between 1941 and 1953, progressed from a traditional, wholly subjective treatment of aspects of the myth to a more profound interpretation which emphasized social awareness and concern. This process mirrored his own personal development. I shall also argue that the rewritten and new poetry of the "Seconda forma de *La meglio gioventú* (1974)" (*LNG*, 159–227) and "Tetro entusiasmo (Poesie italo-friulane, 1973–74)" (*LNG*, 229–59) demonstrate the continuing importance of the myth of Narcissus in both his life and his work. Indeed Pasolini cleverly and carefully exploited the myth both implicitly and explicitly in a metapoetic and metalinguistic exercise which—contrary to the view of most Pasolini critics—was not a destructive negation of his earlier work but rather a serious and sincere project demonstrating his continuing *impegno*.

NARCISSUS, THE POET AND THE WORLD

Freud's development of the concept of absolute primary Narcissism, which exists before the self is able to distinguish between the ego and external objects, encompassing "the 'environment', integrating the narcissistic ego with the objective world", explains that aspect of continuing Narcissism which gives rise to the feeling of "oneness with the universe". This interpretation is at odds with the self-preoccupation and denial of reality which are usually associated with the myth, and "reveals the new depth of the conception: beyond all immature auto-eroticism, Narcissism denotes a fundamental relatedness to reality which may generate a comprehensive existential order."[6]

Yet if this psychoanalytic interpretation is not the one we usually associate with the myth, it is an aspect of the Narcissus theme which has been frequently exploited in literature. In particular, the Symbolists and Decadents, who had developed the motifs from the myth very fully, had used this idea. Joachim Gasquet wrote that "Le monde entier me renvoie mon image" ["The whole world gives me back my own image"].[7] Thus, to use Bachelard's terms, "Narcissisme individuel" ["individual Narcissism"], which is a kind of aesthetic solipsism, progresses to "Narcissisme cosmique" ["cosmic Narcissism"].[8] This is because contemplation embraces both watching and meditation. Whereas in Ovid's myth action destroys the image—when Narcissus reaches for the beautiful stranger, he disturbs the surface of the water and his lover vanishes—, Gide's Narcissus realizes that "le baiser est impossible... Que faire? Contempler" ["a kiss is impossible... what shall I do? Contemplate"].[9] Schopenhauer states that in the act of contemplation "the perceiver [... and] the perception [...] have become one, because the whole consciousness is filled and occupied with one single sensuous picture [...] and, therefore, he who is sunk in this perception is no longer individual, for in such perception, the individual has lost himself."[10] Bachelard similarly writes: "Sa propre image est le centre d'un monde. Avec Narcisse, pour Narcisse, c'est toute la forêt qui se mire, tout le ciel qui vient prendre conscience de sa grandiose image" ["His own image is the centre of a world. With Narcissus, in Narcissus's opinion, it is the entire forest that reflects him, and the whole sky becomes aware of his grandiose image"], and "Le Narcissisme, première conscience d'une beauté, est donc le germe d'un pancalisme" ["Narcissism, the first awareness of beauty, is thus the seed of Pancalism"].[11]

Pasolini's *Narcís tal Friúl* has much in common with his literary antecedents in the development of a "Narcissisme cosmique". In the earliest Friulan poetry ("Poesie a Casarsa" and "Suite furlana", *LNG*, 7–81), Narcissus/the poetic self is self-engrossed,[12] yet finds his image returned by characters, landscape and sound, as well as by direct reflection. All nature reflects the image of Narcissus and is reflected in him. Pasolini's mythical Friulan landscape is full of natural mirrors: the village fountains ("Dedica", "Ciant da li ciampanis", "La not di maj" III, *LNG*, 7, 19, 47); the evening shadows ("Il nini muàrt", *LNG*, 8); the fields ("Ciants di un muàrt" IX, *LNG*, 43). There is a close identification of Narcissus/the poetic self with the external world. In "Colàt dal còur...", "il còur di un zovinút/[...] vistút/di un ciant massa lizèir" ["the heart of a young man/(...) dressed/in a song which is too light"] belongs to the poetic self, with the poetic voice becoming the breath of life itself—if the poet's song should end, life too will be extinguished:

> Oh ciant, oh ciant lizèir,
> tra il còur e il còur dal sèil
> se tu i ti tas li sèjs
> da la vita a si sièrin.
> (*LNG*, 68)

[Oh song, oh song of lightness,/between your heart and heaven's heart/if you fall silent the eyelids/of life close.]

Narcissus is born "tal spieli da la roja" ["in the mirror of the canal": "O me donzel", *LNG*, 11]; the poetic self desires to be a part of nature—"i vorès essi il vint" ["I should like to be the wind": "Tornant al país", *LNG*, 17]—; the whole of nature is part of his being, integral and without constraints:

> sintínt in tal to cuàrp
> la ciera cialda e scura

> e il fresc, clar sèil.
> ("A Rosari", *LNG*, 44)

[feeling in your body/the warm dark earth/and the cool, clear sky.]

It is a relationship the poet describes as love:

> La domenica mattina a Casarsa costituí per lungo tempo uno dei momenti piú luminosi e trepidanti della mia esistenza di innamorato. Amore, si intende, come incarnazione nel mondo intorno a me (il cielo, le case, la strada di asfalto, i vestiti domenicali) della mia floridezza giovanile.[13]

> [For a long time, Sunday mornings at Casarsa were one of the most luminous yet apprehensive periods of my existence as a lover. Love, that is, as the embodiment in the world around me (the sky, the houses, the ashphalted road, the Sunday clothes) of my florescent youth.]

Narcissus's self-love thus extends to the world around him—"il mond/che a Ciasarsa al ardeva" ["the world/which blazed at Casarsa": "Un rap di ua", *LNG*, 88]—, in which he is mirrored and with which he identifies to the extent of losing his own identity. He describes his love for Friuli in similar terms to those he uses for his self-love or image-(object)-love: "un inossènt e pur/amòur" ("an innocent and pure/love": "Cansiòn", *LNG*, 99).[14]

It seems fairly natural that a poet should take on the persona of Narcissus. Creative art, requiring to some extent an externalization of the artist's personality, must involve a certain degree of self-observation, self-absorption and even self-obsession. "Come sappiamo," writes Santato, "i poeti sono egocentrici"; and he quotes Saba: "Per essi, il mondo esterno *esiste*; solo gira esclusivamente intorno alla loro persona" ["As we know, poets are egocentric"; "For them the external world *exists*; only it revolves exclusively around their person"].[15] Pasolini's earliest Friulan poetry is certainly centred around the self—and with the myth of Narcissus as its leitmotif it could hardly be otherwise.

In his review of Pasolini's first Friulan poems, Contini described the poet's "Narcisismo" as a "posizione violentemente soggettiva" ["violently subjective position"].[16] But, as we have seen, the early solipsism of "Narcissisme individuel" can progress to "Narcissisme cosmique", and perhaps to "a fundamental relatedness to reality".[17] In other words, a greater degree of self-concern and self-love can develop into greater concern/interest/ love or *impegno* (call it what you will) for the wider world. Pasolini's Friulan poetry certainly does progress in this way. The earliest poems (in particular, the first two sections of *La nuova gioventú*, "Poesie a Casarsa" and "Suite furlana", *LNG*, 5–35 and 37–81) are characterized by the almost complete subjectivity of the poetic self, enclosed within the experiences of myth and the remote, mythical landscape. This first, self-engrossed stage is followed, in "Appendice (1950–53)" (*LNG*, 83–100), written after the poet had left Friuli, by a transitional phase of looking back at the Friulan experience. The poet then adopts a somewhat more objective, historically and politically aware perspective in the poems of "El testament Coràn (1947–52)" (*LNG*, 103–33) and "Romancero (1953)" (*LNG*, 135–53), written in the late Friulan/early Roman years. In these last two sections, the poet widens the scope of his work geographically, historically and linguistically: he experiments with other varieties of Friulan and Venetian spoken in the region,[18] and confronts social and political factors as diverse as the atrocities of war, the exploitation of Friulan young people, and emigration. Yet it is still very much a personal endeavour. The section "I Colús" (*LNG*, 137–47) deals with family history (or, rather, moments of history seen from the perspective of earlier members of his mother's family); and Friuli and Friulans (especially the Friulan youth now of an age to work and be exploited, who has evolved into a Communist Narcissus) continue to be at the heart of the poetry. The theme of Narcissus remains, however, although now a secondary motif. For example, the poor "biel zuvinín" ["beautiful youngster"], who has only his youth, his beauty and his health, until the bourgeois "paròn" ["boss"] takes even these away from him, has curls which shine in the sun "coma il flòur dal narcís" ["like the narcissus flower": "Biel zuvinín", *LNG*, 129]. A further example is found in the story of the sixteen-year-old murdered by German soldiers, who had

> un cuòr rugio e pothale
> cui vuoj coma rosi rovani
> e i ciavièj coma chej de me mare.
> ("El testament Coràn", *LNG*, 117)[19]

[a rough, undisciplined heart/with eyes like flaming roses/and hair like my mother's.]

Despite the continuing presence in the poetry of motifs from the myth of Narcissus, the poet's new socio-political concerns—arising at this stage from his involvement with the local communities and a new awareness of their problems, his membership of the local Communist Party, and his work with the Movimento Popolare Friulano for Friulan autonomy—had set him on the path that he would follow in his later work, as a concerned and committed intellectual, determined to comment critically and constructively on the age, society and culture in which he lived. This may be seen as a progression from the self-confessed, egocentric Narcissism of his early years to an outward projection of his own kind of "Narcissisme cosmique".[20]

THE POET AND THE METAPOETICAL MIRROR

The "Seconda forma de *La meglio gioventú* (1974)" (the revised and rewritten versions of some of the early Friulan poems) and the new poems of "Tetro entusiasmo (Poesie italo-friulane, 1973–74)" are usually mentioned in very negative terms by Pasolini critics. Rinaldi refers to "un'operazione depressa e priva di ambizioni" ["a joyless project without any purpose"]; Santato writes of "anti-poesia della disperazione" ["anti-poetry of despair"]; Sehrawy describes the later poetry as an "implacable parody, [...] a bitter disavowal"; while Fortini calls the work "[il] libro atroce di un 'morto vivente'" ["(the) atrocious work of a 'zombie'"].[21] In fact Pasolini's critics have seen his "remake" (*LNG*, 263) as simply a destructive and futile exercise, the result of a desire by the poet to shock. Such a violent and instinctive reaction to the later versions would seem to suggest either that the earlier poetry had been perceived as being overwhelmingly positive in nature, or that, because the early poetry was judged to be so beautiful (Asor Rosa stated that "fra tutti i poeti dialettali del Novecento, Pasolini è quello che raggiunge il massimo grado di squisitezza letteraria" ["among all the dialect poets of the twentieth century, Pasolini is the one who achieves the highest level of literary exquisiteness"]),[22] the tone of the revisions was so shocking that they could only be seen as negating and destroying Pasolini's earlier work.[23] Another possibility is that the critics have not appreciated what the poet was trying to do.

Pasolini constantly reworked his poetry, narrative and essays, carrying themes from one area of his literary and artistic production to another. For example, an earlier version of "Le albe", the first prose-poem in the collection of Italian poems, *L'usignolo della Chiesa Cattolica*,[24] had previously appeared in Friulan in the first issue of *Stroligút*.[25] Similar themes are present both in the early Friulan poetry and in *L'usignolo della Chiesa Cattolica*, with a stronger mythical bias in the former and a stronger religious emphasis in the latter. Both works also feature guilt, inner conflict and the pure/impure polarity as motifs.[26] The socio-political themes of "El testament Coràn"—the struggle to find work and fair wages, the need to go abroad to find work, the growth of political awareness—are also the main themes of *Il sogno di una cosa*.[27] The most complete example of this approach is *Teorema*, which appeared as a book and as a film; and Pasolini also produced essays discussing his theoretical approach underlying the work. Thus, the reworking of his writings—in this case, his dialect poetry—was not in itself a new phenomenon.[28]

There do seem to be two elements in Pasolini's "remake" of the poetry, however, which make it a unique endeavour, and which suggest that the poet's intentions were more complex than what Mengaldo describes as "la dolorosa pulsione masochistica a ferire la propria immagine giovanile, come di un pittore che s'induca a sfregiare i suoi antichi dipinti" ["the painful, masochistic compulsion to wound his own youthful image, like a painter who is led to slash his early paintings"].[29] The first of these is the poet's attitude to what he was doing; and it is interesting to note that he refers to himself as a "Zujadòur" ["Player": "Li letanis dal biel fí" III, *LNG*, 174], and does not use a more negative term, such as "destroyer": his new and rewritten poetry is "la Planta dal Zòuc" ["the Plant of the Game": "Variante", *LNG*, 164], and the game he is playing is one with a very serious purpose.[30] Not only does the poet identify himself as the "Zujadòur", he also invites the reader to participate in the game and compare the new poems with the originals—"se vuole"—["if s/he so wants": "Nota (1974)", *LNG*, 263]. Moreover, he suggests what type of reader—a "fantàt fuàrt e líbar" ["a free and strong youth": "Introduzione", *LNG*, 162]—will be able to understand what he wants to achieve with "chistu libri scrit dos voltis" ["this twice-written book": "Introduzione", *LNG*, 162]. The second element is the similarity of the themes of the two sections of *La nuova gioventú* (discussed below). These two aspects of the poet's "remake" of his dialect poetry continue the play on the myth of Narcissus and the theme of the mirror, and the project is even described in terms appropriate to the myth—"chistu libri scrit dos voltis/vivút and rivivút, cuàrp drenti un cuàrp" ["this twice-written book,/lived and relived, body within a body": "Introduzione", *LNG*, 162].

The Narcissus theme continues to be important and is apparent in the very ordering of the poetry in *La nuova gioventú*, with the later versions placed opposite the original ones, thereby offering a distorted mirror image of them—an arrangement which also signals the metapoetic function of the later work; and since in "Tetro entusiasmo" the poet chooses to write some of the poems in Friulan, some in Italian, and others in a mixture of the two, there is also a metalinguistic aspect to consider. The "Seconda forma de *La meglio gioventú*" may be seen as metapoetry precisely because the poet, in revising and rewriting the earlier poems, is highlighting— or placing a mirror in front of—his previous work and calling into question the nature of that poetry; and it is interesting to note that the poems he chooses to rewrite, taken from the first two sections ("Poesie a Casarsa" and "Suite furlana"), are among the most mythical and enchanting and least historically based. Here, in a play on the reflection motif, we have a triple mirror—of art (the early poetry) reflecting myth, of art (the later poetry) reflecting life, and also of art reflecting art.[31]

Sehrawy sees the later work as a repudiation of the earlier poetry, and as a rejection of a linguistic experiment.[32] Others share this view because many of the later poems negate, contradict or replace the earlier ones.[33] Pasolini, however, is assessing his life and work in the light of changes in society in the 1960s and early 1970s, and the later work is a critique of that "modern" society in comparison to his youthful Friulan experience and the work of those years. The poems in "Appendice", written in the years immediately following the poet's departure from Friuli, are tinged with personal bitterness and are surely—in their content—more critical of the Friulan years than the later work. Rather than indicating a rejection of his earlier work, the placing of the two collections side by side is designed to invite a comparison, yes, of the poetry, but also of the changed society depicted in the later work: the underlying realities of his mythicized Friuli are put into historical context by a comparison with modern life. The poet's idealistic view of the past is held in check by his acknowledgement of the myth: the game he is playing now "mirrors" the earlier game, when he played at being a "zòvin puarèt" ["poor youth": "O me donzel", *LNG*, 171]: it was a trick he played on himself and his readers. He acknowledges the "zòuc tal zòuc" ["game within the game"], yet he would still choose to be part of that world rather than of the real, historical present—"i maledís la storia/ch'a no è in me ch'i no la vuej" ("I curse history,/which is not in me which I don't want": "Tornant al país" ɪɪ, *LNG*, 181]. His real rejection is of modern society, not his early poetry.

The metalinguistic aspect of the poetry is also interesting. The Italo-Friulan poems have two functions in this regard. Firstly, in relation to the poet's experience, they may be seen as representing the mythical past (Friulan) and the historical present (Italian), especially as the two parts of the poems are separated not only by their linguistic form but by the contradictory nature of their content. For example, the Romantic picture presented of the effects of recession, depicted in terms of the poet's mythical and idealized view of the past—"a varàn li musis di 'na volta,/cui ciaviej curs e i vuj di so mari" ("they'll have the faces of long ago,/with short hair and their mother's eyes"]—is written in Friulan,[34] but the last stanza, in Italian, brings the focus sharply back onto the present: "basta con questo film neorealistico" ["enough of this Neo-realist film"], says the poet; the only worthwhile reason to relive the past is to do things differently the second time—"Rifarne esperienza val la pena solo/se si lotterà per un mondo davvero comunista" ["It's worth living through it again only/if we'll fight for a truly Communist world": "La recessione", *LNG*, 243–44]. Rather than being a rejection of either his own work of the 1940s and 1950s, or a negation of the ideals he had held then (and still held), this is obviously a criticism of present-day society, which had failed to develop in the way he had envisaged (as is made clear in his journalistic writings of the time).[35] Secondly, the poems which begin in Friulan and end in Italian, or *vice versa*, which have also been seen as a rejection of the dialect, reflect rather what was happening to the dialects in Italy at that time. Dialects were becoming less widely spoken as mass culture, education, television and the other mass media spread the national language as the main vehicle of communication in all areas of life: to put it simply, dialect speakers were turning to Italian. Likewise, the Friulan of the later poems has more Italianisms than the original poetry, also reflecting the changes in dialect culture (see "Nota (1974)", *LNG*, 264). Pasolini was not rejecting Friulan, or the use of dialects in Italy, as may be seen in the last poem in the collection, wholly written in Friulan (nor do I think that this fact or the poem's position in the book is fortuitous) and in which he defends dialect culture—"ama i puòrs: ama la so diversitàt./[...]/ama il so dialèt inventàt ogni matina" ["love the poor: love their otherness./(...)/ love their dialect, which is invented every morning": "Saluto e augurio", *LNG*, 258]. True, he also states that this will probably be his last dialect poem, but Pasolini feared that the dialects were disappearing from the country, and, while this poem is a strong protest by the poet, it also documents his increasing pessimism. It is obvious that Pasolini did not intend the Italo-Friulan poetry in "Tetro entusiasmo" to be a rejection of dialect.[36]

Whereas the theme of Narcissus was in itself the leitmotif of the early poetry, in the later poetry motifs from the myth are closely interwoven into the poet's message, in an obsessive explication of his perception of the sameness and superficiality of modern society. Thus in the first poem the motif of the double is applied to "i zòvins/comunis'c" ["the young/Communists"] and "i zòvins fassis'c" ["the young Fascists"] who have become identical because of the homogenizing effects of modern mass culture, so that they are both "fassis'c ta l'anima *e tal cuàrp*" ["Fascist in their soul and *in their body*": "Introduzione", *LNG*, 161]. In fact, while once only God was One, now everybody and everything is the same:

> Doma Diu Un.
> Vuej Fogolars
> Òmis e Diu
> a son 'na sola
>
> forma par ducius.
> ("La domènia uliva", *LNG*, 201)

[Only God was One./Today Hearths,/Men and God/have just one//form for all.]

Only the poetic self is determined to preserve variety, both in himself—

> Nat par essi Un,
> i sarài Dopli,
> mut e nut ma Dopli,
> forèst a dut ma Dopli

[Born to be One, / I will be Double, / silent and naked but Double, / a stranger to everything but Double]

—and in his poetry: "I libris? / [...] UN E DOPLI!" ("Books? / [...] ONE AND DOUBLE!": "La domènia uliva", *LNG*, 199). This is in keeping with his earlier poetry, where, although Narcissus sought oneness with the Friulan landscape, nature and his environment, the themes of metamorphosis and of the inverted double ensured continued diversity.[37] The very idea of a double suggests an *identical* copy;[38] but conversely, what most interests Pasolini (in his early and later Friulan poetry, and also in much of his other work) is conflicts and contradictions, and the underlying dual nature of the self. Here he uses the concept of the double to suggest variety as a contrast to the sameness of modern society.

The reflection motif is frequently used, but the image is distorted or changed: thus instead of the conventional image of the poetic self as a young man at first and later as an older man, it is the world that is seen as having been young in the early poetry and now having grown old ("Variante", "Li letanis dal biel fí" I and II, *LNG*, 163, 172–73). Similarly, emphasizing the changing perspective of the poetic self over the period of time that has elapsed between the writing of the early poetry and the "remake", the poet's early work is described as "la Planta da la Passion" ["the Plant of Passion"], and the "remake" as "la Planta dal Zòuc" ["the Plant of the Game": "Variante", *LNG*, 164). It is also possible to look at the older poetic self as the metamorphosed (by age) reflection of the younger Narcissus self: for example, the "Diàul peciadòur" ["Devil sinner"] has become the "Diàul Zujadò" ["Devil Player"], but his fascination with his own reflection remains (see "Li letanis dal biel fi" III, *LNG*, 14–15, 174–75). The motif of the divided self is also featured, even in the poet's desire for his later work to be both the same as the first, and yet different:

Plantànd chista seconda planta
chel che pí i bramavi, a era
ch'a fos identica a la prima;
e chel che pí a mi scrussiava

a era ch'a essi diviersa a no podeva.
("Variante", *LNG*, 164)

[In planting this second plant/that which I wanted most/was
that it should be the same as the first one;/and that which
tormented me most//was that it couldn't be different.]

The poet considers the "novitàt" ["newness"] of his "remake" to be
"obediensa/e disobediensa, insièmit" ["obedience/and disobedience, together": "Introduzione", *LNG*, 162].

The content of the rewritten and new poetry largely mirrors the
themes of the poems written in the 1940s and 1950s: death, illusion,
myth, religion, social inequalities (and, indeed, the same concerns
continued to feature prominently in Pasolini's work thereafter).
The themes, however, and the poet's treatment of them, have
progressed and the emphasis has changed, reflecting the conditions of 1970s society. By the time Pasolini left Friuli in January
1950, many of the younger people had emigrated to find work
abroad or gone to other parts of the country, against their will
because "lòur/a son doma che di chista ciera" ["they/are only of
this land": "Viers Pordenon e il mont", *LNG*, 132]. By the early
1970s many villages were almost empty (some entirely abandoned).
Pasolini complains that "Li ciampanis ch'a sunin/nissún li scolta
pí" ["The bells which ring,/nobody listens to them any more":
"Aleluja" vi, *LNG*, 190] and that "a làssin la ciasa ai usièj" ["they
leave their home to the birds": "Ciants di un muàrt" vii, *LNG*, 208].
What is left is "un muart país" ["a dead village": "Ploja fòur di dut",
LNG, 169], and those who do return—Pasolini's "sottoproletariato/
[…]/ha finito col diventare/una riserva della piccola borghesia"
["underclass/(…)/has ended up becoming/a preserve of the *petite
bourgeoisie*": "Versi sottili come righe di pioggia", *LNG*, 252]—
build anonymous "ciasis novis" ["new houses": "Ploja four di
dut", *LNG*, 169]. The people no longer belong to the land, to a
particular area: they move away and lose all sense of their origins:

al dis li so peràulis e al sparís,
e no coma 'na volta
ch'al entrava, al zeva fòur, al tornava entrà,
encia dopu muàrt!
("Ciants di un muàrt" III, *LNG*, 206)

[they say their words and disappear,/and not like at one time/
when they would come in, go out, come back in again,/even after
death!]

Their relationship to the world is thus one of alienation: "i vuàrdi
la ploja/dal mond e di nissún" ["I look at the rain/of the world and
of nobody": "Li letanis dal biel fí" III, *LNG*, 175]. The original rustic
fountain of love is now a "Fontana di amòur par nissún" ["Fountain of love for nobody": "Dedica", *LNG*, 167], reflecting the new
attitudes of society—"Fí, no ti impuàrta/se un forèst al mòur"
["Son, you don't care/if a stranger dies": "Li letanis dal biel fí" III,
LNG, 175]. Thus the mythical element is smaller, and the social
comment stronger.

While the poet describes what he is doing as a game—and there
is an element of humour,[39] despite the seriousness of his aims and
the bleakness of many of the changes—his purpose is to present a
message to his readers: the poet is disillusioned with politics and
society, which are conspiring to produce a bland, mass, bourgeois
culture, losing the diverse traditions, customs and languages which
had previously enriched the nation. Shortly before his death Pasolini
wrote:

La classe dominante, il cui nuovo modo di produzione ha creato
una nuova forma di potere e quindi una nuova forma di cultura,
ha proceduto in questi anni in Italia al piú completo e totale
genocidio di culture particolaristiche (popolari) che la storia
italiana ricordi. I giovani sottoproletari romani hanno perduto
(devo ripeterlo per l'ennesima volta?) la loro "cultura", cioè il
loro modo di essere, di comportarsi, di parlare, di giudicare la
realtà: a loro è stato fornito un modello di vita borghese (consumistico): essi sono stati cioè, classicamente, distrutti e borghesizzati
[…]. La cultura delle classi subalterne non esiste (quasi) piú.[40]

[The dominant class, whose new mode of production has created
a new form of power and therefore a new form of culture, has
proceeded in this period in Italy towards the most complete and

total genocide of particularistic (popular) cultures recorded in Italian history. The young members of the Roman sub-class (must I repeat this for the umpteenth time?) have lost their "culture", that is, their way of being, of behaving, of speaking, of judging reality: a model of bourgeois life (of the consumer society) has been provided for them: they have been, that is, destroyed and made to become bourgeois—classically (…). The culture of the lower classes (almost) no longer exists.]

Pasolini's own personal concept of Communism would not have resulted in the lower classes being absorbed into an expanded bourgeoisie:

> I comunisti […] lottano per i diritti civili in nome di una *alterità*. Alterità (non semplice alternativa) che per sua stessa natura esclude ogni possibile assimilazione degli sfruttati con gli sfruttatori.
> La lotta di classe è stata finora *anche* una lotta per la prevalenza di un'altra cultura. (*LL*, 190)

> [The Communists (…) are fighting for civil rights in the name of an *otherness*. Otherness (not simply an alternative) that by its very nature excludes any possible assimilation of the exploited by the exploiters.
> Class war has been up to now *also* a war for the predominance of another culture.]

Despite his own middle-class family background, and his acknowledgement that he had played at being "un zòvin puarèt" ["a poor youth"], Pasolini continued to identify himself with "the people", the poor of the rural communities and the urban proletariat—"I borghèis/a àn un cuàrp maledèt" ["The bourgeois/have a cursed body": "O me donzel", *LNG*, 171]. The poet still identifies himself with the young, poor Narcissus of his early poetry:

> No è cambiàt nuja:
> mi jot enciamò coma puarèt
> e zòvin; e i ami doma
> chej coma me.
> ("O me donzel", *LNG*, 171)

> [Nothing has changed:/I still see myself as poor/and young; and I love only/those who are like me.]

In "Appunto per una poesia in terrone", he sets out his griev-
ances—where he thinks society has erred—and his suggestions for
the future:

> Perché avete lasciato che i nostri figli fossero educati dai borghe-
> si? Perché avete permesso che le nostre case fossero costruite dai
> borghesi? Perché avete tollerato che le nostre anime fossero
> tentate dai borghesi? Perché avete protestato solo a parole mentre
> pian piano la nostra cultura si andava trasformando in una
> cultura borghese? [...]
> Bisognerà tornare *indietro*, e ricominciare daccapo. [...]
> [...] Viva la povertà. Viva la lotta comunista per i beni
> necessari. (*LNG*, 245–46)

> [Why have you allowed the middle classes to teach our children?
> Why have you permitted the middle classes to build our homes?
> Why have tolerated that the middle classes should tempt our
> souls? Why have you only protested in words while our culture
> was gradually changed into a bourgeois culture? (...)
> We need to go *back*, and start again from the beginning. (...)
> (...) Long live poverty. Long live the Communist struggle for
> what is necessary.]

His suggestion is that people look to the past for the values they
have lost. The turning upside-down/making a distorted image of
his early poetry is thus also a reflection of what he feels has
happened to the values of modern society. The message of the
revised and rewritten poetry is the same as that in his essays and
journalistic writings of the time; and if his method seems extreme,
we have only to think of *Salò* to see that, in the cinema too, he was
resorting to more extreme forms of expression to get his message
across to a world which did not want to listen. His use of poetry as
a double mirror contrasts past illusions with present disillusionment. The "Seconda forma de *La meglio gioventú*" and "Tetro
entusiasmo" are thus both further evidence of his "Narcissisme
cosmique", or *impegno*, and not just a game in which he ruthlessly
and obsessively develops motifs from the Narcissus myth.

Mengaldo points out that the use of the Narcissus myth in
Pasolini's early poetry is a key autobiographical motif for the
poet—"una tematica che contiene in embrione moltissimo del
Pasolini futuro" ["a theme which contains in embryo very much of

the future Pasolini"].[41] And we have seen that this is true: the poet fully and skilfully exploits *topoi* from the myth while placing his Narcissus in a mythicized Friuli with its musical language which adapts so well to his poetic use and mythical theme. Yet while the setting of the poetry and the Narcissus myth itself have personal meaning for Pasolini, they become integrated into his own developing social and political awareness, and aspects of both continue to be essential factors underpinning his work throughout his artistic career. Returning to the language, structures and themes of his early poetry—and especially the "game" which plays on motifs from the myth of Narcissus—Pasolini completes the circular formula which is highly appropriate to myth and is echoed in his other work (for example, in *Teorema*: the desert as a symbol of mythical prehistory and also as the point one must reach in life to know oneself, thereby returning to one's origins). In a sense, it is both appropriate and yet paradoxical that an experimental poet, writer and film-maker like Pasolini should look to his past to frame his concerns for the present and future. Yet despite the great variety and breadth of his work, common themes, interests and motifs (including many from the Narcissus myth) recur. The poet states, "i ài sempri chel stes valòur" ["I have always the same value": "Li letanis dal biel fí", *LNG*, 172]; and, consistent with the dual nature of his "remake" project, the last poem in the collection is both pessimistic and yet an offering of hope, even if the poet knows it is unlikely that his advice will be followed:

> dis
> di no essi borghèis, ma un sant
> o un soldàt: un sant sensa ignoransa,
> un soldàt sensa violensa.
> ("Saluto e augurio", *LNG*, 258)

[say/that you are not bourgeois, but a saint/or a soldier: a saint who is not ignorant,/a soldier who is not violent.]

The saint and the soldier constitute a further inconstant double, echoing the Narcissus theme. The final lines are a declaration of intent on the poet's part not to change, to keep the same values, ideals and desires:

E jo i ciaminarai
lizèir, zint avant, sielzínt par sempri

la vita, la zoventút.
("Saluto e augurio", *LNG*, 259)

[And I will walk/lightly, going forwards, always choosing//life, youth.]

NOTES

1   This essay is based on my undergraduate dissertation (Reading, 1994), and is dedicated to *me mari*, Maria Venturini Meekins, whose love for Friuli and pride in its language first led me to read Pasolini's Friulan poetry. I should like to thank Zygmunt Barański and Giulio Lepschy for their help, patience and encouragement. All quotations from Pasolini's Friulan poetry are taken from *La nuova gioventú* (Turin, Einaudi, 1975).

2   In many ways, from the Friulan poetry onwards, the poet continued to be his own main point of reference for his later work, creatively interpreting life and the society in which he lived in the light of his own feelings, his personal history and his political beliefs and perceptions, thereby giving all his work a subjective and autobiographical bias (implicit or explicit). Diary notebooks (the "Quaderni rossi", written in 1946–47) and poetic and literary diaries were sources for his creative output: for example, *Dal Diario (1945–1947)* (Caltanissetta, Sciascia, 1954); *Roma 1950 diario* (Milan, Scheiwiller, 1960); *Amado mio; Atti impuri* [1982], third edition (Milan, Garzanti, 1993), though it is not known if he intended to publish these two prose works. The last of these "diaries" actually bore the title "Il romanzo di Narciso": see N. Naldini, *Nei campi del Friuli* (Milan, Scheiwiller, 1984), p. 14. *Topoi* taken from the myth and used as themes in literature have included reflection, repetition (visual or aural), the unattainability of the loved one, frustrated love, homosexuality, beauty, vanity and pride, self-recognition or its lack, self-obsession, self-delusion, illusion and reality, impermanence, the double or shade, the divided self, death, and metamorphosis (this being Ovid's preferred leitmotif with three instances of transformation occurring within his Narcissus story; see *Metamorphoses*, III. 341–510). All these themes appear in Pasolini's Friulan poetry, and many are featured in his later work. Just a few examples are: beauty in *Teorema* (book, Milan, Garzanti, 1968; film, Italy, 1968); homosexuality in *Amado mio, Atti impuri* and *Teorema*; excessive love, especially for the mother figure, in "Appendice alla 'religione': una luce", in *La religione del mio tempo* [1961] (Milan, Garzanti, 1976), p. 99. The reflection theme is present in much of Pasolini's work, often associated with the motif of the mirror or the double. The themes of metamorphosis and death are also found. That motifs from the myth of Narcissus continued to be exploited by the writer is

apparent from the incomplete, posthumously published *Petrolio* (Turin, Einaudi, 1992), which prominently features the theme of the double. In *Bestia da stile*, where the double is also a key motif, Pasolini writes that "lo Sdoppiamento del personaggio in due personaggi/è la piú grande delle invenzioni letterarie": *Porcile; Orgia; Bestia da stile* (Milan, Garzanti, 1979), p. 268. Both *Petrolio* and *Bestia da stile* were stated by their author to be autobiographical in nature (see *P*, 569; *Bestia da stile*, 195).

3   In particular, the myths of Narcissus and Oedipus. In a letter to Contini dated 23 July 1947, Pasolini wrote: "Questi campi solitari sono ormai saturi di quelli che Lei chiamava i miei 'complessi', d'altra parte l'affetto che mi lega ad essi è ormai una malattia inguaribile: mortale. L'ultimo stadio del mio narcisismo era dunque l'indifferenza!": *Lettere (1940–1954)*, edited by N. Naldini (Turin, Einaudi, 1986), pp. 307–08. With regard to his film *Edipo re* (Italy, 1967), Pasolini stated: "In *Edipo* io racconto la storia del mio complesso di Edipo. Il bambino del prologo sono io, suo padre è mio padre, ufficiale di fanteria, e la madre, una maestra, è mia madre. Racconto la mia vita, mitizzata naturalmente; [... è] il piú autobiografico dei miei film": quoted in L. De Giusti, *I film di Pier Paolo Pasolini* [1983], third edition (Rome, Gremese, 1990), p. 85.

4   *Poesie a Casarsa* (Bologna, Libreria Antiquaria, 1942; then in *LNG*, 5–35). Contini's review of *Poesie a Casarsa* appeared in the *Corriere del Ticino* on 24 April 1943, now in *Pagine ticinesi di Gianfranco Contini* (Bellinzona, Arti Grafiche A. Salvioni, 1981), pp. 110–15. For discussions of Pasolini's Friulan poetry see G. C. Ferretti, *Letteratura e ideologia* (Rome, Editori Riuniti, 1964); A. Asor Rosa, *Scrittori e popolo: il populismo nella letteratura italiana contemporanea*, third edition (Rome, Samonà and Savelli, 1969); T. Anzoino, *Pasolini* (Florence, La Nuova Italia, 1971); E. Guagnini, "*La nuova gioventú* e l'esperienza friulana di Pier Paolo Pasolini", *La Battana* [Fiume], 13, xxxix (May 1976); G. Santato, *Pier Paolo Pasolini: l'opera* (Vicenza, Neri Pozza, 1980); F. Brevini, *Per conoscere Pasolini* (Milan, Mondadori, 1981); R. Rinaldi, *Pier Paolo Pasolini* (Milan, Mursia, 1982). See also M. Sehrawy, "The Suffering Text: *Poesie a Casarsa* and the Agony of Writing", *The Italianist*, 5 (1985), 9–35. In the present essay I use the phrases "the early Friulan poetry" and "the early poetry" to refer to Pasolini's Friulan poetry written between 1941 and 1953 and contained in *La meglio gioventú (1941–53)*, including, in "Parte prima": "Poesie a Casarsa (1941–43)", "Suite furlana (1944–49)" and "Appendice (1950–53)"; and, in "Parte seconda": "El testament Coràn (1947–52)" and "Romancero (1953)" (*LNG*, 3–153.) I use the phrase "the later poetry" to refer to the rewritten Friulan poems in the "Seconda forma de *La meglio gioventú* (1974)", and the new poems in "Tetro entusiasmo (Poesie italo-friulane, 1973–74)" (*LNG*, 159–259).

5   L. Vinge, *The Narcissus Theme in Western European Literature up to the Early Nineteenth Century* (Lund, Gleerups, 1967) is an excellent study. D. Lesko Baker, *Narcissus and the Lover* (Stanford, ANMA Libri, 1986), which discusses the Narcissus theme in Scève's *Délie*, and N. Segal, *Narcissus and Echo: Women in the French Récit* (Manchester, Manchester University Press, 1988) also provide useful insights. Many influences on Pasolini's poetry have been identified. These include the Provençal poets, the Decadents and Symbolists, and the Hermeticists (see F. Brevini, *Per conoscere Pasolini*, p. 36; G. Santato, *L'opera*, pp. 6, 9, 11). Pasolini, however, particularly in his early Friulan period, chose to associate himself with the Decadents and Symbolists, stating

that he shared their conception of poetry as mythical and metaphysical. This is confirmed by the fact that he embraced the myth of Narcissus as a principal theme, since, as Guy Michaud wrote in *Message poétique du Symbolisme*, 4 vols (Paris, Nizet, 1947), I, 34 n. 74: "C'est le mythe de Narcisse, que nous retrouverons à chaque instant dans l'histoire du Symbolisme." The musicality of the poetry is a further and deliberate link to the Symbolist movement and its objective of bringing poetry closer to music—seeking "una 'melodia infinita'" (letter dated 3 November 1945 to Franco De Gironcoli, in Pasolini, *Lettere 1940–1954*, pp. 209, 210); see Z. G. Barański, "Pasolini: Culture, Croce, Gramsci", in *Culture and Conflict in Postwar Italy*, edited by Z. G. Barański and R. Lumley (Basingstoke–London, Macmillan, 1990), p. 143. Pasolini, however, also described himself as a *"pasticheur"*, adding: "I use the most disparate stylistic material—dialect poetry, decadent poetry, certain attempts at socialist poetry; there is always a stylistic contamination in my writings" (O. Stack, *Pasolini on Pasolini* [London, Thames and Hudson/BFI, 1969], p. 28).

6   H. Marcuse, *Eros and Civilization* (London, Sphere, 1970), pp. 137–38. The Narcissism of first infancy (absolute primary Narcissism) is a stage in which the ego cannot differentiate between self and its environment. Vestiges of this experience can continue, however, as Marcuse points out: "Narcissism survives not only as a neurotic symptom but also as a constitutive element in the construction of reality, coexisting with the mature reality ego. Freud describes the 'ideational content' of the surviving primary ego-feeling as 'limitless extension and oneness with the universe'" (p. 138). Freud's main discussions of Narcissism are found in *The Standard Edition of the Complete Psychological Works of Sigmund Freud*, 24 vols (London, Hogarth Press, 1953–74): "On Narcissism: An Introduction" (XIV, 67–102); "Beyond the Pleasure Principle" (XVIII, 1–64). See also "Some Neurotic Mechanisms in Jealousy, Paranoia and Homosexuality" (XVIII, 230–32); "Psycho-analytic Notes on an Autobiographical Account of a Case of Paranoia (Dementia Paranoides)" (XII, 3–82). On absolute primary Narcissism see "Outline of Psycho-analysis" (XXIII, 150); and on "oceanic feeling", see "Civilization and its Discontents" (XXI, 64–73, especially p. 68).

7   J. Gasquet, *Narcisse* (Paris, Librairie de France, 1931), p. 262. Gasquet also wrote: "La terre est une bonne mère pour toi [...]. Le monde est fait à ton image [...]. Tu représentes le monde. Miroir vivant!" (pp. 272–73). Compare also "La Jeune Parque" by Paul Valéry, *Œuvres*, 2 vols (Paris, Gallimard, 1957), I, 97. L. M. Wills, *Le Regard contemplatif chez Valéry et Mallarmé* (Amsterdam, Rodopi, 1974), p. 20, points out that the fountain-as-mirror in the Narcissus myth is a microcosm of the cosmos. The self-as-mirror-of-the-world is an extremely common literary motif, and not only among the Symbolists. Biagio Marin provides a further example in dialect poetry: "E me son l'aqua che fa specio terso/e l'órdola che canta 'l sovo ben,/e me son l'aria e son el canto perso/che fa trema fin l'erba sul teren" ["I am the water that forms a clear mirror/and the lark which sings its joy,/and I am the air and the lost song/that makes even the grass on the ground tremble": "L'ora granda", in P. V. Mengaldo, *Poeti italiani del Novecento* (Milan, Mondadori, 1981), p. 510; from B. Marin, *Sénere colde* (Rome, Il Belli, 1953)].

8   G. Bachelard, *L'Eau et les rêves: essai sur l'imagination de la matière* (Paris, José Corti, 1942), pp. 36–40.

9   Quoted in R. Robidoux, *Le Traité du Narcisse (théorie du symbole) d'André Gide* (Ottawa, Éditions de l'Université d'Ottawa, 1978), pp. 120–21. Gide's work was originally published as *Le Traité du Narcisse (théorie du symbole)* (Paris, Librairie de l'Art Indépendant, 1891).

10   A. Schopenhauer, *The World as Will and Idea*, 3 vols (London, Trübner, 1883), vol. I, Book III, p. 231.

11   G. Bachelard, *L'Eau et les rêves*, pp. 36, 38.

12   In Pasolini's Friulan poetry, as in much of his other work, there is often no clearly discernible boundary between the author and the poetic self. The distinction is blurred even further by the poet's self-confessed Narcissism. See nn. 2 and 3 above.

13   P. P. Pasolini, *Un paese di temporali e di primule*, edited by N. Naldini (Parma, Guanda, 1993), p. 149.

14   Narcissus/the poetic self finding his image in the world around him is an outward manifestation of his dual (interior) nature, and of the struggle to find a balance between the innocence and purity which he associates with *fanciullezza* and the guilt of awakening sexuality, and also the publicly unacknowledged homosexuality of the poet himself. The sensual "pavea di vilút" ["velvet butterfly"] that "mi svuala dal sen a li cuessis" ["flies from my breast to my thighs"] is thus also "un mostru" ["a monster"] and "al sporcia i flòurs di me frut" ["dirties my young boy's flowers": "Mostru o pavea?" III and IV, *LNG*, 62]. The emphasis on the purity/impurity polarity is a legacy of Catholicism; it also owes much, however, to the Decadents and Symbolists (see G. Santato, *L'opera*, pp. 18–19).

15   G. Santato, *L'opera*, p. 12. The quotation is taken from Umberto Saba, *Scorciatoie e raccontini* (Milan, Mondadori, 1963), p. 136.

16   G. Contini, *Pagine ticinesi*, p. 111.

17   G. Bachelard, *L'Eau et les rêves*, pp. 36–40; H. Marcuse, *Eros and Civilization*, p. 138.

18   While most of the early poetry was written in the Friulan of Casarsa, Pasolini also wrote poetry in other local dialects: "Mi contenti" (*LNG*, 109) in the Friulan of Valvasone; "I dis robàs" (*LNG*, 110) in the Friulan of Cordenons; "Arba pai cunins" (*LNG*, 111) in the Friulan of Cordovado; "La giava" (*LNG*, 112) in the Friulan of Gleris; "Bel coma un ciaval" and "El testament Coràn" (*LNG*, 113 and 117) in the Friulan of Bannia; "Vegnerà el vero Cristo" (*LNG*, 114) in the Venetian dialect of Pordenone; and "El cuòr su l'aqua" (*LNG*, 115) in the Venetian dialect of Caorle. See "Nota (1954)" in *LNG*, 157.

19   Apart from Narcissus himself, the most striking motif taken from the Narcissus myth, and one which recurs frequently in Pasolini's Friulan poetry, is the image of the mother. For a discussion of the association of the mother figure with the myth of Narcissus, see N. Segal, *Narcissus and Echo*, pp. 8–9, 13. See also S. Freud, *Collected Papers*, IV, 398–99; *The Standard Edition of the Complete Psychological Works of Sigmund Freud*, XIV, 87–90, and XVIII, 230–32. In Pasolini's poetry the mother figure is associated with: water as the source of life ("O me donzel", *LNG*, 11); death ("Il nini muàrt", *LNG*, 8); memory (as a mirror) ("Il nini muàrt", "Aleluja", *LNG*, 8, 22); Narcissus and the mother figure reflected in each other ("Suite furlana", *LNG*, 53–54); metamorphosis ("Pastorela di Narcís", *LNG*, 60); myth and religion, as well as sacred and profane love ("La domènia uliva", "Suite furlana", "Pastorela di Narcís", *LNG*, 30–35, 53–54, 60). Throughout the poetry there are references to

Narcissus/the child resembling the mother ("Pastorela di Narcís", "El testament Coràn", *LNG*, 60, 117).

20 I would point out, however, that "Narcissisme cosmique" is still a form of Narcissism. The "self" remained the crucial point of reference in Pasolini's work (see nn. 2 and 3 above).

21 R. Rinaldi, *Pier Paolo Pasolini*, p. 359; G. Santato, *L'opera*, p. 305; M. Sehrawy, "The Suffering Text", p. 10; F. Fortini, *I poeti del Novecento* (Rome–Bari, Laterza, 1977), p. 188.

22 A. Asor Rosa, *Scrittori e popolo*, p. 352.

23 I think it is simplistic to see the "remake" as an entirely negative and destructive process. The original poetry, despite the enchantment of its language, themes and imagery and Pasolini's great skill as a poet, is certainly not positive or optimistic; and the themes treated in the later revisions and additions are in fact very similar to those of the earlier poetry, insofar as the poet's concerns and objectives have not changed, despite his increased pessimism.

24 *L'usignolo della Chiesa Cattolica* [1958] (Turin, Einaudi, 1976).

25 *Stroligút di cà da l'aga* [S. Vito al Tagliamento], Apr. 1944.

26 See n. 14 above.

27 *Il sogno di una cosa* [1962] (Milan, Garzanti, 1989).

28 Z. G. Barański, "Pasolini, Friuli, Rome", in the present volume, also comments on Pasolini's textual reworkings. He points out Pasolini's use of similar themes in the late Friulan and early Roman period, stating: "A sense of continuity, rather than of conflict, marks Pasolini's Friuli and Rome during 1950–51" (p. 256). He also describes the "tormented elaboration" of *Il sogno di una cosa* and *Amado mio*, parts of both texts appearing separately as short stories (pp. 270–72 nn. 22 and 23). Similarities in the style and content of the last poem in *La nuova gioventú* ("Saluto e augurio", *LNG*, 255–59) and the last poem in the Appendix to *Bestia da stile* ("Frammento vi: Praga" iv, pp. 302–07) further illustrate the poet's "recycling" of his work, especially as *Bestia da stile* also strongly features themes from the Narcissus myth. See also P. P. Pasolini, *Volgar' eloquio* (Rome, Editori Riuniti, 1987), pp. 23–25.

29 P. V. Mengaldo, *Poeti italiani del Novecento*, p. 785.

30 The purpose of the game was to provide another vehicle for Pasolini's opinions on the ills of society. It was particularly effective because he was able to contrast his own work "then and now" (the early and later poetry) with the changes in society over the same period, specifically through his "game", by employing those same motifs from the Narcissus myth (especially the reflection motif) which he had exploited so fully in the early Friulan poetry. The message of the rewritten and new poetry of the "Seconda forma de *La meglio gioventú*" and "Tetro entusiasmo" was in effect identical to that of his journalistic writings and film-making of the same period. Compare, in particular, the articles collected in *Scritti corsari* [1975] (Milan, Garzanti, 1993) and *Lettere luterane* [1976] (Turin, Einaudi, 1991) and his film *Salò o le 120 giornate di Sodoma* (Italy/France 1975). See also below, pp. 241–43 and n. 40.

31 In the early poetry, too, Pasolini included Italian versions of the poems, at the foot of each page, providing a linguistic "mirror image" of the Friulan verse. He also stated that the Italian versions "fanno parte insieme, e qualche volta parte integrante, del testo poetico" ("Nota [1954]", *LNG*, 157). One language can, of course, be a mirror or double of another, providing an "image" which

is on the whole the same in substance, yet at the same time a distorted reflection. This is because a text acquires nuances of meaning and subtle differences in the new language. Thus no translation can be an exact copy. In relation to the translation of poetry from Italian and other languages into Friulan, Pasolini wrote: "Non si tratterebbe di trasferire la materia da un piano superiore (la lingua) a un piano inferiore (il friulano), ma di trasporla da un piano all'altro a parità di livello." He went on to describe Friulan as "il duplicato che serba il valore dell'oggetto autentico, dal punto di vista sentimentale" (*Un paese di temporali e di primule*, pp. 225, 238).

32   M. Sehrawy, "The Suffering Text".
33   G. Santato describes *La nuova gioventú* as a palimpsest and palinode (*L'opera*, p. 309), while R. Rinaldi sees Pasolini's "remake" as a negation and neutralization of the earlier work (*Pier Paolo Pasolini*, p. 359). Pasolini, however, not only rewrote some of the poems and added those in "Tetro entusiasmo", but also inserted poems from his early Friulan period which had previously been published separately but properly form part of the collected work (see "Nota [1974]", *LNG*, 263). This, together with the fact that he included the early poetry and did not just publish the later work, suggests that he still felt pride in his early Friulan poetry. I do not believe he was negating or rejecting his earlier work.
34   See n. 19 above.
35   See n. 30 above.
36   Pasolini was not against change, which is a natural process in language and society. He did not, however, want to see the dialects, or the diverse cultures of which they formed a part, obliterated by a different (bourgeois) culture which judged itself to be superior. He wrote: "Non nascondo che sono disperatamente pessimista. Chi ha manipolato e radicalmente (antropologi-camente) mutato le grandi masse contadine e operaie italiane è un nuovo potere che mi è difficile definire: ma di cui sono certo che è il piú violento e totalitario che ci sia mai stato" ("11 luglio 1974: ampliamento del 'bozzetto' sulla rivoluzione antropologica in Italia", in *SC*, 57–58). Discussing young people's use of dialect, Pasolini stated: "Lo fanno perché anche a loro è arrivata, magari non con estrema consapevolezza, ma esistenzialmente, la necessità di lottare contro questo nuovo fascismo che è l'accentramento, che è l'accentramento linguistico e culturale del consumismo"; and he insisted on the importance of retaining cultural diversity: "Questa lotta per il separati-smo non è altro che la difesa di quel pluralismo culturale, che è la realtà di una cultura" (*Volgar' eloquio*, pp. 79, 32).
37   See, for example, "Pastorela di Narcís" and "Mostru o pavea?", *LNG*, 59–60, 61–62.
38   Paradoxically, however, the motif of the double in the literary tradition frequently stresses difference: for example, Oscar Wilde's *The Picture of Dorian Gray* or R. L. Stevenson's *The Strange Case of Dr Jekyll and Mr Hyde*.
39   Humour is subjective, and while others have spoken to me in great serious-ness about Pasolini's "remake", I am sure I cannot be alone in appreciating the humour and self-mockery with which he "sends up" his earlier work and attacks current society. The humour is best appreciated through a direct comparison of the rewritten poems with the original versions. Compare, for example, the two versions of "Li letanis dal biel fí" III (*LNG*, 14–15, 174–75), where the young, laughing "Diàul peciadòur" ["Devil sinner"] of the original

poem becomes the older, sleeping "Diàul Zujadòur" ["Devil Player"] in the second version, thinking not about "frutíns" ["children"] but "nevòus" ["grandchildren"]. The solemn assertion of self-fascination in the poet's first explication of Narcissism—"I vuàrdi il me cuàrp/di quan' ch'i eri frut" ["I look at my body/from when I was a boy"]—gives way to simple habit—"I vuàrdi il me cuàrp/sensa etàt nè pudòur,/[...]/davant e indavòur" ["I look at my body/without age or shame,/[...]/in front and behind"]. The two versions of "Ciants di un muàrt" v (*LNG*, 41, 207), on the other hand, enable the poet to display his dismay at the desertion of village and countryside. In the original poem we have the image of a boy newly dead, and the spirit trying to understand that it is now outside the body: "sint, Stièfin, sint,/zà sentenàrs di àins o za un momènt/jo i eri in te./Drenti, e no fòur,/[...]/i no sint il zenoli/nè il cialt dal me cuàrp" ["listen, Stièfin, listen,/hundreds of years or a moment ago/I was in you./Inside, and not outside,/(...)/I cannot feel my knee/nor the warmth of my body"]. In the revised version, the village has been deserted by the young people, and only a few older people are left. In effect, the whole village is dead: "Contadíns di Chia!/Zà sentenàrs di àins o zà un momènt,/jo i eri in vu./Ma vuei che la ciera/a è bandunada dal timp,/vu i no sèis in me./Qualchidún/al sint un cialt tal so cuàrp/'na fuarsa tal zenoli.../Cui èisia?" ["Peasants of Chia!/Hundreds of years or a moment ago,/I was in you./But today with the land/having been abandoned for a long time,/you are not in me./Someone/feels a warmth in his body,/some life in his knee.../Who is it?"]. This mockery of his early poetry is thus also turned outwards as a critique of modern society. I do not consider the fact that Pasolini could use humour against himself in this way to be equivalent to a rejection of his early poetry.

40 "Le mie proposte su scuola e tv", *Corriere della sera*, 29 Oct. 1975, then in *LL*, 176. See also Pasolini's articles "9 dicembre 1973: acculturazione e acculturazione" and "8 luglio 1974: limitatezza della storia e immensità del mondo contadino" (*SC*, 22–25, 51–66).

41 P. V. Mengaldo, *Poeti italiani del Novecento*, p. 780.

PASOLINI, FRIULI, ROME (1950–1951): PHILOLOGICAL AND HISTORICAL NOTES

Zygmunt G. Barański

Roma nella mia narrativa ha quella fondamentale importanza
[…] in quanto *violento trauma e violenta carica di vitalità*, cioè
esperienza di un mondo e quindi in un certo senso *del* mondo.
Nella narrativa Roma è stata la protagonista diretta non solo
come oggetto di descrizione o di analisi, ma proprio come necessità
testimoniale.[1]

[In my narrative, Rome has that fundamental importance (…) of
acting as *a violent trauma and a violent charge of vitality*, that is, of
acting as experience of a world and thus, in a certain sense, of *the*
world. In my narrative, Rome has been the direct protagonist not
only as object of description and analysis, but also precisely as a
mark of my need to bear witness.]

Pasolini arrived in Rome, accompanied by his mother, on 28
January 1950. They were escaping the furore in Casarsa caused at
the end of October 1949 by the revelation of his homosexuality.
Rome offered the possibility of a new start;[2] it is unlikely, however,
that during his first winter in the capital Pasolini could have had
even the slightest intimation of the radical effects that Rome was to
have on his life and career. Critics, on the other hand, with the
benefit of hindsight and spurred on by Pasolini's own subsequent
declarations on the subject, consider his departure from Friuli to
have marked the beginning of a fundamental moment in his
artistic, intellectual and emotional development. According to
Pasolini and his readers, his fascination with Rome was rapid and
all-embracing; the city quickly cut him off from the "ispirazione
[…] sensuale-stilistica" ["sensual and stylistic inspiration"] offered
by Friuli, and instead stimulated an "ispirazione […] naturalistico-

documentaria" ["naturalistic and documentary inspiration"].[3] His discovery of Rome demanded all his attention, and so Friuli inevitably had to be "rejected". Siciliano dramatically expresses this state of affairs: "Pasolini rifiutava il Friuli [...]; tutto è sprofondato in un passato col quale c'è un tenue legame: un ricordo felice; ma ormai la vita è 'violenta'" ["Pasolini rejected Friuli (...); everything had sunk into a past with which there was a fragile bond: a happy memory; but now life was 'violent'"].[4] Evidence for such an interpretation of the effects on Pasolini of his encounter with Rome is strong; in particular, stress is laid on his immediate artistic effort to come to terms with his new surroundings. He thus began to write *Ragazzi di vita* very soon after his arrival. During 1950–51 he also composed a number of notable prose pieces on Roman subjects, which he subsequently collected in *Alí dagli occhi azzurri*.[5] These "fragments" have been seen as "i primi appunti e studi sull'ambiente popolare, che costituiscono l'abbozzo preparatorio al piú largo respiro della vicenda romanzesca" ["the first notes and studies of the popular environment, which constitute the preparatory sketch for the more broadly based perspective of the novels"].[6] Such conclusions regarding Pasolini's reactions to Rome are obviously valid. They are, however, based on a partial knowledge of his artistic and intellectual attitudes during 1950–51. In addition, the writer's vigorous concentration on Rome throughout the 1950s, which culminated at the beginning of the next decade in the films *Accattone* (1961), *Mamma Roma* (1962) and *La ricotta* (1962), has further encouraged belief in the "violent trauma" of his first response to the city, and has thus helped to conceal some of the nuances of Pasolini's shift from Friuli to Rome.

It is not just Pasolini's first years in Rome which have not been satisfactorily studied. In general, any attempt to examine the progress of Pasolini's artistic career is beset by difficulties. Robert Gordon has convincingly demonstrated the mystificatory character of Pasolini's self-presentations and assessments of his own past.[7] Thus it suited Pasolini's sense of the dramatic and of his own self-importance to aggrandize all that linked him to the capital (his is the provincial's mesmerized awe when confronted with the "excesses" of the big city, that same awe which, *mutatis mutandis*, also determined Fellini's relationship to Rome). In addition, until a reliable critical edition of Pasolini's "complete works" is prepared, most claims regarding his literary and ideological development should be tempered with caution. The canon of his *œuvre* is still far from established. Unknown texts continue to be unearthed, and in some cases published.[8] Equally, since his death editions—of varying philological rigour and efficacy—of known yet previously unpublished or partially published works have appeared with monotonous (yet bewildering) regularity.[9] Furthermore, little work has been done on his autographs,[10] which, however, promise to yield a wealth of fascinating new information.[11] Therefore, given the generally confused, problematic and fragmentary nature of the Pasolinian textual tradition, it is odd that accessible published works, which can help cast further light on the writer's work during his first couple of years in the capital, have been little used by scholars. In particular, these texts, nearly fifty newspaper articles,[12] offer a possible novel perspective on Pasolini's attitudes to Friuli and Rome at this time. Whatever their intrinsic merits, these articles do represent the greater part of Pasolini's published work during 1950 and 1951,[13] and it is thus even more surprising that they should have been either ignored or misrepresented.

Until very recently the majority of Pasolini's newspaper articles belonging to this period remained uncollected, which explains in part why these valuable pieces have been largely "invisible" to scholars. In addition, most of the articles that have been anthologized since Pasolini's death have been included in three wide-ranging collections which have brought together occasional pieces written and published over many years.[14] As a result, none of the anthologies gives particular emphasis to the 1950–1951 writings; if anything, by associating them with texts composed at other times, their significance for charting Pasolini's first encounter with Rome is minimized.[15]

The articles may be divided into two main groups: thirty-one "creative" fictional pieces and seventeen non-fictional pieces (a mixture of literary criticism, travelogues, and articles on general cultural trends and events).[16] Pasolini published these articles in a wide range of newspapers, though, astonishingly, he wrote the largest number for *Il quotidiano*, the Curia-run paper. During 1951 he signed all his work for *Il quotidiano* with the pseudonym Paolo Amari; it is not clear whether he did this to conceal his involvement with a religious newspaper, or whether, as Laura Betti suggested to me, it might have been dictated by contractual obligations to another newspaper. Pasolini's poverty at the time would make such manoeuvring extremely plausible. In fact those scholars who mention these writings tend to dismiss them as merely revenue-raising exercises—the inevitable, albeit unwelcome distraction from his work on an embryonic *Ragazzi di vita* and on the pieces later to appear in *Alí dagli occhi azzurri*.[17] And it is true that once Pasolini's financial situation began to improve in 1951, his journalistic activity decreased.

It is, however, reductive to regard Pasolini's early Roman journalism as the product of simple expediency. This becomes quickly apparent when it is remembered that Pasolini's way of working during 1950 and 1951 was not unusual but mirrored what he had already been doing for several years in Friuli.[18] He submitted short pieces for publication in the press, while concentrating on more ambitious projects: in Friuli, *Atti impuri*, *Amado mio* and the early versions of *Il sogno di una cosa*;[19] in Rome, the trilogy.[20] In the capital, however, he did not just concentrate on his Roman novels. Tellingly, he continued to elaborate his Friulan books: he revised the first part and sketched a second part of *Amado mio*,[21] and began to give *Il sogno di una cosa* the shape in which it was finally to appear in 1962.[22] Some of Pasolini's newspaper contributions of the time are tangible evidence of his continuing work on this Friulan material even after his self-imposed exile, and, more importantly, they also help cast new light on the genesis of *Il sogno di una cosa*.[23] Other pieces show his desire to carry on dealing with Friulan themes,[24] or with topics which belong to a Friulan matrix of inspiration.[25] Taken together, these thirteen articles form a larger group than that which is made up of published stories with explicit Roman settings.[26] Furthermore, "Ragazzo e Trastevere" and "La bibita", both written in the first person, while ostensibly describing Roman vignettes, are much closer in tone to the autobiographical lyricism of Pasolini's Friulan novels and short stories.[27] They repeat a standard motif of this literature: the first-person narrator's encounter with a younger male character belonging to a lower social class. A sense of continuity, rather than of conflict, marks Pasolini's Friuli and Rome during 1950–51.

The mutual interrelationship, even balance, between Pasolini's two worlds is emblematically captured in another newspaper short story, "Castagne e crisantemi", published in *La libertà d'Italia* on 3 April 1951. This piece fuses the lyricism and innocence of the rural with the naturalism and experience of the urban.[28] Although such a perspective smacks of cliché, it nevertheless seems to offer an accurate record of Pasolini's situation during this period. The story describes a moment of equilibrium between the two worlds in which neither appears to hold sway:

> Da Chieti, raccolta nel sole, giú al Campo dei Fiori mattutino, quanto odore di castagne: non ricordava forse, il piccolo venditore, in tutto piú di una decina di autunni, ma era cosí fuso nel loro odore—di castagne e di fuoco—che non se ne distingueva. Dove terminava il ragazzo e dove cominciava l'odore dei suoi frutti? Erano uno dentro l'altro, solidi e vivi, una sola creatura. [...]
>
> La vecchia venditrice dei crisantemi, che si serviva da Belli Capelli, sceso giú a Roma col carretto, al contrario del venditore di caldarroste, di quanti Autunni, o Estati di San Martino, o Ognissanti aveva memoria nella sua fantasia trasteverina? Ma dal loro profumo lei era ben distinta: il dialetto con cui pensava le cose non le ricreava piú; il suo vecchio romanesco era inaridito: prosa, vecchiaia. [...]
>
> Anche il dialetto meridionale del giovinetto di Chieti si sarebbe invecchiato nel cuore: ecco con quale avidità fin da ora intasca il denaro e calcola le lire di guadagno. Nei suoi piccoli occhi azzurri pieni dell'espressione che può brillare in un grano d'uva, si fissa già il solo pensiero che lo spoglierà dei segreti e lo farà adulto. Egli si presta al tradimento con un'innocenza che ora lo fa perdonare. Fra altri dieci o dodici autunni sarà come la vecchia venditrice dei fiori: non riuscirà difficile condannarlo: sarà cosí chiaramente uomo, cosí tediosamente uomo. Ma quello che fra dieci, dodici, cento autunni resterà uguale, sarà l'odore dei crisantemi, delle castagne. Mistero fisso, mistero fossilizzato, garante di immutabilità. La Specie potrà sempre ricercarvi il suo tempo perduto. (*SCD*, 28–30)

[From Chieti, huddled in the sunshine, down to the Campo dei Fiori in the early morning, what a smell of chestnuts: he didn't recall perhaps, the young seller, more than a total of ten or so autumns, but he had become so merged with their smell—of chestnuts and smoke—that he was indistinguishable from them. Where did the boy end and where did the smell of the fruit begin? One was inside the other, solid and alive, a single creature. (...)

The old woman selling chrysanthemums, who bought them from Belli Capelli (Pretty Hair), who had come down to Rome on his cart, contrary to the roast chestnut seller, how many Autumns, or Indian Summers, or All Saints did she remember in her Trastevere imagination? But she was quite separate from their smell: the dialect with which she thought about things no longer recreated them: her old Roman dialect had become withered: prose, old age. (…)

The southern dialect of the Chietian youth will also age in the soul: look at the greed with which he already pockets money and counts the lire he makes. In his small blue eyes full of the expression which can shine in a grape, the single thought is already settling which will deprive him of his secrets and turn him into an adult. He lends himself to the betrayal with an innocence which for now allows him to be forgiven. In another ten or twelve autumns he will be like the old flower-seller: it won't be difficult to condemn him: he will be so clearly a man, so tediously a man. But what in ten, twelve, a hundred autumns will remain the same will be the smell of the chrysanthemums, of the chestnuts. A fixed mystery, a fossilized mystery, guarantor of immobility. The Species will always be able to seek there its lost age.]

The predominantly lyrical register in which this *racconto*, "Ragazzo e Trastevere" and "La bibita" are written is unusual in Pasolini's evocations of Rome.[29] There is little doubt that, in general, the city did make a quick and recognizable impact on his linguistic sensibilities. It is not the fact of this impact that I am questioning, but its relative force during Pasolini's first couple of years in the capital. The stylistic anomalousness of the three stories is especially evident when measured against the language of *Ragazzi di vita*. It is misleading, however, to compare these stories with the novel's much revised 1955 text. By using this as a yardstick, as is often done in discussions of Pasolini's first encounters with Rome, what is lost is a sense of the progressive nature of Pasolini's shift to the dialectal and orally-based plurilingualism of *Ragazzi di vita*, as well as of the debts which the slums of Rome owe the countryside of Friuli. Until such time as the *inediti* discussed by de Nardis are made public, and these are brought together with the texts in the two *cartelle* belonging to 1950–51 held in the Gabinetto Vieusseux—the second of which was labelled by Pasolini himself *Il Ferrobedò (e altri appunti e racconti, passati in parte in "Ragazzi di vita") (1950–1951)—*,[30] an idea of the degree and significance of Pasolini's lingering lyricism, and hence of the relationship during these years between his "Friulan" and "Roman" styles, can only really come from looking both at the other prose fragments on Roman subjects, namely the remaining newspaper articles and the pieces published in *Alí dagli occhi azzuri*, and at the 1951 *Paragone* version of "Il Ferrobedò", an early draft of the novel's opening chapter.[31] Siciliano, attenuating in this instance his thesis of the Roman "trauma", points out that the end of "Il Ferrobedò" translates the end of "La rondinella del Pacher".[32] Friuli and Rome merge; and in fact it has been shown that, stylistically, the whole of "Il Ferrobedò" occupies an intermediate position between the plurilingual expressionism of the finished novel and the more academically literary and monolingual tones of the Friulan writings.[33]

The remaining Roman stories similarly mark different moments of this stylistic development, and none does so more effectively than "Domenica al Collina Volpi". It has hitherto remained unnoticed, even by Siti, who reprints the story (*SCD*, 24–27) and appears to have been accorded special access to Pasolini's 1950 and 1951 typescripts, that this story, which appeared on 14 January 1951, not only contains the first draft of a piece later included in *Ragazzi di vita* but is also the earliest published example of any part of the novel. Its closing section reappears in the opening pages of *Ragazzi di vita* (pp. 7–8), and thus is also an earlier version of part of "Il Ferrobedò" (p. 60). These three passages offer an invaluable insight into the progressive "lowering" of Pasolini's stylistic register; particularly noticeable is his growing confidence in using Roman dialect features and, more generally, elements belonging to oral and popular forms:

> [...] col pallone tra i piedi;[34] formarono un piccolo quadrilatero, elastico come una gomma, e cominciarono a fare del palleggio. Colpivano la palla col collo del piede, in modo da farla scorrere raso terra, senza effetto, molto veloce. Dopo poco erano tutti zuppi di sudore, ma non volevano togliersi le giacche della festa—o le maglie di lana celeste con le striscie nere o gialle—a causa del carattere del tutto casuale e scherzoso della loro esibizione. La massima preoccupazione loro era quella di non parer fanatici: e poiché—a dire il vero—un poco fanatici lo erano, giocando sotto quel sole, cosí vestiti, avevano sfoderato un'allegria rumorosa e minacciosa, da togliere qualsiasi voglia di trovar qualcosa da ridire nei loro riguardi. Tra i passaggi e gli stop, chiacchieravano tra loro. "Ammazzalo quant' era moscio oggi Alvaro" disse un moro, tutto carico di brillantina.
>
> "Le donne," aggiunse poi, rovesciando.

"Macché donne!" gli gridò un altro, con un'espressione da incenerire l'eventuale contraddittore "quello è suonato, quello."

"A maschio!" gridò poi, a un ragazzino, perché questi rilanciasse loro il pallone rotolato al di là del recinto. Egli infatti, conversando, nel tentare uno sprezzante e audace colpo di tacco, aveva fatto un buco, il cui esito negativo, però, non fu preso in nessuna considerazione. Gli altri ragazzi già si erano rivestiti, stando seduti sotto il muretto bruciato dal sole, sull'erba sporca. (*SCD*, 26–27)

[(...) with the ball at their feet; they formed a small quadrilateral, as elastic as a rubber, and they began to pass the ball. They hit the ball with the instep, in order to make it run along the ground, without bending, very fast. After a short while they were dripping with sweat, but they didn't want to take off their Sunday jackets—or their blue woollen pullovers with the black or yellow stripes—on account of the entirely casual and playful character of their exhibition. Their utmost preoccupation was not to seem uncool: and since—to be honest—they were somewhat over-the-top, playing under that sun, dressed like that, they had displayed a noisy and threatening merriment, which took away any wish to find something to criticize about them. Whilst passing and trapping, they chatted among themselves. "Shit, Alvaro was a real wimp today," said a lad with dark hair all covered in brilliantine.

"Women," he then added, reverse passing.

"What women?" another one shouted at him, with a look to reduce to ashes anyone who would contradict him; "he's crazy, he is."

"Hey, mate!" he then shouted to a young lad, so that he might throw them back the ball which had rolled to the other side of the fence. In fact, chatting, while trying a disdainful and audacious back heel, he had screwed up; the negative result, however, was completely ignored. The other young men had already put their clothes back on, while sitting under the low wall burnt by the sun, on the dirty grass.]

[. . .] col pallone tra i piedi. Formarono un cerchio e cominciarono a fare del palleggio, colpendo la palla col collo del piede, in modo da farla scorrere raso terra, senza effetto, molto forte. Dopo un po' erano tutti bagnati di sudore, ma non volevano togliersi le giacche della festa o i maglioni di lana azzurra con le grandi striscie nere o gialle, a causa del carattere tutto casuale e scherzoso del loro gioco. Ma siccome i ragazzini che stavano lí intorno, avrebbero potuto forse pure pensare di loro che erano fanatici a giocare sotto quel sole, cosí vestiti, ridevano e si sfottevano in modo però da far passare agli altri qualsiasi voglia di scherzare. Tra i passaggi e gli stop chiacchieravano. "Ammazzete quanto sei moscio oggi Alvà" gridò un moro carico di brillantina. "Le donne" disse poi, facendo una rovesciata. "Vaff…o" gli rispose Alvà, mentre cercava di colpire il pallone di tacco. Ma fece un buco e il pallone rotolò lontano verso Lucià, e gli altri che stavano sbragati e sudati sull'erba sozza. Agnolo si alzò e rilanciò il pallone verso i giovanotti. "Mica se vole sprecà sa'" gridò Rocco "stasera ce stanno da incollà i quintali." ("Il Ferrobedò", p. 60)

[(…) with the ball at their feet. They formed a circle and began to pass the ball, hitting the ball with the instep, in order to make it run along the ground, without bending, very fast. After a while they were completely soaked in sweat, but they didn't want to take off their Sunday jackets or their heavy blue woollen pullovers with the broad black or yellow stripes, on account of the entirely casual and playful character of their game. But since the kids who were hanging around there could have perhaps also thought of them that they were fanatical playing under that sun, dressed like that, they laughed and took the piss out of each other, in such a way however as to make no one else feel like cracking a joke. While passing and trapping, they chatted. "Shit, you're a real wimp today Alvà," shouted a dark-looking lad covered in brilliantine. "Women," he then said, giving a reverse pass. "F… off," replied Alvà, while he was trying to hit the ball with a back heel. But he screwed up and the ball rolled far away towards Lucià and the others who were lying around trouserless and sweaty on the filthy grass. Agnolo got up and threw the ball back towards the young men. "He dun't wanna knacker himself you know," shouted Rocco; "there's a ton of stuff to carry tonight!"]

[…] col pallone tra i piedi. Formarono un cerchio e cominciarono a fare del palleggio, colpendo la palla col collo del piede, in modo da farla scorrere raso terra, senza effetto, con dei bei colpetti secchi. Dopo un po' erano tutti bagnati di sudore, ma non si volevano togliere le giacche della festa o i maglioni di lana azzurra con le striscie nere o gialle, a causa dell'aria tutta casuale e scherzosa con cui s'erano messi a giocare. Ma siccome i ragazzini che stavano lí intorno avrebbero forse potuto pensare che facevano i fanatici a giocare sotto quel sole, cosí vestiti, ridevano e si sfottevano, in modo però da togliere qualsiasi voglia di scherzare agli altri.

Tra i passaggi e gli stop si facevano due chiacchiere. "Ammazzete quanto sei moscio oggi, Alvà!" gridò un moro, coi capelli infracicati di brillantina. "'E donne," disse poi, facendo una

rovesciata. "Vaffan…," gli rispose Alvaro, con la sua faccia piena
d'ossa, che pareva tutta ammaccata, e un capoccione che se un
pidocchio ci avesse voluto fare un giro intorno sarebbe morto di
vecchiaia. Cercò di fare una finezza colpendo il pallone di tacco,
ma fece un liscio, e il pallone rotolò lontano verso il Riccetto e gli
altri che se ne stavano sbragati sull'erba sozza.

    Agnolo il roscetto si alzò e senza fretta rilanciò il pallone
verso i giovanotti. "Mica se vole sprecà, sa'," gridò Rocco riferen-
dosi a Alvaro, "stasera ce stanno da incollà li quintali." (*Ragazzi
di vita*, pp. 7–8)

[(…) with the ball at their feet. They formed a circle and began to
pass the ball, hitting the ball with the instep, in order to make it
run along the ground, without bending, with nice sharp shots.
After a while they were completely soaked in sweat, but they
didn't want to take off their Sunday jackets or their heavy blue
woollen pullovers with the broad black or yellow stripes, on
account of the entirely casual and playful manner in which they
had started playing. But since the kids who were hanging around
there could have perhaps thought that they were being fanatical
playing under that sun, dressed like that, they laughed and took
the piss out of each other, in such a way as to make no one else
want to crack a joke.

    While passing and trapping they chatted about this and that.
"Shit, you're a real wimp today, Alvà," shouted a dark-looking
lad, whose hair was soaked with brilliantine. "Women," he then
said, giving a reverse pass. "Fuc…," replied Alvaro, with his face
full of bones, so that it looked all bashed up, and a huge noggin
which if a louse had wanted to go for a walk round it it would
have died of old age. He tried to be fancy hitting the ball with his
heel, but he messed up, and the ball rolled far away towards
Riccetto (Curly), and the others who were lying around trouserless
on the filthy grass.

    Ginger Agnolo got up and without hurrying threw the ball
back towards the young men. "He dun't wanna knacker himself,
you know," shouted Rocco referring to Alvaro; "there's a ton of
stuff to carry tonight!"]

Taken together, the three versions of the "fanatical footballers"
are evidence of the effort Pasolini made to change his style and of
the gradual manner of this process. It is clear that in 1950 and 1951
Friuli, with its strong association with the aulic character of literary
prose in Italian—"un piccolo quadrilatero, elastico come una gom-
ma", "esibizione", "La massima preoccupazione", "avevano sfo-

derato un'allegria rumorosa", "un'espressione da incenerire l'e-
ventuale contraddittore", and so on—, still exerted a sway over
Pasolini's stylistic experimentation and assimilation of the languages of Rome. It was later that he began to achieve linguistic
independence:

> Tra il '53 e il '54 c'è un salto, in effetti: quasi un processo di
> "romanizzazione" della scrittura, di progressivo oggettivarsi del
> linguaggio (documentabile ad esempio in *Mignotta* del '54) che
> sfocerà poi nei *Ragazzi di vita*.[35]

> [Between 1953 and 1954 there is, in fact, a leap: almost a process
> of "Romanization" of his writing, of his language becoming
> progressively more objective (which may be documented, for
> instance, in *Mignotta* of 1954), a process which will then flow out
> into *Ragazzi di vita*.]

Conversely, the contacts with Rome affect the language in which
the Friulan world is evoked:

> Il capitolo 5 [of *Il sogno*] è occupato dalle esperienze di Milio in
> Svizzera, narrate attraverso l'uso di un linguaggio intercalato da
> un parlato dialettale che anticipa certi moduli stilistici dei *Ragaz-
> zi*.[36]

> [Chapter 5 (of *Il sogno*) describes Milio's experiences in Switzer-
> land, which are narrated in a language interpolated with a dialect
> speech which anticipates some of *Ragazzi*'s stylistic features.]

And this was a chapter on which Pasolini was working precisely
during 1950 and 1951.[37] Stylistically, too, the transition from Friuli
to Rome, rather than "traumatic", seems to be carefully and coherently modulated. Again, the fictional pieces having Rome as their
setting which Pasolini published in newspapers offer a vivid
insight into this development.

Although these stories have a strong stylistic affinity with the
ones in *Alí dagli occhi azzurri*, it is important, in general, that the two
groups be not confused.[38] The texts collected in *Alí* are marked by
the "scandalousness" of their content, while the ones published in
the newspapers tend to deal with less extreme representations of
Roman life ("Domenica al Collina Volpi" is a particularly good
example). This more restrained description of Rome has debts to

Pasolini's Friulan narrative perspectives, though in choosing topics suitable for publication in newspapers with large circulations he would obviously have been careful not to offend his readers' sensibilities. Thus the two most extreme pieces, both of which are included in *Alí dagli occhi azzurri*—"Testaccio" and "Impressioni per un racconto romano"—appeared in more specialist journals, *La fiera letteraria* and *Orazio*, respectively. When in 1965 Pasolini decided to bring together a selection of his scattered Roman writings in *Alí*, he seems to have been concerned to bolster the uncompromising "scandalous" image that had been created by *Ragazzi di vita* and *Una vita violenta*. He thus rejected those of his earlier pieces which did not confirm such a sense of his writing. This principle of selection led to the exclusion of nearly all the texts he had published in 1950 and 1951.

Given the overall perspective of *Alí dagli occhi azzurri*, and in particular of the 1950–51 pieces included in it, it is not surprising that critics who base themselves essentially on these (and on an anachronistic use of the 1955 text of *Ragazzi di vita*) should argue that a major fission occurred in Pasolini's writing after his arrival in Rome. My observations in this short study would seem to temper this view by highlighting the complexity, the sense of continuity and measured transition, and the experimental tension—Pasolini's "search for a style"—which are apparent in his journey from Friuli to Rome, a journey whose first difficult steps are especially well recorded in the newspaper articles of 1950 and 1951. At present, there is little doubt that these do constitute the best evidence we have of the ways in which Friuli and Rome, *prosa d'arte* and a new striving for literary realism, poetry and life, had become enmeshed in Pasolini. Thus, as this final suggestive example reveals, Pasolini actually imagined Friulan adventures on the streets of Rome, while at the same time confusing fact and fiction:

> Velino gridò a Erio: "Dove vai?"
>   Erio frenò, e restando a cavalcioni sulla sella, su cui arrivava a stento, disse serio, com' era sempre: "Al Pacher."
>   "Portami," disse Velino, attaccandosi al manubrio della bicicletta. "Monta," gli fece Erio. Velino aveva nove anni. ("La rondinella del Pacher", in *PTP*, 168)[39]

[Velino shouted to Erio: "Where are you going?"

Erio braked, remained astride the saddle, which he barely reached, and said seriously, as he always was: "To the Pacher."

"Take me," said Velino, hanging on to the bicycle's handlebar. "Climb on," said Erio. Velino was nine.]

Sulla Prenestina, un ragazzino di nove anni, con una pignatta. "A moré," mi grida, "me porti, che?" "Come no," gli rispondo, "sali." ("Appunti per un poema popolare", in *Alí*, 101)

[On the Prenestina, a nine-year-old lad, with a pot. "Hey mate," he shouts to me, "take me, hey?" "Of course," I reply to him, "get on."]

C'è nella lingua una piú asciutta aria romanza. Ecco alcuni versi di parlanti modernissimi: correvo in bicicletta sulla Prenestina, quando un ragazzino di nove anni, "A moré" mi gridò "me porti, che?" "Come no" gli risposi. "Sali."[40]

[There is in the language a terser Romance character. Here's a few lines spoken by very modern speakers: I was cycling on the Prenestina when a nine-year-old lad shouted "Hey mate" to me, "take me, hey?" "Of course," I replied to him. "Get on."]

As Pasolini himself explained, after 1949 (after "La scoperta di Marx"), he was already moving in directions which would facilitate in the early 1950s the kind of close integration between Friuli and Rome for which I argue:

Non so se alle origini stesse dell'esperienza, o se nato in un secondo istante, coesisteva al furore stilistico, in quel friulano, un tanto di reale, di oggettivo, per cui il mondo contadino della Bassa friulana in qualche modo affiorava all'espressione. E non per nulla all'interno stesso di quel mio sistema—e non per applicazione—è nata tutta una sezione che si potrebbe anche dire "impegnata", dato l'anno, 1947–48, in cui è stata scritta: *Il testament Coran*, che è una delle parti piú nutrite e forse meglio riuscite del mio libro di versi casarsesi. ("Il metodo di lavoro", p. 213)

[I am not sure whether at the very origins of the experience, or whether it was born at a second moment, there co-existed with the stylistic furore, in that Friulan, a touch of reality, of objectiv-

ity, thanks to which the peasant world of southern Friuli somehow surfaced to express itself. And not by chance, right inside
that system of mine—and not because I had applied myself to
putting it there—there was born a section which could also be
called "committed", given the year, 1947–48, in which it was
written: *Il testament Coran,* which is one of the richest and perhaps
most successful parts of my book of Casarsese verse.]

Ferretti defined this change as follows:

> Si può dire [...] che intorno al 1949 si intrecciano due elementi
> fondamentali di novità: da un lato Pasolini porta alla massima
> tensione morale il suo dramma privato originario [...] e dall'altro
> egli sente piú o meno chiaramente la necessità di misurare questo
> dramma con il mondo sociale e razionale che lo circonda.[41]

> [One might say (...) that around 1949 two new fundamental
> elements become intertwined: on the one hand Pasolini pushes to
> the maximum moral tension his original private drama (...) and
> on the other he feels more or less clearly the need to measure this
> drama against the social and rational world which surrounds
> him.]

This tension between the public and the private, between "Friuli"
and "Rome", which was to become the hallmark of Pasolini's
career, found a second major moment of balance in the years 1950–
51. Indeed, it might be better to argue that the first couple of years
in the capital continued and built on the achievements and insights
of Pasolini's last year in Friuli. The crises which these conflicting
forces were later to release had not yet emerged. It is misleading to
characterize the encounter with Rome as an immediate "violento
trauma". It would be more precise to point to the happy co-
existence between Pasolini's two great sources of inspiration.[42]

NOTES

1   P. P. Pasolini, "Dieci domande a Pasolini" [interview with E. F. Accrocca], *La
     fiera letteraria*, 30 June 1957 (italics in the original).
2   For an account of the circumstances surrounding Pasolini's "flight" from
     Friuli, see N. Naldini, *Pasolini, una vita* (Turin, Einaudi, 1989), pp. 133–41.
     Pasolini's letters of this period give an effective impression of the immediate
     impact of the scandal on him: see P. P. Pasolini, *Lettere 1940–1954*, edited by

N. Naldini (Turin, Einaudi, 1986), pp. 368–75, 384–86. See also E. Siciliano, *Vita di Pasolini* [1978] (Milan, Rizzoli, 1981), pp. 175–82. Siciliano's claim that Pasolini and his mother left for Rome in the winter of 1949 is undoubtedly erroneous: Pasolini's last letters from Casarsa (to Silvana Mauri and to Franco Farolfi) are both dated 27 January 1950, while his first letter from Rome which bears a precise date (again to Silvana Mauri) is of 10 February 1950 (*Lettere 1940–1954*, pp. 384–93). Siciliano's error seems to stem from Pasolini himself: see "Al lettore nuovo", in P. P. Pasolini, *Poesie* (Milan, Garzanti, 1970), pp. 5–14 (p. 9). Nonetheless, imprecision is not atypical of Siciliano's problematic "life". The date 28 January is given by Naldini, who claims to have accompanied Pasolini and his mother to the railway station in Casarsa on the morning of their departure: "Al nuovo lettore di Pasolini", in P. P. Pasolini, *Un paese di temporali e di primule*, edited by N. Naldini (Parma, Guanda, 1993), pp. 5–106 (p. 7).

3 P. P. Pasolini, "Il metodo di lavoro" [1958], in "Appendice" to P. P. Pasolini, *Ragazzi di vita* [1955] (Turin, Einaudi, 1979), pp. 207–38 (pp. 209–13 [p. 213]).

4 This view of the writer's development is well established in Pasolini studies. See, for example, G. C. Ferretti, *Letteratura e ideologia* [1964], second edition (Rome, Editori Riuniti, 1974), p. 203; T. Anzoino, *Pier Paolo Pasolini* [1971], second edition (Florence, La Nuova Italia, 1974), pp. 24, 35–36, 53; S. Petraglia, *Pier Paolo Pasolini* (Florence, La Nuova Italia, 1974), p. 18; F. Muzzioli, *Come leggere "Ragazzi di vita" di Pier Paolo Pasolini* (Milan, Mursia, 1975), p. 19; E. Siciliano, *Vita*, pp. 182–85, 197–211 (the quotation may be found on p. 183); G. Santato, *Pier Paolo Pasolini: l'opera* (Vicenza, Neri Pozza, 1980), pp. 145–46; N. Naldini, *Pasolini*, pp. 143–56, who repeats Pasolini's term "trauma" (p. 143), but transfers it exclusively to his cousin's personal rather than literary encounter with Rome. Naldini further confuses art and life when, in contrast to Pasolini's carefully nuanced assertion quoted at the beginning of the present essay, he reductively claims that for Pasolini "Roma non è solo un oggetto da descrivere ma è un certo senso del mondo" (p. 145). Precision, as the corrective nature of several of the studies in the present volume demonstrates, has not always been a strong point of those who have written on Pasolini. For general assessments of Pasolini and Rome see L. de Nardis, *Roma di Belli e di Pasolini* (Rome, Bulzoni, 1977), and K. Jewell, *The Poesis of History: Experimenting with Genre in Postwar Italy* (Ithaca–London, Cornell University Press, 1992), pp. 23–52. See also M. Konstantarakos, "Time and Space in Pasolini's Roman Prose Works", *The Italianist*, 12 (1992), 59–74.

5 P. P. Pasolini, *Alí dagli occhi azzurri* [1965] (Milan, Garzanti, 1976). The pieces written during 1950–51 are: "Squarci di notti romane" [1950], pp. 5–33; "Il biondomoro" [1950], pp. 34–43; "Gas" [1950], pp. 44–51; "Bounce tempo" [1950], p. 52; "Giubileo (relitto d'un romanzo umoristico)" [1950], pp. 53–63; "Notte sull'es" [1951], pp. 64–79; "Studi sulla vita del Testaccio" [1951], pp. 80–88; "Appunti per un poema popolare" [1951–52 and 1965], pp. 89–102. But see n. 38 below.

6 F. Muzzioli, *Come leggere*, p. 19.

7 R. Gordon, *Pasolini: Forms of Subjectivity* (Oxford, Oxford University Press, 1996).

8 For a recent instance of the publication of hitherto unknown texts, see "Tre framens da Safo: traduzioni inedite in friulano", which appear as an appendix in M. Fusillo, *La Grecia secondo Pasolini* (Scandicci, La Nuova Italia,

1996), pp. 243–45. See also, for example (and the examples could be multiplied without difficulty), *Tuttolibri*, 8 June 1985, in which two articles give information about Pasolinian *inediti* which had surfaced at the time: L. Tornabuoni, "Ecco Renzo e Lucia secondo Pasolini: un inedito per il cinema", p. 1 (and see G. P. Brunetta, "Il viaggio di Pasolini dentro i classici", *Galleria*, 35, i–iv [1985], 67–75); and N[ico] O[rengo], "Ultimi idilli in Friuli", p. 2. During a visit to the Fondo Pier Paolo Pasolini I found a number of unpublished poems: "'Ddio il sole", "Deserto fiore scenderemo dove tu sei", "Giorno di nuvole", "Nascita della poesia" (all in typescript), and a fragment in dialect handwritten on the inside cover of a volume of the periodical *Ce fastu?*, 24, i–iv (31 Aug. 1948). See my "Notes towards a Reconstruction: Pasolini and Rome 1950–51", *The Italianist*, 5 (1985), 138–49 (p. 145). None of the above poems is included in P. P. Pasolini, *Bestemmia: tutte le poesie*, edited by G. Chiarcossi and W. Siti, 2 vols (Milan, Garzanti, 1993).

9   As I suggest in the Introduction to the present volume, the most notorious case of this kind is probably the publication of *Petrolio* in 1992 (Turin, Einaudi). Book-length editions, however, of previously unknown works, of known yet unpublished texts, and of partially published and uncollected works have appeared with almost mechanical regularity since Pasolini's death in 1975. Their number—and I exclude from the following list reprints of books which had first appeared while the author was alive—is impressive: *Lettere agli amici* (1976), *Lettere luterane* (1976), *Volgar' eloquio* (1976), *Affabulazione; Pilade* (1977), *Le belle bandiere* (1977), *Pier Paolo Pasolini e "Il setaccio"* (1977), *San Paolo* (1977), *I disegni 1941–1975* (1978), *Descrizioni di descrizioni* (1979), *Il caos* (1979), *Porcile; Orgia; Bestia da stile* (1979), *Poesie e pagine ritrovate* (1980), *Amado mio preceduto da Atti impuri* (1982), *Appunti per un'Orestiade africana* (1983), *L'Academiuta friulana e le sue riviste* (1983), *Lettere 1940–1954* (1986), *Il portico della morte* (1988), *Lettere 1955–1975* (1988), *I dialoghi* (1992), *Petrolio* (1992), *Antologia della lirica pascoliana* (1993), *Bestemmia: tutte le poesie* (1993), *Un paese di temporali e di primule* (1993), *Romàns* (1994), *Storie della città di Dio* (1995), *Interviste corsare sulla politica e sulla vita (1955–1975)* (1995), *I film degli altri* (1996). Questions cannot but arise concerning the philological efficacy of some of these editions given the difficulties—as I explain in the following note—of consulting the autograph materials which form the basis of the printed texts, and hence of thoroughly evaluating the implications of editorial decisions. This chapter provides evidence of the lack of attention with which some editions of Pasolini's posthumous writings have been prepared.

10 One reason for the poverty of research on Pasolini's manuscripts is that the "carte inedite di Pasolini depositate dalla famiglia presso la Biblioteca Nazionale Centrale di Roma […] non [sono] ancora accessibili agli studiosi": L. de Nardis, "Sulla prima redazione di *Ragazzi di vita* e di *Una vita violenta*", *Revue des études italiennes*, 28, ii–iii (1981), 123–39 (p. 123). As far as I am aware, the situation described by de Nardis in 1981 still holds good today. Restrictions also limit access to those of Pasolini's papers preserved in the Gabinetto Vieusseux in Florence, the other main depositary of Pasolini autographs (see F. Selvatici, "Nasce a Firenze l'Archivio Pasolini", *Repubblica*, 19 Aug. 1989). If anything, since de Nardis wrote his article, the situation has become even more complex and confusing. It is not always clear in which archive Pasolini's various papers are lodged, and whether any are still in the

keeping of his family or elsewhere. It would be extremely useful if a full inventory were drawn up of Pasolini autograph material and its location. To complicate matters further, some editions which make use of autograph papers do not indicate the provenance of the texts they publish.

11 See, for example, L. de Nardis, "Sulla prima redazione di *Ragazzi di vita*", pp. 123–27. De Nardis offers an alluring glimpse of the variety of matter—"numerosi fogli costituenti i 'dossiers' preparatori dei due romanzi, contenenti materiali linguistici, liste lessicali, annotazioni sulla struttura dei capitoli, piccole mappe di quegli angoli di borgata che sono il fondale delle picaresche avventure dei protagonisti"—and the tremendous effort—"Centinaia di pagine dattiloscritte, che lo scrittore ha lavorato accanitamente tra il 1950 e il 1951 [...] e tra il 1955 e il 1959 [...] disseminate di interventi manoscritti: cancellature, soppressioni, sfrondamenti, aggiunte, disarticolazioni, sposta-menti, il tutto segnato nell'interlinea e sui margini" (p. 123; and compare N. Naldini, *Vita*, p. 155)—which went into the writing of the two novels. Together with this material, a future editor of *Ragazzi di vita* will also have to consider the proofs of the novel: "Gli ultimi interventi sul romanzo l'autore li fece addirittura in bozze," it is revealed in a note which precedes the "Appendice" to the Einaudi edition of *Ragazzi di vita* (p. 208). Pasolini appears to have made these changes not for literary reasons but to satisfy his publisher's "moralistic scruples" (letter to V. Sereni of 9 May 1955, in P. P. Pasolini, *Lettere 1955–1975*, edited by N. Naldini [Turin, Einaudi, 1988], p. 63); see also the letter to Livio Garzanti of 11 May 1955, in *Lettere 1955–1975*, pp. 65–66.

12 As far as I am aware all the articles except those listed as I, xix–xxiii in the Appendix to the present essay are accessible in the Fondo Pier Paolo Pasolini in Rome. Of the forty-eight articles, twenty-six have been reprinted, twenty-one of them in the anthologies referred to in n. 14. For further details see the Appendix to the present essay.

13 See *Pier Paolo Pasolini: "una vita futura"*, edited by L. Betti et al. (Milan, Garzanti, 1985), pp. 210–11; R. Rinaldi, *Pier Paolo Pasolini* (Milan, Mursia, 1982), pp. 434, 438, 451. S. Onofri's "Bibliografia; Filmografia; Fonti fotogra-fiche" (in *Pier Paolo Pasolini: "una vita futura"*, pp. 199–240) and R. Rinaldi's "Bibliografia delle opere di Pasolini" (*Pier Paolo Pasolini*, pp. 426–65) are, as far as I know, the fullest lists of Pasolini's vast production at present available. Although both bibliographies are incomplete and contain errors (for ex-ample, both omit a number of the 1950–51 articles [see the Appendix to the present essay]; and see also nn. 23 and 24), and so should be used with caution, they do offer a reliable idea of broad trends in Pasolini's artistic activity.

14 See P. P. Pasolini, *Il portico della morte*, edited by C. Segre (Rome, Associazione Fondo Pier Paolo Pasolini, 1988); P. P. Pasolini, *Un paese di temporali e di primule*, edited by N. Naldini (Parma, Guanda, 1993); P. P. Pasolini, *Storie della città di Dio: racconti e cronache romane (1950–1966)*, edited by W. Siti (Turin, Einaudi, 1995). In addition, Pasolini himself included a few of his 1950–51 newspaper pieces in *Alì* (see n. 38).

15 *Il portico della morte* collects literary criticism written between 1942 and 1971; *Un paese di temporali e di primule* brings together writings on Friuli dating from 1945–51; *Storie della città di Dio*, as its subtitle declares, assembles Roman stories and chronicles of 1950–66.

16 This division underlies the Appendix to the present essay. I shall here concentrate on the "fictional" pieces, since they are the more relevant to the general direction of my argument.

17 As one might expect, Siti takes a rather more positive view of Pasolini's occasional "Roman" writings than has been the norm. Like other critics, however, he fails to recognize both the complexity of the genesis of the writer's 1950–51 pieces and the web of interconnections which, in some instances, unites them to each other and to Pasolini's Friulan and Roman novels (W. Siti, "Nota al testo", in *SCD*, 171–73)—problems which are at the core of the present essay.

18 See *Pier Paolo Pasolini: "una vita futura"*, pp. 207–11; R. Rinaldi, *Pier Paolo Pasolini*, pp. 433–34, 437–38, 451.

19 For Pasolini's work on *Atti impuri* and *Amado mio* see C. D'Angeli, "Nota", in P. P. Pasolini, *Amado mio* (Milan, Garzanti, 1982), pp. 195–202 (pp. 197–202); see also E. Siciliano, *Vita*, pp. 148–55. On the genesis of *Il sogno di una cosa*, see E. Siciliano, *Vita*, pp. 155–63 and R. Rinaldi, *Pier Paolo Pasolini*, pp. 71–78, 91 n. 187; and see also nn. 22 and 23 below. All three novels appear to have been started in the late 1940s. For an important analysis of the novels, see D. Ward, *A Poetics of Resistance: Narrative and the Writings of Pier Paolo Pasolini* (Madison, NJ, Fairleigh Dickinson University Press, 1995), pp. 26–51.

20 "Infatti ho pensato contemporaneamente tre romanzi. *Ragazzi di vita, Una vita violenta* e *Il Rio della grana* (titolo questo, provvisorio, forse sostituito dalla *Città di Dio*) negli stessi mesi, negli stessi anni e insieme li ho maturati e elaborati" (P. P. Pasolini, "Il metodo di lavoro", p. 209).

21 In the first of the three *cartelle* in which the *Amado mio* manuscripts are located, there is also the only existing version of Part II of the novel, which is "ad uno stadio semiabbozzato e incompleta (si interrompe all'inizio del capitolo IV). Essa è stata scritta certamente in anni successivi al trasferimento a Roma, come attestano gli espliciti riferimenti, che il testo contiene, al processo a Rina Fort e all'anno 1950; inoltre vi si trovano già tentativi di esperimenti linguistici in romanesco, che saranno attuati in *Ragazzi di vita*" (C. D'Angeli, "Nota", p. 201). For Pasolini's work on *Amado mio*, *Atti impuri* and *Il sogno di una cosa* during his early months in Rome see his letter to Silvana Mauri of 11 February 1950, in *Lettere 1940–1954*, pp. 400–03, which makes some important points about the interrelationship between Friuli and the capital. See too N. Naldini, *Pasolini*, pp. 142–43; but see also p. 145, which seems to contradict what has previously been said about Pasolini's novel-writing activities.

22 *Il sogno di una cosa* had a tormented elaboration. Pasolini began the novel around 1948–49 with the provisional title *La meglio gioventú* (later transferred to his poetry). This version combined public events, arising from the struggles of the peasantry, with the private dramas of a young homosexual teacher-priest and of a young woman active in the Communist Party, who "sono scopertamente le due facce della figura autoriale, del soggetto autobiografico. Il riepilogo romanzesco insomma è pensato come continuazione dei *Parlanti* e di *Amado mio*, tutto centrato sul soggetto, sulla confessione [...]. Poi il progetto raggiunge un'altra fase. Le controfigure del soggetto scompaiono e potremo ritrovare il prete e la militante solo in un marginale raccontino pubblicato nel '50, *L'accelerato Venezia–Udine*. Il romanzo, col titolo mutato in

I giorni del lodo De Gasperi e poi in quello definitivo, si muove verso una totale rimozione del modello autobiografico" (R. Rinaldi, *Pier Paolo Pasolini*, pp. 71–72). This last phase, as the dust-jacket of the first edition announces (Garzanti, Milan, 1962; I quote from the 1976 Garzanti "I bianchi" edition), is primarily the result of revisions made in Rome: "scritto nel 1949–50 (tranne per l'episodio riguardante Cecilia, che risale al '52)"; for further information on the novel's composition, see the following note. With the recent publication of *Romàns* (P. P. Pasolini, *Romàns*, edited by N. Naldini [Parma, Guanda, 1994]), it emerges that the genesis of *Il sogno di una cosa* was even more complicated than has hitherto been imagined. When Pasolini began work on *La meglio gioventú*, as may be gauged from a comparison of the first chapter of *Romàns* with its reworking as "L'accelerato Venezia–Udine" (see Appendix to the present essay—hereafter "Ap."—, I, iii), the protagonists were at first not Don Paolo and a young woman but Don Paolo and a young man called Renato. There is little doubt that the account of the train journey in *Romàns* precedes that which appeared in *Il mondo*. The more pronounced homoerotic dimension of the former connects it closely to *Amado mio* and *Atti impuri* (see n. 19), while the greater political toughness of the latter would fit in with Pasolini's growing politicization at the end of the 1940s. Naldini does not recognize that "L'accelerato Venezia–Udine" rewrites Chapter 1 of *Romàns*: see "Introduzione", in *Romàns*, pp. 7–19.

23   The publication of parts of the last chapter of *Amado mio* (pp. 180–85 and 190–94) as "Avventura adriatica" (with minor changes; Ap. I, i) and as a section of "I parlanti" (with more significant alterations; Ap. I, xxx) confirms that Pasolini was working on the novel in 1950–51 (Rinaldi in his bibliography does not indicate the connections between these two pieces and *Amado mio*). More significantly, four pieces—"Era l'ora del vespro", "La padroncina impaziente", "Acquarello funebre" and "Apparizione della Svizzera"— provide important clues with which to reconstruct the progress of the "impersonal" version of *Il sogno di una cosa*. These apparently autonomous short stories are early examples respectively of pages 155–59, 77–90, 213–16 and 67–70 of the novel. The last three reveal only minor departures from the 1962 text, and are evidence that as early as the beginning of the 1950s parts of the novel, specifically those dealing with the adventures of the three young men, were close to their definitive versions. In the light of this, it is necessary to modify Rinaldi's apparent suggestion that it was not until the late 1950s that *Il sogno di una cosa* began to take on its final shape (p. 91 n. 187; Rinaldi fails to mention that the first three articles I list are conneted to the novel: p. 434). Similarly, "Acquarello funebre", a fragment from the book's last chapter, in part resolves a problem noted by G. Santato and revises his solution to it: "Rimane il problema di quando sia stato scritto, nella prima redazione e in quella definitiva, il quarto ed ultimo capitolo (la descrizione della morte di Eligio), che è completamente staccato, dal punto di vista delle strutture narrative, sia dalla vicenda della *Parte prima* che dai tre precedenti capitoli della *seconda*. La redazione definitiva comunque è da datare, a nostro avviso, posteriormente alla pubblicazione di *Una vita violenta*" (pp. 100–01 n. 64). The fourth article, "Era l'ora del vespro", is in many ways more interesting than the three fragments just discussed, since it belongs to the Cecilia episode, which is generally thought not to have been begun until 1952

(see Santato, p. 100 n. 64, and n. 22 above). This piece, however, proves that as early as 1950 Pasolini was working on the Faedis family. It shows more significant variants in relation to the 1962 text than the other three articles; these differences are clearly the result of Pasolini's major transformation of Cecilia two years later. Other large sections of earlier drafts of the second part of *Il sogno di una cosa* were also published before 1962: "Lied", *L'approdo letterario*, Apr–June 1954; "Cecilia", *L'illustrazione italiana*, 1 (Jan. 1959), 85–95, and also in *Le più belle novelle di tutti i paesi 1959*, edited by D. Porzio (Milan, Martello, 1959); see also R. Rinaldi, *Pier Paolo Pasolini*, p. 91 n. 187. Rinaldi makes another slip concerning the text of *Il sogno di una cosa* when he suggests that "Serate contadine" is a fragment of the novel (p. 434). Onofri makes the same slip by associating it with "Lied" (p. 211), which—as I have noted—is a draft of part of the novel. Although "Serate contadine" does not appear in *Il sogno*, the extent to which it does read like a passage from the Cecilia part of the book is nevertheless striking. It is likely that the story belongs to the same artistic "laboratory" as "Era l'ora del vespro", especially as the characters Leonina and Ilde appear in both (respectively Cecilia and Ilde in 1962). "Serate contadine" belongs to the jettisoned debris of *Il sogno*, and is thus a valuable document. An even more precious such fragment is "L'accelerato Venezia–Udine" (see Ap. I, iii), the only segment of *La meglio gioventú* which Pasolini published during his own lifetime (*Romàns*, of course, now offers the best idea of the earliest draft of *Il sogno di una cosa*; see N. Naldini, "Introduzione", pp. 12–14). In fact all the specifically Friulan pieces published in 1950–51 share interesting points of contact which I do not have the space to explore here; in particular, they confirm the view, already noted, that *Amado mio, Atti impuri* and *Il sogno di una cosa* emerged from a single well of inspiration and only gradually became separated. In this connection D'Angeli's comment is important: "Il testo di *Atti impuri* esiste in una sola redazione. Nella medesima cartella si trova anche, insieme a pagine sparse del romanzo, altro materiale di difficile collocazione, ma da riferirsi probabilmente a quel corpus confuso e non ancora ben ordinato che fa capo a *Il sogno di una cosa*" ("Nota", p. 197). According to Naldini ("Indicazioni bibliografiche", in *PTP*, 313–14), the previously unpublished short story "Spiritual" (now in *PTP*, 179–81) and the other papers in the folder entitled *Passione e ideologia* (1) are connected both to *Amado mio* and to *Il sogno di una cosa*. The location of the *cartella* is not given.

24 See "La rondinella del Pacher" and "Notte d'avventura" (R. Rinaldi, *Pier Paolo Pasolini*, p. 434, mistakenly lists this as having been reprinted in *Alí dagli occhi azzurri*).

25 See "D'improvviso soffiò la sarneghera", "Notturno sul mare di Terracina" and "Dissolvenza sul mare del Circeo". The last two are important and unusual moments in Pasolini's career as a "realist" writer, since, as far as I know, they are the most overtly Verghian pieces that he wrote: their explicit intertext is *I Malavoglia*. Although, thanks to Siti's work on Pasolini's *cartelle* belonging to 1950–51, we now know that these two articles from *Il quotidiano* were part of the longer story "Terracina" ("Nota al testo", pp. 171–72; and see Ap. I, xix–xxiii), which Pasolini placed in the folder containing material connected to *Ragazzi di vita*, my point regarding their debts to a "Friulan matrix of inspiration" holds good. "Terracina" as a whole is a "Roman"

offshoot of Pasolini's long-standing interest in the sea, which was closely tied to his visits to the north-east of Italy. This fascination was intended to find expression in a complex novel on the sea on which Pasolini was working in the late 1940s and early 1950s. Evidence of this creative effort survives in a collection of typescript papers entitled *Per un romanzo del mare*, from which Naldini has extracted and published *Operetta marina*. Further fragments of this project may be discovered, for instance, in "I parlanti" (pp. 231–34). For some basic facts about *Per un romanzo del mare*, see N. Naldini, "Introduzione", pp. 16–19 (on page 18, he explicitly associates "Terracina" with *Per un romanzo del mare*). Unfortunately, Naldini offers minimal information about the "raccolta di carte [...] intitolata nel dattiloscritto *Per un romanzo del mare*" (p. 17). He does not even indicate its location, while some of the points he makes about the texts connected to *Per un romanzo del mare* are undoubtedly incorrect (see Ap. I, xix–xxiii). *Operetta marina* is in *Romàns*, pp. 109–61.

26 There are eleven of these: "Ragazzo e Trastevere", "La bibita", "Il palombo", "La passione del fusajaro", "Roma allucinante", "Domenica al Collina Volpi", "Castagne e crisantemi", "Il Ferrobedò", "Santino nel mare di Ostia", "Testaccio", "Impressioni per un racconto romano".

27 Pasolini placed the typecripts of both stories in the folder which he labelled *(Articoli saggi ecc.) e raccontini romani 1950*, and which, significantly, Siti describes as containing "i racconti dove è piú forte la volontà di 'leggere nei pensieri' dei ragazzi, con una tensione lirica e introspettiva che li apparenta a un testo dell'epoca friulana come *I parlanti*—e una configurazione stilistica da prosa d'arte" ("Nota al testo", p. 171).

28 This story, too, may be found in *(Articoli saggi ecc.) e raccontini romani 1950* (W. Siti, "Nota al testo", p. 171).

29 W. Siti, "Nota al testo", p. 171.

30 W. Siti, "Nota al testo", p. 171.

31 W. Siti, "Nota al testo", p. 171.

32 E. Siciliano, *Vita*, pp. 202–03. See also Ap. I, v and xvii.

33 "Il capitolo del '51 presenta parecchi cambiamenti: [...] la trascrizione del dialetto appare meno accurata. Il lessico verrà modificato nel senso di una maggiore inserzione dei termini dialettali [...]. La stesura definitiva si arricchisce poi di particolari descrittivi che danno maggiore ampiezza e respiro alla sintassi del periodo" (F. Muzzioli, *Come leggere*, p. 21).

34 The original text has a semi-colon and not a colon as printed in *SCD*, 26.

35 M. Vallora, "*Alí dagli occhi impuri*: come nasce il manierismo nella narrativa di Pasolini", in *Lo scandalo Pasolini*, edited by F. Di Giammatteo (Rome, Bianco e Nero, 1976), pp. 156–204 (p. 159).

36 L. Martellini, *Pier Paolo Pasolini* (Florence, Le Monnier, 1983), p. 75; see also n. 22 above .

37 See "La padroncina impaziente" and "Apparizione della Svizzera"; see also n. 23 above.

38 E. Siciliano is wrong to claim that "quasi tutti gli elzeviri 'romani' usciti fra il 1950 e il 1951 sono stati poi [...] radunati in [...] *Alí dagli occhi azzurri*" (*Vita*, p. 509 n. 5). In fact only "Testaccio" (see Ap. I, xxviii), "Impressioni per un racconto romano", which is the seventh of the "Appunti per un poema popolare" (pp. 96–98; and see Ap. I, xxxi), and four fragments from "Roma allucinante", which are included in "Squarci di notti romane" (pp. 25–26, 27–

28) and in "Gas" (pp. 46, 51), are anthologized by Pasolini in *Alì*. In each case, minor differences exist between the newspaper version and that reprinted in 1965. See also Ap. I, x.

39   There are slight differences between the newspaper version of this story and that reprinted in *PTP*.

40   P. P. Pasolini, "Roma e il Belli", *Orazio*, 4, vi–ix (June–Sept. 1952), 62–64 (p. 64). An earlier Roman version of the exchange between the first-person narrator and the young boy may be found in "Ragazzo e Trastevere" (see Ap. I, ii): "Lo straordinario è che a un certo momento egli mi parla. 'A moro,' dice, 'sai che or' è?'" (*SCD*, 7). As the present essay shows, there are obviously many interconnections between Pasolini's prose writings of the late 1940s and those of the early 1950s. Any history of his early career as a novelist and writer of short stories has to be based on a careful comparison of the many different texts in prose that he wrote during this difficult period.

41   For an excellent survey of this period in Pasolini's life, see G. C. Ferretti, *Letteratura e ideologia*, pp. 185–202; the quotation is from p. 202. Naldini describes *Romàns* as incorporating both a realistic and an autobiographical dimension ("Introduzione", pp. 7 and 9–10).

42   In addition to Pasolini's prose works, support for this position comes from the poetry he wrote during 1950–51: see especially *Roma 1950: diario* (Milan, Scheiwiller, 1960).

APPENDIX
Pasolini's Newspaper Articles (1950–1951)

Given the problems which constrain attempts to reach a proper understanding of the chronology, development and publication history of Pasolini's writings—problems to which I refer in this essay and in the Introduction—, I offer below as full a description as my data allow of his 1950–51 articles. On account of the difficulties involved in consulting archive material, I have had to base several of my annotations on snippets of information made available by scholars who have had some opportunity to consult typescript and other unpublished materials. Despite the patchwork and often second-hand character of my research, what follows is the fullest—and I hope the most accurate—bibliographical presentation of Pasolini's 1950–51 newspaper articles to date. All the pieces in *Il quotidiano* appeared under the pseudonym Paolo Amari. References in this Appendix, and in the foregoing notes, to individual articles are made according to their numbering in this Appendix: for instance "Avventura adriatica" is referred to as "Ap[pendix]. I, i". All quotations from and references to Pasolini's works involve the following editions: *Ragazzi di vita* [1955] (Turin, Einaudi, 1979); *Il sogno di una cosa* [1962] (Milan, Garzanti, 1976); *Alí dagli occhi azzurri* [1965] (Milan, Garzanti, 1976); *Amado mio* (Milan, Garzanti, 1982); *Lettere 1940–1954*, edited by N. Naldini (Turin, Einaudi, 1986); *Il portico della morte* [*PM*], edited by C. Segre (Rome, Associazione Fondo Pier Paolo Pasolini, 1988); *Un paese di temporali e di primule* [*PTP*], edited by N. Naldini (Parma, Guanda, 1993); *Romàns*, edited by N. Naldini (Parma, Guanda, 1994); *Storie della città di Dio: racconti e cronache romane (1950–1966)* [*SCD*], edited by W. Siti (Turin, Einaudi, 1995). Abbreviations: Onofri = S. Onofri, "Bibliografia; Filmografia; Fonti fotografiche", in *Pier Paolo Pasolini: "una vita futura"*, edited by L. Betti et al. (Milan, Garzanti, 1985), pp. 199–240; Rinaldi = R. Rinaldi, "Bibliografia delle opere di Pasolini", in his *Pier Paolo Pasolini* (Milan, Mursia, 1982), pp. 426–65.

I   Fiction

i   "Avventura adriatica", *Il quotidiano*, 31 May 1950. This story, with some alterations, is part of the last chapter of *Amado mio* (pp. 180–85). D'Angeli ("Nota", p. 200) mistakenly refers to this piece as "Avventure adriatiche".

ii   "Ragazzo e Trastevere", *La libertà d'Italia*, 6 June 1950; reprinted in *SCD*, 5–8. Siti assigns this piece to *Il mattino d'Italia*, a phantasmic conflation of the titles of two of the newspapers in which Pasolini published during 1950–51, *La libertà d'Italia* and *Il mattino del popolo*. To judge from a cutting, there is no doubt that "Ragazzo e Trastevere" appeared in the former; its original published version has the same typographical layout as "Castagne e crisantemi", a piece with which it has close narrative and linguistic connections, and whose publication in *La libertà d'Italia* no one disputes; see Ap. I, xiv. Siti, like Rinaldi (p. 434), gives 5 June 1950 as the date of publication, while the copy of the article in the Fondo Pier Paolo Pasolini and Onofri (p. 210) give 6 June 1950 (the Fondo's copy has the date written in pen). I have opted for the Fondo's dating.

iii   "L'accelerato Venezia–Udine", *Il mondo*, 17 June 1950; reprinted in *The Italianist*, 5 (1985), 150–58; and see nn. 22–23 above. This piece corresponds, with some important changes (see n. 22), to the opening chapter of *Romàns* (pp. 23–32), a fact not noted by Naldini in the "Introduzione" to his edition of that text.

iv "La bibita", *Il quotidiano*, 25 June 1950; reprinted in *SCD*, 9–13. Pasolini reprinted this text, with the title "Biciclettone" and with some important variants involving the use of popular Roman forms, in *Racconti nuovi: gli scrittori italiani per i nuovi lettori: i ragazzi e i giovani d'oggi*, edited by D. Rinaldi and L. Sbrana (Rome, Editori Riuniti/Pioniere, 1960), pp. 159–63. Not in Rinaldi.

v "La rondinella del Pacher", *Il quotidiano*, 3 Sept. 1950; reprinted in *PTP*, 168–71; the ending of this piece is adapted to the Roman environment and appears in Ap. I, xvii, p. 71 and with further slight modifications in *Ragazzi di vita*, pp. 20–21. See also Ap. I, xi.

vi "Il palombo", *La libertà d'Italia*, 20 Sept. 1950; reprinted in *SCD*, 14–16.

vii "Era l'ora del vespro", *Il quotidiano*, 1 Oct. 1950. This is an early draft, subsequently much revised, of pages 155–59 of *Il sogno di una cosa* (see n. 23 above).

viii "D'improvviso soffiò la sarneghera", *Il quotidiano*, 17 Oct. 1950.

ix "La passione del fusajaro", *Il popolo di Roma*, 18 Oct. 1950; reprinted in *SCD*, 17–20. Pasolini reprinted this text, with the title "Il Cartina" and with some important variants involving the use of popular Roman forms, in *Galleria Colonna*, 1, i (13 Oct. 1960).

x "Roma allucinante", *La libertà d'Italia*, 9 Jan. 1951; reprinted in *SCD*, 21–23. Siti's note—"cfr. *Squarci di notti romane*, in *Alí dagli occhi azzurri*, Garzanti, Roma [*sic*] 1965. Il testo del giornale contiene brani che sono stati eliminati nell'edizione in volume" (p. 23)—is misleading. Two fragments from "Roma allucinante" are included in "Squarci di notti romane" (pp. 25–26, 27–28), while a further two are included in "Gas" (pp. 46, 51). A few minor changes were introduced into the passages reprinted in 1965.

xi "Domenica al Collina Volpi", *Il popolo di Roma*, 14 Jan. 1951; reprinted in *The Italianist*, 5 (1985), 159–61, and in *SCD*, 24–27, which does not mention the 1985 reprint. Revised versions of part of this text are reprinted in "Il Ferrobedò", p. 60 (see Ap. I, xvii) and in *Ragazzi di vita*, pp. 7–8. This is a key article. It is the first published example of a specifically Roman segment of the novel (compare Ap. I, v).

xii "La padroncina impaziente", *Il mondo*, 27 Jan. 1951. This is an early draft of pages 77–90 of *Il sogno di una cosa*; the differences between the two versions are minimal (see n. 23 above).

xiii "Visioni del sud", *Il quotidiano*, 28 Mar. 1951.

xiv "Castagne e crisantemi", *La libertà d'Italia*, 3 Apr. 1951; reprinted in *SCD*, 28–30. See also Ap. I, ii.

xv   "Notturno sul mare di Terracina", *Il quotidiano*, 19 Apr. 1951. Siti is correct in noting that this is a fragment taken from "Terracina" (*SCD*, 172). The article corresponds, with minimal changes, to *SCD*, 49–52. See also Ap. I, xviii, xix–xxiii, xxvii.

xvi   "Acquarello funebre", *Il quotidiano*, 27 Apr. 1951. This is an early draft of pages 213–16 of *Il sogno di una cosa*; the differences between the two versions are minimal (see n. 23 above).

xvii   "Il Ferrobedò", *Paragone*, 2, xviii (June 1951), 56–71. This is a draft of the opening chapter, "Il ferrobedò", of *Ragazzi di vita*, pp. 3–21; page 60 revises pages 26–27 of "Domenica al Collina Volpi" (see Ap. I, xi), while its close is based on the close of "La rondinella del Pacher" (Ap. I, v).

xviii   "Dissolvenza sul mare del Circeo", *Il quotidiano*, 7 June 1951. As Siti observes, this is an excerpt from "Terracina" (*SCD*, 172); apart from a few minor modifications, it corresponds to *SCD*, 56–59. Siti gives 8 June 1951 as the original date of publication (*SCD*, 172), while Rinaldi simply gives "giugno 1951" (p. 434). I have once again (as with Ap. I, ii) followed the date given by Onofri (p. 210) and the Fondo Pier Paolo Pasolini. See also Ap. I, xv, xix–xxiii, xxvii.

xix–xxiii   "Terracina", *Voce del popolo* [Taranto], published in five parts between 7 July and 4 August 1951. I have not been able to consult either the published originals or copies of these articles, which are not listed by Rinaldi or Onofri. I learned about their existence from the "Nota al testo" to *SCD* (pp. 171–73), and the information given there should probably be treated with caution. Without offering any supporting evidence, Siti writes: "Nel 1950 si teneva a Taranto la terza edizione di un premio letterario per un racconto inedito che avesse 'come protagonista o clima o sfondo il mare'; Pasolini inviò *Terracina*, il racconto non vinse ma fu segnalato dalla giuria e pubblicato parzialmente l'anno successivo sulla *Voce del popolo* di Taranto, in cinque puntate (dal 7 luglio al 4 agosto). Una noterella redazionale nella seconda puntata si duole che 'la lunghezza eccessiva ed una certa qual crudezza di termini sconsiglino la pubblicazione dell'intero lavoro'" (p. 172). Slightly different information about "Terracina" is given by Enzo Golino: "*Terracina*, che Pasolini inviò nel 1950 al Premio Taranto, poi pubblicato in cinque puntate, con lo pseudonimo di Paolo Amari, sul giornale tarantino *La voce del racconto*": *Tra lucciole e Palazzo* (Palermo, Sellerio, 1995), p. 29. Siti does not reprint the *Voce del popolo* articles in *SCD*. Instead, he has published as a free-standing story "Santino nel mare di Ostia", which appeared in *Il quotidiano*, 11 Sept. 1951 (*SCD*, 35–38; see also Ap. I, xxvii), and which he describes (p. 172) as the "reworking" of the first newspaper instalment. In addition, he has included in his anthology "il capitolo del dattiloscritto intitolato *Terracina* [part of the *cartella*, held by the Gabinetto Vieusseux in Florence, entitled by Pasolini himself *Il Ferrobedò (e altri appunti e racconti, passati in parte in "Ragazzi di vita") (1950–1951)*: see W. Siti, "Nota al testo", in *SCD*, 171], che comprende le altre quattro puntate della *Voce del popolo* ma le integra e le completa" (p. 172). Two sections of *Terracina* were published as articles in *Il quotidiano*: see Ap. I, xv and xviii. Confusion surrounds Pasolini and the Taranto literary prize. N. Naldini claims, without providing any evidence, that in May 1952 Pasolini "ottiene il Premio Taranto per il racconto *Terracina: operetta marina*" (*Pasolini, una vita* [Turin, Einaudi, 1989], p. 159; and see also "Cronologia", in *Lettere 1940–54*, pp. xi–cxxxii [p. cxxiv]). Naldini's assertion is almost certainly erroneous; in fact Naldini himself, in the "Introduzione" to *Romàns*, states (p. 18) that "*Terracina*" failed to win the Taranto prize in 1950. In his letters of 1952, Pasolini makes no mention either of submitting the short story or of winning the prize. Given his difficult financial circumstances and the frequent references in his letters to his participation in literary prizes, reticence regarding the Premio Taranto would be unexpected. Naldini may be confusing this prize with the Neapolitan Quattro Arti prize for criticism, to which Pasolini in 1952 submitted an essay on Ungaretti, "Un poeta e Dio" (reprinted in *Passione e ideologia*, edited by C. Segre [Turin, Einaudi, 1985], pp. 309–26). Pasolini asked Giacinto Spagnoletti for help in connection with this prize (letter written in the spring of 1952: *Lettere 1940–1954*, p. 476), of which he was joint winner (letter to Luciano Serra written in the summer of 1952: *Lettere 1940–1954*, p. 492). In the close of a letter to Spagnoletti of January 1952, Pasolini lamented the fact that payment was not forthcoming from Taranto (*Lettere 1940–1954*, p. 463), while in a postscript to a further letter to Spagnoletti of March 1952 he alluded to the fact that "i soldi di Taranto, come saprai da Sereni, non si vedono" (*Lettere 1940–1954*, p. 469). These complaints probably refer to the fee he was expecting for his *Voce del popolo* pieces. In "Introduzione", Naldini further confuses the situation regarding Pasolini's contacts with the Premio Taranto by asserting that in 1951 *Operetta marina* was entered for the prize. There is no evidence, even in Naldini's other writings, for this claim.

xxiv   "Le due Bari", *Il popolo di Roma*, 8 Aug. 1951.

xxv   "Notte d'avventura", *Il quotidiano*, 25 Aug. 1951. Rinaldi is incorrect in stating that this article is reprinted in *Alí* (p. 434).

xxvi "Apparizione della Svizzera", *Il quotidiano*, 26 Aug. 1951. This is an early draft of pages 67–70 of *Il sogno di una cosa*; the differences between the two versions are minimal (see n. 23 above).

xxvii "Santino nel mare di Ostia", *Il quotidiano*, 11 Sept. 1951; reprinted in *SCD*, 35–38. According to Siti this story is a revised version of the first instalment of "Terracina", which appeared in *Voce del popolo*, 7 July 1951 (*SCD*, 172). See Ap. I, xix–xxiii.

xxviii "Testaccio: note per un racconto", *La fiera letteraria*, 6, xxxviii (7 Oct. 1951); reprinted in *Nuovi racconti italiani*, edited by A. Baldini (Milan, Nuova Accademia, 1962); and with the title "Studi sulla vita del Testaccio" in *Alí*, 80–88, as well as in *Racconti italiani del Novecento*, edited by E. Siciliano (Milan, Mondadori, 1983). Not in Rinaldi.

xxix "Serate contadine", *Il quotidiano*, 7 Oct. 1951; reprinted in *PTP*, 176–78. Rinaldi is incorrect in stating that this article is reprinted in *Il sogno di una cosa* (p. 434; and see n. 23 above).

xxx "I parlanti", *Botteghe oscure*, 8 (Nov. 1951), then in "Appendice" to *Ragazzi di vita*, pp. 215–38. The text reprinted with *Ragazzi di vita* bears the date 1948 (p. 238). Various portions, all with significant variants, had previously appeared as parts of newspaper articles: pages 218–19 in "Dopocena nostalgico", *Il mattino del popolo*, 13 Oct. 1948 (reprinted in *PTP*, 152–54); pages 234–35 in "Topografia sentimentale del Friuli", *Avanti cul Brun!* [Udine], 1948 (reprinted in *PTP*, 155–58); pages 235–36 in "Simili ad arcangeli", *Il mattino del popolo*, 29 Oct. 1948 (reprinted in *PTP*, 159–61); and pages 236–37 in "Amado mio", *Il mattino del popolo*, 11 Dec. 1947 (reprinted in *PTP*, 141–43), and subsequently, with further changes, as the ending of *Amado mio* (pp. 190–94), which also incorporates the last section of "I parlanti" (pp. 237–38). Naldini only indicates the connection with "Simili ad arcangeli" ("Indicazioni bibliografiche", in *PTP*, 313–15 [p. 313]). Onofri notes (p. 209) that the following newspaper articles, which I have not been able to consult, also publish sections of this story: "Valvasone", *Il messaggero veneto*, 16 Nov. 1947; "Le soglie di Pordenone", *Il mattino del popolo*, 16 Apr. 1948; "La lingua di San Floreano", *Il mattino del popolo*, 19 June 1948.

xxxi "Impressioni per un racconto romano", *Orazio*, 3, x (Dec. 1951); reprinted as the seventh of the "Appunti per un poema popolare" in *Alí*, 96–98. Not in Rinaldi.

II   Non-fiction

i   "Dittatura in fiaba", *La libertà d'Italia*, 9 Mar. 1950; reprinted in *PM*, 23–25.

ii   "Romanesco 1950", *Il quotidiano*, 12 May 1950.

iii   "Sopra il nostro capo due chilometri di terra", *Il quotidiano*, 22 May 1950; the typescript version corrected by the author and bearing the title "Davide in Belgio" is reprinted in *PTP*, 172–75.

iv   "Un piccolo Werther: Enrico Fracassi (1902–1924)", *La libertà d'Italia*, 1 Aug. 1950; reprinted in *PM*, 27–29, with the typescript title "Enrico Fracassi (1902–1924): un Werther moderno". Not in Rinaldi.

v   "Scompare la selvaggina nella campagna romana", *Il quotidiano*, 9 Aug. 1950.

vi   "Gli appunti di Sandro Penna", *Il popolo di Roma*, 28 Sept. 1950; reprinted in *PM*, 31–34.

vii   "Tramonto di un dopoguerra", *La libertà d'Italia*, 6 Oct. 1950, then in *Corriere della sera*, 31 Oct. 1976. Not in Rinaldi.

viii   "Affrescano in segreto la chiesa di S. Eugenio", *Il quotidiano*, 28 Oct. 1950. Not in Rinaldi.

ix   "L'acqua ha ricamato nel calcare fantastiche grotte di merletto", *Il quotidiano*, 4 Nov. 1950.

x   "I nitidi 'trulli' di Alberobello", *Il quotidiano*, 18 Mar. 1951. Not in Rinaldi.

xi   "Letture di malato", *Il popolo di Roma*, 22 Mar. 1951; reprinted in *PM*, 35–37.

xii   "Dialetto e poesia popolare", *Mondo operaio*, 14 Apr. 1951.

xiii   "Insistenza sulla voce 'Dio' nella nuova poesia italiana", *La fiera letteraria*, 6, xxii (3 June 1951); reprinted in *PM*, 39–43.

xiv   "Il premio Viareggio di Poesia: la capanna indiana", *Il giornale*, 18 Aug. 1951; reprinted in *PM*, 45–48 with the title "La capanna indiana"; on the single surviving sheet of the typescript it is entitled "Una fantasiuccia" (*PM*, 48).

xv   "Referto per *Botteghe oscure*", *Il popolo di Roma*, 15 Sept. 1951; reprinted in *PM*, 49–52; the typescript title is "Referto su *Botteghe oscure*".

xvi   "Voci nella città di Dio", *La fiera letteraria*, 6, xxxvi (23 Sept. 1951); reprinted in *PM*, 53–55; the typescript title is "Una passione religiosa".

xvii   "Tema per Sbarbaro", *Idea*, 3, xxxi (14 Oct. 1951); reprinted in *PM*, 57–59. Not in Rinaldi or Onofri.

THE TEXTS OF *IL VANGELO SECONDO MATTEO*

Zygmunt G. Barański

Il Vangelo secondo Matteo was first screened at the twenty-fifth
Venice Film Festival on the evening of 4 September 1964, only
hours after Pasolini had finished editing it.[1] A few months earlier,
in the spring, he had begun shooting the film in the South of Italy.[2]
Contrary to what these facts may suggest, *Il Vangelo secondo Matteo*
had not been a hurried project. Pasolini had had the first idea about
the film as far back as October 1962. Then, as guest of Pro Civitate
Christiana in Assisi, he had re-read Matthew's Gospel after many
years and had felt "subito il bisogno di 'fare qualcosa': una energia
terribile, quasi fisica" ["immediately the need 'to do something': a
terrible energy, almost physical"].[3] Preparations for the film, however, were beset by problems. Difficulties in raising finance delayed
preliminary work on it until February 1963.[4] Once funding for the
film had been settled, Pasolini concentrated on the screenplay.[5] He
took as his basis the original dialogues in Matthew's Gospel.[6] To
these he added his own detailed portrayals of the characters'
clothing, emotional reactions, movements, and even physical features. Equally precisely, he described the Middle Eastern settings
in which the action was to take place. He also included notes on
possible camera positions and movements, and listed musical
accompaniments for certain scenes. Then, during June and July
1963, Pasolini's plans for *Il Vangelo secondo Matteo* suffered a new
setback. He returned from the Holy Land profoundly disappointed
with what he had seen:

> When I landed at Tel Aviv, naturally, I couldn't make out
> anything. It was night-time. All I could see was an airport and a
> city. I got a car and went in towards the interior. Right at the
> beginning I got a few images of an ancient world, which was

mainly Arab. I thought at first I might be able to use them, but then immediately afterwards the kibbutzim began to appear, and reafforestation works, modern agriculture, light industry, etc. and I realized it was all no use—that was after a few hours' driving.[7]

There followed a lengthy period of inactivity and reflection which culminated in Pasolini's decision to change location and shoot *Il Vangelo secondo Matteo* in Southern Italy.[8] As a result, the film was no longer able to accommodate an important aspect of the screenplay, and this led Pasolini to introduce other significant modifications (I shall return to these in due course).

The tension between the film and its script is not unique in the history of the genesis of *Il Vangelo secondo Matteo*. Incongruities may be noticed between the finished film and many of Pasolini's statements about it. This is not surprising. Throughout much of 1963 and 1964, Pasolini had kept the Italian press informed about the film's progress. After the scandal caused by *La ricotta* (1962),[9] there was considerable public interest in his new film. Speculation abounded as to whether Pasolini would again offend Roman Catholic sensibilities. To defuse the situation, Pasolini released lengthy reassuring declarations to the effect that he would treat Matthew's Gospel with respect. As if to prove that he had nothing to conceal, Pasolini willingly gave interviews about the different stages through which his project was passing. One effect of all this talk about *Il Vangelo secondo Matteo* was that ideas about the film were in circulation long before anyone had even seen it, or indeed before Pasolini had actually started shooting and then editing it. Discrepancies between the film and comments about it were inevitable.

For several months after the film's appearance, however, Pasolini continued to argue in terms which show that he believed his finished film was consistent with his previously expressed views. This claim has led to some critical unease, as efforts have been made to integrate Pasolini's comments on *Il Vangelo secondo Matteo* with the film itself. More significantly, it is these views rather than the film itself which have often been discussed. The film has been lost among its interpretations.

I propose in this essay to try and return to the film, both by re-examining the nature of its relationship with Pasolini's statements about it, and by measuring it against its two principal sources—Matthew's Gospel and its screenplay—, with which it is also confused. My contention is that, given *Il Vangelo secondo Matteo*'s long gestation, it is dangerous to telescope the different moments of its development, especially as Pasolini was prone to change his mind about the aims of his work and his reading of the Gospel (see the following section). The conflicting terms in which the director spoke and wrote about *Il Vangelo secondo Matteo* are evidence not of wilful obscurantism but of the different emotions and ideas which the *making* of the film inspired in him over a period of two difficult years. As a result, since its release Pasolini and most commentators have made the finished film bear more than it can carry. It has had to reconcile years of diverging reflection, which was not only affected by changes in the material conditions of the project itself as it passed through different stages but also influenced by a variety of extratextual factors (Pasolini's support for the *centro-sinistra* and his belief in the need for Roman Catholics and Marxists to communicate,[10] his growing disillusionment with traditional left-wing forms of opposition,[11] and his wish to calm fears about the film). In my opinion, the final version should be seen less as an amalgam of all or the expression of one of these moments than as a single, new moment, in which traces of earlier ideas still persist. It is only in this way that the film may be assessed on its own terms.

SOME CRITICAL INTERPRETATIONS

The all-embracing interpretative formula with which all the stages of *Il Vangelo secondo Matteo* have been traditionally considered is that of "fidelity to their source". Pasolini was consistently adamant about this:

> La mia idea è questa: seguire punto per punto *Il Vangelo secondo San Matteo* senza farne una sceneggiatura o una riduzione. Tradurlo fedelmente in immagini, seguendone senza una omissione o un'aggiunta il racconto. Anche i dialoghi dovrebbero essere rigorosamente quelli di San Matteo, senza nemmeno una frase di spiegazione o raccordo: perché nessuna immagine o nessuna parola inserita potrà mai essere all'altezza poetica del testo. ("Sei lettere", p. 16)

> [My idea is this: to follow St Matthew's Gospel point by point without turning it into a screenplay or an adaptation. I want to translate it faithfully into images, following its story without

omitting or adding anything. The dialogues too should rigorously be St Matthew's, without even a single phrase of explanation
or linkage: because no added image or word could ever be the
poetic equal of the text.]

Infatti devo cominciare a trasporre il testo—senza la mediazione
della sceneggiatura, ma cosí com' è, come se fosse già una
sceneggiatura pronta—in un testo inalterato letteralmente, ma
tecnicizzato. ("Una carica di vitalità")

[In fact I have to start transposing the text—without the mediation of the screenplay, but as it is, as if it were already a finished
screenplay—into a text which is literally unaltered, but which is
adapted to technical demands.]

Non ho nessuna intenzione di proporre interpretazioni teologi-
che. Sarà un Vangelo assolutamente canonico.[12]

[I have no intention of putting forward theological interpretations. It will be an absolutely canonical Gospel.]

Non ho cambiato una parola del testo sacro.[13]

[I haven't changed a single word of the holy text.]

I am not interested in deconsecrating: this is a fashion I hate, it is
petit bourgeois. (*Pasolini on Pasolini*, p. 83)

Pasolini's emphasis on the rigour of his vision was his guarantee of the sincerity of his project. It was a way too of establishing a
direct dialogue with Roman Catholics, many of whom, in the
climate of the Centre-left, confirmed his respectful fidelity to the
original and showered him with prizes and approval.[14] An assessment of the film in these same terms also served the contemporary
political ends of most of the Italian Left.[15] Differences of opinion
about the film between the two groups lay elsewhere. Roman
Catholic criticism emphasized Pasolini's ability to remain faithful
to the Christian spirit of the original and his sensitivity in granting
an aura of religiosity to his film, while left-wing reviewers highlighted the social dimensions of the Gospel which the film underlined, and proclaimed *Il Vangelo secondo Matteo*'s qualities as committed art. As we shall see, both could find support for their
judgements in Pasolini's own comments on the film.

The majority of other reviewers and critics have followed similar lines as regards the excellence of the film and the fidelity of its adaptation; and during the last thirty years this latter position has become just about canonical.[16] This consensus of opinion about *Il Vangelo secondo Matteo*'s faithful imitation of its source is not surprising given the fact that this view is openly supported by the film's dialogue, which, as in the screenplay, normally repeats Matthew's text verbatim. It is difficult, however, to find this definition satisfactory.

Many statements made by Pasolini himself would seem to challenge the idea of the film's fidelity to its model:

> I did not want to reconstruct the life of Christ as it really was, I wanted to do the story of Christ plus two thousand years of Christian translation [...]. My film is the life of Christ plus two thousand years of story-telling about the life of Christ. That was my intention. (*Pasolini on Pasolini*, p. 83)

> La storia di Cristo è fatta di due millenni di interpretazione cristiana. Tra la realtà storica e me si è creato lo spessore del mito. Di qui il carattere composito della ricostruzione.[17]

> [The history of Christ is constructed out of two thousand years of Christian interpretation. The thickness of myth has grown up between historical reality and myself. Hence the composite character of the reconstruction.]

Pasolini normally cited his striking use of visual borrowings from religious art as evidence of the presence in his film of this tradition of "story-telling". These echoes, he explained, introduce a number of important perspectives into his film. They reveal the inspiration provided by the life of Christ. They are the means by which he could insert into the film the point of view of the ordinary believer who visualizes his or her faith in iconographical terms. At the same time, they are the point of contact within the film between his vision (since religious art is also part of his intellectual heritage) and that of "cet homme du peuple qui croit" ["that man of the people who believes"].[18] It is through the film's dual vision that it becomes "un racconto epico-lirico in chiave nazional-popolare" ["an epic-lyrical story in a national-popular key"], since "questo schema è riempito da due specie di religiosità, la mia personale e quella del popolo che segue Cristo" ["this scheme is filled by two types of religiosity, my personal one and that of the people who follow Christ"].[19] The epic leads to the mythic ("I preferred to leave things in their religious state, that is, their mythical state. Epic-mythic": "An Interview with James Blue", p. 26), which is so important for Pasolini in this film: "Ho fatto un film in cui si esprime [...] l'intera mia nostalgia del mitico, dell'epico e del sacro" ["I have made a film in which is expressed (...) my entire nostalgia for the mythic, the epic and the holy": *Il sogno del centauro*, p. 32]. Moreover, the presence of examples of religious art in *Il Vangelo secondo Matteo* leads to "una demistificazione dell'iconografia intesa secondo gli schemi della tradizione [...]; l'iconografia [...] nel Vangelo è stata un pretesto per costruirci sopra qualcosa di antitradizionale" ["a demystification of iconography understood in traditional terms (...); iconography (...) in the Gospel was a pretext on which to build something anti-traditional"].[20]

The main feature of this "something", according to Pasolini, is his use of "analogy", rather than historical "reconstruction", in presenting the world in which Matthew's story takes place: "The whole film was shot in Southern Italy. I would remake the Gospel by analogy. Southern Italy enabled me to make the transposition from the ancient to the modern world without having to reconstruct it either archaeologically or philologically" (*Pasolini on Pasolini*, p. 82). Pasolini argued that such a change was inevitable once he had begun to have doubts about the Holy Land as the setting for his film. He could no longer make a "realistic" film as he had first intended: "Vedrò la vita di Cristo e la Palestina con lo stesso occhio con cui ho visto Roma [...], con l'occhio di un realista" ["I will look at the life of Christ and at Palestine with the same eyes as I have looked at Rome (...), with the eyes of a realist"].[21] He needed to find a new way to approach the Gospel. "Analogy" was the obvious solution, especially as there were hints of this approach already in his screenplay (for example, in the episode of the Massacre of the Innocents: "riprendere le atrocità dei corpicini uccisi, ricordando le atrocità analoghe accadute durante l'ultima guerra, nei campi di sterminio, ecc." ["film the atrocity of the small dead bodies, recalling analogous atrocities which happened during the last war, in the concentration camps, etc.": *V*, 54]). The "realist" bias, however, persisted in some of his later explanations of the film: "Mi pare anzitutto che Matteo sia, di tutti gli evangelisti [...] il piú 'realista', il piú vicino alla realtà contadina in cui comparve Cristo" ["It seems to me that of all the evangelists Matthew is (...)

the most 'realistic', the one who is closest to the peasant reality in which Christ appeared": *Il sogno del centauro*, p. 34). Such a definition obviously jars with the mythic-lyrical qualities he claimed elsewhere for the film and for its source.

Pasolini explained that his decision to locate his film in Southern Italy enabled him to satisfy his political concerns:

> Fino a un certo limite della coscienza, anzi, dentro tutta la mia coscienza è un'opera marxista: e infatti, per darle qualche piccolo esempio, io non potevo girare delle scene senza che in queste scene ci fosse un momento di sincerità, almeno come attualità. E così i soldati di Erode come potevo farli? Potevo farli con dei baffoni, con i denti digrignanti, vestiti con degli stracci, come i cori dell'opera? No, non li potevo fare così, li ho vestiti un po' da fascisti e li ho immaginati come delle squadracce fasciste o come i fascisti che uccidevano i bambini slavi buttandoli per aria. La fuga di Giuseppe e Maria verso l'Egitto come l'ho pensata? L'ho pensata ricordandomi certe fughe, certi sfollamenti di profughi spagnoli attraverso i Pirenei. ("Una discussione del '64", pp. 108–09)

> [Up to a certain limit of my conscience, or rather, within the whole of my conscience, it is a Marxist work: and indeed, to give you some small examples, I couldn't shoot certain scenes without there being a moment of sincerity in these scenes, at least in terms of recent events. And so how could I fashion Herod's soldiers? Could I have created them with great big moustaches, with gnashing teeth, dressed in rags, like in an opera chorus? No, I couldn't have created them like that, I dressed them a bit like Fascists and imagined them to be like Fascist gangs or like the Fascists who used to kill Slav babies by throwing them up into the air. How did I imagine Joseph and Mary's flight into Egypt? I imagined it remembering certain flights, certain evacuations of Spanish refugees across the Pyrenees.]

> Ciò che mi interessava era di creare un equivalente dello strato popolare, della gente semplice, in mezzo alla quale ha vissuto Cristo. E mi è sembrato che i meridionali, pugliesi, calabresi, lucani, fossero i più adatti.[22]

> [What I was interested in doing was creating an equivalent of the popular stratum, of the ordinary people, among whom Christ lived. And it seemed to me that the Southerners, the inhabitants of Puglia, Calabria, Lucania, were the most suitable.]

As a result of this "analogical" approach, especially when coupled to the film's evocation of the Christological tradition in Western culture, Pasolini could not really be said to have been intent on restoring Matthew's text to its original state. Indeed, it is difficult to escape the conclusion that he was openly adding to the myriad interpretations of the Gospel. His purpose in the film would seem to have been to superimpose new layers on the original, rather than to dissolve existing accretions. If what Pasolini claimed in the above statements about his methods corresponds with what may reasonably be found in *Il Vangelo secondo Matteo*, then his artistic and ideological aims were in clear contradiction with the affirmations he also made regarding the film's fidelity to its source. But this is not the only problem which Pasolini's various and varied explanations create: is the film mythic or historical? religious or political? "lyrical" or "realistic"? reverential or blasphemous? His diverging pronouncements do seem to fit in with that general intellectual uncertainty which characterized his thinking during the early to mid-Sixties, as well as with the cultural and political climate of the time. But what connection does this lack of certitude—and the competing claims it appears to have generated—have with the film itself?

THE FILM'S STRUCTURE

All Pasolini's conflicting comments on *Il Vangelo secondo Matteo* essentially revolve around the central question of the nature of its relationship to Matthew's Gospel. If one compares the screenplay to the Gospel, it is clear that the former remains rigorously faithful to the structure of the latter, except for a few minor alterations and excisions. Some changes are dictated by Pasolini's effort to "tidy up" the Gospel: for example, the deletion of repetitions, such as the Pharisees' twice-made request for a sign from Jesus (12. 38 and 16. 1), which in the screenplay appears only once. Others are the result of his attention to the practical needs of the future transition from a written text to an audio-visual one for which the screenplay prepares. For example, the screenplay omits certain details, like the background to John the Baptist's imprisonment and death (14. 1–6), which would be very difficult to reproduce without inserting a lengthy new episode. Narrative formulae which serve to structure the Gospel, such as "Quando Gesú ebbe finito di dare le sue istruzioni ai suoi dodici discepoli, partí di là per insegnare e predicare nelle città loro" ["And it came to pass, when Jesus had made an end of commanding his twelve disciples, he departed thence to teach and preach in their cities": 11. 1],[23] also disappear, as they would be cinematically redundant. In addition, the number of settings is reduced, as a result both of financial considerations and of the structural wish—to which I referred earlier—to give the story greater narrative cohesion. Thus, as regards the structure of his screenplay, Pasolini could claim with considerable justification that it remained faithful to the narrative flow of the Gospel.

It would, however, have been difficult for him to make a similar claim as regards the narrative organization of his film. According to my calculations, approximately sixty per cent of the subject-matter of Matthew's Gospel disappears in the film. Pasolini only really followed the Gospel's structure at the beginning and end of his adaptation—and it is difficult to think how he could have avoided doing this when recounting Christ's life. In the space between Jesus's temptation in the desert and his arrival in Jerusalem (from 4. 12 to 21. 1), however, Pasolini completely subverted the narrative sequence of his source; and he even introduced major changes into Christ's early years and last days.

Pasolini altered the structure of the central panel of the Gospel by omitting whole sections of the original (see the section entitled "The Deletions" and note 32). In other cases, he synthesized a single episode: for example, the Sermon on the Mount (5. 1–7. 29) is reduced to 5. 3–17, 38–39, 43–45, 6. 3–4, 7–13, 19–20, 24–7. 3, 7. 9–14, with the resultant loss of over half of Jesus's words. Most frequently, he modified the chronology of events by bringing together episodes which have little or no connection in the original. For example, *Il Vangelo secondo Matteo* moves backwards from the rich young man (19. 16–24) to Christ and the little children (19. 3–12), and then to John the Baptist's execution (14. 3–12) and to Jesus's instructions on how to follow him (8. 18–22), before going forward once again to Christ's praise of Peter and to his prophecy of the Passion (16. 13–24).

The additions to the Gospel that Pasolini made in his film are structurally more radical than these changes. In just about every case he amplified the episodes he retained: from the emphasis placed on Mary during Christ's speech on the family (12. 47–50) to the concentration on Herod's castle and its life which dominates the sequence of John the Baptist's execution. More significantly still, Pasolini interpolated new episodes (see especially the section entitled "The [Melo]drama of History").

A striking example, which neatly illustrates many of the different kinds of structural alteration which Pasolini introduced into his film, is his adaptation of Matthew 11. 25–12. 21:

[25]In quel tempo Gesú disse ancora: "Io rendo lode a te, Padre, Signore del cielo e della terra, che nascondesti queste cose ai dotti e ai furbi e le rivelasti ai semplici. [26]Sí, Padre, perché cosí ti è piaciuto. [27]Ogni cosa mi è stata data dal Padre mio, e nessuno conosce il Figlio se non il Padre, e nessuno conosce il Padre se non il Figlio e colui al quale il Figlio lo voglia rivelare.

[28]"Venite a me, voi tutti che siete stanchi e oppressi, e io vi darò sollievo. [29]Prendete su di voi il mio giogo e imparate da me che sono mite e umile di cuore, e troverete riposo alle anime vostre; [30]perché il mio giogo è lieve e il mio peso è leggiero."

12

[1]In quel tempo se n'andava Gesú, in giorno di sabato, per i seminati, e i discepoli che avevano fame cominciarono a cogliere spighe e a mangiarle. [2]Ma i Farisei, vedendo, gli dissero: "Ecco, i tuoi discepoli fanno ciò che non si può fare di sabato." [3]Rispose loro: "Non avete letto quel che fece Davide quand' egli e gli altri che erano con lui ebbero fame? [4]Come entrò nella casa di Dio e mangiò i pani della Proposizione che né a lui né a quelli che erano con lui era lecito mangiare, ma ai sacerdoti soltanto? [5]O non avete letto nella Legge come di sabato i sacerdoti nel tempio infrangono il sabato, eppure non sono colpevoli? [6]Ora io vi dico: C'è qui (qualcosa) piú grande del tempio. [7]E se sapeste che cosa significhi: Io voglio misericordia e non sacrificio, non condannereste degli innocenti. [8]Perché il Figlio dell'uomo è signore del sabato."

[9]E partito di là, entrò nella loro sinagoga. [10]C'era là un uomo che aveva una mano inaridita. E interrogarono Gesú per poterlo accusare: "È lecito guarire il giorno di sabato?"

[11]Ma egli rispose loro: "Chi tra voi, avendo una sola pecora, se questa cade di sabato in un fosso, non la prende e la tira fuori? [12]Ora un uomo vale molto piú di una pecora. Dunque è lecito far del bene in giorno di sabato." [13]E rivolto all'uomo disse: "Stendi la tua mano." Quello la stese, e tornò sana come l'altra.

[14]Ma i Farisei, usciti, tennero consiglio contro di lui come farlo morire.

¹⁵Gesú però, saputolo, s'allontanò di là. Molti lo seguirono ed egli tutti guarí, ¹⁶ma ordinò loro di non renderlo manifesto. ¹⁷Cosí si compiva il vaticinio d'Isaia profeta:
¹⁸Ecco il mio Servo, che ho scelto,
il mio diletto nel quale si compiace l'anima mia.
Porrò il mio Spirito sopra di lui,
e annunzierà alle nazioni la giustizia.
¹⁹Non disputerà né griderà,
né udirà alcuno nelle piazze la sua voce.
²⁰Non spezzerà la canna fessa,
né spegnerà il lucignolo fumigante,
finché non abbia fatto trionfare la giustizia.
²¹E nel nome di lui le genti porranno la loro speranza.

[²⁵At that season Jesus answered and said, I thank thee, O Father, Lord of heaven and earth, that thou didst hide these things from the wise and understanding, and didst reveal them unto babes: ²⁶yea, Father, for so it was well-pleasing in thy sight. ²⁷All things have been delivered unto me of my Father: and no one knoweth the Son, save the Father; neither doth any know the Father, save the Son, and he to whomsoever the Son willeth to reveal *him*. ²⁸Come unto me, all ye that labour and are heavy laden, and I will give you rest. ²⁹Take my yoke upon you, and learn of me; for I am meek and lowly in heart: and ye shall find rest unto your souls. ³⁰For my yoke is easy, and my burden is light.

12

¹At that season Jesus went on the sabbath day through the cornfields; and his disciples were an hungred, and began to pluck ears of corn, and to eat. ²But the Pharisees, when they saw it, said unto him, Behold, thy disciples do that which it is not lawful to do upon the sabbath. ³But he said unto them, Have ye not read what David did, when he was an hungred, and they that were with him; ⁴how he entered into the house of God, and did eat the shewbread, which it was not lawful for him to eat, neither for them that were with him, but only for the priests? ⁵Or have ye not read in the law, how that on the sabbath day the priests in the temple profane the sabbath, and are guiltless? ⁶But I say unto you, that one greater than the temple is here. ⁷But if ye had known what this meaneth, I desire mercy, and not sacrifice, ye would not have condemned the guiltless. ⁸For the Son of man is lord of the sabbath.

⁹And he departed thence, and went into their synagogue: ¹⁰and behold, a man having a withered hand. And they asked

him, saying, Is it lawful to heal on the sabbath day? that they might accuse him. ¹¹And he said unto them, What man shall there be of you, that shall have one sheep, and if this fall into a pit on the sabbath day, will he not lay hold on it, and lift it out? ¹²How much then is a man of more value than a sheep! Wherefore it is lawful to do good on the sabbath day. ¹³Then saith he to the man, Stretch forth thy hand. And he stretched it forth; and it was restored whole, as the other. ¹⁴But the Pharisees went out, and took counsel against him, how they might destroy him. ¹⁵And Jesus perceiving *it* withdrew from thence: ¹⁶and many followed him; and he healed them all, and charged them that they should not make him known: ¹⁷that it might be fulfilled which was spoken by Isaiah the prophet, saying,/¹⁸Behold, my servant whom I have chosen;/My beloved in whom my soul is well pleased:/I will put my Spirit upon him,/And he shall declare judgement to the Gentiles./¹⁹He shall not strive, nor cry aloud;/Neither shall any one hear his voice in the streets./²⁰A bruised reed shall he not break,/And smoking flax shall he not quench,/Till he send forth judgement unto victory./²¹And in his name shall the Gentiles hope.]

Pasolini fashioned a single new narrative unit by synthesizing these four discrete yet contiguous episodes (uncharacteristically, however, he included most of the content of the original). In addition, he introduced two major new events and a whole host of minor changes. In the film we see Christ and the apostles travelling through a barren countryside. He instructs them as they walk. While Jesus is still explaining his relationship to the Father, they come across a group of peasants. He finishes his speech (11. 30) as, smiling, he lifts up one of the peasant children. The film then cuts to a close-up of Judas's face. He begins slowly to move away from the other disciples. Taking some money out of his purse he buys some olives from the peasants, which he eats and shares with a few of the apostles, who by now have joined him. In a long shot we see the arrival of a cortège of wealthy and well-dressed horsemen with their servants: they are the Pharisees. Their accusation—uttered in the film by a single Pharisee—and Jesus's reply follow Matthew's text verbatim. At the end of Christ's speech, the film cuts to a middle-distance shot of the arrival of a cripple on crutches. The camera rests on him as he slowly shuffles forward to reach Christ. Again the Pharisee's question (12. 10) and the beginning of Jesus's answer (12. 11–12) repeat the words found in the Gospel. Having reached this point, however, Pasolini had to create a new dialogue to conform to the narrative changes he had made. Echoing similar instructions made to other sick people he cures—for instance, "Alzati [...] prendi il tuo lettuccio e vattene a casa" ["Arise, and take up thy bed, and go unto thy house": 9. 6]—, Christ now says, "Getta le tue stampelle" ["Throw away your crutches"]. The cripple does as he is bidden, and then is admonished by Jesus: "Non farlo sapere ad alcuno della tua guarigione" ["Do not let any one know of your cure"]. Pasolini has here restored 12. 16 to direct speech on the basis of 8. 4: "Bada di non raccontarlo a nessuno" ["See thou tell no man"]. Christ moves off, followed by the apostles, shouting the Isaiah prophecy, which in this way becomes part of his overall message. The sequence closes with a close-up of the face of another Pharisee, previously briefly introduced in a close-up, who announces: "Noi dobbiamo trovare il modo di farlo perire" ["We have to find the way of making him perish"]—a translation into direct speech of the latter part of 12. 14.

Unless one compares this episode with the original in Matthew, the extent of Pasolini's innovation can easily be missed. On the surface, the alterations do not seem to go against the spirit or the accepted content of Gospel narratives. Yet significant changes are introduced. The emphasis on Judas is a characteristic feature of this film (see the section entitled "Of Jesus, Judas and Other Characters"). Similarly, when Christ utters the words from Isaiah, his brusqueness and the tone of his voice are completely at odds with the message of his words. Such ambiguity in his character is another specific concern of Pasolini's film (see the section entitled "'Two Thousand Years of Story-telling'").

It might be claimed that these and the other changes are somehow "inevitable", the result of the transposition of Matthew's Gospel to the screen. There is a certain validity to this claim. The unification of setting and the translation of indirect speech and of segments of narrative into direct speech do appear to be largely dictated by cinematic considerations. The placing of the Pharisee's threat at the end of the sequence and the substitution of a cripple for the man with the withered hand also make good film sense, since they heighten the drama. Yet such operations of montage and *mise-en-scène*, even if simply the necessary result of the film adaptation or introduced purely for aesthetic ends,[24] must necessarily undermine old meanings and insert new ones. To see and hear Christ speak in the cinema involves different communicative effects from reading his words or hearing them in church; while the kind of major narrative alterations I have described—for example, in relation to Jesus and Judas—go far beyond what a more rigorously faithful director might have attempted.

It might also be claimed that such developments in the two characters are consistent merely with Pasolini's admitted aim of showing the cultural accretions which have formed around the original Gospel story. For example, the greater role given to Judas in the film could illustrate the fascination which his figure has exerted on many generations of writers, from the authors of the medieval lives of Judas to a modern novelist like Borges, or a song-writer like Bob Dylan, or a writer of thrillers like Peter Van Greenaway.[25] Similarly, Pasolini's amplification of the events around the birth of Christ and those connected with his Passion could mirror the enormous attention which has been paid to them in Western culture. I do not deny that Pasolini wished to suggest the transformations undergone by the Gospel, though, as I shall argue, I think his interventions are part of a more complex strategy than one of simply trying to point out the "two thousand years of story-telling about the life of Christ". Any changes in a text entail changes in meaning, and when these are as widespread and extensive as Pasolini's, it becomes increasingly difficult not to see his film taking on a dialectical relationship with its source rather than passively repeating its rhythms and its message.

And yet, why is it that so many viewers continue to claim that the film is a respectful and faithful adaptation of Matthew's Gospel? Firstly, it is because its muted tones are so different from the garishness and melodrama of Hollywood and Cinecittà Biblical epics. Pasolini's reticence and sober taste appear to be more in keeping with what is expected from a work dealing with a religious topic. Secondly, the film fulfils the viewer's expectations of the Gospel by reproducing his or her culturally conditioned memories of the New Testament. The dialogue, except in one or two places, is not only that found in Matthew's Gospel, but, as Pasolini himself explained: "[Although] it is slightly antiquated […] it would not seem strange to an average Italian because they are used to religion being in that kind of language: it is normal, like the language of television" (*Pasolini on Pasolini*, p. 95). More importantly, Pasolini retained many of the best-known episodes from Christ's life: not just his birth and death but also his baptism, the calling of the apostles, John the Baptist's story, some miraculous cures, the miracle of the loaves and fishes, the walking on the water, the triumphal entry into Jerusalem, the anointing by Mary of Bethany, the fig tree, the attack on the temple sellers, the Last Supper, the Resurrection. Similarly, many of Jesus's most quoted words remain: the Beatitudes, the Lord's Prayer, the investiture of Peter, and such proverbial speeches as those on an eye for an eye, on the birds of the field, on the mote in the eye, on the width of the gate of destruction, on the hair on the head, on little children, on lost sheep, on wealth and the eye of the needle, and on the tribute owed to Caesar. This massive presence of elements which are central to Western culture's memory of the Gospel creates for the film an aura of fidelity to its source, especially as only three of the best-known episodes are missing: the parables of the sower and of the talents, the *sententia* on pearls and swine, and the Transfiguration.

A final reason for the viewer's impression of the film's "fidelity" is the fact that it is made up of apparently self-sufficient narrative blocks, usually marked off by slow fades to black, which reproduce the episodic quality of Matthew's text. The film, however, is more tightly organized than its source, since it has a quite marked circular structure which the Gospel lacks. At the beginning and end we find similar sequences of events: despair (Joseph's anguish at Mary's pregnancy and the pain of Jesus's followers at his death), which then turns into joy after the intervention of an angel (in the film it is the same angel in both instances). We also find similar uses of character and setting: (*a*) a transition from a private rural scene to (*b*) an urban one full of action and then (*c*) back to the rural, but now in a public dimension: (*a*) Mary and Joseph in their cottage in the countryside and Joseph's walk through the fields to the outskirts of Nazareth parallel Jesus and the apostles walking alone in the hills on their way to Jerusalem; (*b*) the hubbub caused by the arrival of the three kings in Jerusalem parallels Jesus's action-packed arrival in the city;[26] and (*c*) the joyful homage which the three kings and the peasants pay the infant is paralleled by the film's last scene, in which the risen Christ is surrounded by a group of happy disciples and peasants. The film's structural unity gives the Biblical narrative a feeling of cohesion which the original lacks. Pasolini's is a much more controlled episodicity than Matthew's.

He also achieves this by establishing musical links between different episodes in the film: the same music is heard during the Massacre of the Innocents, the execution of John the Baptist and Christ's crucifixion. He ensures similar effects through other kinds of repetition. Pasolini normally arranges for two contiguous yet independent episodes to share a common motif or prominent stylistic feature so as to create a sense of "rhythm" and continuity between the film's different moments. For example, Pasolini moves from a close-up of the calmed faces of the possessed to a close-up of the face of the leper (see the next section). Such devices ultimately distance the model from its source by introducing correspondences which do not exist in the original, just as Pasolini's additions, deletions, syntheses and changes in chronology fashion a new narrative for the film. Such alterations clearly point to the hand of the adapter who, rather than concealing his presence, highlights his own authorship and the control he exerts over the material he has borrowed and is refashioning into a new text. In structuring the film, Pasolini eliminates Matthew and substitutes himself as a new "evangelist" and a source of information about Christ. In the film Matthew is marginalized as a character: he is given less space than any other apostle. Pasolini literally excises him from the text by not including in *Il Vangelo secondo Matteo* the episode of Matthew's calling (9. 9), which he had, however, prepared as an independent moment in his screenplay (*V*, 102). Despite the film's title, it is clearly "un film di Pier Paolo Pasolini".[27]

The Deletions

There is much evidence suggesting that Pasolini shot more material than he included in his finished film. It also appears that on location he followed his screenplay more closely than emerges in the final version. He claimed that the omissions, like his structural alterations, resulted from the application of aesthetic criteria and his wish to keep the length of the film within reasonable limits.[28] These claims are partly true, but they would be more convincing if his deletions did not fit so conveniently into certain consistent patterns, and if his narrative additions and his use of *mise-en-scène* did not also support the ideological presuppositions which appear to lie behind his manipulations of Matthew's Gospel.

When Pasolini adapted the Gospel for the screen he was faced with a major problem. The original text is primarily a collection of Jesus's speeches interspersed with brief moments of activity, such as the movements from one place to the next and the miracles. Matthew uses descriptions of action principally as devices with which to introduce a new set of Christ's sayings. If Pasolini had faithfully followed the original, the film would have consisted mainly of long periods of stasis filled only with monologues. Such a solution would have been at odds with the cinema's visual and active properties, and audiences accustomed to Hollywood-type narratives would have found the film very difficult to watch. As it is, many viewers find *Il Vangelo secondo Matteo* over-long, repetitive, slow and, by the end, somewhat alienating, despite all the director's efforts to "liven up" the Gospel story. Pasolini amplifies episodes by filling them with minor characters, whose appearance and behaviour he then observes. Throughout the film he does the same with Jesus and his disciples. He adds layers to an episode in order to make it more complex and fill it with movement, while his use of landscape similarly serves to introduce variety into the film. As a result, *Il Vangelo secondo Matteo* is filled with long periods of silence as the camera focuses on character and location. This not only goes against the obsessively logocentric nature of Matthew's text, but, more importantly, also occupies film space that could have been filled with Christ's words, which thus have to be omitted. Despite these reservations, Pasolini's explanations of his deletions—that they are the result of artistic and cinematic pressures and do not really affect his film's relationship to Matthew's text—appear, at first sight, to be quite cogent.

Nevertheless, such a conclusion is wholly misleading. Regardless of the obvious predominance of direct speech in the Gospel, there are moments of action in it which Pasolini, following other Biblical epics, could have successfully transferred to the screen but chooses to ignore. These are primarily concentrated around the miracles, the Passion and the Resurrection. Matthew introduces excitement into his narrative by underlining the marvellousness of Jesus's powers. In particular, he describes in detail the different moments of Christ's death and return. Pasolini, however, considerably cuts and modifies all these events. His aim might have been to instil greater movement into his version of the Gospel, but it is evident that he did not always want the action offered by the original.

Pasolini included only six miracles in the film, while in the Gospel there are more than twenty. Of the six he accommodated, four are clearly recognizable as famous moments in Christ's life—the healing of the leper, the walking on the water, the feeding of the five thousand and the Resurrection—, and may be seen principally as forming part of the "necessary" baggage for any presentation of Jesus, while the other two are more problematic. We have already seen that the healing of the cripple is Pasolini's own invention. The sixth miracle is portrayed in the most confusing sequence of the whole film. Only after watching the episode many times and comparing it with the Gospel did I realize that it almost certainly describes a casting out of demons. Pasolini seems to have created an extended version of the early, brief reference to Christ's power over demons—"E la fama di lui corse per tutta la Siria; e gli presentarono tutti i malati colpiti da varie infermità e tormenti: indemoniati [...] e li guarí" ["And the report of him went forth into all Syria: and they brought unto him all that were sick, holden with divers diseases and torments, possessed with devils (...) and he healed them": 4. 24]—, which in Matthew comes immediately after the calling of the first four apostles (4. 18–22). In the film, however, these two episodes are separated by a "new" composite sequence made up of 11. 37–38, 10. 2–3, 16–20, 23, 28–31, 34–37, 39.[29]

The reason why this miracle is so difficult to follow is that the cinematic conventions normally used to create connections between different shots in an episode are either missing (there is no conversation) or are used primarily for expressionist ends (for example, the lighting between shots is not properly matched and the editing often appears arbitrary). As a result, there is no clear explanation of its meaning either from within the sequence itself or from its formal properties, except for the suggestion that some kind of mysterious event is taking place. Nor does exegetical help come from the episodes which precede and follow it—Jesus's instructions to the twelve apostles and the cleansing of the leper.

The miraculous in *Il Vangelo secondo Matteo* is no longer the very stuff of Christ's mission, as it is in Matthew's Gospel, but is presented as something illogical and arbitrary. In fact, given that so many miracles are missing from the film, it would seem that they are marginal to Pasolini's view of Jesus. This is supported by his interpolation of the miracle of the cripple and his reworking of the remaining four miracles in a minor key as compared to their original versions. There is no storm for Christ to calm as he walks the waters, though there is in the screenplay. In the film both the miracle of the leper and that of the loaves are presented in an overtly rhetorical manner ("I did the miracles with artificial aids":

Pasolini on Pasolini, p. 90). They are the results of clearly marked editing techniques—for example, of a reverse angle sequence in close-up: Christ's face, the leper's deformed face, back to Christ's face, and finally the leper's face restored to health. They are film conjuring tricks, rather than a respectful suggestion of the supernatural. Similarly, during Jesus's Passion, Pasolini deletes most of the wondrous occurrences at his death and the fear of the guards at the arrival of the angel to announce the Resurrection; and the sole image of the risen Christ is no different from those found earlier in the film. It is clear that Pasolini is not just rejecting a significant component of the original Gospel story and of the traditional conception of Christ, but also calling it into question. His distaste for the miracles became explicit in later years:

> There are some horrible moments I am ashamed of [in *Il Vangelo secondo Matteo*], which are almost Counter-Reformation Baroque, repellent—the miracles. The miracles of the loaves and the fishes and Christ walking on the water are disgusting pietism [...]. Perhaps I should have tried to invent completely new miracles, miracles which are not miracles, like healing or walking on the water; perhaps I should have tried to convey the sense of miraculousness each of us can experience watching the dawn, for example: nothing happens, the sun rises, trees are lit up by the sun. Perhaps for us this is what a miracle is. (*Pasolini on Pasolini*, pp. 87, 91)

What is openly articulated in 1968 is covertly implied in 1964. Pasolini in his film seems intent on challenging conventional perceptions of the Gospel and more specifically its focus on the "divine", and hence its religious dimension.

This challenge becomes quite clear when we examine the other main category of deletions. Pasolini omits just about all Jesus's speeches on the Kingdom of Heaven (one of the main features of Matthew's Gospel), on the Last Judgement and on salvation. What would appear to be the main exception to this process is in fact the most telling evidence for my argument:

> [STACK:] Am I right in thinking the investiture of Peter wasn't in the original version?[30]
> [PASOLINI:] I shot it with the rest of the film, but then removed it after the first editing. But this caused such grief to my friends in the Pro Civitate Christiana that I put it back again. It was an act

of kindness towards my Catholic friends. (*Pasolini on Pasolini*, p. 96)

Remembering the climate of the Centre-left, Pasolini's own assertions concerning the film's respect for its source, his problems with *La ricotta*, his ambivalent attitude towards the "religious", and his close contacts with members of the Roman Catholic clergy, it is understandable that he should have organized his attack from within a framework which appears to remain faithful to Matthew's Gospel. Yet despite these internal and external constraints the film adopts a polemical stance towards the Gospel and its status as a holy book, given that Pasolini does diminish its eschatological concerns in such a programmed manner. As a consequence, what obviously remains is its more earthly concerns, but even these—as the direction of my argument already implies—are subject to Pasolini's manipulations.[31]

THE DRAMA OF POLITICS

It is nothing new to claim that Pasolini in his film politicizes the Gospel or that he fashions a predominantly "revolutionary" Christ. While obviously concurring with this view, I would argue, however, that this secularization of the Gospel in political terms is not the film's main preoccupation, but only part of a more complex operation.

An effect of Pasolini's changes is to create a text which is narratively more complex than Matthew's. Where the latter strives to concentrate almost exclusively on Christ, in order to prove that he is the Messiah, and so allows no other character to compete with Jesus, Pasolini's film introduces pluralism and tension into the story. Thus the film does not focus just on Christ. A variety of other characters are not merely present, but actually dominate certain sections of the film. Judas is the protagonist or shares the stage with Jesus in a whole series of sequences stretching from the blighting of the fig tree to his horrific lonely suicide. During this same part of the film, and going on as far as Christ's burial, the film's centres of attention are first Peter, through whose eyes, via a "subjective" point-of-view shot, we see Jesus's trial before Caiaphas, and then John, who, thanks to the same device, is our eyes in Pontius Pilate's residence. Similarly, during the Crucifixion Pasolini pays greater attention to Mary's and John's anguish and to the crucifixion of a nameless individual than to Jesus's death. This alternation between different characters at the culmination of Christ's mission is clear evidence of the extent of the director's desire to fragment the film's narrative focus.

Pasolini broadens the perspective of Matthew's text in other ways. He gives faces to the anonymous and ubiquitous crowds of the Gospel. As I have already argued, this is partly inevitable; the frequency, however, with which Pasolini's camera lingers in close-up on the faces of the peasants, soldiers, Pharisees, and so on, gives these an important status within the film. On the one hand, as with the use of different locations, this helps make the story of Christ concrete, and is part of *Il Vangelo secondo Matteo*'s "realist" perspective—a descriptiveness which is completely antithetical to the stylistic procedures of Matthew. On the other hand, this massive entry of people (and of the environment) into the story is necessary for the film's secular interests: not just for the "analogies" Pasolini is striving to suggest, and not just as the necessary background to Christ's essentially "social" message, but also for symbolic ends. Thus it is striking that, unlike his presentation in the original and in the screenplay, Jesus in the film is normally surrounded by relatively few people. Once he enters Jerusalem, however, he is greeted and listened to by huge crowds. It is here that Jesus makes his most overtly anti-materialist, anti-authoritarian and populist speeches. It is here that he defeats the Pharisees in argument and undermines their power. He is a real champion of the people, a great revolutionary leader, and the radicalism of his words and actions meets the approval of the masses, so that even on the road to Calvary they do not abandon him or turn against him, as in the Gospel, but continue to shout their support. By their very presence, in contrast to their virtual absence elsewhere, they stress the socio-political significance of Jesus's behaviour. Pasolini underlined this by shooting the crowds using *cinéma vérité* techniques which echo newsreels of modern demonstrations, and by accompanying these scenes and Jesus's words with Russian revolutionary songs and Prokofiev's music to Eisenstein's *Alexander Nevsky*. This is probably the most telling example which may be adduced to show that Pasolini's faithful transposition of Matthew's dialogues into his film is no guarantee of its fidelity to its source. Christ's words now carry a different message from their original one, owing to the particular constraints created by the new text into which his speeches are inserted.

Pasolini's transformation of Jesus is not surprising, and is consistent with the director's particular brand of populist Communism. What is surprising is how reluctant so many critics have been to acknowledge this. Within the film's structure, Christ's death is unambiguously the result of political machinations. During his trial we hear the interpolated shouts, "Vuole sovvertire la legge!" ["He wants to subvert the law!"], "È un sovvertitore!" ["He is a subverter!"], "Vuole rovesciare la legge e la tradizione!" ["He wants to overthrow the law and tradition!"]. According to Pasolini these are the true reasons for his execution. The Pharisees have to get rid of Jesus because he is a threat to the status quo and to their power. From his first encounter with them Jesus reveals their hypocrisy and the falseness of their values. The Pharisees, like the bourgeoisie elsewhere in Pasolini, are presented as the enemies of progress and emancipation. The conflict between them and Jesus is presented as much as possible in social terms; hence Pasolini omits all the Gospel passages in which their disagreements are predominantly doctrinal.[32] In the film, therefore, the conspiracy against Christ has a clear logic and the Passion, as a result, is politicized. Conversely, in Matthew's Gospel, the reasons for these events are much less clear. Jesus's death has a certain fatalism about it: this is what must happen to the Messiah according to the promises of the Old Testament. Pasolini tends to establish a relationship between cause and effect; and this is obviously another way in which he can both give cohesion to his text and introduce dramatic tension into the story.

Pasolini employed a similar organizational device elsewhere in the film. For example, in treating the virgin conception Pasolini concentrated on its effects on Mary and, in particular, on Joseph. Later, he showed the effects of the arrival of the Magi on the peasants of Bethlehem. Similarly, Christ is shown drawing inspiration for his teachings not from some mysterious, divine source but from the world around him. For example, in the film Jesus's praise of the imprisoned John the Baptist (11. 7–19) seems to be in part inspired by what he sees and hears: Herod's castle, which dominates this episode, may be considered the stimulus behind "Ma quelli che portano morbide vesti stanno nei palazzi dei re" ["Behold, they that wear soft *raiment* are in kings' houses": 11. 8]; while it is strongly suggested that Jesus thinks of the image "Essa è simile ai fanciulli che stanno nelle piazze e gridano ai compagni e dicono: 'Il flauto vi suonammo e non ballaste'" ["It is like unto children sitting in the marketplaces, which call unto their fellows, and say, We piped unto you, and ye did not dance": 11. 17] after seeing and hearing the young dancer and flautist on whom Pasolini's camera has lingered earlier in the episode. In fact, in order to underline this association the sound of the flute returns to accompany these very words. Subsequently, before Jesus talks about the need to imitate and respect little children (18. 1–8) Pasolini focuses his camera on a young child and his older companion. The impression is again given that it is the sight of this pair that inspires his words. This goes against the logic of the Gospel, where it is clear that Jesus already has his answer ready before he calls the child to serve as a visual prop for his lesson:

> In quel momento i discepoli si avvicinarono a Gesú e gli dissero: "Chi è il piú grande nel regno dei cieli?" Chiamato allora un bambino, egli lo pose in mezzo a loro, e disse: "In verità vi dico: se non vi convertite e non diventate come i bambini [...]." (18. 1–3)

> [In that hour came the disciples unto Jesus, saying, Who then is greatest in the kingdom of heaven? And he called to him a little child, and set him in the midst of them, and said, Verily I say unto you, Except ye turn, and become as little children (...).]

It may thus be seen that in his film Pasolini seems more interested in analysing the complex relationship between Christ and his world than in giving a report of his deeds and sayings as in the Gospel.

The (Melo)drama of History

In general, *Il Vangelo secondo Matteo* looks like a filmed investigation—a "drama documentary"—on the nature of Jesus and his times: it looks like "filmed history". This is supported by the fact that Jesus is allowed "to speak for himself", since Pasolini respects the Gospel's dialogues. More specifically, this impression is reinforced in the viewer by Pasolini's considerable reliance on documentary techniques (the sequences in *cinéma vérité* and newsreel style, the use of hand-held camera shots, and the brief shots of

Christ as a toddler in Egypt which look like a piece of unearthed "home movie") and, more importantly, on "realist" practices: the use of non-professional actors, of non-studio locations, of deep-focus long takes, pans and tracks, and of natural light, as well as the "grainy" quality of the black and white film stock. Such conventions distance the film from the glossy fabrications of the Hollywood blockbuster, and instead reinforce the constant impression that one has while watching the film of participating in an act of "observation", of peering through a "window" at a "real" world. This effect must have been even stronger when the film first came out. Since *Il Vangelo secondo Matteo* was part of a national tradition in which Neo-realist sensibilities were still strong in the early Sixties, it is difficult to imagine how it could have been read in other than "realist" terms. As a result, critical comparisons were frequently made at the time with Rossellini's *Francesco giullare di Dio* ("Terza intervista", p. 66). Such a perception would naturally have reinforced, and been reinforced by, the belief that the film was faithful to its source: it is able to present a "real" picture because it follows Matthew, a major authority on Christ.

Il Vangelo secondo Matteo, on account of its style, looks like a philological and archaeological reconstruction, regardless of Pasolini's claims to the contrary (see *Pasolini on Pasolini*, p. 82), in the same way as its dialogue offers an apparently "objective" copy of Matthew. Thus, even though Pasolini did not shoot the film in Palestine, it is not at all clear that it is shot in the South of Italy. The role of "analogy" is actually much less evident than might appear from Pasolini's explanations. As with the locations, so too the regional origins of many of the characters are completely lost, while it is just about impossible to see the Flight into Egypt as reminiscent of the tribulations of present-day refugees. Even the "fascist" soldiers of Herod, despite their fezzes and black shirts, do not look out of place, on account of the overall *mise-en-scène* of the Massacre of the Innocents. Although the echoes of these "analogies" are weak, the emphasis on Christ's political significance does connect the film with the modern world, and not just narrowly in relation to the Centre-left. Through its treatment of the conflict between Jesus and the Pharisees, *Il Vangelo secondo Matteo* highlights Pasolini's preoccupation at the time with the power of neo-capitalism. In this sense the film has a twofold "historical" role, both as a cinematic reconstruction of the past and as a commentary on contemporary affairs. For the viewer to appreciate the "analogies" with the present, however, an interpretative effort is required: they are not an easily accessible feature of the film. Conversely, the "literal" level of the film looks like an account of Jesus in the Palestine of two thousand years ago based on an unimpeachable authority (more support for those propagating the thesis that the film is faithful to Matthew's Gospel).

Because of the film's strong "historical-realist" bias, its presumed "mythical" status is barely perceptible. It possibly emerges in a couple of the more "religious" episodes (the end of the Baptism and the Garden of Gethsemane) and is associated with "expressionist" stylistic devices (artificial lighting, distorting uses of the camera, stark visual contrasts) which are sparingly employed in the film. Lyricism and melodrama are similarly kept in control. They are most striking in Pasolini's presentation of children, and in the "autobiographical" sequences of Mary's anguish first at her son's coldness towards her and then at his death.[33] This is all that remains of a highly marked mythic and lyric-melodramatic dimension in the screenplay: Pasolini's *Il Vangelo secondo Matteo* is "lyric-mythic-epic", but only in its written form. In the screenplay Pasolini's treatment of Jesus is often melodramatic (see the section entitled "Of Jesus, Judas and Other Characters"), while he uses the proposed North African settings for aesthetic effects.[34] The film's particular "historical-realist" perspective is clearly the result of its own concerns and not the culmination of a consistent viewpoint which stretches back to the autumn of 1962. Pasolini's early statements on his aims and his screenplay are evidence of this, since they do show a genuine concern with respecting Matthew's Gospel and presenting Christ from a more traditional angle (see the section entitled "Of Jesus, Judas and Other Characters"). The changes which were then introduced during the shooting of the film and, more especially, during its editing were largely the result of Pasolini's increasing reaffirmation of a secular political commitment during 1964 (see, for example, *Comizi d'amore* and his work on *La Divina Mimesis*), which continued at least until *Uccellacci e uccellini* (1966), and which, in part, attenuated the sense of ideological crisis he had felt during the previous years. The whole history of the making of *Il Vangelo secondo Matteo* is fundamentally marked by this conflict, as Pasolini himself explained in 1965:

un tema [that of Christ] lontanissimo nella mia vita [a reference
to *Poesie a Casarsa*] che ho ripreso, e l'ho ripreso in un momento
di regressione irrazionalistica [early Sixties, in particular 1962] in
cui quello che avevo fatto fino a quel punto non m'accontentava,
mi sembrava in crisi e mi sono attaccato a questo fatto concreto di
fare il Vangelo [...]. Poi naturalmente io nel fare il Vangelo ho
voluto tenermi assolutamente fedele a Matteo [...]; volevo farla [a
life of Christ] veramente con Matteo e sono rimasto fedele a
questa idea [1962–64]. Poi nel farlo io tendevo a forzare la materia
nella direzione dell'attualità e mentre lo facevo credevo che
questo avesse un grandissimo peso [1964]. ("Terza intervista",
pp. 67–68)

[a theme (that of Christ) which goes back a long way in my life (a
reference to *Poesie a Casarsa*) which I took up again, and I took it
up in a moment of irrationalist regression (early Sixties, in
particular 1962), when what I had done until then no longer
satisfied me, it seemed to me to be in a state of crisis and I became
attached to this concrete fact of making *The Gospel* (...). Then,
naturally, in making *The Gospel*, I wanted to remain absolutely
faithful to Matthew (...); I wanted to make (a life of Christ) truly
with Matthew and I remained loyal to this idea (1962–64). Then,
as I made it, I tended to force the subject-matter in the direction
of the present and, as I was doing this, I believed it was something
of great weight (1964).]

OF JESUS, JUDAS AND OTHER CHARACTERS

Nowhere are such changes more apparent than in Pasolini's treatment of Christ. The Jesus of the screenplay is very different from
the one of *Il Vangelo secondo Matteo*; both, in their turn, should not
be confused with Matthew's Jesus. In the screenplay Pasolini
betrayed Matthew by fashioning an exaggeratedly lyrical and
melodramatic portrayal of Christ, while in the film he concentrated
on his human attributes. In his first version Pasolini resorted to a
widely popularized image of Jesus, which is supported only in
passing by the Gospels: he is the "meek, sweet and gentle Jesus" of
so much of the Christian tradition since the nineteenth century.
Although Pasolini's vision is unfaithful to Matthew, however, it
was almost certainly dictated not by polemical intent but, as I
suggested earlier, by a desire to respect his source, since his

presentation of Christ is faithful to an idea widely held among Christians.

In the screenplay Pasolini's descriptions of Christ are normally accompanied by qualifications such as "mite" ["meek": *V*, 99], "umile" ["humble": *V*, 61], "sommesso" ["submissive": *V*, 113]. His mood basically oscillates between sadness and joy (for example, *V*, 130–35), two states which are occasionally combined in a "doloroso sorriso" ["painful smile": *V*, 226); he is frequently moved to tenderness and compassion (for example, *V*, 72, 90, 92, 93, 98–100, 125); he is only very rarely angry (*V*, 186—but note how Pasolini tones down even this outburst: on seeing the temple sellers "gli occhi si empiono lentamente di sublime ira" ["his eyes slowly fill with sublime anger"]—and page 189—the fig tree); and equally rarely is he moved to raise his voice: the first time is merely "per farsi sentire" ["to make himself heard": *V*, 104], while the next, during his teaching in Jerusalem, Pasolini underlines the uniqueness of this behaviour: "per la prima volta, a voce alta, quasi gridando" ["for the first time, raising his voice, almost shouting": *V*, 197]. Nothing could be further from the nervy, irritable, moody, only rarely compassionate Christ of the film, whose angers are swift, as when he attacks the temple sellers, and who often raises his voice, at times without apparent cause—as when he quotes the words from Isaiah which I discussed earlier. Such reactions are in stark contrast to Christ's behaviour in the screenplay, where even his rendering of the most harrowing words is neutralized:

> Poi riprende a parlare: ma non con severità o indignazione, come potrebbe far supporre la lettura di queste parole, ma con la dolcezza di chi dà consigli su cose che fatalmente nel mondo accadono. (Comment on Matthew 18. 8–10: *V*, p. 168)

> [Then he starts to speak again: but not with severity or indignation, as a reading of these words might suggest, but with the sweetness of someone who gives advice on matters that fatefully occur in the world.]

In the film Jesus is humble only at his baptism; he smiles only when he sees children. He is implacable even against his own mother; gone is the "profonda e tragica dolcezza" ["deep and tragic sweetness": *V*, 128] which marks their encounter in the screenplay. He lacks any kind of divine serenity, but is prey to human emotions.

Pasolini's Jesus in the film has lost the calm and stability of his earlier counterpart. Instead he is driven and torn by conflicting powerful passions which are never properly explained. It is not surprising, therefore, that Pasolini's usual presentation of Christ in the film should abandon the melodrama of the screenplay. For example, in the film version of Jesus fasting in the desert, details such as these are missing:

> Cristo [...] sta pregando. È sfinito. (Nel viso scheletrito dal digiuno c'è già come un presagio della crocefissione?) Ma ha ancora la sublime forza di pregare.
> Il Demonio e Cristo si guardano a lungo. Una abietta, disperata ironia guizza nell'occhio del Demonio [...]; Cristo, che non ha quasi piú voce per parlare, e con un eroico sforzo, risponde con una voce appena udibile, rauca. (*V*, 64)

> [Christ (...) is praying. He is worn out. (On his face grown thin from fasting, is there already a forewarning of the Crucifixion?) Yet he still has the sublime strength to pray.
> The Devil and Christ look at each other for a long time. A mean, desperate irony flashes in the Devil's eyes (...); Christ, who barely has the strength to speak, and with a heroic effort, replies with a hoarse, barely audible voice.]

Similarly, Pasolini rejects his earlier lyricism (for example, there are no consoling nightingales during Christ's sufferings in the Garden of Gethsemane (*V*, 232–33).

The new Jesus of the film is the product of a deliberate rejection of the "disgusting pietism" (*Pasolini on Pasolini*, p. 87) of the screenplay's traditional Jesus. It is part of Pasolini's broader rejection of an all-embracing *stile sacrale* for the film, though occasionally it still leaves a mark on the film.[35] Instead Pasolini's aim in his presentation of Christ is, again, to question, dramatize and fragment:

> It is a violently contradictory film, profoundly ambiguous and disconcerting, particularly the figure of Christ—at times he is almost embarrassing, as well as being enigmatic [...]. The jump from [...] holy picture scenes to the passionate violence of his politics and his preaching is so great that the Christ figure in the film is bound to produce a strong sense of unease in an audience. Catholics come out of the film a bit shaken up feeling that I have

made Christ bad. He is not bad in fact, he is just full of contradictions. (*Pasolini on Pasolini*, p. 87)

But it is not just a Roman Catholic cinema audience that is bewildered by Pasolini's Christ. In the film he has a similar effect on
everyone around him. Another of the stimuli behind Pasolini's
decision to develop other characters in his version of the Gospel
story is the change which occurs in his conception of his protagonist. The other characters are necessary foils for the contradictions in
Jesus (it is striking that in the screenplay the secondary characters
are not given the emphasis they receive in the film). Without the
record of their reactions, Christ's ambiguities would be a lot less
evident. Thus Mary is needed to highlight Jesus's apparent in-
sensitivity towards her. Similarly, the camera lingers on the apostles,
either singly or in groups, in order to record their astonishment or
confusion at Christ's words or actions. And nowhere is this tension
more apparent than in the relationship Pasolini fashions between
Jesus and Judas, who, in the transition from screenplay to film,
becomes the film's second most important character.

We see close-ups of Judas's preoccupied or bewildered face at
Christ's withering of the fig tree and at his anointing by Mary of
Bethany. During the first sequence Pasolini establishes explicit
parallels between the two. While the other disciples are asleep,
they are both awake praying in similar positions, and when Christ,
in what is presented as a fit of pique, destroys the tree Judas is
several times framed with him. It is he who asks the question,
"Come mai s'è seccato in un istante?" ["How did the fig tree
immediately wither away?": 21. 20], which in the original is spoken
by the disciples as a group. His astonishment and concern act as a
commentary on Jesus's behaviour. Again, at Jesus's anointing it is
Judas alone, and not all the apostles as in the Gospel, who indig-
nantly says: "A che tanto sciupìo? Si poteva vendere questo un-
guento per molto e darne il ricavato ai poveri" ["To what purpose
is this waste? For this ointment might have been sold for much, and
given to the poor": 26. 8].[36] After Christ's rebuke, now approved by
all the other disciples, in another interpolation, Judas dramatically
leaves the feast and runs off to betray Jesus. Pasolini establishes a
causal connection between the two events, while in Matthew's
Gospel Judas's action is presented as much less justified. In the film
Judas's betrayal is built up throughout the film—we often see him

quizzically gazing at Christ—; and he becomes increasingly troubled by Jesus's behaviour from the moment he kills the fig tree. From Judas's perspective Christ is beginning to act irrationally and to contradict his own teachings: he destroys apparently without reason and, even worse, he undermines his own anti-materialist message by allowing himself to be anointed. According to Pasolini the seeds of Christ's destruction lie in himself, in his own inconsistencies, which alienate and harm even those who, like Judas, are most attentive to his words and actions.

Judas is in fact much more consistent than Jesus, who remains a mystery. Ambiguity is his hallmark in the film; it is not just a psychological ambiguity, but one which involves all his being. Although Pasolini goes out of his way to question Jesus's divinity (and the comparison with Judas is also clearly part of this project), the fact remains that he does present elements of this, which adds a further level of tension and drama to the film. For all its apparent effort to locate Jesus in his world and downgrade his divinity, Pasolini's "investigation" fails to offer any clear interpretation of his status, even though the director does suggest his own personal scepticism about Christ's status as the Son of God, and presents instead his view of him as a secular reformer. Similarly, despite Pasolini's concentration on him, Jesus continues to defy explanation. The director obsessively watches him, employing a variety of camera positions, movements and angles, using lenses of different focal lengths, and establishing different narrative points of view. He isolates him in the frame or immerses him in the environment or among people. He depicts Jesus according to different stylistic conventions, from the expressionism of the Baptism to the *cinéma vérité* treatment of the trials, and from Neo-realism to his own *sacralità frontale*. It is as if Pasolini hopes that one or a combination of all these techniques might offer a definitive insight. Yet no such answer is forthcoming. Whatever the perspective, the focus it offers on Christ is inevitably flawed and limited. There is no such thing as an objective or "total" style. Every style is merely the sum of a set of conventions. Just as the Hollywood epic cannot present the solution, so neither can Pasolini's "filmed documentary", despite all its reliance on a variety of "realist" and newsreel techniques; and in fact neither can Matthew's Gospel, because its vision is equally limited: for example, it has to be supplemented by John's Gospel. The film's marked sense of antithesis, tension and ambiguity is the inevitable result of its formal and ideological eclecticism.

"Two Thousand Years of Story-telling"

Pasolini explained *Il Vangelo secondo Matteo*'s bias towards contrast as follows:

> [The film] è riempito da due specie di religiosità, la mia personale e quella del popolo che segue Cristo: è chiaro che io non immagino certi personaggi come li ho rappresentati—l'angelo, per esempio—ma il popolo li immagina cosí, e quindi mi è sembrato giusto raffigurarli in questo modo.[37]

> [(The film) is filled with two kinds of religious feeling, mine and that of the people who follow Christ: it's obvious that I don't imagine certain characters in the way that I have presented them—the angel, for instance—but the people imagine them like this, and so it seemed right to depict them in this way.]

And, more specifically:

> Solo attraverso un esame stilistico si può capire che una trascrizione del Vangelo [of Matthew] avrebbe supposto una sola dimensione, mentre nel mio film si aprono baratri di dimensioni diverse. In *Accattone* [...] ero io a raccontare; qui no, perché io non credo. Ho dovuto invece narrare il Vangelo attraverso gli occhi di qualcun altro che non sono io, cioè di un credente: ho fatto "un discorso libero, indiretto".[38] Questa "visione indiretta" ha presupposto una contaminazione tra chi crede e chi no, e da essa è nata una confusione magmatica nello stile e nella tecnica [...]. Lo sforzo per mantenere l'equilibrio tra questi due punti di vista ha dato al film una tensione.[39]

> [It would only become clear through a stylistic analysis that a transcription of (Matthew's) Gospel would have entailed a single dimension, while in my film chasms of different dimensions open up. It was I who told the story in *Accattone*; in this film it wasn't, because I'm not a believer. Instead I had to narrate the Gospel through the eyes of someone else who isn't me, namely a believer: I fashioned "a free indirect discourse". This "indirect vision" presupposed a contamination between the believer and

> the non-believer, and from this arose the magmatic confusion of
> style and technique (…). The effort to maintain the balance
> between these two points of view gave the film a tension.]

These statements go some way towards clarifying the film's
conflicting focus. By emphasizing the duality of its vision, however, Pasolini oversimplified *Il Vangelo secondo Matteo's* range,
since the film in fact incorporates a multiplicity of perspectives ("si
aprono baratri di dimensioni diverse"). These are not just the
different "subjective" points of view introduced into the narrative
(for example, Peter's, John's, Judas's or the non-specific one of an
anonymous disciple—this is created with a moving hand-held
camera placed among the apostles following Jesus's back), or the
shifting "objective" points of view outside the story (for example,
that of the newsreel camera which is immersed but does not
participate in the action it observes, or that of the apparently
"neutral" camera which stands outside the events it records). The
film's vision also includes that of the tradition of great religious
painting via its iconographical references, that of religious music
via its soundtrack, which ranges from Bach to spirituals,[40] and that
of other religious texts.[41] This fragmentation of the film's focus goes
well beyond an opposition between the views of a believer and a
non-believer. Pasolini seems rather to be investigating and assessing the sources of our knowledge about Christ, since what unites
the film's conflicting viewpoints is their obsession with Jesus.

During *Il Vangelo secondo Matteo*, Pasolini highlights the presence of the camera. He continually alters the camera's point of
observation, and couples this with such "alienating" devices as the
zoom and the telephoto lens. The viewer is made aware of the fact
that the camera is organizing his or her viewpoint, and that it is
only a limited "eye" on the events shown. In fact it cannot even
offer a single coherent vision, since it oscillates between different
points of view. The narrative changes according to where one is
looking from. The viewer is inevitably disoriented and is given no
privileged position from which to participate in the story he or she
is watching. This confusion is compounded by Pasolini's reluctance to help the viewer find his or her bearings within the film (for
example, the episode of the possessed or the film's opening, which
shows a man and a young woman looking at each other in silence
in a series of reverse angle shots). All these are devices which go
against the conventions of mainstream narrative cinema. Pasolini

does not want his spectators to consume passively what they are being shown. Instead he wants them to realize that what they are watching is a film, so that they are encouraged to think about the epistemological status of what they are seeing. Pasolini is underlining the fact that, like his film, their image of Christ is constructed out of many different perspectives, and that each of these perspectives is governed by its own conventions. Hence the emphasis in the film on the multiplicity of people observing Christ, each one of whom had to have his or her own story to tell (the use of "subjective" points of view is fundamental in establishing this). In this way too Matthew's authority is called into question. The evangelist is merely one spectator among many, but one who had the good fortune that his story managed to survive. Furthermore, we are reminded of the limited and subjective nature of his vision. John's and Peter's "subjective" points of view at the trials emphasize the fact that Matthew was not present at these events and that, therefore, much of his account is necessarily second-hand. Like Pasolini's own ideas about Christ, Matthew's too are the result of an act of selection and elaboration aimed at presenting a particular image of Jesus.

If this is the case, then it is clear why unambiguous explanations about Jesus are not forthcoming. From the very beginning, as the film's changes in style and point of view suggest, he represented different things to the different people who observed him. Subsequently, the "two thousand years of story-telling about the life of Christ" have only exacerbated this state of affairs. Just as *Il Vangelo secondo Matteo* questions the validity of Matthew's text, so it also highlights the artificiality and subjectivity of the Christological cultural heritage: "una demistificazione dell'iconografia intesa secondo gli schemi della tradizione" ["a demystification of iconography as understood in the patterns of tradition"].[42] For example, Pasolini challenges the iconographical traditions not through the use of explicit references, which are in fact few and do not recall specific paintings, but by presenting moments of Christ's life from anti-iconographical perspectives: the Crucifixion shot from behind the cross, or the Last Supper in a series of close-ups so that we never have a panoramic view of the table. Similarly, by accompanying certain of the miracles with the African *Missa Luba* and with spirituals, he suggests that they are all expressions of a primitive religiosity. The film shows how Christ has always been exploited to serve the particular ends of an enormous number of interest groups. Even the fact that the film is faithful to Matthew's dialogue only serves to remind us that the words we hear are not Jesus's but the evangelist's transcription of them. As if to emphasize this, Pasolini mentions in the credits—unusually, since this is the customary practice of Italian cinema—that Enrique Irazoqui's voice is dubbed. Like the actor who plays him, Jesus speaks to us through the mediation of others. The film uncovers the precariousness of our knowledge of Jesus, and in its own political emphasis on Christ it confirms how easily he can be exploited to satisfy individual preferences.

CONCLUSION

This film, which is seen as a faithful adaptation of a Biblical text, not only diverges sharply from its source but actually challenges the status of that source. It is through *Il Vangelo secondo Matteo*'s effort critically to examine Matthew's Gospel, rather than imitate it, that a relationship between them is forged. Pasolini aims to show how the cult of Jesus has been fashioned through different and at times conflicting textual traditions: his is a film not so much about Christ as about texts on Christ. His own attempt to investigate the "reality" of Jesus is doomed to failure, and Pasolini can only honestly resolve this failure by acknowledging that he is adding a new layer to the image of Christ by highlighting the conventionality of his apparently "realistic" film. *Il Vangelo secondo Matteo* is Pasolini's great Godardian moment.[43] To have publicly admitted this in the early to mid-Sixties would almost certainly have been impossible. Pasolini did, however, come very close to doing so when he discussed his reasons for employing iconographical echoes in his film, and when he acknowledged that aspects of it satisfied his political concerns. It is in the relationship which is established between Pasolini's most conspicuous additions to Matthew's Gospel, the "story-telling" and the "analogies"—the fundamental Pasolinian tension between *passione* and *ideologia*—that *Il Vangelo secondo Matteo*'s particularity emerges. What could not be openly spoken is articulated in the film—in its style and structure. And it is arguable that Pasolini himself was not totally aware at the time of the "radicalism" of his operation, since, as he himself admitted in December 1964, when he made *Il Vangelo secondo Matteo* "la ricerca tecnica, l'intuizione stilistica ha preceduto il reale approfondimento ideologico" ["technical research and stylistic intuition preceded the actual ideological investigation"].[44]

NOTES

1   See P. P. Pasolini, "Terza intervista", edited by L. Faccini and M. Ponzi, in *Con Pier Paolo Pasolini*, edited by E. Magrelli (Rome, Bulzoni, 1977), pp. 63–73 (p. 64), originally in *Filmcritica*, 156–57 (Apr–May 1965).

2   On all matters of dating, unless otherwise stated, my sources are E. Siciliano, *Vita di Pasolini*, new edition (Milan, Rizzoli, 1981), and N. Naldini, *Pasolini, una vita* (Turin, Einaudi, 1989). Siciliano gives no date for the start of *Il Vangelo secondo Matteo*, while Naldini asserts that shooting began on 24 April 1964. I am not persuaded by this dating. I suspect that work on the film must have begun before 9 March 1964—the date of a discussion between Pasolini and members of the Centro Sperimentale di Cinematografia at which the director discussed problems relating to the making of the film (see "Una visione del mondo epico-religiosa: colloquio con Pier Paolo Pasolini", *Bianco e nero*, 25, vi (1964), 12–38 [p. 38])—and after 24 February 1964—the date of the last interview in which Pasolini mentioned that he had not yet started to shoot the film (see S. Ascanio, "P. P. Pasolini promette di rispettare il Vangelo", *Il gazzettino*, 25 Feb. 1964). On the film's production see N. Naldini, *Pasolini*, pp. 279–83.

3   P. P. Pasolini, "Una carica di vitalità", *Il giorno*, 6 Mar. 1963. On Pasolini's relationship with Pro Civitate Christiana see S. Rohdie, *The Passion of Pier Paolo Pasolini* (London, BFI, 1995), pp. 161–62. See also E. Golino, *Tra lucciole e Palazzo* (Palermo, Sellerio, 1995), pp. 47–48; N. Naldini, *Pasolini*, pp. 256–57, 266–69.

4   On Pasolini's financial difficulties, see G. Gambetti, "Un film 'difficile'", in P. P. Pasolini, *Il Vangelo secondo Matteo*, edited by G. Gambetti (Milan, Garzanti, 1964), pp. 7–9. The making of *Il Vangelo secondo Matteo* was officially confirmed on 8 February 1963: see D. Argento, "'Vedrò Gesú Cristo come Accattone' ci ha detto Pier Paolo Pasolini", *Paese sera*, 9 Feb. 1963.

5   To judge by the correspondence reproduced in the Garzanti edition of the screenplay (P. P. Pasolini, "Sei lettere", pp. 16–20), this must have been written between February and early May 1963. The relevant letters are also printed in P. P. Pasolini, *Lettere 1955–1975*, edited by N. Naldini (Turin, Einaudi, 1988), pp. 508–10, 514–15.

6   In the film's credits Pasolini mentions that his adaptation is based on the edition of the New Testament published under the auspices of Pro Civitate Christiana. All quotations are from this, *Il Vangelo di Gesú Cristo*, third edition (Assisi, Pro Civitate Christiana, 1963).

7   *Pasolini on Pasolini: Interviews with Oswald Stack* (London, Thames and Hudson/ BFI, 1969), p. 83. See also N. Naldini, *Pasolini*, pp. 270–71.

8   As far as I know, there is no external evidence for Pasolini's claim that it was
     in Palestine that he thought of Southern Italy as the location for his film: see
     "I dodici apostoli al premio Strega", *L'espresso*, 21 June 1964, p. 18. The first
     reference to this that I have found is in S. Ascanio, "P. P. Pasolini promette".

9   See *Pasolini: cronaca giudiziaria, persecuzione, morte*, edited by L. Betti (Milan,
     Garzanti, 1977), pp. 153–64; E. Siciliano, *Vita*, pp. 314–15; N. Naldini, *Pasolini*,
     pp. 262–65.

10   See P. P. Pasolini, "An Interview with James Blue", *Film Comment*, 3, iv (1965),
     25–32 (p. 26); "Una discussione del '64", in *Pasolini nel dibattito culturale
     contemporaneo* by various authors (Pavia–Alessandria, Amministrazione Pro-
     vinciale di Pavia/Comune di Alessandria, 1977), pp. 91–123 (p. 108).

11   For a discussion of this crisis see G. C. Ferretti, *Pasolini: l'universo orrendo*
     (Rome, Editori Riuniti, 1976), pp. 21–59; "Introduzione" in P. P. Pasolini, *Le
     belle bandiere*, edited by G. C. Ferretti (Rome, Editori Riuniti, 1978), pp. 7–39.

12   Quoted in L. Locatelli, "Pasolini col Vangelo alla mano muove gli attori senza
     volto", *Il giorno*, 26 Apr. 1964.

13   Quoted in A. Cambria, "'Non ho cambiato una parola del testo sacro' dice lo
     scrittore", *La stampa*, 5 Sept. 1964.

14   See for example M. Casolaro, SJ, "Spirito e lettera nel film di P. P. Pasolini",
     Cineforum, 40 (1964), 963–68; V. Fagone, SJ, "A proposito del *Vangelo secondo
     Matteo*", *Rivista del cinematografo*, 12 (1964), 552–56. *Il Vangelo* won both the
     O[ffice] C[atholique] I[nternational du] C[inéma] prize offered at the Venice
     Film Festival and the Grand Prix OCIC, the highest Roman Catholic cinema
     award.

15   See for example U. Casiraghi, "A Venezia il *Vangelo secondo Matteo* di
     Pasolini", *L'unità*, 5 Sept. 1964, 7; A. Scagnetti, "È finora il film di più alto
     impegno", *Paese sera*, 6 Sept. 1964, p. 11; A. Trombadori, "Passione e ragione
     secondo Matteo", *Vie nuove*, 10 Sept. 1964; M. Argentieri, "La Mostra di
     Venezia l'ha spuntata sulle polemiche", *Rinascita*, 12 Sept. 1964; F. Chilanti,
     "La serata veneziana di Matteo e Pasolini", *Paese sera*, 22 Sept. 1964; A. Savioli,
     "Il Cristo solitario di Pasolini", *L'unità*, 3 Oct. 1964. For a clear presentation
     of the variety of different reactions which *Il Vangelo secondo Matteo* en-
     gendered see N. Naldini, *Pasolini*, pp. 285–88.

16   See for example L. Locatelli, "Pasolini col Vangelo alla mano"; L. Cardone,
     "Gesú è spagnuolo e la Madonna di Crotone" *Settimana incom*, 24 May 1964;
     G. L. Rondi, "Né sacrilegio, né opera d'arte il *Vangelo secondo Pasolini*", *Il
     tempo*, 5 Sept. 1964; D. Zanelli, "Cristo fra i meridionali", *Il resto del carlino*,
     5 Sept. 1964; L. Miccichè, "Fredda fedeltà a Matteo di Pier Paolo Pasolini",
     L'avanti, 5 Sept. 1964; G. Grazzini, "Il film di Pasolini un'astrazione intellet-
     tuale", *Il corriere della sera*, 5 Sept. 1964; G. M. Guglielmino, "Esaltazione lirica
     e consapevole della figura storica del Cristo", *Gazzetta del popolo*, 5 Sept. 1964;
     A. Scagnetti, "E finora"; "Fedele al racconto, non all'ispirazione del Vangelo
     il film di Pasolini", *L'osservatore romano*, 6 Sept. 1964; A. Gatto, "La parola
     intatta del Vangelo", *L'Europa letteraria*, 30–32 (1964), 112; M. Casolaro,
     "Spirito e lettera", p. 965; P. Baldelli, "Pasolini e 'lo scandalo della contraddi-
     zione'", *Giovane critica*, 6 (1964–65), 29–49 (p. 30); J. Pena, "L'Évangile selon
     Saint Matthieu", *Téléciné*, 19, cxxiii (1965), 3–14 (p. 5); M. Gervais, *Pier Paolo
     Pasolini* (Paris, Seghers, 1973), p. 45; S. Petraglia, *Pier Paolo Pasolini* (Florence,
     La Nuova Italia, 1974), p. 58; E. Maakaroun, "Pasolini face au sacré ou

l'exorciste possédé", in *Pier Paolo Pasolini: le mythe et le sacré*, edited by M. Estève (Paris, Lettres Modernes/Minard, 1976), pp. 32–54 (p. 37); F. S. Gérard, *Pasolini, ou le mythe de la barbarie* (Brussels, Editions de l'Université de Bruxelles, 1981), p. 69; R. Rinaldi, *Pier Paolo Pasolini* (Milan, Mursia, 1982), p. 280; L. De Giusti, *I film di Pier Paolo Pasolini* (Rome, Gremese, 1983), pp. 68–69; N. Greene, *Pier Paolo Pasolini: Cinema as Heresy* (Princeton, Princeton University Press, 1990), p. 73; M. Viano, *A Certain Realism: Making Use of Pasolini's Film Theory and Practice* (Berkeley etc., University of California Press, 1993), pp. 140, 143. Although Viano provides a table showing the correlations between the scenes of the film and passages from Matthew's Gospel—a table which graphically underlines Pasolini's many manipulations of the original—, he insists that the film is faithful to its source (pp. 140, 143, 331–33). Indeed, Viano's whole discussion of *Il Vangelo secondo Matteo* is vitiated by a series of questionable statements, for example, regarding its reception (pp. 133–34), its *provocative* qualities (p. 134), its characters' lack of "individual interiority" (p. 138), Judas's role (p. 139), Pasolini's "in-depth, specialized knowledge" of Matthew's Gospel (p. 141), the film's disclosure of the "phallocentrism" of Christ's story (pp. 142–45). Equally, he fails adequately to explain the relationship between "analogy" and "realism", and how the film could be both faithful to Matthew and "a quintessentially open text, a set of interpretative strategies which are left to the reader" (p. 133), the product of "directorial manipulation" (p. 138), of a "subjective rendering" (p. 140). Since the appearance of the original version of this essay in 1985, several scholars have distanced themselves from the idea of the film's rigid, almost simplistic, fidelity to its source: see B. Testa, "To Film a Gospel… and Advent of the Theoretical Stranger", in *Pier Paolo Pasolini*, edited by P. Rumble and B. Testa (Toronto, University of Toronto Press, 1994), pp. 180–209 (Testa's article offers an excellent analysis of *Il Vangelo secondo Matteo's* stylistic and structural properties); S. Rohdie, *The Passion*, pp. 67, 165; R. Gordon, *Pasolini: Forms of Subjectivity* (Oxford, Clarendon Press, 1996), pp. 209, 224.

17   P. P. Pasolini, *Il sogno del centauro*, edited by J. Duflot (Rome, Editori Riuniti, 1983), p. 33; the original interview was conducted in 1969.

18   "Entretien avec Pasolini par Bernardo Bertolucci et Jean-Louis Comolli", *Cahiers du cinéma, hors série 9: Pasolini cinéaste* (1981), 35–42 (p. 42); the original interview was conducted in 1965.

19   M. Rusconi, "4 registi al magnetofono", *Sipario*, 19, ccxxii (1964), 14–20 (p. 16).

20   M. Rusconi, "4 registi", p. 16.

21   D. Argento, "'Vedrò Gesú Cristo'".

22   A. Cambria, "'Non ho cambiato'".

23   I have used the following English version of the Bible: *The Holy Bible Containing the Old and New Testaments* (London, British and Foreign Bible Society, 1959).

24   See Pasolini's claim that "secondo me i critici hanno avuto ragione di trovare una certa lentezza a metà *Vangelo* perché era veramente una cosa senza ritmo, ma d'altra parte non è dipeso da me in quanto ho finito il film proprio la notte prima della sua presentazione a Venezia e alcune cose sono rimaste un po' inespresse. Dopo ho ritoccato. Cioè dove invece di un ritmo lento c'era solo della brada lentezza ho modificato, ho distribuito le scene in altre parti del

film, ho scisso questo punto lento e ora credo che il film abbia tutto questo ritmo lento, che sia però ritmo insomma. Ho fatto anche dei rifacimenti al doppiaggio" ("Terza intervista", p. 64).

25   See J. L. Borges, "Tres versiones de Judas", in *Ficciones* (Buenos Aires, Emecé, 1956), pp. 169–76; Bob Dylan, "With God on Our Side", on *The Times They Are A-Changin'*" (CBS, 1963); P. Van Greenaway, *Judas!* (London, Gollancz, 1972). One should note in this context that the development of Judas as the bearer of the purse in the episode of the olives is based on a passage in John's Gospel: "Now this he [Judas] said, not because he cared for the poor; but because he was a thief, and having the bag took away what was put therein" (12. 6). John's Gospel is, in fact, an important sub-text in Pasolini's vision of Christ: "Personally, I like John's Gospel even more, but I thought Matthew's was the best for making a film" (*Pasolini on Pasolini*, p. 95). Thus John's presence at the Crucifixion in the film repeats the Evangelist's claim that he witnessed this event (19. 26). I shall note other borrowings from John's Gospel during the course of this essay.

26   Both these sequences are prefaced by the same establishing shot of the market and city-gate.

27   This formula is used in the credits of *Il Vangelo secondo Matteo*.

28   See G. Gambetti, "Un film 'difficile'", p. 7; "An Interview with James Blue", pp. 27, 29; *Pasolini on Pasolini*, pp. 96–97. In the edition of the screenplay, there are a number of stills belonging to episodes which do not appear in the film.

29   Pasolini must have originally conceived and shot the two episodes as contiguous, since the same four apostles are present in both.

30   The version of *Il Vangelo secondo Matteo* shown at the Venice Film Festival was different from the one put into distribution; see n. 24 above.

31   Pasolini also omits certain passages because he would have found them ideologically uncomfortable and because they would have gone against his fashioning of a "radical" Jesus: for example, Christ's attacks on adultery (5. 27–32), on Sodom (11. 23–24), on sex and divorce (19. 1–12), his praise of the good centurion (8. 5–13) and his acknowledgement of the need to pay the temple tribute (17. 24–27).

32   Pasolini omits the passages, for example, in which Jesus and the Pharisees debate the forgiveness of sins (9. 1–8), the casting out of demons (9. 32–34; 12. 25–29), the Last Judgement (12. 33–37) and the commandments (15. 1–9).

33   Pasolini's mother played Mary in *Il Vangelo secondo Matteo*; and see G. Buttafava, "Salò o il cinema in forma di rosa", *Bianco e nero*, 37, i–iv (1976), 33–52 (pp. 36–37).

34   G. Rocha, "Le Christ-Oedipe", in *Pasolini cinéaste*, special unnumbered issue of *Cahiers du cinéma* (Paris, L'Étoile, 1981), pp. 81–82.

35   Pasolini described this development as follows: "Very briefly, this is what happened. Already in *Accattone* my style was religious—I thought it was (although I prefer the word 'reverential' [*sacrale*]), and all the critics thought it was, though they called it 'Catholic' rather than 'religious', which was wrong. But it was religious in the style rather than the content: it is possible to cheat in the content, but you can't cheat in the style. When I started *The Gospel* I thought I had the right formula all ready, and I started out shooting it with the same techniques and style as I used for *Accattone*. But after two days I was in a complete crisis and I even contemplated giving the whole thing up, which had never happened to me in my whole life, except for this

time. Using a reverential style for *The Gospel was* gilding the lily: it came out rhetoric. Reverential technique and style in *Accattone* went fine, but applied to a sacred text they were ridiculous; so I got discouraged and was just about to give the whole thing up, and then when I was shooting the baptism scene near Viterbo I threw over all my technical preconceptions. I started using the zoom, I used new camera movements, new frames which were not reverential, but almost documentary. A completely new style emerged. In *Accattone* the style is consistent and extremely simple, like in Masaccio or in Romanesque sculpture. Whereas the style in *The Gospel* is very varied: it combines the reverential with almost documentary moments, an almost classic severity with moments that are almost Godardian—e.g. the two trials of Christ shot like *cinéma vérité*." / [...] / *"Was the change of technique during the shooting of the baptism partly due to technical difficulties, like the terrain?"* / "No, it was voluntary. I spent one completely sleepless night and then decided to give it up, but then when I went out in the morning I just decided to revolutionize everything: this was a big decision for me, because I was not a professional, in fact I knew nothing at all about cinema techniques when I started *Accattone*, not even what the different lenses were and things like that." / *"Is there anything left of the footage you shot before the change?"* /"Yes, there's Gethsemane and the sermon on the mount. I tried to salvage both these during the montage, but they are not right and I don't like them" (*Pasolini on Pasolini*, pp. 83–84, 86).

36   Judas's transformation here is another echo from John's Gospel: "Judas Iscariot, one of his disciples, which should betray him, saith, Why was not this ointment sold for three hundred pence, and given to the poor?" (12. 4–5). Pasolini had already introduced this change in the screenplay. His treatment of Judas in the episode of the fig tree, however, is solely an acquisition of the film. N. Greene is wrong to talk about "Christ's meek and passive followers" (*Pier Paolo Pasolini*, p. 79). Rather more interesting is Gordon's claim that "the peasants are a correlative to the landscape, and to the historical and mythical elements of the Gospel story" (*Pasolini*, p. 208). Testa's is now the most stimulating discussion of the film's "minor" characters ("To Film a Gospel", pp. 192, 194, 207).

37   M. Rusconi, "4 registi", p. 16.

38   See P. P. Pasolini, "Intervento sul Discorso Libero Indiretto", in *Empirismo eretico* [1972] (Milan, Garzanti, 1981), pp. 81–103.

39   Comments reported in [M-]A. Macciocchi, "Cristo e il marxismo", *L'unità*, 22 Dec. 1964.

40   See P. Baldelli, "Pasolini e 'lo scandalo della contraddizione'", p. 39 n. 5; S. Rohdie, *The Passion*, pp. 47, 60.

41   For example, the interpolated references to Isaiah 14. 31 and 15. 3 which preface the sequence following John the Baptist's execution; the echoes from John.

42   M. Rusconi, "4 registi", p. 16.

43   It is important to note that around the same time as he was shooting and editing *Il Vangelo secondo Matteo* Pasolini was also developing his theory of the "cinema di poesia": "Il 'cinema di poesia'" [1965], in *EE*, 167–87. Stimulated by Godard's pioneering attack on the conventionality of "realist" filmmaking (pp. 182–83), Pasolini defined the "cinema di poesia" as follows: "La formazione di una 'lingua della poesia cinematografica' implica dunque la possibilità di fare, al contrario, degli pseudo-racconti, scritti con la lingua

della poesia: la possibilità insomma, di una prosa d'arte, di una serie di pagine liriche, la cui soggettività è assicurata dall'uso pretestuale della 'soggettiva libera indiretta': e il cui vero protagonista è lo stile./La macchina, dunque, si sente, per delle buone ragioni: l'alternarsi di obbiettivi diversi, un 25 o un 300 sulla stessa faccia, lo sperpero dello zum, coi suoi obbiettivi altissimi, che stanno addosso alle cose dilatandole come pani troppo lievitati, i controluce continui e fintamente casuali con i loro barbagli in macchina, i movimenti di macchina a mano, le carrellate esasperate, i montaggi sbagliati per ragioni espressive, gli attacchi irritanti, le immobilità interminabili su una stessa immagine ecc. ecc., tutto questo codice tecnico è nato quasi per insofferenza alle regole, per un bisogno di libertà irregolare e provocatoria, per un diversamente autentico o delizioso gusto dell'anarchia: ma è divenuto subito canone, patrimonio linguistico e prosodico, che interessa contemporaneamente tutte le cinematografie mondiali" (pp. 185–86). It is obvious that this general definition can also serve equally well as a specific description of *Il Vangelo secondo Matteo*. For an excellent analysis, assessment and critique of Pasolini's film theory see Christopher Wagstaff's contribution to the present volume.

44 Strikingly, it is the two interviews Pasolini gave at the end of the Sixties (Stack and Duflot) that come closest to expressing positions similar to mine in this essay. The Stack interview is particularly significant, because Pasolini there revises some of his earlier views on the film after seeing it afresh: for example, "The whole film is full of my own personal motifs—e.g. all the minor characters from the agricultural and pastoral proletariat of Southern Italy are mine completely, and I only realized this when I saw it again now; and I also realized that the Christ figure is all mine, because of the terrible ambiguity there is in him" (*Pasolini on Pasolini*, p. 77); see also p. 87 (on the miracles) and pp. 94–95 (on history).

PIER PAOLO PASOLINI
AND THE EVENTS OF MAY 1968:
THE "MANIFESTO PER UN NUOVO TEATRO"

David Ward

Even though they took place fewer than thirty years ago, it is easy to forget that for many European intellectuals the events of May 1968 represented a unique occasion. Two and half decades after the fall of the Fascist regimes, the experience of the Resistance movements and the birth of a democratic Europe, a new generation of radicalized students demanded that their father-figures, Europe's post-war left, rethink the political positions and strategies they had elaborated in the immediate post-Fascist period. May 1968 was a moment of great euphoria when, in the words of the film-maker Marco Bellocchio, one of its Italian protagonists, "senza sapere perché, senza ragione, nascevano possibilità di cambiare cose che sembravano immutabili" ["without knowing why, without reason, new opportunities to change things that seemed unchangeable were born"].[1] For many of these young intellectuals the climate in and around May 1968 and the possibility of deep-seated change it promised were akin to an earlier generation's hopes that a new Italy would be born of the ideals and values of the anti-Fascist Resistance movement.

In Italy the events of May 1968 came to a head with the occupation of, and consequent street-fighting around, Rome University's Faculty of Architecture in Valle Giulia. A short while after the skirmishes between police and students, Pasolini published a poem, "Il PCI ai giovani!", in the left-leaning weekly magazine *L'espresso*, that was to add a political dimension to the sexual, literary and cinematic scandal that already surrounded the poet, novelist and film-maker.[2] The scandal was caused by Pasolini's reversing the analysis made by the overwhelming majority of left-wing intellectual opinion: instead of siding with the students against the police, he sided with the police and attacked the students.

The crux of Pasolini's polemic lies in his perception of the student groups' ideological shortsightedness. Far from agreeing with the claim of these groups that they had made a genuine break with the political order established by Italy's historical left, Pasolini viewed the events of Valle Giulia as the continuation of the old struggle between proletarian under-class and bourgeoisie. This time, though, the roles were inverted: the revolutionary students were the bourgeoisie, and the police force, which was composed mostly of Southerners, forced by fear of unemployment to do a job nobody else wanted, were the under-class. Rather than as a turning-point in the history of political action, Pasolini describes the events of May 1968 as a ritualized form of protest, according to which supposedly revolutionary students were called on to play assigned roles in a spectacle whose result was not the weakening of bourgeois power but its reinforcement.

For Pasolini the events and ultimate failure of the May 1968 attempt at revolution were manifestations of the new, far more subtle control that bourgeois codes and practices had taken over all areas of political and social life. In the years following 1968 Pasolini dedicated a great deal of his time to denouncing this new and, as he saw it, dangerous development, which he called simply "Power". By turning to one of his verse tragedies we may see the new form Power has taken. In *Calderon* Pasolini describes Power in a way which echoes Renzo De Felice's distinction between the two phases of Mussolini's Fascist regime: an initial coercive phase of crude violence, followed by a second, more sophisticated phase of respectability, figured as the passage from the "manganello", the "cosh", to the "doppio petto", the "double-breasted jacket".[3] In the play, based loosely on *La vida es sueño*, Power, in the guise of an elegantly dressed gentleman, has reached this second phase:

> MANUEL Si crede che il Potere sia un mostro ottuso... un pancione
>   rincagnato...
> BASILIO E invece?
> MANUEL Egli è estremamente elegante.

> [MANUEL You think Power is a dull monster... with a big flaccid
>   belly...

BASILIO And really?
MANUEL He is extremely elegant.][4]

As Pasolini sees it, Power creates a system of control that has reached such a stage of sophistication that its effects go almost unnoticed. It has succeeded in masking its true oppressive nature so successfully that it no longer needs to exercise its domination through outright coercive means like violence or military threat. Rather, it dominates through consent, a kind of non-coercive coercion which is at its most powerful when at its most invisible.

The students' movement of 1968 failed, Pasolini argues, because its participants were not sophisticated enough to understand the subtle new form taken by the enemy against which they were struggling. Instead of attempting the difficult task of identifying the hidden ramifications of Power in its new guise, the student groups took the easier option of continuing to figure Power in its old form, as the kind of traditional oppressor they identified in the police force composed of the children of the Southern poor. According to Pasolini, the students were unable to see the trap that was being set for them and how Power would immediately co-opt their protest and turn it to its own advantage. On more than one occasion Pasolini speaks of the ways in which Power tolerates a certain amount of protest in order to reinforce itself by showing how it is able to resist and contain such protest. Thus protest against Power works in the interests of Power. In "La poesia della tradizione", part of the collection *Trasumanar e organizzar*, Pasolini writes of the "unlucky generation" of 1968, whose "disobedience" has already been inscribed within the logic of an ultimate "obedience":

> Oh generazione sfortunata!
> [...]
> e cosí capirai di aver servito il mondo
> contro cui con zelo "portasti avanti la lotta":
> [...]
> oh generazione sfortunata, e tu obbedisti disobbedendo![5]

[Oh unlucky generation!/[...]/so you will understand that you have served the world/against which with such energy "you carried forward the struggle":/[...]/oh unlucky generation, and you obeyed disobeying!]

In a television interview for the programme "Controcampo", given in 1973, but republished only fifteen years later in the Roman Catholic youth weekly *Il sabato*, Pasolini made a similar point: "La borghesia crea sempre delle contestazioni per potere superare se stessa e avanzare" ["The bourgeoisie always creates a number of protests in order to go beyond itself and go forward"]. A little earlier in the same interview he offered this damning analysis of the disingenuousness of the student groups: "Se posso usare una parabola, direi che questo famoso Potere, questa 'mente' che dirige il destino della borghesia, ha in un certo senso programmato la rivoluzione del '68" ["If I may use a parable, I would say that this famous Power, this 'mind' which directs the destiny of the bourgeoisie, in a certain sense programmed the 1968 revolution"].[6] And in a long interview with Jean Duflot given around the same time he said of the 1968 generation:

> Questa è la radice del problema: usano contro il neocapitalismo armi che portano in realtà il suo marchio di fabbrica, e sono quindi destinate soltanto a rafforzare il suo dominio. Essi credono di spezzare il cerchio, e invece non fanno altro che rinsaldarlo.[7]

> [That's the crux of the problem: to fight neo-capitalism they use arms which in fact carry its trade mark and which are destined only to reinforce its tyranny. They think they are breaking the circle, and yet they are only reinforcing it.]

The price Pasolini paid for such "political incorrectness" was a massive attack from all quarters. He was accused of being out of step with the course of history, of not understanding the newly created conditions of the class struggle which would make an alliance between students and workers possible, of being a *provocateur* in the service of capitalism and of having opportunistically sold out to the system.[8]

Had he lived, however, Pasolini may well have derived some belated consolation from the knowledge that, in the aftermath of the failure of the May 1968 attempt at revolution, subsequent reflection on its limits went some way towards proving his analysis correct. In the wake of the developments in European thought that theorists like Louis Althusser and Michel Foucault elaborated in the early 1970s, we are now in a better position to see that Pasolini, far from being the anachronistic product of a bygone age he was assumed to be in the late 1960s, was very much in line with these more nuanced forms of political and cultural analysis. Pasolini's perception of how Power absorbs supposedly oppositional practices, for example, anticipates the argument advanced in the "Method" section of the first volume of Foucault's *The History of Sexuality*, where the French thinker writes: "Power is everywhere; not because it embraces everything, but because it comes from everywhere [...]; it is the name that one attributes to a complex strategical situation in a particular society."[9]

As Jonathan Culler has recently pointed out, one of the problems raised by Foucault's definition of the all-encompassing nature of Power is that it seems to offer no systematic way of organizing resistance.[10] For Foucault resistance can only be random and sporadic:

> Where there is power, there is resistance, and yet, or rather consequently, this resistance is never in a position of exteriority in relation to power [...]; points of resistance are present everywhere in the power network. Hence there is no single locus of great Refusal, no soul of revolt, source of all rebellions, or pure law of the revolutionary. Instead there is a plurality of resistances, each of them a special case: resistances that are possible, necessary, impossible; others that are spontaneous, savage, solitary, concerted, rampant or violent; still others that are quick to compromise, interested, or sacrificial [...]. Resistances [...] are distributed in irregular fashion: the points, knots, focuses of resistance are spread over time and space at varying densities, at times modifying groups and individuals in a definitive way, inflaming certain parts of the body, certain movements in life, certain types of behaviour [...]; there is a plurality of resistances, each of them a special case.[11]

In a 1972 article, "I sogni ideologici", published in the monthly review *Nuovi argomenti*, Pasolini too seems to rule out the possibility of organized resistance. Speaking of the ontological deprivation the self undergoes when it is imprisoned in a world created by imposed codes and practices, which he terms the "Gioco della Storia" ["Game of History"], he writes:

> *Che cosa potrebbe essere la vita senza la storia*, è naturalmente impensabile o imparlabile: che cos' altro diavolo potrei fare, la mattina, svegliandomi, se non alzarmi da un letto, leggere dei giornali, avere dei pensieri quotidiani, insomma fare tutto ciò che

la mia qualità di vita ammette e prevede anche come sorprenden-
te e assolutamente desueto? Alternative non ne ho.[12]

[*What could life be without history*? It is, of course, unthinkable or
unspeakable. What the hell else could I do in the morning when
I wake up if not get out of a bed, read a few newspapers, have a
few daily thoughts, in a word, do everything that my quality of
life recognizes and foresees, even as something surprising and
absolutely unusual? I have no alternatives.]

This final statement, however, is to be taken, I believe, with a
pinch of salt, as a hyperbolic moment in Pasolini's writings where
he deliberately overstates his case for rhetorical effect. Few intellectuals on the European scene can have been as dogged as Pasolini
in seeking to discover and build viable modes of resistance. What
makes Pasolini different from Foucault is his continual exploration
of the alternatives to the "processo di omologazione", by which he
means the *embourgeoisement*, or gradual obliteration of regional,
national, class and sexual differences, that was to become the main
subject of the journalistic writings of the final years of his life.[13]

It is in such a context that I should like to consider Pasolini's six
verse tragedies and in particular his "Manifesto per un nuovo
teatro". In what follows, I argue that the "Manifesto" may be seen
as Pasolini's attempt to create the kind of locus of resistance that
Foucault seems to rule out. The dialogical theatrical space that the
"Manifesto" proposes, where a text and a public composed of
intellectuals engage in open-ended debate on specific problems
raised by the text, may be seen as an attempt at establishing just
such a locus of resistance. This claim means that my approach to
Pasolini's "Manifesto" and verse tragedies is very different not
only from that of Enrico Groppali's and William Van Watson's
psychoanalytic studies of these texts, but also from that underlying
Rinaldo Rinaldi's recent work.[14] For Rinaldi Pasolini's theatre
represents a moment of deep and irrecuperable pessimism, typical
of the final years of his career, which was to culminate in the film
Salò. The traditional and beneficial cathartic effect of tragedy—
Rinaldi argues—is no longer possible, and the dialogical mode that
the "Manifesto" theorizes as an antidote to the hypostasis of
bourgeois values turns out to be a self-referential monologue in
which Pasolini talks only to himself. My reading of this text, and of
the place it occupies in the corpus of Pasolini's writings, does not

focus on the extent to which it does or does not achieve what it sets out to do, namely, to create a genuinely dialogical space where intellectuals can gather and contribute to political debate. Rather, my reading places the "Manifesto" in the context of a question that Pasolini had begun to investigate in the 1950s and 1960s with the essays that were later to be collected in the volumes *Passione e ideologia* and *Empirismo eretico*: the possibility of elaborating open-ended political and literary forms. In particular I consider the "Manifesto" an important part of Pasolini's encounter with Marxism.

In other words, my interest lies not in the merits of the single verse tragedies as performed on stage, which, as Van Watson has pointed out, have tended to be wordy and tedious on the few occasions they have been performed.[15] Nor does my interest lie in whether the performance of the plays sets up an actual dialogue between text and public or what the results of such an encounter might be. Rather, my interest lies in the "Manifesto"'s theoretical valorization of open-ended, ongoing dialogue as a way of elaborating possible alternative strategies to combat the impasse the student revolutionaries of May 1968 had found themselves in.

To the best of my knowledge Pasolini did not envisage any practical application for his "Manifesto" and the picture of a "New Theatre" it provides. None of the verse tragedies gives any indication of the conditions in which the dialogue of New Theatre might take place, nor does the "Manifesto" itself indicate any one of the six texts as a blueprint for such an exercise. Rather than that of a guideline for a specific course of action, the "Manifesto" takes the form of a call for greater thoughtfulness. Dispensing with the "azione scenica [...], luci, scenografia, costumi ecc." ["scenic action (...), lights, scenery, costumes etc.": *T*, 716] of conventional theatre, Pasolini's New Theatre offers itself as an oasis of thought. Early in the "Manifesto", first published in *Nuovi argomenti* at the beginning of 1968, we read: "Venite ad assistere alle rappresentazioni del 'teatro di parola' con l'idea più di ascoltare che di vedere (restrizione necessaria per comprendere meglio le parole che sentirete, e quindi le idee, che sono i reali personaggi di questo teatro)" ["Come to the performances of the 'theatre of the word' with the idea of listening more than seeing (this is a necessary constraint in order to understand better the words you will hear, and therefore the ideas, which are the real characters of this theatre)": *T*, 716].

The mistaken primacy of action over thought had been one of Pasolini's main criticisms of the tactics adopted by the student groups in May 1968. To act without first thinking, he states in the Duflot interview, is only to reinforce the deeply rooted codes of behaviour that neo-capitalist Power has thrust into place in the bourgeois consciousness. Blind action—he continues—is ultimately a conservative move because it only confirms one of the lynchpins of bourgeois ideology, the valorization of practicality and utilitarianism: "ed eccoli [the student groups] optare per l'azione e l'utilitarismo, rassegnarsi alla situazione in cui il sistema s'ingegna ad integrarli" ["and here they are opting for action and utilitarianism, resigning themselves to the situation in which the system does all it can to integrate them"].[16]

What would be potentially revolutionary—he suggests—is to reverse the priority of action over thought and elaborate new, as yet unidentified ways of putting up genuine resistance to what, in the same interview, he calls the circle of bourgeois codes and practices. The "Manifesto", then, as I propose to treat it, is Pasolini's contribution to an ambitious project whose aim is to prepare suitable conditions in which to elaborate genuinely disruptive modes of protest. Pasolini's perception of the limits of the students' tactics is mirrored in the critique of avant-garde theatre that takes up the opening sections of the "Manifesto". Already in his introduction to the last of his verse tragedies, the posthumously published *Bestia da stile*, Pasolini had drawn a connection between the current degraded state of Italian avant-garde theatre and the limits of the May 1968 movement. Referring back to the critique of the Neo-avant-garde movement he had set out in the essays collected in *Passione e ideologia*, he finds the avant-garde theatre of the late Sixties just as repulsive as traditional bourgeois theatre.[17] Avant-garde theatre, he writes, is "la feccia della neoavanguardia e del '68" ["the scum of the Neo-avant-garde and of 1968": *T*, 598].

Pasolini's "Manifesto" earlier outlines the existence of two kinds of theatre: a conservative, bourgeois theatre, which he calls the "Teatro della Chiacchiera" ["Theatre of Chatter"] and the avant-garde theatre of protest, which he calls anti-bourgeois theatre or "Teatro del Gesto e dell'Urlo" ["Theatre of the Gesture and the Scream"]. It is important to remember that for Pasolini both kinds of theatre, whether or not they confirm or claim to subvert bourgeois values, are ultimately products of the same bourgeois culture. In the course of the "Manifesto", the Teatro del Gesto e dell'Urlo is also termed "anti-bourgeois bourgeois theatre", meaning a supposedly anti-bourgeois theatre which nevertheless comes from within the bourgeoisie and whose subversive impact is thus lessened. It is for this reason that Pasolini has little time for avant-garde theatre, and rejects the idea that its form of protest has any real worth. He finds a common element in bourgeois and anti-bourgeois theatre: each of them represents for its respective audience a ritual confirmation of the already known. Bourgeois theatre is a ritual in which the bourgeoisie mirrors itself, "piú o meno idealizzandosi, comunque sempre riconoscendosi" ["more or less idealizing itself, at the very least always recognizing itself"]; while avant-garde theatre

> è un rituale in cui la borghesia [...] prova il piacere della provocazione, della condanna e dello scandalo (attraverso cui, infine, non ottiene che la conferma delle proprie convinzioni) [...]. Il Teatro del Gesto e dell'Urlo [...] rappresenta, per i gruppi avanzati che lo producono e lo fruiscono come destinatari [...], una *conferma*, rituale, delle proprie convinzioni antiborghesi: la stessa conferma rituale che rappresenta il teatro tradizionale per il pubblico medio e normale con le proprie convinzioni borghesi. (*T*, 718–19)

> [is a ritual in which the bourgeoisie (...) experiences the pleasure of provocation, of condemnation and scandal (through which, finally, it receives nothing other than the confirmation of its own convictions) (...). The Theatre of the Gesture and the Scream (...) represents for the progressive groups that produce it and enjoy it as addressees (...) nothing more than a ritual *confirmation* of their own anti-bourgeois convictions, the same ritual confirmation of bourgeois convictions as traditional theatre represents for the average, normal public.]

In both cases, the key and negatively coded term is "rituale", "ritual". As we move on into the sketch drawn by the "Manifesto" of what a New Theatre looks like, we find that the term "rituale" is gradually replaced by another, this time positively coded term, "rito", "rite". The New Theatre the "Manifesto" proposes is one that considers theatre no longer a bourgeois or anti-bourgeois ritual but a rite, a "RITO CULTURALE" (*T*, 731). Pasolini does not help us a great deal with this terminology. The matter is complicated by the final pages of the "Manifesto", where he distinguishes the cultural rite he considers New Theatre to be from other kinds of rite—natural, religious, political, social, theatrical. As I understand him, for Pasolini "ritual" stands to "rite" as, in a Gadamerian sense, "convention" stands to "tradition". Whereas the former terms indicate the reproposal and confirmation of what is already acquired (and perhaps sedimented) knowledge, the latter indicate an ongoing process of exploration and discovery of new ground.

The parallels between the "Manifesto"'s critique of the two forms of existing theatre and Pasolini's response to the student protests should—I hope—be clear: the ritualized form of both kinds of bourgeois theatre, but especially anti-bourgeois theatre, is the equivalent of the ritualized form of the protests of the student groups. In fact the metaphor which underlies all Pasolini's writings on May 1968 is that of a play whose participants—the students—are called on to interpret pre-assigned roles. Antonio Prete captures this aspect of May 1968 well when he comments that the students

> étaient [...] des figurants d'une représentation dans le Grand Théatre de la politique: des sujets d'un scénario sans metteur en scène, ou bien des sujets d'une mise en scène multiforme et diffuse, à laquelle on donne le nom abstract de pouvoir. Rêve et récitation d'une différence.[18]

> [were (...) actors in a play in the Great Theatre of politics: subjects from a script without director, or, rather, subjects of a scattered, multiform *mise-en-scène* to which one may give the abstract name "power". The dream and the staging of a difference.]

If what Pasolini means by "ritual", the negative term, is fairly clear, what he means by "rite" is far less so. He certainly does not offer any precise indications as to what New Theatre's cultural rite might be or the results it might produce. His point, of course, is that, as yet, we do not know what those results may be, and that it is precisely the task of New Theatre's dialogical format to elaborate such alternative strategies. All this, to an Anglo-Saxon mind, will sound very wishy-washy, as if Pasolini had whetted our appetites only to reward us with very little. Indeed, if we consider the proposals made by the "Manifesto" in a purely pragmatic light, we are certain to find it wanting. An approach that is more productive, and more generous to Pasolini, is to consider the text in the light of some of the theoretical issues he had debated in the early to mid-

1950s. If such an approach is adopted, the apparent vagueness of what Pasolini means by "cultural rite" can be better understood as a stage in his research into the possibility of open-ended political and literary forms which, like dialogue, keep debate going. Pasolini's aim is to elaborate forms which will stimulate enquiry but at the same time avoid the sedimentation of thought to which rigidly held ideological positions are prone. If we go back to his writings of the mid-1950s, we find, in his relationship with Marxism, an example of Pasolini's distrust of all such forms.

For the first Italian critics to write at length about Pasolini in the mid-1960s, his discovery of Marxism was an important turning-point. They argued that he was no longer a marginal dialect poet and novelist concerned with the ahistorical realities of Friulan village life and the Roman *borgata*. Instead, Pasolini's adherence to Marxism brought him into contact with those political and historical forces which, according to Marxism, determine social reality and must be identified and fought if society is to be changed.[19] More recent studies of Pasolini's relationship with Marxism have, however, revealed a more complicated picture. According to such studies, Pasolini's Marxism, and the influence of Gramsci on his thinking, take second place to the far more marked presence of elements of Crocean aesthetics.[20] By turning to a close examination of some of the essays he wrote in the mid-1950s, we find further evidence that Pasolini's adherence to Marxism is far less conventional than his early critics believed.

Two essays are of particular interest, "Osservazioni sull'evoluzione del '900" (1954) and "La libertà stilistica" (1957), both of which are republished in *Passione e ideologia*. The question that the second of the two essays addresses is the failure of the two leading literary movements of post-war Italian culture to develop a genuinely anti-Fascist aesthetic. What innovations Post-hermeticism promised were ultimately only "audacie collaudate" ["tried and tested acts of daring"], in which "non c'era invenzione per quanto scandalosa e abnorme che non fosse in realtà prevista [...]; il desueto rientrava sempre e comunque nella norma" ["there was not a single invention, no matter how scandalous and abnormal, which had not in fact been foreseen (...); the unusual was always and in all cases reined in by the norm"].[21] As for the Neo-realists, their failure to break with previous practices was involuntary, brought about by their disingenuous attempt to express "contenuti solo surrettiziamente nuovi" ["contents which were only surrepti-

tiously new"], while at the same time taking over "il tono innogra-
fico, profetico, fraternizzante [...], lirico-religioso" of the "nove-
centismo superato" they had inherited ["the hymn-like, prophetic,
fraternizing (...), lyrical-religious tone (...) of a long-outmoded
twentieth-century style": *PI*, 485].

At one stage in the mid-1950s Marxism seemed to Pasolini to
offer a new ideological approach which would allow post-war
Italian culture to achieve the break with those continuities that
Neo-realism and Post-hermeticism had failed to enact. In the 1954
essay "Osservazioni sull'evoluzione del '900" Pasolini writes of
Marxist thought as an already existing potential "nuova cultura,
ossia una nuova interpretazione della realtà" ["new culture; or
better, a new interpretation of reality": *PI*, 330). In "La libertà
stilistica", published three years later, however, the picture changes.
The background to that essay is Pasolini's contention that for a
member of the bourgeoisie, such as himself, it is difficult to adhere
fully to a new ideology like Marxism. Intellectuals like Pasolini find
themselves in a halfway position between ideologies: although
they have turned their back on bourgeois ideology, they are not yet
entirely committed to the tenets of Marxism. This is why Pasolini
can state: "Nessuna delle ideologie 'ufficiali' [...] ci possiede"
["None of the 'official' ideologies (...) possesses us": *PI*, 488].
Pasolini presents his "no longer bourgeois/not yet Marxist" position in defensive terms, as an inevitable transitional phase in a
process which will lead to eventual full adherence to, or, to use his
terms, possession by, the principles of Marxist thought.

We should note, however, that Pasolini places emphasis not so
much on the beneficial results which will come at the end of the
process as on those that come from the process itself. In other
words, the difficult transitional phase of the process, and the self-
questioning it necessitates in the bourgeois consciousness, become
as important as the end-point of the process itself. On closer
inspection it transpires that the break with the cultural practices of
the past is made possible by the "crisi nella società e nell'individuo" ["crisis in society and in the individual": *PI*, 330] which
results when a new ideology erupts into a consciousness previously encrusted by the sedimentations of an old one. The productivity of the position Pasolini elaborates in this essay comes not from
the certainties that would result from full adherence to Marxism
but from the crisis that the move towards the new ideology brings

about. Marxism, then, is of interest to Pasolini not as a totalizing ideology which will provide an ultimate new interpretation of the world: for Pasolini, rather, the new ideology plays an important role as an element of rupture that, first, exposes the lines of least resistance within dominant bourgeois ideology and, second, uses the innovative world view that it generates to produce what he calls a "new poetry", by which he means a genuinely anti-Fascist literary practice avoiding the traps into which Neo-realism and Post-hermeticism have fallen. Referring to such a position, he writes:

> A noi questa situazione in cui viviamo quotidianamente, di scelta non compiuta, di dramma irrisolto […], di falsa "distensione", di scontento per tutto ciò che ha dato una sua pur inquieta pienezza alle generazioni che ci hanno preceduto, sembra sufficientemente drammatica perché possa produrre una nuova poesia. (*PI*, 330)

> [To us who, every day, live this situation of unmade choices, of dramas unresolved out of hypocrisy or weakness (...), of false "tolerance", of discontent with everything that has given even an uneasy sense of plenitude to the generations which have come before us, seems sufficiently dramatic to produce a new poetry.]

And in the later essay we find that Pasolini's declaration of ideological independence also puts the emphasis not so much on certainties as on those elements which rupture previously held convictions. Here again he underlines the "contradictory", "negative", "problematic", "undecided" and "dramatic" qualities of an ideological position that demands "un continuo, doloroso sforzo di mantenersi all'altezza di una attualità non posseduta ideologicamente, come può essere per un cattolico, un comunista o un liberale" ["an ongoing, painful effort to keep oneself on a par with a reality one does not possess ideologically, as would be the case for a Catholic, a Communist or a Liberal": *PI*, 488].

We find in these pages the beginnings of the intellectual itinerary that leads us to the "Manifesto"'s proposal of New Theatre as a cultural rite. Already taking shape in these essays is Pasolini's perception that any rigidly held ideological position is destined to degenerate into a series of dogmatic statements which offer themselves as the single interpretative key with which to understand the complexity of the world. It is important to underline here that

Pasolini is not seeking some extra- or supra-ideological position from which he can have immediate access to the world. Rather, his concern at this stage is to emphasize the disruptive effects that a new ideology, like Marxism, can have on the pillars of bourgeois ideology. Pasolini, then, foregrounds what might be called the productively deconstructive side of Marxist thought and its impact in a society and a self pervaded by bourgeois ideology.

To avoid replacing the sedimentations of one orthodoxy with those of another, Pasolini is aware of the need to prevent the potentially disruptive vocabulary of a new ideology from atrophying into a set of standard terms. On two occasions Pasolini uses the same metaphor to make this point: that of the periscope and the horizon. The position that would be offered by complete adhesion to an ideology is rejected because it would reduce "il mondo al suo angolo visuale, adattando l'orizzonte al periscopio" ["the world to its visual angle, making the horizon fit the periscope": *PI*, 348]. The alternative the two essays offer does not abolish the idea of a subject position ("il periscopio") within ideology, for it is clear to Pasolini that this is not an option. What he proposes is a subject position which is aware of its status as an ideological construct, but whose constitutive element is an acute awareness of the danger of ideological sedimentations or perspectivism: "abolire alle origini ogni forma di 'posizionalismo', in una verifica continua, in una lotta continua contro la tendenziosità: facendo adattare senza pace 'il periscopio all'orizzonte' e non viceversa" ["to abolish at its origins any form of 'perspectivism', in a critical process, in an ongoing struggle against tendentiousness: always striving to make the periscope fit the horizon and not vice versa": *PI*, 490–91].

Pasolini knows that ideologies—all ideologies—tend towards an orthodoxy. His project, as I see it, was to locate himself in the rifts of civil and literary society which new ideological formulations open up, but without ever committing himself fully to a single position within ideology that tends towards becoming another orthodoxy. In other words, Pasolini is willing to stay within Marxism as long as the task it sets itself is that of deconstructing dominant ideology. When, however, Marxism establishes itself to such an extent that it constructs an alternative orthodoxy, then Pasolini is quick to proclaim his ideological independence.

It is important to stress at this point that a change in Pasolini's thinking takes place between the mid-1950s and the late 1960s. If,

in the earlier period, he had held the view that the elaboration of an
alternative ideological stance could dislodge bourgeois ideology
from its position of dominance, by the late 1960s, and particularly
around 1968, he had become much more pessimistic. No longer
one ideology among others, bourgeois ideology had installed itself
so pervasively in the consciousness of all sectors of society that no
alternative seemed possible. In his interview with Duflot he says:
"La borghesia sta trionfando, sta rendendo borghesi gli operai, da
una parte, e i contadini ex-coloniali, dall'altra. Insomma, il neocapitalismo, la borghesia sta diventando la condizione umana" ["The
bourgeoisie is winning, it is turning the workers and the ex-
colonial peasants into the bourgeoisie. In other words, neo-capitalism and the bourgeoisie are becoming the human condition"].[22]

By the late 1960s bourgeois ideology, as Pasolini saw it, had
extended its reach so far that it had succeeded in masking its
specific ideological basis and presented itself in a new guise, as
Power. Certainly, statements like the above left Pasolini open to all
kinds of charges: that his hyperbolic mode of address obscured the
strong points of his argument; that he did not understand the
profound changes a society on the verge of a Post-modern world
was experiencing; that his claim to see the truth of a situation that
had escaped all others was ultimately a form of intellectual arrog-
ance. Yet his perception of the encroachment of Power and the
damaging effects it had on all aspects of both political and personal
life remains at the centre of his attention in both the verse tragedies
and his newspaper writings of the early 1970s.[23] In the journalistic
pieces to which, along with cinema, he was to dedicate much of the
final period of his life, Pasolini writes at length about the pernicious
effects that this new form of Power—which he speaks of in terms
of neo-Fascism and anthropological genocide—was having on
Italy and the Italians.

To form a concrete idea of Pasolini's perception of the hold
Power had taken over both consciousness and our imaginative
faculties we may return to the "Manifesto", and in particular to its
opening paragraph. The overall aim of the "Manifesto" is to outline
a New Theatre, different from both the traditional and avant-garde
theatres of the day. But, as the "Manifesto" immediately makes
clear, to elaborate the new we need to be creative enough to invent
a vocabulary that distinguishes the new from the old. In other
words, the creation of something new requires the kind of imaginat-

ive leap that is the traditional task of the poet. The opening paragraph of the "Manifesto", however, puts the possibility of making such a leap in doubt. How can we imagine and describe a New Theatre when all our vocabulary and reference points are drawn from the world of traditional theatre? How can we even expect a New Theatre when our expectations of the new have already been coded in terms of the old? In the opening paragraph of the "Manifesto" we read:

> Il teatro che vi aspettate, anche come totale novità, non potrà essere mai il teatro che vi aspettate. Infatti, se vi aspettate un nuovo teatro, lo aspettate necessariamente nell'ambito delle idee che già avete; inoltre, una cosa che vi aspettate, in qualche modo c'è già [...]. Oggi, dunque, tutti voi vi aspettate un teatro nuovo, ma tutti ne avete già in testa un'idea, nata in seno al teatro vecchio. (*T*, 713)

> [The theatre you expect, even at its most innovative, will never be the theatre you expect. When you expect a new theatre, you necessarily expect it within the limits of the ideas you already have. Besides, something you expect is, in a sense, already there (...). Today, then, you all expect a new theatre, but you all have in your heads an idea about it which comes from the old theatre.]

Any unprecedented innovation a New Theatre might bring is immediately brought back within the confines of the familiar: "Ma le novità, anche totali [...], sono meschine, seccanti e deludenti: o non si riconoscono o si discutono riportandole alle vecchie abitudini" ["But innovations, even the greatest (...), are miserable, annoying and disappointing: they are either not recognized as innovations or are discussed in such a way that they become once again part of old habits": *T*, 713]. Innovations, then, are either not recognized as such, because we have no language flexible enough to describe them adequately, or are diluted through the filter of previous sentences, old linguistic and conceptual habits. Pasolini's point here is that the space for alternative interpretations of reality and constructions of the future that the new ideological vocabulary supplied by Marxism had made possible in the 1950s no longer exists. Going back to the previously quoted essays from *Passione e ideologia*, we find that for Pasolini Marxist ideology offers the kind of new vocabulary which made possible the imaginative leap and reinterpretation of reality that the "Manifesto" rules out. Marxism is a "nuova [...] misura sociale e morale" ["new (...) social and moral measure"] which makes possible a "nuova configurazione del passato, [... una] nuova prospettiva del futuro" ["a new way of configuring the past, (... a) new perspective on the future": *PI*, 330].

As I see it, the task Pasolini gives to the "Manifesto"'s proposal of New Theatre as a cultural rite is the creation of the conditions in which the kind of imaginative leap Marxism had made possible in the 1950s can once again be achieved. The principal instrument with which Pasolini aims to do this is his proposal of theatre as a place of dialogue. The dialogical relationship set up between text and public is the defining characteristic of New Theatre. The kind of theatre Pasolini has in mind is *"prima di tutto dibattito, scambio di idee, lotta letteraria e politica, sul piano più democratico e razionale possibile"* ["*first of all debate, exchange of ideas, literary and political struggle*, at the most democratic and rational level possible": *T*, 724], "uno scambio di opinioni e di idee, in un rapporto molto più critico che rituale" ["an exchange of opinions and ideas, in a relationship that will be far more critical than ritualized": *T*, 719]. On two occasions Pasolini underlines that the dialogue is "open-ended"— "a canone sospeso" (*T*, 715 and 719)—, and he aims to discuss the "problemi posti o dibattuti [...] dal testo" ["questions raised or debated (...) by the text": *T*, 715], "ma senza pretendere di risolverli" ["but without claiming to offer answers": *T*, 719].

By this, of course, Pasolini does not mean that the dialogue goes nowhere, or that it is simply debate for debate's sake. What he is at pains to avoid is the kind of debate which, informed by rigidly held ideological preconceptions, leads to foregone conclusions and precludes the kind of imaginative leap necessary if new and more effective forms of protest are to be elaborated. The proposal of open-ended dialogue may be seen as Pasolini's most concerted attempt at elaborating the means by which to give form (albeit theoretical form) to the mobile ideological position he had first outlined in "La libertà stilistica".

If open-ended dialogue between text and public is the form that New Theatre's cultural rite is to take, the question of who takes part in the dialogue and the precise nature of the issues to be discussed is far less clear. As to the second point, neither the "Manifesto" itself nor the verse tragedies give us any detailed indication. Both, however, are of some help in identifying the intended participants in the dialogue. The "Manifesto" defines them as the "gruppi avanzati della borghesia" ["progressive groups of the bourgeoisie": *T*, 714]. Another group is formed by individuals drawn from the "élites sopravviventi del laicismo liberale crociano e dai radicali" ["élites who have survived Crocean Liberal lay culture and from the Radicals": *T*, 715]. Although both Pasolini's debt to Croce and Croceanism and his involvement with the Radical Party in the final months of his life have been well documented, these definitions remain too vague if we are to identify the actual audience Pasolini envisaged.[24] We gather as we read on into the "Manifesto" that the members of these groups have an intellectual potential that has yet to be tapped because so far they lack the suitable forum that New Theatre proposes to create. It appears that the only forum currently open to such groups is the kind offered by avant-garde theatre, Il Teatro del Gesto o dell'Urlo, whose ability to work genuine change Pasolini challenges. By drawing these groups away from avant-garde theatre, New Theatre aims to give them an alternative forum where their energies may be put to more productive use. In other words, New Theatre offers itself as a kind of rescue operation for intellectuals in search of a role.

All this is only hinted at in the "Manifesto". If, however, we turn to some of the six verse tragedies we may see in more precise terms the outlines of this operation. First written in April 1966 when Pasolini was confined to bed convalescing after an ulcer, extensively revised in the following years for publication in reviews like *Nuovi argomenti*, but published only posthumously in book form, the six verse tragedies have at least one common element: they are all peopled by characters on the edge of things who seek ways to bring their presence to bear on society. We may also see that all these characters, in one way or another, bear a striking resemblance to Pasolini himself. It seems clear, in fact, that high on Pasolini's list of priorities was the need to create for himself a possible niche within Italian civil society from which he could launch the insights he thought he could bring to intellectual debate. Many of the activities in which Pasolini engaged, above all in the post-1968 years—his hyper-participation in round tables and discussions, the columns he wrote for various reviews and newspapers, including the high-profile articles he wrote for the *Corriere della sera*, later collected in *Lettere luterane*—, may be seen in this light, as attempts to give himself a voice in public debate, like those of the characters in his verse tragedies. Indeed, nobody more than Pasolini fits his own description of the ideal audience for his New Theatre: enlightened, secular, radicalized left-wingers of bourgeois extraction and Crocean training.

The character most closely associated with Pasolini is Pilade, in the play of the same name. *Pilade* takes the form of an easily identifiable allegory of post-1945 Italy, albeit in a Greek context. We can recognize the fall of Fascism, the hopes of post-war renewal, the restoration and the re-emergence of Fascism in the new guise of the business culture that has taken over the country. Pilade, the only character to rebel against the turn events have taken, is banished to the mountains, where he spends his time in reflection and gathering an army of revolutionaries with which he attempts (and fails) to reconquer the country. Reflecting on his defeat, he expresses his paradoxical thanks that the new order he attempted to install was not exposed as just another variant on, and thus a continuation of, the old. His fear is that his victory would only have replaced an old monument with a new one; referring to Oreste, his childhood companion turned enemy, he says to Atena, the new ruler of the land:

> Solamente l'idea di impadronirmi del potere
> (sia pure non per sé)
> è la piú colpevole delle colpe...
> [...]
> Oreste, in nome tuo, ha abbattuto un monumento
> e ne ha eretto un altro: io stavo per fare lo stesso,
> ma il mio monumento, per fortuna, resterà incompiuto.
>
> (*T*, 400–10)

[Simply the idea of seizing power/(even if not as an end in itself)/ is the most sinful of sins.../(...)/Orestes, in your name, has knocked down a monument/and built another: I was about to do the same,/but fortunately my monument will never be built.]

This is one of the clearest and strongest formulations of a question with which Pasolini grappled throughout his artistic career, and which comes to a head in the "Manifesto": how to find ways to intervene in the political and cultural debate of the day in order to have one's say on vital issues and leave a mark by which one's contribution may be known, but without that mark ever constituting itself as an irremovable, permanent monument. The verse tragedies are full of "Pasolini" figures similar to Pilade, all of them dissidents who inhabit the margins and seek (and fail to find) ways of expressing their dissidence. The parts of the tragedies which deal with these characters begin to look like an "unemployment office" for intellectuals in search of a purpose, wandering figures lost in their solipsism. Pilade is certainly one; Julian in *Porcile* is another, a character without a role who is reduced to nothingness, "né ubbidiente né disubbidiente [...] né consenziente, né disconsenziente [...] né morto, né vivo" ["neither obedient nor disobedient (...) neither consenting nor dissenting (...) neither dead nor alive": *T*, 427-42); so too is the Jan (Palach) figure in *Bestia da stile*, as well as Sigismundo and Paolo in *Calderon*, the text which perhaps best illustrates the self-perpetuating nature of Power that Pasolini's theoretical elaborations of the late 1960s sought to expose and contrast. *Calderon* signals the impossibility of change by telling the same story three times in different social environments but in an identical manner. The play's tragic heroine is Rosaura, whose attempts at protecting herself from the influence of the world surrounding her end in defeat as she lapses into the incomprehensibility of aphasia. *Porcile* and *Bestia da stile* also illustrate how silence has taken the place of dialogue. *Porcile*, for example, closes with these lines: "ssssst! Non dite niente a nessuno" ["ssssst! Don't tell anyone anything": *T*, 501], while many sections of *Bestia da stile* are composed of attempts at dialogue which degenerate into monologues, as one of the parties' lines is replaced by a sequence of dots:

SPIRITO DI KAREL   Resto qui, perché devo parlarti.
JAN   ....
SPIRITO DI KAREL   No, no, poi me ne andrò per sempre.

(*T*, 626)

[KAREL'S SPIRIT   I'm staying here because I have to speak to you.
JAN   ....
KAREL'S SPIRIT   No, no, then I'll go away for ever.]

The open-ended dialogical space that New Theatre proposes may be seen as a response to the questions that the characters of the verse tragedies are unable to answer. The "Manifesto", I have been arguing, is an attempt to break the silence, to provide the conditions in which to get the conversation going again. I say "attempt" because there are a number of significant problems which

Pasolini's valorization of dialogue raises but does little to address. We need to ask to what extent dialogue is genuinely open-ended: whether, like all narrative structures, it gathers up a pre-interpretative momentum of its own which leads it in a prefigured direction. If legitimate questions can be raised about the direction dialogue goes in, so too can similar concerns about where it comes from. Dialogue, in fact, has long been appropriated by the kind of bourgeois, humanistic discourse of which Pasolini is wary. As Edward Said has recently suggested, the valorization of dialogue by the likes of Richard Rorty that has marked theoretical discussion in the last few years tends to ignore the discrepancy created by the unequal power dynamic which is bound to obtain in any interchange between partners, whether that interchange take place in the classroom or in a love affair. For Said, the picture conjured up by Rorty's "conversation of humankind" is a distinctly élitist one of "philosophers discoursing animatedly in a handsomely appointed salon".[25]

These are questions that Pasolini does nothing to tackle, either in the "Manifesto" or, to the best of my knowledge, elsewhere. A more specific critique of the "Manifesto" has been advanced by Rinaldo Rinaldi in both his recent book-length studies on Pasolini, studies to which the present essay is greatly indebted. For Rinaldi the dialogue that the "Manifesto" proposes is nothing other than a disguised monologue in which Pasolini talks to and thereby justifies himself. The failure to create a genuinely dialogical space is repeated, he argues, in Pasolini's failure to establish a dialogue with the readers of the various newspapers and magazines for which he wrote. In Rinaldi's view Pasolini's attempts at dialogue become one-way traffic: "una confessione, un monologo, un diario" ["a confession, a monologue, a diary"].[26]

While not denying the pertinence of some of these remarks, my approach has been to consider the "Manifesto" in the light of the questions dramatically raised by the political events which culminated in May 1968, but on which Pasolini had been reflecting since at least the 1950s. I have not been concerned to verify the feasibility of the practical application of the "Manifesto"'s proposals, or to gauge any results the dialogue between text and public may or may not have produced. Rather, my interest in the "Manifesto" has been twofold: firstly, as a stage in the evolution of Pasolini's own intellectual itinerary; and secondly, as an attempt to give answers to the questions raised by the events of May 1968. It is on the "Manifesto"'s status as an "attempt" that I should like to conclude. We see the "Manifesto" in its best light if we think of it as an "attempt" in the French sense, as an *essai*: not as a final word, but as a contribution aiming to stimulate a debate made more urgent by the impasse reached by the political culture of the day.[27] Certainly, the "Manifesto"'s proposals may sound idealistic, naïve and at times vaguely formulated, but it is perhaps only visionary thinking along such utopian lines that will create the conditions for the kind of imaginative leap which is necessary if a radically new form of society is to be envisaged. Despite his critical reception of the events of May 1968, one of its key slogans, "Let's bring the imagination to power", would, I think, have met with Pasolini's approval.

NOTES

1   Interview with M. Bellocchio, "Storia dei giovani: prima, durante e dopo il 68", supplement to *Panorama*, 31 Jan. 1988.
2   Originally published in *L'espresso*, 23 June 1968, the poem is now republished in *Empirismo eretico*, second edition (Milan, Garzanti, 1991), pp. 151–59.
3   R. De Felice, *Interpretations of Fascism*, translated by B. Huff Everett (Cambridge, MA, Harvard University Press, 1977).
4   P. P. Pasolini, *Teatro* (Milan, Garzanti, 1988), p. 135. All further quotations from the six verse tragedies and the "Manifesto per un nuovo teatro" will be taken from this edition. For an English translation of Pasolini's "Manifesto" see "Manifesto for a New Theatre", in *Pier Paolo Pasolini: Contemporary Perspectives*, edited by P. Rumble and B. Testa (Toronto, University of Toronto Press, 1994), pp. 152–70, and D. Ward, *A Poetics of Resistance: Narrative and the Writings of Pier Paolo Pasolini* (Madison, NJ, Fairleigh Dickinson University Press, 1995), pp. 179–91.
5   "La poesia della tradizione", in *Trasumanar e organizzar* (Milan, Garzanti, 1971), pp. 120–21.
6   "Controcampo", broadcast on 20 October 1973, and then printed in *Il sabato*, 13–19 Feb. 1988.
7   *Les Dernières Paroles d'un impie: entretiens avec Jean Duflot*, edited by J. Duflot (Paris, Belfond, 1981), p. 69; published in Italian as *Il sogno del centauro* (Rome, Editori Riuniti, 1983).
8   See "Intervista con Vittorio Foà and Claudio Petruccioli", *L'espresso*, 23 June 1968. See also L. Meneghelli, "La rana populista", *Mondo nuovo*, 23 June 1968; W. Pedullà, "Sempre piú in fretta", *L'avanti!*, 4 July 1968.
9   M. Foucault, *The History of Sexuality*, translated by R. Hurley (New York, Random House, 1980), I, 93.

10   J. Culler, "Political Criticism", in *Writing the Future*, edited by D. Wood (London, Routledge, 1990), pp. 192–204, on which this section of my argument has relied heavily.

11   M. Foucualt, *The History of Sexuality*, I, 95–96.

12   "I sogni ideologici", *Nuovi argomenti*, 22 (Apr–June 1971), 22.

13   See in particular P. P. Pasolini, *Scritti corsari* (Milan, Garzanti, 1975) and *Lettere luterane* (Turin, Einaudi, 1976).

14   The only book-length work in English entirely dedicated to Pasolini's theatre is by William Van Watson, *Pier Paolo Pasolini and the Theatre of the Word* (Ann Arbor, UMI Research Press, 1989). I refer readers to that volume for synopses and fuller descriptions of the verse tragedies than I have space for here. For what I believe is the first attempt in English to treat the verse tragedies seriously, see J. Gatt-Rutter, "Pier Paolo Pasolini", in *Writers and Society in Contemporary Italy: A Collection of Essays*, edited by M. Caesar and P. Hainsworth (Leamington Spa, Berg, 1984), pp. 143–66. See also P. Friedrich, *Pier Paolo Pasolini* (Boston, Twayne, 1982). In Italian see E. Groppali, *L'ossessione e il fantasma: il teatro di Pasolini e Moravia* (Venice, Marsilio, 1979); R. Rinaldi, *Pier Paolo Pasolini* (Milan, Mursia, 1982), pp. 287–325, and *L'irriconoscibile Pasolini* (Foggia, Marra, 1990), pp. 227–40.

15   The exception is *Affabulazione*, which has toured in a production by and with Vittorio Gassman. However, as Watson points out, the performed text differed considerably from Pasolini's original.

16   J. Duflot, *Les Dernières Paroles d'un impie*, p. 68.

17   For a comprehensive account in English of the Italian Neo-avant-garde of the early 1960s see C. Wagstaff, "The Neo-avant-garde", in *Writers and Society in Contemporary Italy*, pp. 35–62.

18   A. Prete, "Pasolini, 1968", in *Pier Paolo Pasolini: séminaire dirigé par Maria Antonietta Macciocchi* (Paris, Grasset, 1980), p. 283.

19   See the chapters dedicated to Pasolini's poetry and novels in A. Asor Rosa, *Scrittori e popolo* (Rome, Samonà and Savelli, 1965); and G. C. Ferretti, *Letteratura e ideologia* (Rome, Editori Riuniti, 1965).

20   See Z. G. Barański, "Pier Paolo Pasolini: Culture, Croce, Gramsci", in *Culture and Conflict in Postwar Italy: Essays on Mass and Popular Culture*, edited by Z. G. Barański and R. Lumley (London, Macmillan, 1990), pp. 139–59. See also Joseph Francese's essay in the present collection.

21   P. P. Pasolini, *Passione e ideologia* (Milan, Garzanti, 1973), pp. 486–87.

22   J. Duflot, *Les Dernières Paroles d'un impie*, pp. 161–62.

23   See John Gatt-Rutter's comments, in "Pier Paolo Pasolini", on the alienating effects advanced neo-capitalism has had on everyday life. In particular, see his distinction between bourgeois "individual" and "unassimilated person": "The 'individual' is seen as an interchangeable part in the machinery of production and in the manipulations of Power [...] whereas the unassimilated 'person' [...] resists the pressures of a dehumanizing 'Reason'. His 1966 works are tragic in showing that, once the bourgeois transformation has taken place, the fleshly 'person' buried in each 'individual' can emerge only at the cost of annihilation" (p. 162).

24   For Pasolini's debt to Croce see Z. G. Barański, "Pier Paolo Pasolini: Culture, Croce, Gramsci", and Joseph Francese's contribution to the present volume. For the text of Pasolini's posthumously delivered address to Italy's Partito Radicale see *LL*, 183–95.

25   E. Said, "Representing the Colonized: Anthropology's Interlocutors", *Critical Inquiry*, 15 (Winter 1989), 198–210 (p. 210); R. Rorty, *Philosophy and the Mirror of Nature* (Oxford, Blackwell, 1980).
26   R. Rinaldi, *Pier Paolo Pasolini*, p. 370.
27   See W. W. Holdheim, "Introduction: The Essay as Knowledge in Progress", in *The Hermeneutical Mode* (Ithaca, Cornell University Press, 1984), pp. 19–32.

CONTAMINATION AND EXCESS:
I RACCONTI DI CANTERBURY
AS A "STRUTTURA DA FARSI"

Patrick Rumble

Gli unici momenti espressivi acuti del film, sono, appunto, le *"insistenze"* delle inquadrature e dei ritmi del montaggio, il cui realismo d'impianto [...] si carica attraverso la durata abnorme di un'inquadratura o di un ritmo di montaggio, fino a esplodere in una sorta di *scandalo tecnico*. Tale insistenza sui particolari, specie su certi particolari degli excursus, è una deviazione rispetto al sistema del film: *è la tentazione a fare un altro film.*[1]

[The only expressively sharp moments of the film are, precisely, the "insistent" pauses of the framing and of the rhythms of the editing. The programmatic realism of these devices (...) is charged during the abnormal duration of a shot or of an editing rhythm until it explodes in a sort of technical scandal. This insistence on particulars, especially on certain details in the digressions, is a deviation in relation to the system of the film: it is the temptation to make another film.]

What most characterizes Pasolini's *Trilogia della vita*, what arguably lends this tripartite work its unity, is the *insistence* of the images on their own materiality, and an insistence, furthermore, on the *beholdenness*, or the *debt*, of Pasolini's images to past figural traditions (from which his films appear to spring). Such debts are revealed throughout the *Trilogia* in moments of what Pasolini calls "technical scandal": when the narrative succession of the episodes that make up these films is exceeded, or ruptured, by an awareness of *style*—of style partially freed from function, set adrift from clear narrative motivation, and thus potentially *useless* and bothersome (or, we might say, *heretical* in relation to the *project* embodied in the plot). I would suggest that this notion of formal excess, which (since Pasolini does not always make his sources explicit) is perhaps derived from a reading of the Russian Formalists (and especially Victor Shklovsky), underpins Pasolini's famous and largely misunderstood essay on the *cinema di poesia* published in *Empirismo eretico* in 1972 (but originally a talk delivered at a film conference in Pesaro in 1965). It is in that essay, which will serve as the basis of my approach to *I racconti di Canterbury*, that Pasolini explains his understanding of the excessive or "poetic" moment of films: "È il momento, cioè, in cui il linguaggio, seguendo un'ispirazione diversa e magari piú autentica, si libera dalla funzione, e si presenta come 'lingua in se stesso', stile" ["It is, in other words, the moment in which language, following a different and possibly more authentic inspiration, frees itself of function and presents itself as 'language as such'—style": *EE*, 187; *Heretical Empiricism*, p. 182].

Throughout the *Trilogia* there is a recurring tension between narrative system and style; between images dominated by a communicative or referential function and images (or elements within those images) that "contaminate" the communication with a surplus of meaning, with a "stain" of what Pasolini calls "other material". The "free indirect" style of the *cinema di poesia* is designed precisely to call up such material, and set loose its force against the narrative film's own progress. As Pasolini remarks elsewhere in *Empirismo eretico*:

> Si opera, violentemente e brutalmente, una dilacerazione, una falla, da cui irrompe l'*altra* materia, quella che compone l'oggettività, il tessuto reale delle cose, sfuggita all'intelletuale-poeta, e sfuggita anche in gran parte all'uomo. (*EE*, 99)

> [A rent, a breach, is effected violently and brutally on such cultured material; from it the *other* material erupts which makes up the objectivity, the real texture of things—which escaped the intellectual poet and also in large part escaped man. (*Heretical Empiricism*, p. 92)]

For Pasolini the problem of excess and contamination, and the "liberation" of style from function, not only carry aesthetic significance but also offer—given his insistence on asserting a homology between narrative and social structure—an allegory of an altered society: what he might call *una società da farsi.*

In *The Decameron* (1971), *The Canterbury Tales* (1972) and *The Arabian Nights* (1974), contamination takes the form of an *insistence* of medieval and Renaissance figural traditions (in the case of the first two films), as well as Persian miniature traditions (in the third).[2] The clearest examples of what I shall call the *effetto dipinto,*[3] or painting effect, in the *Trilogy* are found in *Il Decameron,* where Pasolini himself plays the role of Giotto's "best disciple", thereby introducing a tone of irony that runs throughout the film. In this film Giotto's disciple also has an important narrative function, insofar as his story serves as one of the two frames for the film's other episodes.[4] At the same time, his presence in the diegesis also serves to secure a certain degree of narrative motivation for the presence of visual "quotations" of Giotto's *Last Temptation* and Bruegel's *Battle between Carnival and Lent,* so that the "contamination" of the filmic images with archaic figurative models—it might be argued—serves some narrative purpose. Furthermore, the bipartite structure of *Il Decameron* is reinforced by the opposition between the episodes associated with the Bruegel imagery and those associated with imagery drawn from Giotto.

In the case of *I racconti di Canterbury* the paintings of Bruegel and Bosch serve as the "subterranean" figurative models underlying the film's images, lending them a doubled quality reminiscent of the pastiche-like nature of *Il Decameron.* In *I racconti di Canterbury,* however, the investment in an ideologically motivated presentation of "excess" is not accompanied by structural complexity as in the preceding film. This has led certain critics to attack *I racconti di Canterbury* as a weak sequel to *Il Decameron.* For Sandro Petraglia,

> *Decameron* è un'opera autentica. *I racconti di Canterbury* è un brutto calco divitalizzato [...]. Tutte le storie del primo film si sono coagulate nel secondo in una preziosa ma sottile operazione di rimasticamento.[5]

> [*The Decameron* is an authentic work. *The Canterbury Tales* is an ugly, lifeless copy (...). All the stories of the first film have become coagulated in the second in a precious yet subtle operation of remastication.]

And Bernardo Bertolucci remarks on its lack of inspiration, though this comment seems to account for his attitude towards the entire *Trilogia*, which he deemed the product of a "reactionary poet".[6] And while Pasolini would probably not have had too many problems with the notion of *rimasticamento* (something easily bent into a positive observation within the context of the present discussion), he would certainly have conceded a difference of tone in the second film. Indeed, if *Il Decameron* celebrates "innocent" sexuality and uncorrupted bodies, *I racconti di Canterbury* is far more cynical, dark, pessimistic and non-humorous in its representation of these same themes. Compared to *Il Decameron*, *I racconti di Canterbury* certainly contains a marked lack of "vitality"; and the landscape itself, owing partly to the weather on the days Pasolini was shooting on location in England, appears quite dark and oppressive. It is useful to note Pasolini's own comparison of these first two films of the *Trilogia della vita*:

> The world of Chaucer and Boccaccio hadn't yet experienced industrialization. There wasn't any consumer society, there weren't any assembly lines [...]. Chaucer stands astride two epochs. There is something medieval and gothic about him, the metaphysics of death. But often you get the feeling you are reading Shakespeare or Rabelais or Cervantes. [...]
>
> Chaucer still has one foot in the Middle Ages, but he is not "of the people", even though he took his stories from the people. He is already a bourgeois. He looks forward to the Protestant Revolution, in so far as the two were combined in Cromwell. But whereas Boccaccio, for example, who was also a bourgeois, had a clear conscience, with Chaucer there is already a kind of unhappy feeling, an unhappy conscience.
>
> Chaucer foresees all the victories and triumphs of the bourgeoisie, but he also foresees its rottenness. He is a moralist but he is ironic too. Boccaccio doesn't foresee the future in this way. He catches the bourgeoisie at its moment of triumph, when it was being born.[7]

Thus, while both films are concerned with analogous issues and are similar in structure (given the episodic nature of the original works), there is from the very beginning of the second film an impossibility of the kind of celebration of innocence and popular humour found in *Il Decameron*; indeed, Pasolini remarked that "perhaps humour is a class privilege in England."[8] Furthermore, what Petraglia calls the derivative nature of Pasolini's *I racconti di Canterbury*, as a reworking of materials and themes already found in *Il Decameron*, is inscribed in *I racconti di Canterbury* itself. That is, at a certain point in the film Chaucer, played (again ironically) by Pasolini himself, is seen studying at his desk. He is startled by a shout from his wife and, in an embarrassed gesture, quickly hides the book he was obviously enjoying enormously beneath a pile of other books, and the book is identified in a close-up as Boccaccio's *Decameron*. Thus Chaucer's indebtedness to Boccaccio (and his "anxiety of influence") is registered in the film,[9] and the film itself is presented as a continuation of the first film of the *Trilogia*.

What is continued is the form of subversion found in *Il Decameron*. And again, what is represented thematically is excessive; but what is more important is the excessive manner in which it is represented. As Omar Calabrese remarks in his study of "neo-Baroque" elements in contemporary art, excess (a "baroque" quality he finds characteristic of Post-modern works) is always "distabilizzante" ["destabilizing"] of a given order of things, and usually "qualsiasi azione, opera o individuo eccessivo *vuole* mettere in discussione un qualche ordine, magari distruggerlo o costruirne uno nuovo" ["every excessive action, work or individual *wants* to call into question some kind of order, perhaps to destroy it or to build a new one"].[10] Calabrese's recuperation of the historical Baroque in his studies of contemporary culture seems highly appropriate here given Pasolini's own penchant for reactivating or reanimating in his own films what were apparently superseded moments in the history of art. For the *effetto dipinto* is brought into play in *I racconti di Canterbury* just as it was in *Il Decameron*; and the quotations in the film, often divorced from narrative motivation, are interpretable as destabilizing moments of pure excess. There seem to be few other ways to account for the numerous allusions, to be discussed further below, to Bruegel's *Flemish Proverbs* (1559) and the rather puzzling sequence at the end of the film where we are overwhelmed by the infernal imagery of Hieronymus Bosch.

Calabrese's approach to the problem of excess takes two forms: he distinguishes representations of excess from excess in representation,[11] that is, thematic excess from formal or stylistic excess. The strong moralistic reaction that met the *Trilogia* was caused by excess of the first order: "obscene" representations of nudity, heterosexuality, homosexuality, unethical Franciscan *frati*, and so forth.[12] These transgressive aspects of the *Trilogia*, however, actually interest us relatively little in the present context—that is, unless these thematic excesses are translated into *stylistic* excesses. In *I racconti di Canterbury*, the often transgressively erotic world of the tales is presented in a hybridized visual language—what Pasolini also calls, in a manner peculiarly appropriate to the *Trilogia*, an "overexposed" style. Not only is there a mixing of film genres (most clearly in "The Cook's Tale", which acts as homage to Chaplin, with Ninetto as the Tramp; this homage, however, is also carried over into "The Miller's Tale", where we find Josephine Chaplin as the character May): there is also—just as in *Il Decameron*—a mixing of cinematic and painterly representational models. While in *Il Decameron*, however, the quotations from Bruegel and Giotto have clear narrative motivation—as we have mentioned—, in *I racconti di Canterbury* allusions to Bruegel and Bosch, or literal quotations of their *quadri*, do not have the same narrative legitimacy. Divorced from such motivation, they become pure excess, and, as Costa suggests, draw our attention away from the narrative and towards the enunciation. The *effetto dipinto*, for Costa, stages a confrontation between two semiotic systems or "modelli di rappresentazione"; and it is nearly always "leggibile come una marca d'enunciazione, con accentuazione piú o meno forte, della funzione metalinguistica" ["legible as a mark of enunciation, with an emphasis more or less strong, of the metalinguistic function"].[13] While Costa acknowledges that the *effetto dipinto* is not always "excessive" in the sense we are adopting here, his own attention is drawn more to those moments in certain films when the *effetto dipinto* presents a *conflict* between models of representation, a clashing of systems that draws our attention away from the diegesis and redirects it towards the enunciation.

The "Neo-formalist" theorist Kristin Thompson's understanding of cinematic excess helps further to clarify this point. For her, excess is "an inevitable gap in the motivation for the physical presence of a device; the physical presence retains a perceptual interest beyond its function in the work."[14] Something excessive calls attention only to itself and retains no responsibility to narrative continuity—it falls outside the causal chain of the plot. For Thompson what is always potentially excessive is the very material of the medium, or what Post-structuralist theorists might call a film's *écriture*, which may threaten to break up a film's homogeneity or unity. Homogeneity or unity is the product of a coherent narrative *system*, which, in the classical style, is itself based on conventions of continuity editing. In the classical style, all devices or elements within the frame must have narrative motivation; excess must be kept to a minimum in order to avoid any interruption of narrative flow. The very devices that function to maintain continuity and repress excess, however, by their very physical presence in any work inevitably call attention to a potential heterogeneity within that work. There is always something present in the image that retains connotations irrelevant to the given story. As Stephen Heath writes:

> Just as narrative never exhausts the image, homogeneity is always an *effect* of the film and not the filmic system, which is precisely the production of that homogeneity. Homogeneity is haunted by the material practice it represses and the tropes of that repression, the forms of continuity, provoke within the texture of the film the figures—the edging, the margin—of the loss by which it moves; permanent battle over the resolution of that loss on which, however, it structurally depends, mediation between image and discourse, narrative can never contain the whole film which permanently exceeds its fictions. "Filmic system", therefore, always means at least this: the "system" of the film in so far as the film is the organization of the homogeneity *and* the material outside inscribed in the operation of that organization as its contradiction.[15]

For both Heath and Thompson, alongside any narrative film there exists another, non- or even counter-diegetic film, and as critics they are both sensitive to the forces of unity and disunity in conflict in any given work. Furthermore, certain unorthodox or marginal film-makers may produce films which foreground their stylistic worlds and force the spectator to "skid" in his/her interpretation of the narrative. The idea of "skidding perception" is derived from Roland Barthes's notion of the "third meaning" of an image: the materiality of the signifier (or the image) goes beyond the coherent narrative system of a film, and the image takes on a density or opacity that short-circuits or, as Barthes would say, *subverts* the narrative (without necessarily destroying it).

What is the value of this "skidding perception" brought about by a perception of excess? For Thompson, the spectator is forced to *cope* with the perceptual difficulties brought about by an experience of excess in a way that is traditionally avoided by the classical style, a style which engenders passive viewing habits. In films where style is allowed a great deal of independence *vis-à-vis* narrative functioning—films such as those of the *Trilogia*—the perception of excess leads to a questioning of the viewing procedures necessary to decode the text. For Thompson, the value of films such as these "rests less in their thematic material than in their ability to shift our habitual perceptions of filmic conventions through defamiliarization".[16] And here she reveals her debt to the formulations of Russian Formalism, indeed she cites Shklovsky in particular as her source of inspiration. For Shklovsky asserts, much as Pasolini does in his theories of the "cinema of poetry",[17] the importance of "prolonging" the process of perception in order to "de-familiarize" the spectator with his/her usual viewing habits (what he calls "prose perception"):

> If we start to examine the general laws of perception, we see that as perception becomes habitual, it becomes automatic [...]. Such habituation explains the principles by which, in ordinary speech, we leave phrases unfinished and words half expressed [...]. The object, perceived in the manner of prose perception, fades and does not leave even a first impression; ultimately even the essence of what it was is forgotten [...]. And Art exists to make one feel things, to make the stone *stoney*. The purpose of art is to impart the sensation of things as they are perceived, and not as they are known. The technique of art is to make objects "unfamiliar", to make forms difficult, to increase the difficulty and length of perception because the process of perception is an aesthetic end in itself and must be prolonged.[18]

For Thompson, "this concentration on perceptual difficulty has ideological implications. The perceptual skills necessary for resolving the uncertainty of viewing [excess] relate to social as well as filmic practice."[19] That is, the defamiliarization which occurs in the reception of films invites us to develop a potentially altered perception of our lived environment.

Thompson's approach to excess in narrative films can provide crucial insights into Pasolini's *I racconti di Canterbury*. For the importance of excess in this film appears to be twofold: firstly, as Heath would say, the material of the image, divorced from narrative motivation, exists as a force of potential rupture within the narrative system (the excesses of style introduce what Deleuze calls "a foreign language in a dominant language"),[20] and thus the system's drive to maintain homogeneity is revealed in a "sinister" manner; and secondly, excess throws normal viewing habits into crisis and forces the spectator to consider altered patterns of reception. In order to understand this more clearly it is necessary to locate moments of stylistic excess in *I racconti di Canterbury*.

We shall describe two such moments, one rather subtle and the other not very subtle at all. A subtle form of excess may be detected throughout the film insofar as the *dispositio* of elements within the frame, especially the characters and the architecture, recalls Bruegel's *Flemish Proverbs*. Furthermore, the selection Pasolini makes from Bruegel's episodes seems to be motivated by the lessons they contain. Indeed, the similarities between Pasolini's images and those of Bruegel lend the characters and settings a "doubled" nature: the simple presence of one of Pasolini's Bruegelian characters is "stained" by a sense of derivation from the still space of Bruegel's canvas; the "time" of Pasolini's cinematic universe is infected or ruptured by an "alien" time, what Pasolini calls a "durata abnorme" (*EE*, 185); in fact, the temporal succession of the film seems to fight against a threat of arrest—the sequence of prosaic time of the narratives struggles against the poetic materiality that would tend, in a moment of *scandalo tecnico*, to impede or halt it. In a sense, this is how we should understand Pasolini's belief in the "revolutionary" or "resistant" potential of the past; and this is why he was drawn to film ancient myths and medieval narratives, and why he wanted to save the walls of San'A, in Yemen. As he remarked:

> Adesso, preferisco muovermi nel passato proprio perché ritengo che l'unica forza contestatrice del presente sia proprio il passato: è una forma aberrante ma tutti i valori che sono stati valori nei quali ci siamo formati, con tutte le loro atrocità, i loro lati negativi, sono quelli che possono mettere in crisi il presente.[21]

> [Now I prefer to move in the past precisely because I believe that the past is the only force able to challenge the present: it (the past) is an aberrant form but all the values that have been the values which have shaped us, with all that made them atrocious, with their negative aspects, are the ones that are capable of putting the present into crisis.]

Pasolini contaminated the cinematic code with superseded codes of representation, since, as he believed, every language is always a metaphor of an epoch of history.

The "echo-effect" produced by the *effetto dipinto* is clearly discernible in the film. Besides a general sense of indebtedness to Bruegel's popular and humorous imagery, sensed from the very introduction of the film set in a thirteenth-century market near Canterbury Cathedral, there are moments when the forces of allusion and quotation become the dominant forces within the text.

We thus find an episode from Bruegel's painting translated literally into the film, along with its allegorical lessons, during "The Reeve's Tale". Two young students, Alan and John, set off to visit the Miller, who has been dealing unfairly with their school; they bring corn for the Miller to grind and intend to watch him to make sure he performs the job without "trickery". On arriving at the Miller's home they are met by the vision of two *derrières*, those of the Miller's wife and daughter, issuing from a single window of their home. This detail is not derived from Chaucer but from Bruegel's *Flemish Proverbs*. As the art historian Michael Gibson explains, the significance of this episode in the painting is as follows: literally, two persons defecate from the same aperture, but the lesson contained is that these two are forced to make a virtue of necessity.[22] In the context of Pasolini's episode this original lesson seems quite irrelevant; in fact the motivation for the appearance of these *culi* is not clear, though they may function as an anticipation of the events that follow involving these women and the two students. The image, however, remains ambiguous. Indeed, this clear allusion to Bruegel serves to multiply possible interpretations of the episode: that is, the image's narrative function is exceeded by another content. In the film it portends erotic engagement; in the painting, a lesson concerning survival and dignity. It is thus an image that stages a conflict of contexts, and contributes to the poetic ambivalence of Pasolini's signifiers.

Another example of such ambivalence is found in "The Miller's Tale". Here Nicholas "the Gallant", a poor student-boarder (with certain supernatural and prophetic powers) who resides at a Carpenter's, warns the Carpenter to make Noah-like preparations for an impending flood. This advice, however, is only a ploy to distract the naïve *legnaiuolo* for a while, so that Nicholas might enjoy himself with his landlord's wife. Nicholas has the man suspend three large tubs with ropes from the ceiling of the house, one each for husband, wife and boarder, and advises that they sleep in the tubs lest they be surprised by the flood: once the water level is high enough they will all cut the tubs loose and survive in their tiny "ships". The Carpenter carefully carries out the young man's instructions and, that very night, they all retire to their tubs. Once the old man is asleep, Nicholas and the wife wander off as planned, leaving the Carpenter alone, suspended comically from the rafters. In the end he is woken by noise and, thinking it the sound of the oncoming tide, cuts himself loose and falls to the ground sustaining a variety of injuries.

Compared to the other episodes Pasolini chooses to "adapt" from the original, with which he often takes great liberties, this episode remains unusually faithful to Chaucer. As in "The Reeve's Tale", however, the images here seem highly overdetermined: they contain a "surplus". This is most evident in the precarious image of the Carpenter asleep in the hanging tub. We are presented with a quotation from the same painting by Bruegel, where we find, close to the right-hand edge of the canvas, the image of a man hanging below the ceiling of his house in a basket that is clearly unable to carry his weight. In the painting this appears to represent human existence caught between heaven and earth; the apparently inevitable fall and destruction of the basket signifies that one's chances of transcendence or salvation are ruined. Thus, while the allusion to Bruegel in "The Reeve's Tale" contained little or no narrative motivation, here the original significance of Bruegel's image reinforces that of Chaucer and Pasolini, who present the Carpenter in an attempt to escape a prophesied flood intended to purify the world of corruption. All three artists, Chaucer, Bruegel and Pasolini, present this desire for salvation in a comical fashion (and in Bruegel it is a theme carried over into his later paintings of the tower of Babel); perhaps only in Pasolini's episode, however, is there such a strong suggestion that ascetic rituals of transcendence make pernicious strategies of mystification.

There thus seems to be definite thematic motivation for this allusion to Bruegel. Nevertheless, the image retains the type of doubled nature that we have been describing, though in this case, as we have said, in a rather subtle form. What we are offered is the same theme or lesson, the same image, and the same comical attitude represented in three different media: writing, painting and film. But what is important is not so much the idea of continuity, or of an evolution of techniques, but rather the fact that Pasolini's film here appears to assert itself as the medium able to contain and synthesize those traditional media while never entirely overcoming them. That is, the "surplus" that is lent to the image by the *effetto dipinto* serves as a reminder of cinema's indebtedness to the (incorporated) medium of painting; the *effetto dipinto* constantly reminds us of an internalized but irrepressible structural "otherness". The excess, the echo or the surplus found in Pasolini's images continually reiterates this form of generic indebtedness, which both explains the fragmentary qualities of *I racconti di Canterbury* itself and ultimately leads to an awareness of the very processes of structuration: that is, of how the possibility of structural unity or homogeneity depends on the repression of the history of signifying materials themselves. The excessive materiality of Pasolini's contaminated images presents what he refers to as "una deviazione rispetto al sistema del film" ["a deviation in relation to the film's system": *EE*, 185]. In *I racconti di Canterbury* Pasolini presents systemic, narrative tendencies working towards homogeneity in conflict with the highly overdetermined materiality of the signifiers—a materiality that, in Stephen Heath's words, tends to rupture the organization of the text.[23] The fragmentary nature of the film derives from Pasolini's attempt to present a structure that refuses to repress its own material origins; and thus *I racconti di Canterbury* may be seen as yet another example of Pasolini's habit of producing texts that tend to erase themselves, that continually put themselves into crisis. *I racconti di Canterbury* is thus "una struttura da farsi".[24]

The notion of excess, then, allows us an insight into the allegorical significance of *I racconti di Canterbury*. For if, as many critics suggest, the film continues Pasolini's examination of sexuality and repression—the concern found in all three films of the *Trilogia*—it does not do so in the same manner as *Il Decameron* or *Il fiore delle mille e una notte*. While these films present a celebration of sexuality (and predominantly heterosexuality) as an expression of liberty, in *I racconti di Canterbury* the expression of desire seems highly regulated and bodies are under constant surveillance. Gian Piero

Brunetta considers the film to be closer to *Salò* than to *Il Decameron*.[25] Moreover, the film's sanctioning of forms of sexual expression—the sense of normality attributed to heterosexual coupling—is effected through the repression of non-sanctioned sexualities. An image (or ideology) of sexual homogeneity is produced through the identification and public obliteration of what is other. This is clearly the significance of "The Friar's Tale" in the film, where the energies of voyeurism of the Spy (Franco Citti) are harnessed to the official system of surveillance through the lure of financial gain.[26] The Spy locates and reports homosexuals who, if they cannot afford to bribe the authorities, are to become the victims of public burnings. As Foucault shows in *Discipline and Punish*, public executions such as these served to harness the power of transgression in order to strengthen the image of rule; the punishment of the excesses of sexual "aberrants"— heretics, witches, madmen, criminals—provides the opportunity to re-produce the unity or homogeneity that these outlaws were said to threaten.[27]

Ultimately, the problem of excess in *I racconti di Canterbury*, and the allegory of structuration it reveals, must be related to this political, socio-sexual commentary that forms the film's horrible sub-text, just as the structure of Pasolini's *Orestiade africana* forms an allegory of an African society in transition. Pasolini's message is generally not limited to what he represents but, often more importantly, conveyed by *how* he represents it. And we would not be the first to suggest that Pasolini's own death, and the use to which it was put by the organs of popular culture, seems sickeningly analogous to a public execution of a heretic.[28]

I racconti di Canterbury is an allegory of a community or institution *da farsi*. In Sam Weber's terminology, the film provides an image of "ambivalent demarcation": it forms a system that presupposes rather than occults its relations of indebtedness, and it assumes the ambivalence inherent in its own materiality.[29] Ambivalence arises from a structure that refuses completely to efface its beholdenness to models, though in the very process of being formed it must partially repress these "originating" models. For Pasolini, as for Weber, the possibility of such an "arrested effacement" provides an altered image of social aggregation. This Gramscian "optimism of the will" found in the structural allegory, however, seems to be betrayed by a profound "pessimism of the intellect" at the thematic level, and especially in the film's infernal conclusion.

At this juncture, the figural excesses and the palimpsest-like nature of *I racconti di Canterbury* reach a sort of climax. With the concluding sequence, relating the prologue to "The Summoner's Tale", pastiche and quotation become the dominant forces in the text. As recounted in Chaucer's original, the Summoner relates the story of a friar who has a vision of Hell, in which the friars located there are punished by being kept in Satan's "tail". As in "The Miller's Tale", Pasolini remains fairly close to the letter and spirit of the original; his imagery, however, recalls the infernal imagery of Hieronymus Bosch along with that of Dante's *Inferno*, as well as certain elements from the medieval iconographic tradition:[30] his signs have, again, a hybrid nature. The organization of space and certain punishments found in *I racconti di Canterbury* are highly reminiscent of those in Bosch's *Table of Wisdom* or *The Millennium*, while the posture of Satan, and the imprisoning function of his posterior, seem to be drawn from the left panel of *The Temptation of Saint Anthony*. The location of this episode would indicate a pattern shared by *I racconti di Canterbury* and *Il Decameron*. For like *Il Decameron*, the film concludes with an image of contamination. Whereas, however, in the previous film we find a *mirabile visione* of the Madonna (an unusually optimistic finale), *I racconti di Canterbury* ends on a far more pessimistic note; indeed, the profound sense of degradation running throughout the film, and the sense of defeat offered at the conclusion, would seem to contradict the Gramscian "optimism of the will" we have described in the film's allegory of a structure *da farsi*.

In *I racconti di Canterbury* Pasolini's brand of stylistic contamination is expressed through images that exceed their narrative or rational motivation—images that leave something outside, and thus without a function within, the film's formal system (what Pasolini calls its *sistema grammaticale*). This excess exists as a threat to the work's unity. But whereas films in the classical style attempt to eliminate such excess or, as Kristin Thompson and Stephen Heath have shown, "repress" excess in order to maintain homogeneity, Pasolini refuses this model of textual and, by homology, social organization. Excess is the "political unconscious" of dominant narrative cinema,[31] and Pasolini's film is the stylistic de-negation of this unspeakable "altra materia" that erupts within the text. And thus *I racconti di Canterbury* must be seen as a continuation of Pasolini's determination to speak the unspeakable. That is, excess presents material that seems devoid of rational or narrative motivation within the context of the film: there is something, the Barthesian "third meaning", that does not belong, that remains outside but is apprehensible through the fissured text, with a function that is not readily explainable. Pasolini's films call on the spectator to start searching for that mysterious motivation, to start conceptualizing a function for that material. Unable to deny such material, one is forced to conceive of a "futura possibile" structure that will grant it a place and a function—a "revolutionary" engagement within the *langue*, which, for cinema, says Pasolini, "è la realtà stessa" ["is reality itself": *EE*, 257]. Contamination then, as an ideological form of pastiche, produces in *I racconti di Canterbury* an allegory of a society *da farsi*, as well as an ironic image of Pasolini's life as a poet of the margins:

> Che un individuo, in quanto autore, reagisca al sistema costruendone un altro, mi sembra semplice e naturale; cosí come gli uomini, in quanto autori di storia, reagiscono alla stuttura sociale costruendone un'altra, attraverso la rivoluzione, ossia alla volontà di trasformare la struttura. Non intendo quindi parlare, secondo la critica sociologica americana, di valori e volizioni "naturali" e ontologici: ma parlo di "volontà rivoluzionaria" sia nell'autore in quanto creatore di un sistema stilistico individuale che contraddice il sistema grammaticale e letterario-gergale vigente, sia negli uomini in quanto sovvertitori di sistemi politici. (*EE*, 199)

> [That an individual, as author, reacts to a system by constructing another seems to me simple and natural; in the same way in which men, as authors of history, react to a social structure by building another through revolution, that is, react to the will to transform the structure. I therefore don't want to speak, in the terms of American sociological criticism, of "natural" and ontological values and volitions; but I am speaking of a "revolutionary will", both in the author as creator of an individual stylistic system that contradicts the grammatical and literary-jargon system in force, and in men as subverters of political systems. (*Heretical Empiricism*, pp. 193–94)]

NOTES

1   P. P. Pasolini, "Il 'cinema di poesia'", in *Empirismo eretico* (Milan, Garzanti, 1972), pp. 185–86 (the first and second sets of italics are mine). The translation is adapted from *Heretical Empiricism*, translated by L. Barnett and B. Lawton (Bloomington, Indiana University Press, 1988), p. 180; all translations of passages in *Empirismo eretico* are taken from that edition.

2   For an account of some of the visual sources of several of Pasolini's films, including the *Trilogia*, see the interview with Dante Ferretti, Pasolini's scenographer, in A. Bertini, *Teoria e tecnica del film in Pasolini* (Rome, Bulzoni, 1979), pp. 187–94.

3   I borrow this term, which I have found extremely useful in analysing nearly all Pasolini's films, from A. Costa, "Effetto dipinto", *Cinema e cinema*, 54–55 (Jan–Aug. 1989), 37–48. Costa defines the *effetto dipinto* as follows: "L'inquadratura evoca quindi una pittura: perché la cita esplicitamente, perché ne riproduce determinati effetti luministici, cromatici o di organizzazione spaziale, perché ne imita la staticità o la sospensione temporale o si iscrive nella logica compositiva o iconografica di uno stesso genere (per esempio, la veduta paesaggistica, o il ritratto o il decorativismo astratto)" (p. 42).

4   For a description of narrative framing in Pasolini's *Decameron*, see B. Lawton, "The Storyteller's Art: Pasolini's *Decameron*", in *Modern European Film-makers and the Art of Adaptation*, edited by A. Horton and J. Magretta (New York, Ungar, 1981), pp. 203–21.

5   S. Petraglia, *Pier Paolo Pasolini* (Florence, La Nuova Italia), p. 105.

6   Quoted in J. Michalczyk, *The Italian Political Film-makers* (London–Toronto, Associated University Presses, 1986), p. 99.

7   Pasolini interviewed in *Pier Paolo Pasolini*, edited by P. Willemen (London, British Film Istitute, 1977), pp. 69–70.

8   P. Willemen, *Pier Paolo Pasolini*, p. 71.

9   See H. Bloom, *The Anxiety of Influence* (New York, Oxford University Press, 1973).

10 O. Calabrese, *L'età neobarocca* (Rome–Bari, Laterza, 1989), p. 63.

11 O. Calabrese, *L'età neobarocca*, p. 64.

12 For a detailed account of juridical and journalistic assaults on Pasolini's work, see *Pasolini: cronaca giudiziaria, persecuzione, morte*, edited by L. Betti (Milan, Garzanti, 1977), and especially pp. 186–93 regarding the "caso Canterbury".

13 A. Costa, "Effetto dipinto", p. 48.

14 K. Thompson, *Breaking the Glass Armor: Neo-formalist Film Analysis* (Princeton, Princeton University Press, 1988), p. 259; see also her "The Concept of Cinematic Excess", in *Narrative, Apparatus, Ideology: A Film Theory Reader*, edited by H. Rosen (New York, Columbia University Press, 1986), pp. 130–42.

15 Quoted in K. Thompson, "The Concept of Cinematic Excess", pp. 130–31.

16 K. Thompson, *Breaking the Glass Armor*, p. 251.

17 For a discussion of Pasolini's debt to the Russian Formalists, see N. Greene, *Pier Paolo Pasolini: Cinema as Heresy* (Princeton, Princeton University Press, 1990), p. 110.

18 Quoted in K. Thompson, *Breaking the Glass Armor*, p. 10. For Shklovsky's distinction between cinema of poetry and cinema of prose see his "Poesia e prosa nel film", in *Film segno*, edited by E. Bruno (Rome, Bulzoni, 1983), pp. 23–26.

19 K. Thompson, *Breaking the Glass Armor*, p. 10.

20 G. Deleuze, *Cinema 2: The Time Image*, translated by H. Tomlinson and B. Habberjam (Minneapolis, University of Minnesota Press, 1989), p. 223.

21 Quoted in N. Naldini, *Pasolini, una vita* (Turin, Einaudi, 1989), p. 360. Pasolini's short film *Le mura di Sana'a* (1974) was made as an appeal to UNESCO to help save those ancient walls from demolition. He became aware of this issue during the filming of *Il fiore delle mille e una notte* on location in Yemen.

22 M. Gibson, *Bruegel* (Seacaucus, NJ, Wellfleet Press, 1989), p. 44.

23 Quoted in K. Thompson, "The Concept of Cinematic Excess", pp. 130–31.

24 I find this notion of structure in Pasolini's explanation of his own *Appunti per un film sull'India* and *Appunti per un'Orestiade africana*, both to be considered as "sketches" of a possible film (each of which, moreover, is about a society *da farsi*) whose completion is left to the imagination of the spectator. See N. Naldini, *Pasolini*, pp. 326 and 341. Also interesting in this regard is Pasolini's attitude towards the structure of the screenplay, what he calls "una struttura che vuol essere altra struttura" (see *EE*, 192–201). See also A. Bertini, "La metafora della sceneggiatura", in *Teoria e tecnica*, pp. 71–83; M. Vallora, "Alí dagli occhi impuri: come nasce il manierismo della narratività di Pasolini", *Bianco e nero*, 37, i–iv (1976), 156–204 (p. 177); and P. P. Pasolini, *Lettere 1955–1975*, edited by N. Naldini (Turin, Einaudi, 1988), pp. 600–01, for Pasolini's letters to Fortini, where this notion of a structure *da farsi* is carried over to other forms of organization, insofar as he urges Fortini to join the existing editorial committee of *Nuovi argomenti*, a journal which, in Pasolini's mind, would always remain "una rivista futura possibile".

25 G. P. Brunetta, *Storia del cinema italiano*, 2 vols (Rome, Editori Riuniti, 1979), II, 662.

26 For a discussion of the issue of voyeurism in the film and its problematization of bourgeois morality and sexuality see M. Green, "The Dialectic of Adaptation: The *Canterbury Tales* of Pier Paolo Pasolini", *Literature/Film Quarterly*, 4 (1976), 46–53 (p. 50).

27 M. Foucault, *Discipline and Punish: The Birth of the Prison*, translated by A. Sheridan (New York, Vintage, 1979), especially pp. 3–72.

28 See C. Palumbo, *Assassiniamo il poeta: Pier Paolo Pasolini* (Cosenza, Pellegrini, 1978); and M-A. Macciocchi, "Pasolini: assassinat d'un dissident", *Tel quel*, 76 (Summer 1978).

29 See S. Weber, *Institution and Interpretation* (Minneapolis, University of Minnesota Press, 1987), pp. 132–57.

30 See G. P. Brunetta, *Storia del cinema italiano*, II, 662; and, for a discussion of Bosch in *I racconti di Canterbury*, M. Green, "The Dialectic of Adaptation", p. 51.

31 F. Jameson, *The Political Unconscious: Narrative as a Socially Symbolic Act* (Ithaca, Cornell University Press, 1981).

OUTSIDE THE PALACE: PASOLINI'S JOURNALISM (1973–1975)

Michael Caesar

When Pasolini gathered for publication the polemical newspaper articles and some other pieces he had written between January 1973 and February 1975, he provided instructions for the use of the resulting book.[1] The reader was invited to summon up an un-fashionable "fervore filologico" and to "reconstruct" the book, to piece together the fragments, to make the connections between separate parts, to resolve the apparent contradictions, to eliminate any incoherence, to see where repetition gave way to variation. Pasolini himself contributed some useful pointers. The reader could connect the two unequal halves of the book (the "Scritti corsari" proper and the reviews and miscellanea to which Pasolini gave the label "Documenti e allegati"); she or he could examine the responses of other people to Pasolini's articles, and Pasolini's responses to the responses; she or he could make the link between this text and others.[2] And no doubt, had he lived, Pasolini would have issued a similar invitation, or challenge, to the reader of *Lettere luterane*,[3] the posthumous collection of articles written for *Il mondo* and the *Corriere della sera* between March and October 1975.

In appealing to the reader's readiness to sort and classify, to systematize the confusion of writings produced in the heat of the moment, for a specific purpose, it is as though Pasolini is willing them a second life (and his purpose is certainly different from that of organizing a merely retrospective collection). The immediacy of the debate is quite gone: the polemics and arguments, the anxieties and derision, the sense of expectation which over the months Pasolini's articles built up, the inevitable slight shock they caused, entirely prior to other reactions of irritation, anger, impatience—all this is largely absent from the books. But Pasolini chose not to leave his writings in the cemetery of past polemics; the "Nota introduttiva" shows how he wanted them back, those public statements that he now reclaimed for himself, that he wanted to slot into their proper place in the canon of his work. The writings of *Scritti corsari* and *Lettere luterane*, which are now accessible for practical purposes only in the form of a book, are writings recalled in both senses of the term. In this essay I shall attempt to organize and summarize what seem to me the principal arguments of Pasolini's journalism of the early 1970s—Fascism old and new, sexual politics, the politics of opposition—; but at the end I shall suggest that the political significance of Pasolini's writings lies not so much in the individual positions that he from time to time adopts (important though these are) as in the unusual relations with the reader that his writings suggest.

Pasolini's theme in these pieces is Fascism, the Fascism which recurs in his writings as an obsessive presence and insistent question, and the Fascism too which haunted Europe, and Italy in particular, in the early 1970s. Fascism was not just Pasolini's bogey, it was everyone's in Italy, at a time when not only did self-declared Fascists make themselves physically felt by means of terrorist outrage, but the breakdown of law and order, the threat of an uncontainable economic crisis, the pronounced sharpening of class conflict, all suggested uncanny analogies with the years 1919–22. To these factors was added the presence in other northern Mediterranean states—Spain, Portugal and Greece—of regimes which, if not strictly Fascist, were sufficiently close to suggest themselves as possible models for an "authoritarian solution" to the mounting Italian crisis. Pasolini spoke of and for a common fear, and then, perversely, he cut across it.

In the first place—he argued—Fascism, or rather the Fascist, is not something that you can see with the naked eye. Or rather, you see Fascism, it is all around you, but you cannot distinguish it. All opposites run into one another in consumer capitalism and the Fascist cannot be told apart from the anti-Fascist:

> La matrice che genera tutti gli italiani è ormai la stessa. Non c'è
> piú dunque differenza apprezzabile—al di fuori di una scelta
> politica come schema morto da riempire gesticolando—tra un
> qualsiasi cittadino fascista e un qualsiasi cittadino anti-fascista.
> Essi sono culturalmente, psicologicamente e, quel che è piú
> impressionante, fisicamente, interscambiabili. Nel comportamen-

to quotidiano, mimico, somatico non c'è niente che distingua—
ripeto, al di fuori di un comizio o di un'azione politica—un
fascista da un anti-fascista (di mezza età o giovane: i vecchi, in tal
senso possono ancora esser distinti tra loro). Questo per quel che
riguarda i fascisti e gli anti-fascisti medi. Per quel che riguarda gli
estremisti, l'omologazione è ancor piú radicale.[4]

[Every Italian now comes out of the same mould. There is no
appreciable difference—apart from their choice of politics, which
is so many dead words waiting to be brought to life by people
waving their arms around—between your average Fascist citizen
and your average anti-Fascist citizen. Culturally, psychologic-
ally, and what is even more striking, physically, they are interchangeable. In their daily behaviour, in their gestures, in their
appearance, there is nothing—apart, I repeat, from a rally or a
political action of some sort—nothing that distinguishes a Fascist
from an anti-Fascist (I'm talking about the young and middle-
aged; older people can still be told apart in that sense). This is true
of the average Fascist and the average anti-Fascist. As far as the
extremists are concerned, the identification is even more radical.]

The insistence on this physical interchangeability is of the greatest
importance for Pasolini's argument throughout the *Scritti corsari*
and the *Lettere luterane*: not for its ideological content, which could
easily, though mistakenly, be borrowed for yet another denunciation of the opposite extremes, but for its pure rhetorical excess.
This is one of those statements which are designed to stun and
disorient their audience, to soften it up for the more precisely
aimed blows to follow. It is the reader's carefully arranged perceptions (for Pasolini's readership is of course an anti-Fascist one)
that are blacked out in an instant, and she or he finds herself or
himself not only disoriented, but constituted as disoriented: not
only not knowing where she or he is, but being told that from now
on, with things as they are, she or he has no possibility of knowing
where she or he is.

Having established the basic, corporeal fact of physical interchangeability and therefore indistinguishability, Pasolini can apply
the same principle of rhetorical "invisibility" to Fascism as a
historical phenomenon. The Fascism of today is not that of yester-
year; more to the point, it is not that which you see, the Fascism of
the bombers and paramilitaries. Real Fascism is the Fascism you do
not see:

Nel 1971–72 è cominciato uno dei periodi di reazione piú violenti e forse piú definitivi della storia. In esso coesistono due nature: una è profonda, sostanziale e assolutamente nuova, l'altra è epidermica, contingente e vecchia. La natura profonda di questa reazione degli anni settanta è dunque irriconoscibile; la natura esteriore è invece ben riconoscibile. Non c'è nessuno infatti che non la individui nel risorgere del fascismo, in tutte le sue forme, comprese quelle decrepite del fascismo mussoliniano, e del tradizionalismo clericale-liberale [...]. La restaurazione o reazione reale cominciata nel 1971–72 (dopo l'intervallo del 1968) è in realtà una rivoluzione. Ecco perché non restaura niente e non ritorna a niente; anzi, essa tende letteralmente a cancellare il passato, coi suoi "padri", le sue religioni, le sue ideologie e le sue forme di vita (ridotte oggi a mera sopravvivenza). Questa rivoluzione di destra, che ha distrutto prima di ogni cosa la destra, è avvenuta fattualmente, pragmaticamente.[5]

[In 1971–72 there began one of the most violent and perhaps most decisive periods of reaction in history. It has two natures living side by side. One is deep, substantial and absolutely new; the other is superficial, contingent and old. The deep nature of this reaction of the Seventies is unrecognizable, therefore, while its external nature may easily be recognized. There is nobody who can fail to identify it with the resurgence of Fascism, in all its forms, including those, decrepit as they are, of Mussolinian Fascism and clerical-liberal traditionalism (...). The true restoration or reaction begun in 1971–72 (after the interval of 1968) is in reality a revolution. And that is why it neither restores anything nor returns to anything. On the contrary, it tends literally to wipe out the past, with all its "fathers" and its religions and its ideologies and its ways of life (which are now no more than survivals). This revolution of the right, whose first victim has been the right itself, has taken place on the ground, in practice.]

Pasolini gave various accounts of this shift and its relation to Fascism, the clearest of all perhaps in February 1975 in the article "Il vuoto del potere in Italia", which he was to rechristen "L'articolo delle lucciole". Before the disappearance of the fireflies in the early 1960s—their physical disappearance, annihilated by pollution of the air and water—the continuity between the Fascism of the Fascist regime and that of the Christian Democrats was complete, they were the same thing. Since the disappearance of the fireflies there has been an apparent power vacuum in Italy, though the Christian Democrats have until very recently fondly imagined themselves to be in full control. But vacuums, Pasolini insists, do not occur in history—something or someone is exercising power, and to this phase of Italian history he willingly attaches the attributes of Fascism—"il fascismo di questa seconda fase del potere democristiano ["the Fascism of this second phase of Christian Democrat power"]—as he does to the two preceding phases.[6] But actually he does not know in what the new power consists or what form it will take once it is fully installed. The thing that generically one may call Fascist (provided one distinguishes it from the mere appearance of Fascism, the would-be restoration of an outmoded form) may not be Fascist at all:

> Dunque questo nuovo Potere non ancora rappresentato da nessuno e dovuto a una "mutazione" della classe dominante, è in realtà—se vogliamo conservare la vecchia terminologia—una forma "totale" di fascismo.[7]

> [So this new Power, brought about by a "mutation" in the ruling class and not yet represented by anybody, is in reality—if we want to keep the old terminology—a "total" form of Fascism.]

But the old terminology might not be appropriate to the new masters of consumerism and technology:

> Se il loro fascismo dovesse prevalere, sarebbe il fascismo di Spinola, non quello di Caetano: cioè sarebbe un fascismo ancora peggiore di quello tradizionale, ma non sarebbe piú fascismo. (*SC*, 52)

> [If their kind of Fascism were to prevail, it would be the Fascism of Spinola, not that of Caetano. In other words, it would be an even worse kind of Fascism than the traditional kind, but it would no longer be Fascism.]

This ambiguity at the centre of Pasolini's discourse on the new power—is it Fascist or is it not?—is not a weakness in argument or an oversight in composition, but (ah, that philological fervour) a choice that seems to me conscious and deliberate. Fascism is both there and not there, it both is and is not the name of the new game, it is what you do not see—"Tutti dunque fingono di non vedere (o forse non vedono realmente)" ["So everyone pretends not to see (or perhaps really doesn't see)": *SC*, 22])—or what you see wrongly; it is truly spectral, the ghost in the machine.

Pasolini acknowledges the "apocalyptic" character of his new Power with its face still "blank" (*SC*, 54):

> Di tale "potere reale" noi abbiamo immagini astratte e in fondo apocalittiche: non sappiamo raffigurarci quali "forme" esso assumerebbe sostituendosi direttamente ai servi che lo hanno preso per una semplice "modernizzazione" di tecniche. (*SC*, 164)

> [Our images of this "real power" are abstract and basically apocalyptic: we do not know what "forms" it might assume as it takes over directly from the servants who have read it simply as a "modernization" of techniques.]

But his Fascism is not the apocalypse; or if it is, it is the old, false, artificial "Fascism" of the colonels, Chile, the *coup d'état*, precisely that which Pasolini warns us not to mistake for the real one. Rather than an apocalypse, Pasolini's Fascism represents the uncertain, a state of anxiety or dread. And it may do so, paradoxically, because the notion brings into a vision of the impending future as entirely new, as an unprecedented epoch in human history, and as a *tabula rasa*, an element of the known, so that to the terror of the unknown (if that is not an exaggerated description of Pasolini's vision of the new society) is added the disgust of the familiar.

Thus it is that Pasolini can refer back to the old Fascism, the Fascism of Mussolini and the War and the *doppipetti* of the parliamentary MSI, with a hatred tinged with pity, the pity for things on their way into the dustbin of history. In retrospect, historical Fascism is seen as self-deludingly incompetent, woefully inadequate for the tasks with which its successors in power would be confronted. The only right that Italy has proved capable (hitherto) of producing has been "quella rozza, ridicola, feroce destra che è il fascismo" ["that raw, absurd, ferocious right which is Fascism": *SC*, 48]. The totalitarian ambitions and achievements of the old power pale beside those of the new. "Nessun centralismo fascista è riuscito a fare ciò che ha fatto il centralismo della civiltà dei consumi" ["No Fascist centralism ever succeeded in doing what the centralism of consumer civilization has done"], Pasolini argues in "Acculturazione e acculturazione":

Il fascismo, voglio ripeterlo, non è stato sostanzialmente in grado nemmeno di scalfire l'anima del popolo italiano: il nuovo fascismo, attraverso i nuovi mezzi di comunicazione e di informazione [...] non solo l'ha scalfita, ma l'ha lacerata, violata, bruttata per sempre.[8]

[Fascism, I should like to repeat, was in reality powerless to inflict even so much as a graze on the soul of the Italian people. The new Fascism, through the new means of communication and information (...) has not only grazed it, but torn it, violated it, filthied it for ever.]

Yet the *memory* of the old Fascism seems to remain in a new civilization which otherwise erases all reference to the past other than for purely instrumental purposes and is governed by an unbridled consumerism, facilitated by a conformity and uniformity produced by the triumphant imposition of the mass media, and more broadly of a mass culture, which encourage, or demand, a desacralized view of life and a cult of gratification and enjoyment. This hedonism, as Pasolini calls it, is endorsed by the "repressive tolerance" of power, in other words, the ability of power to tolerate everything and allow nothing. On the social plane, the old historic classes—notably the peasantry, the petty bourgeoisie, the "paleo-industrial" bourgeoisie, the subproletariat and, marginally, the industrial proletariat, never a very visible component of society in Pasolini's perspective—tend to be engulfed by the new, lay, technological bourgeoisie; and this all-embracing *embourgeoisement* is matched on the political level by the superseding or bypassing of the parties of the previous age. (The first process is illustrated by the case of the DC, the second by that of the PCI.) The notions of *embourgeoisement*, of repressive tolerance, of the levelling effect of technology on a previous diversity of culture, and much else of this sociology are (and were) immediately traceable to the Frankfurt School and Marcuse in particular. But it is not with origins that we are concerned here. What sticks in the mind is Pasolini's conviction that an event of cataclysmic proportions has occurred or is occurring: "Il mondo contadino, dopo circa quattordicimila anni di vita, è finito praticamente di colpo" ["The peasant world, after fourteen thousand years of life, has ended practically at a stroke"];[9]

I "ceti medi" sono radicalmente—direi antropologicamente—
cambiati: i loro valori positivi non sono piú i valori sanfedisti e
clericali ma sono i valori (ancora vissuti solo esistenzialmente e
non "nominati") dell'ideologia edonistica del consumo e della
conseguente tolleranza modernistica di tipo americano. (*SC*, 47–
48)

[The "middle classes" have changed radically, I would say
anthropologically. Their values are no longer clerical and reactionary, but are those belonging to the hedonistic ideology of consumption and the American-style modernistic tolerance that
flows from it (even if, for the moment, these values are only lived
and not yet "named").]

The most obvious place in which this transformation could be
seen in the early 1970s was not in the economy, and still less in the
political sphere, but in the general area of *costume*, and specifically
in sexual and family relations, on the shifting borderland between
the private and the public. Between 1974 and 1975 we may perceive
a complication of these questions occurring in the course of public
debates on divorce and abortion. Pasolini, like most other commentators, saw the divorce referendum of 1974 largely in terms of its
political implications: what it indicated about the relative electoral
strength of the PCI and the DC, what it said about the progressive
"secularization" of the Italian state, and so on. The question of
abortion, which entered the political agenda in the early months of
1975, led him straight into the personal and into sexual politics.
Pasolini was uncomfortable there; he tried to generalize the issue
and keep it on a "public" plane, but he was almost forced in the end
to acknowledge that by so doing he had not fully addressed the
problem.[10]

In taking up the challenge posed by the Radicals' demand to
legalize abortion, Pasolini honourably acknowledged a personal
hostility to abortion that is total and unconditional: as far as he
personally is concerned, the foetus lives, its overwhelming will to
live "ha qualcosa di irresistibile e perciò di assoluto e di gioioso"
["possesses something irresistible and therefore absolute and joyful"];[11] abortion is tantamount to murder. He acknowledges too the
right of the mother to choose; even though, in his eyes, abortion is
in principle "colposo", "blameworthy", if not "colpevole", "guilty",
in practice he too would endorse and has endorsed that "colpa",

"blame/guilt". But this is a moral, and therefore (Pasolini insists) a private question, between the people concerned, in which Pasolini as a thinker does not want to be involved: his concern is with the juridical aspects of the matter (*SC*, 135).

Despite this assertion, Pasolini does not indicate clearly how he would regulate "juridically" the control and termination of pregnancy, except to suggest that it might properly be seen as a form of euthanasia, subject in the courts to a series of attenuating circumstances "di carattere ecologico" ["of an ecological character"]—a confusion that might be the delight of lawyers but hardly alleviates the position of the person who has to decide whether or not to abort.[12] Pasolini in fact admits that his perspective virtually excludes that of women—almost as though women and their "practical" problems, to be resolved in the light of their and their partners' personal morality, should be removed from the public arena in which matters of principle, and of the law, are to be discussed and decided. And since Pasolini during these years (1974–75) was becoming increasingly explicit about the difficulties and rights of homosexuals, it might be concluded that he was advancing the cause of gay men at the expense of heterosexual women. But the argument should be taken forward more slowly.

Pasolini was facing a proposal to abrogate a (Fascist) law which forbade the practice of abortion in all circumstances. In absolute terms, which were the only ones in which he was prepared to argue in public, this meant for him a legal endorsement, the most comprehensive hitherto, of the climate of sexual freedom that had overtaken Italy in the previous ten years. But this sexual freedom was the supreme example of the repressive tolerance of the new consumerism. It was not something that had been willed from below, but something imposed from the top. This in itself was enough to make it suspect. But worse still was the fact that liberated sex was of a restricted variety: sexual freedom, approved and encouraged by consumerism, is limited to the heterosexual couple, coupling. Hence the startling but polemically effective claim that the problem of abortion is really a problem of coitus, and the disarming conclusion to Pasolini's first intervention on abortion (*SC*, 126) that the problem of unwanted pregnancy might be solved or avoided by better contraceptive education.

This social-worker solution to the question is a rather oblique and, as Pasolini might put it, "diplomatic" approach to the problem

372   *Michael Caesar*

as he defines it. One cannot see how the spread of contraceptive devices alongside the joys of sex—"tecniche amatorie diverse" ["different techniques of love-making"]—, especially if propagated by the most powerful instrument of consumerism, television, could do anything but reinforce the monolithic culture of heterosexual couples that Pasolini deplores. But elsewhere Pasolini is both more angry and more specific. The thesis that the sexual freedom of consumerism is both an imposition and an exclusion, a false tolerance masking a real intolerance, is nowhere more forcibly expressed than in an article published some months before the abortion issue came to the fore:

> La tolleranza del potere in campo sessuale è univoca (e quindi in sostanza piú che mai repressiva): essa concede molti piú diritti che in passato alla coppia eterosessuale, anche al di fuori della convenzione matrimoniale: ma, prima di tutto, tale "coppia" viene presentata come un modello ossessivamente obbligatorio, esattamente alla stregua, per esempio, della coppia consumatore-automobile.
>
> Non possedere un'automobile e non essere in coppia, là dove tutti "devono" avere un'automobile e "devono" essere in coppia (bifronte mostro consumistico), non può essere considerata che una grande disgrazia, una intollerabile frustrazione. Cosí l'amore eterosessuale—talmente consentito da diventare coatto—è divenuto una sorta di "erotomania sociale". Inoltre tanta libertà sessuale non è stata voluta e conquistata dal basso, ma è stata, appunto, concessa dall'alto (attraverso un falso cedimento del potere consumistico e edonistico alle vecchie istanze ideali delle *élites* progressiste). Infine, "tutto ciò riguarda solo la maggioranza". Le minoranze—piú o meno definibili—sono escluse dalla grande, nevrotica abbuffata. Quelli che sono ancora classicamente "poveri", molte categorie di donne, i brutti, gli ammalati e, per tornare al nostro discorso, gli omosessuali, sono esclusi dall'esercizio della libertà di una maggioranza che, pur approfittando, per sé, di una tolleranza sia pur illusoria, non è mai stata in realtà cosí intollerante.[13]

[The tolerance shown by power in the field of sexual relations is one-sided (and therefore in practice it is more repressive than ever). It allows many more rights than it did in the past to the heterosexual couple, even outside the conventions of marriage. But first and foremost, the heterosexual couple is presented as an obsessively coercive model, exactly along the lines, for example, of the pairing between consumer and motor car.

Not to own a car, and not to be in a couple, when everyone "must" have a car and "must" be in a couple (the two-headed monster of consumerism), can only be regarded as a great misfortune, an unbearable frustration. Thus heterosexual love, so widely tolerated as to become obligatory, has become a sort of "social erotomania". What is more, this sexual freedom has not been fought for and conquered from below so much as granted from above (with consumerist and hedonist power making false concessions to demands long made in an idealistic spirit by the progressive élites). And finally, "this only concerns the majority". Minorities—more or less definable—are excluded from the great, neurotic blow-out. Those who are still classically "poor", many categories of women, the ugly, the ill, and to return to our subject, homosexuals, are debarred from the exercise of the freedom of a majority, which, while it makes the most for itself of the tolerance with which it is regarded, however illusory that might be, has never itself been more intolerant.]

A little later that month, April 1974, the same idea, that "essere in coppia è *ormai* per un giovane non piú una libertà ma un obbligo" ["being part of a couple is no longer a freedom for a young person but an obligation"] is reiterated,[14] and the occasion of these statements indicates that the later issue of abortion is not, for Pasolini, the central one. Indeed, the question of abortion got him into deep water, where his ignoring or dismissal of the demands of women could not but cause offence. But, vice versa, his stand on that very public issue did effectively smoke out distinctly hostile attitudes towards homosexuality from such liberals as Umberto Eco. Ignoring Pasolini's concrete proposals on attenuation of the crime and contraceptive advice, Eco seized on a manifestly ironical and paradoxical suggestion that in the present state of over-population it is the homosexual rather than the heterosexual couple that should be privileged, to ironize ponderously in his turn:

Se ne deduce che egli pensa ad una società in cui pochi schiavi eterosessuali, a cui viene proibito l'aborto, dovranno continuare a partorire degli eletti di classe superiore a cui sia invece consentita la libera e aristocratica pratica dell'omosessualità.[15]

[One concludes that he is thinking of a society in which a few heterosexual slaves, denied the right to abortion, shall continue to give birth to the elect of the higher classes, to whom shall be granted the free and aristocratic practice of homosexuality.]

Pasolini's replies to his critics on abortion are to a considerable extent a protest against the misrepresentation of homosexuality, whether unconscious as in the "innocent" Natalia Ginzburg's reference to the "squalor" of gay relations, or deliberate as in the case of Eco and others. For the question of abortion to become the question of homosexuality, it had to pass through the crucible of Pasolini's polemic, where neo-capitalism, consumerism, hetero-sexuality, hedonism and repression are all aspects of the same essential, bad thing at the centre of our lives. And inevitably attention shifted from the original issue to the speaker, Pasolini as a homosexual man, and *his* right to speak; his critics, Pasolini concludes,

> hanno finto per inciso una comprensione, puramente verbale, per le minoranze sessuali: in realtà consistente nell'idea di conce-dere, a tali minoranze, un ghetto dove darsi alle loro pratiche (con chi?), ma da cui sia proibito esprimere pubblicamente un'opinio-ne anche vagamente influenzata dallo "stato d'animo" che fatal-mente nasce vivendo appunto un'esperienza minoritaria. Il "punto di vista" deve essere per forza maggioritario, anche sentimental-mente.[16]

> [have incidentally feigned understanding, purely at the level of words, for sexual minorities. This understanding actually con-sists in the idea of allowing these minorities a ghetto where they can give themselves over to their practices (who with?), but whence it is forbidden to express publicly any opinion that is even vaguely affected by the "state of mind" that comes into being inevitably when one is living a minority experience. The "point of view" has to be a majority one, and that goes for feelings as well.]

Pasolini may have accepted being in a minority, but he had no desire to be politically isolated, and it is characteristic of the writings of 1973–75 that the question of alliances, even if only ideal ones, keeps cropping up. If there is a new power, there must also be a new opposition; it is to be sought among the least comprom-ised of the political forces currently in play. Thus one other aspect of Pasolini's statements on abortion that has to be borne in mind is that which concerns his evolving relationship with the Radical Party, a relationship which in turn affects his position *vis-à-vis* other political groupings, notably the PCI. Pasolini declares on several occasions during 1974 and 1975 his sympathy with, even his identification with, the Partito Radicale and with Marco Pannella in particular. It is not so much the specific issues that draw them together—on the most important of the eight referenda proposed by the Radicals in the spring of 1974, Pasolini is, as we have seen, at odds with at least the implications of the Party's proposal to abrogate the 1930 law on abortion. It is rather the Radical style of politics, the purity of Radical principles, Pannella's "scandalous" respect for the person, his and his party's moral non-violence, their rejection of all moralism and their refusal of all forms of power, not in a quixotic fashion, but in a way which Pasolini sees as absolutely realistic.[17] For in Pasolini's view, the Radicals are the real winners of the divorce referendum of May 1974, being the only politicians who truly wanted it and accurately foresaw the result. Pannella, the Partito Radicale and the LID (Lega per l'Istituzione del Divorzio) coincide, as Pasolini puts it,

> con la presa di coscienza di una nuova realtà del nostro paese e di una nuova qualità di vita delle masse, che è finora sfuggita sia al potere che all'opposizione. (*SC*, 83–84)

> [with the awareness of a new reality in our country and of a new quality of life of the masses, which has hitherto escaped both those in power and the opposition.]

This reference to "the masses" is purely rhetorical; that is, there is no sign in Pasolini's writings that he expects the masses of consumer capitalism to take any active, let alone progressive role in national politics. They are there to lend some legitimacy to a political initiative that otherwise may indeed look quixotic. But the real, profound strength of the Radicals appears to lie in the incontaminable purity of their principles and the almost ascetic optimism with which they pursue them. More than anything else they recall, in Pasolini's account, an early Christian community, living in apostolic poverty. Pasolini invokes just such a type of community a few months later in the context of an appeal to the Church itself to "pass over to the opposition". The future of the Church, he argues, is urban, not rural, and that urban priesthood, which must take its distance from the holders of state power (the police and military, bureaucrats and industrialists), will lead a Church that if it is to survive "non può [...] che abbandonare il potere e abbracciare quella cultura—da lei sempre odiata—che è per sua stessa natura libera, antiautoritaria, in continuo divenire, contraddittoria, collettiva, scandalosa" ["cannot (...) but abandon power and embrace that culture which it has always hated, that culture which is by its own nature free, anti-authoritarian, constantly developing, contradictory, collective, and scandalous"].[18]

In the Radicals and in this kind of contemporary "primitive Christianity" (imaginary, as he knows; or at least he does not show any acquaintance with any actual communities of this kind), Pasolini embodies two, overlapping, forms of libertarian opposition to the new power. The question of opposition preoccupies him during these months, especially, as is understandable, at voting time, after the divorce referendum of 12 May 1974, and the regional and provincial elections of 15–16 June 1975. Pasolini shies away from the explicit formulation of questions one might expect him to ask. What is or can be the form of the opposition? Is it a purely intellectual one, whose function is to denounce (to whom? to itself?) the ills of consumerism, the abuses of power? Does it, should it have access to effective levers of counter-power, through parliament, through the courts? Is it a moral opposition, whose protest may consist primarily in withdrawal from the political process altogether? How far does the political process, as it exists or as it might be modified in the future, bear any relation to power? To what degree may the opposition compromise with that which it opposes? Pasolini does not offer answers to these unasked questions. He is not a politician, he says, he is not embedded in the "pragma"; his business is principles. Yet as a journalist he cannot but respond to events as they occur, and in practice he tries his hand (on paper) at different kinds of opposition. Pasolini sticks to his principles, and the basic framework of his analysis of Italian society is clear, but he is nimble-footed too, and above all does not want to deny himself opportunities, or be compelled to identify exclusively with one group or ideology. This pluralism, which safeguards his own freedom of movement, has the disadvantage, of course, of rendering him vulnerable to attack from all sides.

Pasolini goes a long way towards identifying with the Radicals—even if, at the end, adopting a tone of stern anxiety as he delivers the terrible warning that their struggle for civil rights is in danger of being "reabsorbed" and becoming the new conformism of the left:

Contro tutto questo voi non dovete far altro (io credo) che continuare semplicemente a essere voi stessi: il che significa a essere continuamente irriconoscibili. Dimenticare subito i grandi successi: e continuare imperterriti, ostinati, eternamente contrari, a pretendere, a volere, a identificarvi col diverso; a scandalizzare; a bestemmiare.[19]

[Against all this all you need to do (I believe) is simply to continue being yourselves, which means being continuously unrecognizable. Forget your triumphs straightaway; and carry on regardless, obstinately, always on the opposite side; carry on demanding, willing, identifying with the other, scandalizing, blaspheming.]

He also summons up the figure of a primitive, but no longer rural, Church, uncoupled from its sordid links to power and wealth. But at the same time Pasolini must confront his "ever-present interlocutor", the political force that actually claims the leadership of the opposition, the PCI. The relations between Pasolini and the Party during these years were marked by mutual embarrassment. An attractive cultural openness was one of the hallmarks of the PCI during the early 1970s, and to that extent those parts of Pasolini's argument that ran counter to Party thinking were not openly or violently denounced. On the other hand, it is difficult not to see Pasolini as one of the targets of Berlinguer's denunciation of the mounting tide of cultural "irrationalism" in his Central Committee report in preparation for the fourteenth Congress of December 1974:

Vi sono [...] atteggiamenti di reazione romantica allo sviluppo capitalistico e di contrapposizione disperata di un mitico passato a uno sviluppo storico, che si svolge in modi necessariamente tumultuosi e contraddittori, ma che comunque va avanti.[20]

[There are (...) attitudes of Romantic reaction against capitalist development and the despairing alternative of a mythical past being set up against a historical development, which is necessarily taking place in tumultuous and contradictory ways, but which is neverthelss going ahead.]

The theme of "Romantic reaction", that of an anachronistic celebration of the values of the rural past, was indeed one of the

principal routes along which Pasolini was attacked by PCI intellectuals and others not out of sympathy with the Party (for example, Calvino). A typical example is Giorgio Napolitano's reply
to Pasolini's contribution to a round table discussion at the provincial Festival dell'Unità at Milan in September 1974:

> Non in tutto il discorso di Pasolini, ma in certi momenti del suo
> intervento, è riaffiorata a mio avviso una rappresentazione, se
> non idilliaca, quasi totalmente acritica del passato precapitalisti-
> co, o premonopolistico, del mondo contadino e popolare, delle
> sue tradizioni culturali, della cultura che abbiamo chiamato
> orale.[21]

> [There were certain parts of Pasolini's talk, though not the whole
> of it, where it seems to me there emerged a representation which,
> if not idyllic, was almost wholly uncritical, of the pre-capitalist,
> or pre-monopolistic, past, of the world of the peasants and the
> people, of its cultural traditions, and of what we have called oral
> culture.]

But this was only the most obvious, and not necessarily the most
important part of Pasolini's argument, as Berlinguer and Napolitano
were probably well aware. Pasolini's recurrent concern was with
power relations in the here and now, and these the Party was not
very willing to discuss, certainly not (understandably) on Pasolini's
terms. Pasolini, for his part, could not make up his mind whether
to regard the PCI as no less a political dinosaur than the DC, plodding
about in the old history and blind and deaf to the "anthropological
mutation" that has taken place around it; or whether to celebrate its
"uprightness",[22] the fact that, alone among their contemporaries,
the members of the FGCI had escaped the degradations visited upon
youth by consumer society. In the first mood, he lectures the Party
for getting it wrong about the modernity of contemporary Italy,
miscalculating the divorce issue, sending out the wrong signals
about the Brescia bombing, and falling into complacency about its
electoral support. In the second, he goes so far as to speculate about
the possibility of the PCI achieving a new cultural hegemony
comparable in scope if not in substance to that which it exercised
in the 1950s.[23] There is enough of a family likeness between certain
attitudes of Pasolini and certain positions of the Party (for example
the latter's suggestion, adumbrated from late 1973 onwards, of a
"new development model" involving the switching of resources

from private to public consumption) to ensure that they do not drift apart altogether.[24] But the *forma mentis* is fundamentally different: to mention just one aspect, the policies of the Party throughout this period tend to remain rigidly centralist (thus, for example, the crisis in cultural values is seen primarily as a problem of *education*), exactly at the point where Pasolini tends towards libertarian solutions.

A fourth and final form of opposition for Pasolini, and the one that made most impact at the time, is that afforded him by his role as a campaigning journalist, and it takes the form in the late summer of 1975 of a call for the impeachment of the leadership of the Christian Democrats. In a characteristic move (reminiscent of the opening of *Scritti corsari*, which has Pasolini the film director sitting in a hotel foyer in Prague meditating on the language of long hair), he begins by establishing his credentials: sitting on the beach at Ostia, *L'espresso* in his hand, he contemplates the "folla infimo-borghese", the incarnation of the "rivoluzione antropologica di cui tanto scrivo" ["the lower-middle-class crowd (…), the anthropological revolution which I write so much about"],[25] and suddenly understands that the *other* journalists, who write so differently about the same things, live in a different place from him and these real flesh-and-blood bathers: they live in the Palace, they are, in short, accomplices of power. Pasolini, unsullied, is free to demand a trial, a Russell tribunal, a process like that submitted to by Papadopoulos or (almost) by Nixon. Andreotti, Fanfani, Rumor and a dozen other "potenti democristiani" should stand trial for:

> indegnità, disprezzo per i cittadini, manipolazione del denaro pubblico, intrallazzo con i petrolieri, con gli industriali, con i banchieri, connivenza con la mafia, alto tradimento in favore di una nazione straniera, collaborazione con la Cia, uso illecito di enti come il Sid, responsabilità nelle stragi di Milano, Brescia e Bologna (almeno in quanto colpevole incapacità di punirne gli esecutori), distruzione paesaggistica e urbanistica dell'Italia, responsabilità della degradazione antropologica degli italiani (responsabilità, questa, aggravata dalla sua totale inconsapevolezza), responsabilità della condizione, come suol dirsi, paurosa, delle scuole, degli ospedali e di ogni opera pubblica primaria, responsabilità dell'abbandono "selvaggio" delle campagne, responsabilità dell'esplosione "selvaggia" della cultura di massa e dei mass-media, responsabilità della stupidità delittuosa della televisione, responsabilità del decadimento della Chiesa, e infine,

oltre a tutto il resto, magari, distribuzione borbonica di cariche pubbliche ad adulatori.[26]

[unworthiness of the office which they hold, contempt for the citizens, manipulation of public money, corrupt dealings with oil companies, industrialists and bankers, connivance with the Mafia, high treason in favour of a foreign nation, collaboration with the CIA, illicit uses of bodies such as the secret services, responsibilities connected with the terrorist outrages in Milan, Brescia and Bologna (at least to the extent of a guilty inability to punish the perpetrators), destruction of the countryside and the cities of Italy, responsibility for the anthropological degradation of the Italians (a responsibility aggravated by its being completely unconscious), responsibility for what is habitually called the fearful condition of schools, hospitals and all the other primary public services, responsibility for the "wild" explosion of mass culture and the mass media, responsibility for the criminal stupidity of television, responsibility for the decline of the Church, and finally, on top of everything else, why not?, the distribution of public offices to lickspittles, as if we were still living under the Bourbons.]

It is clear that the trial would have a demonstrative, not a punitive purpose; its aim would be to unmask and to expose to public ridicule and contempt the institutions of Italian *malgoverno*.

The proposed trial, along with Pasolini's theses on Fascism and anti-Fascism (and the "mutazione antropologica"), and his stand on abortion, aroused strong and sometimes vehement reactions on the part of readers, or rather on the part of other intellectuals speaking on behalf of particular constituencies. But it is important to point out that the issues in dispute were different in nature from each other and therefore allowed of a different kind of response from Pasolini's critics and in turn from Pasolini himself. Abortion and the trial were both matters which involved simultaneously a question of principle and a question of practice, and Pasolini could hold firm on the first while leaving himself room for manoeuvre on the second. Thus, while abortion is to be regarded as "una colpa" ["a crime"], "la pratica consiglia di depenalizzarla" ["practice counsels that it be depenalized": *SC*, 145]. The notion of the trial can veer between something very generic, something that would provide a Synthesis, as Pasolini puts it, of the events of the last ten years (but also a kind of visible proof of his own thesis), and lists of specific charges, to read which, or many of which, is almost to read an *Unità* leader recast as a criminal indictment. On these matters Luther can be diplomatic, and to some extent negotiate with his adversaries.

But on the question of Fascism Pasolini is intransigent, and necessarily so, for it is here that he furnishes absolute definitions which run counter to all the assumptions of the left. His challenge to the myth of anti-Fascism, to the belief, sincerely held but in practice leading only to complacency, that the enemy was a resurgence of the old Fascism to be confronted and defeated in the spirit of the wartime Resistance, is one which strikes at the heart of the Italian left, both inside and outside the PCI of the early 1970s. The charge that the left is stirring up false emotions, a false rage, a false indignation, even a false fear, in the name of a misdirected struggle and a refusal, conscious or unconscious, to confront the truth that is concealed by that falsehood, is not something negotiable: you have either to dispute it or accept it: submission or defensiveness seems the only possible response. Pasolini certainly gives his critics enough weapons with which to fend him off, yet there is something magnificent in this rage against those (respectable) men and women of the left who do not or pretend not to see what several times Pasolini refers to as "genocide", attributing the idea, somewhat misleadingly, to the *Communist Manifesto* (*SC*, 159). The inverted commas around the word "genocidio" in this passage should be taken to indicate that Pasolini is interpreting rather than quoting Marx. The *Manifesto* does not use the notion of genocide (the term itself was first used in English in 1944), nor anything that is strictly analogous to it. What it does describe is how the bourgeoisie has destroyed, ripped apart, drowned, stripped bare, torn away (*zerstört, zerriffen, ertränkt, entkleidet, abgeriffen*) the social relations and the self-image of the feudal era. One might almost read the articles of 1973–75, especially the "Scritti corsari", as a kind of *Communist Manifesto* without the Communism, that is, without the strategies of revolutionary politics mapped out in Marx and Engels's text. The *Manifesto* is structured as a vivid and absolute denunciation, whose emphasis is on the speed, violence and overwhelming thoroughness of the victory of the bourgeoisie. But here, in the *pars destruens*, the similarity ends. Pasolini's attachment to peasant culture, though not as absolutely determining as his Communist critics made out, is quite at variance with the *Manifesto*'s view of "the idiocy of rural life".[27] And there is hope in the *Manifesto*, represented by the dialectic, the idea that "what the bourgeoisie [...] produces, above all, is its own grave-diggers" (p. 35). This dialectic is absent in Pasolini, because the proletariat is absent, as from all his work. Pasolini's articles could scarcely point a new way forward. Even the call for *buongoverno*, in many respects the most positive of Pasolini's interventions, is more the claim of an aspirant (an intellectual on the fringes of power) than a proposal for political change. But what his writings could do, and did effectively, was to press on the insecurity and the guilt of the "traditional" left, which was perhaps becoming too settled in its ideas and for which the myths of anti-Fascism and the Resistance were functioning more and more as emotional props in the confusion of those years. And to those who dismissed his "nostalgia" or his "Romanticism", Pasolini might well object that they had not taken to heart the meaning of his regret:

> [...] I plans un mond muàrt.
> Ma i no soj muàrt jo ch'i lu plans.
> Si vulín zí avant bisugna ch'i planzíni
> il timp ch'a no'l pòs pí tornà, ch'i dizíni di no
>
> a chista realtàt ch'a ni à sieràt
> ta la so preson...[28]

[I weep for a dead world./But I who weep am not dead./If we wish to go forward we must weep/for the time which cannot return, we must say no//to this reality which has closed us/in its prison...]

Then a sliding door opened, like a curtain revealing a stage. In the background could be seen a large dinner table littered with the remains of a meal. Into the footlights one by one stepped a woman, then the Nobel prizewinning author Gabriel Marquez, of Colombia, then Castro himself.

Castro was dishevelled. Kinnock was in a bantering mood, opening with: "I would always put a poet before a politician." Castro topped that with: "In history poets can't live without politicians, but without poets the world cannot go on."[29]

The occasion is striking, not for its contribution to the debate on the relation between aesthetics and politics, but for its atmosphere of male camaraderie, represented visually in other reports by pictures of Castro clasping Kinnock round the shoulders or jabbing two fingers and a cigar into his chest, while the "poet", like the "woman" who preceded him, is clearly an appurtenance of power, a hanger-on, a courtier, a clearer of the way. The old bear and the eager-to-learn young cub hug each other's egos in affectionate embrace and make it round the pitfalls of the conversation's start with the sentimental thought that representatives of humanity's higher spiritual self can harmonize with the toughies who make things happen "in history". Of course neither of the two bleary-eyed protagonists—it is two o'clock in the morning and there has been a big party—believes a word of what he is saying. It is all for the television cameras, and it signifies something like peace, the lion lying down with the lamb. It is also a boring reiteration, and reinforcement, of one of the hoariest traditions in European Socialism, that there is a special relation between "poetry" and politics, often asserted by politicians to suggest they are human, and sometimes by poets to suggest they are powerful.

Did Pasolini subscribe to this myth? Did he ever fantasize Berlinguer telling Brezhnev over the twiglets, "That Pasolini's a pain in the ass, but by God we need him, to make the world go round"? Sometimes, in his "corsair" and "Lutheran" writings, it seems that Pasolini did see himself in this way. The "piccolo poeta civile degli Anni Cinquanta" ["the little civic poet of the Fifties": *La Divina Mimesis*, p. 16] makes his reappearance as a "committed" writer, *impegnato* now in the early 1970s when there is a real need for intervention, as against 1968 when there were no objective reasons for the student movement and its intellectual fellow-travellers.[30] This writer asserts his right to "esercitare la mia critica" ["carry on my critique"], with all due respect for the rights of the politicians to operate within their sphere: "Ormai è passato quasi un mese da quel felice 12 maggio [1974] e posso perciò permettermi di esercitare la mia critica senza temere di fare del disfattismo inopportuno" ["Nearly a month has passed since that happy day, 12 May (1974), and I can therefore allow myself to carry on my critique without fear of being inopportunely defeatist": *SC*, 47]. More frequently, it is the other face of this connivance between politics and culture that Pasolini lives and expresses, the alienation of the intellectual from power, his degradation at the hands of a violent counterforce, the *patetismo* of his condition, the poet as sufferer: "È in queste condizioni, ambigue, contraddittorie, frustranti, ingloriose, odiose che l'uomo di cultura deve impegnarsi alla lotta politica" ["It is in these ambiguous, contradictory, frustrating, inglorious, odious conditions that the man of culture must engage in the political struggle": *SC*, 33]. But whether listened to with respect, or scorned and even hated, whether as *vates* or victim, the man of culture, and especially the civic poet, who makes himself visible to politicians, continues to enjoy a special relation with power.

Yet all this in Pasolini, at any rate in the later Pasolini, is only scenery, or, to put it less fancifully, it belongs to the first of what appear to be two positions from which to read his text. As the reader of a newspaper or magazine, engaged with the issues of the day, provoked by what Pasolini has to say, one begins by reading his articles as one would any leader or feature article written by someone whose views are almost bound to be controversial. At this level, the reader is solely and directly receiving, and reacting to, the opinion that is being expressed at that particular moment. It is a question of understanding the argument, agreeing with it or disagreeing. Is he right about Fascism? Do I agree with him about abortion? Is the DC really as catastrophic as that, and for those reasons? It is a naive reading, and an absolutely necessary one, but sooner or later it is likely to run into some equivocation and irritation on the part of the reader, for it supposes a kind of dialogue between reader and author, which cannot take place. The naïve reader in us may be plain frustrated if Pasolini claims he knows the names of those who have been responsible for the terrorist outrages of the past five years…, but cannot state them in print.[31] She or he may react violently to Pasolini's suggestion that the question of abortion is *really* a question of coitus. If a dialogue is begun, it is strictly on the author's terms: for example, in Pasolini's replies to his critics. This is the level of "Pasolini's views on", "Pasolini's attitude to" one issue or another. Pasolini is seen as a coherent subject confronting a coherent object and destined himself to become a coherent object (or a coherently incoherent one) in the reader's eyes.

Then there is another position, whose existence may be suspected even by the naïve reader, and which is much more difficult to define than the first. This is where the reader is not quite sure what he or she is reading, except that the words are clearly only in part and only apparently about what they say they are about. The context of *this* discourse, it seems, is not, or not only, the immediate references, but appears to come from somewhere deeper in the subject himself. The text supposes a pre-text, in which certain words—such as "popolo" ["people"] or "ragazzo" ["youth"], to take obvious general examples, but also more specific images such as "capelli" ["hair"] or "notte" ["night"]—have already crystallized and themselves are determining the present discourse (rather than, or as much as, the immediate context "outside"). This corresponds to the sense that in this immediacy, this present, there is a past constantly thrusting itself forward and "resurfacing". At this level the actual text becomes a prism through which to read the whole text which it has itself pointed out: it is consecrated as a moment of the total discourse which is Pasolini. And now the temptation is to flatten out the immediacy of the discourse altogether, to read the text as though it were written in a kind of second-order language, one that is not related to objects "outside" itself, but rather one that is principally, and indifferently, perpetuating itself. And in this case the reader is aware, not that the language is talking directly to her or him as in the first case, but that it is already directed back to Pasolini, prefiguring that "recall" to which I alluded at the beginning of this essay.

It is from this second position that one perceives, more clearly I think than from the first, the "political" Pasolini. For the self thus revealed is experienced as an integral part of that reality to which Pasolini directs our attention. Pasolini insists on his own physical immersion in the reality of things: that Jekyll-and-Hyde existence which allows him not only to live the intellectual life but also to be part of a corporeal, existential reality among people to which by implication most of his literary colleagues, for example Moravia, do not have access:[32]

> Il consumismo consiste infatti in un vero e proprio cataclisma antropologico: e io *vivo*, esistenzialmente, tale cataclisma che, almeno per ora, è pura degradazione: lo vivo nei miei giorni, nelle forme della mia esistenza, *nel mio corpo*.[33]

> [Consumerism consists in nothing less than an anthropological cataclysm, and I *live*, existentially, this cataclysm, which, for the moment at least, is pure degradation. I live it in my days, in the forms of my existence, *in my body*.]

But what counts more for the reader than this claim to authenticity is the realization that Pasolini uses language not to record experience, authentic or otherwise, but to expand metaphorically certain essential images without which it would be impossible for him to write, or to exist. Thus the writer transcends his journalistic role as opinion-maker, or guide,[34] and thus too his role as the interlocutor of power, to become, through his utterance and in the transparency of his speech, the very thing that he is talking about. Pasolini's speaking of the crisis *is* the crisis, it is the crisis at the moment that it is recognized.

In this extraordinary feat of mimetization, in his embodiment through language of the crisis through which he saw himself and his contemporaries living, lies Pasolini's exceptional position in post-war Italian culture. A year after Pasolini's death, Paolo Volponi tried to explain his appeal in the following terms:

> Perché c'è tanta attenzione sul "fatto Pasolini"? Evidentemente la figura di Pasolini è quella di un intellettuale che ha toccato profondamente molti problemi della nostra società. Questo è stato avvertito anche a livello popolare. Io non credo sia soltanto, come alcuni dicono, per lo scandalo della sua morte. Di scandali come il suo se n'è avuti tanti e non hanno provocato tanto clamore perché sono ricaduti all'interno dello scandalo; soprattutto non hanno provocato tanta riflessione, tanta smania di conoscere il personaggio, di leggere i suoi messaggi, di capire il senso del suo lavoro, di poter ancora dialogare con colui che aveva evidentemente un'idea molto diversa della società italiana e che sapeva esprimerla in modo poetico e popolare. E perché c'è oggi questa grande attenzione anche nei confronti degli intellettuali e c'è questo grande rapporto nuovo fra gli intellettuali e le masse popolari? Non soltanto perché gli intellettuali hanno capito certe cose, e molte volte in ritardo, ma perché le masse popolari, sentendosi ormai portatrici di una cultura nuova, di un disegno nuovo, o per lo meno di un'ansia nuova, vogliono un confronto con quelle persone che si dicono e appaiono depositarie di certe conoscenze politiche, tecniche, letterarie, amministrative, perché vogliono vedere in che modo quella loro cultura e ansia possano essere organizzate, chiarite e introdotte nel disegno di una società diversa. È per questo che oggi c'è ancora una grande "attesa" nei confronti di Pasolini, del suo lavoro, e c'è anche questo rimpianto e sbigottimento nei confronti della sua morte.[35]

[Why is so much attention being paid to the case of Pasolini? Pasolini was clearly an intellectual who touched deeply on many of our society's problems. This was also understood by people who were not intellectuals. I do not think, as some have stated, that it is just because of the scandal of his death. There have been plenty of scandals like the one which befell Pasolini, and they did not cause such a furore because they were in the end contained within the limits of the scandal itself. Above all, they did not provoke such intensity of reflection, such a desire to know the person, to read his messages, to understand the sense of his work, to be able to go on discussing with someone who clearly had a very different idea of Italian society and was able to express it in a poetic and popular way. And why is there so much attention being paid today to intellectuals in general, and this great new relationship between intellectuals and the popular masses? Not only because the intellectuals have understood certain things, often belatedly, but because the popular masses, who now feel themselves to be the bearers of a new culture, a new design, or at the least a new desire, wish to talk with those people who claim, and appear, to be the repositories of certain kinds of political, technical, literary and administrative knowledge, because they wish to know how their culture and their aspirations can be organized, clarified and brought into the design of a different society. It is for this reason that there is such "expectation" of Pasolini and his work today, and this sadness and confusion in the face of his death.]

Whatever doubts one may have about Volponi's optimistic (and un-Pasolinian) assessment of the expectations of the "masse popolari", he is surely right in suggesting that Pasolini stood for something more than just one viewpoint among others. It is in fact not so much his undoubted dogmatism as his extraordinary "availability" that finally remains with the reader of *Scritti corsari* and *Lettere luterane*; something that resembles a sheet of paper on which others may inscribe themselves, as Dominique Fernandez does in his "fictional biography" of Pasolini recounted in Pier Paolo's "own" voice, that is, in Fernandez's convincing imitation of it.[36] To speak through Pasolini, rather than of him, is a temptation to which I have found myself succumbing more than once, *mio malgrado*, in this study.

NOTES

1   *Scritti corsari* [1975] (Milan, Garzanti, 1981). For Pasolini's "instructions", see his "Nota introduttiva", pp. 1–2.

2   The reader is directed in particular to the "Italo-Friulan" poetry written in 1973–74 and published in *La nuova gioventú* (Turin, Einaudi, 1975). One group of poems in particular ("Significato del rimpianto", "Poesia popolare", "Appunto per una poesia in lappone", "La recessione" and "Appunto per una poesia in terrone"), first published in part in *Paese sera* on 5 January 1974, is cited as "un nesso essenziale non solo tra le due 'serie' ma anche all'interno della stessa 'serie' prima [i.e. the "Scritti corsari" proper], cioè del discorso piú attualistico di questo libro" (*SC*, 2).

3   *Lettere luterane* (Turin, Einaudi, 1976). Alongside the more organically conceived and arranged "trattatello pedagogico" entitled "Gennariello", this volume too includes a number of essays and "interventions" whose ends are no less untied than those of the *Scritti corsari*. By the time the *Lettere* were published, the "philologist" had a good deal more work to do: the screenplay *Il padre selvaggio* was published in February 1975 (Turin, Einaudi), *Salò o le 120 giornate di Sodoma* was finished at the end of October (see E. Siciliano, *Vita di Pasolini* [Milan, Rizzoli, 1978], p. 381) and *La Divina Mimesis* (Turin, Einaudi, 1975), which had been written on and off during the 1960s, was published a few weeks after Pasolini's murder, "per far dispetto ai miei 'nemici'" ("Prefazione", n.p.). To these titles should be added the substantial number of book reviews written between November 1972 and January 1975, and later collected under the title *Descrizioni di descrizioni* (Turin, Einaudi, 1979).

4   "Studio sulla rivoluzione antropologica in Italia", in *SC*, 46–52 (pp. 49–50); originally in *Corriere della sera*, 10 June 1974 with the title "Gli italiani non sono piú quelli".

5   "La prima, vera rivoluzione di destra", in *SC*, 20–26 (pp. 20–21); originally in *Tempo illustrato*, 15 July 1973 with the title "Pasolini giudica i temi di italiano".

6   "L'articolo delle lucciole", in *SC*, 156–64 (p. 161); originally in *Corriere della sera*, 1 Feb. 1975 with the title "Il vuoto del potere in Italia".

7   "Il vero fascismo e quindi il vero antifascismo", in *SC*, 53–59 (p. 54); originally in *Corriere della sera*, 24 June 1974 with the title "Il Potere senza volto".

8   "Acculturazione e acculturazione", in *SC*, 27–30 (pp. 27, 30); originally in *Corriere della sera*, 9 Dec. 1973 with the title "Sfida ai dirigenti della televisione".

9   "Vuoto di carità, vuoto di cultura: un linguaggio senza origini", in *SC*, 40–45 (p. 41); originally Preface to *Divorziare in nome di Dio*, edited by F. Perego (Venice, Marsilio, 1974).

10 All parties were agreed on the need to abolish the 1930 law which forbade abortion under all circumstances. They were not agreed on how to replace it. The DC and MSI would consider only abortion in cases of rape or where the mother's life was in danger. The PCI and the smaller lay parties wanted economic and social circumstances to be taken into account. The PSI pressed for abortion on demand, the choice being left to the woman. In June 1975, a

Radical-sponsored petition for a referendum to abolish the 1930 law was handed in, and in early November the Supreme Court declared its validity, containing as it did more than the required 500,000 valid signatures. If Parliament did not approve a new law by mid-April 1976, the referendum would be called within two months. On 1 April the Chamber narrowly approved a bill along DC–MSI lines. The Socialists strengthened their opposition and threatened new elections. Since the bill was not approved by Parliament as a whole by mid-April, President Leone fixed the referendum for 13 June. This was superseded, however, by the collapse of the government and the holding of new elections on 20–21 June 1976.

11   "Thalassa", in *SC*, 134–39 (p. 136); originally in *Paese sera*, 25 Jan. 1975 with the title "Una lettera di Pasolini: 'opinioni' sull'aborto".

12   "Il coito, l'aborto, la falsa tolleranza del potere, il conformismo dei progressisti", in *SC*, 119–27 (p. 123); originally in *Corriere della sera*, 19 Jan. 1975 with the title "Sono contro l'aborto".

13   "Il carcere e la fraternità dell'amore omosessuale", in *SC*, 243–49 (pp. 246–47); originally in *Il mondo*, 11 Apr. 1974.

14   Review of M. Daniel and A. Baudry, *Gli omosessuali* (Milan, Vallecchi, 1974), in *SC*, 250–58 (p. 255); originally in *Tempo*, 26 Apr. 1974.

15   Dedalus [U. Eco], "Le ceneri di Malthus", *Il manifesto*, 21 Jan. 1975.

16   "Cani" [February 1975, not previously published], in *SC*, 140–47 (pp. 145–46).

17   See "Il fascismo degli antifascisti", in *SC*, 78–85; originally in *Corriere della sera*, 16 July 1974.

18   "Nuove prospettive storiche: la Chiesa è inutile al potere", in *SC*, 100–06 (pp. 105–06); originally in *Corriere della sera*, 6 Oct. 1974 with the title "Chiesa e potere".

19   "Intervento al congresso del Partito Radicale", read out to the Congress in Florence on 4 November 1975, two days after Pasolini's murder, in *LL*, 185–95 (p. 195).

20   E. Berlinguer, "Per uscire dalla crisi, per costruire un'Italia nuova", now in E. Berlinguer, *La "questione comunista" 1969–1975*, edited by A. Tatò, 2 vols (Rome, Editori Riuniti, 1975), II, 823–966 (p. 913).

21   "Ideologia e politica nell'Italia che cambia: dibattito tra Roberto Guiducci, Renato Guttuso, Giorgio Napolitano e Pier Paolo Pasolini", *Rinascita*, 27 Sept. 1974, pp. 19–22 (p. 22).

22   "Un paese pulito in un paese sporco, un paese onesto in un paese disonesto, un paese intelligente in un paese idiota, un paese colto in un paese ignorante, un paese umanistico in un paese consumistico": "Il romanzo delle stragi", in *SC*, 107–13 (p. 110); originally in *Corriere della sera*, 14 Nov. 1974 with the title "Che cos' è questo golpe?"

23   "L'ignoranza vaticana come paradigma dell'ignoranza della borghesia italiana", in *SC*, 114–18 (p. 118); originally in *Epoca*, 25 Jan. 1975.

24   Even if Pasolini's comment on the "new development model" is characteristically dismissive—it is ridiculous either to accept or to reject the existing "development model" because it is "quello voluto dalla società capitalistica che sta per giungere alla massima maturità"—, he does not entirely exclude an alternative kind of development, one which the Communists would be particularly well qualified to propose: "E allora—almeno i comunisti—potranno far tesoro dell'esperienza vissuta: e, poiché si dovrà ricominciare

daccapo con uno 'sviluppo', questo 'sviluppo' dovrà essere totalmente diverso da quello che è stato" ("Appunto per una poesia in lappone", in *LNG*, 241).

25   "Fuori dal Palazzo", in *LL*, 92–98 (p. 92); originally in *Corriere della sera*, 1 Aug. 1975.

26   "Bisognerebbe processare i gerarchi dc", in *LL*, 107–13 (p. 113); originally in *Il mondo*, 28 Aug. 1975.

27   K. Marx and F. Engels, *Manifesto of the Communist Party* (London, Lawrence and Wishart, 1983), p. 19.

28   "Significato del rimpianto", in *LNG*, 237.

29   W. Ellsworth-Jones, reporting from Managua, *The Sunday Times*, 13 Jan. 1985, 1.

30   See "Gli intellettuali nel '68: manicheismo e ortodossia della 'rivoluzione dell'indomani'", in *SC*, 31–33; originally in *Dramma*, Mar. 1974.

31   "Il romanzo delle stragi", in *SC*, 107–13. The impossibility for the writer to name names is linked with the bourgeoisie's conferment on the intellectual of a "mandato falsamente alto e nobile, in realtà servile: quello di dibattere i problemi morali e ideologici" (p. 110). The whole essay is structured around the principle of anticlimax.

32   For Pasolini's "Jekyll-and-Hyde existence" see his "Limitatezza della storia e immensità del mondo contadino", in *SC*, 60–65 (p. 61); originally in *Paese sera*, 8 July 1974 with the title "Lettera aperta a Italo Calvino: Pasolini: quello che rimpiango".

33   "Sacer", in *SC*, 128–33 (p. 130; Pasolini's italics); originally in *Corriere della sera*, 30 Jan. 1975 with the title "Pasolini replica sull'aborto".

34   To guide is the role of the "piccolo poeta civile degli Anni Cinquanta": "Era misero, minuto, il mio soccorritore: non era padre, non era fratello maggiore, non aveva l'imponenza consolatrice di chi rappresenta l'autorità; poteva essere tutt' al piú una guida di montagna" (*La Divina Mimesis*, p. 15).

35   P. Volponi, "Pasolini maestro e amico", in *Perché Pasolini: ideologia e stile di un intellettuale militante*, edited by G. De Santi, M. Lenti and R. Rossini (Florence, Guaraldi, 1978), pp. 15–28 (pp. 22–23).

36   D. Fernandez, *Dans la main de l'ange* (Paris, Grasset, 1982).

BIBLIOGRAPHY OF CRITICAL WRITING

The following list comprises all the works not by Pasolini referred to during the course of this collection. Works by Pasolini are excluded because, given the many different editions of his major texts now in circulation, it would have been unreasonable to require all the contributors to use the same editions. Each author, in his or her footnotes, cites the editions to which he or she makes reference. Where appropriate, after the first full reference, Pasolini's works are cited in those footnotes in a standardized manner according to the abbrevations listed at the beginning of this volume.

Anon., "Fedele al racconto, non all'ispirazione del Vangelo il film di Pasolini", *L'osservatore romano*, 6 Sept. 1964

Anon., "Un poeta traduttore", *Il mulino* (Dec. 1961), 961–64

Abruzzese, A., "Scrittura, cinema, territorio", in *Cinema e letteratura del neorealismo*, edited by G. Tinazzi and M. Zancan (Venice, Marsilio, 1990)

Ajello, M., "Riscritti corsari", *Panorama*, 3 Oct. 1993, 134–43

Albini, U., "Tradurre i greci", in *La traduzione dei classici greci e latini in Italia oggi: problemi, prospettive, iniziative editoriali*, edited by P. Janni and I. Mazzini (Macerata, Pubblicazioni della Facoltà di Lettere e Filosofia, 1991), pp. 11–16

Anzoino, T., *Pier Paolo Pasolini* [1971], second edition (Florence, La Nuova Italia, 1974)

A partire da "Petrolio": Pasolini interroga la letteratura, edited by C. Benedetti and M. A. Grignani (Ravenna, Longo, 1995)

Arbasino, A., "Bruciare *Petrolio*?", *Repubblica*, 27 Oct. 1992, 27

Argentieri, M., "La Mostra di Venezia l'ha spuntata sulle polemiche", *Rinascita*, 12 Sept. 1964

Argento, D., "'Vedrò Gesú Cristo come Accattone' ci ha detto Pier Paolo Pasolini", *Paese sera*, 9 Feb. 1963

Aristarco, G., "Dal neorealismo al realismo", *Cinema nuovo*, 4, liii (25 Feb. 1955)

Aristarco, G., "E realismo", *Cinema nuovo*, 4, lv (24 Mar. 1955)

Aristarco, G., "Senso", *Cinema nuovo*, 4, lii (10 Feb. 1955)

Ascanio, S., "P. P. Pasolini promette di rispettare il Vangelo", *Il gazzettino*, 25 Feb. 1964

Asor Rosa, A., "Il neorealismo o il trionfo del narrativo", in *Cinema e letteratura del neorealismo*, edited by G. Tinazzi and M. Zancan (Venice, Marsilio, 1990)

Asor Rosa, A., "La crisi del populismo: Pasolini", in his *Scrittori e popolo: il populismo nella letteratura italiana contemporanea* [1965], third edition (Rome, Samonà and Savelli, 1969), pp. 349–449

Asor Rosa, A., "Pasolini il veggente", *Rinascita*, 11 Nov. 1990, 60–61

Bachelard, G., *L'Eau et les rêves: essai sur l'imagination de la matière* (Paris, Corti, 1942), pp. 36–40

Baldelli, P., "L'elegia dissimulata di Pasolini", in *Pier Paolo Pasolini: materiali critici*, edited by A. Luzi and L. Martellini (n.p., Argalia, 1972–73), pp. 361–77

Baldelli, P., "Pasolini e 'lo scandalo della contraddizione'", *Giovane critica*, 6 (1964–65), 29–49

Barański, Z. G., "Notes towards a Reconstruction: Pasolini and Rome 1950–51", *The Italianist*, 5 (1985), 138–49

Barański, Z. G., "Pier Paolo Pasolini: Culture, Croce, Gramsci", in *Culture and Conflict in Postwar Italy*, edited by Z. G. Barański and R. Lumley (Basingstoke, Macmillan, 1990), pp. 139–59

Barański, Z. G., "Pier Paolo Pasolini: teoremi e teorie", in *Lezioni su Pasolini*, edited by T. De Mauro and F. Ferri (Ripatransone, Sestante, 1997), pp. 99–112

Barański, Z. G., "The Power of Influence: Aspects of Dante's Presence in Twentieth-century Italian Culture", *Strumenti critici*, new series 1 (1986), 343–76

Bàrberi Squarotti, G., "L'anima e la letteratura, il teatro di Pasolini", *Critica letteraria*, 8 (1980), 645–80

Bàrberi Squarotti, G., "La poesia e il viaggio a ritroso nell'io", in *Pier Paolo Pasolini: l'opera e il suo tempo*, edited by G. Santato (Padua, CLEUP, 1983), pp. 206–26

Bàrberi Squarotti, G., *Le maschere dell'eroe: dall'Alfieri a Pasolini* (Lecce, Milella, 1990)

Barnett, L. K., and B. Lawton, "Introduction", in P. P. Pasolini, *Heretical Empiricism*, translated by L. K. Barnett and B. Lawton (Bloomington–London, Indiana University Press, 1988), pp. xiii–xxviii

Barnstone, W., *The Poetics of Translation* (New Haven–London, Yale University Press, 1993)

Bassnett-McGuire, S., "Introduction", in *Translation, History and Culture*, edited by S. Bassnett and A. Lefevere (London–New York, Pinter, 1990), pp. 1–13

Bassnett-McGuire, S., *Translation Studies* (London, Methuen, 1980)

Bazin, A., "Parlatorio", *Cinema nuovo*, 5, lxxxix (10 Sept. 1956)

Bazin, A., *Qu'est-ce que le cinéma?*, vol. IV: *Une Esthétique de la réalité: le néoréalisme* (Paris, Cerf, 1962)

Bazin, A., *What is Cinema?*, vol. II, edited and translated by H. Gray (Berkeley, University of California Press, 1971)

Beccaria, G. L., "Con Pier Paolo linguista", *La stampa*, 29 Sept. 1972

Bellezza, D., *Il poeta assassinato: una riflessione, un'ipotesi, una sfida sulla morte di Pier Paolo Pasolini* (Venice, Marsilio, 1996)

Bellezza, D., *Morte di Pasolini* (Milan, Mondadori, 1981)

Bellocchio, M., "Storia dei giovani: prima, durante e dopo il 68", supplement to *Panorama*, 31 Jan. 1988

Bellocchio, P., "L'autobiografia involontaria di Pasolini", in his *Dalla parte del torto* (Turin, Einaudi, 1989), pp. 145–66

Berardinelli, A., "La poesia: l'area sperimentale", in *Manuale di letteratura italiana, IV: Dalla unità d'Italia alla fine del Novecento*, edited by F. Brioschi and C. Di Girolamo (Turin, Bollati Boringhieri, 1996), pp. 460–71

Berlinguer. E., *La "questione comunista" 1969–1975*, edited by A. Tatò, 2 vols (Rome, Editori Riuniti, 1975)

Bertini, A., *Teoria e tecnica del film in Pasolini* (Rome, Bulzoni, 1979)

Bertolucci, A., Interview with Portia Prebys, Rome, 21 Oct. 1991 (unpublished)

Bettarini, M., "Pasolini, le culture e noi", in *Perché Pasolini: ideologia e stile di un intellettuale militante*, edited by G. De Santi, M. Lenti and R. Rossini (Florence, Guaraldi, 1978), pp. 215–23

Bloom, H., *The Anxiety of Influence: A Theory of Poetry* (New York, Oxford University Press, 1973)

Bonanno, M. G., "Pasolini e l'*Orestea*: dal 'teatro di parola' al 'cinema di poesia'", in *Pasolini e l'antico: i doni della ragione*, edited by U. Todini (Naples, ESI, 1995), pp. 45–66

Bondanella, P., *Italian Cinema: From Neorealism to the Present* (New York, Continuum, 1990)

Bongie, C., *Exotic Memories: Literature, Colonialism, and the Fin de Siècle* (Stanford, Stanford University Press, 1991)

Bordini, C., "Un coraggio a metà", in *Per Pasolini*, by various authors (Milan, Gammalibri, 1982), pp. 29–36

Borgese, G., "Pasolini bocciato dallo Stato, salvato dal Campidoglio", *Corriere della sera*, 2 July 1997, 23

Borgese, G., "Pasolini, l'archivio conteso", *Corriere della sera*, 1 July 1997

Borghese, L., "Tia Alene in bicicletta: Gramsci traduttore dal tedesco e teorico della traduzione", *Belfagor*, 36 (1981), 635–65

Branigan, E., *Point of View in the Cinema* (Berlin–New York–Amsterdam, Mouton, 1984)

Brevini, F., "La lingua che più non si sa: Pasolini e il friulano", *Belfagor*, 34 (1979), 397–409

Brevini, F., *Per conoscere Pasolini* (Milan, Mondadori, 1981)

Briamonte, N., *Saggio di bibliografia sui problemi storici, teorici e pratici della traduzione* (Naples, Libreria Sapere, 1984)

Brunetta, G. P., "Il viaggio di Pasolini dentro i classici", *Galleria*, 35, i–iv (1985), 67–75

Brunetta, G. P., *Storia del cinema italiano*, 2 vols (Rome, Editori Riuniti, 1979)

Bruno, G., "Heresies: The Body of Pasolini's Semiotics", *Cinema Journal*, 30, iii (1991), 29–42

Bruno, G., "The Body of Pasolini's Semiotics: A Sequel Twenty Years Later", in *Pier Paolo Pasolini: Contemporary Perspectives*, edited by P. Rumble and B. Testa (Toronto, University of Toronto Press, 1994), pp. 88–105

Buttafava, G., "Salò o il cinema in forma di rosa", *Bianco e nero*, 37, i–iv (1976), 33–52

Calabrese, O., *L'età neobarocca* (Rome–Bari, Laterza, 1989)

Cambria, A., "'Non ho cambiato una parola del testo sacro' dice lo scrittore", *La stampa*, 5 Sept. 1964

Camon, F., *Il mestiere di poeta* (Milan, Lerici, 1965)

Camon, F., "PPP contro PPP", *Panorama*, 3 Oct. 1993, 135–36

Cardone, L., "Gesú è spagnuolo e la Madonna di Crotone", *Settimana incom*, 24 May 1964

Carpi, F., "Finita l'inchiesta si trova il romanzo", *Cinema nuovo*, 3, xxxiv (1 May 1954)

Casi, S., *Pasolini: un'idea di teatro* (Udine, Campanotto, 1990)

Casiraghi, U., "A Venezia il *Vangelo secondo Matteo* di Pasolini", *L'unità*, 5 Sept. 1964, 7

Casolaro, M., SJ, "Spirito e lettera nel film di P. P. Pasolini", *Cineforum*, 40 (1964), 963–68

Chiarini, L., "Tradisce il neorealismo", *Cinema nuovo*, 3, lv (25 Mar. 1955)

Chilanti, F., "La serata veneziana di Matteo e Pasolini", *Paese sera*, 22 Sept 1964

Chiurlo, B., *Antologia della letteratura friulana* (Udine, Libreria Editrice Udinese, 1927)

Ciceri, A., *I contemporanei* (Aquileia, Tolmezzo, 1975)

Cigni, F., "Né timor di me ti prenda…", in *Desiderio di Pasolini: omosessualità, arte e impegno intellettuale*, edited by S. Casi (Turin, Sonda, 1990), pp. 119–48

Clément, C., "La Cantatrice muette ou le maître chanteur démasqué", in *Pasolini: séminaire*, edited by M. A. Macciocchi (Paris, Grasset, 1980), pp. 265–68

Codacci-Pisanelli, A., "Pasolini: giudicato dagli scrittori under 30: non chiamatelo Maestro", *L'espresso*, 22 Oct. 1995, 26–28

Coletti, V., "La letteratura dialettale e le preoccupazioni unitarie della storiografia e della critica letteraria", in *I dialetti e le lingue delle minoranze di fronte all'italiano*, by various authors, 2 vols (Rome, Bulzoni, 1977), I, 655–66

Con Pier Paolo Pasolini, edited by E. Magrelli (Rome, Bulzoni, 1977)

Contini, G., "Al limite della poesia dialettale", *Corriere del Ticino*, 24 Apr. 1943; reprinted in G. Contini, *Pagine ticinesi*, edited by R. Broggini, second edition (n.p., Salvioni, 1986), pp. 116–21

Contini, G., *Pagine ticinesi di Gianfranco Contini* (Bellinzona, Salvioni, 1981)

Contini, G., "Preliminari sulla lingua del Petrarca" [1951], in his *Varianti e altra linguistica* (Turin, Einaudi, 1970), pp. 169–92

Contini, G., "Testimonianza per Pier Paolo Pasolini", in *Pier Paolo Pasolini: testimonianze*, edited by A. Panicali and P. Sestini (Florence, Nuova Salani, 1982), pp. 13–15; reprinted in Contini's *Ultimi esercizî ed elzeviri (1968–1987)* (Turin, Einaudi, 1988), pp. 389–95

Costa, A., "Effetto dipinto", *Cinema e cinema*, 54–55 (Jan–Aug. 1989), 37–48

Culler, J., "Political Criticism", in *Writing the Future*, edited by D. Wood (London, Routledge, 1990), pp. 192–204

Da Accattone a Salò, edited by V. Boarini, P. Bonfiglioli and G. Cremonini (Bologna, Tipografia Compositori, 1982)

D'Angeli, C., "Nota", in P. P. Pasolini, *Amado mio* (Milan, Garzanti, 1982), pp. 195–202

David, M., *La psicanalisi nella cultura italiana* (Turin, Boringhieri, 1970)

De Angelis, E., "Corpi simbolici", *L'indice dei libri del mese*, 2 Feb. 1993, 6–7

Dedicato a Pasolini, by various authors (Milan, Gammalibri, 1976)

De Felice, R., *Interpretations of Fascism*, translated by B. Huff Everett (Cambridge, Mass., Harvard University Press, 1977)

De Giusti, L., *I film di Pier Paolo Pasolini* (Rome, Gremese, 1983)

de Lauretis, T., "Re-reading Pasolini's Essays on Cinema", *Italian Quarterly*, 21–22 (1980–81), 159–66

Deleuze, G., *Cinéma 1: L'image-mouvement* (Paris, Minuit, 1983)

Deleuze, G., *Cinema 2: The Time Image*, translated by H. Tomlinson and B. Habberjam (Minneapolis, University of Minnesota Press, 1989)

De Lutiis, G., *Storia dei servizi segreti in Italia* (Rome, Editori Riuniti, 1984)

De Mauro, T., "Anonimo Romano e la nuova poesia dialettale italiana", in Anonimo Romano, *Er communismo co' la libbertà*, edited by M. Ferrara (Rome, Editori Riuniti, 1979), pp. xi–xl

De Mauro, T., "La ricerca linguistica (di Pasolini)", *Nuova generazione*, 19 (1976), 23–24

De Mauro, T., "La stampa italiana e Pasolini", in *Pasolini: cronaca giudiziaria, persecuzione, morte*, edited by L. Betti (Milan, Garzanti, 1977), pp. 246–75

De Mauro, T., *Le parole e i fatti* (Rome, Editori Riuniti, 1977)

De Mauro, T., "Pasolini critico dei linguaggi", *Galleria*, 35, i–iv (1985), 7–30

De Mauro, T., "Per l'osservatorio linguistico e culturale: apologia di un ritardo", *Linguaggi*, 1 (1984), 7–13

De Mauro, T., *Storia linguistica dell'Italia unita* (Bari, Laterza, 1963)

De Mauro, T., "Un osservatorio della lingua", *Paese sera*, 25 May 1973

De Melis, F., "L'abiura del corsaro", *Il manifesto*, 24 Oct. 1993

de Nardis, L., *Roma di Belli e di Pasolini* (Rome, Bulzoni, 1977)

de Nardis, L., "Sulla prima redazione di *Ragazzi di vita* e di *Una vita violenta*", *Revue des études italiennes*, 28, ii–iii (1981), 123–39

Desiderio di Pasolini: omosessualità, arte e impegno intellettuale, edited by S. Casi (Turin, Sonda, 1990)

Devoto, G., *Fondamenti della storia linguistica* (Florence, Sansoni, 1951)

Devoto, G., *Profilo di storia linguistica italiana*, second edition (Florence, La Nuova Italia, 1964

Dombroski, R. S., *Antonio Gramsci* (Boston, Twayne, 1989)

Eco, U., *A Theory of Semiotics* (Bloomington, Indiana University Press, 1979)

Eco, U., *La struttura assente* (Milan, Bompiani, 1968)

Eco, U. [Dedalus], "Le ceneri di Malthus", *Il manifesto*, 21 Jan. 1975

Eco, U., *Segno* (Milan, ISEDI, 1973)

Eliade, M., *Le Mythe de l'éternel retour* (Paris, Gallimard, 1949)

Even-Zohar, I., *Polysystem Studies* = *Poetics Today*, 11, i (Spring 1990)

Fagone, V., SJ, "A proposito del *Vangelo secondo Matteo*", *Rivista del cinematografo*, 12 (1964), 552–56

Fernandez, D., *Dans la main de l'ange* (Paris, Grasset, 1982); Italian translation *Nelle mani dell'angelo* (Milan, Bompiani, 1983)

Ferrara, M., "I connotati di un potere reale", *L'unità*, 27 June 1974

Ferrara, M., "I pasticci dell'esteta", *L'unità*, 12 June 1974

Ferretti, G. C., "Introduzione", in P. P. Pasolini, *Le belle bandiere*, edited by G. C. Ferretti (Rome, Editori Riuniti, 1978), pp. 7–39

Ferretti, G. C., *Letteratura e ideologia: Bassani, Cassola, Pasolini* [1964], second edition (Rome, Editori Riuniti, 1974)

Ferretti, G. C., "'Mio padre, quando sono nato…'", *Galleria*, 35, i–iv (1985), 85–105

Ferretti, G. C., *Pasolini: l'universo orrendo* (Rome, Editori Riuniti, 1976)

Ferretti, G. C., "Saggio introduttivo", in *"Officina": cultura, letteratura e politica negli anni cinquanta*, edited by G. C. Ferretti (Turin, Einaudi, 1975), pp. 3–123

Fido, F., "Pasolini e il dialetto", *Italian Quarterly*, 21–22 (1980–81), 69–78

Film Reader 5 (Evanston, Ill., Northwestern University Press, 1979)

Firpo, L., "Quel reazionario di Pasolini", *La stampa*, 31 Aug. 1975

Folena, G., "La storia della lingua oggi", in *Lingua, sistemi letterari, comunicazione sociale*, by various authors (Padua, CLEUP, 1977), pp. 109–36

Fortini, F., *Attraverso Pasolini* (Turin, Einaudi, 1993)

Fortini, F., *I poeti del Novecento* (Rome–Bari, Laterza, 1977)

Fortini, F., "Le poesie italiane di questi anni" [1960], in *Tra continuità e diversità: Pasolini e la critica*, edited by P. Voza (Naples, Liguori, 1990), pp. 98–103

Fortini, F., *L'ospite ingrato* (Bari, De Donato, 1966)

Fortini, F., *Nuovi saggi italiani* (Milan, Garzanti, 1987)

Fortini, F., *Saggi italiani* (Bari, Laterza, 1974)

Fortunato, M., "Pasolini, avanti gli eredi", *L'espresso*, 15 Sept. 1985, 30–31

Foucault, M., *Discipline and Punish: The Birth of the Prison*, translated by A. Sheridan (New York, Vintage, 1979)

Foucault, M., *The History of Sexuality*, translated by R. Hurley (New York, Random House, 1980)

Francescato, G., "Considerazioni per una storia del friulano letterario", *Atti dell'Accademia di scienze, lettere e arti di Udine*, seventh series 1 (1957–60), 1–23

Francescato, G., and F. Salimbeni, *Storia, lingua, società in Friuli* (Udine, Casamassima, 1976)

Francese, J., *Il realismo impopolare di Pier Paolo Pasolini* (Foggia, Bastogi, 1991)

Francese, J., "Pasolini's 'Roman Novels', the Italian Communist Party, and the Events of 1956", in *Pier Paolo Pasolini*, edited by P. Rumble and B. Testa (Toronto, University of Toronto Press, 1993), pp. 22–39

Freud, S., *Collected Papers* (London, Hogarth Press, 1925)

Freud, S., *The Standard Edition of the Complete Psychological Works of Sigmund Freud*, 24 vols (London, Hogarth Press, 1953–74)

Friedrich, P., *Pier Paolo Pasolini* (Boston, Twayne, 1982)

Fusillo, M., *La Grecia secondo Pasolini: mito e cinema* (Scandicci, La Nuova Italia, 1996)

Galleria, 35, i–iv (1985) [special number dedicated to Pasolini and edited by R. Tordi]

Galli, G., *L'Italia sotterranea* (Bari, Laterza, 1983)

Galli de' Paratesi, N., *Lingua toscana in bocca ambrosiana* (Bologna, Mulino, 1984)

Gallo, I., "Pasolini traduttore di Eschilo", in *Pasolini e l'antico: i doni della ragione*, edited by U. Todini (Naples, ESI, 1995), pp. 33–43

Gambetti, G., "Un film 'difficile'", in P. P. Pasolini, *Il Vangelo secondo Matteo*, edited by G. Gambetti (Milan, Garzanti, 1964), pp. 7–9

Garin, E., "Quindici anni dopo", appendix to his *Cronache di filosofia italiana 1900/1943* (Bari, Laterza, 1966)

Garroni, E., "Popolarità e comunicazione nel cinema", *Filmcritica*, 175 (1967); reprinted in *Film segno*, edited by E. Bruno (Rome, Bulzoni, 1983), pp. 27–56

Garroni, E., *Semiotica ed estetica* (Bari, Laterza, 1968)

Gasquet, J., *Narcisse* (Paris, Librairie de France, 1931)

Gatto, A., "La parola intatta del Vangelo", *L'Europa letteraria*, 30–32 (1964), 112

Gatt-Rutter, J., "Pier Paolo Pasolini", in *Writers and Society in Contemporary Italy*, edited by M. Caesar and P. Hainsworth (Leamington Spa, Berg, 1984), pp. 143–65

398   Bibliography

Genette, G., *Introduction à l'architexte* (Paris, Seuil, 1979)
Gensini, S., *Elementi di storia linguistica italiana* (Bergamo, Minerva Italica, 1982)
Gérard, F. S., *Pasolini, ou le Mythe de la barbarie* (Brussels, Editions de l'Université de Bruxelles, 1981)
Gervais, M., *Pier Paolo Pasolini* (Paris, Seghers, 1973)
Gibson, M., *Bruegel* (Seacaucus, NJ, Wellfleet Press, 1989)
Giordana, M. T., *Pasolini: un delitto italiano* (Milan, Mondadori, 1994)
Golino, E., *Pasolini: il sogno di una cosa* (Bologna, Mulino, 1985)
Golino, E., *Tra lucciole e Palazzo: il mito Pasolini dentro la realtà* (Palermo, Sellerio, 1995)
Gordon, R., "Identity in Mourning: The Role of the Intellectual and the Death of Pasolini", *Italian Quarterly*, 32 (1995), 61–75
Gordon, R., *Pasolini: Forms of Subjectivity* (Oxford, Oxford University Press, 1996)
Gordon, R., "Recent Work on Pasolini in English", *Italian Studies*, 52 (1997), 180–88
Gordon, R., "Tradizione e metafora: lingue e dialetto in Pasolini", in *Poesia dialettale e poesia in lingua*, edited by A. Dolfi (Milan, Scheiwiller, 1994), pp. 35–50
Grazzini, G., "Il film di Pasolini un'astrazione intellettuale", *Corriere della sera*, 5 Sept. 1964
Green, M., "The Dialectic of Adaptation: The *Canterbury Tales* of Pier Paolo Pasolini", *Literature/Film Quarterly*, 4 (1976), 46–53
Greene, N., *Pier Paolo Pasolini: Cinema as Heresy* (Princeton, Princeton University Press, 1990)
Grignani, M. A., "Questione di stile?", in *A partire da "Petrolio": Pasolini interroga la letteratura*, edited by C. Benedetti and M. A. Grignani (Ravenna, Longo, 1995), pp. 137–51
Groppali, E., *L'ossessione e il fantasma: il teatro di Pasolini e Moravia* (Venice, Marsilio, 1979)
Guagnini, E., "*La nuova gioventú* e l'esperienza friulana di Pier Paolo Pasolini", *La battana*, 13, xxxix (May 1976), 5–29
Guglielmino, G. M., "Esaltazione lirica e consapevole della figura storica del Cristo", *Gazzetta del popolo*, 5 Sept. 1964
Gundle, S., "Cultura di massa e modernizzazione, *Vie nuove* e *Famiglia cristiana* dalla guerra fredda alla società dei consumi", in *Nemici per la pelle, sogno americano e mito sovietico nell'Italia contemporanea*, edited by P. D'Attore (Milan, Angeli, 1991), pp. 235–68
Herczeg, G., *Lo stile indiretto libero in italiano* (Florence, Sansoni, 1964)
Holdheim, W. W., "Introduction: The Essay as Knowledge in Progress", in *The Hermeneutical Mode* (Ithaca–London, Cornell University Press, 1984), pp. 19–32
Il sogno del centauro: see *Les Dernières Paroles d'un impie*

Intertextuality: Theories and Practices, edited by M. Worton and J. Still (Manchester, Manchester University Press, 1990)

Isenghi, M., "Pasolini giornalista", in *Pier Paolo Pasolini: l'opera e il suo tempo*, edited by G. Santato (Padua, CLEUP, 1983), pp. 153–67

Jacobitti, E., "Hegemony before Gramsci: The Case of Benedetto Croce", *Journal of Modern History*, 52 (1980), 66–84

Jacqmain, M., "Appunti sui glossari pasoliniani", *Linguistica Antwerpiensa*, 4 (1970), 109–54

Jameson, F., *The Political Unconscious: Narrative as a Socially Symbolic Act* (Ithaca–London, Cornell University Press, 1981)

Jewell, K., *The Poesis of History: Experimenting with Genre in Postwar Italy* (Ithaca–London, Cornell University Press, 1992)

Konstantarakos, M., "Time and Space in Pasolini's Roman Prose Works", *The Italianist*, 12 (1992), 59–74

Kristeva, J., *La Révolution du langage poétique* (Paris, Seuil, 1974)

Larivaille, P., "Autobiografia e storia nella poesia di Pasolini", *Galleria*, 35, i–iv (1985), 106–45

Larrain, J., *Marxism and Ideology* (London, Macmillan, 1983)

Lawton, B., "Boccaccio and Pasolini: A Contemporary Reinterpretation of *The Decameron*", in *The Decameron*, edited by M. Musa and P. Bondanella (New York, Norton, 1977), pp. 306–22

Lawton, B., "The Storyteller's Art: Pasolini's *Decameron*", in *Modern European Film-makers and the Art of Adaptation*, edited by A. Horton and J. Magretta (New York, Ungar, 1981), pp. 203–21

Lefevere, A., "Why Waste Our Time on Rewrites?", in *The Manipulation of Literature*, edited by T. Hermans (New York, St Martin's Press, 1985), pp. 215–43

Lepschy, G., "Metalingua", *Delta*, 7 (1967), 1–4

Lepschy, G. and A. L., *The Italian Language Today* (London, Hutchinson, 1977)

Les Dernières Paroles d'un impie: entretiens avec Jean Duflot, edited by F. Duflot (Paris, Belfond, 1981); Italian version *Il sogno del centauro* (Rome, Editori Riuniti, 1983)

Lesko Baker, D., *Narcissus and the Lover* (Stanford, ANMA Libri, 1986)

Letteratura italiana: il letterato e le istituzioni, edited by A. Asor Rosa (Turin, Einaudi, 1982)

Locatelli, L., "Pasolini col Vangelo alla mano muove gli attori senza volto", *Il giorno*, 26 Apr. 1964

Lo Giudice, A., "Pound e Pasolini: viaggio verso il padre", *Letteratura italiana contemporanea*, 12, xxxiv (1991), 33–64

Lo Piparo, F., *Lingua, intellettuali, egemonia in Gramsci* (Bari, Laterza, 1979)

Luperini, R., *Gli intellettuali di sinistra e l'ideologia della ricostruzione nel dopoguerra* (Rome, Edizioni di Ideologie, 1971)

Luperini, R., *Il Novecento* (Turin, Loescher, 1981)

MacCabe, C., "Realism and the Cinema", *Screen*, 15 (1974), 7–27

Maakaroun, E., "Pasolini face au sacré ou l'exorciste possédé", in *Pier Paolo Pasolini: le Mythe et le Sacré*, edited by M. Estève (Paris, Lettres Modernes/Minard, 1976), pp. 32–54

Macciocchi, M-A., "Cristo e il Marxismo", *L'unità*, 22 Dec. 1964

Macciocchi, M-A., "Pasolini: assassinat d'un dissident", *Tel quel*, 76 (Summer 1978)

Manacorda, G., *Storia della letteratura italiana contemporanea (1940–1975)* (Rome, Editori Riuniti, 1977)

Manganelli, G., "Risposta a Pasolini", *Corriere della sera*, 22 Jan. 1975

Marcuse, H., *Eros and Civilization* (London, Sphere, 1970)

Martelli, S., "Dal 'linguaggio tecnologico' al 'volgar eloquio' (questioni e nuove questioni linguistiche di Pasolini)", *Misure critiche*, 7 (1977), 55–74

Martellini, L., *Pier Paolo Pasolini* (Florence, Le Monnier, 1983)

Martinet, A., *Eléments de linguistique générale* (Paris, Colin, 1960)

Mauro, S., "Una vita futura che inizia adesso", *Il mattino di Padova*, 12 Oct. 1985

Mengaldo, P. V., *La tradizione del Novecento: nuova serie* (Florence, Vallecchi, 1987)

Mengaldo, P. V., *Poeti italiani del Novecento* (Milan, Mondadori, 1981)

Meo Zilio, G., "Andrea Zanzotto: come un poeta veneto traduce se stesso (per una critica stilistica della traduzione)", *Quaderni veneti*, 14 (1991), 95–107

Metz, C., "The Cinema: Language or Language System?", in his *Film Language* (New York, Oxford University Press, 1974), pp. 31–91

Micciché, L., "Fredda fedeltà a Matteo di Pier Paolo Pasolini", *L'avanti*, 5 Sept. 1964

Michalczyk, J., *The Italian Political Film-makers* (London–Toronto, Associated University Presses, 1986)

Michaud, G., *Message poétique du Symbolisme*, 4 vols (Paris, Nizet, 1947)

Micocci, E., "Musica, poesia, e aggregazione giovanile", in *L'industria della canzone*, edited by M. Gaspari (Rome, Editori Riuniti, 1981), pp. 138–44

Mioni, A. M., and L. Renzi, "Introduzione", in *Aspetti sociolinguistici dell'Italia contemporanea*, edited by R. Simone and G. Ruggiero, 2 vols (Rome, Bulzoni, 1977), I, 1–8

Monti, R., "Lineamenti di una ricerca linguistica dal Friuli alle *Ceneri di Gramsci*", *Galleria*, 35, i–iv (1985)

Monti, R., *Pier Paolo Pasolini linguista e filologo*, unpublished dissertation, University of Rome "La Sapienza", 1982

Moscati, I., *Pasolini e il teorema del sesso: 1968: dalla Mostra del cinema al sequestro: un anno vissuto nello scandalo* (Milan, Saggiatore, 1995)

Muzzioli, F., *Come leggere "Ragazzi di vita" di Pier Paolo Pasolini* (Milan, Mursia, 1975)

Naldini, N., "Introduzione", in P. P. Pasolini, *Romàns* (Parma, Guanda, 1994), pp. 7–19

Naldini, N., Letter to John P. Welle, 4 Oct. 1991

Naldini, N., *Nei campi del Friuli (la giovinezza di Pasolini) e una conversazione di Andrea Zanzotto* (Milan, All'Insegna del Pesce d'Oro, 1984)

Naldini, N., *Pasolini, una vita* (Turin, Einaudi, 1989)

"Officina": cultura, letteratura e politica negli anni cinquanta, edited by G. C. Ferretti (Turin, Einaudi, 1975)

O'Neill, T., "*Il filologo come politico*: Linguistic Theory and its Sources in Pier Paolo Pasolini", *Italian Studies*, 25 (1970), 63–78

O'Neill, T., "*Passione e ideologia*: The Critical Essays of Pier Paolo Pasolini within the Context of Post-war Italian Criticism", *Forum for Modern Language Studies*, 9, iv (1973), 346–62

O'Neill, T., "Pier Paolo Pasolini's Dialect Poetry", *Forum Italicum*, 9 (1975), 343–67

Onofri, S., "Bibliografia; Filmografia; Fonti fotografiche", in *Pier Paolo Pasolini: "una vita futura"*, edited by L. Betti, G. Raboni and F. Sanvitale (Milan, Garzanti, 1985), pp. 199–240

Orengo, N., "Ultimi idilli in Friuli", *Tuttolibri*, 8 June 1985, 2

Palumbo, C., *Assassiniamo il poeta: Pier Paolo Pasolini* (Cosenza, Pellegrini, 1978)

Paris, R., "Viva Moravia, abbasso Pasolini", *L'espresso*, 3 May 1992, 84–86

Parlangeli, O., *La "nuova" questione della lingua* (Bari, Facoltà di Lettere e Filosofia, 1969; reprinted Brescia, Paideia, 1971)

Pasolini: cronaca giudiziaria, persecuzione, morte, edited by L. Betti (Milan, Garzanti, 1977)

Pasolini e "Il setaccio", edited by M. Ricci (Bologna, Cappelli, 1977)

Pasolini in Friuli 1943–1949, by various authors (Udine, Arti Grafiche Friulane, 1976)

Pasti, D., "L'inferno di Pier Paolo", *Repubblica*, 27 Oct. 1992, 27

Paternostro, R., *Critica, marxismo, storicismo dialettico: due note gramsciane* (Rome, Bulzoni, 1977)

Patrizi, G., "*Petrolio* e la forma romanzo", in *A partire da "Petrolio": Pasolini interroga la letteratura*, edited by C. Benedetti and M. A. Grignani (Ravenna, Longo, 1995), pp. 15–25

Pelosi, G., *Io, Angelo Nero* (Rome, Sinnos, 1995)

Pena, J., "L'Evangile selon Saint Matthieu", *Téléciné*, 19, cxxiii (1965), 3–14

Perché Pasolini: ideologia e stile di un intellettuale militante, edited by G. De Santi, M. Lenti and R. Rossini (Florence, Guaraldi, 1978)

Per conoscere Pasolini, by various authors (Rome, Teatro Tenda/Bulzoni, 1978)

Pertile, L., "The Italian Novel Today: Politics, Language, Literature", in *The New Italian Novel*, edited by Z. G. Barański and L. Pertile (Edinburgh, Edinburgh University Press, 1993), pp. 1–19

Petraglia, S., *Pier Paolo Pasolini* (Florence, La Nuova Italia, 1974)

Pier Paolo Pasolini, edited by P. Willemen (London, British Film Istitute, 1977)

Pier Paolo Pasolini: A Future Life, edited by L. Betti and L. Gambara Thovazzi (Rome, Associazione Fondo Pier Paolo Pasolini, 1989)

Pier Paolo Pasolini: Contemporary Perspectives, edited by P. Rumble and B. Testa (Toronto, University of Toronto Press, 1994)

Pier Paolo Pasolini: corpi e luoghi, edited by M. Mancini and G. Parrella (Rome, Theorema, 1981)

Pier Paolo Pasolini: il cinema di poesia, edited by L. De Giusti [1983], third edition (Rome, Gremese, 1990)

Pier Paolo Pasolini: l'opera e il suo tempo, edited by G. Santato (Padua, CLEUP, 1983)

Pier Paolo Pasolini: testimonianze, edited by A. Panicali and S. Sestini (Florence, Nuova Salani, 1982)

Pier Paolo Pasolini: "una vita futura", edited by L. Betti, G. Raboni and F. Sanvitale (Milan, Garzanti, 1985)

Pitiot, P., "Bernardo Bertolucci s'explique", *Cinéma* [Paris], 472 (Dec. 1990)

Poesia straniera del Novecento, edited by A. Bertolucci (Milan, Garzanti, 1958)

Prete, A., "Pasolini, 1968", in *Pier Paolo Pasolini: séminaire dirigé par Maria Antonietta Macciocchi* (Paris, Grasset, 1980)

Raboni, G., "Poeta senza poesia", in *L'espresso*, 22 Oct. 1995, 25

Rinaldi, R., *L'irriconoscibile Pasolini* (Rovito, Marra, 1990)

Rinaldi, R., *Pier Paolo Pasolini* (Milan, Mursia, 1982)

Rinascita: dialogo con Pasolini; scritti 1957–1984, edited by A. Cadioli, supplement to *Rinascita*, 9 Nov. 1985

Ritratti su misura di scrittori italiani, edited by E. F. Accrocca (Venice, Sodalizio del Libro, 1960)

Rizzolati, P., "Pasolini e i dialetti del Friuli occidentale", *Diverse lingue*, 6 (1986), 27–38

Robidoux, R., *Le Traité du Narcisse (théorie du symbole) d'André Gide* (Ottawa, Editions de l'Université d'Ottawa, 1978)

Rocha, G., "Le Christ-Œdipe", in *Pasolini cinéaste*, special unnumbered issue of *Cahiers du cinéma* (Paris, Editions de l'Etoile, 1981), pp. 81–82

Rohdie, S., *The Passion of Pier Paolo Pasolini* (London, British Film Institute; Bloomington, Indiana University Press, 1995)

Romanò, A., "Introduzione", in E. Siciliano, *Vita di Pasolini* (Milan, Rizzoli, 1981), pp. 5–13

Roncaglia, A., "Nota filologica", in *Petrolio* (Turin, Einaudi, 1992), pp. 567–81

Rondi, G. L. "Né sacrilegio, né opera d'arte il *Vangelo* secondo Pasolini", *Il tempo*, 5 Sept. 1964

Ronsisvalle, V., "Pasolini e Pound", *Galleria*, 35, i–iv (1985), 168–74

Rorty, R., *Philosophy and the Mirror of Nature* (Oxford, Blackwell, 1980)

Rossi-Landi, F., *Marxism and Ideology*, translated by R. Griffin (Oxford, Clarendon Press, 1990)

Rumble, P., *Allegories of Contamination: Pier Paolo Pasolini's "Trilogy of Life"* (Toronto, University of Toronto Press, 1996)

Rumble, P., "Introduction", in *Pier Paolo Pasolini: Contemporary Perspectives*, edited by P. Rumble and B. Testa (Toronto, University of Toronto Press, 1994), pp. 3–13

Rusconi, M., "4 registi al magnetofono", *Sipario*, 19, ccxxii (1964), 14–20

Russo, V., "Riappropriazione e rifacimento: le traduzioni", in *Pasolini e l'antico: i doni della ragione*, edited by U. Todini (Naples, ESI, 1995), pp. 117–43

Said, E., "Representing the Colonized: Anthropology's Interlocutors", *Critical Inquiry*, 15 (1989), 198–210

Santato, G., "La poetica dialettale di Pasolini", *Sigma*, 14, ii–iii (1981), 3–24

Santato, G., *Pier Paolo Pasolini: l'opera* (Vicenza, Neri Pozza, 1980)

Savioli, A., "Hanno detto sí a Pasolini" [review of *Uccellacci e uccellini*], *L'unità*, 14 May 1966

Savioli, A., "Il Cristo solitario di Pasolini", *L'unità*, 3 Oct. 1964

Savioli, A., "*Il Vantone*: da Plauto al Sor Capanna", *L'unità*, 13 Nov. 1963

Scagnetti, A., "È finora il film di piú alto impegno", *Paese sera*, 6 Sept. 1964, 11

Scalia, G., *La mania della verità* (Bologna, Cappelli, 1978)

Schopenhauer, A., *The World as Will and Idea*, 3 vols (London, Trübner, 1883)

Segal, N., *Narcissus and Echo: Women in the French Récit* (Manchester, Manchester University Press, 1988)

Segre, C., "Io faccio autocritica ma gli altri stanno zitti", *L'espresso*, 21 Feb. 1988, 102–03

Segre, C., "La nuova questione della lingua", *La battana*, 3, vii–viii (1966), 37–48

Segre, C., "Prefazione", in P. P. Pasolini, *Il portico della morte*, edited by C. Segre (Rome, Associazione Fondo Pier Paolo Pasolini, 1988), pp. ix–xxvii

Sehrawy, M., "The Suffering Text: *Poesie a Casarsa* and the Agony of Writing", *The Italianist*, 5 (1985), 9–35

Selvatici, F., "Nasce a Firenze l'Archivio Pasolini", *Repubblica*, 19 Aug. 1989

Serri, M., "Un governissimo per Pier Paolo: se lo contendono tutti, dal Msi al Pds", *L'espresso*, 3 May 1992, 88

Shklovsky, V., "Poesia e prosa nel film", in *Film segno*, edited by E. Bruno (Rome, Bulzoni, 1983), pp. 23–26

Siciliano, E., "L'odiato Pasolini", *Il mondo*, 14 July 1972

Siciliano, E., "Non cercava la morte", *L'espresso*, 22 Oct. 1995, 34–35

Siciliano, E., *Vita di Pasolini* [1978] (Milan, Rizzoli, 1981)

Sillanpoa, W. P., "Pasolini's Gramsci", *Modern Language Notes*, 96 (1981), 120–37

Siti, W., "Nota al testo", in P. P. Pasolini, *Bestemmia: tutte le poesie*, edited by G. Chiarcossi and W. Siti, 2 vols (Milan, Garzanti, 1993), I, xxv–xxx

Siti, W., "Nota al testo", in P. P. Pasolini, *Storie della città di Dio* (Turin, Einaudi, 1995), pp. 171–73

Stack, O., *Pasolini on Pasolini* (London, Thames and Hudson/British Film Institute, 1969)

Storia d'Italia: intellettuali e potere, edited by C. Vivanti (Turin, Einaudi, 1981)

Terracini, B. A., "Come parleremo domani", *Fiera letteraria*, 7 Mar. 1965, 6–7

Terracini, B. A., "Lingua e dialetti", *Ce fastu?*, 39 (1963), 8–13

Testa, B., "To Film a Gospel... and Advent of the Theoretical Stranger", in *Pier Paolo Pasolini*, edited by P. Rumble and B. Testa (Toronto, University of Toronto Press, 1994), pp. 180–209

Thompson, K., *Breaking the Glass Armor: Neoformalist Film Analysis* (Princeton, Princeton University Press, 1988)

Thompson, K., "The Concept of Cinematic Excess", in *Narrative, Apparatus, Ideology: A Film Theory Reader*, edited by H. Rosen (New York, Columbia University Press, 1986), pp. 130–42

Tinazzi, G., "Un rapporto complesso", in *Cinema e letteratura del neorealismo*, edited by G. Tinazzi and M. Zancan (Venice, Marsilio, 1990)

Todini, U., "Pasolini e Plauto", *Galleria*, 35, i–iv (1985), 52–63; reprinted as "Sotto il segno di Molière: il latino di Pasolini", in *Pasolini e l'antico: i doni della ragione*, edited by U. Todini (Naples, ESI, 1995), pp. 145–63

Tornabuoni, L., "Ecco Renzo e Lucia secondo Pasolini: un inedito per il cinema", *Tuttolibri*, 8 June 1985, 1

Tra continuità e diversità: Pasolini e la critica, edited by P. Voza (Naples, Liguori, 1990)

Tradizione traduzione società, edited by R. Luperini (Rome, Editori Riuniti, 1989)

Translation/History/Culture: A Sourcebook, edited by A. Lefevere (London–New York, Routledge, 1992)

Trombadori, A., "Passione e ragione secondo Matteo", *Vie nuove*, 10 Sept. 1964

Turigliatto, R., "La tecnica e il mito", in *Lo scandalo Pasolini*, edited by F. Di Giammatteo = *Bianco e nero*, 37, i–iv (1976), 113–55

Vacca, G., "Alcuni temi della politica culturale di Togliatti", in P. Togliatti, *I corsivi di Roderigo* (Bari, De Donato, 1976), pp. 5–18

Valentini, C., "Scandaloso Pier Paolo", *L'espresso*, 1 Nov. 1992, 74–77

Valesio, P., "Pasolini come sintomo", *Italian Quarterly*, 21–22 (1980–81), 29–42

Vallora, M., "Alí dagli occhi impuri: come nasce il manierismo nella narrativa di Pasolini", in *Lo scandalo Pasolini*, edited by F. Di Giammatteo = *Bianco e nero*, 37, i–iv (1976), 156–204

Vannucci, S., *Pier Paolo Pasolini: il colore della poesia* (Rome, Associazione Fondo Pier Paolo Pasolini, 1985)

Van Watson, W., *Pier Paolo Pasolini and the Theater of the Word* (Ann Arbor, UMI Research Press, 1989)

Vassalli, S., "Avrebbe aperto un ristorante...", *Panorama*, 3 Oct. 1993, 139–41

Viano, M., *A Certain Realism: Making Use of Pasolini's Film Thory and Practice* (Berkeley–Los Angeles–London, University of California Press, 1993)

Vignuzzi, U., "Discussioni e polemiche novecentesche sulla lingua italiana", in *Letteratura italiana contemporanea*, edited by G. Mariani and M. Petrucciani (Rome, Lucarini, 1982), pp. 709–36

Vinci, E., "Pasolini, si riparte: oggi la decisione", *Repubblica*, 4 Sept. 1995

Vinge, L., *The Narcissus Theme in Western European Literature up to the Early Nineteenth Century* (Lund, Gleerups, 1967)

Vitale, M., *La questione della lingua*, second edition (Palermo, Palumbo, 1978)

Volponi, P., "Pasolini maestro e amico", in *Perché Pasolini: ideologia e stile di un intellettuale militante*, edited by G. De Santi, M. Lenti and R. Rossini (Florence, Guaraldi, 1978), pp. 15–28

Wagstaff, C., "Reality into Poetry: Pasolini's Film Theory", *The Italianist*, 5 (1985), 107–32

Wagstaff, C., "The Neo-avantgarde", in *Writers and Society in Contemporary Italy*, edited by M. Caesar and P. Hainsworth (Leamington Spa, Berg, 1984), pp. 35–62

Ward, D., *A Poetics of Resistance: Narrative and the Writings of Pier Paolo Pasolini* (Madison, NJ, Fairleigh Dickinson University Press, 1995)

Weber, S., *Institution and Interpretation* (Minneapolis, University of Minnesota Press, 1987)

Wills, L. M., *Le Regard contemplatif chez Valéry et Mallarmé* (Amsterdam, Rodopi, 1974)

Zanelli, D., "Cristo fra i Meridionali", *Il resto del carlino*, 5 Sept. 1964

Zanzotto, A., "Pasolini nel nostro tempo", in *Pier Paolo Pasolini: l'opera e il suo tempo*, edited by G. Santato (Padua, CLEUP, 1983), pp. 235–39

Zanzotto, A., "Pedagogia", in *Pasolini: cronaca giudiziaria, persecuzione, morte*, edited by L. Betti (Milan, Garzanti, 1977), pp. 361–72

Zavattini, C., "Diario", *Cinema nuovo*, 4, liv (1955)

Zigaina, G., *Hostia: trilogia della morte di Pasolini* (Venice, Marsilio, 1995)

Zigaina, G., *Pasolini e la morte* (Venice, Marsilio, 1987)

Zigaina, G., "Pier Paolo Pasolini e il dialetto", *Italian Quarterly*, 21–22 (1980–81), 79–84

INDEX OF REFERENCES TO PASOLINI'S WORKS

INDEX OF NAMES